Copyright © 2013 by Dennis J. Prutow
All Rights Reserved.

Unless otherwise noted, Scripture quotations are from
the New American Standard Bible.
Copyright © 1960, 1962, 1968, 1971, 1972, 1973, 1975, 1977, 1995
by The Lockman Foundation. Used by permission.

No part of this publication may be reproduced, stored in a retrieval system or transmitted, in any form, or by any means, electronic, mechanical, photocopying, recording or otherwise, without the prior permission of the author.

ISBN 978-0-9885215-1-3 (print)

ISBN 978-0-9885215-2-0 (ePub)

ISBN978-0-9885215-3-7 (kindle)

Library of Congress Control Number: 2012953500

Printed in the United States of America
at McNaughton & Gunn, Inc., Michigan

Cover Art: Nicora Gangi
Cover and Book Design: Eileen Bechtold

Public Wo
101

An Introduction to the Biblical Theolo
the Elements of Worship, Exclusive
and A Cappella Psalmod

Dennis J. Pruto

RPTS Press
Reformed Presbyterian Theological Semina
7418 Penn Avenue
Pittsburgh, Pennsylvania 15208

In Memory of
Robert Bruce Tweed
Counselor, Mentor, Colleague, Brother, and Friend

Table of Contents

Forward	*vii*
Introduction and Preface	*xi*
Part One: The Theology of Worship	
Chapter 1: What Is Worship?	3
Chapter 2: What Is the Church?	21
Chapter 3: What Is the Sabbath?	47
Chapter 4: Who Regulates How We Worship?	71
Part Two: The Scriptural Elements of Worship	
Chapter 5: The Elements of Worship: Temple and Synagogue	97
Chapter 6: The Scriptural Elements of Worship	125
Chapter 7: Preaching as Shepherding	153
Chapter 8: The Sacraments	173
Chapter 9: Baptism	183
Chapter 10: The Lord's Supper	203
Part Three: The Element of Praise: Psalmody	
Chapter 11: The Element of Praise: Psalmody	231
Chapter 12: Psalmody and Psalter Expectations	261
Chapter 13: Objections to Exclusive Psalmody	275
Chapter 14: A Brief History of Psalmody: The First Five Centuries	309
Chapter 15: A Brief History of Psalmody: Medieval Declension and Reformation Restoration	335
Part Four: Instrumental Music In Worship	
Chapter 16: Instrumental Music: Laying the Foundation	371

Chapter 17: Instrumental Music: The Historical Perspective from Adam to Augustine — 391

Chapter 18: Instrumental Music: The Historical Perspective from Cassiodorus to Girardeau — 419

Chapter 19: Instrumental Music: The Typological Perspective — 441

Chapter 20: Instrumental Music: Basic Objections — 457

Chapter 21: Instrumental Music: Thesis Confirmed — 477

SUMMING-UP — 487

BIBLIOGRAPHY — 493

INDEX OF PERSONS — 509

INDEX OF SCRIPTURES — 517

INDEX OF SUBJECTS — 531

Foreword

Several months ago, my family was on a trip over the Lord's Day and worshipped at a large evangelical church that had a "traditional" worship service. When the senior pastor came forward for the sermon, he introduced his message by playing a video clip from a recent Hollywood movie (rated PG13). As the dramatic scene (complete with a daring and violent rescue) unfolded, my family was headed for the exits. As far as I could tell, no one else at the service had any qualms about it. We have reached a point in our society at which there really is no telling what might happen in a worship service. Churches themselves are often divided over the content and form of their worship services. It seems unlikely that we will come to any kind of consensus on the matter any time soon, because we cannot agree, in the first place, on what worship *is*.

The Book of Revelation shows us not only that worship is important, but that, in one sense, it is the central activity of the universe. John is shown a vision of the world from the perspective of heaven, and that perspective reveals an occupied throne at the center of all things. Angels and a heavenly host surround the glorious triune God, who rules all things. This host ceaselessly declares, "Holy, holy, holy, is the Lord God Almighty, who was and is and is to come" (Revelation 4:8 ESV)! Worship is not just a part of the Christian life; it is at the heart of the Christian life. For it is only when we see God as He is and take our place worshipping Him as such, that we can have the proper perspective needed to live faithfully as His servants.

Sadly, we live in an age that is dominated by a view of God captured well by the movie version of Frank Baum's *The Wizard of Oz*. The all-powerful wizard turns out to be an unimpressive, old man, who does little more than validate the deeds that Dorothy and her friends have already accomplished.[1] When the prevailing view in the church is that God exists to make me feel better about myself, it is no wonder that we are confused about worship. If we are going to recapture something of the awe that we should have in worship, we need to start by coming to terms with what worship really is. We also need to learn what the Bible says about how our God wants to be worshipped.

I was first introduced to the material presented in *Public Worship 101* when I was a student at the Reformed Presbyterian Theological Seminary in Pittsburgh, Pennsylvania. Professor Prutow's systematic approach to the theology and practice of public worship revolutionized my understanding of entering into the presence of God in the assembly of His people. I have tried to incorporate Dr. Prutow's teaching in my own ministry over the years and have seen God's profound blessing on our congregation as a result. Since this material has been an invaluable resource to my church family and to me personally, I am very happy that Dr. Prutow has taken the time to repackage his work into book form and make it available to a wider audience.

In this volume, Dr. Prutow has done painstaking historical research that greatly strengthens his original lectures. By tracing worship practices from the early church to the present day, Dr. Prutow shows that there has been a surprising level of agreement on how God should be worshipped in all branches of the church throughout much of history. Although he writes from a confessionally reformed perspective, his work will be helpful to Christians from a variety of backgrounds. This text is not a sectarian book! In fact, it is one of those rare books that will actually make a difference in how you think about worship.

---

1. See Dennis Johnson's insightful comments on this in his *Triumph of the Lamb* (Phillipsburg, NJ: P & R Publishing, 2001), 95-96.

A greater appreciation for God's purposes in worship will change the expectations of those who come to worship. A better understanding of the Biblical and historical method of worship will strengthen our confidence that we are, indeed, worshipers who worship in spirit and in truth. Time invested in studying the topic of public worship with Dr. Prutow will pay wonderful dividends. Be warned, though, your thinking about worship is going to be challenged! My prayer for you is that this book may help you draw closer to our sovereign, triune God!

Richard Holdeman, Ph.D.
Bloomington, Indiana
December 1, 2012

Introduction and Preface

*On the other hand, a better hope is introduced,
through which we draw near to God.*
~ Heb. 7:19, ESV

When Jesus Christ appeared in fulfillment of all the Old Testament prophecies, types, and shadows, the Christian era dawned. The Old Testament temple, sacrifices, and high priest were a mere copy and shadow of heavenly things (Heb. 8:5). The substance belonged to Christ (Col. 2:17). He introduced a better hope (Heb. 7:19). Now there is a new temple. The believers at Corinth are, in part, this temple, as Paul declares, "We are the temple of the living God" (2 Cor. 6:16). The Apostle Peter adds, "As living stones, [we] are being built up as a spiritual house for a holy priesthood, to offer up spiritual sacrifices acceptable to God through Jesus Christ" (1 Pet. 2:5). Coming together for worship as this spiritual house, believers have the privilege of drawing near to God. At the same time, God commits Himself to draw near to them. "Draw near to God and He will draw near to you" (Jam. 4:8).

> Therefore, brethren, since we have confidence to enter the holy place by the blood of Jesus, by a new and living way which He inaugurated for us through the veil, that is, His flesh, and since *we have* a great priest over the house of God, *let us draw near* with a sincere heart in full assurance of faith, having our hearts sprinkled *clean* from an evil conscience and our bodies washed with pure water (Heb. 10:19-22, italics added).

The burden of *Public Worship 101* is to display the great privilege the people of God have of drawing near to God in corporate, public worship. In corporate, public worship, God is also pleased to draw near to His people to renew His covenant with them and to assure them that they belong to Him and that He is indeed their God. These coordinate facets of public worship are part of the Biblical theology of worship and form the foundation for a proper understanding of the Biblical elements of worship, including exclusive a cappella Psalmody. The plan is for a four-part study: The Theology of Worship; The Elements of Worship; The Element of Praise, Psalmody; and The Element of Praise, Instrumental Music.

Part One, the Theology of Worship, seeks to answer 4 questions: What is worship? What is the church? What is the Sabbath? Who prescribes how we worship? The Biblical answers to these questions gives us our *theology* of worship.

On one hand, worship is the reverent fear and awe of God expressed by God's people. They bow to Him in heart and soul and determine to serve Him because He alone is worthy. The Father seeks such worship as a response to His worthiness as the only Creator and Redeemer. In spiritual worship, God's people approach the Father, through the Son, by the power of the Spirit. They delight in God and He delights in them. They enjoy Him and pause to find rest in Him. *In this facet of corporate, public worship, God's people have the privilege approaching Him.*

On the other hand, the church assembled for worship is the New Testament temple in which God graciously dwells. As citizens of heaven, God's people form embassies of heaven in this world. God commits himself to these worshiping assemblies for the purpose of renewing His covenant with His people. As God meets with his people, they enjoy His gracious presence and enter into and taste of heaven. *This aspect of worship is God's approach to His people as they gather before Him in sacred assembly.*

As there is a *stated place* for public worship, the gathered church, the Biblical data shows that there is a *stated day* for public worship, the Christian Sabbath. Sabbath rest is a perpetual, moral obligation, and God changes the Sabbath from the seventh to the first day of the week. In a proper use of the Sabbath, God pledges to assure His people that they belong to Him and that He is indeed their God.

This *theology* of worship derives from the temple and the Sabbath and leads to the following syllogism:

> Major Premise: God prescribers how we enter heaven;
>
> Minor Premise: Public worship is an entrance into and a taste of heaven;
>
> Conclusion: God prescribes how we worship.

The syllogism restates the regulative principle of worship: In worship, whatever God does not command, He forbids.

The alternative is the normative principle: In worship, whatever God does not forbid He permits. The normative principle is the default position of many, if not most, churches. However, since a proper theology of worship is based upon stated, heaven-directed temple worship and upon the Sabbath, the regulative principle of worship holds. Christian worship is not based upon the occasional, culturally-conditioned, celebrations found in the the Old Testament. The beauty and power of stated, corporate, Sabbath worship is its connection to heaven and its distinctiveness from prevalent cultural influences.

Part Two, The Elements of Worship, undertakes a study of the Biblical components of worship. While the theology of worship arises from the *temple* and the *Sabbath*, the elements of worship, or its constituent parts, come from the *temple* and the *synagogue*.

As will be shown, New Testament Psalmody stems from praise in the Old Testament temple, to which there is a direct exegetical connection to New Testament praise, the fruit of lips giving thanks to God. The offering and benediction also trace back to the temple. Other elements of worship spring from the synagogue, which was the teaching institution in Israel. There, the people confessed their faith with the *Shema*, recited prescribed prayers, heard the Scriptures read, and also heard an exhortation based upon Moses as seen through the eyes of the prophets. The New Testament evidences other elements of worship including the sacraments of baptism and the Lord's Supper.

Although the New Testament does not set forth a formal order of worship, Old Testament temple worship offers a pattern for approaching God. This approach to God recognizes sin, confesses sin, trusts the promised Savior seen in His sacrifice, and receives cleansing from sin. Since, in worship, God renews His covenant with His people and they respond to Him, worship is dialogical. Praise is one of the means of response. Given the nature of worship, the approach of God's people to Him in worship, and the individual elements of worship, "by good and necessary consequence," an order of worship "may be deduced from Scripture" (Westminster Confession of Faith 1:6).

PART THREE, THE ELEMENT OF PRAISE: PSALMODY, develops the element of praise, argues for the propriety of Psalmody and exclusive Psalmody, answers objections to Psalmody, completes a brief historical review of Psalmody, and examines both the *subjective element* and the *eschatological thrust* of the Psalms. Psalmody has a venerable history of some 3000 years. Those who reject Psalmody ignore this history. Those who reject Psalmody also very likely overlook the heartfelt eschatological longing expressed in the Psalms.

PART FOUR, INSTRUMENTAL MUSIC: The thesis for this part of the study is that instrumental music is not integral to Biblical worship but, when introduced, it is incidental, typical, and temporary. Validation of this thesis begins with a brief review the theology of worship and a short study of music and emotions. From the beginning, worship required faith in the promised Savior and the atoning sacrifice prescribed by

God. This faith was expressed through prayer, praise, and thanksgiving. Instrumental music was never integral to worship.

In addition, God takes His people through various transitions in worship. He introduced more regulated ceremonial worship with Moses, Psalmody with various instruments with David, and then abrogated the sacrificial system with the once for all sacrifice of Christ. God set aside the use of instruments in worship when He set aside the ceremonial sacrifices. They were temporary, because they were typical. Psalmody continues because God commands it in the New Testament. That instrumental music was typical and therefore temporary confirms the fact that it is incidental to worship, not integral to it. A historical review will show that a cappella worship was the standard approach in the church for over eighteen hundred years.

The purpose of *Public Worship 101* is to demonstrate that, in Biblical worship, God renews His covenant with His people as they draw near to Him in the *place* He prescribes, on the *day* He prescribes, in the *manner* He prescribes, with the *elements* He prescribes, including the *praise* He prescribes both in content, *exclusive Psalmody*, and manner, *a cappella Psalmody*, using an *order* properly deduced from Scripture. Since I am known as a proponent of one-point sermons, it is difficult for me to avoid distilling this project into this single purpose statement. Whether I have accomplished this purpose or not is for you, the reader, to judge.

Crown and Covenant Publications produced Part Four of this study in a different form under the title of *Joyful Voices*. I am grateful for their permission to use this material in *Public Worship 101*. I am also grateful to the congregation of Rose Point Reformed Presbyterian Church near New Castle, Pennsylvania. While without a pastor, this congregation patiently listened to sermons from Chronicles dealing with worship and was a great encouragement in developing these materials.

My appreciation also goes to the members of Sterling Reformed Presbyterian Church, Sterling, Kansas, where I was privileged to serve as pastor for fourteen years. Much of what you read here, the congregation first heard in sermon form over the course of my ministry there. During this period, the congregation encouraged me in further study. The Doctor of Ministry project I completed at Reformed Theological Seminary in Orlando, Florida, helped clarify my thinking, and the fruit of those earlier labors is also found in this present volume.

For over a decade it has been my duty and privilege to teach the Ministry of Worship class at the Reformed Presbyterian Theological Seminary. I am grateful to God for the students who patiently listened, struggled with the concepts presented in class, and continue to wrestle with Scripture. Others embraced the regulative principle and exclusive, a cappella Psalmody or were confirmed in their positions. God be praised. The basic outline for this volume comes from my class notes. My deep appreciation also goes to Dr. Jerry O'Neill, President of RPTS, for his encouragement to write and for RPTS Press for publishing this volume. Lee Troup edited the manuscript. Our faithful Seminary Librarian, Tom Reid, proofread the text and developed the indexes. Thanks to both of them. Errors of any kind that remain are my own. Thanks to Pastor Rich Holdeman for his kindness in writing the Preface.

The Reverend Doctor Robert Bruce Tweed administered my theology exam when I was received into the Midwest Presbytery of the Reformed Presbyterian Church of North America from the Orthodox Presbyterian Church. Bob and I became fast friends. Our high school and college age children enjoyed one another's friendship and company. Bob and I were often on the phone together or in face-to-face conversation as I sought counsel from my friend and mentor. I affectionately dedicate this book to my counselor, mentor, colleague, brother, and friend.

Dennis J. Prutow,
January 1, 2013

Public Worship 101

PART ONE:

The Theology of Worship

1
WHAT IS WORSHIP?

> *But an hour is coming, and now is, when the true worshipers will worship the Father in spirit and truth; for such people the Father seeks to be His worshipers.* ~ JOHN 4:23

WHAT IS WORSHIP? The answer to this question is basic as we begin this study. First, there are three terms our English Bibles translate *worship*. Second, the English term worship points to God's ultimate worth. A comparison of proper, true, and spiritual worship with improper, false, and carnal worship logically follows. Third, the characteristics of proper, true, and spiritual worship include joy, delight, and rest in the Lord.

THREE ASPECTS OF WORSHIP

Biblical worship involves fear, reverence, and awe. The Greek verb in question is *sebō*. For example, Gentiles attending synagogue worship are called *God-fearers* or *worshipers of God*. Acts 13:43 says, "Now when the meeting of the synagogue had broken up, many of the Jews and of the *God-fearing* [*sebomenōn*] proselytes followed Paul and Barnabas, who, speaking to them, were urging them to continue in the grace of God" (italics added). Compare Acts 16:14. "A woman named Lydia, from the city of Thyatira, a seller of purple fabrics, a *worshiper* of God [*sebomenē*], was listening; and the Lord opened her heart to respond to the things spoken by Paul." God-fearers are God-worshipers.

Compare Acts 17:4 and 18:7. "And some of them were persuaded and joined Paul and Silas, along with a large number of the *God-fearing* [*sebomenōn*] Greeks and a number of the leading women" (italics added). "Then he left there and went to the house of a man named Titius Justus, a *worshiper* of God [*sebomenou*], whose house was next to the synagogue." God-fearers are God-worshipers.

Scripture also uses the word, translated either God-fearer or worshiper, in a negative sense. In Matthew 15:8-9, Christ upbraids the Scribes and Pharisees. "THIS PEOPLE HONORS ME WITH THEIR LIPS, BUT THEIR HEART IS FAR FROM ME. BUT IN VAIN DO THEY WORSHIP [*sebontai*] ME TEACHING AS DOCTRINES THE PRECEPTS OF MEN." Although vain and empty worship is possible, such worship is outward display. There is no fear, reverence, or awe for God in the heart.

Our Lord quotes Isaiah 29:13. "Then the Lord said, 'Because this people draw near with their words and honor Me with their lip service, but they remove their hearts far from Me, and their reverence [*fear* (KJV, ESV) *sebontai* (LXX)] consists of tradition learned by rote.'" They are acting. They are hypocrites (Matt. 15:7). Hypocritical worship is common.

Psalm 1 uses similar language to describe the wicked and the ungodly. Verse 1 declares, "How blessed is the man who does not walk in the counsel of the wicked [*asebōn* (LXX)]." Verse 4 indicates these wicked are the ungodly [*asebeîs* (LXX)]. Note the alpha privative meaning *not* godly or wicked; these people are without godly fear.

The principal aspect of worship seen here is *fear*. The one who has a proper fear, reverence and awe of the Creator and Redeemer is the believer (Prov. 1:7; 9:10).

Next, worship involves bowing before the Lord. The Greek word [*proskuneō*] is often associated with falling down. When the wise men came into the presence of the Christ-child, "they fell to the ground and worshiped [*prosekunēsan*] Him" (Matt. 2:11). The posture is that of kneeling and bowing forward. The word "designate[s] the custom of prostrating oneself before a person and kissing his feet, the hem of his garment, the ground, etc."[1]

Genesis 22:5 relates that, "Abraham said to his young men, 'Stay here with the donkey, and I and the lad will go over there; and we will worship [*proskunēsantes* (LXX)] and return to you.'" Revelation 4:10 presents a similar picture: "The twenty-four elders will fall down before Him who sits on the throne, and will worship [*proskunēsousin*] Him who lives forever and ever."

As Revelation 13:4 shows men and women easily turn to worship the devil and his minions. "They worshiped [*prosekunēsan*] the dragon because he gave his authority to the beast; and they worshiped [*prosekunēsan*] the beast, saying, 'Who is like the beast, and who is able to wage war with him?'" Revelation 13:8 identifies these worshipers. "All who dwell on the earth will worship [*proskunēsousin*] him, everyone whose name has not been written from the foundation of the world in the book of life of the Lamb who has been slain."

John 4:21-24 uses the same word.

> Jesus said to her, "Woman, believe Me, an hour is coming when neither in this mountain nor in Jerusalem will you worship [*proskunēsete*] the Father. You worship [*proskuneîte*] what you do not know; we worship [*proskunoûmen*] what we know, for salvation is from the Jews. But an hour is coming, and now is, when the true worshipers [*proskunetai*] will worship [*proskunoûntas*] the Father in spirit and truth; for such people the Father seeks to be His worshipers. God is spirit, and those who worship [*proskunoûntas*] Him must worship [*prokuneîn*] in spirit and truth."

In this light, what was the principal difference between Cain and Abel? "The LORD had regard for Abel and for his offering; but for

---

1. William Arndt and F. Wilbur Gingrich, *A Greek-English Lexicon of the New Testament* (Grand Rapids: Zondervan, 1963), 723.

Cain and for his offering He had no regard" (Gen. 4:4-5). John Calvin explains God's actions here: "We see he begins with the person and moves to his works, as if saying God does not spend time with appearances, but begins with the more important, the persons."[2] Calvin then makes this application: "So when we want God to approve the acts of worship we offer him, he must first of all approve of us and consider us to be acceptable."[3] On what basis does God accept us? Faith. "By faith Abel offered to God a better sacrifice than Cain, through which he obtained the testimony that he was righteous" (Heb. 11:4). Abel was acceptable to God by grace through faith in the promised Savior. He engaged in truly spiritual worship. After pointing to John 4:24, Calvin says, "Thus God is worshipped today in a spiritual way and in truth ... As we have already pointed out, he looks on the heart, desires truth and integrity, and loathes that appearance which conceals hypocrisy and those affections which are not sincere and pure."[4]

The principal aspect of worship seen here is bowing or prostrating oneself before the Lord. Outward appearance is insufficient. One must bow his or her heart before the Lord.

Finally, worship is a form of service [latreia] *in which we carry out religious duties* [latreuō]. Consider Hebrews 9:1, "Now even the first covenant had regulations of divine worship [*latreias*, service (KJV)] and the earthly sanctuary." Or Hebrews 9:6, "The priests are continually entering the outer tabernacle performing the divine worship [*latreias*, service (KJV)]." And Hebrews 9:9, "Accordingly both gifts and sacrifices are offered which cannot make the worshiper [*latreias*] perfect in conscience."

Exodus 20:3 and 5 connect bowing in worship with service. "You shall have no other gods before Me ... You shall not worship [*proskunēseis* (LXX)] them or serve [*latreusēs* (LXX)] them." Christ

---

2. John Calvin, *Sermons on Genesis Chapters 1-11*, trans. Rob Roy McGregor (Carlisle: Banner of Truth, 2009), 362.
3. Ibid.
4. Ibid., 365.

uses the same language in responding to Satan. "Jesus said to him, 'Go, Satan! For it is written, "YOU SHALL WORSHIP [*proskunēseis*] THE LORD YOUR GOD, AND SERVE [*latreuseis*] HIM ONLY"'" (Matt. 4:10). In Acts 7:42, Stephen points to the idolatrous worship of Israel in the wilderness. "God turned away and delivered them up to serve [*latreuein*] the host of heaven."

When Paul speaks of service, he seems to have in mind worship as all of life. "Therefore I urge you, brethren, by the mercies of God, to present your bodies a living and holy sacrifice, acceptable to God, which is your spiritual service of worship [*latreian*]" (Rom. 12:1). In this study, my interest is public worship rather than private worship or our general Christian duty. When God commissioned Moses, He gave him this promise: "When you have brought the people out of Egypt, you [plural] shall worship [*latreusete* (LXX)] God at this mountain" (Exod. 3:12). Public worship is preparation for service and worship in the world as individuals.

An associated word for service, *leitourgias*, has reference to the service of worship. It is the word from which we derive our English word *liturgy*. Luke 1:23 speaks of Zechariah's ministry in the temple. "When the days of his priestly service [*leitourgias*] were ended, he went back home." In comparison to the Jewish High Priest, Hebrews 8:6 says of Christ, "But now He has obtained a more excellent ministry [*leitourgias*]."

Worship involves the fear of God, reverence for God, and an awe of God. Worship involves bowing or prostrating oneself before God. Worship, therefore, also involves serving God. This worship and service cannot be simply outward, formal, lip service. It must be heartfelt reverence, genuine respect, and willing, humble service for the Lord.

WORTHSHIP

Worship is the proper response to the dignity, honor, and rank of God. Our English word *worship* comes from the archaic English, *woerthscipe*. *Woerth* or *wurth* means *worthy* or *honorable*, that is, having worth from the standpoint of dignity, importance, or rank. God has ultimate worth. He has the highest dignity, honor, and rank. He alone is worthy. Because He is of ultimate worth, believers honor Him only. Using this definition of the English word, a Biblical concept may be developed.

Compare the following texts (italics added). "*Worthy* are You, our Lord and our God, to receive glory and honor and power" (Rev. 4:11). "Who is *worthy* to open the book and to break its seals?" (Rev. 5:2). "Then I began to weep greatly because no one was found *worthy* to open the book or to look into it" (Rev. 5:4). "And they sang a new song, saying, '*Worthy* are You to take the book and to break its seals'" (Rev. 5:9). "*Worthy* is the Lamb that was slain to receive power and riches and wisdom and might and honor and glory and blessing" (Rev. 5:12). Yes, Jesus Christ is worthy of our worship.

This worship is an axiomatic response. The Greek word translated *worthy* is *axios*. It is the term from which we derive our English word *axiom*.[5] An axiom is a self-evident truth; it needs no proof. It is *self-evident* that we ought to fall before God and honor Him. Consider Revelation 5:1-14 as a whole. Note the saving work of the Lamb, His power to unfold God's decrees. Note the response of the elders, the angels, and all creation.

> I saw in the right hand of Him who sat on the throne a book written inside and on the back, sealed up with seven seals. And I saw a strong angel proclaiming with a loud voice, "Who is worthy to open the book and to break its seals?" And no one in heaven or on the earth or under the earth was able to open the book or to look into it. Then I began to weep greatly because no one was found worthy to open the book or to look into it; and one of the elders said to me, "Stop weeping; behold, the Lion that is from the tribe of Judah, the Root of Da-

---

5. F. Wilbur Gingrich, *Shorter Lexicon of the Greek New Testament* (Chicago: University of Chicago Press, 1983), 18.

vid, has overcome so as to open the book and its seven seals." And I saw between the throne (with the four living creatures) and the elders a Lamb standing, as if slain, having seven horns and seven eyes, which are the seven Spirits of God, sent out into all the earth. And He came and took the book out of the right hand of Him who sat on the throne. When He had taken the book, the four living creatures and the twenty-four elders fell down before the Lamb, each one holding a harp and golden bowls full of incense, which are the prayers of the saints. And they sang a new song, saying, "Worthy are You to take the book and to break its seals; for You were slain, and purchased for God with Your blood men from every tribe and tongue and people and nation. You have made them to be a kingdom and priests to our God; and they will reign upon the earth." Then I looked, and I heard the voice of many angels around the throne and the living creatures and the elders; and the number of them was myriads of myriads, and thousands of thousands, saying with a loud voice, "Worthy is the Lamb that was slain to receive power and riches and wisdom and might and honor and glory and blessing." And every created thing which is in heaven and on the earth and under the earth and on the sea, and all things in them, I heard saying, "To Him who sits on the throne, and to the Lamb, be blessing and honor and glory and dominion forever and ever." And the four living creatures kept saying, "Amen." And the elders fell down and worshiped.

Worship honors the Lord and recognizes His worthiness. This worship is a *response* to the supreme dignity of the Triune God. We see the same response in other places in the Bible. "After coming into the house they saw the Child with Mary His mother; and they fell to the ground and worshiped Him. Then, opening their treasures, they presented to Him gifts of gold, frankincense, and myrrh" (Matt. 2:11).

After His resurrection, "behold, Jesus met them and greeted them. And they came up and took hold of His feet and worshiped Him" (Matt. 28:9).

Since worship is an axiomatic response, there are two primary types of worship, worshiping God or worshiping idols. We honor the saving work of Christ or we honor human efforts. We serve good or we serve evil. We respond to God's dignity or we respond to human dignity. Israel responds to and honors God by bowing before Him and worshiping Him.

> Now the Lord said to Aaron, "Go to meet Moses in the wilderness." So he went and met him at the mountain of God and kissed him. Moses told Aaron all the words of the Lord with which He had sent him, and all the signs that He had commanded him to do. Then Moses and Aaron went and assembled all the elders of the sons of Israel and Aaron spoke all the words which the Lord had spoken to Moses. He then performed the signs in the sight of the people. So the people believed; and when they heard that the Lord was concerned about the sons of Israel and that He had seen their affliction, then *they bowed low and worshiped* (Exod. 4:27-31, italics added).

Now compare Exodus 32:8 (with italics added). "They have quickly turned aside from the way which I commanded them. *They have made for themselves a molten calf, and have worshiped it* and have sacrificed to it and said, 'This is your god, O Israel, who brought you up from the land of Egypt!'" The people foolishly sought their own pleasure, and honored the work of their own hands. "They exchanged the truth of God for a lie, and *worshiped* and *served* the creature rather than the Creator, who is blessed forever. Amen" (Rom. 1:25, italics added).

The distinction between worshiping God and worshiping idols is a persistent theme in Scripture from Genesis through Revelation. Abel honored, worshiped, and served God. Cain sought his own pleasure and served himself. Worship in some form is axiomatic. Revelation

What is Worship?

makes the distinction vivid. Some worship the Lamb. See Revelation 7:9-12 (italics added).

> After these things I looked, and behold, a great multitude which no one could count, from every nation and all tribes and peoples and tongues, standing before the throne and before the Lamb, clothed in white robes, and palm branches were in their hands; and they cry out with a loud voice, saying, "Salvation to our God who sits on the throne, and to the Lamb." And all the angels were standing around the throne and around the elders and the four living creatures; and *they fell on their faces before the throne and worshiped God,* saying, "Amen, blessing and glory and wisdom and thanksgiving and honor and power and might, be to our God forever and ever. Amen."

Others worship the dragon and the power of the beast. Compare Revelation 13:1-4 (italics added).

> And the dragon stood on the sand of the seashore. Then I saw a beast coming up out of the sea, having ten horns and seven heads, and on his horns were ten diadems, and on his heads were blasphemous names. And the beast which I saw was like a leopard, and his feet were like those of a bear, and his mouth like the mouth of a lion. And the dragon gave him his power and his throne and great authority. I saw one of his heads as if it had been slain, and his fatal wound was healed. And the whole earth was amazed and followed after the beast; *they worshiped the dragon because he gave his authority to the beast; and they worshiped the beast,* saying, "Who is like the beast, and who is able to wage war with him?"

In the *first* case, there is worship of God and the Lamb. There is worship because all redeemed life comes from God. This worship is a *response* to the power of God. This worship is a response to the *good* use of power in redemption. In the *second* case, there is worship of the power to make war and to destroy. This worship is veneration of the power to do *evil*. We see both types of worship in our world today. Men and women either *honor* good and God, or they *honor* evil and the devil.

All true worship is God-centered. "Whether, then, you eat or drink or whatever you do, do all to the glory of God" (1 Cor. 10:31). "Whom have I in heaven *but You*? And besides You, I desire nothing on earth. My flesh and my heart may fail, but God is the strength of my heart and my portion forever" (Ps. 73:25-26). Worship does not exclude human pleasure, but these texts demonstrate that human pleasure is not the primary focus of worship. The Westminster Shorter Catechism asks this question: "What is the chief end of man?" The answer is: "Man's chief end is to glorify God and to *enjoy him* forever."[6]

In the Old Testament, *glory* refers to weight or weightiness. Gold has glory; it is weighty or heavy. When we recognize the glory of God and do all to the glory of God, He carries weight in our lives. We are in awe of Him and have reverent fear for Him. We see Him alone as worthy. We bow to His will and determine to serve Him. We worship Him. He is the focal point of our lives.

What then is the pleasure we enjoy in worship? We have the pleasure of enjoying God. Consider David's great desire. "One thing I have asked from the Lord, that I shall seek: / That I may dwell in the house of the Lord all the days of my life, / To behold the beauty of the Lord / And to meditate in His temple" (Ps. 27:4). Worship is, therefore, joy, delight, and rest *in the Lord*. All true worship is God-centered.

Since God is the only Worthy One, He seeks worshipers. In John 4:23, Jesus confirms this fact. "But an hour is coming, and now is, when the true worshipers will worship the Father in spirit and truth; for such people the Father seeks to be His worshipers." The grammar

---

6. Italics added. The proof texts are 1 Corinthians 10:31 and Psalm 73:25-26 just quoted.

of the second clause of the text falls out this way: the Father seeks such, those worshiping Him. A. T. Robertson puts it this way, "John pictures the Father as seeking worshippers ... "[7]

We should gather two things from the first clause of Jesus' statement. First, Christ speaks of true worshipers. True worshipers worship *the Father*. They honor *the Father*. They hold *Him* in awe. They do not honor Him with their lips and, at the same time, turn their hearts away from Him. True worship is worship of the Father, through the Son, by the power of the Spirit.

Second, Christ therefore also speaks of worship "in spirit and truth." In verse 24, He says such worship is necessary; we must "worship in spirit and truth." *Spirit and truth* is a hendiadys, a figure of speech for referring to one thing using two nouns connected with *and*. We interpret this hendiadys as *truly spiritual worship*.[8] Such worship is from the heart. Truly spiritual worship *is* worship of the Father, through the Son, by the power of the Spirit.

Christ says, "But an hour is coming, and now is" (John 4:23). Note how Calvin interprets the text:

> When He says that the hour cometh or will come, He teacheth that the order handed down by Moses is not everlasting; when He says that the hour is now come, He puts an end to the ceremonies ... To understand this, we must note the antithesis between the Spirit and external figures, as between the shadow and the substance. The worship of God is said to be in Spirit because it is only the inward faith of the heart that produces prayer and purity of conscience and denial of ourselves, that we may be given up to obedience of God as holy sacrifices ... [9]

---

7. A. T. Robertson, *Word Pictures of the New Testament* (Nashville: Broadman, 1932), 5:67.
8. E. W. Bullinger, *Figures of Speech Used in the Bible Explained and Illustrated* (GrandRapids: Baker, 1968), 657, 664-665. The "spirit and power of Elijah" (Luke 1:17) means the powerful spirit of Elijah
9. John Calvin, *The Gospel According to John*, 1-10, trans. T. H. L. Parker, ed. David W. Torrance and Thomas F. Torrance (Grand Rapids: Eerdmans, 1959), 99.

When Christ speaks of *true worshipers*, Calvin comments,

> He knows that the world will never be free from superstitions, and therefore He separates the godly and true worshippers from the perverted and hypocritical ... What it is to worship God in spirit and truth appears plainly from what has already been said. It is to remove the coverings of the ancient ceremonies and retain simply what is spiritual in the worship of God.[10]

True worshipers worship the Father. They engage in truly spiritual worship. The Father seeks such, "not in the sense that there are individuals who have made themselves such worshipers, and that the Father is, as it were, searching for them; but in the sense that he keeps on intensely yearning for his elect in order that he may make them *such* worshipers."[11]

In review, worship is the reverent fear and awe of God expressed by bowing to Him in heart and soul. Seeing Him alone as worthy, worshipers bow to His will and determine to serve Him. We worship Him as the center and focal point of our lives. We know the Father seeks our worship as a response to His worthiness as Creator and Redeemer. This truly spiritual worship is our public approach to the Father, through the Son, by the power of the Spirit.

WORSHIP IS JOY, DELIGHT, AND REST IN THE LORD

First, Worship is joy and gladness in the Lord. C. S. Lewis critiques the teachers of his day.

> They see the world around them swayed by emotional propaganda—they have learned from tradition that youth are sentimental—and they conclude that the best thing they can do is fortify the minds of young people against emotion. My own experience as a teacher tells

---

10. Ibid., 101.
11. William Hendriksen, *Exposition of the Gospel of John* (Grand Rapids: Baker, 1972), 1:167.

an opposite tale. For every one pupil who needs to be guarded against a weak excess of sensibility there are three who need to be awakened from the slumber of cold vulgarity. The task of the modern educator is not to cut down jungles but to irrigate deserts. The right defense against false sentiments is to inculcate just sentiments. By starving the sensibility of our pupils we only make them easier prey to the propagandist when he comes. For famished nature will be avenged and a hard heart is no infallible protection against a soft head.[12]

Good, wholesome, uplifting, enriching, gracious sentiments are instilled and brought out in worship. Psalm 92 is a "Song for the Sabbath Day." Verse 4 declares, "You, O Lord, have made me glad by what You have done, / I will sing for joy at the works of Your hands." God's sovereign work in sending His Son to die on a cross to pay the penalty due to us for our sins makes us glad. The inner work of God in sending the Holy Spirit into our hearts enabling us to embrace the death and resurrection of Christ makes us glad.

This joy and gladness springs from the depths of our hearts. Deep-seated joy is the response to the work of God. Gladness wells up within us and pervades our thoughts and emotions. Spurgeon counsels, "If we consider either creation or providence, we shall find overflowing reasons for joy; but when we come to review the work of redemption, gladness knows no bounds, but feels that she must praise the Lord with all her might."[13] Calvin concurs, "Those are best qualified for celebrating the praises of God who recognize and feel his fatherly goodness, and can undertake this service with willing and joyful minds."[14] Worship is joy and gladness in the Lord.

Second, worship is delight in the Lord. Psalm 37:4 exhorts, "Delight yourself in the Lord." Delight refers to pleasure, happiness, rapture,

---

12. C. S. Lewis, *The Abolition of Man* (New York: Macmillan, 1966), 24.
13. Charles Spurgeon, *Treasury of David* (Newark: Cornerstone, n.d.), 4:264.
14. John Calvin, *Commentary on the Book of Psalms*, trans. James Anderson (Grand Rapids: Baker, 1979), 3:496.

ecstasy, bliss, joy, gladness, exaltation. As a small boy, I recall going to bed to await the arrival of Santa Claus. What a delight to find the tree and presents on Christmas morning! While a chaplain in Vietnam, it was shear delight to go to Saigon to a clean, cool, air-conditioned restaurant serviced by Americans. As noted before, the Westminster Shorter Catechism asks this question: "What is the chief end of man?" The answer is: "Man's chief end is to glorify God and to *enjoy him forever*." With Scripture, our Catechism calls us to delight in and enjoy God. Our worship includes delight in and enjoyment of God.

While Psalm 37:4 exhorts us to delight in the Lord, Proverbs 3:12 teaches, "For whom the Lord loves He reproves, even as a father, *the son in whom he delights*" (italics added). God promises Israel, "But you will be called, 'My delight is in her,' And your land, 'Married'; For the LORD delights in you" (Isa. 62:4). Yes, God delights in His redeemed people. David experienced this delight. He confesses, "He brought me forth also into a broad place; He rescued me, because He delighted in me" (Ps. 18:19). Moses had wonderful tastes of the power, glory, and grace of God. Beyond doubt, Moses took great delight in the Lord. This delight led him to cry, "I pray You, show me Your glory" (Exod. 33:18). As believers, we taste of the Lord; He is good. There is therefore good reason to delight in Him. When two persons who delight in each other meet, they experience mutual love and compassion. Worship is delight in the Lord.

Finally, worship is rest in the Lord. Psalm 46:10 exhorts, "Be still, and know that I am God: / I will be exalted among the nations, / I will be exalted in the earth." This Psalm was probably composed in answer to some great deliverance experienced by Jerusalem displaying the mighty hand of God, quite possibly when He miraculously delivered Jerusalem from Sennacherib, king of Assyria, in 688 B.C. The Psalm celebrates the power and greatness of God on behalf of His people. It develops this theme in three stanzas punctuated by the word *selah*. *Selah* indicates a *pause* or *musical interlude*. It may be a form of dramatic pause that gives time to reflect on the wonders of

God. It may be a *rest* calling for reflection, reorientation, and rejuvenation.

Verses 1-3 relate the presence of God preserving us in the midst of tumult. "God is our refuge and strength, / A very present help in trouble. / Therefore we will not fear, though the earth should change / And though the mountains slip into the heart of the sea; / Though its waters roar and foam, / Though the mountains quake at its swelling pride. Selah." As a present help, we find God is the shelter and strength we need. We can therefore rest, *selah*. Worship is rest in the Lord.

These verses also remind us of the end of time. "But the day of the Lord will come as a thief, in which the heavens shall pass away with a great noise, and the elements shall be dissolved with fervent heat, and the earth and the works that are therein shall be burned up" (2 Pet. 3:10). God will be exceedingly faithful and will deliver His people. *Selah*. In worship, we rest in and reflect on this hope.

Verses 4-7 turn to the city of God, Jerusalem. "There is a river whose streams make glad the city of God, / The holy dwelling places of the Most High. / God is in the midst of her, she will not be moved; / God will help her when morning dawns. / The nations made an uproar, the kingdoms tottered; / He raised His voice, the earth melted. / The LORD of hosts is with us; / The God of Jacob is our stronghold. Selah." The Psalm portrays God's dealing with His church. God's sanctuary was in the midst of Jerusalem. Similarly, God's presence now abides in His church. He is with His people. Just as Jerusalem was well supplied with conduits bringing water, the church is well supplied with the living waters of Christ. Just as Jerusalem was well protected from the Assyrians, the gates of hell will not prevail against the church. The Lord of Hosts is Messiah Jesus, our Immanuel. *Selah!* Worship is rest in the Lord's secure presence pointing to final heavenly rest:

> And he showed me a river of water of life, bright as crystal, proceeding out of the throne of God and of the Lamb, in the midst of the street thereof. And on this side of the

> river and on that was the tree of life, bearing twelve manner of fruits, yielding its fruit every month: and the leaves of the tree were for the healing of the nations. And there shall be no curse any more: and the throne of God and of the Lamb shall be therein: and his servants shall serve him; and they shall see his face; and his name shall be on their foreheads (Rev. 22:1-4).

Worship is rest in the Lord; we rest in and pause to reflect on this hope.

Verses 8-11 recognize the exaltation of God throughout the whole earth.

> Come, behold the works of the Lord, / Who has wrought desolations in the earth. / He makes wars to cease to the end of the earth; / He breaks the bow and cuts the spear in two; / He burns the chariots with fire. / "Be still and know that I am God; / I will be exalted among the nations, I will be exalted in the earth." / The Lord of hosts is with us; / The God of Jacob is our stronghold. Selah.

God calls both believer and unbeliever to witness His work. He causes wars to cease as Sennacherib and the Assyrians experienced. At the same time the people of Jerusalem were constrained to be still and witness God's deliverance. God was with them. Similarly, Jesus Christ commissions His church and makes a profound promise. "Go ye therefore, and make disciples of all the nations, baptizing them into the name of the Father and of the Son and of the Holy Spirit: teaching them to observe all things whatsoever I commanded you: *and lo, I am with you always, even unto the end of the world*" (Matthew 28:19-20, italics added). Worship is a time of rest to reflect on this promise. *Selah.*

Here again, there is a comparison with the end of the age and the ushering in of the New Heavens and New Earth.

> "For just as the new heavens and the new earth / Which I make will endure before Me," declares the Lord, / "So

your offspring and your name will endure. / And it shall be from new moon to new moon / And from Sabbath to Sabbath, / All mankind will come to bow down before Me," says the Lord. / "Then they will go forth and look / On the corpses of the men / Who have transgressed against Me. / For their worm will not die And their fire will not be quenched; / And they will be an abhorrence to all mankind" (Isa. 66:22-24).

God calls us to be still, outwardly and inwardly. He calls us to cease our striving, turn to Him, and observe His work. *Selah* means rest. When Israel had her back to the Red Sea, "Moses said to the people, 'Do not fear! Stand by and see the salvation of the Lord which He will accomplish for you today; for the Egyptians whom you have seen today, you will never see them again forever. The Lord will fight for you while you keep silent'" (Exod. 14:13-14). Psalm 46:10 applies to past events, "Be still, and know that I am God" (ESV). John relates a similar and remarkable picture in heaven. After he relates the scene of the throne of God on a crystal sea encompassed by a rainbow, four living creatures, twenty-four elders, innumerable angels, and myriads of saints, Revelation 8:1 says, "There was silence in heaven for about half an hour." Psalm 46:10 also applies to future events, "Be still, and know that I am God" (ESV). Jesus Christ calls us to be still and know that He is truly God. This rest is the essence of worship. This is the rest to which God calls us in weekly corporate worship.

WHAT IS WORSHIP?

The answer to this question is personal. Worship is the reverent fear and awe of God we express by bowing to Him in heart and soul. He alone is worthy and we bow to His will and determine to serve Him. He is the focal point of our lives. He alone is worthy of honor and praise. The Father seeks our worship in response to His worthiness as our Creator and Redeemer. In truly spiritual worship, we approach the Father, through the Son, by the power of the Spirit. As we do so, we delight in God and He delights in us. We enjoy Him and pause to find rest in Him.

Worship may be either individual and private, or corporate and public. The focus of this study is public, corporate worship. Psalm 87:2 reminds us, "The Lord loves the gates of Zion more than all the other dwelling places of Jacob." Spurgeon applies these words to the church assembled in public, corporate worship. "God delights in the prayers and praises of Christian families and individuals, but he has a special eye to the assemblies of the faithful, and he has a special delight in their devotions in their church capacity."[15] The focus of this chapter has been the believer's approach to God in worship. Chapter 2 will examine God's approach to us in public worship.

---

15. Spurgeon, *A Treasury of David*, 4:115.

What Is the Church?

We are the temple of the living God.
~ 2 Cor. 6:16

The focus in chapter 1 is upon *our approach* to God in worship. In this chapter we consider *God's approach to us* in worship. Here, we get a glimpse into God's purposes in and for *public* worship. On one hand, worship in God's gathered church is God's special means for communicating His covenant grace. On the other hand, the church assembled for worship is God's special dwelling place. These two co-ordinate points are part of the theology of worship.

WORSHIP IS GOD'S COMMUNICATION OF COVENANT GRACE

In 2 Corinthians 6:16-18, Paul connects New Testament worship of the living God with the covenant promises and themes of the Old Testament.

> For we are the temple of the living God; just as God said, "I will dwell in them and walk among them; and I will be their God, and they shall be my people. Therefore, come out from their midst and be separate," says the Lord. "And do not touch what is unclean; And I will welcome you. And I will be a father to you, And you shall be sons and daughters to Me," Says the Lord Almighty.

Our text is imbedded in 2 Corinthians 6:14-7:1. We will discover that this text is a clearly-defined section of Paul's letter, briefly examine its Old Testament background, and review Paul's use of the Old Testament here to confirm that this worship text teaches God's approach to us in covenant renewal.

Consider 2 Corinthians 6:14-7:1 from a literary perspective. Verse 14 exhorts, "Do not be bound together with unbelievers." Verse 1 of chapter 7 returns to this theme: "Let us cleanse ourselves from every defilement of body and spirit, bringing holiness to completion in the fear of God." This inclusion distinguishes this text from the surrounding context. Also notice how the previous section ends: "I speak as to children—open wide to us also" (2 Cor. 6:13). Paul resumes this same thought in verse 2 of chapter 7, "Make room for us in your hearts." These shifts in theme show that our text falls within a well-defined Scripture portion beginning with the warning of verse 14: "Do not be bound together with unbelievers."

Rhetorical questions follow this warning: "What partnership have righteousness and lawlessness, or what fellowship has light with darkness? Or what harmony has Christ with Belial, or what has a believer in common with an unbeliever? Or what agreement has the temple of God with idols?" (2 Cor. 6:14-16). As Beale and Carson say, "Five antithetical questions strengthen this warning (6:14b-16a), the last of which leads to an application to the *Christian congregation*: 'What agreement has the temple of God with idols? For we are the temple of the living God' (6:16a). This statement is then supported by several *OT quotations* ... "[1] Paul asks the question, "What agreement has the temple of God with idols?" Then he boldly states, "We are the temple of the living God." To support his statement, Paul quotes from Leviticus 26:12 and Isaiah 52:11. He also alludes to 2 Samuel 7:14 and Ezekiel 20:34. As Beale and Carson note, Paul applies these Old Testament passages to the *Christian congregation*.

---

1. G. K. Beale and D. A. Carson, *Commentary on the New Testament Use of the Old Testament* (Grand Rapids: Baker, 2007), 769. Italics added.

Since Paul makes this application, some examination of the Old Testament background is in order. The book of Exodus has three main sections. In chapters 1-18, God redeems Israel from slavery in Egypt. In chapters 19-24, God forms redeemed Israel into a covenant community. Then, in chapters 25-40, God forms Israel into a worshiping community.[2] What is the message of Exodus? God redeems His people to form them into a covenant, worshiping community. God deals with His people in the same way today. He redeems His people to form them into covenant, worshiping communities. The church at Corinth was one of these communities.

Leviticus continues the story. "The bulk of the book of Leviticus contains laws and rituals surrounding the formal worship of Israel."[3] The central theme of Leviticus is holiness. "I am the Lord who brought you up from the land of Egypt to be your God; thus you shall be holy, for I am holy" (Lev. 11:45). Holiness is not simply an individual duty; it is a congregational mandate. "Speak to all the congregation of the sons of Israel and say to them, 'You shall be holy, for I the Lord your God am holy'" (Lev. 19:2). The basic meaning of *holiness* is separateness. "Thus you are to be holy to Me, for I the Lord am holy; and I have set you apart from the peoples to be Mine" (Lev. 20:26). This holiness is epitomized in the tabernacle.

The court of the tabernacle, 100 cubits[4] by 50 cubits, was enclosed with curtains of fine linen five cubits high (Exod. 27:9-18). Fine linen garments set apart priests, nobles, and kings. For instance, Pharaoh clothed Joseph with robes of fine linen (Gen. 41:42). Fine linen also represents the righteousness of the saints (Rev. 19:8). The tabernacle proper was constructed of gold covered boards ten cubits by one and a half cubits. These boards, set upright, formed the walls of the sanctuary thirty cubits long and ten cubits wide. The boards had silver foundations (Exod. 26:15-30).

---

2. Tremper Longman III and Raymond B. Dillard, *An Introduction to the Old Testament* (Grand Rapids: Zondervan, 2006), 70-72.
3. Ibid., 85.
4. A cubit is approximately a foot and a half.

There were four layers of curtain used to cover the sanctuary. The first layer was woven of "fine twisted linen and blue and purple and scarlet material; you shall make them with cherubim, the work of a skillful workman" (Exod. 26:1). "This curtain was the one that could be seen from inside the tabernacle. Its sky-like color and the presence of the heavenly creatures on it demonstrate that the tabernacle was considered to be heaven on earth."[5] The second curtain was a protective layer of goat hair, "the down or the finest part of the hair,"[6] probably black.[7] The third curtain was a layer of "rams' skin dyed red" (Exod. 26:14). The top layer, more exposed to the elements, was water-resistant and "a covering of porpoise skins" (Exod. 26:14).

Israel camped around the tabernacle. "The center of the camp, according to Near Eastern tradition, was the place for the king's tent. Since God was king of Israel, His tent was rightly in the center."[8] In addition, "As the place of God's special presence, the tabernacle was holy ground ... Outside the camp was the realm of the Gentiles and the unclean ... The camp itself was close to the presence of God and was the place where all Israelites in covenant with the Lord dwelt."[9]

We may picture Israel encamped around the tabernacle in the Sinai desert. During the day, the Levites could pull back the curtains covering the sanctuary to reveal the gleaming gold boards, silver foundations, and the contrasting colors of blue, black, and scarlet. Sunlight reflected from the gold, silver, blue, and scarlet could be seen for miles. The dazzlingly white linen curtains of the tabernacle court also shimmered in the bright desert sun. Thus the camp was dramatically separated from its surroundings. In the camp itself, the tents of the people faced the tabernacle. The center and focal point of the life of the people, of their separateness from the world, and of their holiness,

---

5. Longman and Dillard, *An Introduction to the Old Testament*, 78.
6. George Bush, *Commentary on Exodus* (Grand Rapids: Kregel, 1993), 378.
7. W. S. McCullough, "Goat," *The Interpreter's Dictionary of the Bible* (New York: Abington, 1962), 2:407.
8. Longman and Dillard, *An Introduction to the Old Testament*, 6.
9. Ibid., 77.

was the tabernacle and worship.[10] In a similar way, the focal point of present day holiness, of separateness from the world, is public, corporate worship. Corporate worship is one of the places the church most visibly exhibits its separateness from the world as a body.

Given this background, note how Paul uses the Old Testament to confirm his statement: "We are the temple of the living God" (2 Cor. 6:16). Remember, the people do not receive Paul's letter via email or through social media networks as they sit in their homes before their computers. The church at Corinth hears the words of Paul as they assemble together to listen to his Letter read to them. Paul addresses the church at Corinth as a body (2 Cor. 6:1, 11, 12, 13, and 14). He then declares to the church assembled, "We are the temple of the living God." *Paul validates his declaration by quoting from God's covenant promise in Leviticus 26:11-12.* "Moreover, I will make My dwelling among you, and My soul will not reject you. I will also walk among you and be your God, and you shall be My people."

Taken as a whole, Leviticus 26 has reference to tabernacle worship. This chapter uses the term *covenant* eight times. Remember, God redeemed the people of Israel to make them into a covenant, worshiping community. Since the tabernacle was the forerunner of the temple, it is appropriate for Paul to refer to Leviticus 26. Leviticus 26 is also a worship text. Verse 1 is a reference to the Second Commandment. "You [plural] shall not make for yourselves [plural] idols, nor shall you [plural] set up for yourselves [plural] an image or a sacred pillar, nor shall you [plural] place a figured stone in your [plural] land to bow down to it; for I am the Lord your [plural] God." Verse 2 adds references to the Sabbath and the sanctuary, that is, the tabernacle. "You [plural] shall keep My sabbaths and reverence My sanctuary; I am the Lord."

> God established the Sabbaths and the sanctuary, so that through them he could dwell with his people and lavish

---

10. Understanding public worship as the "focal point" of holiness places worship as all of life (Romans 12:1-2) in proper perspective.

his blessings upon them ... The sanctuary was the sacred area around the altar for burnt offering and the tent of meeting ... It was the place for the performance of the divine service, the place where God met twice each day to receive his people and to bless them.[11]

This covenant worship text continues in verses 3-13. Verse 3 is a conditional clause, "*If you walk* in My statutes and keep My commandments so as to carry them out ..." Note the added italics. Verse 13 announces God's blessing, "I am the Lord your God, who brought you out of the land of Egypt so that you would not be their slaves, and I broke the bars of your yoke and *made you walk erect.*" Again, note the added italics. This inclusion indicates that God's gracious work in the context of worship causes the *walk* He requires.

The text Paul quotes falls within this inclusion. Leviticus 26:11-12 reads, "Moreover, I will make My dwelling among you, and My soul will not reject you. I will also walk among you and be your God, and you shall be My people." Here are Paul's words in 2 Cor. 6:16, "For we are the temple of the living God; just as God said, 'I WILL DWELL IN THEM AND WALK AMONG THEM; AND I WILL BE THEIR GOD, AND THEY SHALL BE MY PEOPLE.'" Paul's words involve covenant worship.

With the declaration, "I will be your God," our Lord recalls His promise to Abraham. "I will establish My covenant between Me and you and your descendants after you throughout their generations for an everlasting covenant, *to be God to you and to your descendants after you*" (Gen. 17:7, italics added). John Kleinig says, "God's foundational promise in Gen 17:7-8 that he would be a God for Abraham and his descendants is fulfilled with the establishment of the divine service (Exod. 29:44-45)."[12] Note that Exodus 29:44-45 connects the promise with the tabernacle: "I will consecrate the tent of meeting and the altar; I will also consecrate Aaron and his sons to minister as priests to Me. *I will dwell among the sons of Israel and will be their*

---

11. John W. Kleinig, *Leviticus* (St. Louis: Concordia, 2003), 573.
12. Ibid., 560.

God" (italics added). Here again we have the twin themes of covenant and worship.

The covenant declaration of Leviticus 26:12 continues with the words, "You shall be my people." God recalls entering into covenant with His people at Sinai. The people respond by confessing, "All that the Lord has spoken we will do; and we will be obedient" (Exod. 24:7). Finally, when the covenant declaration states, "I will make my dwelling among you," God more specifically recalls the worship of Israel. "Let them construct a sanctuary for Me, that I may *dwell* among them" (Exod. 25:8, italics added). God redeemed His people to form them into a covenant, worshiping community.

Paul affirms that the New Testament church is God's temple by applying God's three-part covenant declaration to the Christian congregation in Corinth: I will be your God; you shall be my people; I will dwell among you. What is the significance of this declaration? When the assembled people of God hear this word regarding themselves, God is assuring them that they belong to Him, that He is indeed their God, and that He will dwell in their midst. God is renewing His covenant with His people. God extending covenant assurance and affecting covenant renewal is part of His covenant purpose for worship.

Paul adds a quotation of Isaiah 52:11. He does so to confirm his application of God's covenant to the Corinthian Christians. He declares, "Therefore, 'COME OUT FROM THEIR MIDST AND BE SEPARATE,' says the Lord. 'AND DO NOT TOUCH WHAT IS UNCLEAN'" (2 Cor. 6:17). Isaiah 52:11 addresses Israel and exhorts, "Depart, depart, go out from there, / Touch nothing unclean; / Go out of the midst of her, purify yourselves, / You who carry the vessels of the Lord." Isaiah looks ahead, not only to the captivity of Israel, but also to the release of the people from Babylon. "Having proclaimed the Gospel ['Your God reigns' (Verse 7)], Isaiah now commands the people to believe and to manifest their trust in departing from Babylon."[13]

---

13. Edward J. Young, *The Book of Isaiah* (Grand Rapids: Eerdmans, 1981), 3:332.

The people must leave the idolatry and false worship of Babylon and come out of that pagan land. The "vessels of the Lord" are the "vessels of the Sanctuary which were taken to Babylon when the Temple was destroyed and brought back (cf. Ezra 7:1ff) by the returning exiles."[14] Those who carry these vessels "must undergo the legal requirements of purification."[15] The reason for departing from Babylon is to return to Jerusalem, rebuild the temple, and reinstitute the Biblical worship of God (Ezra 1:3, 5). As E. J. Young says, "Calvin suggests that the address is basically to the priests and Levites who officiate in the divine services, and that they stand by way of eminence for the whole people."[16] Young continues, "This may be correct; it is certainly the people in the aspect of worshiping God officially that is in view here."[17]

On what basis does God call Israel out of Babylon to return to Jerusalem and reestablish true Biblical worship? We find the answer in Leviticus 26:43-45:

> They rejected My ordinances and their soul abhorred My statutes. Yet in spite of this, when they are in the land of their enemies, I will not reject them, nor will I so abhor them as to destroy them, breaking My covenant with them; for I am the Lord their God. But I will remember for them the covenant with their ancestors, whom I brought out of the land of Egypt in the sight of the nations, that I might be their God. I am the Lord.

Thus, Isaiah 52:11 advances the themes of redemption, covenant, and worship. Isaiah 52:11 is a worship text reinforcing covenant renewal. From a contemporary and personal perspective, we too must separate ourselves from the influences of the world in both our thinking and conduct. And we must align ourselves with God's church, the covenant and worshiping community of Jesus Christ.

---

14. I. W. Slotki, *Isaiah* (New York: Soncino, 1983), 259-260.
15. Carl Wilhelm Eduard Nägelsbach, *The Prophet Isaiah*, trans. Samuel Lowrie and Dunlop Moore (Grand Rapids: Zondervan, 1960), 565.
16. Young, *The Book of Isaiah*, 3:333.
17. Ibid.

Paul next alludes to Ezekiel 20:34 and 2 Samuel 7:14 in writing to the Corinthians. "And I will welcome you. And I will be a father to you, And you shall be sons and daughters to Me, Says the Lord Almighty" (2 Cor. 6:17-18). The first Old Testament text Paul has in mind is Ezekiel 20:34, God's promise to the exiles in Babylon. "I will bring you out from the peoples and gather you from the lands where you are scattered, with a mighty hand and with an outstretched arm and with wrath poured out." The Septuagint version of this verse reads, "And I will lead you out from the peoples *and I will welcome you* from the land" (italics added). In keeping with his theme of calling the church out of the world and to covenant worship before God, Paul applies this short clause, "And I will welcome you," to the church at Corinth. As the Corinthian Christians, with all their baggage of corruption and sin, separate themselves from the world and join themselves to God's church in worship, God promises to welcome them. Similarly, as we heed God's call to separate ourselves from the world and unite with His covenant and worshiping community, God promises to welcome us.

The second Old Testament text Paul has in mind is God's covenant promise to David in 2 Samuel 7. Here is God's word to David through Nathan the prophet:

> Thus says the Lord of hosts [*Lord Almighty* (LXX)] ... When your days are complete and you lie down with your fathers, I will raise up your descendant after you, who will come forth from you, and I will establish his kingdom. He shall build a house for My name, and I will establish the throne of his kingdom forever. *I will be a father to him and he will be a son to Me* ... Your house and your kingdom shall endure before Me forever; your throne shall be established forever (2 Sam. 7:8, 12-14, 16, italics added).

In 1 Chronicles 22:6-11, David applies this promise, *I will be a father to him and he will be a son to Me*, to his son Solomon. However, Hebrews 1:5 applies this promise to Christ. How do we resolve this seeming contradiction? Remember, we are talking about the corporate body assembled in worship. Paul is arguing that the church is God's temple. In the Old Testament, Solomon's temple was a "type and shadow" pointing to the "true reality [which] would appear in all perfection."[18] Calvin compares the reality with the type:

> But here is a kind of house which is far more perfect than the building which was on the mountain of Zion. It is a temple in which so many men and women who have been converted to the faith of the Gospel are like numerous stones which have been assembled so that God might dwell throughout all the earth, so that his name might be honored and worshiped by all, and so that everyone might offer him a free-will sacrifice.[19]

"Thus Paul applies a promise originally uttered for David's royal house—and through it for the whole chosen people—to the new people of God (to whom the Christians in Corinth belong)."[20] That is, Paul applies God's covenant promise to the Corinthian Christians: "I will be a father to you, and you shall be sons and daughters to me" (2 Cor. 6:18). Assembled as God's New Testament temple, God welcomes us into His presence. He also applies His word to us to confirm that He is our Father and we are indeed His children through Jesus Christ. Paul adds God's own guarantee, the opening words of the prophet Nathan to David, "Thus says the Lord of hosts" (2 Sam. 7:8). As shown above, the Septuagint renders the text, "Says the Lord Almighty." Here is our text, 2 Corinthians 6:14-16, once again:

> For we are the temple of the living God; just as God said, "I WILL DWELL IN THEM AND WALK AMONG THEM; AND I WILL BE THEIR GOD, AND THEY SHALL BE MY PEOPLE. Therefore, COME OUT FROM THEIR MIDST AND BE SEPARATE," says the Lord. "AND DO NOT TOUCH WHAT IS UNCLEAN; And I will welcome you.

---

18. John Calvin, *Sermons on 2 Samuel, Chapters 1-13*, trans. Douglas Kelly (Carlisle: Banner of Truth, 1992), 327.
19. Ibid., 328.
20. Beale and Carson, *Commentary on the New Testament Use of the Old Testament*, 771.

And I will be a father to you, And you shall be sons and daughters to Me," Says the Lord Almighty.

The application of Old Testament covenant worship texts to the New Testament church teaches that God's primary purpose in public worship is to communicate covenant grace. Public worship is a setting in which God condescends to meet with His people to express and affect His covenant with His people. Remember the Westminster Confession of Faith and the words of Geerhardus Vos:

> The distance between God and the creature is so great, that although reasonable creatures do owe obedience unto Him as their Creator, yet they could never have any fruition of Him as their blessedness and reward, but by some voluntary condescension on God's part, which He hath been pleased to express by way of covenant (Westminster Confession of Faith 7:1).
>
> The covenant is neither a hypothetical relationship, nor a conditional position; rather it is the fresh, living fellowship in which the power of grace is operative ... The covenant is the totality from which no benefit can be excluded.[21]

God calls His people out of the world and redeems them to form them into covenant, worshiping communities. God freely condescends and purposes to graciously apply all the benefits of His covenant to His people. This application of covenant benefits is God's purpose in worship. Worship in God's gathered church is God's special means for communicating His covenant grace. Understanding worship as God's communication of covenant grace is an important facet of the theology of worship.

There are therefore two sides to the dynamic of public worship. On one side, worship is a service of covenant renewal. God redeems

---

21. Geehardus Vos, "The Doctrine of the Covenant in Reformed Theology," *Redemptive History and Biblical Interpretation*, ed. Richard B. Gaffin (Phillipsburg: Presbyterian and Reformed, 1980), 256.

a people for Himself and forms them into covenant and worshiping communities. He pledges to meet with His assembled people to fulfill and apply His covenant promises to their lives both individually and corporately. On the other side, in public worship, believers respond to God with holy reverence and awe. They bow in their hearts before Him. They serve and honor Him as their Creator and Redeemer because He is worthy of all praise, honor, and glory.

THE CHURCH IS GOD'S SPECIAL DWELLING PLACE

The New Testament builds on the imagery of the Old Testament tabernacle and temple in its understanding of the church and worship. Further study of the tabernacle and the temple fills out our theology of the church and her God given purpose. In 2 Corinthians 6:16, Paul declares, "For we are the temple of the living God." This section of this study will confirm this truth. As God manifested His gracious presence in the temple, He now does so in the New Testament church. As a result, as the temple was an extension of heaven, the New Testament church now is. In public worship, pastors and elders have the privilege of leading men and women into the gracious heavenly presence of God. Finally, quotes from several theologians will validate this view of the church. God *graciously dwells* within His gathered church to renew His covenant with His people.

Scripture confirms the truth that the church is the New Testament temple of God. The basic text is 2 Corinthians 6:16, "For we are the temple of the living God." The corporate emphasis of this text and its context has already been discussed. Several other texts confirm this idea. Consider Ephesians 2:19-22:

> So then you are no longer strangers and aliens, but you are fellow citizens with the saints, and are of God's household, having been built on the foundation of the apostles and prophets, Christ Jesus Himself being the corner stone, in whom the whole building, being fitted together, is growing into a holy temple in the Lord, in

whom you also are being built together into a dwelling of God in the Spirit.

Paul encourages the Ephesian Christians, telling them that they have been brought out of the world. They have been incorporated into God's spiritual house, His temple. This temple is the church universal. Paul does not stop here. The local church in Ephesus is also a special dwelling place of God in the Spirit. God is building the Ephesian Christians into a special dwelling place. In like manner, God is building congregations today into His dwelling places in the Spirit.

Think about 1 Corinthians 3:9-17:

> For we are God's fellow workers; *you are* God's field, *God's building*. According to the grace of God which was given to me, like a wise master builder I laid a foundation, and another is building on it. But each man must be careful how he builds on it. For no man can lay a foundation other than the one which is laid, which is Jesus Christ. Now if any man builds on the foundation with gold, silver, precious stones, wood, hay, straw, each man's work will become evident; for the day will show it because it is to be revealed with fire, and the fire itself will test the quality of each man's work. If any man's work which he has built on it remains, he will receive a reward. If any man's work is burned up, he will suffer loss; but he himself will be saved, yet so as through fire. Do you not know that *you are a temple of God* and that the Spirit of God dwells in you? If any man destroys the temple of God, God will destroy him, *for the temple of God is holy, and that is what you are* (italics added).

The church at Corinth is likened to a building, a temple. Regarding this text, D. A. Carson observes, "God cares about his church, and he holds his leaders accountable for how they build it."[22]

---

22. D. A. Carson, *The Cross and Christian Ministry* (Grand Rapids: Baker, 2002), 75.

Peter also uses the Old Testament temple imagery to describe God's purpose for the Christians to whom he is writing. They are being built into a spiritual house, a temple, to offer spiritual sacrifices to the Lord. "And coming to Him as to a living stone which has been rejected by men, but is choice and precious in the sight of God, *you also, as living stones, are being built up as a spiritual house* for a holy priesthood, to offer up spiritual sacrifices acceptable to God through Jesus Christ" (1 Pet. 2:4-5, italics added).

An objection to this interpretation is that the Bible teaches that *our bodies* are temples of the Spirit. Paul notes that the individual bodies of Christians are temples of the Holy Spirit in 1 Corinthians 6:18-20. "The immoral man sins against his own body. Or do you not know that your body is a temple of the Holy Spirit who is in you, whom you have from God, and that you are not your own? For you have been bought with a price: therefore glorify God in your body." Clearly Paul has the individual in mind. However, Paul also applies temple imagery to the local church. "We are the temple of the living God" (2 Cor. 6:16).

A second objection is that Scripture designates Christ as the temple. John 2:18-21 connects Christ's resurrection body to the temple in Jerusalem in a debate Christ has with the Jews.

> The Jews then said to Him, "What sign do You show us as your authority for doing these things?" Jesus answered them, "Destroy this temple, and in three days I will raise it up." The Jews then said, "It took forty-six years to build this temple, and will You raise it up in three days?" But He was speaking of the temple of His body.

You see, the objection goes, Christ is the temple, not the church. Compare, however, another statement of the Apostle John, found in Revelation 13:6. "And he opened his mouth in blasphemies against God, to blaspheme His name and His tabernacle, that is, those who dwell in heaven." The body of believers who dwell in heaven compose God's tabernacle. Think about collective singular nouns in English. "A collective noun is the name of a group, class, or multitude, and not of a single person, place or thing ... The same noun may be abstract in one of its meanings, collective in another."[23] The word *seed* is a collective, singular noun. It may refer to one seed or a large bag of seed. Genesis 3:15 uses a collective, singular noun. "I will put enmity / Between you and the woman / And between your seed and her seed." Seed is a collective, singular noun. It may refer to an individual, Christ. It may also refer to the succeeding generations of the children of God and the children of the devil as we see them interact throughout the book of Genesis. The word *seed*, therefore, has what can be called a combined referent. The word *body*, when speaking of the body of Christ, is similar. *Body* may refer to the physical *body* of Christ (John 2:19-21). The body of Christ may also refer to the church (Eph. 4:11-12). The temple may therefore point to Christ. At the same time, the temple may point to the church. Paul properly says, "We are the temple of the living God."

The next step is to see that God manifests what we call His gracious presence in the Old Testament tabernacle, the temple, and later, within His church. Remember, God redeems Israel to form His people into a covenant and worshiping community. As a part of His covenant with Israel, God declares, "I will make My dwelling [*mishkani*] among you" (Lev. 26:11). Originally, God's special dwelling place was the tabernacle. God commanded Moses, "Let them construct a sanctuary for Me, that I may dwell [*shachanti*] among them" (Exod. 25:8). He then adds, "According to all that I am going to show you, as the pattern of the tabernacle [*mishkan*] and the pattern of all its furniture, just so you shall construct it" (Exod. 25:9).

The Hebrew root for both *dwell* and *tabernacle* is the verb *shachan*. Sound it out, "*shachan*." Do you hear another familiar term? It is *Shekinah*. The term *Shekinah* is not in the Bible, but the reality is. "Then the

---

23. George Lyman Kittredge and Frank Edgar Farley, *Advanced English Grammar* (New York: Ginn and Company, 1913), 29.

cloud covered the tent of meeting, and the glory of the Lord filled the tabernacle. Moses was not able to enter the tent of meeting because the cloud had settled on it, and the glory of the Lord filled the tabernacle" (Exod. 40:34-35). The *Shekinah* Glory is the tabernacled glory of God. Although God is essentially present everywhere, He displays or manifests Himself in this glory cloud in the tabernacle. The *Shekinah* Glory is God's special, gracious presence in His sanctuary.

Fast forward to the dedication of Solomon's temple. "In Solomon's day God manifested his *gracious presence* in the temple by a cloud, 1 Kings viii, 10."[24] The *Shekinah* Glory is God's gracious presence. Later, Ezekiel predicted the departure of God's glory from the temple. Westminster Divine, William Greenhill, comments on the prospect of God's glorious, gracious presence departing the temple as prophesied by Ezekiel:

> We may hold to the words, and understand thereby some visible sign of the *gracious presence* of God ... Because he was to pronounce sentence against this wicked, idolatrous, oppressing people, which he would not do in sancto sanctorum, or in the temple, which was the place of his *gracious presence*, and a type of Christ, and mercy by him ... The Lord's way of manifesting his *gracious presence* in his church, was by some notable sign or other. All those visible signs before mentioned were the glory of the Lord; so the Spirit is pleased to call the sign of God's *gracious presence* ... God's withdrawing the signs of his *gracious presence* from his church and people, is a forerunner of heavy judgments.[25]

To understand the distinction between the *essential* presence and the *gracious* presence of God, look at Psalm 139:7-8. "Where can I go from Your Spirit? / Or where can I flee from Your presence? / If I ascend to heaven, You are there; / If I make my bed in Sheol [hell

---

24. William Greenhill, *Exposition of Ezekiel* (Carlisle: Banner of Truth, 1994), 214. Italics added.
25. Ibid.

(KJV)], behold, You are there." Plumer comments: "Both in heaven and in hell is God's essential presence. In heaven they have his gracious presence. In hell they feel his wrathful presence."[26] God manifests the greatness of His love in heaven. He manifests Himself in frightful, awful wrath in hell. Since He is *essentially* present everywhere, God is pleased to manifest Himself differently at different times, in different places, and on different occasions.

Pentecost is a good example. God is omnipresent; He is essentially present everywhere. "It is correct then to say that on the Day of Pentecost the Holy Spirit 'came from heaven,' but it is erroneous to think of His coming as a moving from one place to another. Rather His coming means a special manifestation of His presence."[27]

A proper interpretation of 2 Thessalonians 1:9 depends on understanding the distinction between God's essential presence, gracious presence, and wrathful presence. Paul writes that unrepentant unbelievers "will pay the penalty of eternal destruction, away from the presence of the Lord and from the glory of His power" (2 Thess. 1:9). If God is present everywhere, including hell, what does "eternal destruction away from the presence of the Lord" mean? Here, the "presence of the Lord" refers to His gracious presence. Men and women will be eternally separated from His gracious presence, "from the manifestation of his power in the glorification of his saints."[28] These people will experience God's frown "which will be turned toward them in a threatening, penal, terrible manner; that mere look destroys them."[29]

A. A. Hodge sums up our discussion about God's presence:

> As to his self-manifestation, and the exercise of his power, his presence differs endlessly in different cases in degree and mode. Thus God is present to the church

---

26. William S. Plumer, *Psalms* (Carlisle: Banner of Truth, 1975), 1162.
27. James Oliver Buswell, *A Systematic Theology of the Christian Religion* (Grand Rapids: Zondervan, 1972), 1:116.
28. Henry Alford, *Alford's Greek Testament* (Grand Rapids: Guardian Press, 1976), 3:286.
29. C. A. Auberlen and C. J. Riggenbach, *The Two Epistles of Paul to the Thessalonians*, trans. John Lillie (Grand Rapids: Zondervan, 1960), 118.

as he is not to the world. Thus he is present in hell in the manifestation and execution of righteous wrath, while he is present in heaven in the manifestation and communication of gracious love and glory.[30]

Since the temple is the place of God's gracious presence, and since the church is the New Testament temple of the living God, the church gathered for worship is a place of God's gracious presence. "For we are the temple of the living God; just as God said, 'I WILL DWELL IN THEM AND WALK AMONG THEM; AND I WILL BE THEIR GOD, AND THEY SHALL BE MY PEOPLE'" (2 Cor. 6:16).

As a result, the Old Testament temple was, and the New Testament church is, an extension of heaven. The writer to the Hebrews teaches that believers are connected to heaven when they gather for worship.

> But you have come to Mount Zion and to the city of the living God, the heavenly Jerusalem, and to myriads of angels, to the general assembly and church of the firstborn who are enrolled in heaven, and to God, the Judge of all, and to the spirits of the righteous made perfect, and to Jesus, the mediator of a new covenant, and to the sprinkled blood, which speaks better than the blood of Abel (Heb. 12:22-24).

As the church of the firstborn enrolled in heaven, believers are heirs of God and joint heirs with Christ. They are connected to the church triumphant already in heaven. They are united to Christ who is their great high priest in heaven and who is King and Lord of all.

In addition, Paul uses ambassadorial language concerning the church and the ministry. He declares of Christians living in this world, "Our citizenship is in heaven, from which also we eagerly wait for a Savior, the Lord Jesus Christ" (Phil. 3:20). Heaven is our home. We are not citizens of this world. We are on an official mission representing our King. Our churches are like embassies. Paul develops this compar-

---

30. A. A. Hodge, *Outlines of Theology for Students and Laymen* (Grand Rapids: Zondervan, 1976), 141.

ison in Ephesians 6:20: "I am an ambassador in chains." Dispatched by King Jesus, he carries the message of His Sovereign. Paul includes his fellow laborers in this high calling. "Therefore, we are ambassadors for Christ, as though God were making an appeal through us; we beg you on behalf of Christ, be reconciled to God" (2 Cor. 5:20).

There are two main definitions of an *embassy*. First, an embassy is "a person or group sent on an official mission to a foreign government."[31] Second, an embassy is "the official residence or offices of an ambassador [the head of the mission] in a foreign land."[32] The building or property assumes the name of the people who occupy it. The same is true with the church, since a building takes on the designation for the people who worship in it. To draw out the comparison, the property in which the embassy lives and works belongs to the nation the embassy represents. When American citizens repair to an American embassy in a foreign land, they stand in America. Believers gathered for worship as Christ's body and church are an embassy of heaven. God is committed to graciously dwell in and with His embassy to apply His covenant, the laws of His heavenly land, to the lives of His people living in hostile territory.

That believers are citizens of heaven and form embassies of heaven makes the church gathered for worship an entrance into and a taste of heaven. The writer to the Hebrews describes the experience of those who become part of the worshiping body of believers: they "have once been enlightened and have tasted of the heavenly gift and have been made partakers of the Holy Spirit, and have tasted the good word of God and the powers of the age to come" (Heb. 6:4-5). Worshipers receive several benefits.[33] They receive real light from and partake of the Holy Spirit. They taste the Word of God. They taste heaven. They taste the powers of the age to come. The worshiping

---

31. *Webster's New World Dictionary of the English Language* (New York: World Publishing, 1951), 473.
32. Ibid.
33. Amazingly, that worshipers may receive the benefits mentioned is true even though they may later repudiate Christ's church, walk away from her, and blaspheme the Spirit by calling His work in the bosom of the Church the work of the devil (Heb. 6:6 with 1 John 5:16-17 and Matt. 12:22-32).

assembly is an embassy of heaven. It is an outpost of heaven. Yes, the church gathered for worship is an entrance into and a taste of heaven.

This leads to an important question: Where do we anticipate our most profound encounters with God? Our individualistic culture presses for the answer, "In my prayer closet as I read my Bible and engage in private prayer." In recent decades, evangelistic meetings have been designed to usher individuals into the hands of counselors where they may experience a more personal and profound encounter with Christ. Compare the scene in heaven.

> Then I looked, and I heard the voice of many angels around the throne and the living creatures and the elders; and the number of them was myriads of myriads, and thousands of thousands, saying with a loud voice, "Worthy is the Lamb that was slain to receive power and riches and wisdom and might and honor and glory and blessing." And every created thing which is in heaven and on the earth and under the earth and on the sea, and all things in them, I heard saying, "To Him who sits on the throne, and to the Lamb, be blessing and honor and glory and dominion forever and ever" (Rev. 5:11-13).

This scene is anything but private and individual. Participation in this heavenly, corporate setting will be the most profound and deeply-held encounter with God and with Christ imaginable. This idea of corporate encounter with Christ carries over to the local church in Corinth. "But if all prophesy, and an unbeliever or an ungifted man enters, he is convicted by all, he is called to account by all; the secrets of his heart are disclosed; and so he will fall on his face and worship God, declaring that God is certainly among you" (1 Cor. 14:24-25). The church gathered for worship is an entrance into and a taste of heaven.

Finally, in public worship, pastors and elders have the privilege of leading men and women into the gracious presence of God. For example, Psalm 95:1-2 is often used as a call to worship, "O come, let us sing for joy to the Lord, / Let us shout joyfully to the rock of our salvation. / Let us come before His presence with thanksgiving, / Let us shout joyfully to Him with psalms." God calls His people into His presence to sing and to give thanks to Him. The church is the New Testament temple of God where He commits Himself to graciously dwell, to meet with His people, to renew His covenant with them, and to apply His covenant to them. God calls His people into His gracious presence to worship Him, not metaphorically nor symbolically, but really. In response, join in David's cry,

> How lovely are Your dwelling places, O Lord of hosts! / My soul longed and even yearned for the courts of the Lord; / My heart and my flesh sing for joy to the living God. / The bird also has found a house, / And the swallow a nest for herself, where she may lay her young, / Even Your altars, O Lord of hosts, / My King and my God (Ps. 84:1-3).

Psalm 100:1-4 is another call to worship. What is the basic point of Psalm 100? Worship the Lord because He is your creator and redeemer. We are enjoined to come before the Lord. Who is the Lord? From the New Testament perspective, Jesus is Lord (Rom. 10:9-13). He is the Divine being in human form. He is God. We worship Him.

> Shout joyfully to the Lord, all the earth. / Serve the Lord with gladness; / Come before Him with joyful singing. / Know that the Lord Himself is God; / It is He who has made us, and not we ourselves; / We are His people and the sheep of His pasture. / Enter His gates with thanksgiving / And His courts with praise. / Give thanks to Him, bless His name. / For the Lord is good; / His lovingkindness is everlasting / And His faithfulness to all generations.

Understand the Old Testament imagery and apply God's call to worship in the church today. Answer the summons to worship Him and to worship His Son, Jesus Christ.

With a similar understanding, the invitation of Matthew 11:28-30 may be a call to worship. "Come to Me, all who are weary and heavy-laden, and I will give you rest. Take My yoke upon you and learn from Me, for I am gentle and humble in heart, and YOU WILL FIND REST FOR YOUR SOULS. For My yoke is easy and My burden is light." Respond to this invitation and enter into God's presence with thanksgiving. In the same light, what does James 4:8 mean in the context of worship? "Draw near to God and He will draw near to you." God commits himself to graciously meet with His people in worship and to graciously draw near to them. The church of Jesus Christ gathered for worship is no ordinary meeting. It is a special place to draw near to God.

D. A. Carson objects to the idea of the special presence of God and leading people into the presence of God.

> It is not uncommon to hold that "worship leads us into the presence of God"... or the like. There is a way of reading those statements sympathetically ... but taken at face value they are simply untrue ... I doubt that it is helpful to speak of such matters in terms of worship "leading us into the presence of God": not only is the term *worship* bearing too narrow a meaning to be useful, but the statement is in danger of conveying some profoundly untrue notions.[34]

In taking this position, Carson runs counter to the Biblical witness, and to many other theologians as the following quotations display.

> The outward provision of the visible church of Christ is mysteriously impregnated with Divine grace. The church itself is, in an especial and supernatural man-

---

34. D. A. Carson, *Worship by the Book* (Grand Rapids: Zondervan, 2002), 50-51. Carson's accent in worship seems to be on the transition away from the Old Testament "cultus" to individuals in the New Testament. "The language of worship, so bound up with the temple and the priestly system under the old covenant, has been radically transformed by what Christ has done. We see the change in a well-known passage like Romans 12:1-2. To offer our bodies as 'living sacrifices, holy and pleasing to God' is our 'spiritual act of worship'" (37). Carson then links Romans 12:1-2 with John 4:24. He also seems to contradict himself, "So there is a narrower sense of worship, it appears; and this narrower sense is bound up with corporate worship, with what the assembled church does in the pages of the New Testament" (49). And, "We long to meet, corporately, with the living and majestic God and offer Him the praise that is due" (59).

ner, the residence of the Holy Spirit; and in the right and faithful use of the ordinances the spirit of man meets the Spirit of God, and finds a blessing beyond the reach of ordinances (James Bannerman).[35]

Good men have not only the essential presence, which is common to all, but his gracious presence; not only the presence that flows from his nature, but that which flows from his promise; his essential presence makes no difference between this and that man ... His nature is the cause of the presence of his essence; his will, engaged by his truth, is the cause of the presence of his grace (Stephen Charnock).[36]

The gospel church is called *mount Zion, the heavenly Jerusalem, which is free*, in opposition to mount Sinai, which tendeth to bondage, Gal. 4:24. This was the hill on which God set his king the Messiah. Now, in coming to mount Zion, believers come into heavenly places, and into a heavenly society.

1. Into heavenly places. (1.) *Unto the city of the living God.* God has taken up his gracious residence in the gospel church, which on that account is an emblem of heaven. There his people may find him ruling, guiding, sanctifying, and comforting them; there he speaks to them by the gospel ministry; there they speak to him by prayer, and he hears them; there he trains them up for heaven, and gives them the earnest of their inheritance. (2.) To the heavenly Jerusalem as born and bred there, as free denizens there. Here believers have clearer views of heaven, plainer evidences for heaven, and a greater meetness and more heavenly temper of soul.

---

35. James Bannerman, *The Church of Christ* (Carlisle, PA: The Banner of Truth Trust, 1960), 1:89.
36. Stephen Charnock, *The Existence and Attributes of God* (Minneapolis: Klock and Klock, 1977), 176.

2. To a heavenly society. (1.) *To an innumerable company of angels,* who are of the same family with the saints, under the same head, and in a great measure employed in the same work, ministering to believers for their good, keeping them in all their ways, and pitching their tents about them. These for number are innumerable, and for order and union are a company, and a glorious one. And those who by faith are joined to the gospel church are joined to the angels, and shall at length be like them, and equal with them. (2.) *To the general assembly and church of the first-born, that are written in heaven* (Matthew Henry).[37]

When God's people assemble for worship they enter into the places where God dwells. God meets them, and they meet God. They find themselves face to face with none other than God himself. Their worship is an intimate transaction between them and their God. If the church were fully conscious of that truth, what dignity and reverence would characterize its worship (R. B. Kuiper)![38]

Worship is not only an expression of gratitude, but also a means of grace whereby the hungry are fed, so that the empty are sent away rich. For 'there is in worship an approach of God to man.' 'God's presence in his ordinances' is a reality; God is essentially present in the world, graciously present in his church (J. I. Packer).[39]

"Worship is *special* ... The distinction between general service and specific worship can be illustrated by the fact of God's special presence" (Frank J. Smith).[40]

God is far off from the wicked (as to the special presence

---

37. Matthew Henry, *Matthew Henry's Commentary on the Whole Bible* (Grand Rapids: Fleming H. Revell, 1985), 6:959.
38. R. B. Kuiper, *The Glorious Body of Christ* (Carlisle: Banner of Truth, 1967), 347.
39. J. I. Packer, *A Quest for Godliness: The Puritan Vision of the Christian Life* (Wheaton: Crossway, 1990), 252.
40. Frank J. Smith, *Worship in the Presence of God*, ed. Frank J. Smith and David Lachman (Greenville, SC: Greenville Seminary Press, 1992), 12.

of his favor and grace), but is always present with them by his general presence of essence. Where God is, there indeed is his grace originally and subjectively, but not always effectively because its exercise is perfectly free ... Although he is differently in heaven and in hell (here by grace, there by justice; here as blessing, there as punishing), yet he can be in both places as to the immensity of his essence (Francis Turretin).[41]

    The gathered church is God's temple. It is the place of His special dwelling. It is an embassy and outpost of heaven. There, believers have the privilege of drawing near to Him. As they gather in sacred assembly, God commits Himself to draw near to them to confirm and renew His covenant with them. There He reaffirms that He is their God and that they are His people.

---

41. Francis Turretin, *Institutes of Elenctic Theology*, trans. George Musgrave Giger, ed. James T. Dennison (Phillipsburg: Presbyterian and Reformed, 1992), 1:200.

3

What Is the Sabbath?

*So there remains a Sabbath rest for
the people of God.* ~ Heb. 4:9

Here is a refined summary of chapters 1 and 2. The first question was: *What is worship?* Worship is a service of covenant renewal in which God, who redeems a people for Himself and forms them into covenant and worshiping communities, pledges to graciously meet with His assembled people to fulfill and apply His covenant promises in their lives individually and corporately.

Worship is the proper human response to the worthiness of God. In worship, God's people ascribe honor, glory, and majesty to Him, fear and reverence Him, bow before Him in body and heart, and seek to serve Him. Worship is the creature's act of giving honor and glory to God through Jesus Christ, the Son, by the power of the Holy Spirit because the Triune God is worthy of such praise, honor, and glory.

The second question was: *What is the church?* The church, the assembly of God's people, is a special dwelling place of God, the New Testament counterpart to the Old Testament tabernacle and temple. In that assembly, God's people anticipate meeting the special, gracious presence of God, who draws near to them to fulfill His covenant promises among them and in them.

The assembly of God's people gathered for worship is the principal place of public worship. It is in public worship where God's people corporately meet with God to honor Him openly. God promises to graciously meet with them, fulfill his covenant promises to them, give them a taste of heaven, and make them embassies of heaven in this world.

A third question now beckons: *What is the Sabbath? The Christian Sabbath is a means of grace giving us a taste of the rest we will experience in heaven.* This short answer will be fleshed out by exploring some basics, noting the connection of the Sabbath and worship, considering Sabbath rest, and investigating the change of the day.

SOME SABBATH BASICS

The Sabbath is a creation ordinance and therefore perpetual. Genesis 2:1-3 shows us that the Sabbath is part of God's created order. "Thus the heavens and the earth were completed, and all their hosts. By the seventh day God completed His work which He had done, and He rested on the seventh day from all His work which He had done. Then God blessed the seventh day and sanctified it." Sabbath rest originates in creation not in the Ten Commandments. The Sabbath is a creation ordinance. Moses confirms this truth in Exodus 16:26 and 29, when God gives directions concerning the collection of manna in the wilderness. "Six days you shall gather it, but on the seventh day, the Sabbath, there will be none … See, the Lord has given you the Sabbath; therefore He gives you bread for two days on the sixth day. Remain every man in his place; let no man go out of his place on the seventh day." Israel must observe the Sabbath in the wilderness *before* the giving of the Ten Commandments.

In the same way, marriage and work are creation ordinances.

> God created man in His own image, in the image of God He created him; male and female He created them. God blessed them; and God said to them, Be fruitful and multiply, and fill the earth, and subdue it; and rule over the

fish of the sea and over the birds of the sky and over every living thing that moves on the earth (Gen. 1:27-28).

God gave Adam and Eve to each other in marriage, and He gave them the work of building a Godly culture and society in His world. Marriage, work, and the Sabbath are integral to creation. As creation ordinances, they are in force as long as this present creation continues to exist. They are perpetual.

As a creation ordinance that is perpetual, the Sabbath recalls both creation and redemption.

> Remember the Sabbath day, to keep it holy. Six days you shall labor and do all your work, but the seventh day is a Sabbath of the Lord your God; in it you shall not do any work, you or your son or your daughter, your male or your female servant or your cattle or your sojourner who stays with you. *For in six days the Lord made the heavens and the earth, the sea and all that is in them,* and rested on the seventh day; therefore the Lord blessed the Sabbath day and made it holy (Exod. 20:8-11, italics added).

God sanctifies the Sabbath day; He sets it apart from the rest. "He consecrated it as a day of holy rest and worship; as a season set apart for the devout contemplation of the Creator's works ... "[1] It is a special day of reflection.[2]

> Observe the Sabbath day to keep it holy, as the Lord your God commanded you. Six days you shall labor and do all your work, but the seventh day is a Sabbath of the Lord your God; in it you shall not do any work, you or your son or your daughter or your male servant or your female servant or your ox or your donkey or any of your cattle or your sojourner who stays with you, so that your male servant and your female servant may rest as well

---

1. George Bush, *Notes on Genesis* (Minneapolis: James Family, 1979), 1:47.
2. John Calvin, *Sermons on Genesis 1-11*, trans. Rob Roy McGregor (Carlisle: Banner of Truth, 2009), 126-129.

as you. *You shall remember that you were a slave in the land of Egypt, and the Lord your God brought you out of there by a mighty hand and by an outstretched arm*; therefore the Lord your God commanded you to observe the Sabbath day (Deut. 5:12-15, italics added).

The day ought to be used as a time to reflect not only on God's greatness in creation but also God's goodness in redemption. Deuteronomy renews the covenant at the end of Israel's 40-year journey in the wilderness. The setting apart of the Sabbath "corresponds significantly to the national character of Israel ... The sanctification of the Sabbath is indeed a national confession.[3] In what specific sense? "To the reason for the institution on the part of God [His recognition as Creator] there is added now a special reason for its observance on the part of the people, who therein confess that they are redeemed, and thus distinguished above the nations ... "[4]

Bear in mind these two referents. The purpose of the Christian Sabbath is to remember both creation and redemption, and to reflect upon the Creator and Redeemer.

Since the Sabbath points to our creation and redemption, the Sabbath is also covenantal. As already seen, Exodus presents God redeeming His people and forming them into a *covenant* community and a worshiping community at Sinai. In Deuteronomy, we have the "covenant between God and Israel made at Sinai and renewed on the plains of Moab before Moses' death ... "[5]

The Ten Commandments are integral to God's covenant. "So He declared to you His covenant which He commanded you to perform, that is, the Ten Commandments; and He wrote them on two tablets of stone" (Deut. 4:13). "There is a partial identification here of the covenant and the ten words. The covenant is, however, wider than

---

3. Wilhelm Julius Schroeder, *Deuteronomy*, trans. A. Gosman (Grand Rapids: Zondervan, 1960), 89.
4. Ibid., 89-90.
5. Tremper Longman III and Raymond B. Dillard, *An Introduction to the Old Testament* (Grand Rapids: Zondervan, 2006), 114.

the covenant stipulations."[6] That the Ten Commandments are part of God's covenant is an example of synecdoche, the part for the whole. The Fourth Commandment is a part of the Ten Commandments, which represent the totality of the God's covenant with His people. The celebration of the Sabbath was, therefore, a covenantal responsibility, as Moses makes clear. "So the sons of Israel shall observe the Sabbath, to celebrate the Sabbath throughout their generations as a perpetual covenant" (Exod. 31:16). As will be seen, Sabbath observance remains a covenantal responsibility in the New Testament era.

At the same time, the Sabbath is a sign. Circumcision was also a sign and a covenant. God charged Abraham, "Now as for you, you shall keep My covenant, you and your descendants after you throughout their generations. This is My covenant, which you shall keep, between Me and you and your descendants after you: every male among you shall be circumcised" (Gen. 17:9-10). Circumcision is not a separate covenant; it is the sign of the covenant. "You shall be circumcised in the flesh of your foreskin, and *it shall be the sign of the covenant between Me and you*" (Gen. 17:11, italics added). In verse 10, the sign, circumcision, is put in the place of the thing signified, the covenant, which is an example of metonymy, the sign put in the place of the thing signified.

In a similar way, the Sabbath is a sign. "The Lord spoke to Moses, saying, 'But as for you, speak to the sons of Israel, saying, "You shall surely observe My sabbaths; for this is a sign between Me and you throughout your generations, that you may know that I am the Lord who sanctifies you"'" (Exod. 31:12-13).

> The institution of the weekly Sabbath as a *sanctified* season, was an expressive indication of the character of the covenant which was to subsist between God and Israel. They were continually reminded by it that they were

---

6. J. A. Thompson, *Deuteronomy* (London: Inter-Varsity, 1974), 105.

to be a *sanctified* people, chosen, separated, and distinguished from the rest of the world ... [7]

In the observance of the Sabbath, God's people set themselves apart from their regular daily activities just as God set apart the Sabbath day from the other days of the week. Sabbath observance signifies God setting apart His people for His purposes to enjoy His rest. The Sabbath therefore signifies sanctification. More particularly, Sabbath worship, as the focal point of sanctification, signifies separateness from the world. From this perspective, Sabbath observance and Sabbath worship are a testimony to a watching world.

Furthermore, in the proper use of this sign, there is a strong element of assurance. "You shall surely observe My Sabbaths; for this is a sign between Me and you throughout your generations, *that you may know that I am the Lord who sanctifies you*" (Exod. 31:13, italics added). Observe the Sabbath. Why? "That you may know that I am the Lord who sanctifies you." God, it appears, commits himself to use this day to assure His people that He is indeed the Lord who sets them apart for His purposes and "that He who began a good work in you will perfect it until the day of Christ Jesus" (Phil. 1:6). "If God by his grace incline our hearts to keep the law of the fourth commandment, it will be an evidence of a good work wrought in us by his Spirit. If we sanctify God's day, it is a sign between him and us that he has sanctified our hearts ... "[8]

As God says through Ezekiel, "I gave them My Sabbaths to be a sign between Me and them, that they might know that I am the Lord who sanctifies them." And again, "Sanctify My Sabbaths; and they shall be a sign between Me and you, that you may know that I am the Lord your God" (Ezek. 20:12, 20). "Sabbaths, if duly sanctified, are the means of our sanctification; if we do the duty of the day, we shall find, to our comfort, it is the Lord that sanctifies us, makes us

---

7. George Bush, *Commentary on Exodus* (Grand Rapids: Kregel, 1993), 504.
8. Matthew Henry, *Matthew Henry's Commentary on the Whole Bible* (Grand Rapids: Fleming H. Revell, 1985), 1:405.

holy (that is, truly happy) here, and prepares us to be happy (that is, perfectly holy) hereafter."[9]

THE SABBATH AND WORSHIP

The Sabbath means worship. Leviticus 23 lists the feast days, the special days of worship, on which God requires His people to meet. The first day God requires Israel to set apart for public worship is the weekly Sabbath. As will be seen later, this command is likely the origin of the synagogue.

> The Lord spoke again to Moses, saying, "Speak to the sons of Israel and say to them, 'The Lord's appointed times which you shall proclaim as holy convocations—My appointed times are these: For six days work may be done, but on the seventh day there is a Sabbath of complete rest, a holy convocation. You shall not do any work; it is a Sabbath to the Lord in all your dwellings'" (Lev. 23:1-3).

The Westminster Confession of Faith 21:7 applies this Scriptural principle.

> As it is the law of nature, that, in general, a due proportion of time be set apart for the worship of God; so, in His Word, by a positive, moral, and perpetual commandment binding all men in all ages, He hath particularly appointed one day in seven, for a Sabbath, to be kept holy unto Him: which, from the beginning of the world to the resurrection of Christ, was the last day of the week; and, from the resurrection of Christ, was changed into the first day of the week, which, in Scripture, is called the Lord's Day, and is to be continued to the end of the world, as the Christian Sabbath.

The Sabbath is for worship. God blesses the Sabbath as a sign. He

---

9. Ibid., 4:865-866.

promises to use the Sabbath to assure His people that they belong to Him and that He is the Lord who sanctifies them. God blesses the Sabbath and it is a blessing.

The Sabbath also means the cessation of work. "Remember the Sabbath day, to keep it holy. Six days you shall labor and do all your work, but the seventh day is a Sabbath of the Lord your God; in it you shall not do any work" (Exod. 20:8-10). In response, this question often comes first, "What may I do or not do on the Sabbath?" But to ask this question is to begin on the wrong foot. Why? Personal desires are immediately put first rather than considering God's will and His desires first. In this light, reflect on Isaiah 58:13-14.

> If because of the Sabbath, you turn your foot / From doing your own pleasure on My holy day, / And call the Sabbath a delight, the holy day of the Lord honorable, / And honor it, desisting from your own ways, / From seeking your own pleasure / And speaking your own word, / Then you will take delight in the Lord, / And I will make you ride on the heights of the earth; / And I will feed you with the heritage of Jacob your father, / For the mouth of the Lord has spoken.

God ordains the Sabbath as a day of rest and worship. Cessation from work opens the door to worship, to reflection on redemption, to delighting in God, and to needed covenant assurance.

Scripture also connects rest in the promised land with worship. On one hand, Israel must enter the land to find rest. See how Joshua charges the tribes on the east side of the Jordan (Josh. 1:12-15, italics added).

> To the Reubenites and to the Gadites and to the half-tribe of Manasseh, Joshua said, "Remember the word which Moses the servant of the Lord commanded you, saying, '*The Lord your God gives you rest and will give you this land.*' Your wives, your little ones, and your cattle shall remain in the land which Moses gave you beyond the Jordan,

> but you shall cross before your brothers in battle array, all your valiant warriors, and shall help them, *until the Lord gives your brothers rest*, as He gives you, and they also possess the land which the Lord your God is giving them. Then you shall return to your own land, and possess that which Moses the servant of the Lord gave you beyond the Jordan toward the sunrise.

When Israel obtains their rest, Joshua sends the Reubenites, the Gadites, and the half-tribe of Manasseh back to their homes with these words, "And now *the Lord your God has given rest to your brothers*, as He spoke to them; therefore turn now and go to your tents, to the land of your possession, which Moses the servant of the Lord gave you beyond the Jordan" (Josh. 22:4, italics added). The land is Israel's rest.

On the other hand, God ties entering this rest, the rest of the land, with worship. Read Deuteronomy 12:10-11 and this connection becomes clear.

> When you cross the Jordan and live in the land which the Lord your God is giving you to inherit, and He gives you rest from all your enemies around you so that you live in security, then it shall come about that *the place in which the Lord your God will choose for His name to dwell, there you shall bring all that I command you: your burnt offerings and your sacrifices*, your tithes and the contribution of your hand, and all your choice votive offerings which you will vow to the Lord (italics added).

The Sabbath means rest and worship.

THE SABBATH AND HEAVENLY REST

The rest of the Sabbath day, and rest in the promised land, picture Sabbath rest in heaven. To grasp this connection, requires a review of an extended passage, Hebrews 3:1-4:11. The writer to the Hebrews compares Moses and Jesus, and also compares ancient Israel and the church. This comparison recognizes that Moses is a type of Christ. Moses was a servant in his house, Old Testament Israel. Christ is the Son over His house, the church. The writer to the Hebrews adds that believers are this church.

> Therefore, holy brethren, partakers of a heavenly calling, consider Jesus, the Apostle and High Priest of our confession; He was faithful to Him who appointed Him, as Moses also was in all His house. For He has been counted worthy of more glory than Moses, by just so much as the builder of the house has more honor than the house. For every house is built by someone, but the builder of all things is God. Now Moses was faithful in all His house as a servant, for a testimony of those things which were to be spoken later; but Christ was faithful as a Son over His house—whose house we are, if we hold fast our confidence and the boast of our hope firm until the end (Hebrews 3:1-6).

The Hebrews must hold fast to their confidence in Christ. They must not turn away from Christ and turn back to Judaism. "The prevailing view up to fairly recent times was that the epistle was directed to Hebrew Christians who were in danger of apostatizing."[10] This continues to be the case. "All agree that the book is written to Christians, who are urged to maintain their confession (e.g., 3:6, 14; 4:14; 10:23) … [A]postasy is only a whisker away."[11] The writer of Hebrews, therefore, refers his readers to Psalm 95, to remind them of Israel's apostasy in the wilderness (Heb. 3:7-11).

> Therefore, just as the Holy Spirit says, "TODAY IF YOU HEAR HIS VOICE, DO NOT HARDEN YOUR HEARTS AS WHEN THEY PROVOKED ME, AS IN THE DAY OF TRIAL IN THE WILDERNESS, WHERE YOUR FATHERS TRIED *Me* BY TESTING *Me*, AND SAW MY WORKS

---

10. Everett F. Harrison, *Introduction to the New Testament* (Grand Rapids: Eerdmans, 1964), 347.
11. D. A. Carson and Douglas J. Moo, *An Introduction to the New Testament* (Grand Rapids: Zondervan, 2005), 609, 612.

FOR FORTY YEARS. THEREFORE I WAS ANGRY WITH THIS GENERATION, AND SAID, 'THEY ALWAYS GO ASTRAY IN THEIR HEART, AND THEY DID NOT KNOW MY WAYS'; AS I SWORE IN MY WRATH, 'THEY SHALL NOT ENTER MY REST.'"

The author of Hebrews then applies the lesson of the wilderness. He compares the ancient generation in the wilderness not entering the rest of the promised land to the church which has the promise of the rest of heaven. Members of that past generation did not enter their rest because of unbelief. Members of the present generation may also fail to enter their rest because of unbelief. And so the writer to the Hebrews issues this warning: Do not step back away from Christ in unbelief.

> Take care, brethren, that there not be in any one of you an evil, unbelieving heart that falls away from the living God. But encourage one another day after day, as long as it is still called "Today," so that none of you will be hardened by the deceitfulness of sin. For we have become partakers of Christ, if we hold fast the beginning of our assurance firm until the end, while it is said, "TODAY IF YOU HEAR HIS VOICE, DO NOT HARDEN YOUR HEARTS AS WHEN THEY PROVOKED ME." For who provoked Him when they had heard? Indeed, did not all those who came out of Egypt led by Moses? And with whom was He angry for forty years? Was it not with those who sinned, whose bodies fell in the wilderness? And to whom did He swear that they would not enter His rest, but to those who were disobedient? So we see that they were not able to enter because of unbelief (Heb. 3:12-19).

Calvin interprets this text in the following way. "We see, then, that the land of Canaan was a rest, but one of shadow, beyond which believers ought to progress ... Christ does not stretch out His hand to lead us round by figures but to take us from this world and raise us to heaven."[12] Canaan points to heaven and God's ultimate rest. F. F. Bruce writes, "The meaning of that 'rest' was not exhausted by the earthly Canaan … the spiritual counterpart of the earthly Canaan is the goal of the people of God today."[13] Yet, this rest "is not simply to be identified with heaven … "[14] How so? "We who have believed enter that rest" (Heb. 4:3). We do so now. "Believers, because of firm faith, enter God's rest, which is a spiritual state of being in the presence of God."[15] As Calvin says, "The highest human good is therefore simply union with God."[16] In other words, we enter what Psalm 95:11 and Hebrews 3:11, 4:3, and 4:5 call "My rest" and Hebrews 3:18, 4:1, and 4:10 call "His rest." "In proof of this, the inspired writer carries his readers back to the creation of the world, and shows how, by the sanctification and blessing of the seventh day, it was from the first, man's calling and destination to share in God's rest."[17]

> Therefore, let us fear if, while a promise remains of entering His rest, any one of you may seem to have come short of it. For indeed we have had good news preached to us, just as they also; but the word they heard did not profit them, because it was not united by faith in those who heard. For we who have believed enter that rest, just as He has said, "As I swore in My wrath, 'They shall not enter my rest,' although His works were finished from the foundation of the world. For He has said somewhere concerning the seventh day: "And God rested on the seventh day from all His works"; and again in this passage, "They shall not enter my rest" (Heb. 4:1-5).

The writer to the Hebrews therefore shows us that the weekly Sabbath rest, and the rest of Canaan, foreshadow the rest of heaven. We

---

12. John Calvin, *The Epistle of Paul the Apostle to the Hebrews and The First and Second Epistles of St Peter*, trans. William B. Johnston, ed. David W. Torrance and Thomas F. Torrance (Grand Rapids: Eerdmans, 1970), 48.
13. F. F. Bruce, *The Epistle to the Hebrews* (Grand Rapids: Eerdmans, 1964), 72.
14. Patrick Fairbairn, *The Typology of Scripture* (Welwyn: Evangelical Press, 1975), 1:420.
15. Simon Kistemaker, *Exposition of the Epistle to the Hebrews* (Grand Rapids: Baker, 1984), 109.
16. Calvin, *Hebrews*, 48.
17. Fairbairn, *Typology*, 1:420.

have a foretaste of this rest now through faith in Jesus Christ, the Lord of the Sabbath (Heb. 4:1-2; 6:4-5). Therefore, the writer to the Hebrews declares, "So there remains a Sabbath rest for the people of God. For the one who has entered His rest has himself also rested from his works, as God did from His" (Heb. 4:9-10). "This rest which is reserved for the people of God is properly called a 'Sabbath rest' —a *sabbatismos* or 'Sabbath keeping'—because it is a participation in God's own rest."[18] The shadow, the Sabbath and Sabbath keeping, will give way to the reality. "When God completed His work of creation, He 'rested'; so his people, having completed their service on earth, will enter into His rest."[19]

"Therefore, right from the beginning, all history was moving toward the consummation—the state of living beyond the possibility of sin and death and sharing God's Sabbath rest with him forever."[20] The Sabbath, therefore, looks back, and also looks forward.

> The ordinary week is a microcosm of God's "time" just as the temple in Jerusalem was a microcosm of God's heavenly "place." Like the week, history has a beginning and an ending. The Sabbath is the weekly link to both past creation and future consummation. Thus, it keeps us anchored to the order that God established before the fall as creatures who share his image as well as stretch our necks forward, longing for our full entrance into the Sabbath day the Second Adam already enjoys with God. The Sabbath keeps us navigationally fixed to these two points—what is built into creation (Alpha) and what is still awaiting us in the future in the new creation (Omega). It gives us the tempo of belonging to the One *by* whom we exist and *for* whom our existence is directed.[21]

Sabbath rest is Sabbath keeping. To see that Sabbath rest is Sabbath

---

18. Bruce, *Hebrews*, 77.
19. Ibid.
20. Michael Horton, *A Better Way* (Grand Rapids: Baker, 2003), 195.
21. Ibid., 196.

keeping, take a closer look at the Biblical terminology. Consider Leviticus 26:34-35. "Then the land will enjoy its Sabbaths all the days of the desolation, while you are in your enemies' land; then the land will rest and enjoy its Sabbaths. All the days of its desolation it will observe the rest which it did not observe on your Sabbaths, while you were living on it."

Verse 34 uses a particular verb and reads, "The land will *enjoy its Sabbaths* [*sabbatiei*, (LXX)]." Verse 35 uses the same verb two additional times and then a related noun. "All the days of its desolation it will *observe the rest* [*sabbatiei* (LXX)] which it did not *observe* [*sabbatisen* (LXX)] on your sabbaths [*sabbatois* (LXX)]. Notice the translations. Enjoying Sabbath *is* observing rest and observing Sabbath.

Compare 2 Chronicles 36:20-21, which uses similar language.

> Those who had escaped from the sword he carried away to Babylon; and they were servants to him and to his sons until the rule of the kingdom of Persia, to fulfill the word of the Lord by the mouth of Jeremiah, until the land had enjoyed its sabbaths. All the days of its desolation it kept sabbath until seventy years were complete.

Verse 21 uses the same verb as Leviticus 26:34-35. "The land had *enjoyed its sabbaths* [*sabbatisen* (LXX)]." In an emphatic form, verse 21 then uses both the verb and the noun. "*It kept sabbath* [*esabbatisen sabbata* (LXX)]." Again, notice the translations. To enjoy the Sabbath *is* to keep the Sabbath.

Hebrews 4:9 uses a noun form of the same word. "So there remains a *Sabbath rest* [*sabbatismos*] for the people of God." From the use of the term in the Old Testament, Sabbath rest *is* Sabbath observance or Sabbath keeping. The text may therefore be translated, "There remains a Sabbath keeping for the people of God."[22] Reference has been made to the Septuagint, the Greek version of the Old Testament, because of the linguistic connection with the New Testament.

---

22. Joseph A. Pipa, *The Lord's Day* (Fearn: Christian Focus, 1997), 115-119 reviews the argument leading to the suggested translation.

Exodus 31:16 confirms this line of thought. "So the sons of Israel shall observe the sabbath, to celebrate the sabbath throughout their generations as a perpetual covenant." The Hebrew is quite clear. "Israel shall observe [*shamar, keep*] the Sabbath [*shabbat*], to celebrate [*'asah, do*] the Sabbath [*shabbat*]." Observing or keeping the Sabbath is celebrating the Sabbath. The definition of *sabbatismos* in *The Analytical Greek Lexicon* is, "to cease or rest from labor, and thus to keep Sabbath," and "a keeping of a Sabbath; a state of rest, a Sabbath-state, Heb. 4:9."[23] Sabbath rest *is* Sabbath keeping.

The Sabbath certainly does mean the cessation of work.

> Remember the Sabbath day, to keep it holy. Six days you shall labor and do all your work, but the seventh day is a Sabbath of the Lord your God; *in it you shall not do any work*, you or your son or your daughter, your male or your female servant or your cattle or your sojourner who stays with you. For in six days the Lord made the heavens and the earth, the sea and all that is in them, and rested on the seventh day; therefore the Lord blessed the Sabbath day and made it holy (Exod. 20:8-11, italics added).

Here is part of Calvin's comments on Exodus 20:8. (A few statements are emphasized with added italics.) Read what Calvin says with the following in mind: The Sabbath is a foretaste of heaven. Entrance into heaven is by grace through faith. Sabbath rest testifies to this truth by setting aside personal *work* to enjoy Sabbath *rest*. Thus God's people testify that they do not trust their own works to open the doors of heaven for them. Rather they trust God's grace.

> [I]t is not without good cause that God has appointed a special place to the Sabbath as well as to the other festivals; and although there is a connection between the observance of the Sabbath and the tabernacle with its

---

23. Harold K. Moulton, *The Analytical Greek Lexicon Revised* (Grand Rapids: Zondervan, 1977), 361.

sacrifices, and the priesthood itself, still it was advisedly done that the festivals should be separately appointed, that by their aid the people might be the more encouraged to maintain the unity of the faith and to preserve the harmony of the Church. *Meanwhile, the mutual connection between the sanctuary and the Sabbath is evident from what has been already said. God indeed would have it to be a notable symbol of distinction between the Jews and heathen nations.* Whence, too, the devil, in order to asperse pure and holy religion with infamy, has often traduced [blasphemed] the Jewish Sabbath through froward tongues. But the better to show what there is peculiar in this Commandment, and what is its difference from the First, we must remember the spiritual substance of the type; for not only did God prescribe certain days for the holding of assemblies, in which the people might give attention to sacrifices, prayers, and the celebration of His praise; but *He placed before their eyes as the perfection of sanctity that they should all cease from their works.* Surely God has no delight in idleness and sloth, and therefore there was no importance in the simple cessation of the labors of their hands and feet; nay, it would have been a childish superstition to rest with no other view than to occupy their repose in the service of God. *Wherefore, lest we should make any mistake in the meaning of this Commandment, it is well to remember its analogy and conformity with the thing it signifies; i.e., that the Jews might know that their lives could not be approved by God unless, by ceasing from their own works, they should divest themselves of their reason, counsels, and all the feelings and affections of the flesh.* For they were not forbidden without exception from the performance of every work, since they were required both to circumcise their children, and to bring the victims into the court, and to offer them in sacrifice on that day; but they were only called away from their own works, that, as if dead to themselves and to the world, they might wholly devote themselves to God. *Wherefore, since God declares elsewhere by Moses, and again by Ezekiel, that the Sabbath is a sign between Him and the Jews that He sanctifies them (Exodus 31:13; Ezekiel 20:12), we must see what is the sum of this sanctification, viz., the death of the flesh, when men deny themselves and renounce their earthly nature, so that they may be ruled and guided by the Spirit of God.*

Although this is sufficiently plain, still it will be worth while to confirm it by further statements. And first of all, that this was a ceremonial precept, Paul clearly teaches, calling it a shadow of these things, the body of which is only Christ (Colossians 2:17). But if the outward rest was nothing but a ceremony, the substance of which must be sought in Christ, it now remains to be considered how Christ actually exhibited what was then prefigured; and this the same Apostle declares, when he states that "our old man is crucified with Christ," and that we are buried with Him, that His resurrection may be to us newness of life (Romans 6:4). It is to be gathered without doubt from many passages, that the keeping of the Sabbath was a serious matter, since God inculcates no other commandment more frequently, nor more strictly requires obedience to any; and again, when He complains that He is despised, and that the Jews have fallen into extreme ungodliness, He simply says that His "Sabbaths are polluted," as if religion principally consisted in their observance (Jeremiah 17:24; Ezekiel 20:21; 22:8; 23:38). Moreover, if there had not been some peculiar excellency in the Sabbath, it might have appeared to be an act of atrocious injustice to command a man to be put to death for cutting wood upon it (Numbers 15:32). Wherefore it must be concluded that the substance of the Sabbath, which

Paul declares to be in Christ, must have been no ordinary good thing. Nor does its excellency require much eulogium [praise], since spiritual rest is nothing else than the truly desirable and blessed death of man, which contains in it the life of God, even as Paul glories that he is as it were dead, because Christ liveth in him (Galatians 2:20). The Apostle in the epistle to the Hebrews argues more subtilely, that true rest is brought to us by the Gospel, and that it is rejected by unbelievers, (Hebrews 4:3;) for although he mixes up some allegorical matter with it, he still retains the genuine reason of the Commandment, viz., *that we should rest from our works "even as God from His" (Hebrews 4:10)*. On this ground Isaiah, when he reproves the hypocrites for insisting only on the external ceremony of rest, accuses them of "finding their own pleasure" on the Sabbath (Isaiah 58:13); as much as to say, that *the legitimate use of the Sabbath must be supposed to be self-renunciation, since he is in fact accounted to cease from his works who is not led by his own will nor indulges his own wishes*, but who suffers himself to be directed by the Spirit of God. *And this emptying out of self must proceed so far that the Sabbath is violated even by good works*, so long as we regard them as our own; for rightly does Augustin remark in the last chapter of the 22d book, *De Civitate Dei* — "*For even our good works themselves, since they are understood to be rather His than ours, are thus imputed to us for the attaining of that Sabbath*, when we are still and see that He is God; for, if we attribute them to ourselves, they will be servile, whereas we are told as to the Sabbath, Thou shalt not do any servile work in it."[24]

To cease daily work and enter weekly Sabbath rest is to witness to the truth that salvation is by grace not by works. Sabbath rest is a tes-

---

[24]. John Calvin, *Commentaries on the Four Last Books of Moses Arranged in the Form of a Harmony*, trans. Charles William Bingham (Grand Rapids: Baker, 1979), 2:433-436.

timony to the truth that entrance into heaven is by grace through faith and not by works. Sabbath rest points to heavenly rest. The Seventh Day Sabbath *looked back* at creation and the Redemption from Egypt. It also foreshadowed the Last Days and the rest of God we now experience through Christ. The First Day Sabbath, while celebrating our arrival at the beginning of the Last Days through the resurrection of Jesus Christ, also *looks ahead* to the consummation and our eternal Sabbath rest.

THE CHANGE OF THE DAY

God abrogates or sets aside the Seventh Day Sabbath. Zacharius Ursinus discusses this change in his exposition of the Fourth Commandment.

> The Fourth Commandment consists of two parts—a *commandment and the reason of the commandment*. The commandment is, *Remember the Sabbath day to keep it holy; in it thou shalt do no manner of work, &c.* Of this, again, there are two parts—the *one* moral and perpetual, as that the Sabbath be kept holy; the *other* ceremonial and temporary, as that the seventh day be kept holy.

> That the first part is moral and perpetual, is evident from the end and the causes of the commandment, which are perpetual in their character. The *end* or design of the commandment is the maintenance of the public worship of God in the church ... [25]

On the moral and perpetual side, Ursinus lists several of God's objectives for the commandment. Among them are: "That he may be publicly praised and worshipped in the world ... That the church may be visible in the world, and be distinguished from the rest of mankind."[26] Remember Leviticus 26:3 and the connection of the Sab-

25. Zacharius Ursinus, *The Commentary on the Heidelberg Catechism* (Phillipsburg: Presbyterian and Reformed, 1985), 557.
26. Ibid.

bath with public worship. "You shall keep My Sabbaths and reverence My sanctuary; I am the Lord." Ursinus then distinguishes the ceremonial and temporary side of the commandment from the moral and perpetual. Note again the connection he makes between Sabbath and public worship. At the same time, recall that keeping Sabbath foreshadows entrance into heaven by grace and not by works.

> That the other part of the commandment is ceremonial, and not perpetual, is evident from the fact that the Sabbath of the seventh day was, in the promulgation of the law, instituted of God *for the observance of the Mosaic worship*, and given to the Jews as a sacrament or *type of the sanctification of the church by Messiah*, who was to come … Hence the Sabbath, in as far as it has respect to the seventh day, was, together with the other ceremonies and types, fulfilled and abolished by the coming of the Messiah.[27]

God abolished the *seventh day* Sabbath upon the coming of Christ, because it was ceremonial and typical. "It would seem, therefore, that the Lord through the seventh day has sketched for his people the coming perfection of his Sabbath in the Last Day, to make them aspire to this perfection by unceasing meditation upon the Sabbath throughout life."[28] This typical and ceremonial aspect of the Sabbath must pass away with the coming of Christ. So it is that Calvin interprets Colossians 2:16-17. "Therefore no one is to act as your judge in regard to food or drink or in respect to a festival or a new moon or a Sabbath day—things which are a mere shadow of what is to come; but the substance belongs to Christ."

> But there is no doubt that by the Lord Christ's coming the ceremonial part of this commandment was abolished. For he himself is the truth, with whose presence

---

27. Ibid., 557-558. Italics added.
28. John Calvin, *Institutes of the Christian Religion*, trans. Ford Lewis Battles, ed. John T. McNeill (Philadelphia: Westminster, 1960), 1:396.

all figures vanish; he is the body at whose appearance the shadows are left behind. He is, I say, the true fulfillment of the Sabbath ... For this reason the apostle elsewhere writes that the Sabbath [Col. 2:16] was "a shadow of what is to come; but the body is Christ" [Col. 2:17], that is, the very substance of truth, which Paul well explained in that passage ... Christians ought therefore to shun completely the superstitious observance of days.[29]

Paul sets aside the ceremonial aspects of the Sabbath in Colossians 2:16-17, not the Sabbath in its entirety. "What he had previously said of circumcision [Col. 2:11-12] he now extends to the discrimination of meats and days. For circumcision was the initiation [doorway] into the observance of the law, other things [ceremonies] then followed."[30] Unclean *foods* (Leviticus 11), sacrificial *drinks* (Leviticus 23), *festival days* (Leviticus 23), and *new moons* (Numbers 29:6) are all aspects of the ceremonial law. Paul adds "a Sabbath day" to this list of the ceremonial stipulations. "[T]he apostle discharges Christians from the observance of Sabbath-days, not in a false and improper sense, but in the very sense in which they were shadows of good things to come, placing them on a footing in this respect with distinctions of meat and drink."[31] Colossians 2:16-17 does not abrogate the moral and perpetual requirement of Sabbath rest (Gen. 2:2-3). "There remains a Sabbath keeping for the people of God" (Heb. 4:9).

God now appoints the First Day as the Christian Sabbath rest. Some argue that there is no positive command for this change. However, Hebrews 4:9 points in the direction of a perpetual and moral obligation to keep the Sabbath in our age: "There remains a Sabbath keeping for the people of God." Also, consider the Westminster Confession of Faith 1:6.

---

29. Ibid., 397.
30. John Calvin, *The Epistles of Paul the Apostle to the Galatians, Ephesians, Philippians and Colossians*, trans. T. H. L. Parker, ed. David W. Torrance and Thomas F. Torrance (Grand Rapids: Eerdmans, 1972), 316.
31. Fairbairn, *Typology*, 2:125.

> The whole counsel of God concerning all things necessary for His own glory, man's salvation, faith and life, is either expressly set down in Scripture, or *by good and necessary consequence may be deduced from Scripture*: unto which nothing at any time is to be added, whether by new revelations of the Spirit, or traditions of men (italics added).

What are the good and necessary consequences deduced from Scripture concerning the Sabbath? Consider the feast of first fruits, the beginning of the barley harvest, which is on the day after the Sabbath, the eighth day. It is an eighth day feast.

> Then the Lord spoke to Moses, saying, "Speak to the sons of Israel and say to them, 'When you enter the land which I am going to give to you and reap its harvest, then you shall bring in the sheaf of the first fruits of your harvest to the priest. He shall wave the sheaf before the Lord for you to be accepted; *on the day after the Sabbath the priest shall wave it*'" (Lev. 23:9-11, italics added).

Paul connects the waving the sheaf of barley before the Lord, the first fruits, with the resurrection of Christ on the first day of the week, the day after the Sabbath, the eighth day.

> But now Christ has been raised from the dead, the first fruits of those who are asleep. For since by a man came death, by a man also came the resurrection of the dead. For as in Adam all die, so also in Christ all will be made alive. But each in his own order: Christ the first fruits, after that those who are Christ's at His coming (1 Cor. 15:20-23).

As Matthew Henry therefore recognizes, "This sheaf of first-fruits was typical of our Lord Jesus, who has risen from the dead as *the first-fruits of those that slept*, 1 Cor. xv. 20."[32] John Lightfoot also develops this truth:

---

32. Henry, *Commentary on the Whole Bible*, 1:537.

> Although the resurrection of Christ, compared with *first-fruits* of any kind, has very good harmony with them, yet it more especially agrees with the offering of the *sheaf*, commonly called [omer], not only as the thing itself, but also as to the circumstances of the time. For, first, there was the Passover, and the day following was a sabbatic day; and on the day following that were *the first-fruits offered*. So "Christ our passover was sacrificed." The day following his crucifixion was the sabbath, and the day following that, He, *the first-fruits of them that slept*, rose again.[33]

The Law of Moses foreshadowed the resurrection of Christ in the feast of first fruits on the eighth day, which is the first day of the week. Scripture often mentions the eighth day. For example, compare John 20:1, 19, and 26. "Now *on the first day of the week* Mary Magdalene came early to the tomb, while it was still dark, and saw the stone already taken away from the tomb" (vs. 1, italics added). A week later, the risen Christ visits the disciples. Thomas was absent. "So when it was evening on that day, *the first day of the week*, and when the doors were shut where the disciples were, for fear of the Jews, Jesus came and stood in their midst and said to them, 'Peace be with you'" (vs. 19, italics added). After another week passes and Thomas is present, Jesus again appears to the assembled disciples. "*After eight days* His disciples were again inside, and Thomas with them. Jesus came, the doors having been shut, and stood in their midst and said, 'Peace be with you'" (vs. 26, italics added). It is not insignificant that John mentions the eighth day. A. T. Robertson interprets "After eight days" in this way: "That is the next Sunday evening, on the eighth day in reality just like 'after three days' and 'on the third day.'"[34]

Since the eighth day is the first day of the week, Christians began

---

33. John Lightfoot, *A Commentary on the New Testament from the Talmud and Hebraica* (Peabody, MA: Hendrickson, 2003), 4:269.
34. A. T. Robertson, *Word Pictures of the New Testament* (Nashville: Broadman, 1932), 5:315.

meeting for public worship on the first day of the week to commemorate their redemption in the resurrection of Christ, as the Fourth Commandment requires (Deut. 5:15). Acts 20:7 is an example, "On the first day of the week, when we were gathered together to break bread, Paul *began* talking to them, intending to leave the next day, and he prolonged his message until midnight." Another example is 1 Corinthians 16:2, "On the first day of every week each one of you is to put aside and save, as he may prosper, so that no collections be made when I come." The Sabbath even has a new name: the Lord's Day (Rev. 1:10).

SUMMARY

What is the Christian Sabbath? The Christian Sabbath, the first day of the week, is a covenant sign and means of grace wherein we worship and taste the *rest* of heaven, and whereby God assures us He is sanctifying us. Setting aside their regular labors, believers gather on the Christian Sabbath to testify that they have access to heaven by grace and not because of their own works. As the visible church or covenant assembly of God's people is the *place* of worship, the Christian Sabbath is the covenant *day* of worship. As God fulfills His covenant promises to His people in the context of corporate worship by His gracious presence, so He assures His people that He sanctifies them on the day of worship. If God's people desire to meet with God, they will approach the place of worship on the day of worship. Pastors and elders will also teach God's people to use this means of grace and cherish this institution.

4

WHO REGULATES HOW WE WORSHIP?

Let them construct a sanctuary for Me, that I may dwell among them. According to all that I am going to show you, as the pattern of the tabernacle and the pattern of all its furniture, just so you shall construct it. ~ EXOD. 25:8-9

WHERE WE ARE AND WHERE WE ARE GOING

SO FAR, THREE QUESTIONS have been considered: What is worship? What is the assembly of God's people gathered for worship? What is the Christian Sabbath? After a brief review, question four will be answered: Who regulates how we worship?

What is worship? Worship is a service of *covenant renewal* in which God, who redeems a people for Himself and forms them into covenant and worshiping communities, pledges to meet with His assembled people to apply His covenant promises in their lives individually and corporately.

True worship is the creature's act of giving honor and glory to God through Jesus Christ by the power of the Holy Spirit. The Triune God is worthy of such praise, honor, and glory. Worship is the human response to the divine worthiness of God ascribing honor, glory, and majesty to Him, reverencing and fearing Him, bowing before Him, and serving Him.

What is the assembly of God's people gathered for worship? The assembly of God's people, God's *covenant assembly*, is the special dwelling place of God, the New Testament counterpart to the tabernacle, and later the temple, in the Old Testament. In this assembly, God's people experience God's gracious presence, and He fulfills His covenant promises to His people. Through this assembly, God's people enter the precincts of heaven and taste the good things of the world to come. In the context of public corporate worship and meeting with God, His people publicly give Him the honor He is due.

What is the Christian Sabbath? The Christian Sabbath is a covenant sign and means of grace wherein the people of God worship Him, taste the rest of heaven, and are assured that God is sanctifying them. The Christian Sabbath is an institution His people should cherish.

As the assembly of God's people is the *place* of worship, the Sabbath is the *day* of worship. As God fulfills His covenant promises to His people in public worship by His gracious presence, He also assures His people He sanctifies them on the day of worship. If God's people desire to meet with Him, they avail themselves of the place of worship and the day of worship. They will use the means of grace.

These three questions and answers logically lead to the following question: *Who prescribes how we worship?* Given the above discussions, the proposed answer to this question is a simple syllogism.

> Major Premise: God prescribes how we enter heaven and His presence.
>
> Minor Premise: Worship is an entrance into God's presence and a taste of heaven.
>
> Conclusion: God prescribes how we worship Him.

VALIDATING THE SYLLOGISM

The Major Premise: God prescribes how we enter heaven and His presence. For those holding to the inerrancy of Scripture and the gospel of grace, the major premise is self-evident. God prescribes how we enter heaven; God prescribes how any person may enter His presence. Scripture is clear on this point; Jesus Christ is clear. There is one way into the presence of the Father. "I am the way, and the truth, and the life; no one comes to the Father but through Me" (John 14:6). Jesus Christ is the only way into heaven and into the Father's presence. "There is salvation in no one else; for there is no other name under heaven that has been given among men by which we must be saved" (Acts 4:12). Our Lord also acknowledges that this way is narrow. "Enter through the narrow gate; for the gate is wide and the way is broad that leads to destruction, and there are many who enter through it. For the gate is small and the way is narrow that leads to life, and there are few who find it" (Matt. 7:13-14). Biblical Christians do not complain that there is only one way to heaven and that this way is narrow. On this important matter, Bible believers do not complain that God is too narrow or that the Bible is too narrow. It is clear that God prescribes how we enter heaven.

In this light, consider Genesis 28:10-17.

> Then Jacob departed from Beersheba and went toward Haran. He came to a certain place and spent the night there, because the sun had set; and he took one of the stones of the place and put it under his head, and lay down in that place. He had a dream, and behold, a ladder was set on the earth with its top reaching to heaven; and behold, the angels of God were ascending and descending on it. And behold, the Lord stood above it and said, "I am the Lord, the God of your father Abraham and the God of Isaac; the land on which you lie, I will give it to you and to your descendants. Your descendants will also be like the dust of the earth, and you will spread out to the west and to the east and to the north and to the south; and in you and in your descendants shall all the families of the earth be blessed. Behold, I am with you and will keep you wherever you go, and will bring you back to this land; for I will not leave you until I have done what I have promised you." Then Jacob

awoke from his sleep and said, "Surely the Lord is in this place, and I did not know it." He was afraid and said, "How awesome is this place! This is none other than the house of God, and this is the gate of heaven."

Note two things. First, the ladder is Christ. Here is Calvin's interpretation of the text. He refers to John 1:51. "Truly, truly, I say to you, you will see the heavens opened and the angels of God ascending and descending on the Son of Man."

> It is Christ alone, therefore, who connects heaven and earth: he is the only Mediator who reaches from heaven down to earth: he is the medium through which the fullness of all celestial blessings flows down to us, and through which we, in turn, ascend to God. He it is who, being the head over angels, causes them to minister to his earthly members. Therefore, (as we read in John 1:51), he properly claims for himself this honor, that after he shall have been manifested in the world, angels shall ascend and descend. If, then, we say that the ladder is a figure of Christ, the exposition will not be forced.[1]

Second, Jacob's confession confirms that Christ alone connects us to heaven. He exclaims, "How awesome is this place! This is none other than the house of God, and this is the gate of heaven." George Bush observes, "He had laid him down to sleep, as on common ground, but he found that it was a consecrated place, hallowed by the presence of God himself in this blessed vision of the night. It seemed a lone and uninviting spot, but it had proved to be a magnificent temple."[2] How so? "He had seen in it a glorious presence of God, with his attendant retinue: and the gates of heaven itself had, as it were, been opened to his view."[3] God prescribes Jesus Christ as the only way into heaven.

---

1. John Calvin, *Commentaries on the Book of Genesis*, trans. John King (Grand Rapids: Baker, 1979), 2:113.
2. George Bush, *Notes on Genesis* (Minneapolis: James Family, 1979), 2:110
3. Ibid.

Esther's experience adds to the picture, though a human comparison. She reflects on the prospect of entering the royal Persian throne room and the king's presence without his summon or command.

> All the king's servants and the people of the king's provinces know that for any man or woman who comes to the king to the inner court who is not summoned, he has but one law, that he be put to death, unless the king holds out to him the golden scepter so that he may live. And I have not been summoned to come to the king for these thirty days (Esther 4:11).

However, Esther did seek an audience with the king. "When the king saw Esther the queen standing in the court, she obtained favor in his sight; and the king extended to Esther the golden scepter which was in his hand. So Esther came near and touched the top of the scepter" (Esther 5:2). The word *favor* means *grace*. "If a heathen king can willingly grant such grace, how much more willing is the most faithful Lord to receive all poor destitute sinners coming to Him in faith ... "[4] As Ahasuerus prescribed how Esther might enter his presence, so God prescribes how we may enter His presence. These texts validate the major premise: God prescribes how we enter heaven and enter His presence.

The Minor Premise: Worship is an entrance into God's presence and a taste of heaven. The second chapter on the nature of the church validates this minor premise. The church assembled for worship is a temple built of living stones (2 Cor. 6:16; 1 Pet. 2:5). God commits Himself to graciously dwell within this temple (Ephesians 2:21-22). His purpose is to apply and renew His covenant with His people (2 Cor. 6:16). The people of God are also citizens of heaven (Phil. 3:20) and form embassies of heaven in this world (2 Cor. 5:20; Eph. 6:20). The argumentation of chapter 2 need not be repeated. *Worship is an entrance into and a taste of heaven.*

---

4. W. Schultz, *The Book of Esther*, trans. James Strong (Grand Rapids: Zondervan, 1960), 68.

Conclusion: God prescribes how we worship Him. Since the worshiping assembly is a special dwelling place of God where we enter into and taste of heaven, we must build the worshiping assembly in which God dwells *as God prescribes.* (1) God prescribes how we enter heaven and His presence. (2) Worship is entering into God's presence and tasting heaven. (3) God prescribes how we worship Him.

FURTHER BIBLICAL AND CONFESSIONAL VALIDATION

For further Biblical validation of the syllogism, consider the following texts. God Commands His covenant people: "Let them construct a sanctuary for Me, that I may dwell among them" (Exod. 25:8). Speaking of the sanctuary furnishings, God says, "See that you make them after the pattern for them, which was shown to you on the mountain" (Exod. 25:40). The writer to the Hebrews explains the importance of God's command. "Now if He were on earth, He would not be a priest at all, since there are those who offer the gifts according to the Law; who serve *a copy and shadow of the heavenly things,* just as Moses was warned by God when he was about to erect the tabernacle; for, 'SEE,' He says, 'THAT YOU MAKE ALL THINGS ACCORDING TO THE PATTERN WHICH WAS SHOWN YOU ON THE MOUNTAIN'" (Heb. 8:4-5, italics added). The tabernacle and later the temple were copies of heavenly things. In this sense, entering into the tabernacle, especially entering the most holy place, the location of God's throne, was an entrance into heaven. Since the church is now the temple of God, the place of His special presence, *God prescribes how we worship Him.*

Add the Great Commission to these Old Testament texts.

> Jesus came up and spoke to them, saying, "All authority has been given to Me in heaven and on earth. Go therefore and make disciples of all the nations, baptizing them in the name of the Father and the Son and the Holy Spirit, *teaching them to observe all that I commanded you;* and lo, I am with you always, even to the end of the age" (Matt. 28:18-20, italics added).

Christ commissions His apostles, and through them His church, telling His people "to observe all that I commanded." Are believers to carry out all that Christ commands *except in worship*? No! Christ's commission includes worship. Our syllogism holds. Scripture validates the conclusion.

Support also comes from a part of the definition of worship. Worship is *service*. Believers regularly speak of the *Worship Service* or a *Service of Worship*. Exodus 30:6-9 describes the service involving the altar of incense in the tabernacle.

> You shall put this altar in front of the veil that is near the ark of the testimony, in front of the mercy seat that is over the ark of the testimony, where I will meet with you. Aaron shall burn fragrant incense on it; he shall burn it every morning when he trims the lamps. When Aaron trims the lamps at twilight, he shall burn incense. There shall be perpetual incense before the Lord throughout your generations. You shall not offer any strange incense on this altar, or burnt offering or meal offering; and you shall not pour out a drink offering on it.

Numbers 18:7 connects this service with the priesthood. "You and your sons with you shall attend to your priesthood for everything concerning the altar and inside the veil, and *you are to perform service*" (italics added). The Septuagint reads *leitourgēsete tas leitourgias*, literally, *You are to serve the service*. As chapter 1 observed, worship is a form of service.

When Aaron's own sons failed to properly carry out their service at the altar of incense, the consequences were swift and devastating. Aaron had no response to God's judgment except silence. Lev. 10:1-3 relates the scene.

> Now Nadab and Abihu, the sons of Aaron, took their respective firepans, and after putting fire in them, placed incense on it and offered strange fire before the Lord, which He had not commanded them. And fire came out

from the presence of the Lord and consumed them, and they died before the Lord. Then Moses said to Aaron, "It is what the Lord spoke, saying, 'By those who come near Me I will be treated as holy, And before all the people I will be honored.'" So Aaron, therefore, kept silent.

Zechariah, the father of John the Baptist, faithfully performed this same *service*. "When the days of his priestly service [*leiturgias*] were ended, he went back home" (Luke 1:23). Worship is service prescribed by God.

Also consider Acts 13:2 and the church at Antioch. "While they were ministering [*leitourgountōn*] to the Lord and fasting, the Holy Spirit said, 'Set apart for Me Barnabas and Saul for the work to which I have called them.'" Worship is service. In this same light, Christ is also a servant. "Now the main point in what has been said is this: we have such a high priest, who has taken His seat at the right hand of the throne of the Majesty in the heavens, a minister [*leitourgos*] in the sanctuary and in the true tabernacle, which the Lord pitched, not man" (Heb. 8:1-2). These texts confirm this point: *God prescribes how we worship Him.*

The Westminster Standards also validate the syllogism: (1) God prescribes how we enter heaven and His presence. (2) Worship is an entrance into God's presence and a taste of heaven. (3) God prescribes how we worship Him. This syllogism restates what is called the regulative principle of worship, which is taught in the Westminster Standards. Their authors maintained that the Second Commandment indicates *how* we should worship. The Westminster Shorter Catechism 49 reads as follows:

> Which is the second commandment? Answer: The second commandment is, Thou shalt not make unto thee any graven image, or any likeness of any thing that is in heaven above, or that is in the earth beneath, or that is in the water under the earth: Thou shalt not bow down thyself to them, nor serve them: for I the Lord thy God am a

jealous God, visiting the iniquity of the fathers upon the children unto the third and fourth generation of them that hate me; and showing mercy unto thousands of them that love me, and keep my commandments.

Westminster Shorter Catechism 50: "What is required in the second commandment? Answer: The second commandment requireth the receiving, observing, and keeping pure and entire, all such religious worship and ordinances as God hath appointed in his word." God appoints how believers are to worship; their duty is to keep His worship pure and entire.

Westminster Shorter Catechism 51: "What is forbidden in the second commandment? Answer: The second commandment forbiddeth the worshipping of God by images, *or any other way not appointed in his word*" (italics added). In worship, whatever God does not appoint, He forbids. This statement is the regulative principle of worship. *God prescribes how we worship.*

AN ALTERNATIVE POSITION

The alternative to the regulative principle of worship is the normative principle. "Roman Catholics, Episcopalians, and Lutherans have taken the position that we may do anything in worship except what God forbids."[5] The normative principle states: *Whatever God does not forbid, He permits*. Many churches hold this view. Compare the two positions. The regulative principle may be stated positively or negatively. Positive statement: In worship, whatever God appoints, He permits. Negative statement: In worship, whatever God does not appoint, He forbids. Compare the normative principle: In worship, whatever God does not forbid He permits. Remember the syllogism: (1) God prescribes how we enter heaven and His presence. (2) Worship is an entrance into God's presence and a taste of heaven. (3) God prescribes how we worship Him. Which position best represents the

---

5. John M. Frame, *Worship in Spirit and Truth* (Phillipsburg: P & R, 1996), 38.

syllogism? The regulative principle of worship does.

Although some within Presbyterian and Reformed circles profess adherence to the regulative principle, their implementation of it leads them into a practice of the normative principle. Professor John Frame appears to be a prominent example. Professor Frame expresses his views on worship as follows: "Typically, Scripture tells us what we should do in general and then leaves us to determine the specifics by our own sanctified wisdom, according to the general rules of the Word. Determining the specifics is what I call 'applications.'"[6] Professor Frame says that, "the sphere of application includes some matters that are 'common to human actions and societies' and some matters that are not."[7] He adds this footnote, "I do subscribe to the confession's teaching at this point; I wish only to supplement it. I agree with the confession that we must use our own prudence in areas 'common to human actions and societies.' But I believe that we must use our prudence in other areas as well."[8]

Professor Frame means that our only task is to *apply* the commands of Scripture to specific situations.[9] Further, he holds that it is in the *context of application* that we should understand the regulative principle.

> Thus understood, the regulative principle for worship is no different from the principles by which God regulates all of life. That is to be expected, because, as we have seen worship is, in an important sense, all of life. In both cases, "whatever is not commanded is forbidden"—everything we do must be done in obedience to God's commands. In both cases, application determines the specifics in accordance with the general principles of the word.[10]

---

6. Ibid., 41.
7. Ibid. Westminster Confession 1.6 defines the circumstances of worship as matters "common to human actions and societies," such as heating, lighting, seating, and the location and times of meetings.
8. Ibid., 48, n. 5.
9. Ibid., 43.
10. Ibid., 42.

However, when Professor Frame illustrates the application in accordance with the general principles of the word, he illustrates the *normative principle*—whatever God does not forbid, He permits—not the regulative principle—whatever God does not command, He forbids. Listen to Professor Frame: "*Scripture does not, for example, explicitly forbid juggling exhibitions at worship meetings.* But Scripture does set forth the purposes of worship meetings; and entertainment—even though lawful at other times, is not normally consistent with those purposes."[11] Professor Frame says of his position, "My own formulation does not contradict the confession, but goes beyond it."[12] In other words, he claims to be operating within the framework of the Confession while, by his own admission, he operates beyond, outside the limits of, the Confession. If you follow Professor Frame, you quite probably embrace the normative principle.

Does the regulative principle apply to all of life as Professor Frame alleges? A moment's reflection reveals that it does not. Scripture does not give explicit commands concerning all aspects of life. If it did, no library could contain the books that would be needed. If, in all of life, whatever God does not command is forbidden, a host of things we commonly use would be forbidden. We would not drive cars, fly in airplanes, or use computers. Scripture never commands the use of these things. At the same time, Professor Frame is correct in saying that we must take care to properly apply the commands of Scripture. "Human wisdom may never presume to *add* to its commands. The only job of human wisdom is to *apply* those commands to specific situations."[13]

In applying the commands of Scripture, the Westminster Confession does not place all of life under the rubric of the regulative principle. Specifically, it does not do so in its section on Oaths and Vows. Here is Westminster Confession of Faith 22.4 (italics added).

---

11. Ibid. Italics added.
12. Ibid., 43.
13. Ibid.

> An oath is to be taken in the plain and common sense of the words, without equivocation, or mental reservation. *It cannot oblige to sin; but in anything not sinful being taken, it binds to performance,* although to a man's own hurt; nor is it to be violated, although made to heretics or infidels.

The Confession's position may be stated this way: Regarding oaths and vows, whatever God does not forbid, He permits. In anything not sinful, a vow binds to performance. This statement is the normative principle. We take oaths and vows in many different circumstances that cover vast areas of life. Examples are vows taken when entering marriage, public office, the military, church membership, the pastorate, the eldership, or the diaconate, when being baptized, and more narrowly, when testifying in court or serving on a jury. These vows touch all areas of life. They are not subject to the regulative principle.

Westminster Confession of Faith 22.1 does say, "A lawful oath is a part of religious worship." The prooftext is Deuteronomy 10:20, "You shall fear the Lord your God; you shall serve Him and cling to Him, and you shall swear by His name." A. A. Hodge interprets the Confession, with its prooftext, as follows: "Hence an oath is an act of supreme religious worship, since it recognizes the omnipresence, omniscience, absolute justice and sovereignty of the Person whose august witness is invoked, and whose judgment is appealed to as final."[14] Oaths and vows cover vast areas of life and therefore fall under the category of worship as all of life. They may or may not be a part of public worship. The regulative principle does not govern all of life as Professor Frame alleges.

Worship as all of life and regular public worship differ. If the regulative principle does not govern all of life, worship as all of life and regular public worship must differ in significant ways. This idea Professor Frame rejects, saying,

> I therefore reject the limitation of the regulative principle

---

14. A. A. Hodge, *The Confession of Faith* (Carlisle: Banner of Truth, 1978), 287.

to official worship services ... It is a doctrine about worship, all forms of worship. It governs all worship, whether formal or informal, individual or corporate, public or private, family or church, broad or narrow. Limiting the doctrine to officially sanctioned worship robs it of its biblical force.[15]

D. A. Carson seems to agree with Professor Frame. He says that, in the New Testament documents, "worship *language* moves the locus away from a place or time to all of life ... It is for all the people of God at all times and places, and it is bound up with how they live (e.g. Rom. 12:1-2)."[16] However, if the theology of worship presented above is correct and is rooted in the Old Testament tabernacle, temple, and Sabbath, Carson is not entirely correct. There are stated times for public worship, the Sabbath, and a place for public worship, God's assembled people, the New Testament temple. Carson goes on to say,

> But one of the entailments [inevitable consequences] is that we cannot imagine that the church gathers for worship on Sunday morning[,] if by this we mean that we then engage in something that we have not been engaging in the rest of the week. New covenant worship terminology prescribes *constant* "worship."[17]

Believers can indeed imagine that, even though they may engage in private and family worship, they also engage in something different when they gather in corporate assembly, as a New Testament temple, to enjoy the gracious presence of God. The next chapter will examine the Biblical understanding of *constant* or *continual* worship. As will be seen, Biblically, continual worship does not necessarily refer to worship *occurring continuously over a period of time*.

Frame and Carson err. Recall that chapter 2 discussed public worship as the focal point of sanctification. *To sanctify* means *to set aside*

---

15. Frame, *Worship in Spirit and Truth*, 44-45.
16. D. A. Carson, *Worship by the Book* (Grand Rapids: Zondervan, 2002), 24.
17. Ibid.

for the purposes of God or to consecrate something. The camp of Israel with the tabernacle, in all its distinctiveness, surrounded by the tents of Israel, stood out as utterly separate from its surroundings and portrayed Israel's separateness from the world. The focal point of this separateness was the tabernacle and the worship of the people. There, God tightly regulated the public worship carried out in the center of the camp. God permitted only what He commanded. How the people lived their daily lives also displayed their separateness from the world. All of life reflected their devotion to God. However, although daily life was profoundly affected by public worship, it was not regulated in the same way.

The situation is similar for God's people today. Stated, public worship is the focal point of their sanctification, their separateness from the world. As indicated in chapters 1 through 3, in public worship, God's people gather in His special presence on His special day. God commits Himself to them as His assembled people to apply and renew His covenant with them and to assure them that they belong to Him. God prescribes this worship. Whatever He does not command, He forbids. Renewed in their covenant life, believers depart from worship to serve before their God each day. Their devotion to God is on display in every area of life.

As outlined above, understanding that stated public worship is the *focal point* of sanctification helps in understanding that the regulative principle does not govern all of life. The following word study will assist in assessing the distinctiveness of stated, weekly public worship, its detachment from worship as all of life, and its separateness from the culture.

OCCASIONAL CELEBRATIONS VS. STATED PUBLIC WORSHIP

A development of the regulative principle inevitably evokes questions about so-called "contemporary worship." The following Old Testament word study gives perspective on contemporary worship questions. The title of this section contrasts celebration and worship. In this context, *celebration* refers to *occasional culturally-conditioned worship settings*. *Worship* refers to *structured, heaven-directed worship settings*. The former arise occasionally in response to prominent events. The latter are regular, stated meetings for public worship.[18] The following study supports this distinction and adds to our understanding of the implementation of the regulative principle.

The Hebrew word *tof*, used seventeen times in the Old Testament, is translated either tambourine(s) or timbrel(s) in the New American Standard Version. The references are: Genesis 31:27; Exodus 15:20; Judges 11:34; 1 Samuel 10:5; 18:6; 1 Chronicles 13:8; Job 21:12; Psalm 81:2; 149:3; 150:4; Isaiah 5:12; 24:8; 30:32; Jeremiah 31:4; and Ezekiel 28:13.

The first mention of tambourines is Genesis 31:27. Jacob's father-in-law, Laban, complains that he was not given an opportunity to properly send away his daughters with a banquet. "Why did you flee secretly and deceive me, and did not tell me so that I might have sent you away with joy and with songs, with timbrel and with lyre?" The typical banquet or wedding feast of the time featured singing and dancing with timbrels and lyres.

Job 21:12 speaks similarly of the revelry of unbelievers. "They sing to the timbrel and harp and rejoice at the sound of the flute." This text pictures a secular, cultural celebration. Israel was prone to engage in such revelry and to ignore God. "Their banquets are accompanied by lyre and harp, by tambourine and flute, and by wine; but they do not pay attention to the deeds of the Lord, nor do they consider the work of His hands" (Isa. 5:12). Contemporary culture celebrated various events with banquets, singing, and playing various instruments; such activities are not sinful in themselves. The problem in Israel was a failure to acknowledge God. The result was judgment.

---

18. I am grateful to Reformed Presbyterian Pastor, William Edgar, Ph.D., for his suggestion that the proper distinction is between occasional celebrations and stated public worship.

When judgment comes, "The gaiety of tambourines ceases, the noise of revelers stops, the gaiety of the harp ceases" (Isa. 24:8). Judgment cuts off joy, celebration, banquet, and party. On the other hand, when Israel's enemies face God's judgment, it is time to celebrate. Israel will rejoice at the demise of Assyria. "Every blow of the rod of punishment, which the Lord will lay on him, will be with the music of tambourines and lyres" (Isa. 30:32). In like manner, the restoration of Israel from exile meant the restoration of banquet, joy, celebration, and party. "Again you will take up your tambourines, and go forth to the dances of the merrymakers" (Jer. 31:4). These texts are all descriptions of culturally-conditioned, secular celebrations.

Given the common use of tambourines in the culture of the time, it is not surprising that Miriam takes up the timbrel to celebrate the crossing of the Red Sea and the destruction of the Egyptians. The people would naturally celebrate a great occasion in this way. "Miriam the prophetess, Aaron's sister, took the timbrel in her hand, and all the women went out after her with timbrels and with dancing" (Exod. 15:20). In this case, Miriam gave thanks to the Lord. "Miriam answered them, 'Sing to the Lord, for He is highly exalted; the horse and his rider He has hurled into the sea'" (Exod. 15:21).

This celebration has a worshipful component. However, it differs from the tabernacle worship and temple worship later ordained by God. This difference is crucial. We derive our theology of worship from the temple and the Sabbath. Regular, stated worship each Sabbath or Lord's Day is *God-ordained* and *heaven-directed*. The regulative principle applies to it. It, therefore, bears the marks of heaven and offers a taste of heaven. Miriam's celebration, occasioned by God's deliverance, was a one-time event. In addition, it was *culturally-conditioned*. We ought not to use this culturally-conditioned celebration as the pattern for New Testament worship. The church should be "a communion that is a contradiction to society."[19] It should be a

---

19. Marva Dawn, *Reaching Out Without Dumbing Down* (Grand Rapids: Eerdmans, 1995), 131.

counter-culture. "The only way to offer the world an alternative, the moral foundation of God's truth, is if the Church and its members are distinctly different."[20]

Continuing the discussion of culturally-conditioned, occasional celebrations, look at Judges 11:34. "When Jephtha came to his house at Mizpah, behold, his daughter was coming out to meet him with tambourines and with dancing." Here, Jephtha's daughter celebrates his victory in battle over Ammon. Scripture records a similar circumstance regarding David: "It happened as they were coming, when David returned from killing the Philistine, that the women came out of all the cities of Israel, singing and dancing, to meet King Saul, with tambourines, with joy and with musical instruments" (1 Sam. 18:6). As in the case of Miriam, these celebrations involve special circumstances, rather than regular, stated meetings established by God. Further, these are *culturally-shaped* celebrations. Too often the church uses these culturally-shaped, occasional celebrations as the rationale for its worship. "The result is that congregations no longer are 'contrast-societies but mirrors of the individualistic society that surrounds and infects them.'"[21] In contrast, the true theology of worship grows out of the fertile soil of the tabernacle, temple, and Sabbath. Regular, stated tabernacle worship was *God-directed* and *heaven-filled*. New Testament, stated, weekly Sabbath, worship ought to reflect heaven, rather than the surrounding culture.

There are two other important incidents manifesting the air of celebration and having worshipful components. The first is 1 Chronicles 13:8 where David is celebrating the return of the ark of God from the Philistines. "David and all Israel were celebrating before God with all their might, even with songs and with lyres, harps, tambourines, cymbals and with trumpets." David engages in a *culturally-shaped* celebration. As in the case of Miriam, this celebration involves a special circumstance; it is occasional. It differs from the regular, stated

---

20. Ibid., 114.
21. Ibid., 133.

meetings established by God. As a *culturally-shaped* celebration, it stands in sharp contrast to the regular, stated worship of God in the tabernacle and temple. The latter is specifically *God-ordained* and *heaven-directed*.

In 1 Samuel 10:5, Saul meets a band of prophets prophesying and using tambourines and other instruments. Samuel made this prediction: "You will come to the hill of God where the Philistine garrison is; and it shall be as soon as you have come there to the city, that you will meet a group of prophets coming down from the high place with harp, tambourine, flute, and a lyre before them, and they will be prophesying." The prophets were prophesying; "they were in a condition of ecstatic inspiration, in which, singing or speaking, with accompaniment of music, they gave expression to the overflowing feeling with which their hearts were filled from above by the controlling Spirit."[22]

These ministers of God are singing with musical accompaniment; they are doing so under the influence of the Spirit. On one hand, they combine instruments and singing as found in the temple. However, as will be observed in a following chapter, the musical instruments are typological. They point to Spirit empowered proclamation and praise, the exact circumstance of 1 Samuel 10:5. On the other hand, the celebratory activity of the prophets is clearly shaped by their *contemporary culture*. This occasional celebration stands in contrasts to the regulated, God-ordained stated worship of the tabernacle and the temple prescribed to reflect *heaven*.

The temple and its services, not the occasional celebrations of the Old Testament, form the basis for New Testament worship. The New Testament repeatedly compares the church with the temple (2 Cor. 6:16; Eph. 2:21-22; 1 Pet. 2:5). The temple was the Old Testament designated place for regular, stated corporate worship. Today, the church assembled is the designated place for regular, stated corporate wor-

---

22. David Erdman, *The Books of Samuel*, trans. C. H. Toy and John A. Broadus (Grand Rapids: Zondervan, 1960), 153.

ship. It is an embassy of heaven. The characteristics of this embassy "transcend the particular colors and forms of the local culture because the community [of the church] is centered on Christ, the universal Head."[23]

The occasional celebrations of Miriam, Jephtha's daughter, David, and Saul do not provide the pattern for New Testament worship. These celebrations are culturally-conditioned and -shaped. These celebrations involve special circumstances and not stated meetings. Scripture shows them to be distinct from the regular, stated worship instituted by God in the tabernacle and temple. *Culturally-shaped* celebrations, patriotic remembrances, special banquets, and weddings are also a part of contemporary life. However, these celebrations are quite distinct from the regular, stated worship of God.

There is a place for occasional celebrations; but they differ from stated worship. The difference between them should be understood and taught. Again, the theology of worship is built upon the formal, stated Old Testament worship of the temple rather than upon the pattern of Old Testament occasional celebrations. In the Reformed tradition, for example, weddings are not considered worship services. They are not stated meetings, but occasional, culturally-conditioned celebrations with worshipful elements.

The church's aim should be to draw people toward heaven and away from the world through heaven-directed worship. The church ought not to *culturally* condition her worship. The church must not be more concerned about being connected to the culture than to being connected to heaven.

The stated meetings of Old Testament temple worship provide the theological and Biblical foundation for the stated meetings of worship in the church. The syllogism with which this chapter begins holds: God prescribes how we enter heaven; worship is an entrance into and a taste of heaven; God prescribes how we worship. This syl-

---

23. Dawn, *Reaching Out*, 138.

logism is simply a different formulation of the regulative principle of worship. In worship, whatever God does not command, He forbids.

CONTEMPORARY WORSHIP AND CONTEMPORARY CHRISTIAN MUSIC

Like it or not, one of the tensions within the church has to do with so-called contemporary worship (CW) and contemporary Christian music (CCM). Against the backdrop of the above discussions of worship, the church, the Sabbath, and the regulative principle, a brief look at this tension is in order. Here are some telling comments by Dan Lucarini in *Why I Left the Contemporary Christian Music Movement*:

> How important has CCM become in churches? When asked what one thing he would do differently if he could start his own church all over again, here is what Rick Warren (the well-known pastor of Saddleback Community Church in California, USA, mentioned earlier) had to say: "From the first day of the new church I'd put more energy and money into a first-class music ministry that matched our target. In the first years of Saddleback, I made the mistake of underestimating the power of music so I minimized the use of music in our services. I regret that now."[24]

Here, Rick Warren is quoted as desiring a music ministry matching the church's target demographic. He appears to desire to link the church with the culture. However, God's plan is to link worshiping assemblies to heaven.

Lucarini also quotes Pastor Warren as saying, "The style of music you choose to use in your service will be one of the most critical (and controversial) decisions you make in the life of your church. It may also be *the* most influential factor in determining who your

---

24. Dan Lucarini, *Why I left the Contemporary Christian Music Movement* (Webster, NY: Evangelical Press, 2002), 45.

church reaches for Christ and whether your church grows."[25] Marva Dawn responds to this kind of thinking. "What is faulty *is* churches' assumption that if we choose the right *kind* of music people will be attracted to Christ. It is idolatry to think our work makes the difference. Christ himself draws people to believe in him through the Holy Spirit."[26]

More will be said about style in the more detailed discussion of music in chapter 16. Here, the question has to do with the desire to connect to the culture. T. David Gordon raises the issue by asking why the term *sacred music* is disappearing from use. "Why? Because sacred music in our day does not wish to sound different from secular music; to the contrary, it intentionally emulates it, and attempts to sound exactly like it. But if worship is a sacred task, what is wrong with the musical aspects of our worship sounding sacred?"[27] Indeed! Because of the Biblical theology of worship discussed above, churches ought to be more concerned in public worship with connecting with heaven than with linking with the culture.

Marva Dawn speaks about this disparity in worship under the heading, "Narcissism in Contemporary Society and Worship" and says, "Perhaps the most dangerous of the subtle influences on contemporary worship practices is the self-centered bent of the modern world ... The Church must combat the constant influence of this cultural mind-set on our character and its subtle expression in Christian worship."[28]

Michael Horton correctly states that

> we need to ask about the theological rationale for church music in the first place. What is its role? What is the significance of the shift from viewing music as a means of inculcating sound doctrine (Col. 3:16) and communal response to God's action (Eph. 5:19-20) to seeing it as "the

---

25. Ibid., 46.
26. Dawn, *Reaching Out*, 192.
27. T. David Gordon, *Why Johnny Can't Sing Hymns* (Phillipsburg: P&R, 2010), 75.
28. Dawn, *Reaching Out*, 107-108.

worship time"? Is the implication that while we continue to tip our hat to the ministry of the Word, we believe that the main event is really about expressing ourselves, even if it is in an attitude of praise?[29]

Hart and Muether address the issue from the perspective of language.

> Consider, for example, the use of the term *worship experience*. This phrase threatens to eclipse the older expression, *worship service*. What difference does it make? We believe the difference is enormous. Service is the work and duty of a servant to and for a superior, and good service is that which pleases the superior. The word *experience* redirects the goal of worship, from God-centeredness to man's pleasure.[30]

"[S]hould worship be simply what we want, and should the Church be like the culture around it?"[31] From all that has been said, the answer is a resounding, No! "We do not come to church to affirm *our* faithfulness, *our* devotion, *our* praise, and *our* up-to-the-minute emotional state but to be addressed, undressed, and redressed by God. Only when this fact is central are we in any position to faithfully praise God as 'our *reasonable* service.'"[32]

What is the answer? "We need to ... rediscover the biblical, confessional, theological warp and woof of worship."[33] To rediscover the Biblical, confessional, and theological underpinnings of public, corporate worship has been the burden of the first section of our study. Four questions have been answered: What is worship? What is the church? What is the Sabbath? Who regulates how we worship? The answers to these questions lead us to the regulative principle of worship and the distinctiveness of public worship over against the con-

---

29. Michael Horton, *A Better Way* (Grand Rapids: Baker, 2002), 179.
30. D. G. Hart and John R. Muether, *With Reverence and Awe* (Phillipsburg: P & R, 2002), 17.
31. Dawn, *Reaching Out*, 166.
32. Horton, *Better Way*, 180.
33. Ibid., 181.

temporary culture. In summary, the *theology* for worship is derived from the temple and the Sabbath. The next section of this study seeks to show that the *elements* of worship are derived from the temple and the synagogue.

PART TWO:

The Scriptural Elements of Worship

5

The Elements of Worship:
Temple and Synagogue

*Through Him then, let us continually offer up a
sacrifice of praise to God, that is, the fruit of lips
that give thanks to His name.*
~ Heb. 13:15

INTRODUCTION

After formulating a basic definition of worship, chapters 2-4 developed a theology of public worship. Worship is covenant renewal. The church assembled is God's temple indwelt by His gracious presence. God commits Himself to His assembled church to apply His covenant word to the hearts of His people and to renew His covenant with them. As His people gather for worship on the Sabbath Day, He commits Himself to both the day and the assembly of His people, to assure them that they belong to Him. The emphasis in public worship is therefore upon what God does. He acts to renew His covenant with His people. They respond to Him in worship, adoration and praise. In the words of John, "We love, because He first loved us" (1 John 4:19).

As the New Testament temple and outpost of heaven, believers order the church assembly and their worship as God directs: God prescribes how we enter heaven. Worship is an entrance into and taste of heaven. God prescribes how we worship. This syllogism is the regulative principle of worship. Whatever God does not command,

He forbids. Following God's prescriptions for worship, believers anticipate meeting with Him in public worship, enjoying His gracious presence, and being assured that they belong to Him.

As seen above, the *theology* of New Testament worship comes from the temple and the Sabbath. In this chapter, it will be seen that the principal *elements* of New Testament worship come from both the temple and the synagogue. First, this chapter examines the sacrificial worship of the temple, and the connection between the blood sacrifices and New Testament sacrifices of praise. Second, an examination of the origin, purpose, and worship of the synagogue will show that the public prayer, Scripture readings, preaching, and benedictions of New Testament worship derive from the synagogue.

TEMPLE WORSHIP

After the time of David, worship in the temple included praise, along with the use of instruments added to the two silver trumpets appointed by Moses. Perhaps the prime Biblical description of temple worship is found in 2 Chron. 29:25-28.

> He then stationed the Levites in the house of the Lord with cymbals, with harps and with lyres, according to the command of David and of Gad the king's seer, and of Nathan the prophet; for the command was from the Lord through His prophets. The Levites stood with the musical instruments of David, and the priests with the trumpets. Then Hezekiah gave the order to offer the burnt offering on the altar. When the burnt offering began, the song to the Lord also began with the trumpets, accompanied by the instruments of David, king of Israel. While the whole assembly worshiped, the singers also sang and the trumpets sounded; all this continued until the burnt offering was finished.

The trumpets to be blown over the sacrifices were ordained by God through Moses (Num. 10:1, 10). By the command of the Lord (2

Chron. 29:25), David added singing and the use of cymbals, harps, and lyres to the service of sacrifice.

> David and the commanders of the army set apart for the service some of the sons of Asaph and of Heman and of Jeduthun, who were to prophesy with lyres, harps and cymbals ... All these were under the direction of their father to sing in the house of the Lord, with cymbals, harps and lyres, for the service of the house of God (1 Chr. 25:1, 6).

The Babylonian Talmud, Mishnah, tractate Tamid, chapter 7, paragraph 3 relates the order of the daily sacrificial service.[1] In reading this description, it is helpful to note that the altar in Solomon's temple was 20 cubits by 20 cubits and ten cubits high or a height of 15 feet (2 Chron. 4:1). The altar in use in the following description was in Herod's temple. Its foundation was 32 cubits by 32 and one cubit high. There was then a one cubit wide step, and the altar rose an additional five cubits. Then there was another cubit wide step enabling the priests to walk around the altar that then rose another three cubits. The horns of the altar extended up another cubit making ten cubits in all.[2] The priests used the steps to work around the altar. With this explanation, M Tamid 7, 3 gives the following explanation:

> WHEN THE HIGH PRIEST DESIRED TO BURN THE OFFERINGS, HE USED TO GO UP THE ASCENT WITH THE DEPUTY PRIEST AT HIS RIGHT HAND, AND WHEN HE REACHED THE MIDDLE OF THE ASCENT THE DEPUTY TOOK HIS HAND AND HELPED HIM UP. THE FIRST [OF THE OFFICIATING PRIESTS] THEN HANDED TO HIM THE HEAD AND THE FOOT OF THE SACRIFICE AND HE LAID HIS HANDS ON THEM AND THREW THEM [ON THE ALTAR FIRE]. THE SECOND THEN HANDED

---

1. The Mishnah was a series of tractates and collections of exegetical material containing the oral tradition of the Jewish law. "The Hebrew Mishnah, redacted in about A.D. 200, was followed by two extended Aramaic commentaries, one compiled in Palestine and one in Babylonia each referred to as Gemara. The Mishnah together with the Palestinian Gemara, redacted in the fourth century, is called the Jerusalem Talmud, and the Mishnah with the Babylonian Gemara, redacted in the fifth century, is called the Babylonian Talmud." James W. McKinnon, "On the Question of Psalmody in the Ancient Synagogue," *Early Music History* 6 (1986): 161, n. 5.
2. Mishnah, tractate Middoth, chapter 3, paragraph 1, with n. b (4), (5).

> TO THE FIRST THE TWO FORE LEGS, AND HE HANDED THEM TO THE HIGH PRIEST WHO LAID HIS HANDS ON THEM AND THREW THEM [ON THE FIRE]. THE SECOND THEN SLIPPED AWAY. IN THE SAME WAY ALL THE OTHER LIMBS WERE HANDED TO HIM AND HE LAID HANDS ON THEM AND THREW THEM [ON THE ALTAR FIRE]. IF HE PREFERRED, HE COULD LAY ON HANDS AND LET OTHERS THROW ON THE FIRE. WHEN HE CAME TO GO AROUND THE ALTAR FROM WHERE DID HE COMMENCE? FROM THE SOUTH-EASTERN CORNER. FROM THERE HE WENT TO THE NORTH-EASTERN. THEN TO THE NORTH-WESTERN AND THEN TO THE SOUTH-WESTERN. THEY THERE HANDED TO HIM WINE FOR LIBATION. THE DEPUTY HIGH PRIEST STOOD ON THE HORN OF THE ALTAR WITH THE FLAGS IN HIS HAND, AND TWO PRIESTS ON THE TABLE OF THE FAT WITH TWO TRUMPETS IN THEIR HANDS. THEY BLEW A TEKI'AH, A TERU'AH, AND A TEKI'AH. AND THEN WENT AND STOOD BY BEN AZRA. ONE ON HIS RIGHT HAND AND ONE ON HIS LEFT. WHEN HE WENT DOWN TO MAKE THE LIBATION THE DEPUTY HIGH PRIEST WAVED THE FLAGS AND BEN AZRA STRUCK THE CYMBALS AND THE LEVITES CHANTED THE PSALMS.[3]

A careful study by James W. McKinnon gives a commentary on Tamid 7, 3 and several other Midrash references.[4] "The participants in the Temple liturgy were representatives from the twenty-four regions of Israel who twice yearly served for a week in the Temple."[5] The Gospel of Luke testifies to these arrangements where Zacharias, father of John, is seen serving in the temple "in the appointed order of his division" (Luke 1:8).

> During their stay in the Temple, they were supervised by resident staff. There was the High Priest, of course, and a sort of executive officer, the *segan*, who deputized for him during the daily services, and several lesser officers with

---

3. *Hebrew-English Edition of the Babylonian Talmud: Tamid*, trans. Maurice Simon, ed. I. Epstein (London: Soncino, 1989), 7, 3.
4. See note 1.
5. McKinnon, "On the Question," 161.

authority in specific areas: among these were one who was "over the cymbals" and another "over the singing."[6]

"The service proper began when the 'eastern sky was alight as far a Hebron.' The priests blew three blasts on their silver trumpets, the great gate of the sanctuary was opened, the lamb was slaughtered and its limbs made ready for the sacrifice."[7] These trumpet blasts appear to have announced the breaking of day and the opening of the temple. The participants in the service retired to the Chamber of Hewn Stone where they recited the Ten Commandments, the Shema, "Hear O Israel," and a number of benedictions or prayers.[8] "The latter two, the Shema and Tefillah [prayer], eventually came to constitute the core of the synagogue liturgies, and indeed many scholars have tended to view the interlude just described as a synagogue service within the Temple service and similarly speak of a synagogue within the temple precincts."[9]

"The service continued as two priests chosen by lot went to the Sanctuary for the solemn incense offering before the Holy of Holies."[10] After a prescribed signal, "the Levite musicians assembled on the *duchan*, a platform adjoining the people's portion of the inner court toward the east."[11] The position of the Levites was therefore "east of the altar" (2 Chron. 5:12). "The most likely interpretation of this is that the singers faced the altar, while the trumpeters stood between them and the altar facing the congregation. Thus as the singers performed their ministry they stood before the altar and faced it."[12] The singers, therefore, stood on a platform just inside the temple court.

While the priests performed the incense offering, the people gathered outside the temple court engaged in prayer (Luke 1:10). As these priests completed their work, they retired from the scene.

---

6. Ibid. "The Temple officers and the individuals who held them in the last years of the Temple are given in M. Shekalim 5." n. 6. The reference, in standard form, refers to Mishnah, tractate Shekalim, chapter 5.
7. Ibid., 162. Note 8 refers to M. Sukkah 5, 5.
8. Ibid.
9. Ibid.
10. Ibid.
11. Ibid.
12. John W. Kleinig, *The Lord's Song* (Sheffield: Sheffield Academic Press, 1993), 72-73.

> The limbs of the lamb were then carried up the altar ramp and cast on the fire. Two priests gave three blasts on their trumpets [*a tiki'ah, a teru'ah,* and *a tiki'ah,* that is, a plain, broken, and plain blast[13]], the *segan* waved a cloth, the Temple officer who was "over the cymbals" clashed them together, and as the libation wine was poured on to the fire the Levites sang a psalm accompanied by the string instruments *nevel* and *kinnor* [probably the harp and kithara (or lyre)].[14] The morning service—and the afternoon service as well—ended with the conclusion of the psalm.[15]

Given this review of the temple service based on 2 Chronicles 29:25-28 and Tamid 7, 3, note the close association of the sacrifice and the singing of the Levites.

> The most remarkable feature in the institution by David of sacred song was its deliberate synchronization with the presentation of the public burnt offering on the altar … The narrative … states that the song of the Lord began when the burnt offerings began, and ended when they ended. These two activities were then synchronized exactly with each other.[16]

The same or a similar service accompanied, not only the whole burnt offerings, but also the thank-offerings. "This is confirmed by 2 Chron. 31.2, where the ministry of the Levites in performing thanks and praise is associated with both the burnt offerings and the peace offerings."[17] Note that thank-offerings were peace offerings (Lev. 7:13, 15).[18] Grasping this connection is important as the next section moves

---

13. James W. McKinnon, "The Exclusion of Musical Instruments from the Ancient Synagogue," *Journal of the Royal Musical Association* 106 (1979): 77. For a more detailed musical description of these trumpet blasts, see, Frances L. Cohen, "Ancient Musical Traditions of the Synagogue," *Journal of the Royal Musical Association* 19 (1892): 139-140.
14. McKinnon, "The Exclusion," 77
15. McKinnon, "On the Question," 163. See also, John Lightfoot, *The Works of the Reverend and Learned John Lightfoot* (London: Robert Scot, 1684), 2:922-923.
16. Kleinig, *Lord's Song*, 108-109.
17. Ibid., 123, n. 1.
18. The two other peace offerings were the votive and the freewill offerings (Lev. 22:21).

ahead to show that praise in the New Testament church comes from temple psalmody.

SACRIFICIAL LANGUAGE AND THE COMMAND FOR PRAISE

The writer to the Hebrews clearly uses sacrificial language in commanding praise. "Through Him then, let us continually offer up a sacrifice of praise to God, that is, the fruit of lips that give thanks to His name" (Heb. 13:15). The phrase *sacrifice of praise* in Greek is *thusian aineseōs*. The word *continually* translates the Greek prepositional phrase, *dia pantos*. The following study examines the use of these terms in the Greek Old Testament (LXX) by first looking at the language of the Old Testament peace offerings, specifically the thank-offerings.

Leviticus 7, complementing Leviticus 3, gives additional directions for peace offerings and thank-offerings. Verse 12: "If he offers it by way of thanksgiving [*aineseōs*], then along with the *sacrifice of thanksgiving* [*tês thusias tês aineseōs*] he shall offer unleavened cakes … " Verse 13: "With the *sacrifice* [*thusiai*] of his peace offerings for *thanksgiving* [*aineseōs*], he shall present his offering with cakes of leavened bread." Verse 15: "Now as for the flesh of the sacrifice [*thusias*] of his thanksgiving [*aineseōs*] peace offerings, it shall be eaten on the day of his offering."

The writer to the Hebrews uses the language of the bloody Old Testament thank-offering, but he redefines this sacrifice of thanksgiving as "the fruit of lips" that gives thanks to God. The bloody sacrifices become songs of praise. This redefinition of *thusian aineseōs*, sacrifice of thanksgiving, is understandable given the close connection between the animal sacrifice and the psalmody of the Levitical choirs.

Given this connection, compare several of the Psalms using the same language. "Offer to God a *sacrifice of thanksgiving* [*thusian aineseōs*] and pay your vows to the Most High" (Psalm 50:14). The Greek Old Testament (LXX) uses the same two words picked up by the writer to the Hebrews. The text also speaks of two of the peace offerings, the thank-offering and the votive offering. Verse 23 is similar. "He who offers a sacrifice of thanksgiving [*thusia aineseōs*] honors Me." A contemporary reading of these verses, and others like them, leads one to think of songs of praise. In the Old Testament context however, Psalm 50:14 and 23 refer to the animal sacrifices in the temple. Hebrews 13:15 leads the way in making a shift in thinking from animal sacrifices to songs of praise.

Consider Psalm 107:22, "Let them also offer *sacrifices of thanksgiving* [*thusian aineseōs*], and tell of His works with joyful singing." This psalm also uses the language picked up by Hebrews 13:15. The word translated *offer* is *thusatōsan* and the text says literally, "Let them sacrifice sacrifices of thanksgiving." This reference to the animal sacrifice of the thank-offering is also coupled with "joyful singing," no doubt a reference to the scene at the altar where the Levitical choir accompanies the sacrifice. Given the conjunction of the blood sacrifice with the singing of praise, it is easy to see how the writer to the Hebrews makes the sacrifice of thanksgiving the fruit of lips giving praise to God. Therefore, it seems that New Testament praise arises from the temple.

Psalm 116:17 is another example using the language of Hebrews 13:15. "To You I shall offer a sacrifice of thanksgiving [*thusian aineseōs* (LXX)], and call upon the name of the Lord." In this case, the language of the thank-offering picked up by the writer to the Hebrews is linked with calling on the name of the Lord. That is, the blood sacrifice is the only basis for a sinner to approach God. The writer to the Hebrews tells us the same thing. "Through Him then, let us continually offer up a sacrifice of praise to God, that is, the fruit of lips that give thanks to His name" (Heb. 13:15). It is through Christ and His sacrifice of Himself for sinners that they may approach the Father and rightly give Him the praise He is due.

The clear and easy transition from the blood sacrifice of the thank-offering to the sacrifice of thanksgiving, which is New Testament praise, occurs because of the close connection between the sacrifice on the altar and Levitical psalmody next to the altar. So it is clear that the language of Hebrews 13:15 indicates that New Testament psalmody derives from the temple.

What about the synagogue? Did the New Testament church not derive the element of psalmody from the synagogue? This position is the majority report. However, Alfred Edersheim emphatically states, "There was no service of 'praise' in the synagogues."[19] Why the popular view then? James McKinnon answers the question:

> That psalmody flourished in the ancient synagogue is a notion created by Christian liturgical and musical historians ... [I]t was probably that group of Anglican liturgical historians writing in the second quarter of the [twentieth] century—W.O.E. Oesterley, Clifford Dugmore and Dom Gregory Dix—who did the most to popularize the view among English speaking scholars."[20]

McKinnon adds that it appears these scholars were "in search of Jewish precedents" and made a grand "assumption based upon its supposed appropriateness"; they did so "without the benefit of primary sources" and with a clear "lack of documentary evidence."[21] On the other hand, musicologist John Smith adds, "No contemporary sources make any mention of singing in the synagogue during the first [century A.D.] ... Nor in early rabbinical documents which might, in places, have bearing on the period is there any mention of singing in the ancient synagogue."[22] Smith continues, "More recently the point has been underlined by Sigmund Mowinckel: 'The synagogue service was in ancient times always songless', and further:

---

19. Alfred Edersheim, *Sketches of Jewish Social Life in the Days of Christ* (Grand Rapids: Eerdmans, 1993), 268.
20. McKinnon, "On the Question," 181. McKinnon cites: Oesterley, *The Jewish Background of the Christian Liturgy* (London, 1925), 75; Dugmore, *The Influence of the Synagogue on the Divine Office* (London, 1944), 8, 80-81; Dix, *The Shape of the Liturgy*, 2nd ed. (London, 1945); 45; and *Jew and Greek* (London, 1953), 92-93.
21. Ibid., 180-182.
22. John Smith, "The Ancient Synagogue, the Early Church and Singing," *Music and Letters* 65 (1984), 5. Smith cites, "Mishna, the Tosefta (completed A.D. c. 250), the Jerusalem Talmud (completed A.D. c. 400), and the Babylonian Talmud (completed A.D. c. 500)." See his notes 26, 27, and 28.

'Nor before mediaeval time did synagogal poetry and singing come into existence.'"[23] More recently, Christopher Page, speaking of the Mishnah, redacted around 200 A.D., says, "there is no mention of synagogue music in that compilation … "[24] All of this data serves to vindicate Edersheim.

Returning to Hebrews 13:15, what does the word *continually* mean, as used in this text? The text says, "Through Him then, let us *continually [dia pantos]* offer up a sacrifice of praise to God, that is, the fruit of lips that give thanks to His name." The directions for the daily burnt offerings are found in Numbers 28:3-4. "This is the offering by fire which you shall offer to the Lord: two male lambs one year old without defect as a *continual* burnt offering every day. You shall offer the one lamb in the morning and the other lamb you shall offer at *twilight*" (italics added). In the context of these sacrifices, continual means daily, morning and evening.

The offerings were doubled on the Sabbath. "Then on the sabbath day two male lambs one year old without defect, and two-tenths of an ephah of fine flour mixed with oil as a grain offering, and its drink offering: This is the burnt offering of every sabbath in addition to the *continual [dia pantos* (LXX)] burnt offering and its drink offering" (Num. 28:9-10). Here, we find the same expression that Hebrews 13:15 uses. Again, in this context, *continual* means daily, morning and evening. Numbers 29: 16, 19, 22, 25, 28, 31, 34, 38 all speak of the *continual* burnt offering. In each case, the LXX reads, *dia pantos*. Again, as Numbers 28:4 indicates, these sacrifices were daily offerings, morning and evening. Clearly, there were regular stated times for these sacrifices.

Matthew Henry comments on the daily sacrifices, each morning and each evening:

> The particular law of the daily sacrifice, a lamb in the

---

23. Smith, 5, "The Ancient Synagogue," in Mowinckel, *The Psalms in Israel's Worship* (New York: Abingdon Press, 1962), 1:4.
24. Christopher Page, *The Christian West and Its Singers* (New Haven: Yale University Press, 2010), 42.

morning and a lamb in the evening, which, for the constancy of it as duly as the day came, is called a continual burnt-offering (v. 3), which intimates that when we are bidden to pray always, and to pray without ceasing, it is intended that at least every morning and every evening we offer up our solemn prayers and praises to God.[25]

What about the Sabbath and the doubling of the sacrifices? "This teaches us to double our devotions on Sabbath days, for so the duty of the day requires."[26] The duty enjoined includes morning and evening prayers and Sabbath worship. The traditional rationale for churches having both morning and evening worship services was found in the morning and evening sacrifices.

Matthew Henry takes a similar approach concerning the command: "Pray without ceasing" (1 Thessalonians 5:17). "The way to rejoice evermore is to pray without ceasing. We should rejoice more if we prayed more. *We should keep up stated times for prayer,* and continue instant in prayer" (italics added).[27] The word *continual*, in Hebrews 13:15, refers to worship maintained at stated intervals, morning and evening. That Hebrews 13:15 contemplates worship at stated intervals mirroring the stated times of worship in the temple also confirms the argument that the New Testament praise enjoined in Hebrews 13:15 comes from the temple. Other elements of worship are derived from the synagogue. The next step this study is to examine the origin and purpose of the synagogue.

THE ORIGIN OF THE SYNAGOGUE

The ancient, traditional view is that the synagogue originated with Moses. However, the modern, academic perspective is decidedly different. As the *New Bible Dictionary* states, "Before the Babylonian

---

25. Matthew Henry, *Matthew Henry's Commentary on the Whole Bible* (Grand Rapids: Fleming H. Revell, 1985), 1:698.
26. Ibid., 1:699.
27. Ibid., 6:790.

captivity, worship was centered at the Temple in Jerusalem. During the Exile, when worship at Jerusalem was an impossibility, the synagogue arose as a place for instruction in the Scriptures and prayer."[28] The mid-seventeenth century seems to have been the turning point. "The idea that the 'synagogue' originated with Moses was held by many scholars after the rabbis. One of the last scholars to keep a firm hold on this long held 'consensus' was the oft-cited Grotius, writing in 1644."[29] This long consensus of holding the traditional position is regrettably no more. "Attributions of the origin of the 'synagogue' to the patriarchal period and to Moses belong to the past."[30]

The traditional position links the Sabbath and the synagogue. Leviticus 23:2-4 is a key text that shows the principal holy convocation or sacred assembly appointed by God was the weekly Sabbath.

> The Lord's appointed times which you shall proclaim as holy convocations—My appointed times are these: For six days work may be done, but on the seventh day there is a Sabbath of complete rest, a holy convocation. You shall not do any work; it is a Sabbath to the Lord in all your dwellings. These are the appointed times of the Lord, holy convocations which you shall proclaim at the times appointed for them.

John Lightfoot (1602-1675) asks, "How was it possible that the Jews should keep the Sabbath according to the injunction laid upon them of having every seventh day a holy meeting or convocation, Leviticus 23:3, 4[,] if they had not in all times their Synagogue meetings or particular congregations ... [?]"[31] Here Lightfoot refers to Psalms 26:12 and 68:26 to validate "the plural number used of *Assemblies* or *Congregations*."[32] Psalm 26:12 reads, "My foot stands on a level place;

---

28. C. L. Feinberg, "Synagogue," *New Bible Dictionary*, ed. J. D. Douglas (Grand Rapids: Eerdamns, 1962), 1227.
29. Anders Runesson, *The Origins of the Synagogue: A Socio-Historical Study* (Stockholm: Almqvist and-Wiksell, 2001), 86.
30. Ibid., 87.
31. Lightfoot, *Works*, 1:609.
32. Ibid.

/ In the congregations [plural] I shall bless the Lord."[33] And Psalm 68:26 follows suit. "Bless God in the congregations [plural], / *Even the Lord, you who are* of the fountain of Israel." Henry Hammond (1605-1660) appears to hold the traditional position regarding the ancient synagogue, that Moses mandated weekly meetings. Hammond applies Psalm 68:26, making a comparison with the church, "As all Christians shall be obliged solemnly to magnify the name of Messias, and to that end frequently assemble together."[34]

To bolster the traditional position, Lightfoot adds an argument from Psalm 74:8. The Authorized Version reads, "They said in their hearts, Let us destroy them together: / They have burned up all the synagogues of God in the land." Lightfoot interprets the text.

> It is said expressly according as our English utters it, Psal. 74.4 [8], that the enemy had burnt all the *Synagogues of God* in the land. Which although the *Chaldee* render it of the Temple only, and *Rabbi Solomon* of *Shiloh* and the first and second Temple only, yet both the plural number used, and the context it self inforceth it, to be interpreted of more conventions than only in one place.[35]

Henry Hammond views the text similarly as speaking of God's enemies and the destruction of local synagogues: "And that they might make one work of it, to root out all religion both from the present and future ages, burning down and destroying all sorts of sacred assemblies, oratories, or synagogues all the nation over."[36] Thomas Godwyn (1587-1643) adds regarding synagogues, "That they were in David's time appeareth; They have burnt all the Synagogues of God in the land, Psal. 74.8."[37]

The Hebrew betrays a striking linguistic connection between Leviticus 23:2 and 4 and Psalm 74:8. The "appointed times" of Leviticus

---

33. The LXX reads *en ekklesias* in both Psalms following the plural in the Hebrew.
34. Henry Hammond, *A Paraphrase and Annotations upon the Book of Psalms* (London: R. Norton, 1659),330.
35. Lightfoot, *Works*, 1:608.
36. Hammond, *Paraphrase and Annotations*, 364.
37. Thomas Godwyn, *Moses and Aaron* (London: R. Rayston, 1631), 79.

23:2 and 4 and the "meeting places" or "synagogues" of Psalm 74:8 render the same Hebrew word. "Speak to the sons of Israel and say to them, 'The Lord's appointed times [*mo'ed*] which you shall proclaim as holy convocations—My appointed times [*mo'ed*] are these'" (Lev. 23:2). "These are the appointed times [*mo'ed*] of the Lord, holy convocations which you shall proclaim at the times appointed for them" (Lev. 23:4). "They have burned all the meeting places [*mo'ed*] of God in the land" (Ps. 74:8).

Finally, Lightfoot asks this question: "What can we make of these High places that are so often mentioned in Scripture in a commendable sense: as 1 Sam. 9.19 & 10:5, 1 Kings 3.4. &c. other, than that they were Synagogues or places of publick worship for particular congregations?"[38] Speaking of the ancient Jews, Godwyn makes the same point. "As they had *Synagogues,* so likewise *Schooles,* in every City and Province, and these were built also upon hills. There is mention of the hill *Moreh,* Judges 7.1. that is, *the Hill of the Teacher.*"[39] The clear implication of these texts is that synagogues were also located on high places. Lightfoot understands that synagogues were located on high places during the times of the Kings of Israel. "Only the high places were not taken away; the people still sacrificed and burned incense on the high places" (2 Kings 12:2, 14:4, and 15:4). Lightfoot says,

> *But the high places were not taken away,* nor that they should have been destroyed for being places of worship or of publick Assemblies, but the text expresseth still what was their abuse and what should have been removed, namely that the people should not have sacrificed and burnt incense there, which part of worship was only confined to *Jerusalem.*[40]

And so the traditional view of the origin of the synagogue goes back to Leviticus 23:2-3 and links the synagogue and the Sabbath. The

---

38. Lightfoot, *Works,* 1:608.
39. Godwyn, *Moses and Aaron,* 82.
40. Lightfoot, *Works,* 1:609.

Westminster Annotations concur, giving these comments on Leviticus 23:3. "The observation of the Sabbath, was not only in the Sanctuary, as other Feasts were, but in private habitations, tents or houses, as other Feasts were not: for that purpose there were built divers[e] Synagogues, not only in Jerusalem, but divers[e] other Cities ... "[41] Acts 15:21 seems to confirm the ancient existence of these gatherings. "Moses from ancient generations has in every city those who preach him, since he is read in the synagogues every Sabbath." The origin of these gatherings therefore seems to be very ancient.

THE PURPOSE OF THE SYNAGOGUE

Teaching was associated with the synagogue and the Levitical teaching priests from the time of Moses. He declared of the Levites, "They shall teach Your ordinances to Jacob, / And Your law to Israel" (Deut. 33:10). Preaching on this text, Calvin boldly asserts,

> Here we see that because the worlde is so weake, and so easily turned away from God & the right way, it is requisite that God's word should be preached, and that there should be men appointed thereunto ... Moreover, for the better maintaining of the pure Religion, it behooveth them to have zeale of God's honour; they must all their life long indeavour to maintaine the doctrine, and therewithal they must have their mouths open to preach the worde that is committed unto them, to the end that that treasure bee not lost or buried, but that all men may bee made partakers thereof. *They shall preach thy law then unto Jacob, and thy doctrine unto Israel.*[42]

God appointed the Levites as teachers and preachers in Israel. To this end, the tribe of Levi was scattered like salt throughout the land. "I will disperse them in Jacob, / And scatter them in Israel" (Gen.

---

41. *Annotations Upon All the Books of the Old and New Testament* (London: Evan Tyler, 1657), Leviticus 23:3.
42. John Calvin, *Sermons on Deuteronomy*, trans. Arthur Golding (Carlisle: Banner of Truth, 1987), 1205, 1206.

49:7). Although these words were uttered as a curse, "this dispersing of theirs was converted into a blessing, for they were consecrated to teach Jacob God's Judgments, and Israel his Law, Deut. 33.10. So the people had the benefit of their instruction … "[43] So also, Calvin argues concerning Genesis 49:7,

> But God, who in the beginning had produced light out of darkness, found another reason why the Levites should be dispersed abroad among the people—a reason not only free from disgrace, but highly honourable—namely, that no corner of the land might be destitute of competent instructors.[44]

There is a logical connection between the weekly Sabbath required of the people throughout the land and the settling of the Levites to teach throughout the land. Lightfoot makes this connection in his discussion of the synagogue under the heading "*Of their Preachers.*"

> From the very first platforming of the Church of *Israel*, the tribe of Levi was set a part for the publick ministry, to attend upon the Altar at *Jerusalem*, and to teach the people up and down the Nation, *Deut.* 33:10. *Mal.* 2.7. and for the better fitting of them for teaching, they had eight and forty cities allotted them, *Josh.* 21. in which they dwelt together, as in so many Universities, studying the Law, that they might be able in time to be Preachers in the Synagogues and Teachers in the schools up and down the Land.[45]

This connection between weekly Sabbath convocations and the scattering of teaching priests throughout the land is a "good and necessary consequence … deduced from Scripture."[46]

---

43. *Annotations Upon All the Books of the Old and New Testament*, Genesis 49:7.
44. John Calvin, *Commentaries on the First Book of Moses Called Genesis*, trans. John King (Grand Rapids: Baker, 1979), 2:448.
45. Lightfoot, *Works*, 1:612.
46. Westminster Confession of Faith, 1:6.

But the preachers and teachers of Israel failed in their duties. This failure was particularly acute when the kingdom was divided. "For many days Israel was without the true God and without a teaching priest and without law" (2 Chron. 15:3). Because of the failure of the teaching priests, the people were without God and without His Word, and, as Calvin says, there was no "maintaining of the pure Religion."[47] There is also an important connection between teaching and law in 2 Chronicles 15:3. "The Hebrew root of both words is the same. A function of the priest was to give teaching (*moreh*) in matters relating to the law (*Torah*)."[48] Recall the "hill of Moreh" (Judg. 7:1) or "the hill of the teacher."

After the restoration of Jerusalem and the rebuilding of the temple, Malachi deplores the lack of adequate teaching. "For the lips of a priest should preserve knowledge, and men should seek instruction from his mouth; for he is the messenger of the Lord of hosts" (Mal. 2:7). The teaching priest is God's messenger, the "interpreter of God's will, in teaching and governing the Church."[49] Calvin confirms this interpretation with his comments on Malachi 2:7.

> What the Prophet has said of the first priests he extends now to the whole Levitical tribe, and shows that it was a perpetual and unchangeable law as to the priesthood. He had said that Levi had been set over the Church, not to apply to himself the honor due to God, but to stand in his own place as the minister of God, and the teacher of the chosen people. The same thing he now confirms, declaring it as a general truth that *the lips of the priest ought to retain knowledge*, as though he had said, that they were to be the store-house from which the food of the Church was to be drawn. God then did appoint the priests over his chosen people, that the people might seek their food from them as from a store-room, according to what we

---

47. Calvin, *Deuteronomy*, 1206.
48. I. W. Slotki, *Chronicles* (New York: Soncino, 1985), 226.
49. *Annotations Upon All the Books of the Old and New Testament*, Malachi 2:7.

find to be the case with a master of a family, who has his store of wine and his store of provisions. As then the food of a whole family is usually drawn out from places where provisions are laid up, so the Prophet makes use of this similitude—that God has deposited knowledge with the priests, so that the mouth of every priest might be a kind of store-house, so to speak, from which the people are to seek knowledge and the rule of a religious life: *Keep knowledge* then *shall the lips of the priest, and the law shall they seek from his mouth.*[50]

What about the relationship between the two functions of priests? "Usually people think of the priests as specialists in bringing sacrifices, and indeed, that does seem to be their characteristic function in the time long after the return from exile. Nevertheless, the OT ideal of the priesthood was different. The teaching function precedes the sacrificial function in Deut. 33:8-10 and 2 Chr. 15:3."[51]

Questions may arise concerning the difference between prophet and priest. The difference must

> be sought in the manner in which priest and prophet both received and dispensed the revelation. The prophet is the man of the *dāḇār*, which was given him in a direct and personal manner by way of special revelation. The priest, on the other hand, is the man of the *tôrâ*, which is handed down to him either in written or in oral form, and which he communicated by means of instruction in the context of his priestly function (cf. Hag. 2:10-14).[52]

In summary, taking the traditional position, rather than the modern, academic position, yields the following. The synagogue was an institution of Moses associated with the Sabbath in his command for

---

50. John Calvin, *Commentaries on the Twelve Minor Prophets*, trans. John Owen (Grand Rapids: Baker Book House, 1979), 527.
51. Pieter A. Verhoef, *The Books of Haggai and Malachi* (Grand Rapids: Eerdmans, 1987), 257.
52. Ibid., 258.

weekly holy convocations given in Leviticus 23:2-3.[53] The Levitical priests were the *ordinary* teachers and preachers of the old economy. Their task was to teach and expound the written word of God in the local assemblies. The principal purpose of the Old Covenant synagogue was teaching God's Law.

THE WORSHIP OF THE SYNAGOGUE

"In *Hypothetica*, vii. 13, Philo [of Alexandria (20 B.C.-c. 50 A.D.)], after scribing the institution of the synagogue to Moses, gives the following account of the typical Sabbath service:"[54]

> And indeed they [the Jews] do always assemble and sit together, most of them in silence except when it is the practice to add something to signify approval of what is read. But some priest who is present or one of the elders reads the holy laws to them and expounds them point by point till about late afternoon, when they depart having gained both expert knowledge and considerable advance in piety.[55]

As will be seen, Philo's statement corroborates the New Testament accounts of the synagogue service and no doubt predates those accounts. If Luke and Acts were written in the early 60s, before the burning of Rome in 64, Philo's description of synagogue services certainly does predate Luke's.[56] Although Philo seems to describe the synagogue services in Alexandria alone,

> the same author gives a similar account of the synagogue service of the Essenes of Palestinian Syria. Philo says that on the Sabbath day the Essenes " ... abstain from all work and proceed to sacred spots which they

---

53. The traditional position appears to be the stance of the Orthodox Jewish community. This anecdotal evidence comes from my colleague, Professor C. J. Williams, Ph.D., and his discussion of these matters with his Orthodox Jewish professors while pursuing his doctoral studies.
54. Smith, "The Ancient Synagogue," 4.
55. Ibid. Quoted from, Philo, *Volume IX, Every Good Man Is Free*, trans. F. H. Colson (London: Loeb Classical Library, 1941), 433.
56. Everett F. Harrison, *Introduction to the New Testament* (Grand Rapids: Eerdmans, 1964), 229-228.

call synagogues. There, arranged in rows according to their age, the younger below the older, they sit decorously as befits the occasion with attentive ears. Then one takes the books and reads aloud and another of special proficiency comes forward and expounds what is not understood."[57]

Josephus (37-c. 100) comments similarly and indicates that Moses

> demonstrated the law to be the best and most necessary instruction [by] permitting the people to leave their other employments, and to assemble together for the hearing of the law, and learning it exactly, and this not once or twice, or oftener, but every week; which thing all other legislators seem to have neglected.[58]

Synagogue gatherings included Scripture readings and exhortations. The New Testament indicates the presence of the same reading and the teaching of the word of God in the synagogue services. Acts 13:14-15 outlines the procedure which was followed.

> But going on from Perga, they arrived at Pisidian Antioch, and on the Sabbath day they [Paul and Barnabas] went into the synagogue and sat down. After the reading of the Law and the Prophets the synagogue officials sent to them, saying, "Brethren, if you have any word of exhortation for the people, say it."

F. F. Bruce makes these comments.

> After the appropriate prayers had been recited and the two scripture lessons read—one from the Pentateuch and the other from some place in the prophetical books bearing some relation to the subject of the Pentateuchal reading—an address was normally delivered by some suitable member of the congregation. It was part of the

---

57. Smith, "The Ancient Synagogue," 4.
58. Flavius Josephus, *The Works of Flavius Josephus*, trans. William Whiston (Grand Rapids: Baker, 1974), 4:221. The passage is found in "Against Apion," II, 18.

The Elements of Worship: Temple and Synagogue

duties of the "rulers of the synagogue" to appoint someone to deliver the address. On this occasion they sent to the two strangers who had come to their city synagogue, inviting them to speak a word of exhortation to the gathering.[59]

To discuss the phrase, *word of exhortation*, in Acts 13:15, Bruce refers to Hebrews 13:22, "I urge you, brethren, bear with this word of exhortation, for I have written to you briefly," commenting, "The expression 'a word of exhortation' [*logos paraklēseōs*] was perhaps a synagogue term for the sermon which followed the Scripture readings (cf. Heb. 13:22)."[60] Lane says that this expression is "an idiomatic designation for the homily or edifying discourse that followed the public reading from the designated portions of Scripture ... "[61]

Luke's gospel reveals the same procedure when Christ worshiped in the synagogue.

> And He came to Nazareth, where He had been brought up; and as was His custom, He entered the synagogue on the Sabbath, and stood up to read. And the book of the prophet Isaiah was handed to Him. And He opened the book and found the place ... And He closed the book, gave it back to the attendant and sat down; and the eyes of all in the synagogue were fixed on Him. And He began to say to them ... (Luke 4:16-21).

Commenting on this text, Lightfoot says, "*Moses* and the Prophets were read in their Synagogues every Sabbath day, Acts 13.15 & 15.21."[62] Then Lightfoot describes the procedure as follows.

> The reader of the *Haphtoroth* or portion out of the Prophets, was ordinarily one of the number of those that had read the Law: he was called out to read by the Minister of the Congregation, he went up into the desk, had the

---
59. F. F. Bruce, *Commentary on the Book of Acts* (Grand Rapids: Eerdmans, 1970), 267-268.
60. Ibid., 268, n. 24.
61. William Lane, *Word Biblical Commentary: Hebrews 9-13* (Dallas: Word Books, 1991), 568.
62. Lightfoot, *Works*, 1:614.

book of the Prophet given him, began with Prayer, and had an interpreter, even as it was with them that read the Law.

And under these Synagogue rulers are we to understand Christ's reading in the Synagogue at this time: namely, as a member of the Synagogue, called out by the Minister, reading according to the accustomed order, the portion in the Prophet when the Law was read (and it is like[ly] he had read some part of the Law before) and having an Interpreter by him to render into *Syriack* the Text he read: he then begins in *Syriack* to preach upon it.[63]

Worship in the synagogue involved a reading from Moses, a corresponding reading from one of the prophets,[64] and then an exhortation or sermon. A reading from the prophets illuminating the portion read from the Pentateuch provided opportunity for the exhortation to look at Moses through the eyes of the prophet and make application to the contemporary situation. Something similar is done today when worship services have an Old Testament reading, a New Testament reading, and then a sermon looking at the Old Testament through the lens of the New Testament to apply God's truth to the congregation.

Scripture readings and exhortations or sermons were not the only parts of the synagogue service. Bruce also refers to appropriate prayers as a part of synagogue worship. As indicated above, after twilight and the sounding of the trumpet, the participants in the temple sacrifices retired to the Chamber of Hewn Stone where they recited the Ten Commandments, the Shema, "Hear O Israel," and a number of benedictions or prayers.[65] As McKinnon suggests, "The latter two, the Shema and Tefillah [prayer], eventually came to constitute the core of the synagogue liturgies, and indeed many scholars have tended to view the interlude just described as a synagogue service within the

---

63. Ibid., 615.
64. McKinnon, "On the Question," 188.
65. Ibid., 162.

Temple service and similarly speak of a synagogue within the temple precincts."[66] Quoting Isaiah 56:7, it may be the above-described practice to which Christ refers when He calls the temple a house of prayer. "He began to teach and say to them, 'Is it not written, "MY HOUSE SHALL BE CALLED A HOUSE OF PRAYER FOR ALL THE NATIONS"'" (Mark 11:17)? Also, note Acts 3:1, "Now Peter and John were going up to the temple at the ninth hour, the hour of prayer"; and Acts 22:17, where Paul says, "It happened when I returned to Jerusalem and was praying in the temple, that I fell into a trance."

After the destruction of the temple, the Shema and Tefillah were "to be recited at the same times of the day and the week as the sacrificial rites had been performed in the Temple."[67] McKinnon argues that Gamaliel II became the leader of the Sanhedrin after the destruction of the temple, arranged the "eighteen benedictions," and regularized the synagogue liturgy in about 80 A.D.[68] It is, therefore, quite conceivable that less than fifty years earlier the synagogues of Judea and Galilee followed a very similar pattern of prayers. Edersheim gives this description:

> Public worship commenced on ordinary occasions with the so-called "Shema," which was preceded in the morning and evening by two "benedictions" and succeeded in the morning by one and in the evening by two, benedictions; the second being strictly speaking an evening prayer. The "Shema" was a kind of "belief" or "creed" composed of these three passages of Scripture: Deut. vi. 4-9; xi. 13-21; Num. xv. 37-41. It obtained its name from the initial word, "shema" : "Here, O Israel," in Deut. vi. 4. From the Mishnah (*Ber. i. 3*), we learn that this part of the service existed before the time of our Lord ...

---

66. Ibid.
67. Ibid., 176.
68. Ibid., 175-176.

The following are the "benedictions" before the "Shema"...

I. *Blessed be Thou, O Lord, King of the world*, who formest light and createst the darkness, Who makest peace and createst everything; Who, in mercy, givest light to the earth and to those who dwell upon it, and in Thy goodness day by day and every day renewest the works of creation. Blessed be the Lord our God for the glory of His handiwork and for the light-giving lights which He has made for His praise. Selah! *Blessed be the Lord our God*, Who hath formed the lights.

II. With great love hast Thou loved us, O Lord our God, and with much overflowing pity hast Thou pitied us, our Father and our king. For the sake of our fathers who trusted Thee, and Thou taughtest them the statutes of life, have mercy upon us and teach us. Enlighten our eyes in Thy law; cause our hearts to cleave to Thy commandments; unite our hearts to love and fear Thy name, and we shall not be put to shame, world without end. For Thou art a God Who preparest salvation, and us hast chosen from among all the nations and tongues, and hast in truth brought us near to Thy great Name—Selah —that we may lovingly praise Thee and Thy Oneness. *Blessed be the Lord Who in love chose his people Israel ...*

The prayer after the "Shema" was as follows:

True it is that Thou art Jehovah our God and the God of our fathers, our Savior and the Savior of our fathers, our Creator, the Rock of our salvation, our Help and our deliverer. Thy Name is from everlasting, and there is no God beside Thee. A new song did they that were delivered sing to Thy Name by the seashore; together did all praise and own Thee King, and say, Jehovah shall reign world without end! *Blessed be the Lord Who saveth Israel!*[69]

The Shema and the accompanying benedictions were recited at the lectern in the synagogue. Mishna *Meggilah* iv. 3 speaks of the leader of the devotions need "to step before the *Tebah*."[70] "'[T]o step before the *Tabah*' (the Ark of the Torah scroll) is a common phrase in rabbinic literature indicating the recitation of the Tephilah; it refers to a member of the congregation rising and standing before the Ark for the recitation."[71] The Tephilah, or prayer, consisted of the eighteen benedictions, in part, listed above.[72] Edersheim records the first three and the last three and the second reads as follows:

> Thou, O Lord art mighty forever; Thou, Who quickenest the dead, art mighty to save. In Thy mercy Thou preservest the living; Thou quickenest the dead; in Thine abundant pity Thou bearest up those who fall, healest those who are diseased, and loosest those who are bound, and fulfillest Thy faithful word to those who sleep in the dust. Who is like unto Thee, Lord of strength, and who can be compared to Thee, Who killest and makest alive, and causest salvation to spring forth? And faithful art Thou to give life unto the dead. *Blessed be Thou Jehovah, Who quickenest the dead!*[73]

This prayer, benediction, or eulogy is quite striking. Note the words placed in italics in the "benedictions" or prayers quoted above. Edersheim observes,

> Another fact, hitherto, so far as we know, unnoticed, requires here to be mentioned. It invests the prayers just quoted with a new and almost unparalleled interest. According to the Mishnah (Megillah, iv. 5), the person who

---

69. Edersheim, *Sketches*, 268-271. Italics added.
70. McKinnon, "On the Question," 173.
71. Ibid., 173. Edersheim, *Sketches*, 272.
72. Ibid., 169.
73. Edersheim, *Sketches*, 273. Italics added.

> read[s] in the synagogue the portion from the prophets was also expected to say the "Shema," and to offer the prayers which have been quoted. It follows that in all likelihood, our Lord Himself had led the devotions in the synagogue of Capernaum on that Sabbath when He read the portion from the prophesies of Isaiah which was that day "fulfilled in their hearing" (Luke iv. 16-21). Nor is it possible to withstand the impression, how specially suitable to the occasion would have been the words of these prayers ... [74]

Scripture readings, exhortations, prescribed prayers and a final benediction were all part of synagogue worship. As noted earlier, designated priests make the morning and evening incense offerings in the temple. "After performing the offering, the chosen priests withdrew from the Sanctuary and together with the other priests blessed the people from the sanctuary steps."[75] Regarding the synagogue, "The liturgical service concluded with the priestly benediction (Num. vi. 23, 24), spoken by the descendants of Aaron."[76] This concluding benediction seems to mirror the priestly blessing in the temple.

Now notice the words in italics in the "benedictions" quoted above: *Blessed be Thou, O Lord, King of the world ... Blessed be the Lord our God ... Blessed be the Lord Who in love chose his people Israel ... Blessed be the Lord Who saveth Israel! Blessed by Thou Jehovah, Who quickenest the dead!* And then compare Eph. 1:3; 2 Cor. 1:3; and 1 Pet. 1:3, which all read, "Blessed be the God and Father of our Lord Jesus Christ ... " Thinking particularly of 2 Corinthians, Paul seems to borrow language from the synagogue in uttering these blessings.[77] If so, there is little reason to fail to see that Paul leans on synagogue procedure when he pronounces his benedictions. As discussed above,

---

74. Ibid., 275.
75. McKinnon, "On the Question," 163.
76. Edersheim, *Sketches*, 275.
77. C. K. Barrett, *The Second Epistle to the Corinthians* (New York: Harper and Row, 1973), 58. Paul Barnett, *The Second Epistle to the Corinthians* (Grand Rapids: Eerdmans, 1997), 66.

when he writes, Paul is "conscious that his letter will be read aloud to the congregation assembled for worship ... "[78] As the blessing at the beginning of the letter reflects the synagogue, it is quite likely that the benediction closing the letter also reflects the synagogue. The apostolic benediction is therefore appropriate for the close of New Testament worship.

CONCLUSIONS

It seems clear from the discussion of the temple sacrifices that the New Testament worship element of praise derives from the temple. The writer to the Hebrews shows the transition from blood sacrifices of thanksgiving to sacrifices of thanksgiving as the fruit of lips giving praise to God (Hebrews 13:15). Paul clearly extends this praise to the New Testament church (Eph. 5:19; Col. 3:16). Praise as an element of worship will be discussed in Part Three.

The synagogue was the local assembly in which the people heard the reading, explanation, and application of Scripture. Our Lord and the apostles affirmed the synagogue practices of prayer, Scripture reading, and exhortation, with their attendance and active participation in the worship of the synagogue. Therefore, it seems likely that the worship elements of reading Scripture and preaching come into the New Testament church from the synagogue. The practice of prayer in New Testament worship and the practice of closing New Testament worship with the Aaronic benediction or an apostolic benediction derive from both the temple and the synagogue. Paul extends these practices into the New Testament church (1 Tim. 2:1; 3:15; and 4:13).

The next steps are to fill out the elements of worship set forth in Scripture, explore the rationale behind an order of worship, and to begin a more specific discussion of each element of worship.

---

78. Barnett, 68.

The Scriptural Elements of Worship

They were continually devoting themselves to the apostles' teaching and to fellowship, to the breaking of bread and to prayer. ~ Acts 2:42

INTRODUCTION

THE PLAN FOR THIS CHAPTER is as follows: First, there are some general observations about the elements of worship and their placement in an order of worship and into the covenantal outlook on worship set forth in Part One. Second, there follows a discussion of the individual elements of worship to establish their propriety more firmly, and to make practical suggestions as to their use. A discussion of preaching related to covenant renewal is reserved for chapter 7. A discussion of the sacraments of baptism and the Lord's Supper will also come later in chapters 8 through 10.

The element of praise will be discussed in Part Three of this study. We then set forth the Biblical position for exclusive psalmody, and answer objections to this position. In Part Four, we discuss instrumental music in worship.

GENERAL OBSERVATIONS

In looking at the elements of worship, consider the Reformation and John Calvin.

The order of public worship in Calvin's congregation at Strassburg was as follows:—

> The service began with an invocation, a confession of sin and a brief absolution. Then followed reading of the Scriptures, singing, and a free prayer. The whole congregation, male and female, joined in chanting the psalms, and thus took an active part in public worship, while formerly they were but passive listeners or spectators. This was in accordance with the protestant doctrine of the general priesthood of believers. The sermon came next, and after it a long general prayer and the Lord's prayer. The service closed with singing and the benediction.[1]

The order of worship in Calvin's Geneva congregation was not substantially different. Referring to the 1542 Geneva service book, T. H. L. Parker describes the "ordinary Sunday morning service" as follows:

> The minister began with a set confession of sin in the name of the congregation, adding some verses of Scripture as he thought good, and then pronouncing the absolution in the form: "To all those who in this way repent and seek Jesus Christ for their salvation, I pronounce absolution in the name of the Father, and of the Son, and of the Holy Spirit. Amen." Hereupon the congregation sang the first four commandments and the minister prayed that these laws might be "written in our hearts so that we may seek only to serve and obey thee." The rest of the commandments were sung as the minister entered the pulpit. He prefaced his sermon with the set prayer leading into the Lord's Prayer. Before the sermon began, however, the congregation sang a psalm

---

1. Philip Schaff, *History of the Christian Church* (Grand Rapids: Eerdmans, 1958), 8:372.

and the minister prayed an extemporary prayer. After the sermon an extemporary bidding prayer (which for Calvin began: "Now let us fall down before the majesty of our good God, praying him that he will give his grace not only to us but also to all peoples and nations of the earth ... ") led into a long prayer beginning "Almighty God, heavenly Father, thou hast promised to hear our requests that we make to thee in the name of thy Son Jesus Christ, the well-beloved of the Lord," and praying for rulers, for pastors and the church, for the salvation of all men, for those in affliction and especially for the persecuted under the Papacy, and for the salvation and sanctification of our own souls. The minister then gave a short explanation of the Lord's Prayer, and after the singing of another psalm, dismissed the congregation with the Aaronic blessing. Apart from the singing and the sermon, the service was short, occupying less than a quarter of an hour.[2]

Moving forward a century, the Westminster Confession of Faith 21:5 briefly summarizes the elements of worship recognized by the Westminster Divines.

> The reading of Scriptures with godly fear; the sound preaching, and conscionable hearing of the Word, in obedience unto God, with understanding, faith, and reverence; singing of Psalms with grace in the heart; as also, the due administration and worthy receiving of the sacraments instituted by Christ; are all parts of the ordinary religious worship of God ...

Scripture clearly commands certain elements of worship: prayer (1 Tim. 2:1 and 3:14-15); reading Scripture (Neh. 8:1-8; Acts 15:21; 1 Tim. 4:13; Rev. 1:3); preaching (Neh. 8:1-8; Rom. 10:14; 2 Tim. 4:2); praise

---

2. T. H. L. Parker, *John Calvin: A Biography* (Philadelphia: Westminster Press, 1975), 86-87.

(Ps. 22:3; Col. 3:16; Heb. 13:15); and the sacraments of baptism and the Lord's Supper (Acts 2:41-42; Matt. 28:19-20; 1 Cor. 11:23-26). Scripture also evidences other elements: call to worship (Ps. 95:6; James 4:8); salutation (Eph. 1:2; Rev. 1:4-6); invocation (2 Cor. 6:16 with 1 John 5:14-15; 1 Kings 8:22-30); offering (Gen. 14:18-19; 1 Cor. 16:2); and benediction (Num. 6:24-27; 1 Cor. 13:14; Heb. 13:20-21).

It is important to distinguish the *circumstances* of worship from the elements of worship. The Westminster Confession of Faith 1:6 says,

> The whole counsel of God, concerning all things necessary for His own glory, man's salvation, faith and life, is either expressly set down in Scripture, or by good and necessary consequence may be deduced from Scripture: unto which nothing at any time is to be added, whether by new revelations of the Spirit, or traditions of men. Nevertheless, we acknowledge the inward illumination of the Spirit of God to be necessary for the saving understanding of such things as are revealed in the word; *and that there are some circumstances concerning the worship of God, and government of the Church, common to human actions and societies, which are to be ordered by the light of nature, and Christian prudence, according to the general rules of the word, which are always to be observed* (italics added).

Scripture commands the elements of worship. The circumstances of worship are matters the church shares with other organizations and societies. Like the Kiwanis Club, the church has a meeting place. The meeting place has heating, air conditioning, seating, and lighting. These are circumstances of worship. Scripture does not command the type of meeting place, heating or cooling, seating, or lighting. We use common sense and wisdom to determine these things.

There are other circumstances more closely related to worship in the church. For example, many churches make Bibles available for people to use. Scripture does not command the presence of Bibles nor does Scripture command what version they must be. Common sense dictates that they ought to be in the common language of the people. Similarly, congregations often use songbooks or Psalters. Scripture commands praise but does not command the use of hymnals or Psalters. Common sense guides the church to use a book of hymns or Psalms to keep the congregation together during praise. These are circumstances of worship. What about instrumental accompaniment? Later, it will be shown that instrumental accompaniment is not a circumstance of worship, and that Scripture commands a cappella praise.

The order of the elements of worship mirrors God's covenant dealings with His people as they enter into the presence of the covenant God. The figures and symbolism of the temple help us here. Worshipers were glad to respond to the call to come before their God. "I was glad when they said unto me, / 'Let us go to the house of the Lord'" (Ps. 122:1). God's house was His dwelling place (Exod. 25:8, Lev. 26:11-12). Entrance into God's house was by way of confession and sacrifice. The worshiper "shall lay his hand on the head of the burnt offering, that it may be accepted for him to make atonement on his behalf" (Lev. 1:4). "This meant transmission and delegation, and implied representation; so that it really pointed to the substitution of the sacrifice for the sacrificer. Hence it was always accompanied by confession of sin and prayer."[3] Atonement means covering. "Its predominant usage is in relation to the *reconciliation* effected between God and sinner, in which sense *atonement for sin* is the *covering* of sin..."[4] As Psalm 32:1 declares, "How blessed is he whose transgression is forgiven, whose sin is covered!"

Moreover, there was also a large laver or sea "between the tent of meeting and the altar" (Exod. 30:18). The priests washed their hands and feet (Exod. 30:19), not *in* the laver, but with water drawn *from* the laver, perhaps "from cocks or spouts."[5] This washing was required

---

3. Alfred Edersheim, *The Temple: Its Ministry and Services* (Peabody: Hendrickson, 1994), 81. See also John W. Kleinig, *Leviticus* (St. Louis: Concordia, 2003), 53-54.
4. George Bush, *Notes, Critical and Practical, on the Book of Leviticus* (Minneapolis: James Family, 1979), 15.
5. George Bush, *Commentary on Exodus* (Grand Rapids: Kregel, 1993), 496.

when the priests entered the tabernacle (Exod. 30:20). In addition, "the lower legs and intestines [of each animal sacrifice] had to be washed so that they were clean before they could be burnt on the altar."[6] See Leviticus 1:9.

When the priests entered the Holy Place, the candlestick was to their left and the table of bread was to their right (Exod. 26:35). The altar of incense was before them in front of the veil, separating them from the Most Holy Place or throne room of God (Exod. 40:5). "Ancient symbolism, both Jewish and Christian, regarded the 'bread of the Presence' as an emblem of Messiah."[7] The bread

> meant that the Covenant-people owned "His Presence" as their bread and life; the candlestick, that He was their Light-giver and Light; while between the table of shewbread and the candlestick burned the incense on the golden altar, to show us that life and light are joined together, and come to us in fellowship with God and prayer.[8]

Worshipers called to enjoy fellowship with God and to enjoy His presence, confess their sins, receive forgiveness and cleansing through sacrifice, and confess Messiah as their Light and Life. From the vantage point of believers under the New Covenant, an order of worship might look like this:

Call to worship	Prayer for Enlightenment
Invocation	Proclamation of the Word
Salutation	Prayer
Praise	Praise in Response to the Word
Reading of the Law	Presentations of Tithes and Offerings
Prayer of Confession	Prayer for the Church and the World
Assurance of Pardon	Praise
Praise	Benediction
Reading of Scripture	

---

6. Kleinig, *Leviticus*, 62.
7. Edersheim, *Temple*, 144.
8. Ibid.

This order of worship is also dialogical in nature. God speaks to His people, and they respond. God calls them to worship, they pray that He will dwell with them, and God greets them as they enter His presence. God then speaks to them in His word, they confess their sins, and He declares He forgives them. They also enter into this dialogue with their praise. They may use praise as a proper response to God. The covenantal perspective imbedded in the order of worship regularly reminds God's people that their standing before God is by grace alone through Christ alone.

This order of worship arises from a proper understanding of the covenantal context of worship, the nature of worship, and the elements of worship. Believers are responsible for the clear implications arising from the direct teachings of Scripture, that which we learn by "good and necessary consequence," as well as the direct teachings themselves. The Westminster Confession of Faith 1:6 teaches, "The whole counsel of God, concerning all things necessary for His own glory, man's salvation, faith and life, is either expressly set down in Scripture, or *by good and necessary consequence may be deduced from Scripture*: unto which nothing at any time is to be added … " (italics added). With these general remarks, a closer look at the respective elements of worship is next.

DISCUSSION OF THE ELEMENTS OF WORSHIP

When you lead the congregation through the order of worship, be deliberate. This is not a time for casual talk. Lead the people through the elements without making announcements or comments. You need not tell people what you and they are going to do. If explanations are needed or helpful, make them brief. Worship is a time for God to deal with His people. God is graciously present in corporate public worship to apply His covenant word to the hearts of His covenant people and to assure them that He is their God and they are His people. Given this foundation, when you participate in worship or lead in worship you should understand God's purposes. You should lead and be led into God's gracious presence.

Call God's people to worship. Purposefully call the covenant assembly to enter God's covenant presence. Call the people to draw away from the world. Not only so, lead them away from the world. Worship is heavenly refreshment not worldly pleasure. Remember that leading in worship is a shepherding activity. Call God's people into God's presence. Lead them into His presence. Listen to our Lord Jesus Christ, our great Shepherd. "Come to Me, all who are weary and heavy-laden, and I will give you rest. Take My yoke upon you and learn from Me, for I am gentle and humble in heart, and you will find rest for your souls" (Matt. 11:28-29).

When you call God's people to worship, you do not issue an order or give a command. The Biblical metaphor is not that of a military commander but of a shepherd. When you lead in worship, you speak for Christ and invite those present to come to Him. You base the call upon God's goodness and grace. Listen to Psalm 100.

> Shout joyfully to the Lord, all the earth.
> Serve the Lord with gladness;
> Come before Him with joyful singing.
> Know that the Lord Himself is God;
> It is He who has made us, and not we ourselves;
> We are His people and the sheep of His pasture.
> Enter His gates with thanksgiving
> And His courts with praise.
> Give thanks to Him, bless His name.
> For the Lord is good;
> His lovingkindness is everlasting
> And His faithfulness to all generations.

Although the call may be in the imperative, it expresses a plea. Take Psalm 95:1-2 for example.

> O come, let us sing for joy to the Lord,

> Let us shout joyfully to the rock of our salvation.
> Let us come before His presence with thanksgiving,
> Let us shout joyfully to Him with psalms.

You are inviting the people into the God's gracious presence. Scripture promises, "Draw near to God and He will draw near to you" (James 4:8). As already discussed, God commits Himself to meet with His people. Trust Him to do so.

Invoke or summon the presence of God. After calling God's people into God's presence, summon the good God of the covenant to fulfill his promise, to join His people, and to bless them with His covenant presence. The essence of the invocation is to call upon God to dwell with His people as promised. God assured Moses, "My presence shall go with you, and I will give you rest" (Exod. 33:14). Moses responded,

> If Your presence does not go with us, do not lead us up from here. For how then can it be known that I have found favor in Your sight, I and Your people? Is it not by Your going with us, so that we, I and Your people, may be distinguished from all the other people who are upon the face of the earth? (Exod. 33:15-16)

How is the local congregation gathered for worship distinguished from other meetings carried out in the community? Is it simply the fact that God's people sing religious songs and use the Bible as the basis for their teaching and instruction? No! They are distinguished from other gatherings by God's gracious presence. There is therefore a sense in which pastors and elders leading in worship are in a position similar to that of Moses. They seek God's gracious presence.

Therefore, the invocation is *not* a prayer of confession. In some Reformed circles, the invocation is a plea for acceptance despite sinfulness. "Lord, we realize we are unworthy of You. Our sin separates us from You. We dare not lift our eyes toward heaven. We plead with you to accept us because of Christ. We plead with you to find our worship acceptable in your sight because of Jesus Christ our Lord." A confession of sin is *not* an invocation. Save such words for the time of confession after the reading of God's Law.

In addition, the invocation is *not* the pastoral prayer. The invocation is not the place to lay congregational petitions before the Lord. It is not the time to seek healing and comfort for the suffering within the flock. Nor is it the time to recite the reasons for congregational praise. Save these matters for the pastoral prayer. Petition God's presence, help, and support. Seek God's gracious presence to open ears, to enlighten eyes, and to apply His covenant word to the people's hearts. Pray something along these lines:

> Great God of Heaven, thank you for calling your people together for worship. Be pleased to meet now with us as your people assembled before you. Manifest your gracious presence in our midst. Apply your covenant word to our hearts. Open our eyes to see you in your word. Open our ears to hear you speak to us from your word. Fill us with your Spirit to sing your praise and to cry out to you in our prayers. Fulfill your covenant promise to us to be our God through Jesus Christ and assure us that we are indeed your people through the work of your Son and our only Savior, Jesus Christ the Lord. Hear us in His great name we pray. Amen.

Greet the people on behalf of their God. Think of the epistles and letters of the Bible. They were written to be read to various congregations and groups of people. They are forms of oral communication. Paul's famous run-on sentences betray his oral emphasis. Note these Pauline greetings. "Grace to you and peace from God our Father and the Lord Jesus Christ" (Rom. 1:7; 1 Cor. 1:3; 2 Cor. 1:2; Gal. 1:3; Eph. 1:3; Phil. 1:2; and 2 Thess. 2:2). "Grace to you and peace from God our Father" (Col. 1:2). "Grace to you and peace" (1 Thess. 1:1). Note John's beautiful greeting in Revelation 1:4-6.

> Grace to you and peace, from Him who is and who was

and who is to come, and from the seven Spirits who are before His throne, and from Jesus Christ, the faithful witness, the firstborn of the dead, and the ruler of the kings of the earth. To Him who loves us and released us from our sins by His blood—and He has made us to be a kingdom, priests to His God and Father—to Him be the glory and the dominion forever and ever. Amen.

These greetings are in keeping with God's commitment to worship. Remember 2 Corinthians 6:16-17. Refer to the earlier exposition arguing that this passage deals with worship.

> For we are the temple of the living God; just as God said, "I WILL DWELL IN THEM AND WALK AMONG THEM; AND I WILL BE THEIR GOD, AND THEY SHALL BE MY PEOPLE." Therefore, "COME OUT FROM THEIR MIDST AND BE SEPARATE," says the Lord. "AND DO NOT TOUCH WHAT IS UNCLEAN." *And I will welcome you* (2 Cor. 6:16-17, italics added).

The people of Israel returned to Jerusalem from Babylon with the vessels of the Lord to reinstitute the Biblical worship of God. Paul quotes from Isaiah 52:11 to this end. In the New Testament context, God promises to welcome His people as they approach Him in worship, having been invited by Him. The greetings, exemplified in the epistles, express this welcome. The pastor or elder leading in worship has the privilege of issuing this welcome. It is perfectly appropriate at this time in the service for the people, having been welcomed into God's gracious presence, to offer Him the praise He is due.

Read God's Law. The Ten Commandments are the center, focus, and face of God's covenant. "So [Moses] was there with the Lord forty days and forty nights; he did not eat bread or drink water. And he wrote on the tablets the words of the covenant, the Ten Commandments [lit. *ten words*]" (Exod. 34:28). As Milton Terry indicates, "Thus the Decalogue, the totality and substance of the whole Torah, or Law, is spoken of as *the ten words* (Exod. xxxiv, 28; Deut. iv, 13; x, 4)."[9] The Ten Commandments stand in the place of and represent God's covenant as a whole. Putting it confessionally, "The moral law is summarily comprehended in the ten commandments" (WSC 41). A. A. Hodge, therefore, says, "Every specific duty taught in any portion of the Scriptures may more or less be referred to one or other of the general precepts taught in the Decalogue."[10] What then do you have when you add up the Ten Commandments? "The sum of the ten commandments is, to love the Lord our God with all our heart, with all our soul, with all our strength, and with all our mind; and our neighbor as ourselves" (WSC 42). The Apostle Paul confirms this confessional statement, "For this, 'You shall not commit adultery, You shall not murder, You shall not steal, You shall not covet,' and if there is any other commandment, it is summed up in this saying, 'You shall love your neighbor as yourself'" (Rom. 13:9). Our Lord also confirms this. "On these two commandments depend the whole Law and the Prophets" (Matt. 22:40).

Rather than repeatedly rehearsing the Ten Commandments, other portions of God's covenant word will suffice under this element of worship. Read from the writings of Moses. For instance, Numbers 14:1-4 gives opportunity to seek forgiveness and cleansing for our own rebel hearts and love for the things of the world rather than our love for God and His word.

> Then all the congregation lifted up their voices and cried, and the people wept that night. All the sons of Israel grumbled against Moses and Aaron; and the whole congregation said to them, "Would that we had died in the land of Egypt! Or would that we had died in this wilderness! Why is the Lord bringing us into this land, to fall by the sword? Our wives and our little ones will become plunder; would it not be better for us to return

---

9. Milton Terry, *Biblical Hermeneutics* (Grand Rapids: Zondervan, 1974), 383.
10. A. A. Hodge, *The Confession of Faith* (Carlisle: Banner of Truth, 1978), 252.

to Egypt?" So they said to one another, "Let us appoint a leader and return to Egypt."

Read from the writings of Prophets. Malachi 3:6-12 prepares us to seek God's forgiveness for misplaced priorities in giving and the kind of testimony the church bears to others in the community.

> "For I, the Lord, do not change; therefore you, O sons of Jacob, are not consumed. From the days of your fathers you have turned aside from My statutes and have not kept them. Return to Me, and I will return to you," says the Lord of hosts. "But you say, 'How shall we return?' Will a man rob God? Yet you are robbing Me! But you say, 'How have we robbed You?' In tithes and offerings. You are cursed with a curse, for you are robbing Me, the whole nation of you! Bring the whole tithe into the storehouse, so that there may be food in My house, and test Me now in this," says the Lord of hosts, "if I will not open for you the windows of heaven and pour out for you a blessing until it overflows. Then I will rebuke the devourer for you, so that it will not destroy the fruits of the ground; nor will your vine in the field cast its grapes," says the Lord of hosts. "All the nations will call you blessed, for you shall be a delightful land," says the Lord of hosts.

Read from the Psalms. Psalm 2 opens the door to pray for the nation, to seek the gift of repentance for government leaders and the people at large, to beg God's forgiveness for the nation, and to pray for renewed national allegiance to Christ.

> Why are the nations in an uproar
> And the peoples devising a vain thing?
> The kings of the earth take their stand
> And the rulers take counsel together
> Against the Lord and against His Anointed, saying,
> "Let us tear their fetters apart

And cast away their cords from us!"
He who sits in the heavens laughs,
The Lord scoffs at them.
Then He will speak to them in His anger
And terrify them in His fury, saying,
"But as for Me, I have installed My King
Upon Zion, My holy mountain.
I will surely tell of the decree of the Lord: He said to Me,
'You are My Son, Today I have begotten You.
Ask of Me, and I will surely give the nations as Your inheritance,
And the very ends of the earth as Your possession.
You shall break them with a rod of iron,
You shall shatter them like earthenware.'"
Now therefore, O kings, show discernment;
Take warning, O judges of the earth.
Worship the Lord with reverence
And rejoice with trembling.
Do homage to the Son, that He not become angry, and you perish in the way,
For His wrath may soon be kindled.
How blessed are all who take refuge in Him!

Read from the Gospels. Matthew 13:18-23 accentuates the need to pray for open ears and hearts and to bear the fruit of the Spirit that defines us at followers of Christ and members of His kingdom.

> Hear then the parable of the sower. When anyone hears the word of the kingdom and does not understand it, the evil one comes and snatches away what has been sown in his heart. This is the one on whom seed was sown beside the road. The one on whom seed was sown on the rocky places, this is the man who hears the word and immediately receives it with joy; yet he has no firm root in himself, but is only temporary, and when affliction or persecution arises because of the word, immediately he

> falls away. And the one on whom seed was sown among the thorns, this is the man who hears the word, and the worry of the world and the deceitfulness of wealth choke the word, and it becomes unfruitful. And the one on whom seed was sown on the good soil, this is the man who hears the word and understands it; who indeed bears fruit and brings forth, some a hundredfold, some sixty, and some thirty.

Read from the Epistles. Galatians 5:19-21 simply sets forth the fruit of an unacceptable life and the propriety of seeking God's forgiveness for living after the flesh.

> Now the deeds of the flesh are evident, which are: immorality, impurity, sensuality, idolatry, sorcery, enmities, strife, jealousy, outbursts of anger, disputes, dissensions, factions, envying, drunkenness, carousing, and things like these, of which I forewarn you, just as I have forewarned you, that those who practice such things will not inherit the kingdom of God.

The procedure is simply to read and pray. Read selected texts highlighting sin, lead the congregation in prayers of confession, and inform them that Christ is the answer to their sins.

Offer assurance of pardon. John's First Epistle has assurance as its purpose. "These things I have written to you who believe in the name of the Son of God, so that you may know that you have eternal life" (1 John 5:13). This assurance is also God's purpose. How do God's people know that they have eternal life? They must experience God's forgiveness through Jesus Christ. The Good God guides His people to such assurance through the words of the apostle. "If we confess our sins, He is faithful and righteous to forgive us our sins and to cleanse us from all unrighteousness" (1 John 1:9). Read words of assurance from Scripture such as 1 John 1:9 or Romans 5:1-2. "Therefore, having been justified by faith, we have peace with God through our Lord

Jesus Christ." Offer God's people God's assurance according to God's word. "To all those who in this way repent and seek Jesus Christ for their salvation, I pronounce absolution in the name of the Father, and of the Son, and of the Holy Spirit. Amen."[11] Many passages point to Christ and offer members of the congregation assurance of pardon for their sins. After this assurance of pardon, it is again appropriate for God's people to lift their voices in praise.

Read the Scriptures. Read God's covenant word to His covenant people. Reading the Scripture text before the sermon is one purpose for the reading of Scripture. However, the call to worship, the salutation, the reading of the law, the assurance of pardon, in addition to the reading before the sermon, are all Scripture readings. Each reading has a specific purpose in worship.

Scripture reading is commanded. "Moses from ancient generations has in every city those who preach him, since he is read in the synagogues every Sabbath" (Acts 15:21). Our Lord approved of such reading by His active participation in the synagogue worship. "He came to Nazareth, where He had been brought up; and as was His custom, He entered the synagogue on the Sabbath, and stood up to read. And the book of the prophet Isaiah was handed to Him" (Luke 4:16-17). When Paul directs Pastor Timothy concerning the life of the church (1 Tim. 3:15), he gives this positive command, "Until I come, give attention to the public reading of Scripture, to exhortation and teaching" (1 Tim. 4:13).

Since Paul associates the public reading of Scripture with "exhortation and teaching" (1 Tim. 4:13), the Scripture reading is normally thought of as the reading of a text before the sermon. However, as seen above, the Bible exemplifies different purposes in different books and displays different purposes in different texts. Some Scriptures call God's people to worship (Ps. 149:1). Other Scriptures wel-

---

11. Parker, *Calvin*, 86.

come them into God's presence (Isa. 9:1-2). Some Scriptures present God's Law (Exod. 20; Deut. 5). Other Scriptures are confessions of sin (Ps. 51). Happily, some Scriptures assure God's people of pardon and forgiveness (Ps. 32:1-2). God commands the public reading of His word. God also commands the reading of various Scripture texts for the purposes He designs in the respective texts themselves.

Keeping in mind God's purpose in respective texts when reading them in public worship assures both pastor and people that God will use both the reading and hearing of Scripture as a means of grace. Paul reminds Timothy, "From childhood you have known the sacred writings which are able to give you the wisdom that leads to salvation through faith which is in Christ Jesus" (2 Tim. 3:15). John indicates there is blessing associated with the public reading and hearing of Scripture. "Blessed is he who reads and those who hear the words of the prophecy, and heed the things which are written in it; for the time is near" (Rev. 1:3). The assembly of God's people is an optimum place to read Scripture. God commits Himself to this worshiping assembly to apply and confirm His covenant in the hearts of His people. Practice is, therefore, required. Read purposefully and prayerfully without rushing. Read naturally, with appropriate emphasis. Read with faith that God will carry out His purposes by the power of the Spirit in and through His word.

Pray publicly and seek God's covenant blessings. Paul directs Timothy on how to pursue his ministry within the church. "I write so that you will know how one ought to conduct himself in the household of God, which is the church of the living God, the pillar and support of the truth" (1 Tim. 3:14-15). Given this purpose statement, when Paul writes of prayer, he has in mind public prayer. "First of all, then, I urge that entreaties and prayers, petitions and thanksgivings, be made on behalf of all men, for kings and all who are in authority, so that we may lead a tranquil and quiet life in all godliness and dignity" (1 Tim. 2:1-2). Scripture commands public prayer.

As in the case of the public reading of Scripture, public prayer is for different purposes according to God's will. "This is the confidence which we have before Him, that, *if we ask anything according to His will*, He hears us" (1 John 5:14, italics added). God's will is to graciously dwell with His assembled, worshiping people. Pray according to God's will and invoke God's presence. Confession of sin is prayer according to God's will. Lead God's people in confessing your sins and their sins.

When praying according to God's will, pray *with confidence*. "*This is the confidence which we have before Him*, that, if we ask anything according to His will, He hears us" (1 John 5:14, italics added). Pray *with faith*. "All things you ask in prayer, believing, you will receive" (Matt. 21:22). Pray *with fervency, heartiness, and strength*. "The effectual fervent prayer of a righteous man availeth much" (James 5:16, KJV). Pray *with persistence*. "I say to you, ask [and keep on asking], and it will be given to you; seek [and keep on seeking], and you will find; knock [and keep on knocking], and it will be opened to you" (Luke 11:9).

In pastoral prayer, begin with praise. "Pray, then, in this way: 'Our Father who is in heaven, / Hallowed be Your name'" (Matt. 6:9). Consider other facets of our Lord's model prayer (Matt. 6:9-15). Include confession of sin and words of comfort if these are not separate elements in the service of worship. Finish with needs. "Therefore let us draw near with confidence to the throne of grace, so that we may receive mercy and find grace to help in time of need" (Heb. 4:16). People in the congregation will learn from your prayers. "It happened that while Jesus was praying in a certain place, after He had finished, one of His disciples said to Him, 'Lord, teach us to pray just as John also taught his disciples'" (Luke 11:1). In addition, feel free to prepare your prayers in writing. Thoughtful, written prayers are often more effective than unprepared, extemporaneous prayers. The pastoral prayer ought always to be a prepared, thoughtful, purposeful, trusting approach to God through Christ.

Remember that the assembly of God's people is an optimum place to pray. God is graciously present. Prayer is a means of grace. God is pleased to use the prayers of His people as the means to accomplish His purposes in their lives. William Greenhill offers this reminder to trust God in the use of His means:

> We must not neglect means, and leave all to God, that is tempting the Most High; neither must we trust to means when used, that is to idolize the creature: but we must use means, and look to God to be all in them (for without him nothing is done); and if we make him all in the means, we shall make him all after them.[12]

Receive gifts and tithes and offerings from God's people. Although some doubt that offerings are an element of worship,[13] God does command the receiving of tithes and offerings. Andrew Quigley writes:

> God has never left us in any doubt as to how we should worship him. In fact he has given specific instructions which preclude us from doing what we think is best. One aspect of these instructions relates to the matter of giving to him. " ... No man should appear before the Lord empty-handed: Each of you must bring a gift in proportion to the way the Lord your God has blessed you" (Deuteronomy 16:16, 17).
>
> This instruction in turn formed the basis for Paul's direction to the church at Corinth, "on the first day of every week, each one of you should set aside a sum of money in keeping with his income ... " (1 Corinthians 16:2).[14]

---

12. William Greenhill, *An Exposition of Ezekiel* (Carlisle: Banner of Truth, 1994), 741.
13. For example, the Westminster Confession of Faith 21:5 does not list offerings among the "parts of the ordinary religious worship of God."
14. Andrew Quigley, *Giving in the Church* (Airdrie: In the Pew Publications, 1997), 6.

Pastor Quigley connects the public offerings commanded in the Old Testament to Paul's command in 1 Corinthians 16:2. Does 1 Corinthians 16:2 refer to weekly offerings received as a part of public worship? Charles Hodge argues that it does. First the text: "On the first day of every week each one of you is to put aside and save, as he may prosper, so that no collections be made when I come." As Hodge says, "The direction is nothing more definite than, *let him place by himself*, i.e. let him take to himself what he means to give."[15] The NASB then uses the term *save*. The original language is a present participle, *thesaurizōn*, treasuring. This word "means *putting into the treasury*, or *hoarding up*, and is perfectly consistent with the assumption that the place of deposit was some common treasury, and not every man's own house."[16]

The question then arises, "If Paul directed this money to be laid up *at home*, why was the first day of the week selected?" As Hodge goes on to say, "The only reason that can be assigned for requiring the thing to be done on the first day of the week, is, that on that day the Christians were accustomed to meet, and what each one had laid aside from his weekly gains could be treasured up, i.e. put into the common treasury of the church."[17]

Since Paul's request was "that no collections be made when I come," Hodge argues, "The probability is, therefore, Paul intended to direct the Corinthians to make a collection every Lord's day for the poor, when they met for worship."[18] Leon Morris concurs, "But as Paul expressly deprecates the collecting of the money when he arrives (which would be necessary if they all had it laid by at home) it is perhaps better to think of it as being stored in the church treasury."[19] In summary, "Paul instructs each member of the church in Corinth individually to donate to the common fund on the first day of the

---

15. Charles Hodge, *An Exposition of the First Epistle to the Corinthians* (Grand Rapids: Eerdmans, 1965), 364.
16. Ibid.
17. Ibid.
18. Ibid.
19. Leon Morris, *The First Epistle of Paul to the Corinthians* (Grand Rapids: Eerdmans, 1979), 238.

week ... "[20] Commenting on this text, Ralph Martin adds, "Money which had been honestly gained in the toil of the week is to be brought to the assembly of the church and thus made part of the Sunday worship."[21]

What about the propriety of tithing, the practice of giving one tenth of our income to the church? After Abraham rescued his nephew, Lot, from the four kings who overthrew Sodom and Gomorrah, Melchizedek, priest of God Most High, met him. When Melchizedek blessed Abraham, "He gave him a tenth of all" (Gen. 14:19). The Apostle Paul declares, "It is those who are of faith who are sons of Abraham" (Gal. 3:7). He says "to those who are of the faith of Abraham" that Abraham "is the father of us all" (Rom. 4:16). Since Abraham is the father of our faith, it makes sense that we ought to follow him in tithing.

Tithing, practiced long before Moses (Gen. 14:20; 28:22), was later institutionalized by God's command.

> You shall seek the Lord *at the place which the Lord your God will choose* from all your tribes, to establish His name there for His dwelling, and there you shall come. There you shall bring your burnt offerings, your sacrifices, *your tithes*, the contribution of your hand, your votive offerings, your freewill offerings, and the firstborn of your herd and of your flock. There also you and your households shall eat before the Lord your God, and rejoice in all your undertakings in which the Lord your God has blessed you (Deut. 12:5-7, italics added).

The place of God's choosing was Zion, where Solomon built the temple. It was to this place of assembly that God commanded the people to bring their tithes. Malachi repeats the command during the time of the second temple. "'Bring the whole tithe into the storehouse, so that there may be food in My house, and test Me now in this,' says the Lord of hosts, 'if I will not open for you the windows of heaven

---

20. David Downs, *The Offering of the Gentiles* (Tübingen: Mohr Siebeck, 2008), 128.
21. Ralph P. Martin, *Worship in the Early Church* (Westwood, NJ: Fleming H. Revell, 1964), 80.

and pour out for you a blessing until it overflows'" (Mal. 3:10). The temple, as already seen, foreshadowed the church (2 Cor. 6:16). A basic Reformed hermeneutical principle is that Old Testament commands remain valid and binding unless specifically abrogated in the New Testament.[22] Therefore, tithing remains a valid principle for the New Testament church, since the command to tithe has never been abrogated.

The case of tithing is *similar* to that of the Sabbath. As already discussed, early Sabbath practice was incorporated into the Ten Commandments. There was, therefore, both a moral and a ceremonial aspect to the Sabbath. The abrogation of the ceremonial law did not set aside the moral requirement of the Sabbath. Although *similar*, the case for tithing is not the *same* as that for the Sabbath. Pastor Quigley observes, "Whilst it is true that tithing was an ancient custom, which Abram observed and which Jacob vowed to observe, and that it was subsequently embraced within the ceremonial Law, the matter of whether or not it is a creation ordinance is open to discussion."[23] Although tithing may not be a creation ordinance, and although there were ceremonial aspects to tithing, the abrogation of the ceremonial law does not necessarily set aside the principle followed by Abraham. As Andrew Quigley says,

> In addressing the hypocrisy of the Pharisees, the Lord Jesus commanded that tithing be observed as well as the 'more important matters.' "Woe to you, teachers of the law and Pharisees, you hypocrites! You give a tenth of your spices—mint, dill and cumin. But you have neglected he more important matters of the law—justice, mercy and faith. You should have practiced the latter without neglecting the former (*reference to things tithed*)" (Matthew 23:23).[24]

---

22. Hodge, *Confession*, 255.
23. Quigley, *Giving*, 14.
24. Ibid., 13.

Tithing is a principle incorporated into the ceremonial law. Justice, mercy, and faith are also principles incorporated into the ceremonial law. Christ commends *both*. Justice, mercy, and faith are not abrogated with the setting aside of the ceremonial law. As a principle preceding the ceremonial law, neither is tithing.

Part of the beauty of tithing is God's genius in requiring this specific amount. For most people, taking the first ten percent of their gross income requires them to adjust their lifestyle to fit the other ninety percent. In other words, when they give the first ten percent to the Lord, He then governs the use of their entire income. The tithe is also based upon gross income. The idea is not to deduct living expenses (food, clothing, rent, taxes, etc.) and then tithe on the net. When believers tithe on their gross income, they give God the glory He is due by recognizing that all their income belongs to the Lord.

Add to tithing the fact that under the Old Testament economy, God required tithes *and* offerings. "Will a man rob God? Yet you are robbing Me! But you say, 'How have we robbed You?' *In tithes and offerings*" (Mal. 3:8, italics added). Tithes and offerings were to be given in accord with God's blessing (Deut. 16:10, 17, 1 Cor. 16:2). The tithe should, therefore, be the beginning of individual and family giving. God calls for giving generously beyond the tithe.

The New Testament upholds the principle of generosity. For this reason, Paul commends the churches of Macedonia: "For I testify that according to their ability, and beyond their ability, *they gave* of their own accord" (2 Cor. 8:3). He reminds believers, "Each one *must do* just as he has purposed in his heart, not grudgingly or under compulsion, for God loves a cheerful giver" (2 Cor. 9:7). He also exhorts the people of God to "remember the words of the Lord Jesus, that He Himself said, 'It is more blessed to give than to receive'" (Acts 20:35).

Finally, the manner in which the churches receive the gifts and tithes of God's people varies. The command is to "bring the whole tithe into the storehouse" (Mal. 3:10). Passing offering plates or offering bags is common. Some churches place offering boxes in their worship area.

Worshipers may place their offerings in these boxes at a designated time during worship service.[25] Giving is an *element* of worship. The manner of receiving such gifts is a *circumstance* of worship.

Pronounce the benediction. God commands the benediction (Num. 6:22-27).

> Then the Lord spoke to Moses, saying, "Speak to Aaron and to his sons, saying,
>> 'Thus you shall bless the sons of Israel.
>> You shall say to them:
>> The Lord bless you, and keep you;
>> The Lord make His face shine on you,
>> And be gracious to you;
>> The Lord lift up His countenance on you,
>> And give you peace.'
>
> So they shall invoke My name on the sons of Israel, and I then will bless them."

Numbers 6:22-27 is an Old Testament benediction. Are benedictions commanded in the New Testament? Remember the "benedictions" used in the synagogue quoted above in chapter 5: *Blessed be Thou, O Lord, King of the world ... Blessed be the Lord our God ... Blessed be the Lord Who in love chose his people Israel ... Blessed be the Lord Who saveth Israel! Blessed by Thou Jehovah, Who quickenest the dead!* Then compare these blessings with the salutations in Eph. 1:3; 2 Cor. 1:3; and 1 Pet. 1:3, which all read, "Blessed be the God and Father of our Lord Jesus Christ ... " Paul seems to borrow language from the worship of the synagogue in uttering these blessings.[26] If so, Paul very likely leans on synagogue procedure when he also pronounces his benedictions. As the blessings at the beginning of His let-

---

25. Churches that encourage worshipers to place their tithes and offering in offering boxes before or after the worship service may hold that giving is not an element of worship.
26. C. K. Barrett, *The Second Epistle to the Corinthians* (New York: Harper and Row, 1973), 58. Paul Barnett, *The Second Epistle to the Corinthians* (Grand Rapids: Eerdmans, 1997), 66.

ters reflect synagogue blessings, it is quite likely that the benedictions closing his letters also reflect synagogue worship. At the same time, when he writes, Paul is "conscious that his letter will be read aloud to the congregation assembled for worship ... "[27] The benediction is, therefore, appropriate for the close of New Testament worship.

A *benediction* is *good speaking*. A *blessing*, in the Greek of the Septuagint, is also a *good word*. To *bless*, in the Greek, is to *speak well of*. Here, God commands the priests to pronounce a blessing upon the people. At the same time, God Himself promises He will bless, speak well of, the people. What God says, He brings to pass. Calvin therefore says,

> The promise, which is finally subjoined, gives assurance that this was no empty or useless ceremony, when He declares that He will bless the people. And hence we gather, that whatsoever the ministers of the Church do by God's command, is ratified by Him with a real and solid result; since He declares nothing by His ministers which He will not Himself fulfill and perform by the efficacy of His Spirit. But we must observe that He does not so transfer the office of blessing to His priests, as to resign this right to them; for after having entrusted this ministry to them, He claims the accomplishment of the thing for Himself alone.[28]

The blessing of Numbers 6:22-27 is threefold. First, "The Lord bless you, and keep you." This "first blessing forms not only the general foundation of the whole benediction, of the entire salvation of revelation, but is at the same time the first special blessing."[29] In the second blessing, "The Lord make His face shine on you, / And be gracious to you," we are confronted with "the Light of the knowledge of the glory

---

27. Barnett, 68.
28. John Calvin, *Commentaries on the Last Four Books of Moses*, trans. Charles William Bingham (Grand Rapids: Baker, 1979), 2:247.
29. John Peter Lange, *Numbers*, trans. Samuel T. Lowrie and A. Grosman (Grand Rapids: Zondervan, 1960), 43.

of God *in the face of Christ*" (2 Cor. 4:6). In the third blessing, "The Lord lift up His countenance on you, / And give you peace," the Lord lifts His countenance upon believers. God's blessing reverses the effects of sin. God asked Cain, "Why are you angry? And why has your countenance fallen?" (Gen. 4:6). Sin, working from within, affects the face. On the other hand, the Spirit's fruit, growing from within, lifts the countenance. "In these three blessings most of the fathers and earlier theologians saw an allusion to the mystery of the Trinity ... "[30] As Keil and Delitzsch go on to say,

> Not only does the name Jehovah denote God as the absolute Being, who revealed Himself as Father, Son, and Spirit in the historical development of His purpose of salvation for the redemption of fallen man; but the substance of this blessing, which He caused to be pronounced upon His congregation, unfolded the grace of God in the threefold way in which it is communicated to us through the Father, Son, and Spirit.[31]

Perhaps the threefold benediction of Numbers 6:22-26 is the basis for Paul's threefold Trinitarian benediction. "The grace of the Lord Jesus Christ, and the love of God, and the fellowship of the Holy Spirit, be with you all" (2 Cor. 13:14).

Notice verse 27 following the benediction itself; here, the word translated *invoke* means *to place upon*. God's *name* is associated with His *character*. When God places His name upon believers, he invests them with His character.[32] Believers, therefore, have the privilege of being a people called by His name (2 Chron. 7:17, Dan. 9:19). As a result, they should recognize that the benediction is a means of grace, not a perfunctory act marking the end of worship. When the pastor pronounces a Biblical benediction, he engages in another presenta-

---

30. C. F. Keil and F. Delitzsch, *Biblical Commentary on the Old Testament, The Pentateuch*, trans. James Martin (Grand Rapids: Eerdmans, 1981), 3:41.
31. Ibid., 42.
32. J. A. Motyer, "Name," *The New Bible Dictionary*, ed. J. D. Douglas (Grand Rapids: Eerdmans, 1962), 862-863.

tion of Scripture to the congregation. In this case, he follows God's will and carries out God's purposes by pronouncing His blessing upon His covenant people using His words. The pastor ought to be deliberate in pronouncing the benediction, taking his time, surveying the congregation and looking at God's people as he pronounces the benediction. The pastor ought to expect God's blessing, and thus teach God's people also to expect God's blessing.

Some pastors add conditions or limitations to the benediction by saying, "To all those who sincerely acknowledge Jesus Christ and have the hope of eternal life, hear the blessing God gives to you." In Numbers, the blessing is pronounced upon the members of the visible church. Beyond doubt, Israel was a mixed multitude, ethnically and spiritually (Exod. 12:38). They were a people created from a "diverse mingling of other nations who joined the Israelites,"[33] and the latter especially were "the occasion of various sins within Israel."[34] Yet God commands this benediction without conditions.

Similarly, the Corinthian church had its problems. In his introduction to 2 Corinthians, Calvin notes "that some wicked men were still refusing to acknowledge Paul's authority and persisting in their obstinacy."[35] Yet, the apostle Paul ends his Epistle with these familiar words, "The grace of the Lord Jesus Christ, and the love of God, and the fellowship of the Holy Spirit, be with you all" (2 Cor. 13:14). Paul speaks to the visible body. He adds no conditions or limitations. Do the same; simply pronounce the benediction.

CONCLUSION

Remember, the elements of worship are means of grace. The believer's posture before God is to enter His presence as He prescribes, and to reverently use His designated means. The term *means* is used here in a sense more broad than the traditional *means of grace*. Westmin-

---

33. J. Rabbinowitz, *The Book of Exodus, The Soncino Chumash*, ed. A. Cohen (New York: Soncino, 1993), 396.
34. R. Alan Cole, *Exodus* (Downers Grove: Inter-Varsity, 1973), 113.
35. John Calvin, *The Second Epistle of Paul to the Corinthians and the Epistles to Timothy, Titus, and Philemon*, trans. T. A. Smail, ed. David W. Torrance and Thomas F. Torrance (Grand Rapids: Eerdmans, 1973), 3.

ster Shorter Catechism 88 asks, "What are the outward means whereby Christ communicateth to us the benefits of redemption?" Answer: "The outward and ordinary means whereby Christ communicateth to us the benefits of redemption, are his ordinances, especially the word, sacraments, and prayer; all which are made effectual to the elect for salvation." What are the ordinances? They are the elements of worship that God prescribes. God Himself is pleased to make these elements effectual to His elect for salvation.

God is present in worship to bless His people and to renew His covenant with them. Worship is a time to draw near to God and to seek His face, as believers are exhorted in Isaiah 55:6, "Seek the Lord while He may be found / Call upon Him while He is near." In doing so, God's people fulfill the purpose for which they were made, as the Apostle Paul explains, "He made from one man every nation of mankind to live on all the face of the earth, having determined their appointed times and the boundaries of their habitation, that they would seek God ... " (Acts 17:26-27). Those who lead in worship ought to lead God's people into God's gracious presence to seek His face and to meet with Him and His Son, Jesus Christ.

7

PREACHING AS SHEPHERDING

Be on guard for yourselves and for all the flock, among which the Holy Spirit has made you overseers, to shepherd the church of God which He purchased with His own blood. ~ ACTS 20:28

INTRODUCTION

UNDERSTANDING THE COVENANT NATURE of worship, that is, God actively renewing His covenant with His people, this chapter considers *preaching* as an element of worship. In his charge to the pastor, a seasoned elder wisely counseled a young home missionary, "Remember, you're a shepherd not a cowboy." The elder, doing some cattle business himself, knew how truckers drive livestock out of a truck with shouts and electric cattle prods. The cattle virtually stampede out of the truck with clattering hooves, butting one another, heaving themselves on top of and over one another, and hoarsely bellowing all the while. Shepherds, in contrast, stand before their flocks and lead their sheep. Congregations are not herds of cattle; they are flocks of sheep. Christ calls elders and pastors to be shepherds.

Worship is a shepherding activity. Those who stand before the congregation in worship must lead God's people into His presence to meet with Him. Preaching also is a shepherding activity. In what follows, the shepherding model in preaching will be emphasized. This chapter also will validate the Biblical propriety of preaching, discuss the distinction between preaching and teaching, emphasize the importance of application, and draw out the shepherding temperament.

PREACHING IS SHEPHERDING

Christ commands preaching. Paul urges young pastor Timothy, "I solemnly charge you in the presence of God and of Christ Jesus, who is to judge the living and the dead, and by His appearing and His kingdom: preach the word; be ready in season and out of season; reprove, rebuke, exhort, with great patience and instruction" (2 Tim. 4:1-2). The Savior's commission to His apostles is, "Go into all the world and preach the gospel to all creation" (Mark 16:15). The commission is to gospel preaching. The Apostle Paul affirms this commission and says, "I aspired to preach the gospel" (Rom. 15:20). The commission also means preaching Christ. Paul declares, "We preach Christ crucified" (1 Cor. 1:23).

The gathered church is a primary venue for such preaching. Paul's purpose for writing Timothy has to do with the conduct of church affairs. "I write so that you will know how one ought to conduct himself in the household of God, which is the church of the living God, the pillar and support of the truth" (1 Tim. 3:15). Paul, therefore, urges public prayer (1 Tim. 2:1). He commends the public reading of Scripture and links it to preaching. "Until I come, give attention to the public reading of Scripture, to exhortation and teaching" (1 Tim. 4:13).

The Apostle Paul already exemplified this God-ordained procedure. When a mission church sprang up in Antioch, Barnabas sought out the apostle. "And he left for Tarsus to look for Saul; and when he had found him, he brought him to Antioch. And for an entire year they met with the church and taught considerable numbers; and the disciples were first called Christians in Antioch" (Acts 11:25-26). Paul followed this procedure in Corinth when opposition arose to his preaching in the local synagogue. "Then he left there and went to the house of a man named Titius Justus, a worshiper of God, whose house was next to the synagogue ... And he settled there a year and six months, teaching the word of God among them" (Acts 18:11). Sailing from Philippi, Paul met with the church at Troas. "On the first day of the week, when we were gathered together to break bread, Paul began talking to them, intending to leave the next day, and he prolonged his message until midnight" (Acts 20:7). Paul taught in Ephesus "publicly and from house to house" (Acts 20:20). At his last meeting with the Ephesian elders, Paul charged them, "Therefore be on the alert, remembering that night and day for a period of three years I did not cease to admonish each one with tears" (Acts 20:31).

Paul's practice is based upon his Biblical-theological understanding. The gathered church is the place of God's gracious presence. While the whole church, "being fitted together, is growing into a holy temple in the Lord," Paul wrote to the Ephesians, "you also are being built together into a dwelling of God in the Spirit" (Eph. 2:21-22). God is present in worship to reaffirm and assure His people, "I will dwell in them and walk among them; and I will be their God, and they shall be my people" (2 Cor. 6:16). Corporate worship is, therefore, an optimum context for preaching. Here we pray for and expect the outcome Westminster Shorter Catechism 89 relates. "The Spirit of God maketh the reading, but especially the preaching of the word, an effectual means of convincing and converting sinners, and of building them up in holiness and comfort, through faith, unto salvation."

Preaching is, therefore, the primary means of grace. Romans 10:14 asks, "How then will they call on Him in whom they have not believed? How will they believe in Him whom they have not heard? And how will they hear without a preacher? (Rom. 10:14). John Murray comments on the second question. "There is no need to insert the preposition 'in' before 'him.'"[1] Professor Murray translates the question: "How shall they believe him whom they have not heard?"[2] He then says, "A striking feature of this clause is that Christ is represent-

---

1. John Murray, *Epistle to the Romans* (Grand Rapids: Eerdmans, 1980), 2:58, n. 16.
2. Ibid, 58.

ed as being heard in the gospel when proclaimed by sent messengers. The implication is that Christ speaks in the gospel presentation."³ As a result, Paul speaks of his preaching as the word of God, "When you received the word of God which you heard from us, you accepted it not as the word of men, but for what it really is, the word of God" (1 Thess. 2:13).

How can preaching be called the word of God? William Gouge, a Westminster Divine, answers, "That which ministers do or ought to preach is styled the word of God in a fourfold respect."⁴ First, after dealing with extraordinary ministers, Gouge says, "As for ordinary ministers, they have God's word written and left upon record for their use ... They therefore that ground what they preach upon the Scripture, and deliver nothing but what is agreeable thereunto, preach the word of God."⁵ In addition, when men preach what is agreeable to the word of God, it necessitates a high regard for "the subject-matter which they preach, which is the will of God," a high regard for "the end of preaching, which is the glory of God, and making known 'the manifold wisdom of God,' Eph. iii. 10," and a high regard for "the mighty effect and efficacy thereof, for preaching God's word is 'the power of God unto salvation, Rom i. 16.'"⁶ Preaching is therefore designated, or as Gouge says, "styled," the word of God, when it is agreeable to Scripture and sets forth the will of God, for the glory of God, in the power of God.

The minister is the servant of God and the people. Some people take what seems to be a very straightforward position. "When the robed pastor is prominent, the people are left in no doubt that God is speaking and acting through the instrumentality of the office of the Ministry to deliver His gifts to the congregation."⁷ It is not the presence of the robed minister, but God's gracious presence, that assures God's

---

3. Ibid.
4. William Gouge, *Commentary on Hebrews* (Grand Rapids: Kregel Publications, 1980), 1072.
5. Ibid.
6. Ibid, 1072-1073.
7. Jeffrey J. Meyer, *The Lord's Service* (Moscow, ID: Canon Press, 2003), 99.

people He is speaking to them. When Paul preached at a place of prayer in Philippi, "A woman named Lydia, from the city of Thyatira, a seller of purple fabrics, a worshiper of God, was listening; and the Lord opened her heart to respond to the things spoken by Paul" (Acts 16:14). While members of the congregation sit and listen, Jesus Christ reaches down from heaven to operate upon and open the hearts of men and women to respond to the preaching of the word. The Westminster Confession of Faith 1:5 describes the work of Christ, "[O]ur full persuasion and assurance of the infallible truth, and divine authority thereof, is from the inward work of the Holy Spirit, bearing witness by and with the word in our hearts."

Preaching may be defined as follows: "Preaching is God—Father, Son, and Holy Spirit—communicating His truth in our world to people in the pews ... " When presenting this definition in class for the first time, a student asked, "Where is the preacher?" Good question! When Peter introduces his letter, he introduces himself, "Peter, an apostle of Jesus Christ" (1 Pet. 1:1). So it is with Paul, "Paul, an apostle of Christ Jesus" (2 Cor. 1:1; Eph. 1:1; 1 Tim. 1:1; 2 Tim. 1:1; compare Gal. 1:1 and Col. 1:1). God communicates His truth through Spirit-inspired human instruments. In preaching and teaching, God also communicates His truth through very fallible human instruments. Therefore, this phrase, *through human instruments*, was added to the definition.

However, by his tone, the student seemed to exaggerate the importance of the minister. In preaching and teaching, the minister is a very *human* instrument, a messenger. "In this form of communication, the Sender of the message comes first in importance, and after him the substance of the message. Next in importance are the people to whom the message is addressed. The preacher comes fourth in importance."[8] For this reason, preachers and teachers must know their place as messengers, servants, and instruments. The above

---

8. H. Grady Davis, *Design for Preaching* (Philadelphia: Fortress, 1958), 110.

quote speaking of the prominence of the "robed pastor" speaks of the "office of the Ministry" with a capital "M." In the New Testament, *ministry* is *service*, like waiting on tables.⁹ The word is lower case.

Preachers are weak, human instruments. They have their our own biases, presuppositions, and agendas, none of which are important. R. C. Sproul warns his students about a danger for them:

> Don't ever, ever, ever, ever, preach your own anger. If you are angry about something, recuse yourself from preaching on that issue. Don't ever use the pulpit as your personal soapbox. If you want to proclaim the wrath of God, you'd better make sure it's God's wrath and not your own. You should be clear that your concern is the honor of Christ and not your own.¹⁰

There is a philosophy of ministry here. Preachers are shepherds; preaching is shepherding. There are two sides to this preaching activity, *what* preachers say and *how* they say it. The accent in the Scriptural qualifications for elders and pastors is on the latter. Listen to the Apostle Paul.

> An overseer, then, must be above reproach, the husband of one wife, temperate, prudent, respectable, hospitable, able to teach, not addicted to wine or pugnacious, but gentle, peaceable, free from the love of money (1 Tim. 3:2-3). The Lord's bond-servant must not be quarrelsome, but be kind to all, able to teach, patient when wronged, with gentleness correcting those who are in opposition, if perhaps God may grant them repentance leading to the knowledge of the truth, and they may come to their senses and escape from the snare of the devil, having been held captive by him to do his will (2 Tim. 2:24-26). Preach the word; be ready in season and out of season;

---

9. F. Wilber Gingrich, *Shorter Lexicon of the Greek New Testament* (Chicago: University of Chicago, 1983), 46.
10. R. C. Sproul, "The Teaching Preacher," *Feed My Sheep: A Passionate Plea for Preaching* (Orlando: Reformation Trust Publishing, 2008), 79.

reprove, rebuke, exhort, with great patience and instruction (2 Tim. 4:2).

Paul speaks of being temperate, prudent, respectable, hospitable, able to teach ... gentle, peaceable (1 Tim. 3:2-3). Perhaps the words *able to teach* can be translated *teachable*.[11] The series of descriptives would therefore require pastors to be temperate, prudent, respectable, hospitable, *teachable* ... gentle, peaceable. To teach, preachers must be taught. To be taught, preachers must be teachable. Preachers must be open to correction and admonition. If preachers expect congregation members to open their hearts to them, they must open their hearts to the members of the congregation. A teachable spirit invites openness. When preachers are not teachable, they tend to be impatient, rigid, and demanding. They feed strife and contention.

In 2 Timothy 2:24, Paul reminds preachers that they are servants. "Paul's train of thought is as follows, 'The servant of God must stand aloof from contentions; but foolish questions are contentions [verse 23]; therefore everyone who wishes to be reckoned a servant of God [including elders and pastors] must shun them.'"[12] Kindness, patience, and gentleness must accompany correction. Pastors must exhibit the fruit of the Spirit when pressing the claims of Christ. God uses *fruit-adorned instruction* to evoke repentance leading to the knowledge of the truth.

At the same time, Paul uses strong language in 2 Timothy 4:2 to describe pastoral work. The preacher must reprove (*convict* and *correct*) and rebuke (*warn* and *censure*); he must exhort (*summon, invite, call to one's side*).[13] While Paul describes *what* Timothy must do; yet, he also advises Timothy *how* to carry out his duties. He must do so *with great patience and instruction*. Timothy must mix his instruction, however severe it is at times, with all patience. Preaching, then, ought not to have "an edge" and "zeal should be tempered with longsuffer-

---

11. The lexicons and versions all translate the Greek adjective, *didaktikon*, "able to teach."
12. John Calvin, *The Second Epistle of the Apostle Paul to the Corinthians and the Epistles to Timothy, Titus, and Philemon*, trans. T. A. Smail, ed. David W. Torrance and Thomas F. Torrance (Grand Rapids: Eerdmans, 1973), 320.
13. Gingrich, *Shorter Lexicon*, 62, 76, 148.

ing gentleness."[14] Pastors ought to set forth the truth and patiently summon, invite, and call the people of the congregation to their side. Preachers are shepherds. They lead the people into God's truth.

Remembering how God deals with him will help the local pastor. Paul asks, "Do you think lightly of the riches of His kindness and tolerance and patience, not knowing that the kindness of God leads you to repentance?" (Rom. 2:4). When God deals kindly and patiently with pastors, He is leaving room for their repentance. He is also teaching them to deal gently, kindly, and patiently with God's people, and to leave room for their repentance. In doing so, he does not force the truth upon them. He leads them into God's truth; he shepherds them.

This philosophy of ministry agrees with a covenantal understanding of worship. God is graciously present in worship to renew His covenant with His people and assure them He is indeed their God. In the context of Christian worship, grace is a more powerful motivator than law. Leading people into a vision of the multifaceted love of God in Christ and gratitude for what God has done in Christ is powerful motivation for them to live for Christ. It is a much better motivator than guilt. Heaping extra-Biblical requirements upon people yields guilt. "If you don't knock on fifty doors per week, you are not faithful." "If you don't witness to someone once a day you are not a good disciple." The Bible sets no such standards. Law is the way of the cowboy. Grace is the way of the shepherd. Embrace the way of a shepherd. Lead people into the green pastures of God's truth.

PREACHING IS GOAL-ORIENTED SHEPHERDING PROCLAMATION

The essence of preaching is proclamation. The primary Greek term for the work of the preacher is *kerugma*, meaning *"proclamation, preaching."*[15] The verb form is *kerussō*, *"proclaim aloud, announce, mention publicly, preach* most often in reference to God's saving

---

14. Calvin, *Second Epistle*, 333.
15. Gingrich, *Shorter Lexicon*, 108.

action."[16] A worldly example of such proclamation is found in 2 Chronicles. 36:22. "Now in the first year of Cyrus king of Persia—in order to fulfill the word of the Lord by the mouth of Jeremiah—the Lord stirred up the spirit of Cyrus king of Persia, so that he sent a proclamation throughout his kingdom." In the Greek version of the Old Testament (LXX), the words *sent a proclamation* are literally *commanded to proclaim* [*parenggeilen keruxai*].

Matthew 4:17 declares, "From that time Jesus began to preach [*kerussein*] and say, 'Repent, for the kingdom of heaven is at hand.'" In Luke 4:16-18, Christ describes His ministry by quoting from Isaiah 61:1, "The Spirit of the Lord God is upon me, / Because the Lord has anointed me to bring good news to the afflicted; / He has sent me to bind up the brokenhearted, / To *proclaim* [*keruxai* (LXX)] liberty to captives / And freedom to prisoners" (italics added). Paul asks this question, "How will they preach [*keruxōsin*] unless they are sent?" (Rom. 10:15). He also exhorts Timothy, "Preach [*keruxon*] the word" (2 Tim. 4:2).

Preaching is, therefore, declarative in nature. The messenger declares the words of the King. Isaiah 52:7 is a good example. "How lovely on the mountains / Are the feet of him who brings good news, / Who announces peace / And brings good news of happiness, / Who announces salvation, / And says to Zion, 'Your God reigns!'" Preaching announces Good News. Isaiah looks ahead, not only to the captivity in Babylon, but also to Israel's restoration. The message the captives in Babylon need is a simple one, "Your God reigns!" Nebuchadnezzar does not reign. God reigns. Paul declares the same message in Romans 10:9, "That if you confess with your mouth *Jesus as Lord*, and believe in your heart that God raised Him from the dead, you will be saved" (italics added). Christ is King; He reigns, is the basic message we proclaim. The accent in preaching is, therefore, upon declaring good news.

---

16. Ibid.

Preaching differs from teaching. While the essence of preaching is proclamation, teaching is the methodical impartation of information. The modern educational heresy is that if teachers give people enough information and the proper information, they will make the right decisions. Our job is to give them the information they need. The procedure, in this case, is lecturing.

Jay Adams draws out the distinction by speaking about the stance of the preacher and the stance of the lecturer. "The lecturer speaks *about* the Bible; the pastoral preacher speaks *from* the Bible about the congregation."[17] Furthermore, the "Lecturer talks to the congregation *about* the Bible, about what God did long ago and far away to the Israelites, in 3rd person (he, they), in unemotional, uninvolved reporting style."[18] On the other hand, the "Preacher talks to the congregation about themselves from the Bible, about what [God] is doing and what they ought to be doing, in 2nd person (you), in an emotionally involved but controlled style."[19] Adams goes on to explain, "Everything the lecturer says may be quite true, but if that truth doesn't come to grips with the congregation in such a way that it can change their lives in accordance with the purpose of the Holy Spirit, it may be lecturing, but it isn't preaching."[20] This distinction leads to another important characteristic of preaching.

Preaching is application. R. C. Sproul writes, "I make a distinction between preaching—which involves exhortation, exposition, admonition, encouragement, and comfort—and teaching, which involves the transfer of information."[21] As just noted, those who view preaching as imparting information take the posture of modern education: *give people the proper information and they'll make the correct decisions.* Yet, "there is more to preaching than imparting information ... "[22]

---

17. Jay E. Adams, *Preaching With Purpose* (Grand Rapids: Zondervan, 1982), 43.
18. Ibid.
19. Ibid.
20. Ibid, 44.
21. R. C. Sproul, "The Teaching Preacher," 73.
22. Derek W. H. Thomas, "Expository Preaching," *Feed My Sheep, A Passionate Plea for Preaching* (Orlando: Reformation Trust, 2008), 38.

Application is essential. "For the Reformers, the whole sermon was application ... "[23] Calvin is no exception. "From the very outset of a sermon, Calvin was applying the teaching of the passage to the experience and life of the congregation."[24] T. H. L. Parker explains it this way: "Expository preaching consists in the explanation *and application* of a passage of Scripture. Without explanation it is not expository; without application it is not preaching."[25]

Pastors do teach when they preach; and as preachers at heart, pastors do some preaching when they teach. Preaching is unavoidable when rightly explaining the Scriptures. As Parker says, explanation cannot stand alone. Consider the approach of the Apostle Paul. "We proclaim Him [Christ], admonishing every man and teaching every man with all wisdom, so that we may present every man complete in Christ" (Col. 1:28). Preaching involves counseling [*nouthetountes*] and teaching [*didaskontes*]. *To counsel and admonish from the pulpit is to apply the Scriptures to the lives of those listening.*

God's pastor-shepherds, counsel, admonish, and apply God's truth *with all wisdom*. Wisdom requires tact, that is, sensitivity in dealing with others and with difficult issues.[26] Having sensitivity means exercising patience, kindness, and gentleness. For example, the Ninth Commandment requires telling the truth. Doing so, preachers follow the law of love. "For the commandments, 'You shall not commit adultery, You shall not murder, You shall not steal, You shall not covet,' and any other commandment, are summed up in this word: 'You shall love your neighbor as yourself'" (Rom. 13:9, ESV). The stance of pastor-shepherds is not truth at any price. *How* they present and maintain the truth is of great importance. If telling the truth is the loving thing to do, they must remember 1 Corinthians 13:4, "Love is patient, love is kind and is not jealous; love does not brag and is not

---

23. Jay E. Adams, *Essays on Biblical Preaching* (Grand Rapids: Zondervan, 1983), 78.
24. David J. Engelsma, "Forward," *Sermons on Election and Reprobation by John Calvin* (Audubon, NJ: Old Paths, 1996), viii.
25. T. H. L. Parker, *Calvin's Preaching* (Louisville: Westminster/JohnKnox, 1992), 79. Emphasis added.
26. *Webster's New World Dictionary of the American Language* (New York: World Publishing, 1958), 1483.

arrogant." The wise shepherd patiently and humbly leads his congregation into God's truth, by "speaking the truth in love" (Eph. 4:15).

Shepherding proclamation has a great goal. Pastor-shepherds seek to "present [*parastesōmen*] every man complete in Christ" (Col. 1:28). *Present* also means *place beside*. It is the same word Paul uses in Ephesians 5:25-27.

> Husbands, love your wives, just as Christ also loved the church and gave Himself up for her, so that He might sanctify her, having cleansed her by the washing of water with the word, *that He might present* [parastese] *to Himself the church* in all her glory, having no spot or wrinkle or any such thing; but that she would be holy and blameless.

Our Savior is at work preparing the church, His bride, for the great wedding feast to come when He will *present* the church to Himself. In a preeminent work of love, He will *place beside* himself the church cleansed and sanctified. The task of the preacher and shepherd is to prepare the bride, and in the end, to "present every man complete in Christ." This task is a preeminent work of love on the part of pastors. To carry out this work, pastors must "shepherd the church of God which He purchased with His own blood" (Acts 20:28). Week by week, God's under-shepherds must lead God's people to Christ, preparing them for the great wedding feast of the Lamb (Rev. 19:7; 21:2).

Goal-oriented, shepherding proclamation imparts self. Witness the work of our Lord. After sending the Twelve on a preaching mission and hearing their subsequent reports, Jesus and the disciples went by boat to a secluded place (Mark 6:32). However, the people of that region saw them and followed them, running along the shore (Mark 6:33). "When Jesus went ashore, He saw a large crowd, and He felt compassion for them because they were like sheep without a shepherd; and He began to teach them many things" (Mark 6:34).

The text says that Jesus began to teach [*erxato didaskein*]. But Jesus does not engage in traditional teaching, as we understand it. Christ does not begin a lecture as though He is in a classroom. His teaching is preaching. How so? Consider the size of the crowd. The context is the feeding of the five thousand. Verse 44 says, "There were five thousand men who ate the loaves." Counting women and children (Matt. 14:21), there may have been upwards of fifteen thousand people. Speaking to such a crowd requires huge effort and energy. It is exhausting. Listen to John Broadus, "I think it absolutely necessary, if we would interpret aright the teachings of our Lord, to remember that he spoke not as a scientific lecturer but as a *preacher*, a preacher for the most part to the common people, an open air preacher ... "[27]

The people in the crowd "were like sheep without a shepherd" (Mark 6:34). Matthew 9:36 adds to the picture: "They were distressed and dispirited like sheep without a shepherd." Because these people manifested the characteristics of lost sheep, "Jesus felt compassion [*esplanxnisthe*] for them." He had a visceral gut reaction to them. He empathized with them. They were immediate objects of His affection. He therefore poured out His heart to them in His preaching. "And so in him we see, as we see in all his more worthy followers, that materials of preaching are important, and methods of preaching are important, but that most important of all is personal character and spirit."[28] Goal-oriented, shepherding proclamation means to share in the personal character and Spirit of Christ.

To share in the personal character and Spirit of Christ, in turn, means preachers must imbibe, absorb, and assimilate the truth, spirit, and emotion of the texts they preach. As they study preaching portions, they must prayerfully seek Christ and imbibe His Spirit.

> We must meditate on his perfect fidelity to truth, and yet perfect courtesy and kindliness; his severity in rebuking, without any tinge of bitterness; his directness and simplicity, and yet his tact—wise as a serpent, with the simplicity of the dove; his complete sympathy with man,

---

27. John A. Broadus, *Lectures on the History of Preaching* (New York: A. C. Armstrong and Son, 1893), 33.
28. Ibid., 35-36.

and also having complete sympathy with God—bringing heaven down to earth, that he might lift up earth to heaven.[29]

More particularly, as pastors study their preaching portions, they must imbibe and assimilate the emotion of the texts they preach. For example, God declares, "When Israel was a youth I loved him, and out of Egypt I called My son" (Hosea 11:1). God had already declared, "Israel is My son, My firstborn" (Exod. 4:22). God is like a father who has great care and great hopes for his son. Yet, his son spurns him and fails to see or even acknowledge his father's love and care for him. Hosea 11:2-5 begins to fill out the picture.

> The more they [the prophets] called them [the people of Israel],
> The more they went from them;
> They kept sacrificing to the Baals
> And burning incense to idols.
> Yet it is I who taught Ephraim to walk,
> I took them in My arms;
> But they did not know that I healed them.
> I led them with cords of a man, with bonds of love,
> And I became to them as one who lifts the yoke from their jaws;
> And I bent down and fed them.
> They will not return to the land of Egypt;
> But Assyria—he will be their king
> Because they refused to return to Me.

Grasping the context, the preacher senses the pathos and poignancy of the tragedy, the utter failure of Israel, God's son. He feels the pain. The preacher who suffers the excommunication of his own unrepentant, adulterous son, knows the emotional pain. But then he sees that Matthew quotes Hosea 11:1 as *fulfilled* in Christ. How so? The failure of Israel is replaced with the success of Jesus, the Son. All the plans and purposes of the Father sadly left unfulfilled by Israel give way to a new hope-filled future in Jesus Christ. The preacher feels the pathos

---

29. Ibid., 35.

and grief give way to joy in the text. "So Joseph got up and took the Child and His mother while it was still night, and left for Egypt. He remained there until the death of Herod. This was to fulfill what had been spoken by the Lord through the prophet: 'Out of Egypt I called My Son'" (Matt. 2:14-15). Ah, now all the plans and purposes for Israel, spurned by God's rebel son, come into view and are fulfilled in the Son. To grasp the emotion of the text is to more fully grasp the meaning of the text. To grasp the emotion of the text is to begin to share in the personal character and Spirit of Christ.

Once preachers imbibe the truth, spirit, and emotion of a text, they may adequately express that truth; they may passionately preach the truth. As they preach, they express the fruit of the Spirit in the tenor and character of the message. They also convey the truth with the passion and emotion born of the text itself. Doing so, preachers transparently open their hearts to God's people. They exhibit both passion and compassion. When pastors have passion, they preach; they lead God's people into the truth. When preachers have compassion for God's people, they shepherd them and point them to "the great Shepherd of the sheep" (Heb. 13:20).

WHAT ABOUT CHILDREN'S CHURCH, CHILDREN'S SERMONS AND OBJECT LESSONS?

Children's church is popular. Yes, it is popular in many circles to separate young children from the rest of the worshiping congregation before the sermon to allow them to attend children's church. There they have a Bible lesson suited to their age and capacity. What about this practice?

First, there is no Biblical command nor is there any Biblical precedent for separating any specific age group from the worshiping congregation to provide age-specific worship or Bible lessons. The worshiping congregation is just that, God's gathered, called-out people. All ages are included.

Second, some pastors may find it easier to gear their sermons for older members of the congregation. Ushering children off to children's church might assist the pastor. He need not "water down" his message, but he ensures that the young people and adults in the congregation receive the "meat" they need and deserve. His ministry is therefore "more effective." However, there is no Biblical warrant for thus dividing the congregation. In addition, it is the duty of the pastor to preach for the benefit of all age levels in the congregation. Word definitions and explanations can be briefly directed to children, then to young people, and then to adults. Illustrative material should shed light on word meanings and explanations for all age levels. In fact, simple explanations geared for the ears of children are at the same time often better suited for adult hearts and minds. Haddon Robinson warns about the use of technical theological language in the pulpit.

> While it takes three years or more to get through seminary, it can take you ten years to get over it. If you pepper your sermons with words like *eschatology, angst, pneumatology, exegesis, existential, Johannine, the Christ-event,* you throw up barriers to communication. Jargon combines the pretentiousness of big words with the deadness of cliché, and it is often used to impress rather than to inform an audience.[30]

Third, although the younger members of the congregation may at first lack the self-discipline to sit through the worship service, they will learn to their profit from it. Wait! Are not age-specific meetings and teaching sessions more effective? Age-specific teaching sessions may or may not be more effective depending upon the goals and ultimate objectives. Within the church, the primary objective is to see children and young people remain in the church and become active adult members of the visible body of Christ.

---

30. Haddon W. Robinson, *Biblical Preaching* (Grand Rapids: Baker, 2001), 190-191.

A startling study done by the [Uniting] Church of Australia documented the long-term impact of dividing the church into age-specific groups. The researchers discovered that people who grew up in church attending worship and not Sunday school were much more likely to be involved in church as adults than those young people who had attended only Sunday school without attending worship.[31]

The implication is that children who stay in church as youngsters, sit with their parents throughout worship, and learn to listen to the sermon, are more likely to stay in church as adults. Over the long haul, children's church, although preferred by many children and appreciated by many adults, may be counter-productive. "Resist excluding them [children] from times of corporate worship because they learn much from watching the faith community sing, pray, give, testify and participate in the ordinances of the church."[32]

Children's sermons and object lessons are also popular. First, consider the idea of the children's sermon. The objective is to provide a special time to address children within the context of congregational worship. The advantage is that pastors or elders may gear a message specifically for the children *while they remain in congregational worship.* The other so-called advantage is that when the children have been addressed, the pastor may concentrate on feeding the adult members of the congregation. In this case, although there is no spatial exclusion of children from worship, there is, what can be called, liturgical separation. There is a sermon for children; then, there is a sermon for the adults. However, there is no Biblical warrant for this type of separation within the context of corporate worship. It is curious that some who hold tenaciously to the regulative principle of worship insist upon considering a children's sermon an element of worship. Pastor-

---

31. Mark DeVries, *Family Based Youth Ministry* (Downers Grove: InterVarsity Press, 1994), 64.
32. Cheryl L. Fawcett, *Understanding People* (Wheaton: Evangelical Training Association, 2001), 39.

shepherds should address the entire congregation in their sermons. If pastors are capable of effectively addressing children during one portion of worship and then addressing adults of various ages in another portion of our worship, surely they are capable of addressing all ages, young and old, in one sermon. If pastors are incapable of speaking to a span of ages in the congregation, they fail as shepherds.

Second, an object lesson is often the center and core of a children's sermon. An object lesson uses a simple object to teach an abstract principle. In the case of the children's sermon, there is some "obvious" connection between the object and the abstract spiritual principle. For example, take Genesis 28:12 and Jacob's ladder as the text to explore with the children: "He had a dream, and behold, a ladder was set on the earth with its top reaching to heaven; and behold, the angels of God were ascending and descending on it." The *object* is a ladder. The *abstract principle* is that Jesus is like a ladder; He is the way to heaven. The object lesson might be like the following:

> Look children, I brought this ladder to church this morning and put it up against the wall. We can use this ladder to climb way up to the top of the wall. If we put the ladder against the wall outside the church you could climb up on the roof. But your mom and dad probably wouldn't like you doing that. Some fire engines have long ladders that help firefighters climb way up above a building so they can spray water down on top of a fire. Ladders help you get up to very high places. Hmm, heaven is a place that is up very high. When Jacob had his dream, he saw a ladder reaching all the way up to heaven. Wow! That ladder really must have been big. You know, children, Jesus is *like* that ladder. Jesus connects us to heaven. He is our way to heaven. And so, to get to heaven, you must believe in Jesus. Jesus is your way to heaven.

The lesson connects the object, a ladder, to the abstract idea that Jesus is the way to heaven. The Bible makes this connection and the connection seems obvious. Here is the difficulty. "The two- to seven-year-old child judges things by how they look to him rather than on the basis of mental operation. He is dependent upon appearance."[33] Such children are full of questions. "Parents frequently are overwhelmed by the questions that are voiced by the preschooler. 'Where is Jesus?' 'Who is God?' 'Where does He live?' 'Where is heaven?'"[34] These children are gathering facts. The best approach to them is to give them facts. The *Catechism for Young Children* is, therefore, an excellent tool to use with these children.[35] However, these children are not prepared to deal with abstract concepts. They are not prepared to perform the mental operations required to connect an object, such as a ladder, to a principle, like Jesus is our way to heaven. "The clear implication is that using object lessons is inappropriate when the abstract truth is not within the grasp of the student."[36]

It is also significant that adults love object lessons. The adults see the wide-eyed children looking at the lights, colored balls, balloons, bottles of water changing color, and the other things used in the object lessons. Since the adults readily make the connections intended by the object lessons, they register their approval and delight, but fail to understand the capacities of the children. Older children also begin to make these connections. "It is sad that most Christian educators quit telling object lessons at the very age when they could possibly be understood."[37] Since object lessons are ineffective with the young, one of the most common arguments for a children's sermon is invalid. Moreover, as already indicated above, the Bible gives no support to age-specific sermons within worship.

---

33. Joanne Brubaker, Robert Clark, Roy Zuck, *Childhood Education in the Church* (Chicago: Moody Press, 1975), 70.
34. Ibid., 352.
35. *Catechism for Young Children: An Introduction to the Shorter Catechism* (Philadelphia: Board of Christian Education, 1936); *First Catechism: Biblical Truth for God's Children*, ed. Thomas R. Patete and Thomas A. Nichols (Suwanee, GA: Great Commission Publications, 1996).
36. Fawcett, *Understanding People*, 39.
37. Ibid., 52.

SUMMARY AND CONCLUSION

Preaching is a shepherding activity that Christ commands. The gathered church is the primary venue for such preaching. Paul's practice evidences this, and is based upon his Biblical-theological understanding that the church is the New Testament temple, a special dwelling place of God in the Spirit. God is graciously present to renew and apply His covenant word to the hearts of His people. Preaching in the gracious presence of God is, therefore, a primary means of grace.

The pastor is God's instrument, servant, and shepherd. The philosophy of ministry and of preaching is that of *shepherding*. Pastors lead the people into God's gracious presence and into His truth, believing He will meet with them and apply His covenant word as He promises.

At the same time, the essence of preaching is *proclamation*, the declaration of God's truth. Preaching also requires *application*. The separation of certain age groups from corporate worship during the sermon is unwarranted. The liturgical separation of age groups within the congregation during worship is also unwarranted. We Preachers must apply God's truth to the whole congregation, young and old.

The goal of preaching is to prepare the bride of Christ for the wedding feast of the Lamb. This preparation means shepherding all the sheep, lambs, ewes, and rams of the congregation. Such goal-oriented, shepherding proclamation means sharing in the personal character and Spirit of Christ. To share in the personal character and Spirit of Christ requires pastors to imbibe the truth, spirit, and emotion of the texts they preach and results in the impartation of self. As a result, pastors may better preach with passion and compassion and lead people to Christ and into the truth. They shepherd the church of the living God.

The Sacraments

*For as often as you eat this bread and
drink the cup, you proclaim the Lord's
death until He comes.* ~ 1 Cor. 11:26

INTRODUCTION

THE TREATMENT OF THE ELEMENTS of worship, except for the element of praise, will now be completed with an analysis of the sacraments. In this chapter, sacraments will be defined, their Biblical warrant given, their nature as signs and seals of covenant renewal discussed, their prophetic, symbolic character presented, and their shepherding role set forth. Baptism in particular will be considered in chapter 9. The administration of the Lord's Supper and questions regarding this sacrament will be explored in chapter 10.

DISCUSSION

Christ commands the sacraments. Broadly put, the word sacrament refers to something dedicated to *sacred use*.[1] However, "It is to be remembered that the term 'sacrament' does not occur in the Bible."[2] At the same time, the "ordinances which are 'universally recognized' as sacraments are baptism and the Lord's Supper."[3] These sacraments

---

1. A. A. Hodge, *Outlines of Theology* (Grand Rapids: Zondervan, 1976), 588.
2. Ibid., 589.
3. Ibid., 590.

are ordinances or religious practices commanded by Christ. Westminster Shorter Catechism 92 asks, "What is a sacrament?" The answer begins, "A sacrament is an holy ordinance instituted by Christ … " Christ clearly commands the making of disciples by means of baptism: "Make disciples of all the nations, baptizing them in the name of the Father and the Son and the Holy Spirit" (Matt. 28:19). Christ also commands believers to remember Him by eating bread together and drinking wine together: "This is My body, which is for you; do this in remembrance of Me … This cup is the new covenant in My blood; do this, as often as you drink it, in remembrance of Me" (1 Cor. 11:24-25).

The sacraments employ outward, visible signs ordained by Christ. Both Matthew 28:19 and 1 Corinthians 11:24-25 speak of outward, visible signs which signify inward, spiritual grace. In the case of these sacraments, Christ establishes the relationship between the sign and the thing signified; He unites them.[4] John Dick explains: "From this union arises what has been called sacramental phraseology, or certain expressions in which the names of the sign and the thing signified are exchanged."[5] The Westminster Confession of Faith 27:2 therefore states, "There is, in every sacrament, a spiritual relation, or sacramental union, between the sign and the thing signified: whence it comes to pass, that *the names and effects of the one are attributed to the other*" (italics added). The language of the Confession refers to a figure of speech known as *metonymy*. Metonymy "indicates such relations as cause and effect, progenitor and posterity, subject and attribute, sign and thing signified."[6] The sacraments fall into the category of sign and thing signified. It is important to keep in mind that the so-called *sacramental language* is also common *figurative language*. As Bullinger's *Figures of Speech in the Bible* rightly observes, "'This is my body,' has been forced to teach false doctrine when translated literally."[7]

---

4. Louis Berkhof, *Summary of Christian Doctrine* (Grand Rapids: Eerdmans, 1969), 165-166.
5. John Dick, *Lectures on Theology* (New York: M. W. Dodd, 1850), 4:118, quoted by Robert Shaw, *Exposition of the Westminster Confession of Faith* (Fearn: Christian Focus, 1998), 335.
6. Louis Berkhof, *Principles of Biblical Interpretation* (Grand Rapids: Baker, 1964), 83.
7. E. W. Bullinger, *Figures of Speech Used in the Bible* (Grand Rapids: Baker, 1968), 738.

The sacraments are both signs and seals. The Westminster Confession of Faith 27:1 describes the difference. Note the italics.

> Sacraments are holy signs and seals of the covenant of grace, immediately instituted by God, to *represent Christ and His benefits*; and to *confirm our interest in Him*: as also, to put a visible difference between those that belong unto the Church and the rest of the world; and solemnly to engage them to the service of God in Christ, according to His Word.

Signs represent Christ and His benefits. *Seals* confirm our interest in Him. A seal is an authenticating mark. God places the seal of His Spirit upon believers to mark them as His children. "In Him, you also, after listening to the message of truth, the gospel of your salvation—having also believed, you were sealed in Him with the Holy Spirit of promise, who is given as a pledge of our inheritance" (Eph. 1:13-14). God, therefore, uses the sacraments to assure believers that they do indeed belong to Him. Through them, He renews His covenant with believers. That the sacraments are signs and seals of the covenant will be shown in the following chapters that deal with them individually.

The sacraments also exhibit or apply the benefits of Christ. "The sacraments of the Old Testament in regard to the spiritual things thereby signified and *exhibited*, were, for substance, the same with those of the new" (WCF 27:5, italics added). "The word [exhibit] is derived from the Latin word 'exhibeo' which bore the twofold sense of *conveying* and *disclosing*."[8] Westminster Larger Catechism 162 uses the words *signify, seal,* and *exhibit*.

> A sacrament is an holy ordinance instituted by Christ in his church, to *signify, seal,* and *exhibit* unto those that are within the covenant of grace, the benefits of his mediation; to strengthen and increase their faith, and all other

---

8. Hodge, *Outlines of Theology*, 591.

graces; to oblige them to obedience; to testify and cherish their love and communion one with another; and to distinguish them from those that are without (italics added).

Westminster Shorter Catechism 92 parallels Westminster Larger Catechism 162: "A sacrament is an holy ordinance instituted by Christ, wherein, by sensible signs, Christ, and the benefits of the new covenant, are *represented, sealed, and applied to believers*" (italics added). To *signify* means to represent the reality; to *seal* means to authenticate; to *exhibit* means to convey and apply the truth. The confession teaches that the sacraments signify, authenticate, and convey the truth. This line of thinking is pursued further in what follows.

The sacraments are instruments of grace. Keeping in mind the idea of sacramental union, the concept of a seal, and the teaching that the sacraments convey and apply the truth of Christ, carefully note what the Westminster Confession of Faith 27:3 says.

> The grace which is exhibited in or by the sacraments rightly used, is not conferred by any power in them; neither does the efficacy of a sacrament depend upon the piety or intention of him that does administer it: but upon the work of the Spirit, and the word of institution, which contains, together with a precept authorizing the use thereof, a promise of benefit to worthy receivers.

The grace exhibited or applied in the sacraments depends solely upon the work of the Holy Spirit. There is no power in the sacraments themselves; they are instruments or means. "The sacramental union, therefore, between the sign and the thing signified is (1.) Symbolical and representative—the one symbolizes and so represents the other; and (2.) Instrumental, because by divine appointment, through the right use of the sign, the grace signified is really conveyed."[9] Speaking of the sacraments as instruments of grace is close to the question

---

9. A. A. Hodge, *The Confession of Faith* (Carlisle: Banner of Truth, 1978), 329.

of the presence of Christ in the sacraments. How is this question to be answered?

The sacraments are prophetic, symbolic acts. Christ was the great prophet foretold by Moses (Deut. 18:15; Acts 3:22). He prescribed certain actions: baptism with water, eating bread, and drinking wine. The Apostle Paul interprets these acts when he declares, "For as often as you eat this bread and drink the cup, you proclaim the Lord's death until He comes" (1 Cor. 11:26). It is not in the elements, but in the actions, that the presence of Christ is found. To help understand this idea, go back to the prophet Ezekiel. "Ezekiel employed four different modes to communicate his message: oracles delivered orally, visions, symbolic actions, and prophetic discourse."[10] One way in which Ezekiel declared God's truth was through prophetic, symbolic actions.

> Now you son of man, get yourself a brick, place it before you and inscribe a city on it, Jerusalem. Then lay siege against it, build a siege wall, raise up a ramp, pitch camps and place battering rams against it all around. Then get yourself an iron plate and set it up as an iron wall between you and the city, and set your face toward it so that it is under siege, and besiege it. This is a sign to the house of Israel (Ezek. 4:1-3).

Ezekiel proclaims the approaching fall of Jerusalem through his prophetic actions. These prophetic acts are as efficacious as the spoken, prophetic word.

> In a similar manner, we may approach the [Lord's Supper]. In Luke 9:22 we find Jesus says, "The Son of Man must suffer many things, and be rejected by the elders and chief priests and scribes and be killed, and on the third day be raised." We hear similar words in Matthew 16:21 and Mark 8:21. The institution of the Lord's Supper is no less a proclamation. And it is in this institution that

---

10. C. Hassell Bullock, *An Introduction to the Old Testament Prophetic Books* (Chicago: Moody, 2007),281.

we "proclaim the Lord's death until he comes." Taken in this light, the [Lord's Supper] is not simply a symbol intended to bring out the meaning of oral preaching; it is in fact an intensified form of that oral preaching setting forth a predictive word and containing the same unction as the oral presentation.

Reflecting on Ezekiel's "siege of Jerusalem" we can see that emphasis is [placed] upon Ezekiel's actions; the materials used by Ezekiel are important only insofar as they aid in the carrying out of the symbolic actions. We can in no way say that the brick upon which the city is portrayed is, in a literal fashion, Jerusalem. But as the brick *is* Jerusalem, so the bread which is broken *is* the body of Christ. Similarly, when Ezekiel sets his face toward the brick and lets the *city* be in a state of siege, we cannot say that Ezekiel is in fact laying siege to Jerusalem. But we can say that in the same manner as *Ezekiel lays siege* on Jerusalem, the body of Christ *is* received by us in the breaking and the eating of the bread.

… As Ezekiel's siege is a [prophetic] predictive word, so the Lord's breaking of bread is a prophetic act which is inextricably bound to the actual sacrifice through the bridge of the prophetic, Spirit embodied, word. Thus, our Lord proclaimed his own death on that night in the upper room.

It is this aspect of the proclamation about which the apostle speaks when he says, "You proclaim the Lord's death until he comes." The Lord is present in his word, this we cannot deny. In like manner, the Lord is present in the prophetic act, the [Lord's Supper]. And in this act he stretches forth his arm as he stretches forth his arm through the spoken word.[11]

---

11. Dennis J. Prutow, "The Eucharist at Corinth," (paper, submitted to Dr. George Eldon Ladd, Fuller Theological Seminary, Pasadena, CA, May 16, 1968), 19-20.

Understanding prophetic, symbolic acts explains the presence of Christ in the sacraments. Berkhof gives this summary definition. "A sacrament is a holy ordinance instituted by Christ, in which by sensible signs the grace of God in Christ is represented, sealed, and applied to believers, and they, in turn, express their faith and obedience to God."[12] Once again, the sacraments are means of grace like the spoken word is a means of grace. Remember what William Greenhill wrote:

> We must not neglect means, and leave all to God, that is tempting the Most High; neither must we trust to means when used, that is to idolize the creature: but we must use means, and look to God to be all in them (for without him nothing is done); and if we make him all in the means, we shall make him all after them.[13]

Understanding the sacraments as prophetic, symbolic acts explains the presence of Christ in the sacraments. In the same way He is present in his word to perform it, Christ is present in the prophetic, symbolic acts of baptism and the Lord's Supper.

Words of explanation always accompany the elements in the sacraments. Following the model of prophetic symbolic actions, interpretive statements always accompany the symbolic acts. "In these actions message and messenger were combined into one inseparable mode of communication. Constantly some words of interpretation accompanied them ... "[14] Compare Christ's institution of the Lord's Supper and how His explanation accompanied His actions.

> And when He had taken some bread and given thanks, He broke it and gave it to them, saying, "This is My body which is given for you; do this in remembrance of Me." And in the same way He took the cup after they had eaten, saying, "This cup which is poured out for you is the new covenant in My blood" (Luke 22:19-20).

---

12. Berkhof, *Summary*, 166.
13. William Greenhill, *An Exposition of Ezekiel* (Carlisle: Banner of Truth, 1994), 741.
14. Bullock, *Introduction*, 282-283.

In a similar way, the apostles accompany explanation with baptism:

> Peter said to them, "Repent, and each of you be baptized in the name of Jesus Christ for the forgiveness of your sins; and you will receive the gift of the Holy Spirit. For the promise is for you and your children and for all who are far off, as many as the Lord our God will call to Himself" (Acts 2:38-39).

Calvin quotes Augustine to make this point. "Let the word be added to the element and it will become a sacrament."[15] Then Calvin himself goes on to say, "You see how the sacrament requires preaching to beget faith."[16]

Words of explanation accompanying the elements lead the people to Christ. Adding explanations to the signs and symbols of the sacraments employs the shepherding model. Calvin leads us to this conclusion.

> You see how the sacrament requires preaching to beget faith. And we need not labor to prove this when it is perfectly clear what Christ did, what he commanded us to do, what the apostles followed, and what the purer church observed. Indeed, it was known even from the beginning of the world that whenever God gave a sign to the holy patriarchs it was inseparably linked to doctrine, without which our senses would have been stunned in looking at the bare sign. Accordingly, when we hear the sacramental word mentioned, let us understand the promise, proclaimed in a clear voice by the minister, *to lead the people by the hand wherever the sign tends and directs us.*[17]

The proper administration of the sacraments shepherds God's people and leads them to Christ.

---

15. John Calvin, *Institutes of the Christian Religion*, ed. John T. McNeill, trans. Ford Lewis Battles (Philadelphia: Westminster Press, 1960), 1279.
16. Ibid.
17. Ibid., 1279-1280. Italics added.

The sacraments are elements of public worship. The outcome of Peter's preaching on the Day of Pentecost seems clear. "The three thousand converts were then formed into a distinct community, the apostolic fellowship, constituted on the basis of the apostolic teaching. The apostolic teaching was authoritative because it was the teaching of the Lord communicated *through* the apostles."[18] As Calvin puts it, these converts "were joined to the disciples of Christ, or ingrafted into the same Body, and continued in their doctrine."[19] Converts became part of the visible body through the doorway of baptism (Acts 2:41). *The Geneva Bible of 1599* renders Acts 2:41, "Then they that gladly received his word, were baptized: and the same day there were added to the Church about three thousand soules." These baptisms were undoubtedly performed in public.

Luke immediately records the character of the public meetings of this first New Testament Christian Church.[20] "They were continually devoting themselves to the apostles' teaching and to fellowship, to the breaking of bread and to prayer" (Acts 2:42). The people sat under the teaching of the apostles. They shared "a common religious experience."[21] The people joined in the breaking of bread. "This is Luke's term for what Paul calls the Lord's Supper."[22] Calvin adds, "The reason why I would rather have the breaking of bread to be understood here of the Lord's Supper is because Luke is recording those things which constitute the form of the church visible to the public eye."[23] Luke adds the element of prayer also offered in public assembly.[24] "As for public prayers, there are two kinds: the ones with the word only, the others with song. And this is not a thing invented a short time ago. For from the first origin of the church, this has been

---

18. Ibid., 1279.
19. John Calvin, *The Acts of the Apostles*, trans. John Fraser and W. J. G. McDonald, ed. David W. Torrance and Thomas F. Torrance (Grand Rapids: Eerdmans, 1973), 1:84.
20. F. F. Bruce, *The Acts of the Apostles: The Greek Text with Introduction and Commentary* (Grand Rapids: Eerdmans, 1968), 99.
21. I. Howard Marshall, *The Acts of the Apostles* (Grand Rapids: Eerdmans, 1982), 83.
22. Ibid. See also J. A. Alexander, *Acts of the Apostles* (Carlisle: Banner of Truth, 1980), 1:91.
23. Calvin, *Acts*, 1:85.
24. Ibid., 86.

so, as appears from the histories."[25] In summary, Luke includes baptism and the Lord's Supper as parts of the public worship of the early church.

CONCLUSION

Christ commands the sacraments of baptism and the Lord's Supper. These sacraments employ outward, visible signs also ordained by Christ. As a result, the sacraments are both signs and seals. The sacraments also exhibit or apply the benefits of Christ. They are, therefore, instruments or means of grace. The sacraments are prophetic, symbolic acts and Christ is present in these acts as He is present in the spoken word. Words of explanation accompanying the elements lead the people to Christ. Finally, the sacraments are elements of public worship.

---

25. John Calvin, "Epistle to the Reader," 1565 *Genevan Psalter*, in Charles Garside, *The Origin of Calvin's Theology of Music: 1536-1543* (Philadelphia: American Philosophical Society, 1979), 32.

BAPTISM

> *When they believed Philip preaching the good news about the kingdom of God and the name of Jesus Christ, they were being baptized, men and women alike.* ~ ACTS 8:12

INTRODUCTION

THIS CHAPTER BEGINS by considering Christ's command to baptize and the significance of Trinitarian baptism. The discussion then turns to baptism's relationship to the visible church, the mode of baptism, the propriety of infant baptism, an examination of what constitutes a valid Christian baptism, and concludes with practical points to remember and a brief summary.

TRINITARIAN BAPTISM

Christ commands water baptism symbolizing Spiritual baptism. "Go therefore and make disciples of all the nations, baptizing them in the name of the Father and the Son and the Holy Spirit" (Matt. 28:19). Baptism with water is an outward visible sign. The inner grace signified is "the washing of regeneration and renewing by the Holy Spirit" (Tit. 3:5). Scripture often unites the two. "I baptized you with water; but He will baptize you with the Holy Spirit" (Mark 1:8). "John baptized with water, but you will be baptized with the Holy Spirit not many days from now" (Acts 1:5). "Surely no one can refuse the water for these to be baptized who have received the Holy Spirit just as we did, can he?" (Acts 10:47). "I remembered the word of the Lord, how He used to say, 'John baptized with water, but you will be baptized with the Holy Spirit'" (Acts 11:16).

"For by one Spirit we were all baptized into one body, whether Jews or Greeks, whether slaves or free, and we were all made to drink of one Spirit" (1 Cor. 12:13). When speaking of baptism, the thought of water baptism comes first; the figurative use of the term is secondary.[1] Here, Calvin says, "Paul of course is speaking about the baptism of believers, which is efficacious through the grace of the Spirit. For to many people baptism is merely a formality, a symbol without any effect; but believers actually do receive the reality with the sacrament."[2] Water baptism symbolizes the work of the Spirit. Here, Paul connects the two.

Baptism in the name of the Trinity emphasizes God's work. Christ commands baptism "in the name of the Father and the Son and the Holy Spirit" (Matt. 28:19). What about baptism "in the name of Jesus Christ" (Acts 2:38; 10:48)? These words are not a reference to the formula of baptism but rather to baptism by the authority of Christ.[3] The Trinitarian formula directs attention away from the subjects of baptism and to the acts of God that save them. Baptism is not so much about what the recipients of baptism have done or will do but what is done to them and for them. Action is taken upon the recipients of baptism; they *are baptized*.

"Baptism in the name of God the Father declares to us the supreme fact that God has a purpose of love for us."[4] As Paul confirms, "In love He predestined us to adoption as sons through Jesus Christ to Himself, according to the kind intention of His will" (Eph. 1:4-5). "Baptism in the name of God the Son declares to us that God has

---

1. F. Wilbur Gingrich and Frederick W. Danker, *Shorter Lexicon of the Greek New Testament* (Chicago: University of Chicago Press, 1983), 33.
2. John Calvin, *The First Epistle of Paul the Apostle to the Corinthians*, trans. John W. Fraser, ed. David W. Torrance and Thomas F. Torrance (Grand Rapids: Eerdmans, 1973), 265.
3. J. A. Alexander, *Acts of the Apostles* (Carlisle: Banner of Truth, 1980), 1:85.
4. G. W. Bromiley, *The Baptism of Infants* (London: Church Book Room Press, 1955), 11.

indeed fulfilled His purpose of grace for us ... "[5] Here again is Scripture's confirmation: "In Him we have redemption through His blood, the forgiveness of our trespasses, according to the riches of His grace" (Eph. 1:7). "Baptism in the name of the Holy Spirit declares to us the supreme fact that the fulfillment of the divine purpose in Jesus Christ is appropriated to us individually in the power of the Holy Spirit."[6] Scripture again confirms, "In Him, you also, after listening to the message of truth, the gospel of your salvation—having also believed, you were sealed in Him with the Holy Spirit of promise, who is given as a pledge of our inheritance" (Eph. 1:13-14).

The Trinitarian formula points to God's plan and purpose to save, Christ's accomplishment of the Father's plan to save, and the Spirit's application of Christ's work to save. Baptism is, therefore, decidedly God-centered. "We are not directed to ourselves and our faith and our confession of faith. We are directed to God, and to what God has done for us in Jesus Christ and will do with us by the Holy Ghost. Only in that context can we think of the necessary response of faith as the personal entry into the saving work of God."[7] And that faith rests upon grace. "For by grace you have been saved through faith; and that not of yourselves, it is the gift of God" (Eph. 2:8).

BAPTISM AND THE VISIBLE CHURCH

Water baptism begins the discipleship process. Christ commands His church to make disciples, "Go therefore and make disciples of all the nations." He then describes the two-step process: (1) *"baptizing* them in the name of the Father and the Son and the Holy Spirit"; and (2) *"teaching* them to observe all that I commanded you; and lo, I am with you always, even to the end of the age" (Matt. 28:19-20). Para-church organizations that engage in discipleship programs make converts and then go on to teach them. However, they neglect to fol-

---

5. Ibid., 14.
6. Ibid., 18.
7. Ibid., 10.

low the specific command of Christ to baptize. Biblically speaking, water baptism begins the discipleship process.

This process may be described as an apprenticeship. An apprentice attaches himself to a skilled craftsman for a fixed period of time to learn a trade. Disciples are apprentices of Jesus Christ. They attach themselves to Him to learn His way of life. Once baptized, the apprenticeship begins, and the task is to learn to do all that Christ commands from Genesis to Revelation. This apprenticeship calls for lifelong learning, training, and practice.

Water baptism also begins discipleship by associating converts with the visible church. That association occurred on the Day of Pentecost. "So then, those who had received his word were baptized; and that day there were added about three thousand souls" (Acts 2:41). The response to Peter's preaching was positive. Three thousand were baptized. To what were they added? They were added to the visible fellowship of believers, the visible church. "[B]aptism in water continued to be the external sign by which individuals who believed the gospel message, repented of their sins, and acknowledged Jesus as Lord, were publicly incorporated into the Spirit-baptized fellowship of the new people of God."[8]

The work in Antioch is a case study of this association. The church began with a preaching mission resulting in a group of *converts*. "The hand of the Lord was with them, and a large number who believed turned to the Lord" (Acts 11:21). The church at Jerusalem sent Barnabas to Antioch. He enlisted the help of Paul. "For an entire year they met with the *church* and *taught* considerable numbers; and the *disciples* were first called *Christians* in Antioch" (Acts 11:26, italics added). This church is formed following Christ's command. Acts 11:26 connects the church with discipleship, teaching, and the title, Christian. The presence of *disciples* indicates that the converts were baptized and made part of a visible body. Paul and Barnabas then *taught* these

---

8. F. F. Bruce, *The Book of Acts: The English Text with Introduction, Exposition and Notes* (Grand Rapids: Eerdmans, 1970), 77.

baptized converts or new *disciples*. For the first time, the title Christian is applied to baptized disciples who are members of the visible church in Antioch.

Water baptism is, therefore, an ordinance of the visible church administered by Christ's ministers. How so? The church is God's household [*oikeioi*] (1 Tim. 3:15). Paul is an administrator, manager, or steward [*oikonomos*] in God's house (1 Cor. 4:1). "Stewards [*oikonomoi*] were generally slaves appointed as managers or overseers. It was their business to direct the affairs of the household, and dispense its provisions. It is as *dispensers* that ministers are here called *stewards*."[9] Paul also sees himself as a Christ-appointed steward. "I was made a minister [*diakonos*] according to the stewardship [*oikonomian*] from God bestowed on me for your benefit" (Col. 1:25). His work was to further the administration [*oikonomia*] of God (1 Tim. 1:4).

Paul indicates that ministers, stewards, and overseers, are shepherds. "Be on guard for yourselves and for all the flock, among which the Holy Spirit has made you *overseers*, to *shepherd* the church of God which He purchased with His own blood" (Acts 20:28, italics added). The apostle Peter agrees. "I exhort the elders among you, as your fellow elder and witness of the sufferings of Christ, and a partaker also of the glory that is to be revealed, *shepherd* the flock of God among you, *exercising oversight* ... " (1 Pet. 5:1-2, italics added). In keeping with this oversight, Christ originally gives the command to baptize to the apostles, His designated representatives (Matt. 28:19).

Barnabas and Paul, official representatives of the church in Jerusalem, it appears, baptize the converts in Antioch, form them into a visible body, and teach the members of this new church.[10] In like manner, the Westminster Confession of Faith 27:4 teaches, "There are only two sacraments ordained by Christ our Lord in the Gospel; that is to say, Baptism, and the Supper of the Lord: *neither of which may*

---

9. Charles Hodge, *An Exposition of the First Epistle to the Corinthians* (Grand Rapids: Eerdmans, 1965), 64.
10. Bruce, *Acts: English Text*, 240-241.

be dispensed by any, but by a minister of the Word lawfully ordained" (italics added).

As an ordinance of the visible church, public confession accompanies adult baptism. When the apostle addresses the organized church at Philippi, he writes, "Paul and Timothy, bond-servants of Christ Jesus, To all the saints in Christ Jesus who are in Philippi, including the overseers and deacons" (Phil. 1:1). How was this church formed? Paul spoke to a small group gathered for prayer. "A woman named Lydia, from the city of Thyatira, a seller of purple fabrics, a worshiper of God, was listening; and the Lord opened her heart to respond to the things spoken by Paul. And when she and her household had been baptized ... " (Acts 16:14-15). "Lydia believed what they said and acknowledged Jesus as Lord. She thus became Paul's first convert in Europe."[11] She was baptized upon her confession of faith. The practice of the New Testament church from the beginning was to baptize adults upon confession of faith (Acts 2:38).

Christ required public confession of faith: "Therefore everyone who confesses Me before men, I will also confess him before My Father who is in heaven" (Matt. 10:32). Since the sacraments are elements of public worship, since instruction accompanies the sacraments, since water baptism is, therefore, an ordinance of the visible church administered by Christ's ministers, and since water baptism begins discipleship by associating converts with the visible church, such a confession *before men* naturally occurs in the context of public worship. "This means that faith was registered by confession, and the criterion by which the church exercised its administrative responsibility in the admission of members was confession."[12]

Water baptism is a covenant sign and seal. The outward Old Testament sign of the covenant was circumcision (Gen. 17:10-11). This outward sign was also a seal. "He received the sign of circumcision, a seal of the righteousness of the faith which he had while uncircumcised"

---

11. Ibid., 331.
12. John Murray, *Christian Baptism* (Philadelphia: Presbyterian and Reformed, 1972), 38-39.

(Rom. 4:11). The outward sign signified inner grace, the circumcision of the heart. "He is a Jew who is one inwardly; and circumcision is that which is of the heart, by the Spirit" (Rom. 2:29; Deut. 30:6). Water baptism is the outward New Testament sign, signifying inner grace, "the washing of regeneration and renewing by the Holy Spirit" (Tit. 3:5).

Paul makes a similar comparison and shows that baptism replaces circumcision in the New Covenant. "In Him you were also circumcised with a circumcision made without hands, in the removal of the body of the flesh by the circumcision of Christ" (Col. 2:11). Here, the outward sign, circumcision, is connected with inner grace, circumcision made without hands, the circumcision of the heart (Deut. 30:6). Paul defines this circumcision of heart as baptism. Believers are circumcised with a *circumcision made without hands, having been buried with Him in baptism*" (Col. 2:12).

Clearly, Paul relates circumcision and baptism by telling Christians they too were circumcised. How so? It was through burial with Christ in baptism. Spiritual circumcision is the circumcision of the heart (Rom. 2:28-29). Physical circumcision is a sign pointing to the work of the Holy Spirit in the heart. Inner baptism is the baptism of the Spirit. Water baptism is a sign pointing to this work of the Holy Spirit. Paul tells us that believers were circumcised when they were baptized. Christian baptism replaces Old Testament circumcision. Baptism, therefore, becomes the New Testament sign and seal of the covenant.

THE MODE OF BAPTISM

The Greek words baptizō *and* baptismos *do not always mean dip, plunge, or immerse.* If the New Testament uses of the noun *baptismos* to refer to sprinkling just once, it can be argued that it does not always mean dip, plunge or immerse. Hebrews 9:6-14 offers such an example. Verse 10 speaks of various Old Testament *washings* or *baptisms* which are regulations for the body. Verse 13 indicates that these *baptisms* include a *sprinkling* for the cleansing of the flesh. The text reads as follows:

Now when these things have been so prepared, the priests are continually entering the outer tabernacle performing the divine worship, but into the second, only the high priest enters once a year, not without taking blood, which he offers for himself and for the sins of the people committed in ignorance. The Holy Spirit is signifying this, that the way into the holy place has not yet been disclosed while the outer tabernacle is still standing, which is a symbol for the present time. Accordingly both gifts and sacrifices are offered which cannot make the worshiper perfect in conscience, since they relate only to food and drink and various washings [*baptismois*], regulations for the body imposed until a time of reformation. But when Christ appeared as a high priest of the good things to come, He entered through the greater and more perfect tabernacle, not made with hands, that is to say, not of this creation; and not through the blood of goats and calves, but through His own blood, He entered the holy place once for all, having obtained eternal redemption. For if the blood of goats and bulls and the ashes of a heifer sprinkling [*rantizousa*] those who have been defiled sanctify for the cleansing of the flesh, how much more will the blood of Christ, who through the eternal Spirit offered Himself without blemish to God, cleanse your conscience from dead works to serve the living God?

Other ceremonial washings confirm that baptism does not always mean dip, plunge, or immerse. For example, the laver in the Old Testament tabernacle was for washing. "Aaron and his sons shall wash their hands and their feet from it" (Exod. 30:19). This washing was through pouring. "It [the laver] took the form of a large pot with spouts through which water was poured."[13] Mark 7:3 notes,

---

13. J. Rabbinowitz, *The Book of Exodus: The Soncino Chumash,* ed. A. Cohen (New York: Soncino, 1993), 541.

"The Pharisees and all the Jews do not eat unless they carefully wash their hands." Mark 7:4 calls this washing a baptism. "And when they come from the market place, they do not eat unless they cleanse [*baptisōntai*] themselves." *The Babylonian Talmud*, tractate Tohoroth, stipulates that this baptism was accomplished by pouring. "Hands become unclean and are made clean as far as the wrist. How so? If he poured the water over the hands as far as the wrist and poured the second water over the hands beyond the wrist and the latter flowed back to the hands, the hands nevertheless become clean."[14] Baptism does not always mean dip, plunge, or immerse.

Pouring or sprinkling are proper modes of baptism. The Westminster Confession of Faith 28:3 says, "Dipping of the person into the water is not necessary; but Baptism is rightly administered by pouring, or sprinkling water upon the person." Pouring is in keeping with the symbolism of water baptism. Acts 2:17-18 reads, "I WILL POUR FORTH OF MY SPIRIT ON ALL MANKIND ... I WILL IN THOSE DAYS *POUR FORTH* OF MY SPIRIT" (Italics added). Acts 2:33 says, "Therefore having been exalted to the right hand of God, and having received from the Father the promise of the Holy Spirit, He *has poured* forth this which you both see and hear" (Italics added). Acts 10:45 records, "All the circumcised believers who came with Peter were amazed, because the gift of the Holy Spirit had been *poured out* on the Gentiles also" (Italics added).

INFANT BAPTISM

The children of believers are privileged. Paul notes the privileged position of the Jews. "What advantage has the Jew? Or what is the benefit of circumcision? Great in every respect. First of all, that they were entrusted with the oracles of God" (Rom. 3:1-2). Children born into Christian homes have a similar advantage. They are born into the covenant community. As a result, they are in homes where their parents value the Scriptures, hope in Christ, take them to public worship,

---

14. Quoted by William Hendricksen, *Exposition of the Gospel According to Mark* (Grand Rapids: Baker, 1976), 272-273.

and teach them the way of salvation through Christ. They are not like the children of unbelieving parents who have no interest in the Bible, disdain Christ, and use His name as an expletive.

Peter makes it clear that children born into Christian homes within the visible church are heirs of promise: "Repent, and each of you be baptized in the name of Jesus Christ for the forgiveness of your sins; and you will receive the gift of the Holy Spirit. For the promise is for you *and your children* and for all who are far off, as many as the Lord our God will call to Himself" (Acts 2:38-39, italics added). These children are born into homes where they have the opportunity to hear the promises of God and come to faith in Christ. As Norman Harper observes, "It is important at this point to distinguish between being an heir of the covenant promise and an heir of salvation."[15] Harper quotes Pierre Marcel,

> ... children born in the covenant are *heirs*. But their heritage is that of the promise, of which the Holy Spirit is the pledge. We can never insist too much on this point in opposition to those who obstinately maintain that according to us the heritage has to do with salvation. These children do not inherit salvation and eternal life. Salvation is not hereditary. They inherit only the promises. It behooves them thereafter to receive the *content* of the promise by faith and repentance, and thus by regeneration and conversion, and to live a life consecrated to the Lord. Then, and then only, will they be heirs *of the things promised*. The heritage is only communicated to the heir who receives the promise with faith.[16]

Harper goes on to say, "According to this view the advantage of the covenant child is not in the presumption of his salvation but in the assurance of his privilege as an heir of the promise together with his

---

15. Norman E. Harper, *Making Disciples* (Memphis: Christian Studies Center, 1981), 42.
16. Pierre Marcel, *The Biblical Doctrine of Infant Baptism* (London: James Clark, 1953), 107-108. Quoted by Harper, *Making Disciples*, 42-43.

corresponding obligation."[17] It is clear that not all Abraham's children were among God's elect nor were all his children regenerate believers (Rom. 9:6-8). They were covenant children born into the covenant community. In like manner today, covenant parents ought not to hold to presumptive election, presumptive regeneration, or presumptive salvation. Covenant parents in the Reformed Presbyterian Church of North America, upon the baptism of their infant children, take this vow: "Do you promise to teach him/her of his/her sinful nature, of the plan of salvation which centers in Jesus Christ, and his/her own personal need of a relationship with Christ?" The presumption is that the child will hear the promises of God in Christ and be encouraged to trust Christ. Covenant children are members of the covenant community where they are privileged to hear the promises of the gospel and respond in faith.[18]

The children of believers are proper recipients of baptism. Since circumcision, the sign and seal of the covenant, was applied to infants in the Old Testament (Gen. 17:10-12), and since baptism replaces circumcision as the sign and seal of the covenant in the New Testament (Col. 2:11-12), and since the infants of believers are privileged as heirs of God's promise (Acts 2:38-39), the children of believers should receive the sign and seal of the covenant, and be baptized.

"If infants are excluded now, it cannot be too strongly emphasized that this change implies a complete reversal of the divinely instituted practice."[19] We find no such reversal in the New Testament. "More pointedly, does the New Testament revoke or does it provide any intimation of revoking so expressly authorized a principle as that of the inclusion of infants in the covenant and their participation in the covenant sign and seal?"[20] The answer is, "No."

---

17. Harper, *Making Disciples*, 43.
18. Compare the vows of two other Presbyterian and Reformed denominations. First: "Do you believe that your children, though sinful by nature, are received by God *in* Christ as members of His covenant and therefore ought to be baptized?" (italics added). Second: "Do you acknowledge that, although our children are conceived and born in sin and are therefore subject to condemnation, they are *holy in Christ*, and as members of his church ought to be baptized?" (italics added). Both of these vows appear to presume union with Christ as the basis for baptism.
19. Murray, *Christian Baptism*, 52.
20. Ibid.

Francis Schaeffer asks us to "place ourselves in the position of a Jew who has been saved in the early Christian era."[21]

> [I]t would be impossible for the saved Jew not to expect that, as in the Old Testament the Covenant sign was applied to the believer's child, so also the sign of his faith, baptism, should likewise be applied to his child. Why should he expect less in this dispensation of fullness than he would have possessed in the Old Testament era?
>
> ... [H]e would expect his child to be baptized. If it were refused, what would you have done in his place? You would have asked the Apostles the reason why. So would the thousands of Christian Jews in that day. The question would have been asked in a hundred meetings; and Peter, John, Paul, and the others would have sat down and written in their Epistles to clear up the matter, just as they answered other questions that arose. The New Testament would have contained the clear answer as to why in the Old Testament the Covenant sign was applied to the infants of believers, but in the New Testament it was to be withheld from them.
>
> *The only reason possible for the New Testament not dealing with this problem is that the problem did not exist. The only possible reason that there was no problem in the Jews' minds was that the believing Jews did apply the covenant sign to their children. They baptized their babies as they had circumcised them in the Old Testament dispensation.*[22]

What about women and girls? Philip preached the gospel in Samaria with good results. "When they believed Philip preaching the good news about the kingdom of God and the name of Jesus Christ, they were being baptized, men and women alike" (Acts 8:12). If women were baptized and Schaeffer's argument holds, little girls were

---

21. Francis A. Schaeffer, *Baptism* (Wilmington: TriMark, 1976), 12.
22. Ibid., 18-19, italics added.

also baptized. Calvin puts it this way, "Men and women could not have been baptized without making open confession of their faith; but they were admitted to baptism on this condition, that their families were consecrated to God at the same time. For the covenant is in these terms, 'I will be thy God and the God of thy seed.'"[23]

Adult baptism is primary and infant baptism follows. Because infant baptisms are the usual occurrence in most Reformed and Presbyterian churches, and adult baptisms are unusual, infant baptism is often seen as normative or standard. Remember that infants are eligible to the outward sign of baptism because of their birth to believing parents. That is, only when one or both parents are baptized, confessing members of the visible church may their infant children be baptized. Note Paul's affirmation in 1 Cor. 7:14: "For the unbelieving husband is sanctified through his wife, and the unbelieving wife is sanctified through her believing husband; for otherwise your children are unclean, but now they are holy." The children are not holy in the sense "that they are rendered inwardly holy."[24] As already discussed, the children of believers are privileged. They are outwardly set apart from the world or made holy. They have a relationship with the church and access to the means of grace because their parents are believers and members of the church. It would serve the church well to see more adult conversions, more frequent confessions of faith, and thus, more frequent adult baptisms.

Baptism has an evangelistic office. Baptism "has an evangelistic office as an adjunct to the word."[25] It always calls those who have been baptized to live according to its meaning. Westminster Larger Catechism 167 speaks of this under the heading of "improving our baptism." Baptism calls children baptized in infancy to confess faith in Christ and receive the forgiveness and cleansing symbolized in their baptism. Baptism calls adults to live in the holiness of grace and

---

23. John Calvin, *The Acts of the Apostles*, trans. John Fraser and W. J. G. McDonald, ed. David W. Torrance and Thomas F. Torrance (Grand Rapids: Eerdmans, 1973), 1:232.
24. Hodge, *First Corinthians*, 116.
25. Bromiley, *Baptism of Infants*, 22.

to pursue the sanctification and purity symbolized in their baptism. Baptism also looks ahead to its ultimate fulfillment, final and complete cleansing experienced by "the spirits of just men made perfect" (Heb. 12:23).

> We begin with His death and resurrection for us. We end with our death and resurrection with Him at the last day. The attainment of that end is the miraculous work of the Spirit attested in baptism and expressed already in conversion and sanctification. Only when we have attained that end can we say that by this work of the Spirit we have fully entered into the baptism of Christ. But then the attestation of the sacrament will no longer be necessary.[26]

VALID BAPTISMS

What constitutes a valid baptism? A. A. Hodge indicates there are three basic requirements for a valid sacrament, the proper matter, form, and intention.[27] In baptism, the proper *matter* is the use of water in sprinkling, pouring, or immersion to signify the work of the Spirit. The proper *form* is the use of the Trinitarian formula added to the *matter* in its administration in order to constitute the sacrament. Right *intention* is "the serious design of doing what Christ commanded in the institution of the rite."[28] The Westminster Confession of Faith 27:3 seems to contradict Hodge and states, " ... neither doth the efficacy of a sacrament depend upon the piety or intention of him that doth administer it: but upon the work of the Spirit, and the word of institution ... " This stipulation is directed against the Catholic doctrine of baptismal regeneration and "the fact that the administrator exercises at the moment of administration the secret 'intention' of doing thereby what the [Roman Catholic] Church intends in the definition of the

---

26. Ibid., 24.
27. A. A. Hodge, *Outlines of Theology* (Grand Rapids: Zondervan, 1976), 598.
28. Ibid.

sacrament."[29] The Confession indicates that the validity of a baptism is *not* affected by this specific intention.

The Westminster Confession of Faith 28:2 speaks of the *matter* and *form* but also refers to baptism as an ordinance of the church. "The outward element to be used in this sacrament is water, wherewith the party is to be baptized, in the name of the Father, and of the Son, and of the Holy Ghost, *by a minister of the Gospel, lawfully called thereunto*" (italics added). Since baptism is an ordinance of the church, and as has been argued, an element of public worship, the impropriety of private baptisms, and baptisms performed by para-church organizations, is evident.

Given the standard of proper *matter*, *form* and *intention*, baptisms performed by non-Trinitarian denominations, Jesus Only churches, or Unitarians, are invalid. Included among non-Trinitarian churches are those having aberrant views of the person of Christ and of the Holy Spirit such as Jehovah's Witnesses and Mormons. Although using water, they may not use the Trinitarian formula or may lack the Biblical understanding of the Trinity necessary to use the Trinitarian formula as Christ commands. Some churches seeking political correctness have changed the formula and baptize in the name of God the Creator, God the Redeemer, and God the Sanctifier. This avoidance of the Biblical formula clearly calls into question the intent of the person administering the sacrament.

If a baptism is invalid, proper Christian baptism is in order. Acts 19:2-5 is the Biblical example.

> Paul passed through the upper country and came to Ephesus, and found some disciples. He said to them, "Did you receive the Holy Spirit when you believed?" And they said to him, "No, we have not even heard whether there is a Holy Spirit." And he said, "Into what then were you baptized?" And they said, "Into John's

---

29. A. A. Hodge, *The Confession of Faith* (Carlisle: Banner of Truth, 1978), 333.

baptism." Paul said, "John baptized with the baptism of repentance, telling the people to believe in Him who was coming after him, that is, in Jesus." When they heard this, they were baptized in the name of the Lord Jesus.

Bruce indicates, "This is the only account of re-baptism that we find in the NT."[30] Marshall adds, "This is the only case recorded in the New Testament of people receiving a second baptism, and it took place only because the previous baptism was not Christian baptism in the name of Jesus."[31] Christian baptism signifies and seals the work of the Holy Spirit. The baptismal formula is Trinitarian. Hearing of their clear lack of knowledge of the Holy Spirit, Paul inquires regarding the baptism of these Ephesians. "They were therefore baptized again in a Christian sense ... "[32] Valid baptism requires the Trinitarian formula and a proper Biblical understanding of the Trinity.

What about Roman Catholic baptisms? John Calvin was baptized as an infant in the Roman Catholic Church in Noyon, France, shortly after his birth, on July 10, 1509.[33] The Council of Trent began meeting in 1547 and published the church's position regarding baptism on March 3, 1547. Calvin published his *Antidote to Trent* on November 21, 1547. Given Trent's position on baptism and his repudiation of the superstitious additions to it, Calvin bluntly states, "That Baptism is not to be repeated the pious are sufficiently agreed."[34]

Later, Francis Turretin (1623-1687) argues for the validity of Catholic baptisms.

> The truth of the doctrine concerning baptism may be regarded either as to essence, or as to its accidents, or the rites and ceremonies employed in it. In the former sense, we acknowledge that by the singular providence

---

30. Bruce, *Acts: English Text*, 386.
31. I. Howard Marshall, *The Acts of the Apostles* (Grand Rapids: Eerdmans, 1982), 307.
32. Bruce, *Acts: English Text*, 386. Recall that the words, *in the name of the Lord Jesus*, are not a reference to the formula of baptism, but rather to baptism by the authority of Christ (Alexander, Acts, 1:85).
33. T. H. L. Parker, *John Calvin: A Biography* (Philadelphia: Westminster, 1975), 2.
34. John Calvin, *Selected Works of John Calvin: Tracts and Letters*, ed. and trans. Henry Beveridge (Grand Rapids: Baker, 1983), 3:176.

of God that the true doctrine of baptism remains in the church of Rome because in it is retained the matter of true baptism (to wit, water and the formula prescribed by Christ, according to which it is administered in the name of the Trinity). For this reason, baptism performed in that church is considered valid and is not repeated.[35]

Some disagree with Calvin and Turretin and argue against the truth of Romanist religion and, therefore, question the validity of its baptism. In response, Turretin draws an analogy with the religion of the Pharisees and Sadducees and the validity of their administration of the Old Testament sacrament of circumcision.

> The doctrine of the Romanists concerning baptism can be called true and false [*kat' allo kai allo*] in different respects. True, as to the essence of the institution, the visible elements and the word of institution. False as to accidental opinions and rites. Nor because it is considered to be true baptism is the truth of the Roman religion on that account rightly proven, no more than the doctrine of the Pharisees and Sadducees was true because they lawfully administered the external right of circumcision.[36]

Therefore, Turretin concludes, "Hence we properly gather that Roman baptism is not to be repeated. (1) The essence of baptism still remains entire within it. (2) The power of baptism is not dependent upon an erring minister or heretic, but on Christ (Mt. 3:11; 1 Cor. 3:5)."[37]

There is at present great disparity among Reformed churches in their approach to Roman Catholic baptisms.

> A 1980 paper adopted by the Southern California Presbytery of the OPC [Orthodox Presbyterian Church] states that an individual baptized in infancy as a Roman

---

35. Francis Turretin, *Institutes of Elenctic Theology*, trans. George Musgrave Giger, ed. James T. Dennison (Phillipsburg: P & R Publishing, 1997), 3:405.
36. Ibid., 3:409.
37. Ibid.

Catholic should not be baptized when joining one of their churches. It concludes that "his baptism was with water, in the name of the Triune God, with the intention of doing what Christ commanded, and was, therefore, a valid baptism."[38]

In this case, the presbytery judged that the baptism in question met the requirements of matter, form, and intent. A 1983 Presbyterian Church in America committee paper states, "The Romish communion is not a true church and therefore, its sacraments cannot be true and valid sacraments."[39] In 1985, the Synod of the RPCNA adopted the following recommendation, "That we uphold the present practice of requiring baptism of Roman Catholic converts seeking entrance into the RPCNA."[40] The Synod later faced the situation of someone transferring membership from another Reformed church where his Roman Catholic baptism was accepted as valid. Synod adopted a special resolution including the following statement, "Therefore, Synod declares that its decision [regarding converts from Roman Catholicism] is for the general guidance of our sessions, and is not to be regarded as the inviolable rule of the church."[41] Written counsel to seminary students in the RPCNA concludes, "This understanding is viewed as consistent with our practice of session-controlled communion where local sessions judge the credibility of one's profession of faith."[42]

PRACTICAL POINTS

It is important to instruct candidates for baptism in the vows they will take. Pastors and elders ought to assure themselves that adults standing before the congregation are able to intelligently make their

---

38. Reformed Presbyterian Church of North America, *1985 Minutes of the Synod and Yearbook* (Pittsburgh: Board of Education and Publication, 1985), 40.
39. Ibid.
40. Ibid., 42.
41. Ibid., 52.
42. Jerry O'Neill, *Roman Catholic Baptism*, Memorandum to Reformed Presbyterian Students Under Care of Presbytery, April 2011. The propriety of session-controlled communion is discussed in chapter 10.

profession of faith and take their vows. They will do this in two ways. First, they will instruct candidates for baptism in the vows they will take. Second, it is their duty, meeting as sessions or boards, to examine individuals for church membership.

It is also important to instruct parents of infants to be baptized concerning their responsibilities and vows. A primary responsibility of parents is to teach their children the way of salvation in Christ, and to encourage them to make public profession of faith in the church. In other words, parents ought to take the evangelistic office of baptism seriously. Pastors and elders ought to teach parents to do so. When baptisms take place before the congregation, pastors ought to remind each member and child in the congregation to recall his or her baptism. Pastors can take the occasion to teach children to improve their baptism, to live in accord with its meaning, and to profess their faith in Christ.

In infant baptism, ministers often hold the child. Since infants are baptized because they are part of covenant families, my preference is to encourage the parents who present their children for baptism to hold them. They may hold the child over the baptismal font, and the pastor may easily apply the water to the child's head. This practice has two practical advantages. First, the infant is not placed in the hands of someone strange to him or her, so the peace and tranquility of the child is more likely preserved. Second, in the case of twins or triplets, the baptism will go much more smoothly without the transfer of the children between parents and pastor.

As a practical matter, the water used in baptism should be at room temperature. Do not place ice water on the brow or head of an infant. Do not use cold water in an adult baptism. You do not want to startle the infant or adult. Watch how you apply the water. You may want to use a quantity of water. Do not splash or inadvertently throw water into the face of an adult. Do not pour water in the face of an infant. Maintain the dignity and decorum of the occasion.

SUMMARY

Christ commands the sacraments of baptism and the Lord's Supper. These sacraments employ outward visible signs commanded by Christ proclaiming Him and the work of His Spirit. The sacraments are both signs *and* seals. As authenticating marks and means of grace, they exhibit and apply the benefits of Christ. Sacraments do so because they are prophetic, symbolic acts. Like the prophetic, symbolic acts of the Old Testament, words of explanation always accompany the elements and actions. These actions and words lead people to Christ and shepherd them as the sacraments are administered in the context of public worship.

Christ commands water baptism as an outward sign of the work of the Spirit. He also commands baptism in the name of the Trinity to emphasize God's work in salvation. Baptism is a sign *and* seal assuring God's people of God's promises. Water baptism unites adults with the visible church by confession of faith and is an ordinance of the visible church administered by ordained pastors only. Baptism does not always mean dip, plunge, or immerse. Sprinkling and pouring are proper modes of baptism. Born within the pale of the visible church, the children of believers are in a privileged position. As heirs of God's promise, both boys and girls are to be baptized. Finally, the validity of the baptisms of various sects, cults, and churches ought to be judged, based upon the matter, form, and intention of baptism outlined in Scripture.

The Lord's Supper

This is My body, which is for you; do this in remembrance of Me ... This cup is the new covenant in My blood; do this, as often as you drink it, in remembrance of Me. ~ 1 Cor. 11:24-25

INTRODUCTION

THIS CHAPTER TURNS to a discussion of the Lord's Supper in four parts. One: there is a brief examination of the historical background of the sacrament, of Christ's command to celebrate the sacrament, and of Christ's presence in the sacrament. Two: there is a treatment of issues involving access to the sacrament including the requirements for church membership, voting membership, session-controlled communion, and paedocommunion. Three: there is a consideration of practical matters touching on the administration of the sacrament such as the definition of worthy receivers, fencing the table, the frequency of communion, the use of wine or grape juice, the use of a common cup or of individual communion cups, and the practice serving both wine and grape juice. Four: there is a discussion of the Lord's Supper as covenant renewal and a shepherding activity, and of preparation for the Lord's Supper.

BACKGROUND TO THE LORD'S SUPPER

Communion or the Lord's Supper grew out of the Passover. Although the roots of the Lord's Supper may be well-known, a short review is in order. On the first day of Jesus' final week of ministry in Jerusalem, He entered the city with the shouting of the crowds and the words of Psalm 118 on their lips, "Hosanna to the Son of David, 'BLESSED IS HE WHO COMES IN THE NAME OF THE LORD;' Hosanna in the highest" (Matt. 21:9). Once in the city, "Jesus entered the temple and drove out all those who were buying and selling in the temple, and overturned the tables of the money changers and the seats of those who were selling doves" (Matt. 21:12). He then retreated to Bethany (Matt. 21:17).

On Tuesday, Jesus again ventured into the temple to teach. He explained Isaiah's parable of the vineyard (Isa. 5:1-7). The chief priests and Pharisees realized that He identified them as the rebellious vine-growers (Matt. 21:43). Jesus also made Himself the Son of the landowner killed by the rebellious vine-growers (Matt. 21:45). In this context, Jesus applied Psalm 118 to Himself. "THE STONE WHICH THE BUILDERS REJECTED, THIS BECAME THE CHIEF CORNER *stone*; THIS CAME ABOUT FROM THE LORD, AND IT IS MARVELOUS IN OUR EYES" (Ps. 118:22-23). Later that day, Jesus, God's glory incarnate, departed from the temple with the words of a curse, "Behold, your house is being left to you desolate" (Matt. 23:38). He again quoted Psalm 118, "For I say to you, from now on you will not see Me until you say, 'Blessed is He who comes in the name of the Lord'" (Matt. 23:39, Ps. 118:26). He then retired to the Mount of Olives for a long discourse (Matt. 24-25) and finally back to Bethany. The next day, Wednesday, a woman anointed Jesus for His burial (Matt. 26:6-13), and Judas plotted His betrayal (Matt. 26:3-5, 14-16).

On Thursday, "Jesus sent Peter and John, saying, 'Go and prepare the Passover for us, so that we may eat it'" (Luke 22:8). Part of this preparation was slaying the Passover lamb in the temple. Edersheim rehearses the scene for us. He says in part,

> The worshipers were admitted in three divisions within the Court of the Priests. When the first company had entered, the massive Nicanor Gates—which led from the Court of the Women to that of Israel—and the other

side-gates into the Court of the Priests, were closed. A threefold blast from the Priests' trumpets intimated that the lambs were being slain. This each Israelite did for himself. We can scarcely be mistaken that Peter and John would be in the first of the three companies into which the offerers were divided ... Peter and John had slain the lamb ... While all of this was going on, the *Hallel* [Ps. 113-118] was being chanted by the Levites. We remember that only the first line of every Psalm was repeated by the worshipers; while to every other line they responded by a *Hallelujah,* till Ps. cxviii, was reached, when, besides the first, these three lines were also repeated:

> Save now, I beseech Thee, Lord;
> O Lord, I beseech Thee, send now prosperity.
> Blessed be He that cometh in the Name of the Lord.

As Peter and John repeated them on that afternoon, the words must have sounded most deeply significant. But their minds must have also reverted to that triumphal Entry into the City a few days before, when Israel greeted with these words the Advent of their King. And now—was it not, as if it had only been an anticipation of the Hymn, when the blood of the Paschal Lamb was being shed?[1]

Although Peter and John physically slew the Passover lamb, as the head of the company of those celebrating the Passover together, Jesus was considered to be the one sacrificing the Passover. On earlier occasions, He would have been the guest at the table of someone else. Then, in the first year of His public ministry, Jesus was in Jerusalem for Passover (John 2:13, 23). It does not appear that the Twelve were gathered then.[2] During His second year of public ministry, Jesus remained in Galilee (John 6:4). "Thus, the first, the last, the only sacrifice which

---

1. Alfred Edersheim, *The Life and Times of Jesus the Messiah* (Peabody: Hendrickson, 2000), 2:487-488.
2. Ibid., 491.

Jesus offered was that in which, symbolically, He offered Himself."[3]

"The Pascal Supper itself commenced by the head of 'the company' taking the first cup of wine in his hand and 'giving thanks' over it ... "[4] It is to this cup that Luke 22:17 refers. "And when He had taken a cup and given thanks, He said, 'Take this and share it among yourselves.'" As the disciples drank from this cup, our Lord added these words: "I say to you, I will not drink of the fruit of the vine from now on until the kingdom of God comes" (Luke 22:18). "The next part of the ceremonial was for the Head of the Company to rise and 'wash hands.'"[5] These actions were the preliminaries.

Then the leader of the feast "took some herbs, dipped them in salt water, ate them, and gave [them] to the others."[6] "Next, he would break one of the unleavened cakes ... half of which was put aside for after supper."[7] As the bitter herbs remind the participants of the bitterness of bondage in Egypt, so the bread is specifically designated the bread of *poverty*, *misery*, or *affliction*. "This is the bread of misery which our fathers ate in the land of Egypt."[8] These actions and statements evoked a question. "The son asks, 'Why is this night distinguished from all other night?'"[9] Then the father, host, or "head of the house," in this case our Lord, "was to relate the whole national history, commencing with Terah, Abraham's father, and telling of his idolatry, and continuing in due order, the story of Israel, up to their deliverance from Egypt and the giving of the Law; and the more fully he explained it all, the better."[10] After the recitation of Israel's history, those participating in the feast sang Psalms 113 and 114, the first part of the *Hallel*, and drank of the second cup of wine.[11]

---

3. Ibid.
4. Alfred Edersheim, *The Temple* (Peabody: Hendrickson, 2009), 187. For outlines of the Passover Feast, see also, F. L. Godet, *Commentary on the Gospel of Luke* (Grand Rapids: Zondervan, 1956), 2:286-287; William Hendricksen, *Exposition of the Gospel According to John* (Grand Rapids: Baker, 1972), 1:121; and John Lightfoot, *A Commentary on the New Testament from the Talmud and Hebraica* (Peabody: Hendrickson, 2003), 2:346-356.
5. Edersheim, *Life and Times*, 497.
6. Edersheim, *The Temple*, 188-189.
7. Edersheim, *Life and Times*, 504.
8. Ibid.
9. Edersheim, *The Temple*, 189.
10. Ibid.
11. Ibid., 190.

The Lord's Supper

The main part of the feast followed. "The lamb forms the principal dish. The conversation is free. It closes with the distribution of the third cup, called the *cup of blessing*, because it was accompanied with the giving of thanks by the father of the house."[12] "At this point, Passover passes over into the Lord's Supper; for it was while, toward the end of the Passover meal ... that Jesus instituted the new sacrament that was to replace the old."[13] Matthew 26:26 therefore says, "While they were eating, Jesus took some bread." This was the bread already designated the bread of poverty or the bread of affliction. Recall Isaiah 53:4, "Yet we ourselves esteemed Him stricken, / Smitten of God, and afflicted," and Isaiah 53:7, "He was oppressed and He was afflicted, / Yet He did not open His mouth; / Like a lamb that is led to slaughter." Our Lord was indeed "the Lamb of God who takes away the sin of the world" (John 1:29). As a result, Matthew 26:26 goes on to record, "And after a blessing, He broke it and gave it to the disciples, and said, 'Take, eat; this is My body.'" Now the old, bloody sacrifice of the Passover lamb was giving way to the new. The old was about to be fulfilled "in the blood shed on Calvary."[14]

"In the same way He took the cup also after supper, saying, 'This cup is the new covenant in My blood; do this, as often as you drink it, in remembrance of Me'" (1 Cor. 11:25). This cup is the third one, "the cup of blessing which we bless," as the Apostle Paul declares (1 Cor. 10:16). It was so called "partly because it and the first cup required a special 'blessing,' and partly because it followed the 'grace after meat' [prayer after the meal]."[15]

Then, there is a final and fourth cup, "over which the second portion of the 'Hallel' was sung, consisting of Psalms 115, 116, 117, and 118 ... "[16] The disciples heard Psalm 118 sung days before upon Jesus' entry into Jerusalem. They heard Jesus quote Psalm 118 in response to

---

12. Godet, *Gospel of Luke*, 2:287.
13. William Hendriksen, *Exposition of the Gospel According to Matthew* (Grand Rapids: Baker, 1973), 908.
14. William Hendriksen, *Exposition of the Gospel According to Luke* (Grand Rapids: Baker, 1978), 961.
15. Edersheim, *The Temple*, 192.
16. Ibid.

the challenges of the Pharisees two days before. Peter and John heard the familiar words of Psalm 118 that afternoon when they were in the temple. Now they sang Psalm 118. Psalm 115-118 constituted the "hymn" sung by the disciples as they conclude their meal together and go to the Mount of Olives (Matt. 26:30, Mark 14:26).

The Lord's Supper grows out of the Passover. The Apostle Paul makes the connection clear. "Christ our Passover also has been sacrificed" (1 Cor. 5:7). "[B]y historically linking Passover and the Lord's Supper, so closely together, Jesus also made clear that what was essential in the first was not lost in the second. Both point to *him*, the only and all sufficient sacrifice for the sins of his people."[17]

Christ commands believers to observe this rite. The sacrifice of the Passover lamb pointed to Christ and eating the Passover *in faith* indicated the participant's *trust* in His sacrifice. Christ took physical elements from the Passover to represent the same spiritual realities. The bread broken represents Christ giving Himself for salvation of His people. The cup, containing the fruit of the vine, signifies Christ's blood ratifying God's covenant with His people. Eating and drinking *in faith* signify the participation of believers in the work of Christ *by faith*. "Is not the cup of blessing which we bless a sharing in the blood of Christ? Is not the bread which we break a sharing in the body of Christ?" (1 Cor. 10:16). Calvin states it this way,

> Now, of course I agree that the reference to the cup as a communion is a figure of speech, but only so long as the truth which the figure conveys is not destroyed; in other words, provided that the reality itself is also present, and the soul receives the communion in the blood, just as much as the mouth tastes the wine.[18]

Christ also commands the perpetual remembrance of His death using prescribed elements He takes from the previously commanded

---

17. Hendriksen, *Luke*, 961.
18. John Calvin, *The First Epistle of Paul to the Corinthians*, trans. John W. Frazer, ed. David W. Torrance and Thomas F. Torrance (Grand Rapids: Eerdmans, 1973), 216.

Passover meal. "This is My body, which is for you; do [*poieite*] this in remembrance [*anamnesin*] of Me" (1 Cor. 11:24). "This is my body, which is given for you. Do [*poieite*] this in remembrance [*anamnesin*] of me" (Luke 22:19). "*This do*: the Holy Communion is a perpetual institution."[19] Hodge says, "*This* do, i.e. 'Do what I have just done; take bread, consecrate it, break it, distribute and eat it. *In remembrance of me*, i.e. that I may be remembered as he who died for your sins."[20] Calvin adds, "The Supper is therefore a memorial [*mnemosunon*] provided to assist our weakness; for if we were otherwise sufficiently mindful of the death of Christ, this help would be superfluous. This applies to all sacraments, for they help us in our weakness."[21]

As seen here and in the previous discussion of the sacraments, the Lord's Supper fits the definition of a sacrament. "A sacrament is a holy ordinance instituted by Christ, in which by sensible signs the grace of God in Christ is represented, sealed, and applied to believers, and they, in turn, express their faith and obedience to God."[22] A discussion of the frequency of the administration of the Lord's Supper will follow.

What about the presence of Christ in the sacrament? Again, recall the discussion in chapter 8. The Lord's Supper is a prophetic, symbolic act. The significance of the sacrament is not only in the elements but also in the actions, the distribution of the elements, and the eating and drinking of them. As a prophetic, symbolic action, the Lord's Supper is also a form of proclamation. Note Paul's affirmation: "For as often as you eat this bread and drink the cup, you *proclaim* the Lord's death until He comes" (1 Cor. 11:26, italics added). "Taken in this light, the Eucharist is not simply a symbol intended to bring out the meaning of oral preaching; it is, in fact, an intensified form of that oral preaching ... containing the same unction as the oral presentation."[23] In oth-

---

19. F. W. Grosheide, *Commentary on the First Epistle to the Corinthians* (Grand Rapids: Eerdmans, 1972), 270
20. Charles Hodge, *An Exposition of the First Epistle to the Corinthians* (Grand Rapids: Eerdmans, 1965), 226.
21. Calvin, *First Corinthians*, 248.
22. Louis Berkhof, *Summary of Christian Doctrine* (Grand Rapids: Eerdmans, 1969), 166.
23. Dennis J. Prutow, "The Eucharist at Corinth," paper submitted to Dr. George Eldon Ladd, Fuller Theological Seminary, Pasadena, CA, May 16, 1968.

er words, Christ is present in the Lord's Supper in the same way He is present in the spoken word.

ACCESS TO THE LORD'S SUPPER

Who may receive the Lord's Supper? This question raises the issues of the qualifications for communicant church membership and therefore the requirements for communing, the tiered membership of some churches, session-controlled communion, and paedocommunion.

The requirement for communicant church membership is a credible confession of faith. All Reformed congregations and denominations follow this requirement. It is quite clear that the apostles admitted new converts into the fellowship of believers upon confession of their faith. John Murray indicates, "What we find in the New Testament is that the constituting bond of communion was common faith in Christ and that the condition of admission to the fellowship was this same faith (cf. Acts 2:38-42; 8:13, 35-38; 10:34-38; 16:14, 15, 31-33)."[24] Murray goes on to say, "[F]aith was registered by confession, and the criterion by which the church exercised its administrative responsibility in the admission of members was confession. In its essence this confession was that Jesus was the Christ, the Son of God, and that he was the Lord."[25] Acts 2:38-42 reads as follows,

> Peter said to them, "Repent, and each of you be baptized in the name of Jesus Christ for the forgiveness of your sins; and you will receive the gift of the Holy Spirit. For the promise is for you and your children and for all who are far off, as many as the Lord our God will call to Himself." And with many other words he solemnly testified and kept on exhorting them, saying, "Be saved from this perverse generation!" So then, those who had received his word were baptized; and that day there were added about three thousand souls.

---

24. John Murray, *Christian Baptism* (Philadelphia: Presbyterian and Reformed, 1972), 38.
25. Ibid., 38-39.

Conversion consists of repentance and faith: "repent and believe the gospel" (Mark 1:15). Registering their repentance and faith, these converts were baptized and admitted into the membership of the visible church. Inner faith must be expressed or confessed.

Regeneration or the new birth is not the criterion for church membership, as in many fundamentalist churches and denominations. Why? You cannot see or detect the work of the Spirit. "The wind blows where it wishes and you hear the sound of it, but do not know where it comes from and where it is going; so is everyone who is born of the Spirit" (John 3:8). You do not see the wind. You see the results of the wind, leaves fluttering and trees swaying. Similarly, you cannot see the Spirit. You see the results of His work. He produces the inner faith that believers confess. "The church is therefore circumscribed by the facts of regeneration and faith, facts which in themselves are spiritual and invisible. For this reason, no man or organization of men is able infallibly to determine who are regenerate and who are not, who are true believers and who are not."[26] Therefore, the Biblical criterion for church membership is a credible (believable) confession of faith.

What are the requirements for admittance to the Lord's Supper? Communion is open to those who have made a public profession of their faith, are baptized, and are members of a local Bible-believing congregation. God set forth the criterion for eating the Passover. It was clearly for members of the covenant community set apart from the world by the rite of circumcision.

> This is the ordinance of the Passover: no foreigner is to eat of it; but every man's slave purchased with money, after you have circumcised him, then he may eat of it. A sojourner or a hired servant shall not eat of it ... All the congregation of Israel are to celebrate this. But if a stranger sojourns with you, and celebrates the Passover to the Lord, let all his males be circumcised, and then let

---

26. Ibid., 34.

him come near to celebrate it; and he shall be like a native of the land. But no uncircumcised person may eat of it (Exod. 12:43-48).

Calvin comments on this text as follows:

> We know that among the Gentiles none but the initiated were admitted to their sacred rites. This was an absurd imitation of this true and lawful ordinance [the Passover]; because such a condition is only applicable to the institution of God, lest strangers should promiscuously usurp the testimonies of His grace, with which He honors His Church alone. For circumcision was then like a hedge, which should distinguish heathen nations from the holy race of Abraham; if, then, any should wish to celebrate the Passover together with the elect people, it was necessary that he should be circumcised, so as to attach himself to the true God; though God did not merely refer to the outward sign, but to the object, viz., that all who were circumcised should promise to study sincere piety.[27]

Similarly, baptized members of local congregations who make public profession of their faith are admitted to the Lord's Supper. After directing attention to His body "given for you" and to "the new covenant in My blood," Jesus directs, "Do this in remembrance of Me" (Luke 22:19-20; 1 Cor. 11:24-25). Paul adds that, in such eating and drinking, "You proclaim the Lord's death until He comes" (1 Cor. 11:26). Only men and women who are disciples of Christ by way of public confession of faith and baptism, and who also enjoy union with Christ by faith, are eligible for the sacrament. These individuals are those who recognize Christ's body *given for them*, embrace Christ's blood as the *blood of the covenant*, purposefully engage in the sacrament to *remember Christ's work* for them, and sincerely desire to *proclaim Christ's death*.

---

27. John Calvin, *The Last Four Books of Moses Arranged in the Form of a Harmony*, trans. Charles William Bingham (Grand Rapids: Baker, 1979), 1:467-468.

Who determines the eligibility of a person to partake of the Lord's Supper? Session-controlled communion is the position of the Reformed Presbyterian Church of North America. Its "Directory for the Public Worship of God," Chapter 3, Paragraph 11, reads in part,

> Only those who have been baptized and are communicant members in good standing in a true branch of Christ's visible church are to partake of the Lord's Supper ... Those who desire to commune, who are not members of the Reformed Presbyterian Church, are to be interviewed by the elders as to their personal faith and commitment to Christ, their church membership and their Baptism. The church's practice of session-controlled Communion should be clearly explained to visitors, preferably by a carefully worded written statement, given out as people enter the service.[28]

Why session-controlled communion? Another question is more pertinent. Who determines the eligibility of a person to partake of the sacrament? Is it the privilege of the individual or is this the responsibility of the church to make this judgment? Open communion means that all those who deem themselves qualified to partake of the sacrament are welcome to do so; the individual makes the determination. However, is such approach to the Lord's Supper really proper?

Remember, the Lord's Supper arises from Passover. Both institutions point to Christ. God specifically limits Passover participants to members of the congregation (Exod. 12:47). As just observed, in like manner, communion is limited to baptized members of local congregations. The local session, composed of the local elders, is the ruling body of the local church. "The elders who rule well are to be considered worthy of double honor, especially those who work hard at preaching and teaching" (1 Tim. 5:17). In the Presbyterian system,

---

28. Reformed Presbyterian Church of North America, *The Constitution of the Reformed Presbyterian Church of North America* (Pittsburgh: Crown and Covenant, 2010), F-13.

when a matter is brought before the church, the matter is brought before the elders. Local elders hear professions of faith and admit men and women and young people into church membership. Such membership is called *communicant* church membership. In other words, membership in the local church carries with it the privilege of the Lord's Supper.

In the disciplinary process of Matthew 18:15-17, if a church member refuses to repent of his or her sin after the matter is brought before the church, Christ says, "Let him be to you as a Gentile and a tax collector." Such a person is removed from the *membership* of the local church and considered to be an unbeliever, a person who is the subject of evangelism. The disciplinary removal of an individual from church membership is called excommunication. In other words, access to Communion, the Lord's Supper, is denied to the excommunicated individual. As A. A. Hodge says, "The officers of the church are the judges of the qualifications of those to be admitted to the sealing ordinances."[29]

Session-controlled communion simply means that the privilege of access to the Lord's Supper is not determined by the individual but by the elders of the local church. The local session, therefore, requires those whom they have not examined to testify "to their personal faith and commitment to Christ, their church membership and their Baptism."[30] Thus members of the local church welcome fellow believers to commune with them.

What about voting membership? Should there be more stringent requirements for voting in the congregation than for partaking of the Lord's Supper? To put it bluntly, is voting on a budget more significant and of greater importance than taking communion? Gary North mounts an argument in favor of more stringent requirements for voting membership, drawing a distinction between the uses of creeds and confessions. The Apostle's Creed and the Nicene Creed are ex-

---

29. A. A. Hodge, *Outlines of Theology* (Grand Rapids: Zondervan, 1976), 645.
30. *Constitution of the RPCNA*, F-13.

amples of the former. The Westminster Confession of Faith and the Belgic Confession are examples of the latter. North then asks, "What is the proper role of historic creeds and confessions in the life of the Presbyterian Church?"[31] He then gives the following answer:

> The creeds—shorter than the confessions—should establish a church's institutional boundaries. Communicant membership should be by confession of faith in the creed. This should not be voting membership, however, lest the lowest common denominator principle be subsidized. Voting membership should require more: affirmation of the full Confession. *Those given the right to impose ecclesiastical sanctions in terms of a confession must be under those sanctions and confession.*[32] Detailed confessions serve as Constitutional law documents of the respective denominations. This law is always subject to the fundamental law of the Bible. Confessions establish boundaries for Church officers, and should also establish boundaries for voting communicant members. Those who lawfully impose Presbyterian Church sanctions—voting in a local election is such a sanction—should be governed by an oath to the Westminster Confession and both catechisms.[33]

In this model, *voting* membership is a higher privilege than participating in the Lord's Supper or *communicant* church membership. There is no Biblical support for this position.

What about paedocommunion? Those who argue in favor of feeding communion to their infant children or small children, so-called paedocommunion, go back to the Passover. Exodus 12 is the primary text.

---

31. Gary North, *Crossed Fingers* (Tyler: Institute for Christian Economics, 1996), 922.
32. In Presbyterian polity, the officers of the church, elders and deacons, subscribe to the Westminster Confession of Faith and Catechisms. The elders alone have the power to sanction members or fellow officers in cases of formal discipline. Although a congregation may request the removal of its pastor, since the presbytery installs pastors, only the presbytery, the elders from various congregations in a prescribed area, may remove a pastor from his charge. Those who vote in a local election at the congregational level do not have this power.
33. North, *Crossed Fingers*, 922.

Speak to all the congregation of Israel, saying, "On the tenth of this month they are each one to take a lamb for themselves, according to their fathers' *households*, a lamb for each *household*. Now if the *household* is too small for a lamb, then he and his neighbor nearest to his *house* are to take one according to the number of persons in them; according to what each man should eat, you are to divide the lamb (Exod. 12:3-4, italics added).

A household refers to "a family group."[34] That is, "The companies were not to be formed arbitrarily, but were to be formed according to families."[35] Compare verse 21, "Go and take for yourselves lambs according to your families, and slay the Passover lamb." God provides that, "more than two families might unite, if some of them were childless."[36] Children were certainly present at the Passover meal. The "children" at the Passover meal, were expected to ask, "What does this rite mean to you?" (Exod. 12:26). This question led to the recitation of the history of Israel behind the Passover.

Proponents argue for paedocommunion by pointing out that, since children partook of the Passover meal, they should have the privilege of receiving the elements of the Lord's Supper. Such theologians add that, since infants receive the sacrament of baptism, they should also be permitted to partake of the Lord's Supper. These proponents of infant-communion also point to Calvin's concession, "This permission was indeed commonly given in the ancient church, as is clear from Cyprian and Augustine ... "[37]

Calvin admits that the Lord sets no definite age for baptism. "But he does not similarly hold forth the Supper for all to partake of, but only for those who are capable of discerning the body and blood of the Lord, of examining their own conscience, of proclaiming the

---

34. J. Rabbinowitz, *The Book of Exodus: The Soncino Chumash*, ed. A. Cohen (New York: Soncino, 1993), 387.
35. John Peter Lange, *Exodus*, trans. Charles M. Meade (Grand Rapids: Zondervan, 1960), 35.
36. Ibid.
37. John Calvin, *Institutes of the Christian Religion*, ed. John T. McNeill, trans. Ford Lewis Battles (Philadelphia: Westminster, 1960), 2:1352.

Lord's death, and considering its power."[38] Calvin then points to 1 Corinthians 11:28, "But a man must examine himself, and in so doing he is to eat of the bread and drink of the cup." He adds, "Self-examination ought, therefore, to come first, and it is vain to expect this of infants."[39]

Infants and children participated in the Passover and that by God's command. However, when we come to the Lord's Supper, God changes the requirements for access to the Supper by His word through the Apostle Paul. God commands self-examination. The English Standard Version reads, "Let a person examine [*dokimazetō*] himself, then, and so eat of the bread and drink of the cup." The verb *examine* is an imperative.

> In other words, let him ascertain whether he has correct views of the nature and design of the ordinance, and whether he has the proper state of mind. That is, whether he desires thankfully to commemorate the Lord's death, renewedly to partake of the benefits of that death as a sacrifice for his sins, publicly to accept the covenant of grace with all its promises and obligations, and to signify his fellowship with his brethren as joint members with himself of the body of Christ.[40]

As indicated above, the local session or board of elders grants initial access to the Lord's Supper by confession of faith in Christ. Subsequently, God calls each participant in the Supper to self-examination, thus confirming the individual's previous confession as he or she communes with Christ and the corporate body. Infants and young children do not meet these qualifications and are thus excluded from the Lord's Supper.

---

38. Ibid., 1352-1353.
39. Ibid., 1353.
40. Hodge, *Corinthians*, 232.

ADMINISTRATION OF THE LORD'S SUPPER

This section turns to the following practical matters regarding the administration of the Lord's Supper: fencing the table, what it means to be worthy receivers, the use of wine versus grape juice, the use of a common cup, individual cups, and split cups, the frequency of celebration, and the actual administration of the sacrament.

Use wisdom when fencing the table. The Biblical approach to the communion table is threefold, words of institution, warning, and invitation. Fencing the table involves the words of warning addressed to those who are already qualified to come to the Lord's Table because of their public profession of faith. Fencing the table does *not* mean rehearsing all the possible sins professing Christians are capable of committing and heaping such guilt upon them so that few feel worthy of partaking of communion. The sacrament is not for perfectly sanctified saints; it is for sinners saved by grace.

Fencing the table means reminding professing Christians of the requirement to "judge the body rightly" (1 Cor. 11:29). The word translated *judge* means to *discern* or to *discriminate,* "in the sense of discriminating one thing from another, or in the sense of estimating aright."[41] The bread and the cup are sacramental symbols in which the sign is put in the place of the thing signified. *This [bread] is My body. This cup is the new covenant in My blood.* These sacramental symbols point to Christ as He Himself refers to them as *My* body and *My* blood. These sacramental symbols also point to the body of believers. "Is not the cup of blessing which we bless a sharing in the blood of Christ? Is not the bread which we break a sharing in the body of Christ? Since there is one bread, we who are many are one body; for we all partake of the one bread" (1 Cor. 10:16-17). Fencing the table means reminding God's people that the *elements* are symbols pointing to *Christ* who died for *them.*

Judging the body has three aspects. First, it means understanding

---

41. Ibid., 233.

the symbolic import of the elements. Second, it means trusting Christ set forth in the sacrament. Third, it means accepting the fact that just as Christ forgives each professing believer, He also forgives all those sitting around him or her. They are bound to forgive each brother and sister in Christ, just as He has forgiven them. Believers fail in these matters regularly. They sin daily in thought, word, and deed. "If we say that we have no sin, we are deceiving ourselves and the truth is not in us" (1 John 1:8). Fencing the table means reminding God's people, "If we confess our sins, He is faithful and righteous to forgive us our sins and to cleanse us from all unrighteousness" (1 John 1:8-9).

If a member of the congregation is engaged in gross or notorious sin, the elders must confront the offender. If this person refuses to repent, the session or board of elders must take formal action, impose suspension, and exclude him or her from the privilege of the sacraments.[42] Church officers ought to take such action, rather than tightly fencing the table, hoping such a one will exclude himself from the sacrament. Fencing the table in this case means exercising formal discipline.

Losing Biblical focus and missing the point occurs when arguing over the content of the cup in communion. While celebrating His final Passover with His disciples, Christ speaks of using the "fruit of the vine" (Matt. 26:29; Mark 14:25; Luke 22:18). He also speaks simply of "this cup" (Matt. 26:39; Mark 14:36; Luke 22:42; 1 Cor. 11:25). "The Biblical language used for the elements of the supper are generic terms, not specifically defined."[43] This lack of specificity is certainly the case. "From this usage we deduce that Jesus indicated to us that the precise nature of the 'fruit of the vine' is not the point."[44] Focusing on the content of the cup, and arguing for fermented wine or unfermented grape juice, misses the point. What then is the point?

---

42. For example, "The Book of Discipline" of the Reformed Presbyterian Church of North America states that suspension "is the temporary exclusion from the privileges of church membership, including participation in the sacraments or from the exercise of ordained office or from both ... "

43. "The Committee to Study the Contents of the Cup in the Lord's Supper," *Minutes of the 2010 Synod of the Reformed Presbyterian Church of North America* (Pittsburgh: Crown and Covenant, 2010), 14.

44. Ibid.

Christ calls us to remember Him and focus on the import of His blood. The sacrament links the blood of grapes with the blood of Christ. Genesis 49:11 speaks of "the blood of grapes." The passage is messianic. Note the parallels in the Hebrew poetry of Genesis 49:10-11:

> The scepter shall not depart from Judah,
> Nor the ruler's staff from between his feet,
> Until Shiloh comes,
> And to him shall be the obedience of the peoples.
> He ties his foal to the vine,
> And his donkey's colt to the choice vine;
> He washes his garments in wine,
> And his robes in the blood of grapes.

Isaiah 63:2 asks, "Why is Your apparel red, / And Your garments like the one who treads in the wine press?" God answers in verses 3-4. Note the power of the Hebrew poetry in this striking portrayal of God's wrath and redemption:

> I have trodden the wine trough alone,
> And from the peoples there was no man with Me.
> I also trod them in My anger
> And trampled them in My wrath
> And their lifeblood [juice] is sprinkled on My garments,
> And I stained all My raiment.
> For the day of vengeance was in My heart,
> And My year of redemption has come.

Isaiah calls to mind the picture of the Savior riding in triumph over His enemies "clothed with a robe dipped in blood" (Rev. 19:13). Why are His garments dipped in blood? Revelation 19:16 answers. "He treads the winepress of the fierce wrath of God, the Almighty."

Now, the tables are turned. The Lord Jesus Christ drinks the cup of God's wrath. He cries to His Father in heaven, being in great torment at the prospect. "Father, if You are willing, remove this cup from Me;

yet not My will, but Yours be done" (Luke 22:42). How awful was the drinking of *this* cup! "My God, My God, Why have you forsaken Me?" (Mark 15:34, quoting Psalm 22:1). He cried these terrible words in great agony, so that those who trust in Him will never have to utter these awful words themselves. He drank the cup of God's wrath for His people. He did so that their blood would not spatter His garments. To argue about the content of the communion cup fixes hearts and minds on the symbol. It diverts attention from the truth to which the symbol points. When communicants drink the fruit of the vine in the Lord's Supper, Christ calls them to remember the winepress of God's wrath, His innocent blood spilled in judgment for them, and their salvation. Focusing on the content of the cup, the symbol, whether it is fermented wine or unfermented grape juice, misses this point.

Focusing on the content of the cup misses the point from another perspective. Listen to the Apostle Paul. "Is not the cup of blessing which we bless a sharing [*koinōnia*] in the blood of Christ? Is not the bread which we break a sharing [*koinōnia*] in the body of Christ? Since there is one bread, we who are many are one body; for we all partake of the one bread" (1 Cor. 10:16-17).

> There are three facets to koinonia in this passage: 1. Koinonia points us to the peaceful unity and fellowship each individual Christian has with Christ ... 2. Koinonia also points us to the peaceful unity and fellowship that we have with one another ... There is a unity among all believers as we eat and drink together. 3. Koinonia then points to the peaceful unity and fellowship that the corporate body of Christ shares with Christ ... We, the body of Christ, enjoy fellowship with and spiritually feed upon our Savior.
>
> This koinonia is inherent to the celebration of the Lord's Supper and it is symbolized in two ways: 1. First, koinonia is symbolized in the singularity of the elements of one loaf and one cup ... [O]ur koinonia as the body of

Christ is represented in that we all partake of one constituent loaf [part of the whole] and one constituent cup [part of the whole]. 2. The second symbol of our unity is the fact that *everyone* actually participates in the supper ... Our unity and fellowship with Christ, our head, is expressed not only in the singularity of the elements of the supper, but also in the fact that we all participate together—we eat and drink *together*.[45]

Here are two clear implications from the above. The use of the so-called split cup, serving fermented wine to some and grape juice to others, undercuts the unity fostered in the sacrament and exacerbates division within the body. What about using individual cups? The point is that believers all drink of the *same fruit of the vine* whether we share from one cup or drink from individual cups. As they drink together the same fruit of the vine, they remember the winepress of God's wrath, His innocent blood spilled in judgment for them, and their salvation. Note the emphasis of the Lord Jesus Christ: "I will not drink of *this fruit of the vine* from now on until that day when I drink it new with you in My Father's kingdom" (Matt. 26:29, italics added). Participants in the Lord's Supper lose Biblical focus and miss the point of *Communion*, when they argue over the specific content of the cup.

The frequency of communion is discretionary or optional. Some churches administer the sacrament weekly, some monthly, some quarterly, some even less often. The Westminster's Assembly's Directory for the Public Worship of God states, "The Communion, or supper of the Lord, is frequently to be celebrated; but how often, may be considered and determined by the ministers, and other church-governors of each congregation, as they shall find most convenient for the comfort and edification of the people committed to their charge."[46] Let wisdom dictate in this matter.

---

45. Ibid., 15-16.
46. *Westminster Confession of Faith* (Glasgow: Free Presbyterian Publications, 1997), 384.

It is true that Calvin earnestly desired to celebrate the sacrament weekly. He argues from Acts 2:42, "They were continually devoting themselves to the apostles' teaching and to fellowship, to the breaking of bread and to prayer," and says, "Thus it became an unvarying rule that no meeting of the church should take place without the Word, prayers, partaking of the Supper, and almsgiving."[47]

In his "Articles Concerning the Church and Worship at Geneva," Calvin says, "It would be well to require that the Communion of the Holy Supper of Jesus Christ be held every Sunday at least as a rule."[48] The Genevan Council declined to approve weekly communion and cut back the compromise for monthly communion to quarterly.[49] The date was January 16, 1537. Later, in 1561, in a treatise on the "true partaking of the flesh and blood of Christ," Calvin clearly states, "The table of the Lord ought to be spread in sacred assembly at least once a week."[50] Although he did not change his position on the frequency of communion, it appears that Calvin did not make this issue *a hill on which to die*. He lived under the constraints imposed upon him. Let us follow Calvin's example and the direction of the Westminster divines.

Make the administration simple, clear, and efficient. As indicated above, the Biblical approach to the communion table is threefold, words of institution, warning, and invitation. The words of institution come from Scripture. Read one of the four passages relating Christ's institution of the Supper, such as 1 Cor. 11:23-26. A simple form, such as the following from the Orthodox Presbyterian Church, will then suffice. This form includes words of explanation, warning, and invitation. Footnotes 51-65 were added to the form to offer definitions and explanations for those who may not be familiar with the language used. If printed as a bulletin insert, this form helps prepare

---

47. Calvin, *Institutes*, 2:1422.
48. John Calvin, *Theological Treatises*, trans. J. K. S. Reid (Philadelphia: Westminster, 1954), 49.
49. T. H. L. Parker, *John Calvin: A Biography* (Philadelphia: Westminster, 1975), 64.
50. Calvin, *Theological Treatises*, 310.

people for the sacrament. People will no doubt read it, review the citations, and reflect on their participation in the Supper.

THE SACRAMENT OF THE LORD'S SUPPER

The Lord's Supper is an ordinance[51] instituted by our Lord Jesus Christ. Until His coming again it is to be observed for a perpetual remembrance of the sacrifice of Himself in His death. The physical elements, representing the broken body and shed blood of the Savior, are received by true believers as signs and seals of all the benefits of His sacrifice upon the cross. They signify and seal remission[52] of sins and nourishment and growth in Christ, and are a bond and pledge[53] of communion of believers with Him and with each other as members of His mystical[54] body. As signs and seals[55] of the covenant of grace[56] they not only declare that God is faithful and true to fulfill the promises of the covenant but they also summon us to all the duties of the children of God, and call us to renewed consecration[57] in gratitude for His salvation.

It is my solemn duty to warn the uninstructed, the profane,[58] the scandalous,[59] and those who secretly and impenitently[60] live in any sin,[61] not to approach the holy table lest they partake unworthily, not discerning the

---

51. A custom established by authority. In this case, the custom is the Lord's Supper; the authority is Christ.
52. Forgiveness, cleansing.
53. Guarantee, security deposit.
54. Believers are united to Christ. He is their representative. He is the head of the body, the church.
55. A seal is a mark showing something is authentic. The Lord's Supper marks us. In their participation, God affirms true believers as authentic members of the body of Christ.
56. The Covenant of Grace is the outworking of the agreement established by God with Christ in which He dies for His people in payment for their sins (Matthew 1:21). The people of God receive forgiveness, the righteousness of Christ imputed to them, eternal life, and heaven all by grace through faith. They, in turn, covenant with God to follow Him.
57. Devotion to Christ.
58. Irreverent, blasphemous, or godless.
59. Disreputable, disgraceful, shameful.
60. Not sorry, obstinate, unrepentant.
61. Offense, wrong-doing.

Lord's body,[62] and so eat and drink condemnation to themselves. Nevertheless, this warning is not designed to keep the humble and contrite[63] from the table of the Lord, as if it were for those who might be free from sin. On the contrary, we who are invited to the supper, coming as guilty and polluted[64] sinners and without hope of eternal life apart from the grace of God in Christ, confess our dependence for pardon and cleansing upon the perfect sacrifice of Christ, base our hope of eternal life upon His obedience and righteousness,[65] and humbly resolve to deny ourselves, crucify our sinful natures, and follow Christ as becomes those who bear His name. Let us therefore in accordance with the admonition of the Apostle Paul, examine our minds and hearts to determine whether such discernment is ours, to the end that we may partake to the glory of God and to our own growth in grace.[66]

After reading the form, it is appropriate to call the congregation to a time of silent prayer and confession. After this time of silent prayer, whoever officiates, may pray, asking the Lord to set apart the bread and the fruit of the vine to its sacred use in the sacrament. Pray that so much of the bread eaten by members of the congregation will be blessed to them as a participation in the body of Christ. Pray that so much of the fruit of the vine received by members of the congregation will be blessed to them as a participation in the blood of Christ.

Let the elders distribute the elements, first the bread and then the cup. Members of the congregation may hold the bread, and then the cup, so that they may all partake together. When the elders have dis-

---

62. The bread and the fruit of the vine represent the Lord's body given for believers on the cross. When they partake of these elements by faith, they partake of the work of Christ. The Lord's body is also found in the church.
63. Sorry, repentant.
64. Contaminated, dirty.
65. Uprightness, ethical correctness.
66. Orthodox Presbyterian Church, *The Standards of Government, Discipline, and Worship of the Orthodox Presbyterian Church* (Philadelphia: Committee on Christian Education, 1965), 77-78.

tributed the bread and take their seats, the pastor may serve them. Serving himself, rather than being served, the pastor may lead the congregation with the simple words, "The body of Christ given for you." In a similar fashion, when all are prepared, the pastor may lead the congregation in partaking of the cup with the simple words, "The blood of Christ poured out for you." A prayer of thanksgiving is appropriate to conclude the communion service.

COVENANT RENEWAL IN COMMUNION

The Lord's Supper is an outward mark or seal of covenant renewal. A seal is an authenticating mark placed upon an official document. For instance, a diploma has the seal of the school from which someone graduates. The seal may be stamped on the paper or embossed in the paper. In either case, the intent is to make a permanent mark linking the individual with the institution from which he or she graduates. Outside of Christ, unbelievers bore the mark of the world, the mark of the beast. "If anyone worships the beast and his image, and receives a mark on his forehead or on his hand ... " (Rev. 14:9). All that unbelievers think and do bears the mark of evil. As Paul puts it, before conversion, unbelievers "walked according to the course of this world, according to the prince of the power of the air, of the spirit that is now working in the sons of disobedience" (Eph. 2:2).

Nothing unbelievers do can remove this mark. Only God has the power to do so. Christ must redeem them. "In Him we have redemption through His blood" (Eph. 1:7). Christ authenticates His redeemed people with the mark or seal of the Holy Spirit. *He is the indelible mark and guarantee of redemption.* "Do not grieve the Holy Spirit of God, by whom you were sealed for the day of redemption" (Eph. 4:30). Baptism is the outward mark or seal corresponding to the inward mark of the Holy Spirit.

As people inwardly marked by the Spirit, outwardly marked by baptism, and publicly confessing their faith in Christ, believers are eligible to come to the Lord's Table. Participation in the Lord's

Supper separates them from the world and marks them as disciples of Jesus Christ. At the same time, Christ assures them that they belong to Him. Think about what takes place as believers participate in the sacrament. As they take the bread in their hands, Jesus Christ says to them, "Take, eat ... This is My body which is given for you; do this in remembrance of Me" (Matt. 26:26; Luke 22:19). When they take the cup in their hands, Jesus Christ says to them, "Drink from it, all of you ... This cup which is poured out for you is the new covenant in My blood" (Matt. 26:27; Luke 22:20). Jesus Christ is renewing His covenant with them. They may also hear these rhetorical questions: "Is not the cup of blessing which we bless a sharing in the blood of Christ? Is not the bread which we break a sharing in the body of Christ?" (1 Cor. 11:16). These questions anticipate an affirmative response. Their hearts leap with joy. Yes, they are marked with the seal of discipleship. Jesus Christ is renewing His covenant with them.

Leading people in the covenant renewal of communion is a shepherding activity. The objective is to lead God's people in the sacrament so that they will experience covenant renewal. Worship itself is covenant renewal. Communion is simply another aspect of this work of God. "Augustine calls a sacrament 'a visible word.'"[67] God not only strikes communicants' ears but also their other senses. They handle the bread and cup with their hands. They taste the bread and the fruit of the vine in their mouths. They unite themselves with Christ by faith. Christ unites with them; they abide in Him. Those who lead in worship and administer the sacrament have the privilege of leading men and women and young people into this fellowship with the Savior. Pastor-shepherds lead God's people through this eating and drinking, so that Christ reaffirms that He is indeed their Savior and that they do belong to Him. Pastors-shepherds lead God's people into and through this simple ceremony where God renews His covenant with them.

---

67. Calvin, *Institutes*, 2:1281.

A perspective on covenant renewal and shepherding alters communion preparation. The accent is not on warning. Yes, Biblical warnings are important and necessary. The Apostle Paul is clear: "Whoever eats the bread or drinks the cup of the Lord in an unworthy manner, shall be guilty of the body and the blood of the Lord" (1 Cor. 11:27). However, the words of the Apostle John must also be taken seriously. "We love, because He first loved us" (1 John 4:19). Believers express love, as Paul declares, "because the love of God has been poured out within our hearts through the Holy Spirit who was given to us" (Rom. 5:5). God's law is best understood in the context of love. "For this is the love of God, that we keep His commandments; and His commandments are not burdensome" (1 John 5:3). The law gives believers the means to express their love for God and for their neighbors.

A weekly rehearsal of God's law, and a companion rehearsal of the gospel of grace in Christ, lead God's people in weekly covenant renewal and prepare them for the Lord's Supper. Week by week, God's people see themselves in the mirror of God's word. Week by week, the gospel of grace assures them that God receives them by faith. Week by week, God restates His love for His people and they restate their love for Him and for one another. Week by week, they are prepared by grace to sit at the table of the Lord. Communion preparation is, therefore, a regular feature of life in the body of Christ, not a special occasion. God's people experience covenant renewal as they sit under the *spoken word* weekly. They also experience covenant renewal as they participate in the *visible word*, whether weekly, monthly, or quarterly. The gracious God draws them out of the world and into His worship for this purpose.

Public Worship 101

PART THREE:
The Element of Praise:
Psalmody

11

THE ELEMENT OF PRAISE: PSALMODY

Let the word of Christ richly dwell within you, with all wisdom teaching and admonishing one another with psalms and hymns and spiritual songs, singing with thankfulness in your hearts to God.
~ COL. 3:16

INTRODUCTION

SOME GENERAL CONSIDERATIONS begin the discussion of the element of praise. A treatment of several topics then follows: King David's introduction of Psalmody into the worship of Israel, the use of Psalms in the New Testament, the Biblical meaning of the terms *psalms*, *hymns*, and *songs*, and the case for the exclusive use of Psalms. The chapter concludes with an analysis of the genius of Psalmody: its special character and use for molding the inner person.

PRAISE: GENERAL CONSIDERATIONS

Recall that the element of praise derives from the Old Testament temple and that Scripture uses sacrificial language to describe New Testament Praise. Hebrews 13:15 is a good example. "Through Him then, let us continually offer up a sacrifice of praise to God, that is, the fruit of lips that give thanks to His name." The phrase *sacrifice of praise* in Greek is *thusian aineseōs*.

Here is a brief examination of the word translated praise. The verb form of this Greek word is found in the following texts. "Give praise [*aineite*] to our God, all you His bond-servants, you who fear Him, the small and the great" (Rev. 19:5). "As soon as He was approaching, near the descent of the Mount of Olives, the whole crowd of the disciples began to praise [*ainein*] God joyfully with a loud voice for all the miracles which they had seen" (Luke 19:37). "And again, 'Praise [*aineite*] the Lord all you gentiles'" (Rom. 15:11). In this last text, Paul is referring to Psalm 117:1, "Praise [*aineite* (LXX)] the Lord, all nations; Laud [*epainesate* (LXX)] Him, all peoples!"

The noun *epainos* and the verb *aineō* appear seventeen times in the New Testament: in praise of men, nine times; in praise of God, six times; in praise of things, one time; and once as a proper name. Note this repetitive use of the term in Ephesians 1:6, 12, and 14: "to the praise [*epainon*] of the glory of His grace ... to the praise [*epainon*] of His glory ... to the praise [*epainon*] of His glory."

This praise is the heart and core of public worship. Remember this definition: Worship is the reverent fear and awe of God expressed in bowing to Him in heart and soul. Worshipers know that God alone is worthy. Therefore, they bow to His will and determine to serve Him. They worship Him as the center and focus of their lives. They know that the Father seeks their worship as a response to His worthiness as their Creator and Redeemer. In truly spiritual worship, they approach the Father, through the Son, by the power of the Spirit. As they do so, they delight in God and He delights in them. They enjoy Him and find rest in Him. Praise is the heart of this worship and the assembly of God's people is the optimum place for praise. "Yet You are holy, / O You who are enthroned upon the praises [*epainos* (LXX)] of Israel" (Ps. 22:3). Note Matthew Henry's reference to God's special gracious presence with His people in worship as they offer Him the praise that He is due.

> "*Thou inhabitest the praises of Israel*; thou art pleased to manifest thy glory, and grace, and special presence with thy people, in the sanctuary, where they attend thee with their praises. There thou art always ready to receive their

homage, and of the tabernacle of meeting thou hast said, *This is my rest for ever.*" This bespeaks God's wonderful condescension to his faithful worshippers—(that, though he is attended with the praises of angels, yet he is pleased to inhabit the praises of Israel) ... [1]

This praise is the believer's sacrifice. "Through Him then, let us continually offer up a *sacrifice of praise* to God, that is, the fruit of lips that give thanks to His name" (Heb. 13:15, italics added). The phrase *sacrifice of praise* in Greek is *thusian aineseōs*. In the Septuagint, Leviticus 7:12-15 uses the same language in giving directions for peace offerings and thank-offerings. Verse 12, "If he offers it by way of thanksgiving [*aineseōs*], then along with the *sacrifice of thanksgiving* [*tês thusias tês aineseōs*] he shall offer unleavened cakes ... " Verse 13, "With the *sacrifice* [*thusia*] of his peace offerings for *thanksgiving* [*aineseōs*], he shall present his offering with cakes of leavened bread." Verse 15, "Now as for the flesh of the sacrifice [*thusias*] of his thanksgiving [*aineseōs*] peace offerings, it shall be eaten on the day of his offering."

Hebrews 13:15 uses the language of the bloody Old Testament thank-offering, redefining this sacrifice of thanksgiving as "the fruit of lips" that give thanks to God. The Old Testament bloody sacrifices become New Testament songs of praise. Recall that this redefinition of *thusian aineseōs*, sacrifice of thanksgiving, is understandable given the close connection between the animal sacrifice and the psalmody of the Levitical choirs. These choirs sang selected Psalms as the sacrifices were in process. This connection was established in chapter 5.

The Biblical principle is to bring the sacrifice God designates. Psalm 50:23 reads, "He who offers a sacrifice of thanksgiving [*thusia aineseōs* (LXX)] honors Me." The Old Testament saints gave honor to God by obeying Him and offering the sacrifices that He commanded. To honor God in the church of the New Testament, believers also bring the sacrifices of thanksgiving, the fruit of lips, that God commands. This

---

1. Matthew Henry, *Matthew Henry's Commentary on the Whole Bible* (Grand Rapids: Fleming H. Revell, 1985), 3:310.

is an expression of the regulative principle. God, therefore, provides the substance and content of this praise. David confesses, "From You comes my praise [*epainos* (LXX)] in the great assembly [*ekklesia* (LXX)]" (Ps. 22:25). Calvin translates this text, "My praise shall proceed from thee," and goes on to say, "I do not reject the other translation; but in my opinion, the Hebrew manner of expression here requires this sense—that David will take the matter of his song of praise from God."[2] That is, the substance and content of David's praise is from God. The Hebrew does use the preposition *from*. Psalm 22:25 is an expression of the regulative principle. These general considerations lead to a discussion of Psalmody.

PSALMODY

David introduced the singing of Psalms before the ark of the covenant in Jerusalem and in the tabernacle in Gibeon. Recall that the Philistines had captured the ark of the covenant (1 Sam. 5:17). They subsequently sent it away and the ark remained in Kiriath-jearim for twenty years (1 Sam. 7:1-2). After a failed attempt to bring the ark to Jerusalem (1 Chron. 13:1-13), David succeeded in doing so and placed the ark in a tent he pitched for it (1 Chron. 16:1). At the same time, the tabernacle was in Gibeon, five or six miles northwest of Jerusalem (1 Chron. 16:39). This anomalous situation existed until Solomon dedicated the temple (2 Chron. 1:3-4; 5:4-5). It was during this period that David introduced Psalmody to Israel. Here is the story, as 1 Chronicles 16 gives it:

> He [David] appointed some of the Levites as ministers before the ark of the Lord, even *to celebrate* [proclaim] and *to thank* and *praise* the Lord God of Israel ... So he left Asaph and his relatives there before the ark of the covenant of the Lord *to minister* before the ark continually, as every day's work required ... He [David] left Zadok the

---

2. John Calvin, *Commentary on the Book of Psalms,* trans. James Anderson (Grand Rapids: Baker, 1979), 1:381-382.

> priest and his relatives the priests before the tabernacle of the Lord in the high place which was at Gibeon… With them were Heman and Jeduthun, and the rest who were chosen, who were designated by name, *to give thanks* to the Lord, because His lovingkindness is everlasting. And with them were Heman and Jeduthun with trumpets and cymbals for those who should sound aloud, and with instruments for the *songs of God* … (1 Chron. 16:4, 37, 39, 41-42, italics added).

The long center section of 1 Chronicles 16, verses 8-36, gives examples of the praise David assigned the Levites. It quotes Psalms 105:1-15; 96:1-13; and 106:1, 46-47. Thus David began Psalmody in Israel's worship. Martin Selman comments on 1 Chronicles 16:37-43.

> This paragraph summarizes the Levites functions (cf. 1 Ch. 23-26). Basically they were in charge of the music (v. 31, cf. v. 32; 'singing', JB, or 'the service of song') and with the duties of the tabernacle (v. 48). 'After the ark rested' (v. 31, RSV), the musicians were divided between the ark in Jerusalem and the Tent of Meeting (v. 32) in Gibeon (cf. 16:1-4, 41-42).[3]

Why did David introduce Psalmody into the worship of Israel? Hezekiah restored God-ordained worship in Israel according to God's command to David: "He [Hezekiah] then stationed the Levites in the house of the Lord with cymbals, with harps and with lyres, according to the command of David and of Gad the king's seer, and of Nathan the prophet; *for the command was from the Lord through His prophets*" (2 Chron. 29:25, italics added). God commanded the addition of praise with Psalms and instrumental accompaniment.

King Hezekiah regularized temple Psalmody. "Moreover, King Hezekiah and the officials ordered the Levites to sing praises to the Lord with the words of David and Asaph the seer" (2 Chron. 29:30). Keil

---

3. Martin J. Selman, *First Chronicles* (Downers Grove: InterVarsity, 2008), 111.

and Delitzsch put it this way, "The king and the princes commanded the Levites to sing praise unto the Lord with the words (psalms) of David and Asaph ... "[4] John Kleinig adds, "If there was no collection of psalms attributed to David and Asaph, this decree would have authorized the preparation of such an edition. These were thereafter to be used to praise the Lord as the public burnt offering was presented at the temple."[5]

The practice of Psalmody continued after the exile. The people offered praise according to the direction of David which God commanded. The sample of praise given in the following quote refers to Psalms 106:1; 107:1; 118:1, 29, or 136:1.

> Now when the builders had laid the foundation of the temple of the Lord, the priests stood in their apparel with trumpets, and the Levites, the sons of Asaph, with cymbals, to praise the Lord according to the directions of King David of Israel. They sang, praising and giving thanks to the Lord, saying, "For He is good, for His lovingkindness is upon Israel forever" (Ezra 3:10-11).

Nehemiah 12:45-46 commends the priests and Levites for their service, hearkens back to the psalmody of David and Asaph, and appears to be a reference to Hezekiah's decree in 2 Chronicles 29:30.

> For they performed the worship of their God and the service of purification, together with the singers and the gatekeepers in accordance with the command of David and of his son Solomon. For in the days of David and Asaph, in ancient times, *there were* leaders of the singers, songs of praise and hymns of thanksgiving to God.

Remember, our argument is that the element of praise and Psalmody derives from the temple. As Edersheim says, "There was no service of 'praise' in the synagogues."[6] Is Edersheim correct? "No contempo-

---

4. C. F. Keil and F. Delitzsch, *The Books of the Chronicles*, trans. Andrew Harper (Grand Rapids: Eerdmans, 1982), 452.
5. John W. Kleinig, *The Lord's Song* (Sheffield: Sheffield Academic Press, 1993), 68.
6. Alfred Edersheim, *Sketches of Jewish Social Life* (Grand Rapids: Eerdmans, 1993), 268.

rary sources make any mention of singing in the synagogue during the first [century A.D.] ... Nor in early rabbinical documents which might, in places, have bearing on the period is there any mention of singing in the ancient synagogue."[7] (As will be seen, the contrary is the case in the early church). "More recently the point has been underlined by Sigmund Mowinckel: 'The synagogue service was in ancient times always songless', and further: 'Not before mediaeval time did synagogal poetry and singing come into existence.'"[8] In a more recent work, Christopher Page, speaking of the Mishnah, redacted around 200 A.D., says that "there is no mention of synagogue music in that compilation ... "[9] Edersheim appears to be correct. *The element of praise comes from the temple and its Psalmody.*

PSALMODY IN THE NEW TESTAMENT

Both Jesus and the disciples sang the Psalms. As indicated in chapter 10, Peter and John sang the Psalms in the temple while they were slaying the Passover lamb. The psalms sung on this occasion were Psalms 113-118, the Egyptian Hallel. As was seen in chapter 10, those celebrating the Passover sang from these same Psalms. This collection of Psalms composed the *hymn* sung by the disciples at the close of the Passover and the institution of the Lord's Supper: "After singing a hymn [*humnesantes*], they went out to the Mount of Olives" (Matt. 26:30, Mark 14:26). Hendriksen comments, "'When they had hymned,' says the original. Since, as has been shown, the Lord's Supper was the natural outgrowth of the Passover, it is probable that the hymns of praise that were lifted up to God were Pss. 115-118."[10] As seen above, Psalms 113-114 were sung earlier in the Passover celebration. Alexander adds, *"When they had sung a hymn,* in Greek a single word, *hymning* (or *having hymned*), referring no doubt to the series

---

7. John Smith, "The Ancient Synagogue, the Early Church and Singing," *Music and Letters* 65 (1984), 5. Smith cites, "Mishna, the Tosefta (completed A.D. c. 250), the Jerusalem Talmud (completed A.D. c.400), and the Babylonian Talmud (completed A.D. c. 500)." See his notes 26, 27, and 28.
8. Smith, 5 cites Mowinckel, *The Psalms in Israel's Worship*, 1:4.
9. Christopher Page, *The Christian West and Its Singers* (New Haven: Yale University Press, 2010), 42.
10. William Hendricksen, *Exposition of the Gospel of Matthew* (Grand Rapids: Baker, 1973), 913.

of psalms usually chanted at the Passover ... "[11] Two important facts are seen here. First, Jesus and the disciples sang the psalms. Second, the psalms *are* Biblical *hymns*.

In this context, Matthew Henry therefore says, "Singing of psalms is a gospel-ordinance. Christ's removing the hymn from the close of the passover to the close of the Lord's supper, plainly intimates that he intended that ordinance should continue in his church, that, as it had not its birth with the ceremonial law, so it should not die with it."[12] Henry also speaks to the appropriateness of Christ's use of the psalms in this circumstance. "It is not unseasonable, no, not in times of sorrow and suffering; the disciples were in sorrow, and Christ was entering upon his sufferings, and yet they could sing a hymn together. Our spiritual joy should not be interrupted by outward afflictions."[13] As will be seen, one of the beauties of Psalmody is that the Psalms are a *divine guide* for the exercise of our inner thoughts and affections.

Paul and Silas also sang the Psalms. "About midnight Paul and Silas were praying and singing hymns [*humnoun*] of praise to God, and the prisoners were listening to them" (Acts 16:25). The verb *humneō* means to *sing hymns*. The *hymns* they were singing were Psalms. "[I]f we are correct in reasoning that the human spirit, under duress and trial, turns instinctively to what is familiar and well-known, there is nothing to deny that the Psalms of the Old Testament rang through the dark prison, greatly to the interest of the missionaries' fellow-captives."[14] Matthew Henry comments on this text. "This proves that the singing of psalms is a gospel ordinance, and ought to be used by all good Christians; and that it is instituted, not only for the expressing of their joys in a day of triumph, but for the balancing and relieving of their sorrows in a day of trouble."[15] J. A. Alexander adds that Paul and Silas were "singing or chanting perhaps one or

---

11. J. A. Alexander, *Commentary on the Gospel of Mark* (Minneapolis: Klock and Klock, 1980), 382.
12. Henry, *Commentary on the Whole Bible*, 5:392.
13. Ibid.
14. Ralph Martin, *Worship in the Early Church* (Westwood, NJ: Fleming H. Revell, 1964), 43.
15. Henry, *Commentary on the Whole Bible*, 6:211.

more [Psalms] of the Book of the Psalms peculiarly adapted and intended for the use of prisoners and others under persecution."[16] Yes, the Psalms are uniquely qualified for such circumstances.

James 5:13 exhorts the singing of Psalms. Compare the King James Version for the more literal translation. "Is any among you afflicted? Let him pray. Is any merry? Let him sing psalms [*psalletō*]." Ralph Martin, who is no friend of exclusive Psalmody, says, "[T]he allusion in James V, 13: 'Is any merry? Let him sing psalms' may be taken to refer to Davidic psalms."[17] Matthew Henry also says here, "[T]he singing of psalms is a gospel ordinance."[18] In this context, Calvin points to the Psalms as a bridling influence guiding our passions and emotions.

> But such is the perverseness of men, that they cannot rejoice without forgetting God, and that when afflicted they are disheartened and driven to despair. *We ought, then, to keep within due bounds,* so that the joy, which usually makes us to forget God, may induce us to set forth the goodness of God, and that our sorrow may teach us to pray. For he has set the singing of psalms in opposition to profane and *unbridled* joy; and thus they express their joy who are led, as they ought to be, by prosperity to God (italics added).[19]

Here is seen, not only the use of Psalms in the New Testament, but also the rationale for the Psalms as a divine guide to inner passions and emotions.

PSALMS, HYMNS, SONGS

Do the three terms, psalms, hymns, and songs, refer to the 150 Psalms? Early Psalters make this connection. The title page for the Sternehold

---

16. J. A. Alexander, *Commentary on the Acts of the Apostles* (Carlisle: Banner of Truth, 1980), 2:121.
17. Martin, *Worship in the Early Church*, 43.
18. Henry, *Commentary on the Whole Bible*, 6:999.
19. John Calvin, *Commentaries on the Catholic Epistles*, trans. John Owen (Grand Rapids: Baker, 1979), 354-355.

Hopkins Psalter, published in England in 1562, bears two Scripture quotes: *If any be afflicted, let him pray: if any by merry, let him sing Psalms; Let the word of God dwell plenteously in you, in all wisdome teaching and exhorting one another, in Psalms, Hymns, and Spiritual Songs, and sing unto the Lord in your heart.*[20] The first book published in America was the so-called "Bay Psalm Book," officially *The Whole Book of Psalms Faithfully Translated into English Metre*, and was printed in Cambridge, Massachusetts, in 1640. The title page quotes Colossians 3:16.[21] But what about the Biblical exegetical case that the three terms, psalms, hymns, and songs, refer to the 150 Psalms?

First, consider the use of the Septuagint. By the beginning of the Christian era, "if the message of the Christian faith could be sent forth in the Greek tongue, which had become the truly international language of the day, the Word could penetrate almost anywhere in the Graeco-Roman world."[22] It is therefore not surprising to see the rise of a Greek version of the Old Testament, the Septuagint (LXX). "The importance of this book, which was the Bible of the apostolic Church, is beyond all exaggeration."[23] The Third Edition (Corrected) of the United Bible Societies *Greek New Testament* indicates seventy-four out of 343 quotations from the Old Testament in the New Testament (over twenty-one percent) are based on the Septuagint.[24] Everett Harrison writes, "As time has passed and investigation has proceeded, the consensus of judgment is that the influence of the Septuagint upon the New Testament is so important as to be crucial in the field of interpretation."[25]

---

20. Thomas Sternehold and John Hopkins, *The Booke of Psalmes Collected into English Meeter*, bound with *The 1599 Geneva Bible, Facsimile Edition* (Ozark, MO: L. L. Brown, 1995).
21. Richard G. Appel, *The Music of the Bay Psalm Book* (New York: Institute for Studies in American Music, 1975), 1.
22. Everett F. Harrison, *Introduction to the New Testament* (Grand Rapids: Eerdmans, 1964), 50.
23. C. K. Barrett, *The New Testament Background: Selected Documents* (London: SPCK, 1961), 208.
24. *The Greek New Testament* (Stuttgart: United Bible Societies, 1983), 899-900. Estimates as to the number of Old Testament quotations in the New Testament vary widely, depending on how quotations are defined and how quotations are distinguished from allusions. Gleason L. Archer and Gregory Chirigchino list 268 out of 410 "quotations [which] consist of reasonably or completely accurate renderings from the Hebrew of the Masoretic Text (MT) into the Greek of the Septuagint (LXX), and from there (apart from word order, which sometimes deviates slightly) into the New Testament passage in which the Old Testament text is cited," *Old Testament Quotations in the New Testament* (Chicago: Moody Press, 1983), xi, n. 1, and xxv.
25. Everett F. Harrison, "The Influence of the Septuagint on the New Testament Vocabulary," *Bibliotheca Sacra* 113 (Jan. 1956): 38.

Septuagint Psalm titles appear to influence Paul's thinking. Remember, these titles or superscriptions are the first verse of each of the psalms in the Hebrew text and in the Septuagint. The superscriptions are part of the now recognized divine text and, as Michael LeFebvre indicates, "evidence seems to increasingly support their ancient provenance … "[26] LeFebvre goes on to show, "Both Biblical and extra-biblical evidences have pointed to the importance of the superscriptions."[27]

Harrison also says, "It is unquestionably true that the use of terms in the New Testament not only reflects Septuagint usage but goes beyond it in some instances."[28] The terms *psalms*, *hymns*, and *songs* fit into this category. From the perspective of the Septuagint, the Psalms of the Old Testament were considered psalms, hymns, and songs. As a result, when Paul refers to singing psalms, hymns, and songs, he is referring to the Psalms of the Old Testament. Here are a few Psalm titles clearly equating psalms, hymns, and songs. MT refers to the Hebrew Masoretic Text, and LXX refers to the Septuagint.

> Psalm 4:1 in the MT is designated as "a psalm belonging to David." The LXX title says, "among the Psalms [*en psalmois*] a song [*ōde*]."

> Psalm 6:1 in the MT is designated as "a psalm belonging to David." The LXX title adds, "among the hymns [*en humnois*]."

> Psalm 61:1 in the MT is designated as "belonging to David." The LXX title adds, "among the hymns [*en humnois*].

> Psalm 65:1 is designated both "a psalm [*psalmos*] of David" and "a song [*ōde*]" in both the MT and the LXX (numbered 64:1).

---

26. Michael LeFebvre, "The Shape of the Psalter" (Paper, International Christian College, 2000), 4.
27. Ibid.
28. Harrison, "Influence of the Septuagint," 39.

Psalm 66:1 is designated both "a song" and "a psalm" in the MT and "a song of a psalm [*ōde psalmou*]" in the LXX (numbered 65:1).

Psalm 67:1 in the MT is designated "a psalm, a song." In the LXX (numbered 66:1), the same psalm is designated as "among the hymns a psalm of a song [*en humnois psalmos ōdes*]."

Psalm 68:1 is designated "a psalm of David, a song" in the MT and "a psalm of a song [*psalmos ōdes*] in the LXX (numbered 67:1).

Psalm 75:1 is designated both "a psalm of Asaph," and "a song" in the MT, and "a psalm of Asaph of a song [*psalmos tōi Asaph ōdes*]" in the LXX (numbered 74:1).

Psalm 76:1 is designated both a "a psalm of Asaph," and "a song" in the MT. The LXX (numbered 75:1) title reads, "among the hymns, a psalm of Asaph, a song [*en humnois psalmos tōi Asaph ōde*]."

Psalm 72:20 marks the end of Book 2 of the Psalter and reads, "The prayers of David the son of Jesse are ended." Psalm 72 may have been penned "for Solomon", when David, just before his death, transferred the kingdom and power to him.[29] Since the Psalter contains several other Psalms of David, Psalm 72:20 appears to reflect the end of David's reign and the beginning of Solomon's. Significantly, the LXX says, "The hymns [*hoi humnoi*] of David the son of Jesse are ended." In other words, the LXX considers the Psalms of David to be hymns.

Properly interpreting Paul requires getting into his head and into his thinking. When Paul refers to psalms, hymns, and songs, what does he mean? Paul used Greek with facility; all his letters are in Greek. Paul was familiar with the Septuagint; for example, he quotes the Septuagint twenty-two times in Romans. The bulk of these quotes

---

29. Mark D. Futato, *Transformed by Praise* (Phillipsburg: P & R, 2002), 116-118.

are from the Psalms and Isaiah. Six of the thirteen quotations from the Psalms come from the Septuagint.[30] As Harrison indicates, the use of terms in the New Testament reflects Septuagint usage. As a result, when Paul thinks of psalms, hymns, and songs, he is thinking of the Psalms of the Old Testament. Therefore, the terms *psalms*, *hymns*, and *songs* used by Paul refer to the 150 Psalms of the Old Testament.

The terms songs *and* hymns *refer to Psalms in other contexts.* First Chronicles 1-9 is a genealogical survey, with historical notes. Chapter 6, verses 31-32 present David's appointments for the service of *song*. "Now these are those whom David appointed over the *service of song* in the house of the Lord, after the ark rested there. They ministered with *song* before the tabernacle of the tent of meeting, until Solomon had built the house of the Lord in Jerusalem" (italics added). It has already been established that David instituted Psalmody in the stated worship of God according to the command of God. In these texts, the term *song* refers to psalms. The same is true in 1 Chronicles 16:42 regarding David's institution of Psalmody. Look at the specific language there. "With them were Heman and Jeduthun with trumpets and cymbals for those who should sound aloud, and with instruments for the *songs* of God" (italics added). Taken in context, the term *songs* refers to David's Psalms.

Next, turn again to Hezekiah and note 2 Chronicles 29:27, "Then Hezekiah gave the order to offer the burnt offering on the altar. When the burnt offering began, *the song to the* Lord also began with the trumpets, accompanied by the instruments of David, king of Israel" (italics added). As seen above, Hezekiah revived the true worship of God, including the singing of Psalms, "praises to the Lord with the words of David and Asaph the seer" (2 Chron. 29:30). Here again, the term *song* refers to Psalms.

Remember Nehemiah 12:46. "In the days of David and Asaph, in ancient times, there were leaders of the singers, *songs* of praise and

---

30. *The Greek New Testament*, 899.

hymns of thanksgiving to God" (italics added). The mention of David and Asaph may hearken back to Hezekiah's decree and the preparation of an edition of the Psalms for singing in the temple.[31] This reference to David and Asaph also indicates that the terms *songs* and *hymns* refer to the Psalms of David and Asaph: not only the Psalm titles give definition to the terms *song* and *hymn*.

Recall the singing of our Lord, the disciples, and Paul and Silas. "After singing a *hymn*, they went out to the Mount of Olives" (Matt. 26:30, Mark 14:26). As seen above, the term *hymn* refers to Psalms. "About midnight Paul and Silas were praying and singing hymns of praise to God" (Act 16:25). As also previously seen, the term hymn in this text refers to Psalms. Not only the Psalm titles but also other Old Testament data indicate that the terms *psalms*, *hymns*, and *songs* refer to the Psalms of the Old Testament. Given all of this data, it is evident that the terms *psalms*, *hymns*, and *songs* used by Paul refer to the 150 Psalms of the Old Testament.

Grammar confirms this line of thinking. Ephesians 5:19 speaks of "psalms *and* hymns *and* songs" (italics added). This expression uses *three words*, in this case nouns, connected with *and*. This grammatical construction is known as a *hendiatris*, one through three. *Hendiatris* uses three similar terms connected with *and* to express one thing.[32] In this case, the three terms do not refer to three different categories of song; rather, they refer to one category of song, the Psalms. Interpreting the *hendiatris*, the three terms, *psalms* and *hymns* and *songs*, used by Paul in Ephesians 5:19 refer to one thing, the 150 Psalms of the Old Testament.

In Greek, *kai* is the word translated *and*. Edward Robson calls this figure the *two-kai configuration*. Professor Robson explains,

> Concerning Eph. 5:19 there is a very simple point to make. If any one of the three terms in Eph. 5:19 is Scripture, all of the terms are the equal of Scripture. This is

---

31. Kleinig, *The Lord's Song*, 68.
32. James D. Hernando, *Dictionary of Hermeneutics* (Springfield: Gospel Publishing, 2005), 117.

what an interpretation of the 2-kai-cnf [configuration] means. Psalms are the O.T. Psalms. Hymns and Songs are made the equal of the Psalms by virtue of being joined with the Psalms in the 2-kai-cnf.[33]

Paul uses a different figure in Colossians 3:16 and packs the three terms more closely together. He strings together the terms *psalms, hymns, songs* without using *and*. He uses the figure of speech *asyndeton*, without conjunctions. It "ordinarily join[s] coordinate words or clauses ... The terseness of expression usually adds effect to the words."[34] In this case, when *psalms, hymns,* and *songs* are joined as one, Paul uses a *conjunctive asyndeton*.[35] Therefore, Bullinger says these three terms are synonyms.[36] These grammatical considerations confirm that the terms *psalms, hymns,* and *songs* used by Paul in Ephesians 5:19 and Colossians 3:16 refer to the 150 Psalms of the Old Testament.

Literally, Ephesians 5:19 reads, "psalms and hymns and psalms spiritual"; Colossians 3:16 reads, "psalms hymns songs spiritual." What about the modifier, *spiritual*? The adjective "'spiritual' means produced by or belonging to the Holy Spirit."[37] B. B. Warfield concurs,

> [O]f the twenty-five instances in which the word occurs in the New Testament, in no single case does it sink even as low in its reference as the human spirit; and in twenty-four of them is derived from [*pneuma*], the *Holy Ghost*. In this sense of belonging to, or determined by, the Holy Spirit, the New Testament usage is uniform ... [38]

Since the two-kai-configuration ties together the three terms, *psalms* and *hymns* and *songs*, the modifier appears at the end of the figure

---

33. Edward A. Robson, "Interpretation of the Two-Kai Configurations of the Greek New Testament," *Semper Reformanda* 7:2 (Summer 1998): 9.
34. Hernando, *Dictionary of Hermeneutics*, 111.
35. E. W. Bullinger, *Figures of Speech Used in the Bible* (Grand Rapids: Baker, 2004), 138.
36. Ibid., 333.
37. John Eadie, *Commentary on the Epistle to the Ephesians* (Minneapolis: James and Klock, 1977), 14.
38. B. B. Warfield, "Pneumatikos and Its Opposites in the Greek New Testament," *The Presbyterian Review* 1:3 (1880): 561.

and applies to all the terms.[39] For example, Paul calls Epaphroditus, "my brother and fellow worker and fellow soldier" (Phil. 2:25). The text literally reads, "brother and fellow-worker and fellow-soldier of me [my]." The modifier *my* appears at the end of the hendiatris and applies to all three terms. As just observed, hymns and songs are made equal to psalms and equal to Scripture because they are joined with the psalms in the two-kai-configuration. That is, these psalms and hymns and songs of the Old Testament, all three, are spiritual because they come from the Holy Spirit; they are inspired by the Spirit. Therefore, the terms *psalms, hymns,* and *songs* used by Paul refer to the 150 Psalms of the Old Testament.

EXCLUSIVE PSALMODY

The first step is to properly understand Colossians 3:16. The text reads as follows in the English Standard Version, "Let the word of Christ dwell in you richly, *teaching and admonishing* one another in all wisdom, *singing* psalms and hymns and spiritual songs, with thankfulness in your hearts to God" (italics added). Paul's basic command is simple, "Let the word of Christ dwell in you richly." Adverbial participles follow. They indicate *how* believers obey the basic command. The participles are *teaching and admonishing* on one hand and *singing* on the other hand. There is a further parallel in the text. Teaching and admonishing should be accomplished in or *with all wisdom* and singing should be done *with thankfulness or grace in our hearts*.

The English versions translate the text in two different ways. Here is the New American Standard Update: "Let the word of Christ richly dwell within you, with all wisdom teaching and admonishing one another *with psalms and hymns and spiritual songs*, singing with thankfulness in your hearts to God" (italics added). This version links psalms and hymns and spiritual songs with teaching and admonishing. Compare the English Standard Version: "Let the word of Christ

---

39. Robson, "Interpretation of the Two-Kai Configurations," 9.

dwell in you richly, teaching and admonishing one another in all wisdom, singing *psalms and hymns and spiritual songs*, with thankfulness in your hearts to God" (italics added). This version links psalms and hymns and spiritual songs with singing. Why the difference?

As just mentioned, the main clause in the text is an imperative, "Let the word of Christ dwell [*enoikeitō*] in you richly." Two participle phrases indicate how the command is to be followed. They are present active participles, indicating contemporaneous action with the main verb, dwell. Literally the text reads: The word of Christ let dwell in you richly (1) with all wisdom teaching [*didaskontes*] and admonishing [*nouthentountes*] one another; (2) with grace singing [*adontes*] with your hearts to God. The words *psalms, hymns, songs spiritual* [*psalmois humnois ōdais pnoimatikais*] are between the two participial phrases. As a result, some versions place these words with teaching and admonishing, as do the Authorized Version and the New American Standard Version. John Eadie voices his objection: "[W]hile metrical or musical compositions are not the common vehicle of instruction or admonition, they are specially connected with sacred song."[40] For this same reason, other versions, such as the New International Version and the English Standard Version, consider it more logical to place *psalms, hymns,* and *songs* with singing. Eadie suggests a similar division of the text.

> Let the Christian truth have its enduring abode "within you" —let it be no stranger or occasional guest in your hearts. Let it not be without you, as a lesson to be learned, but within you, as the source of cherished and permanent illumination ... Different ideas have been formed of the best mode of dividing the following clauses of the verse ... [T]he idea of wisdom is better joined to the following clause, which refers to mutual teaching—"in all wisdom teaching and admonishing one another" ... Our

---

40. John Eadie, *Commentary on the Epistle of Paul to the Colossians* (Grand Rapids: Zondervan, 1957), 252.

translators, too, so point the verse as to make psalms and hymns the material of instruction, whereas, it seems better, and more appropriate, to keep the clause distinct, thus—"Let the word of Christ dwell in you richly; in all wisdom teaching and admonishing one another: in psalms, hymns, and spiritual songs, singing with grace in your hearts unto the Lord."[41]

There is one other consideration in looking at the exegesis of Colossians 3:16. Psalms, hymns, songs spiritual is in the dative case, *psalmois humnois ōdais pnoimatikois*. Lightfoot argues that the datives describe the instruments of the teaching and admonishing.[42] Eadie counters, "The datives, without the preposition denote the materials of song."[43] Eadie's approach and the translation of the English Standard Version are thus preferable.

If this exegesis holds, Paul circumscribes singing more closely than teaching. How so? First, according to Paul, teaching and admonishing with all wisdom is preaching. Paul uses similar language in Colossians 1:28: "We proclaim Him, *admonishing every man and teaching every man with all wisdom*" (italics added). From Paul's perspective wisdom comes from the Scriptures. He reminds Timothy, "From childhood you have known the sacred writings *which are able to give you the wisdom* that leads to salvation through faith which is in Christ Jesus" (2 Tim. 3:15, italics added). When Colossians 3:16 exhorts, "Let the word of Christ dwell in you richly, teaching and admonishing one another in all wisdom," the text exhorts *teaching and admonishing* rooted in Scripture. In other words, preaching must be *Scriptural*.

Second, Paul is more specific when it comes to singing. He not only requires the singing of public worship to be Scriptural, he specifies the Scriptures to be used in this singing; he specifies the psalms, hymns, and songs inspired by the Spirit found in the Book of Psalms.

---

41. Ibid., 251.
42. J. B. Lightfoot, *Saint Paul's Epistles to the Colossians and to Philemon* (Grand Rapids: Zondervan, 1965), 224.
43. Eadie, *Colossians*, 252.

Again, the English Standard Version exhorts, "Let the word of Christ dwell in you richly ... singing *psalms and hymns and spiritual songs*, with thankfulness in your hearts to God" (italics added). What are believers assembled for worship to sing? They are to sing psalms, hymns, and spiritual songs; these are the songs of the 150 Psalms of the Old Testament. In other words, *Paul requires exclusive Psalmody.* He gives these directions to the New Testament church by the power of and under the inspiration of the Holy Spirit. Part Four of this study will investigate the unique power of music. Paul may be mindful of the power of music when he gives the command to exclusively sing the Psalms. However, it is more significant for our present purposes to observe the special character of the Psalms.

The Psalms are God-given inspired songs. We dare not forget that the Psalms are both God-given and inspired. The coordinate truth is that God is most holy, excellent, and good. Jesus Christ goes so far as to say, "No one is good except God alone" (Mark 10:18; Luke 18:19). To be truly good is to be Godlike. At the same time, even believers fall infinitely short of this perfection. They live in a crooked and perverse generation (Acts 2:40; Phil. 2:15). Malcolm Watts therefore says,

> Once this is understood, the question naturally arises: how can men, even with the aid of revelation, set forth in praise the wonders of a Being so illustriously great? He is surely "exalted *above* all blessing and praise" (Neh 9:5, emphasis added), and it must surely follow that our most sublime songs fall unspeakably below His transcendent majesty. The problem, of course, is further aggravated by the fact that men are fallen and therefore subject to sin and error. If the divine glory rises far above the flights of human praise, certain it is that men corrupted in all their faculties of soul, with defective understanding of spiritual things, are altogether incapable of producing material for praise. The general principle lies

in the question, "Who can bring a clean thing out of an unclean?" (Job 14:4; cf. 11:12; Eph. 4:18).[44]

God solves the dilemma. He gives His people a book of praise that He inspires. He gives His people the sacrifice of praise His people may offer to Him. They have the privilege of singing back to Him the praise He condescends to give to them. This position is not new, unusual, or remarkable. Calvin goes back to Augustine to make this point.

> Now what Saint Augustine says is true, that no one is able to sing things worthy of God unless he has received them from Him. Wherefore, when we have looked thoroughly everywhere and searched high and low, we shall find no better songs nor more appropriate to the purpose than the Psalms of David which the Holy Spirit made and spoke through Him.[45]

A criticism may be that those holding to exclusive Psalmody do not sing God's words back to Him; they sing paraphrases of the psalms with rhyme and meter. The response is quite simple. When properly accomplished, a metrical psalter set to music is a version of the Psalms much like the versions of the Bible we commonly use. A version is a translation carried out by committees seeking to be faithful to the original language. Creating a metrical psalter is a similar technical process. It involves the work of translating Hebrew poetic parallelisms into western verse and then setting the verse to music. This process is called prosody, "the science or art of versification, including the study of metrical structure, rhyme, stanza forms, etc."[46] First, the Psalms are translated from Hebrew to English. Then versification (prosody) takes place to produce a metrical version of the Psalms. Finally, the metrical version of each Psalm is matched with a specific tune. The process is designed to produce a metrical version of the

---

44. Malcolm H. Watts, "The Case for Psalmody," *Sing a New Song*, ed. Joel R. Beeke and Anthony T. Selvaggio (Grand Rapids: Reformation Heritage, 2010), 127-128.
45. John Calvin, "'Preface' to the Geneva Psalter (1545)," Charles Garside, *The Origins of Calvin's Theology of Music*, 1536-1543 (Philadelphia: American Philosophical Society, 1979), 33.
46. *Webster's New World Dictionary of the American Language* (Cleveland: World Publishing, 1958), 1169.

Psalms holding as closely to the original text as possible, while rendering the text in a form suitable for placement with music.

The Westminster Standards teach exclusive Psalmody. Westminster Confession of Faith 21.5 lists the ordinary elements of worship.

> The reading of Scriptures with godly fear; the sound preaching, and conscionable hearing of the Word, in obedience unto God, with understanding, faith, and reverence; *singing of psalms with grace in the heart*; as also, the due administration and worthy receiving of the sacraments instituted by Christ; are all parts of the ordinary religious worship of God: besides religious oaths, vows, solemn fastings, and thanksgivings upon special occasions, which are, in their several times and seasons, to be used in an holy and religious manner (italics added).

The proof texts given for the singing of Psalms are Colossians 3:16; Ephesians 5:19; and James 5:13. G. I. Williamson expounds this section of the Confession as follows:

> It will be observed that the Confession does not acknowledge the legitimacy of the use of modern hymns in the worship of God, but rather only the psalms of the Old Testament. It is not generally realized today that Presbyterian and Reformed Churches originally used only the inspired psalms, hymns, and songs of the Biblical Psalter in divine worship, but such is the case. The Westminster Assembly not only expressed the conviction that only the psalms should be sung in divine worship, but implemented it by preparing a metrical version of the Psalter for use in the Churches ... [I]t has never been proved that God has commanded his Church to sing the uninspired compositions of men rather than or along with the inspired songs, hymn, and psalms of the Psalter in divine worship.[47]

---

[47] G. I. Williamson, *The Westminster Confession of Faith for Study Classes* (Philadelphia: Presbyterian and Reformed, 1964), 167.

THE GENIUS OF PSALMODY:
THE SUBJECTIVE ELEMENT

To grasp the genius of Psalmody, we must reorient our approach to the Psalms. Michael LeFebvre points out that we rightly read sixty-five books of the Bible as *God's word to us.* "But the Psalmbook is different: it alone is composed as a collection of *songs from men to God.* They are no less God's inspired word ... but of all the Bible's books, in the Psalms we receive an exceptional gift designed to become *our words to God*" (italics added).[48] LeFebvre adds,

> The Book of Psalms is unique. It is a hymnal. It is the only book of the Bible with God as the audience and God's people as its appointed speakers. This is an important feature of the Psalms with significance for how we should use them in the church today.
>
> The Psalms are words for God's people to sing to Him. This does not mean the Psalms are any less God's word to us than other books of the Bible ... Like the rest of Scripture, the Psalms are fully God's word to us. But unlike the rest of Scripture, the Psalms are further designed to become our words to sing back to God.[49]

The Psalms have a distinctive, subjective element. This *special significance* of the Psalms accompanies God's word given to us to sing back to Him in worship. Geerhardus Vos alerts us to this important aspect of the Psalter. As God's words we sing back to Him, the Psalms, says Vos, are distinguished by a "penetrating subjectiveness."[50] He clarifies what he means by this subjective element.

> The deeper fundamental character of the Psalter consists in this that it voices the subjective response to the objective doings of God for and among his people. *Subjec-*

---

48. Michael LeFebvre, *Sing the Songs of Jesus* (Fearn: Christian Focus, 2010), 15.
49. Ibid., 16-17.
50. Geerhardus Vos, "Eschatology of the Psalter," *The Pauline Eschatology* (Grand Rapids: Baker, 1979), 356-357.

> *tive responsiveness is the specific quality of these songs.* As prophecy is objective, being the address of Jehovah to Israel in word and act, so the Psalter is subjective, being the answer of Israel to divine speech (italics added).[51]

As both God's inspired Word and the believer's subjective response to God and His deeds, the Psalms are the divine guide to the subjective responses His people have to Him and His deeds. As God's people take the words of the Psalms on their lips, God guides them in responding to Him both objectively, in the words they sing, and subjectively, in the feelings and emotions they express. Calvin puts it just this way when he too speaks of this subjective element in the Preface to his *Commentary on the Book of Psalms*. Notice the stress Calvin places on this subjective aspect of the Psalms in giving expression to heartfelt emotions.

> The varied and resplendid riches which are contained in this treasury it is no easy matter to express in words; so much so, that I well know that whatever I shall be able to say will be far from approaching the excellence of the subject. But as it is better to give to my readers some taste, however small, of the wonderful advantages they will derive from the study of this book, than to be entirely silent on the point, I may be permitted briefly to advert to a matter, the greatness of which does not admit of being fully unfolded. *I have been accustomed to call this book, I think not inappropriately, "An Anatomy of all the Parts of the Soul"; for there is not an emotion of which any one can be conscious that is not here represented as in a mirror. Or rather, the Holy Spirit has here drawn to the life all the griefs, sorrows, fears, doubts, hopes, cares, perplexities, in short, all the distracting emotions with which the minds of men are wont to be agitated.* The other parts of Scripture contain the commandments which God enjoined his servants to

---

51. Ibid., 324.

announce to us. But here the prophets themselves, seeing they are exhibited to us as speaking to God, and laying open all their inmost thoughts and affections, call, or rather draw, each of us to the examination of himself in particulars in order that none of the many infirmities to which we are subject, and of the many vices with which we abound, may remain concealed. It is certainly a rare and singular advantage, when all lurking places are discovered, and the heart is brought into the light, purged from that most baneful infection, hypocrisy. *In short, as calling upon God is one of the principal means of securing our safety, and as a better and more unerring rule for guiding us in this exercise cannot be found elsewhere than in The Psalms, it follows, that in proportion to the proficiency which a man shall have attained in understanding them, will be his knowledge of the most important part of celestial doctrine* (italics added).[52]

As believers sing the Psalms, the Holy Spirit probes the anatomy of their souls. He lays bare their raw emotions. He counters their deep-seated, tightly-held hypocrisies. Then, when they cry out to God and vent their own emotions, the Spirit provides them an "unerring rule for guiding [them] in this exercise [which] cannot be found elsewhere than in The Psalms ... "[53]

The subjective element of the Psalter becomes the believers own as they sing the Psalms. As God's word, and as a means of grace, the Psalms are the divine guide for the proper expression of one's emotions. Through the Psalms, God bridles and trains God's people in the inner person. As they mimic the Spirit in His divinely-given guidance, He forms Christ in them.

Ultimately, this subjective element may be the reason the Apostle Paul circumscribes singing more closely than teaching. He knows the subjective element of the Psalter from his own study, experience, and

---

52. John Calvin, "The Author's Preface," *Commentary on the Book of Psalms* (Grand Rapids: Baker, 1979), 1:xxxvii.
53. Ibid.

singing. His experience is deeply rooted in the Old Testament and reverberates with the emotions, heart, and soul of David. Holding this thought, listen to Colossians 3:16 and note Paul's own emphasis on the subjective element. "Let the word of Christ dwell *in you richly*, teaching and admonishing one another in all wisdom, singing psalms and hymns and spiritual songs, with thankfulness *in your hearts* to God" (ESV, italics added).

Calvin's emphasis on the subjective element in the Psalter goes back at least to Athanasius of Alexandria (296-373). Here are excerpts from his "Letter to Marcellinus Concerning the Psalms."

> [A]mong all the books, the Psalter has certainly a very special grace, a choiceness of quality well worthy to be pondered; for, besides the characteristics which it shares with others, it has this peculiar marvel of its own, that within it are represented and portrayed in all their great variety the movements of the human soul. It is like a picture, in which you see yourself portrayed, and seeing, may understand and consequently form yourself upon the pattern given. Elsewhere in the Bible you read only that the Law commands this or that to be done, you listen to the Prophets to learn about the Savior's coming, or you turn to the historical books to learn the doings of the kings and holy men; but in the Psalter, besides all these things, you learn about yourself. You find depicted in it all the movements of your soul, all its changes, its ups and downs, its failures and recoveries. Moreover, whatever your particular need or trouble, from this same book you can select a form of words to fit it, so that you do not merely hear and then pass on, but learn the way to remedy your ill. Prohibitions of evil-doing are plentiful in Scripture, but only the Psalter tells you how to obey these orders and abstain from sin. Repentance, for example, is enjoined repeatedly; but to repent means to

leave off sinning, and it is the Psalms that show you how to set about repenting and with what words your penitence may be expressed. Again, Saint Paul says, Tribulation worketh endurance, and endurance experience, and experience hope, and hope maketh not ashamed; but it is in the Psalms that we find written and described how afflictions should be borne, and what the afflicted ought to say, both at the time and when his troubles cease: the whole process of his testing is set forth in them and we are shown exactly with what words to voice our hope in God. Or take the commandment, In everything give thanks. The Psalms not only exhort us to be thankful, they also provide us with fitting words to say. We are told, too, by other writers that all who would live godly in Christ must suffer persecution; and here again the Psalms supply words with which both those who flee persecution and those who suffer under it may suitably address themselves to God, and it does the same for those who have been rescued from it. We are bidden elsewhere in the Bible also to bless the Lord and to acknowledge Him: here in the Psalms we are shown the way to do it, and with what sort of words His majesty may meetly be confessed. In fact, under all the circumstances of life, we shall find that these divine songs suit ourselves and meet our own souls' need at every turn.[54]

Imagine songs for worship that give believers divinely-inspired words to express all their longings, griefs, sorrows, and praise. Imagine a book designed and edited by God for this purpose. The Psalter is such a book. It is a marvel. Athanasius continues,

[B]ut the marvel with the Psalter is that, barring those prophecies about the Savior and some about the Gen-

---

54. Athanasius, "Letter to Marcellinus Concerning the Psalms," Fisheaters.com, accessed November 15, 2011.

tiles, the reader takes all its words upon his lips as though they were his own, and each one sings the Psalms as though they had been written for his special benefit, and takes them and recites them, not as though someone else were speaking or another person's feelings being described, but as himself speaking of himself, offering the words to God as his own heart's utterance, just as though he himself had made them up. Not as the words of the patriarchs or of Moses and the other prophets will he reverence these: no, he is bold to take them as his own and written for his very self. Whether he has kept the Law or whether he has broken it, it is his own doings that the Psalms describe; every one is bound to find his very self in them and, be he faithful soul or be he sinner, each reads in them descriptions of himself.

It seems to me, moreover, that because the Psalms thus serve him who sings them as a mirror, wherein he sees himself and his own soul, he cannot help but render them in such a manner that their words go home with equal force to those who hear him sing, and stir them also to a like reaction … And every other Psalm is spoken and composed by the Spirit in the selfsame way: just as in a mirror, the movements of our own souls are reflected in them and the words are indeed our very own, given us to serve both as a reminder of our changes of condition and as a pattern and model for the amendment of our lives …

It is possible for us, therefore, to find in the Psalter not only the reflection of our own soul's state, together with precept and example for all possible conditions, but also a fit form of words wherewith to please the Lord on each of life's occasions, words both of repentance and of thankfulness … [55]

---

55. Ibid.

The subjective element and Psalmody are abandoned to the church's peril. As just observed, the subjective element is seen in Paul (early 60s A.D.) as he advocates Psalmody. Athanasius (c. 350 A.D.) carried the subjective element forward in his teaching about Psalmody. Calvin (1543) likely derived his understanding of the subjective element from Athanasius and he too advocated Psalmody. Finally, we see the subjective element in the writings of Geerhardus Vos (1902).

LeFebvre asks a question about the Psalms posed by Dietrich Bonhoeffer (1906-1945): "How did these words which men sang to God come to be regarded as words from God to man? That is, if the Psalms were composed for worshipers to lift their thoughts (by singing) up to God, why do we study them (by reading) as thoughts from God down to us?"[56] The answer to this question is crucial. The subjective element has been dropped. As LeFebvre observes, "We stopped *using* the Psalms as human words to God" (italics added).[57]

For Vos, the subjective element in the Psalter comes into its own in the heart's longing for the life to come. "The Psalter bears eloquent witness to the truth that a hope of infinite perpetuation for the collective body is not enough. It requires the *assurance* of the eternity of religion *in the individual soul* to secure the permanence of religion as such" (italics added).[58] How do believers come to this assurance? "The Psalmists had their faces set toward this [assurance] and through wrestlings of prayer with Jehovah won their way to the light."[59] Believers take the wrestlings of the Psalmists on their own hearts and lips. The psalmist's groaning, seeking, joy, and praise become the believer's groaning, seeking, joy, and praise. Their words from God become the believer's words to God. Vos contrasts God-born, eschatological assurance with modern humanism and skepticism. Believers dare not abandon God-born, Psalmody-instilled eschatological assurance and compromise with humanism or skepticism. "The Church

---

56. LeFevre, *Singing the Songs of Jesus*, 15.
57. Ibid., 27.
58. Vos, "Eschatology of the Psalter," 364-365.
59. Ibid., 365.

by compromising and affiliating with this [humanism or skepticism] would sign her own death-warrant as a distinct institution."[60] To extend the argument, believers stop using the Psalms as their own words to God and they abandon the subjective element in Psalmody to their own peril.

The thread running through objections to Psalmody is the supposed insufficiency of the Psalter for New Testament praise. These objections generally view the Psalms, like the rest of Scripture, as presenting God's word to men. If there is any relevance to the Psalter as the believer's words and the believer's subjective response to God's acts and deeds, as presented above, it is either unknown or studiously avoided. Avoidance of the subjective element, of course, colors expectations when coming to the Psalter or engaging in Psalmody. As will be shown in the next chapter, the problem is not with the Psalms; the problem is with expectations when coming to the Psalms.

---

60. Ibid.

12

PSALMODY AND PSALTER EXPECTATIONS

How long, O LORD? Will You forget me forever?
How long will You hide
Your face from me? ~ Ps. 13:1

PRELIMINARY THOUGHTS

THIS AGE OF INDIVIDUALISM might be waning, but its broad impact is wide and deep. An individualistic approach to Scripture is still pervasive among God's people. Seeking proof-texts is an outgrowth of living in this present age. Dr. Jay E. Adams has referred facetiously to the modern disease of *plaquosis*, putting texts on plaques for wall hangings. He then jests about needing to manufacture contextual wallpaper. Those approaching Psalmody, and exclusive Psalmody in particular, often seek proof texts. However, understanding worship, exclusive Psalmody, and a cappella singing in worship requires careful, Biblical-theological study. The need for such study is frustrating for those who seek simple answers; they want chapter and verse, not chapters and verses. Yet, to answer objections requires some basic Biblical-theological background.

The previous chapter closes with an emphasis on what can be called the *subjective element* in the Psalter. Grasping this subjective element is a key to understanding Psalmody. For this reason, the subject is briefly revisited in this chapter. Another key to appreciating Psalmody is Psalter eschatology. After discussing these two matters, it will be seen that they mesh and deeply affect Psalmody expectations.

REVISITING THE SUBJECTIVE ELEMENT

Grasping the subjective element of the Psalter is a key to understanding Psalmody. What is this subjective element? As already stated, "The deeper fundamental character of the Psalter consists in this that it voices the subjective response to the objective doings of God for and among his people. Subjective responsiveness is the specific quality of these songs."[1] That the Psalms present a divine guide for subjective responsiveness to God is their subjective element.

Geerhardus Vos begins a sermon entitled "Songs from the Soul" with these remarks:

> The Psalter is of all books of the Bible that book which gives expression to the experimental side of religion ... Hence the Psalter has been at all times that part of Scripture to which believers have most readily turned and upon which they have chiefly depended for the nourishment of the inner religious life of the heart ... Our Lord himself, who had a perfect religious experience ... found his inner life portrayed in the Psalter and in some of the highest moments of his ministry borrowed from it the language in which his soul spoke to God, thus recognizing that a more perfect language for communion with God cannot be framed.[2]

Vos' remarks are stunning: A language more perfect than the Psalms for communion with God cannot be framed? How can such perfect language exist? The language of the Psalms is inspired language. The Holy Spirit gives this language to His people for the expression of their hearts and souls. "Here the language of the Bible comes to meet the very thoughts of our hearts before these can even

---

1. Geerhardus Vos, "Eschatology of the Psalter," *The Pauline Eschatology* (Grand Rapids: Baker, 1979), 324.
2. Geerhardus Vos, "Songs from the Soul," *Grace and Glory* (Carlisle: Banner of Truth, 1994), 169-170.

clothe themselves in language and we recognize that we could not have expressed them better than the Spirit has here expressed them for us."[3] The language of the Psalms is therefore useful and suitable and functional for all peoples in all times. Vos continues,

> At first sight, this may easily seem strange to us when we remember that the Psalmists lived under the conditions of a typical and preparatory dispensation; that on many points they saw through a glass darkly, whereas we, who live in the full light of the complete gospel, see face to face. But for the very reason that the Psalms reflect the experimental religion of the heart, which is unvarying at all times and under all circumstances, we need not greatly wonder at this.[4]

Fallen human nature is always the same. The operations of sin within the heart are ever the same. The work of the Spirit within the human heart is ever the same. Since the Psalms are songs especially fit for the expression of the soul and were given by the Spirit for this purpose, they are useful and suitable and functional for all peoples in all ages. Grasping this subjective element is a key to understanding Psalmody.

THE PSALTER'S INDIVIDUAL ESCHATOLOGY

Grasping the personal eschatology of the Psalter is a key to understanding Psalmody. Eschatology is viewed from two perspectives, individual eschatology and cosmic or general eschatology.[5] Both views are in the Psalter. Consider individual eschatology. David declares, "Even though I walk through the valley of the shadow of death, / I fear no evil, for You are with me" (Ps. 23:4). Why this faith? There is the hope of eternal life within him. "The dead do not praise the Lord, / Nor do any who go down into silence; / But as for us, we will bless the Lord

---

3. Ibid., 171.
4. Ibid.
5. Anthony A. Hoekema, *The Bible and the Future* (Grand Rapids: Eerdmans, 1979), 77; Cornelius P. Venema, *The Promise of the Future* (Carlisle: Banner of Truth, 2000), 35.

/ From this time forth and forever" (Ps. 115:17-18). "My flesh and my heart may fail, / But God is the strength of my heart and my portion forever" (Ps. 73:26). Psalm 116:15 therefore exclaims, "Precious in the sight of the Lord / Is the death of His godly ones." What occurs at death? "As for me, I shall behold Your face in righteousness; / I will be satisfied with Your likeness when I awake" (Ps. 17:15).

Speaking of such statements in the Psalms, Vos offers a reminder, "The eschatological state is before all else a state in which the enjoyment of Jehovah, the beatific vision of his face, the pleasures at his right hand, the perpetual dwelling with him in his sanctuary, form the supreme good."[6] The Apostle Paul says the same thing. "We are of good courage, I say, and prefer rather to be absent from the body and to be at home with the Lord" (2 Cor. 5:8). He speaks of "having the desire to depart and be with Christ, for that is very much better" (Phil. 1:23). Augustine also sees this progression to glory.

> For it seems to me not without significance, that the fiftieth [in Latin and fifty-first in Hebrew] is of penitence, the hundredth of mercy and judgment [in Latin and one hundred first in Hebrew], the hundred and fiftieth of the praise of God in His saints. For thus do we advance to an everlasting life of happiness, first by condemning our own sins, then by living aright, that, having condemned our ill life, and lived a good life, we may attain to everlasting life.[7]

THE PSALTER'S COSMIC ESCHATOLOGY

The Psalter also presents a cosmic eschatology. "In the LXX Psalter, this tendency is most readily discernible in its interpretation of headings."[8] For instance, Psalm 4:1 reads, "For the choir director; on stringed instruments. A Psalm of David." The Hebrew term trans-

---

6. Vos, "Eschatology of the Psalter," 349.
7. Saint Augustine, *Expositions on the Book of Psalms* (Oxford: John Henry Parker, 1857), 6:458.
8. David C. Mitchell, *The Message of the Psalter: An Eschatological Programme in the Book of Psalms* (Sheffield: Sheffield Academic Press, 1997), 19.

lated *for the choir director* is translated or interpreted *eis to telos* in the Septuagint. This phrase occurs in fifty-six Psalm titles in the Septuagint. It might be taken as meaning *"for the end or consummation [of the cosmos]"*, suggesting that the LXX "translators interpreted Psalms eschatologically."[9] Also, Psalm titles referring to lilies may have "eschatological implications. For the idea of the transformation of the earth in the spring connotes the image-complex of Passover, new creation and resurrection, for which lilies are an ancient symbol."[10] Finally, three LXX Psalm titles read, *eis to telos uper tōn lenōn* meaning *for the end concerning the winepresses*. The context within the Psalter "suggests that the LXX translators wished to evoke [the image of] the winepress of God's wrath."[11]

What about the Psalter as a whole? "The LXX Psalter, dating probably from the early second century BCE, contains the 150 psalms of the Masoretic Text (MT), in the same sequence ... "[12] Acts 1:20 refers to the Book of Psalms and "seems to regard the MT-type Psalter as definitive."[13] Psalms 1 and 2 form the introduction to the Psalter.[14] "Whereas Psalm 1 describes the two ways open to every man, Psalm 2 describes the two ways open to every nation. Together, the two Psalms introduce the Psalter ... "[15] The struggle between the two ways, individually and nationally, exists within a profoundly important context. "The message of the Psalms is simple: the Lord reigns."[16] The struggle between the two ways leads to praise. "The Psalter also has a conclusion, the great acclamation of Psalms 146-50. This is the only series of psalms in which each psalm features a double *Halleluyah*, one at the beginning and one at the end."[17] Futato claims, "Claus Westermann was the first scholar to draw attention to this

---

9. Ibid.
10. Ibid., 20.
11. Ibid.
12. Ibid., 16, n. 2.
13. Ibid., 26.
14. Mark D. Futato, *Transformed by Praise* (Phillipsburg: P & R, 2002), 53-55.
15. Bill Edgar, "Reformed Systematic Theology Textbooks: Hand Maiden to the Enlightenment Privatization of Faith" (Paper, Reformed Presbyterian Theological Seminary, June 10, 2010).
16. Futato, *Transformed by Praise*, 101.
17. Mitchell, *Message of the Psalter*, 74, see also n. 23.

movement in the macro-structure of the book of Psalms, a movement from lamentation to praise, from suffering to glory."[18] However, as just seen and as Mitchell indicates, Augustine "recognizes a progression to perfection in the whole arrangement [of the Psalms]."[19]

BOOKS 1-3 OF THE PSALTER AND THE DILEMMA

A closer look at this progression is in order. "For a number of reasons, we can divide the Psalms into two large sections, books 1-3 and books 4-5."[20] For example, books 1, 2, and 3 each end with the affirmation, "Amen and Amen" (Ps. 41:13; 72:19; and 89:52). Books 4 and 5 each end with the declaration, "Praise the Lord" (Ps. 106:48 and 150:6). The national struggle between the two ways begins with the coronation of God's messianic king:[21] "I have installed My King Upon Zion" (Ps. 2:6). God then issues this promise, "Ask of Me, and I will surely give the *nations* as Your inheritance, / And the very *ends of the earth* as Your possession" (Ps. 2:8, italics added). Certainly, Messiah asked (John 17:9, 20). The promise is, therefore, in the process of fulfillment. "Go therefore and make disciples of all the *nations*" (Matt. 28:19, italics added). "You shall be My witnesses both in Jerusalem, and in all Judea and Samaria, and even *to the remotest part of the earth*" (Acts 1:8, italics added). Psalm 2 lays out an eschatological agenda. "I am using *eschatological* in the sense of that which pertains to the destiny of the world. The outcome of continued opposition to God's rule is not in doubt."[22]

"Psalm 41 brings book 1 to a close by confirming that the plan for the messianic kingship initiated in Psalm 2 is working out perfectly."[23] Psalm 72 marks the end of book 2 and may have been penned "for Solomon" when David, just before his death, transferred the kingdom and power to him.[24] "The program laid out in Psalms 1 and 2

---

18. Mark D. Futato, *Interpreting the Psalms* (Grand Rapids: Kregel, 2007), 80.
19. Mitchell, *Message of the Psalter*, 34.
20. Futato, *Transformed by Praise*, 114.
21. Ibid., 107.
22. Futato, *Interpreting the Psalms*, 76.
23. Futato, *Transformed by Praise*, 115.
24. Ibid., 116-118.

is working. Psalm 89 brings book 3 to a close."[25] Yet, all along the line, there is conflict. A mournful lament punctuates books 1-3: "How long?" Psalms 6:3; 13:1-2; 35:17; 74:10; 79:5; and 80:4 repeat the plea. Such sorrow comes to a climax in 89:46 and 49, "How long, O Lord? / Will You hide Yourself forever? / Will Your wrath burn like fire? ... Where are Your former lovingkindnesses, O Lord, / Which You swore to David in Your faithfulness?" "The program begun with David in Book 1 and effectively transferred to Solomon in Book 2 seems, at the end of Book 3, to have been aborted."[26]

BOOKS 4-5 OF THE PSALTER, THE DILEMMA ANSWERED

The great question now becomes, How do you live in an era when the Messianic King is apparently absent? "How do you live with the tension that at times exists between what God's Word says and what you experience in life?"[27] Books 4 and 5 provide the answer. "In Books 4 and 5, faith that the Lord is king is coupled with hope that the King is coming. And not just an ordinary king is coming. These Books teach that the divine King is coming, and that the messianic King is coming."[28] Book 4 (Ps. 90-106) begins with "A prayer of Moses" to remind us, "Lord, You have been our dwelling place in all generations" (Ps. 90:1). No matter the time or the season, the Lord is the shelter and dwelling place of His people. Psalm 91:2 continues the theme, "I will say to the Lord, 'My refuge and my fortress, / My God, in whom I trust!'" Not only so, "The Lord reigns" (Ps. 93:1, 96:10, 97:1, and 99:1). He is a refuge for His people; He is the believers' King. The King may be out of our sight. Yet He is still the Lord of all and He is the object of faith and hope. And the message to Christians and to the nations is that the King is coming!

---

25. Futato, *Interpreting the Psalms*, 84.
26. Ibid., 85
27. Futato, *Transformed by Praise*, 121.
28. Futato, *Interpreting the Psalms*, 88..

Say among the nations, "The Lord reigns; / Indeed, the world is firmly established, it will not be moved; / He will judge the peoples with equity." / Let the heavens be glad, and let the earth rejoice; / Let the sea roar, and all it contains; / Let the field exult, and all that is in it. / Then all the trees of the forest will sing for joy before the Lord, for He is coming, / For He is coming to judge the earth. / He will judge the world in righteousness / And the peoples in His faithfulness (Ps. 96:10-13).

Similarly, "Let the rivers clap their hands, / Let the mountains sing together for joy / Before the Lord, for He is coming to judge the earth; / He will judge the world with righteousness / And the peoples with equity" (Ps. 98:8-9). God's eschatological program will not fail.

Book 5 (Ps. 107-150) continues this eschatological theme. At this present time, the Lord is inexorably putting all of His and our enemies under His feet. "The Lord says to my Lord: / 'Sit at My right hand / Until I make Your enemies a footstool for Your feet'" (Ps. 110:1; 1 Cor. 15:27). Book 5 reminds God's people that their Lord's eschatological program will not fail; He will subdue the nations and bring them to glory. Book 5 contains four series of Psalms: the Egyptian Hallel (113-118), Psalm 119 (a series of shorter Psalms on the virtues of love and the law), the Songs of Ascent (120-134), and the Great Hallel (146-150). Derek Kidner says the following about the first series, Psalms 113-118, and notes their eschatological thrust.

> A short run of psalms used yearly at the Passover begins here, and is therefore commonly known as the Egyptian Hallel (Hallel means Praise). Only the second of them (114) speaks directly of the Exodus, but the theme of raising the down-trodden (113) and the note of corporate praise (115), personal thanksgiving (116), world vision (117) and festal procession (118) *make it an appropriate*

> series to mark the salvation which began in Egypt and will spread to the nations.[29]

Psalm 118 is a song of national thanksgiving for redemption.[30] "Give thanks to the Lord, for He is good; For His lovingkindness [covenant love] is everlasting" (Ps. 118:1, 29). Sung at Passover, this Psalm looks back to God's great redemption. This Psalm also looks forward: "Blessed is the one who comes in the name of the Lord" (Ps. 118:26). This King has come. "He is just and endowed with salvation / Humble, and mounted on a donkey / Even on a colt, the foal of a donkey" (Zech. 9:9; Matt. 21:5). "The crowds going ahead of Him [Jesus], and those who followed, were shouting, 'Hosanna to the Son of David; BLESSED IS HE WHO COMES IN THE NAME OF THE LORD; Hosanna in the highest'" (Matt. 21:9). As Christ Himself promises, He will come again: "For I say to you, from now on you will not see Me until you say, 'BLESSED IS HE WHO COMES IN THE NAME OF THE LORD'" (Matt. 23:39). The Egyptian Hallel contributes to the eschatological program of the Psalter.

The Songs of Ascent (120-134) are also eschatological. "They were evidently songs used by the pilgrims on their way up to the Temple at Jerusalem for the feasts."[31] The word translated ascent [*ma'alot*] in the title of these Psalms refers to *going up* to Jerusalem. Psalm 122:4 uses the verb form of the same word. "To which the tribes *go up* ['*alo* from '*alah*], even the tribes of the Lord."

> Similarly, that the ascent of the tribes is *a statute for Israel to thank the name of Yhwh* (122:4) would appear to suggest an association with the appointed feasts ... Several points suggest Ascents were associated not only with the appointed feasts in general, but with the Feast of Sukkoth [Tabernacles] in particular.[32]

---

29. Derek Kidner, *Psalms 73-150* (Downers Grove: Inter-Varsity, 1973), 401. Italics added.
30. A. Cohen, *The Psalms* (New York: Soncino, 1992), 389.
31. Kidner, *Psalms 73-150*, 429.
32. Mitchell, *Message of the Psalter*, 113.

Sukkoth or Tabernacles was a time of harvest and ingathering (Exod. 34:22). "The predominate imagery in the collection is of harvest, vintage, and general fertility ([Ps.] 126.6; 127.3-5; 128.3; 129.6-7; 132.15)."[33] The Talmud indicates that the Songs of Ascent were sung in the temple during Tabernacles. "Likewise, Ps. 134:1 refers to a night service in the temple. The only such service referred to in rabbinic literature took place during Sukkoth (m. Suk. 5.2-4), and Psalm 134 is said to have been sung at that very time."[34] Finally, note that

> Zechariah 14 depicts all nations ascending to celebrate the Feast of Sukkoth in Jerusalem after the eschatological war. Its fivefold use of ['alah] (vv. 16, 17, 18, 18, 19) in connection with threefold reference to Sukkoth (16, 18, 19) shows a connection existed between the ascent motif and the feast in biblical times ... The eschatological tone of Zechariah 14 is striking.[35]

Zechariah 14:16-19 advances to the great eschatological feast of the Lord.

> Then it will come about that any who are left of *all the nations* that went against Jerusalem will *go up* [*'alah*] from year to year to worship the King, the Lord of hosts, and to celebrate the Feast of Booths [*Sukkoth*]. And it will be that whichever of the families of the earth does not *go up* [*'alah*] to Jerusalem to worship the King, the Lord of hosts, there will be no rain on them. If the family of Egypt does not *go up* [*'alah*] or enter, then no rain will fall on them; it will be the plague with which the Lord smites the nations who do not *go up* [*'alah*] to celebrate the Feast of Booths [*Sukkoth*]. This will be the punishment of Egypt, and the punishment of all the nations who do not *go up* [*'alah*] to celebrate the Feast of Booths [*Sukkoth*] (italics added).

---
33. Ibid., 114.
34. Ibid.
35. Ibid., 114-115.

Compare Isaiah 2:2 and Micah 4:1, which also move into "the remote future, when wickedness will disappear and the kingdom of God will be firmly established."[36] Then, "Many peoples will come and say, 'Come, let us go up [*'alah*] to the mountain of the Lord'" (Isa. 2:3; Mic. 4:2). "[W]hen the *ma'alot* [ascent] heading [of Psalms 120-134] is considered in the context of the prophetic writings, the group appears to depict an ascent to Sukkoth, not in historical, but in eschatological time ... "[37] The Psalms of Ascent reflect God's eschatological program.

"The book of Psalms is brought to a close with a grand collection of doxological psalms—Psalms 146-150."[38] Remember Psalm 2:2-3, "The kings of the earth take their stand / And the rulers take counsel together / Against the Lord and against His Anointed, saying, 'Let us tear their *fetters* apart / And cast away their cords from us'" (italics added). The rulers of the nations fail. Psalm 149:6-8 declares, "Let the high praises of God be in their mouth, / And a two-edged sword in their hand, / To execute vengeance on the *nations* / And punishment on the *peoples*, / To bind their kings with *chains* / And their nobles with *fetters* of iron" (italics added). God's eschatological plan is victorious. Psalm 2:8 promises Messiah, "I will surely give the *nations* as Your inheritance" (italics added). God's eschatological plan is victorious. "All *nations* whom You have made shall come and worship before You, O Lord, / And they shall glorify Your name" (Ps. 86:9, italics added). The Psalter closes with eschatological hymns of praise for God on a cosmic scale. Kidner explains the eschatological thrust of the Psalter as a whole: "So in this respect as in many others, the Psalms are a miniature of our story as a whole, which will end in unbroken blessing and delight."[39] Futato makes a similar observation.

We can say the whole Book of Psalms is eschatological. This means, among other things, that the Book of Psalms

---

36. I. W. Slotki and A. J. Rosenberg, *Isaiah* (New York: Soncino, 1983), 10.
37. Mitchell, *Message of the Psalter*, 126.
38. Futato, *Interpreting the Psalms*, 114.
39. Kidner, *Psalms 73-150*, 483.

was driving the original audience forward. One purpose of the Psalms was and is to create a sense of hope that one day the King would come to put everything in our lives and in the world in right order once and for all.[40]

PSALTER ESCHATOLOGY, THE SUBJECTIVE ELEMENT, AND EXPECTATIONS

Individual eschatology and national eschatology combine. The subjective element and Psalter eschatology intertwine and mesh. Carefully reread the above quotes of Kidner and Futato to see this emphasis. Vos also connects Psalter eschatology with its subjective element.

> The trouble with eschatology in the experience of the church has frequently been that it was either dead or overmuch pathologically alive. In the Psalter we can observe what is its normal working. And through observing this we can learn the even more principal [important] lesson, what is the heart and essence of religion, because when eschatologically attuned the religious mind responds to the highest in-working and closest approach to God, and therefore operates up to the fullest potentialities of its own nature.[41]

In other words, a good grasp of both Psalter eschatology and its purpose to guide believers in the proper expression of their hearts and emotions tends to lead them into the fullest potentiality of their own nature as they engage in praise. As Michael LeFebvre puts it, Psalmody, therefore, "involves a fundamentally different 'heart movement' ... than the contemporary worship movement represents."[42] And again, the Psalter is "designed for a different kind of 'heart movement' than churches in the English hymn-writing movement are used to."[43]

---

40. Futato, *Tranformed by Praise*, 131.
41. Vos, "Eschatology of the Psalter," 332.
42. Michael LeFebvre, *Singing the Songs of Jesus* (Fearn: Christian Focus, 2010), 100.
43. Ibid., 111.

Psalmody requires God's people to have Biblical expectations when it comes to the matter of praise. Psalm 1 tells us that the blessed person's "delight is in the law of the Lord." The law is much more than the Ten Commandments. It is Torah; it includes the moral law and much more. It includes the ceremonial law with all of its sacrifices pointing to Christ. Torah contains both law and gospel. To delight in Torah means to find pleasure in both gospel salvation and right living. The blessed person, the happy person, *meditates* on God's salvation and God's right ways. It is the word *meditate* to which Lefebvre draws attention. The Hebrew word is *hagah*. Such meditation is far from silent and can involve singing. "My tongue shall declare [*hagah*] Your righteousness and Your praise all day long" (Ps. 35:28). Why was *hagah* used rather than other words for speech, talk, or song? This particular Hebrew verb brings out what Vos calls the *subjective element* in the Psalter. LeFebvre puts it this way,

> When the verb hagah is used in Hebrew, it is chosen in order to draw attention to the particular quality of a person's speech. The Hebrew linguist, Anastasie Negoiță, provides the following explanation:
>
>> ... hāghāh is not the common word for speaking. Hebrew has other words for this, like 'āmar, dibber, or qāra'. On the other hand, hāghāh is sometimes used to express the feelings of the human soul. With śîach[44] in particular, hāghāh means that a man "is lost in religion," that he is filled with thoughts of God's deeds or his will.
>
> In other words, this verb is used instead of any other speech-verb when the writer wants to draw our attention to the deep internal, wholehearted sentiments involved in that vocalization.[45]

---

44. "I will meditate [*hagah*] on all Your work and muse [*śîach*] on Your deeds" (Ps. 77:12).
45. LeFebvre, *Singing the Songs of Jesus*, 107.

The Psalms are quite unlike traditional hymns and contemporary gospel songs. "There is a lot of moaning and groaning going on in the Psalms."[46] Even so, the Psalter is a book of praise. The Hebrew name for the book, *tehellim,* means *songs of praise.* "The book is called 'Praises' because the nature of the whole collection is to carry us from sorrow to praise."[47] You see, "the book of Psalms is so named because these are sung meditations, which meet us in 'the city of confusion and trouble' where we live and, if we follow them where they take us, they carry us to the 'city of praise and rejoicing.'"[48] That the Psalms set believers on a journey from the city of trouble to the city of rejoicing is true personally, subjectively, and eschatologically.

Geerhardus Vos is correct. Psalter eschatology, individual and national, along with its purpose to guide God's people in the proper expression of their hearts, its subjective element, leads them into the fullest potentiality of their own nature as they engage in praise. Grasping the Psalters eschatology and its subjective element guides believers to approach the Psalms with Psalmody's expectations for them. Psalmody's problem, if there is one, is not with the Psalms; the problem is with improper expectations regarding the Psalms.[49] As will be seen, the objections raised against Psalmody fail because they do not recognize nor do they take into account either the Psalter's subjective element or its vital personal and national eschatological thrust. These objections, therefore, bypass and ignore the central and most dynamic features of the Psalter's use as God ordained praise.

---

46. Ibid., 97.
47. Ibid.
48. Ibid.
49. Ibid., 111.

13

Objections to Exclusive Psalmody

> *Sing to the* LORD *a new song; Sing to the* LORD*, all the earth ... O sing to the* LORD *a new song, For He has done wonderful things.* ~ Ps. 96:1; 98:1

THE INSUFFICIENCY OF THE PSALTER

THE OBJECTIONS TO EXCLUSIVE PSALMODY boil down to one basic complaint: The Psalter is insufficient for New Testament praise. When people exclaim, "But I want to sing about Jesus," they mean, "Psalms are insufficient for my praise." Some also take the position that the Psalms often speak about the Father, but have little reference to the Son. Others point out that the Psalms themselves teach that believers are to sing new songs, and therefore, instruct them not to confine their singing to those old songs. Then too, who wants to sing about Old Testament Types? It is of course far better to sing about the New Testament realities. There are many Scripture songs outside the Psalter, including hymn fragments imbedded in the New Testament. The presence of these hymn fragments shows that New Testament believers ought to sings songs outside the Psalter.

Add to these objections, the fact that Ephesians 5:19 and Colossians 3:16 have nothing to do with public corporate worship. Then too, texts like 1 Corinthians 14:15 and 26 speak about newly-inspired songs sung in the New Testament Church.

Professor Scott Sanborn insists exclusive Psalmody is insufficient for New Testament praise. He writes that the mystery of Gentile inclusion in the church, specifically revealed to the Apostle Paul (Eph. 3:4-6), is not present in the Psalms. Dr. Vern Poythress and Dr. Leonard Coppes insist that the regulative principle is fulfilled in Christ along with other aspects of the ceremonial law. Confining praise to the Psalter is, therefore, outmoded and contrary to Scripture. Dr. T. David Gordon goes a step further. The Psalms themselves command believers to sing about all the deeds of God, which presumably includes the incarnation, crucifixion, and resurrection. Confining worship song to the Psalter is, therefore, positively sinful to Dr. Gordon.

Each of these objections will be answered, seeking to show that the Psalter is sufficient for New Testament praise. Along the way, it will also be shown that these objections fail to appreciate the real beauty of Psalmody, that is, its subjective element meshed with its eschatology.

I WANT TO SING ABOUT JESUS

This objection means, "I want to sing about Jesus *like modern hymns and choruses do*." Of course, the implication is that Psalmody is insufficient. Furthermore, Dr. Leonard Coppes asserts, "The Old Testament psalms focus preeminently on the Father. While it is true that they also speak of the Son, they do not speak of him as pointedly and clearly as does the New Testament."[1] The response is twofold.

Note how the Apostle Paul speaks about Christ. "God highly exalted Him, and bestowed on Him the name which is above every name, so that at the name of Jesus EVERY KNEE WILL BOW, of those who are in heaven and on earth and under the earth and that every tongue will confess that Jesus Christ is Lord" (Phil. 2:9-11). Paul quotes Isaiah 45:23. In context, *Yahweh* declares every knee will bow to Him and every tongue will confess Him.

---

1. Leonard J. Coppes, *Exclusive Psalmody and Doing God's Will as It Is Fulfilled in Christ* (NP: The Author, n.d.), 23.

Is it not I, the LORD [*Yahweh*]? / And there is no other God besides Me, / A righteous God and a Savior; / There is none except Me. / Turn to Me and be saved, all the ends of the earth; / For I am God, and there is no other. / I have sworn by Myself, / The word has gone forth from My mouth in righteousness / And will not turn back, / That to Me every knee will bow, every tongue will swear allegiance [LXX *confess*] (Isa. 45:21-23).

From the apostle's perspective, Jesus is Yahweh; Jesus is Jehovah. He is God Incarnate. Paul brings out this truth with the confession that Jesus Christ is LORD. He also connects Jesus and Jehovah in Romans 10:9 and context, "If you confess with your mouth Jesus as Lord, and believe in your heart that God raised Him from the dead, you will be saved." He goes on in verse 11, quoting from Isaiah 28:16, "For the Scripture says, 'WHOEVER BELIEVES IN HIM WILL NOT BE DISAPPOINTED.'" Paul then quotes Joel 2:32, "WHOEVER WILL CALL ON THE NAME OF THE LORD WILL BE SAVED" (Rom. 10:13). The LORD to whom Paul points in Joel 2:32 is *Yahweh*. Paul calls his readers to confess that Jesus is Yahweh, that Jesus is Jehovah.

From this perspective, when believers sing, "The Lord is King! Let all the earth be joyful,"[2] they follow the Apostle Paul and make the confession that Jesus Christ is Lord. When Christians sing, "The Lord is my Shepherd,"[3] they confess Jesus Christ to be the great and good Shepherd of the sheep (John 10:11, 14, 16). They sing to Him! In doing so, they follow the teaching of the New Testament. They follow the teaching of the Apostle Paul.

Note that the New Testament frequently uses the Psalms to preach Christ. The New Testament quotes the Psalter 82 times.[4] Consider Romans. To accentuate the depth of human depravity in Romans 3, Paul quotes from Psalm 51:4 and Psalm 14:1-3. He adds quotes from

---

2. *The Book of Psalms for Worship* (Pittsburgh: Crown and Covenant, 2009), 97A.
3. Ibid., 23D.
4. *The Greek New Testament* (Stuttgart: United Bible Societies, 1983), 897-898.

Psalms 5:9; 10:7; 36:1; and 140:3. In chapter 4, Paul turns to the subject of justification by grace through faith in Christ and quotes Psalm 32:1-2. He also uses Psalm 117 as part of his rationale for preaching the gospel to the Gentiles (Rom. 15:11).

Elsewhere in the New Testament, Psalm 22 is used to present the details of Christ's crucifixion (Matt. 27:46; Mark 15:34; John 19:24). Psalm 16 is used to preach His resurrection (Acts 2:24-28, 31; 13:35). Psalm 2 is used to explain the opposition of Rome and Israel to Christ and His Kingdom (Acts 4:25-26). Psalm 110 is used to preach Christ's ascension and heavenly reign (Acts 2:34-35). Psalm 68 is also used to proclaim Christ's ascension (Eph. 4:7-8). Psalm 118:26 is used by our Lord to predict His coming again (Matt. 23:39). Hebrews 1 uses Psalms 2:7; 45:6-7; 102:25-27; and 110:1 to present Christ as God and Creator. Hebrews 10 uses Psalm 40:6-8 to present Christ as the once for all sacrifice saving us from our sins.

When believers sing, "Therefore kings now heed this word: Earthly judges, come and hear. Rev'rent worship give the Lord,"[5] they exhort earthly rulers to bow before King Jesus. When Christians sing, "The earth you founded long ago; Your mighty hand the heavens made,"[6] they confess Christ as the Creator (Heb. 1:10). In singing the Psalms, believers do sing about Jesus. The Psalter is quite sufficient for the New Testament age.

Granted, the traditional language of Western hymns is not used in singing the Psalms, nor is the popular language of modern gospel songs and choruses used. The language of Scripture is used, language said to be outmoded and designed for an earlier age. By what standard? A standard designed by those objecting to Psalmody, *a standard foreign to Scripture*. This objection argues that words "made by an act of human will" are superior to, or at least equal with, words not "made by an act of human will, but [by] men moved by the Holy Spirit [who] spoke from God" (2 Pet. 2:21). Words, it must be add-

---

5. *The Book of Psalms for Worship*, 2C.
6. Ibid., 102D.

ed, specifically set forth by the Spirit for singing the public praises of God. On this count, the Reformed Presbyterian Church of North America stands with the venerable Geerhardus Vos with regard to the Psalms and recognizes that "a more perfect language for communion with God *cannot be framed.*"[7]

This objection, settling, as it does, on the *objective* standard of a form of words or language, appears to ignore the *subjective* principle imbedded so deeply in the language of the Psalms. Vos again rightly states "that the Psalms reflect the experimental religion of the heart, which is unvarying at all times and under all circumstances ... [8] The Psalter is, therefore, sufficient for New Testament praise.

THE PSALTER COMMANDS NEW SONGS

The Psalms themselves command believers to sing a new song. "Sing to Him a new song; / Play skillfully with a shout of joy" (Ps. 33:3). "Sing to the Lord a new song; / Sing to the Lord, all the earth" (Ps. 96:1). "Praise the Lord! / Sing to the Lord a new song, / And His praise in the congregation of the godly ones" (Ps. 149:1). Coppes invokes Isaiah 42:1, 9, and 10 to make his case.

> Behold, My Servant, whom I uphold; / My chosen one in whom My soul delights. / I have put My Spirit upon Him; / He will bring forth justice to the nations ... Behold, the former things have come to pass, / Now I declare *new* things; Before they spring forth I proclaim them to you. / Sing to the Lord a *new* song, / Sing His praise from the end of the earth! (italics added).

Pointing to verse 9, Coppes says, "This verse defines 'new' as something that does not yet exist in the Old Testament period."[9] He then maintains that

---

7. Geerhardus Vos, "Songs from the Soul," *Grace and Glory* (Carlisle: Banner of Truth, 1994), 170, italics added.
8. Ibid., 171.
9. Coppes, *Exclusive Psalmody*, 6.

the proper exegesis of Isaiah 42:10 is fixed by Revelation 5:9 where God tells us the saints in heaven are singing "a new song"

> And they sang a new song, saying,
> You are worthy to take the scroll,
> And to open its seals;
> For You were slain,
> And have redeemed us to God by Your blood
> Out of every tribe and tongue and people and nation ...

Thus we see that in heavenly worship, the saints gathered before the throne of God, and hence, within the heavenly holy of holies, are singing a new song as prophesied in Isaiah 42:10 and the words are new words, i.e., words not recorded as one of the Old Testament psalms (cf. Rev. 14:3).[10]

This objection raises three important issues: the Biblical understanding of the term *new*, the interpretation of Isa. 42:10, and our relationship to the praise of God's people portrayed in the Book of Revelation.

What is the Biblical understanding of the terms new *and* newness? George Ladd teaches, "The idea of newness is distinctly eschatological ... The idea of newness preserves its eschatological character in the New Testament."[11] That is, believers live in an era in which the future has dawned. The age to come is pressing into this present age. "Thus," as Vos puts it, "the other world, hitherto future, has become present."[12] This is realized eschatology, the *already* but *not yet*. R. A. Harrisville adds that, "the 'new covenant' is an eschatological concept."[13] Harrisville then rehearses four characteristics of this concept of *newness*. The first is that of *contrast*. "The new covenant exists

---

10. Ibid., 7.
11. George Eldon Ladd, *A New Testament Theology* (Grand Rapids: Eerdmans, 1993), 521-522.
12. Geerhardus Vos, *The Pauline Eschatology* (Grand Rapids: Baker, 1979), 38.
13. R. A. Harrisville, "The Concept of Newness in the New Testament," *Journal of Biblical Literature* 74:2 (June, 1955): 73.

in contrast to the old by the fact that the community founded upon it is no longer ruled by an external authority from without (i.e., the letter of the law), but is motivated by the Spirit of God from within."[14] This distinctive of newness, contrast, or discontinuity, presupposes a second characteristic, "the element of *continuity*. The new covenant does not replace the old, but rather grows out of it and is related to it as fulfillment to promise."[15] The new covenant is in essence one with the old; the new is a new administration of the same covenant of grace.

A third "distinctive feature of the idea" of newness "is its *dynamic element*."[16] This dynamic element is explained by the power of Jesus Christ and his redemptive activity.[17] Newness is seen and experienced in and through texts such a 2 Corinthians 5:17, "Therefore if anyone is in Christ, he is a *new* creature; the old things passed away; behold, *new* things have come" (italics added). The Christian is a *new* creature or a *new* creation. Great change has occurred in the newly-converted person. There is *discontinuity* with the past. The newly-converted person, however, may be readily recognized. There is definite *continuity* with the past. This tension exists because of the *dynamic element* of the power of Christ introduced into the life of the Christian.

The fourth distinctive feature of "new" is *finality*. "The renewal by faith is final; it cannot be repeated because the believer has been placed within the last and final period of God's redemptive activity which hastens to its goal."[18] There is *finality* to newness because as has been observed in the previous chapter, God's eschatological plan will come to fruition. This fourfold distinctiveness of *newness* in Scripture—contrast, continuity, dynamic, and finality—fits well with both the subjective element and the eschatology of the Psalter.

---

14. Ibid.
15. Ibid., 74.
16. Ibid.
17. Ibid., 75.
18. Ibid., 76-77.

From this perspective, it is simplistic to hold that *new* refers to something that does not already exist. John 13:34 is a helpful example: "A new commandment I give to you, that you love one another, even as I have loved you, that you also love one another." Harrisville comments, "The new commandment is thus the rule of the new eschatological community. It is an eschatological commandment ... Thus though the commandment is not new from a purely historical point of view, it is new as given by Jesus."[19]

What is the proper interpretation of Isaiah 42:10? The text reads, "Sing to the Lord a new song, / Sing His praise from the end of the earth!" Isaiah's words are a simple command. He exhorts God's people to sing God's praise. They must sing a *new* song. "*New* is here contrasted with what is Ordinary, and thus he extols the infinite mercy of God, which was to be revealed in Christ, and which ought therefore to be celebrated and sung with the highest praises."[20] The new song is the song of future glory and blessing, sung as though that future glory and blessing were then present. How could believers sing such a song? Calvin answers, "It ought to be observed that this *song* cannot be sung but by renewed men; for it ought to proceed from the deepest feeling of the heart, and therefore[,] we need the direction of the Spirit, that we may sing those praises in a proper manner."[21] Calvin refers to the *subjective element*, which has been discussed above. Calvin goes on to say, "Besides, he does not exhort one or a few nations to do this, but all nations in the world; for to all them Christ was sent."[22] The *eschatological element* comes through strongly in Calvin's exposition. In the case of Isaiah 42:10, the new song may be old songs sung from a new heart. If so, and if guided by the Spirit, the prophetic songs of David and Asaph, with their eschatological thrust and prominent subjective element, comport well with the

---

19. Ibid, 79.
20. John Calvin, *Commentary on the Prophet Isaiah*, trans. William Pringle (Grand Rapids: Baker, 1979), 299.
21. Ibid.
22. Ibid.

command of God through Isaiah. Isaiah 42:10 *does not* command new and different songs with new and different words.

What about the believer's connection with the praise portrayed in Revelation? A more complete discussion of this question awaits analysis of the heavenly worship portrayed in the Book of Revelation and the use of musical instruments in worship. The basic premise is that God commands believers to hold to the principles of worship He sets forth *for the age in which they live*. When God commands the building of the tabernacle and institutes sacrifices in this specific location, He changes worship in Israel. The people are not permitted to use the standards of worship previously followed by Abraham. When David adds singing of the Psalms and additional musical instruments to worship in the tabernacle and in the temple by the command of God, the people are not permitted to revert to the more simplified worship under Moses. Similarly, the people living in the time of David and Solomon could not look ahead and adjust their worship to conform to the new age ushered in by Messiah. They were not permitted to forsake principles of worship ordained by God for their time. In like manner, believers today are required to maintain the standards of worship God gives them for this present age. It is not their prerogative to appropriate into the worship of today aspects of worship from another age, whether earlier or later. This argument is another way of stating the regulative principle of worship.

PSALMODY IS TYPOLOGICAL

I don't want to sing about types; I want to sing about the realities. Dr. T. David Gordon says of exclusive Psalmody, "We may sing of Christ typologically through canonical psalms, but we may not sing of Christ expressly; even though Israel could sing expressly of deliverance from Babylon, and was not restricted to singing of it typologically through Exodus-psalms."[23] It has already been shown, under

---

23. T. David Gordon, "Some Provisional Thoughts on Exclusive Psalmody" (Grove City, PA: The Author, n.d.), 15.

the heading, "I Want to Sing About Jesus," that believers do expressly sing of and to Christ using the Psalms. The matter of typology will be addressed shortly.

Dr. Coppes adds the following regarding exclusive Psalmody,

> God limits us to returning to those types when we sing. We accuse them of this because the 150 Psalms were written to express and facilitate the idea of the Levitical/ Mosaic theology and not to express the theology and ideas of fulfillment in Christ. They are part of the Levitical system. They stand in the same relationship to the new covenant as does the rest of that system ... When some of those songs became officially the hymnbook of the Old Testament church, then they became the type.[24]

The Psalter itself is not a type. It does not fit the definition of a Biblical type. In his *Biblical Hermeneutics*, Milton Terry says, "There must be evidence that the type was designed and appointed by God to represent the thing typified."[25] Scripture nowhere identifies the Psalter as a type. A Biblical type also prefigures something in the future; a Biblical type is prophetic.[26] What does the Psalter prefigure? In addition, Biblical types involve typical persons, typical institutions, typical offices, and typical events.[27] The Psalter fits none of these categories. *The Psalter is not a type.*

Granted, King David associated Psalmody with the typical institution of the ceremonial law (1 Chronicles 16). King Hezekiah also formalized Psalmody in temple worship (2 Chronicles 29:30). This association with the ceremonial law does not necessarily indicate that the Psalter is typological. After all, the Psalter, as we know it, did not come into being until post-exilic times, perhaps through the work of Ezra. "The LXX Psalter, dating probably from the early second century BCE, contains the 150 psalms of the Masoretic Text (MT),

---

24. Coppes, *Exclusive Psalmody*, 4-5.
25. Milton S. Terry, *Biblical Hermeneutics* (Grand Rapids: Zondervan, 1974), 337.
26. Ibid., 338.
27. Ibid., 338-339.

in the same sequence ... "²⁸ Did the Psalter become a type sometime between the time of Ezra and the early second century B.C.? In his Preface to the Bay Psalm Book, Richard Mather speaks directly to this question:

> What type can be imagined in making use of his [David's] songs to praise the Lord? If they [David's psalms] were typical because the ceremony of musical instruments were joined with them, then their prayers were also typical, because they had that ceremony of incense mixed with them: but we know that prayer then was a moral duty, notwithstanding the incense, and so singing those psalms [was a moral duty] notwithstanding their musical instruments. Besides, that which was typical (as that they were sung with musical instruments, by the twenty-four orders of Priests and Levites, 1 Chron. 25:9) must have the moral and spiritual accomplishment in the New Testament, in all the churches of the Saints ... with hearts and lips, instead of musical instruments, to praise the Lord ... ²⁹

Also recall Matthew Henry's observation, "Singing of psalms is a gospel-ordinance. Christ's removing the hymn [Psalms 113-118] from the close of the passover to the close of the Lord's supper, plainly intimates that he intended that ordinance should continue in his church, that, as it had not its birth with the ceremonial law, so it should not die with it."³⁰ Henry acknowledges that Psalmody did not come into existence with the Levitical system. It was added later. To insist that, "the 150 Psalms were written to express and facilitate the idea of the Levitical/Mosaic theology and not to express the theology and ideas of

---

28. David C. Mitchell, *The Message of the Psalter: An Eschatological Programme in the Book of Psalms* (Sheffield: Sheffield Academic Press, 1997), 16, n. 2.
29. Richard Mather, "Preface," *The Whole Booke of Psalmes Faithfully Translated into English Metre* (Cambridge: Riverside Press, 1640), 2. Rendered in modern English.
30. Matthew Henry, *Matthew Henry's Commentary on the Whole Bible*, 6 Vol. (Grand Rapids: Fleming H. Revell, 1985), 5:392.

fulfillment in Christ,"[31] ignores the Psalter's specific Messianic and eschatological character, as already discussed. *The Psalter is not a type.*

It is true that the Psalms use symbolism and typology to speak about the future. Undoubtedly, the Bible in general speaks to God's people about their future in terms of their past or their present. Israel's prophets used imagery from the past or present to discuss the future of God's people. Prophetic portions of the The New Testament do the same.

> Of all the various forms of prophetic thought, few are so common and so helpful in getting a handle on the meaning as a writer's borrowing past events, persons, or expressions to depict the future. The reason for choosing to us what appears at first so strange is simple: no one has ever been in the future, so how can the writer adequately talk about or the reader understand what neither has ever experienced?[32]

The Biblical writers speak about the future using types and symbols, and they do so in the Psalms. New Testament songs use the same procedure. Revelation 5:9-10 is one such song. "And they sang a new song, saying ... "

> Worthy are You to take the book and to break its seals;
> For You were slain, and purchased for God with Your blood
> Men from every tribe and tongue and people and nation.
> You have made them to be a kingdom and priests to our God;
> And they will reign upon the earth.

This song is sung to "the Lion that is from the tribe of Judah, the Root of David" (Rev. 5:5). The apostle John is referring back to the messianic prophecies of Genesis 49:9 and Isaiah 11:1, respectively. The object of praise is also described as "a Lamb standing, as if slain, having seven horns and seven eyes, which are the seven Spirits of

---

31. Coppes, *Exclusive Psalmody*, 4.
32. Walter C. Kaiser, *Back Toward the Future* (Grand Rapids: Baker, 1990), 51.

God, sent out into all the earth" (Rev. 5:6). This picture is thick with symbolism. The song itself speaks of a book or scroll. What is this book or scroll? It is symbolic. The Lamb standing, as if slain, having seven horns and seven eyes, is spoken of as a sacrifice shedding its blood. This description is the characteristic New Testament symbolic representation of Christ. "Behold, the Lamb of God who takes away the sin of the world" (John 1:29). The sacrificial lamb was a type of Christ. The saints in heaven appear to sing about Christ *typologically*. The song gives praise to the Lamb for taking "men from every tribe and tongue and people and nation" and making them into "a kingdom and priests." These lines are a clear reference to Exodus 19:6. The Old Testament priests were types. This New Testament song of the consummation speaks of God's people *typologically*.

Revelation 15:3-4 presents another song. "And they sang the song of Moses, the bond-servant of God, and the song of the Lamb, saying ... "

> A   Great and marvelous are Your works,
> B   O Lord God, the Almighty;
> A´   Righteous and true are Your ways,
> B´   King of the nations!
> C   Who will not fear, O Lord, and glorify Your name?
> D   For You alone are holy;
> C´   For ALL THE NATIONS WILL COME AND WORSHIP BEFORE YOU,
> D´   FOR YOUR RIGHTEOUS ACTS HAVE BEEN REVEALED.

The language in this song is straightforward, like many of the Psalms. This song also reads like a psalm. It has eight lines. As outlined, the first four lines are an alternating parallelism. The second four lines are also an alternating parallelism. The song's very form and language recalls the Psalms and recommends the Psalms. The seventh line of this song is a quotation from Psalm 86:9. The words of the eighth line come from Psalm 98:2. Apparently the Psalms do "express the theology and ideas of fulfillment in Christ." In addition, this song is both the song of Moses and the song of the Lamb, and is one song. "[T]he saints praise the Lamb's victory as the typological fulfillment of that to which the Red Sea victory pointed ... "[33]

Grasping Biblical typology assists in seeing the unity of Scripture, the unity of the gospel, and the unity of the covenant of grace. Far from being a hindrance to gospel singing, an appreciation of Biblical typology assists gospel praise. As just seen, the way the Bible speaks about the future is with the use of symbols and types. From this perspective, the use of types and symbols in Psalmody is natural and expected.

THE REGULATIVE PRINCIPLE IS FULFILLED IN CHRIST

Dr. Vern Poythress, noted Professor of New Testament Interpretation, argues against exclusive psalmody as follows: "The regulative principle of worship finds its final, decisive expression when Christ fulfills the law of Moses and the ordinances of David with superabundant fulfillment and riches."[34] He further states that the fulfillment of the regulative principle "is of a piece with the fulfillment of the priestly, kingly, and prophetic ministry" of the Old Testament: "all is fulfilled in Christ."[35]

Professor Poythress mixes apples and oranges. The regulative principle arises from the Second Commandment; it is part of the moral law, which is perpetual. "You shall not make for yourself an idol, or any likeness of what is in heaven above or on the earth beneath or in the water under the earth. You shall not worship them or serve them ... " (Exod. 20:4-5). "What is forbidden in the second commandment?" Answer, "The second commandment forbiddeth the worshipping of God by images, *or any other way not appointed in his word*" (WSC 51, italics added). Shorter Catechism 51 is a classic statement of the regulative principle of worship. Believers are not to worship in any way God does not command in His word. The Old Testament

---

33. G. K. Beale, *The Book of Revelation: A Commentary on the Greek Text* (Grand Rapids: Eerdmans, 1999), 792.
34. Vern S. Poythress, "Ezra 3, Union with Christ, and Exclusive Psalmody," *Westminster Theological Journal* 37:1 (Fall 1974) 82.
35. Ibid., 82-83.

prophets, priests, and kings were prophetic types pointing forward to Christ and fulfilled in Him. They served under the ceremonial law and the civil law of Israel, which were temporary.

The professor also uses the term *fulfilled* in different ways. The prophetic types of prophet, priest, and king are fulfilled in Jesus Christ, the anti-type. Old Testament ceremonies are fulfilled when Christ sets them aside to establish His own sacrificial work as final (Heb. 10:9). Christ *fulfills* the moral law in a different way. He obeys it. Since the regulative principle is part of the moral law and therefore perpetual, it remains in force. God calls all people to obey it.

Professor Poythress goes on to rightly say, "In our worship we are to strive for complete conformity to the law, bending all our efforts and finding all our joy in fulfilling it (not going beyond it with inventions)."[36] Amen! However, the professor also says, "Moreover, it is conformity which is *internal*."[37] Expressing the need for this internal conformity, he continues, "We must have the mind of Christ ... "[38] How true. What happens when there is failure? "We must see that Christ himself is the definitive embodiment of true righteousness."[39] Christ, therefore, fulfills the regulative principle; "all is fulfilled in Christ."[40] Note the ambiguity, the equivocation. Christ fulfills the regulative principle as a part of the Second Commandment by His perfect obedience. Since the regulative principle is a perpetual and moral principle and not ceremonial, Christ does not fulfill it like the Old Testament sacrifices, which He does set aside.

Conformity to God's moral law is not only internal. Believers must outwardly act according to God's law, including the regulative principle. Yes, believers must have the mind of Christ. There is an internal and subjective aspect to worship as God commands. Calvin, following Athanasius, points in this direction in his Preface to the Psalms,

---

36. Ibid., 83.
37. Ibid.
38. Ibid.
39. Ibid.
40. Ibid.

"[T]here is not an emotion of which any one can be conscious that is not here represented ... "[41] Athanasius teaches "each one sings the Psalms as though they had been written for his special benefit ... " and we sing them "as a pattern and model for the amendment of our lives."[42] The Psalms are a divine guide for the expression of personal thoughts and emotions in worship.

The regulative principle of worship remains in force. Psalmody helps believers fulfill, follow, and obey it. As Christians sing the Psalms in worship, God works internal conformity to His Law in them by training their thoughts and emotions. Holding to the regulative principle of worship, the church continues to sing the Psalms.

PAUL'S MYSTERY NOT IN THE PSALMS

Professor Scott Sanborn argues against exclusive Psalmody by stating that the mystery of Gentile inclusion does not appear within the Psalter. Ephesians 3:4-6 is the text in question.

> By referring to this, when you read you can understand my insight into the *mystery* of Christ, which in other generations was not made known to the sons of men, as it has now been revealed to His holy apostles and prophets in the Spirit; to be specific, *that the Gentiles are fellow heirs and fellow members of the body, and fellow partakers of the promise in Christ Jesus through the gospel* (italics added).

Sanborn states, "[T]he psalms did not reveal this mystery."[43] More emphatically, "No Old Testament revelation (including the Psalter) revealed this mystery."[44] Again, "The wisdom of Christ ... is God's mystery, a mystery that was not revealed to the Old Testament prophets, including the Psalmists."[45] Why this protest? If the Psalms do not

---

41. John Calvin, "The Author's Preface," *Commentary on the Book of Psalms* (Grand Rapids: Baker, 1979), 1:xxxvii.
42. Athanasius, "Letter to Marcellinus Concerning the Psalms," Fisheaters.com, accessed November 15, 2011.
43. Scott F. Sanborn, "Inclusive Psalmody: Why 'Psalms, Hymns, and Spiritual Songs' Refer to More than the Old Testament Psalter," *Kerux* 23:3 (December 2008): 20.
44. Ibid., 34.
45. Ibid., 36

reveal this mystery, they are not sufficient for New Testament worship. Then "it follows that the church *is required* to sing more than the Psalter in public worship."[46] Not only so, "to restrict the church's song to Old Testament revelation in the Psalter is at odds with the Regulative Principle of worship."[47] Earlier in his article, Sanborn says, "By calling us to sing out of this mystery, Paul is surely calling us to sing more than the Psalter."[48]

Psalm 117, among many others, readily answers this objection. "Praise the Lord, all nations; / Laud Him, all peoples! / For His lovingkindness is great toward us, / And the truth of the Lord is everlasting. / Praise the Lord!" Psalm 117, the shortest in the Psalter, is part of the so-called Egyptian Hallel. It is sung at the Jewish Passover in remembrance of Israel's salvation and deliverance from Egypt. Of course, Passover points to Christ. "For Christ our Passover also has been sacrificed" (1 Cor. 5:7).

Rooted in deliverance and pointing to Christ, this Psalm calls "all nations" and "all people" to offer praise and worship to the Lord of glory. Specifically, all Gentile nations and peoples ought to "praise the Lord." The implication is that all nations, Jew and Gentile, will be gathered in one body to worship and serve Jesus Christ. Calvin comments on this Psalm, "It would therefore serve no purpose for the prophet to address the heathen nations, unless they were to be gathered together in the unity of the faith with the children of Abraham."[49] Matthew Henry refers to Ephesians 3:6 in his comments on the Psalm. "[T]he gospel of Christ is ordered to be preached to all nations, and by him the partition-wall is taken down, and those that were *afar off* are made *nigh*. This was the mystery which was hidden in prophecy for many ages, but was at length revealed in the accomplishment, *That the Gentiles should be fellow-heirs*, Eph. iii. 3, 6."[50]

---

46. Ibid., 49, italics added.
47. Ibid., 49.
48. Ibid., 18.
49. John Calvin, *Commentary on the Book of Psalms*, trans. James Anderson (Grand Rapids: Baker, 1979), 4:375.
50. Henry, *Commentary on the Whole Bible*, 3: 679.

Yes, Psalm 117, among others, sets forth "the mystery of Christ, which in other generations was not made known to the sons of men, *as it has now been revealed to His holy apostles and prophets in the Spirit*" (Eph. 3:4-5, italics added). Note the comparison that Paul makes. The mystery was revealed in the Old Testament, but has now been more fully revealed. What is this mystery? "That the Gentiles are fellow heirs and fellow members of the body, and fellow partakers of the promise in Christ Jesus through the gospel" (Eph. 3:6).

Sanborn's protestations are ill-founded. He appears to miss the comparison Paul makes. Paul does not say that the mystery of gentile inclusion was not revealed in the Old Testament. Rather, he pointedly indicates that this mystery was not fully revealed in the Old Testament. Note Paul's comparison once again: "You can understand my insight into the mystery of Christ, which in other generations was not made known to the sons of men, *as it has now been revealed to His holy apostles and prophets in the Spirit*" (Eph. 3:4-5). "As" is a conjunction or particle "denoting comparison."[51] Again, the mystery is, "That the Gentiles are fellow heirs and fellow members of the body, and fellow partakers of the promise in Christ Jesus through the gospel" (Eph. 3:6).

That this mystery is revealed in the Old Testament is clear. Again, Psalm 117, for example, calls the Gentiles to join in the worship of the Lord of glory. This call is rooted in the promise given to Abraham, Isaac, and Jacob, "In your seed all the nations of the earth shall be blessed" (Gen. 22:18). The seed is Christ (Gal. 3:16). The promise is the gospel: "The Scripture, foreseeing that God would justify the Gentiles by faith, preached the gospel beforehand to Abraham, saying, 'ALL THE NATIONS WILL BE BLESSED IN YOU'" (Gal. 3:8). The Father's *eternal* promise to the Son stands behind all of the *temporal* promises: "Ask of Me, and I will surely give the nations as Your inheritance" (Ps. 2:8). The Psalms are full of the gospel of Christ. They are full of the mystery of Gentile inclusion. Believers can sing the Psalms con-

---

51. F. Wilbur Gingrich and Frederick W. Danker, *Shorter Lexicon of the Greek New Testament* (Chicago: University of Chicago Press, 1983), 221.

cerning this mystery. Additional newer songs are not required. *The Psalter is sufficient for New Testament Praise.*

WE MUST SING OF ALL GOD'S DEEDS

The Psalter commands believers to sing about all the deeds of God. "Sing to Him, sing praises to Him; / Speak of all His wonders" (Ps. 105:2, italics added). If all the deeds of God are not recorded in the Psalms, the Psalter is insufficient for New Testament praise, *by its own admission.* Some claim that the Psalter itself, therefore, commands believers to sing more than the Psalms. Professor Poythress properly argues that, "Christ tells the deeds of God in song."[52] He connects Psalms 9, 22, 40, 89, 105, and 107 and says that "in each of the psalms Christ can be regarded as the principle singer."[53] However, Poythress goes on,

> Because of these connections, we feel justified in applying to Christ such exhortations as "sing to him, sing praises to him, tell of *all* his wonderful works" (105:2). Hence we conclude that Christ sings also the New Testament deeds of salvation, including such deeds as his appearance to Thomas, his conversation with Peter in John 21, etc.—deeds not explicitly mentioned in the 150 psalms.[54]

Professor Gordon puts the case more strongly,

> The psalms themselves command us to sing of God's "deeds," which presumably include His incarnate deeds. The psalms themselves tell us to "give thanks" in song, and presumably we may thank Him for giving His Son to die for us. The psalms teach us to "tell of his salvation day by day" in song, and presumably the death and resurrection of Christ constitute part of the biblical message of salvation. The psalms themselves

---

52. Poythress, "Ezra 3," 90.
53. Ibid., 91.
54. Ibid.

teach us to sing to God "because he has done marvelous things," and again, presumably the humiliation and exaltation are reasonably marvelous. The canonical psalms themselves teach us to "tell of *all* his wonderful works," apparently excluding none, and who would wish to deny that the dying and rising of Christ are chief among those wonderful works? *Prima facia*, then, the canonical psalms themselves call the people of God to give thanks and praise to God for all his mighty acts of creation and deliverance.[55]

Professor Gordon ends his paper, "I therefore conclude that exclusive psalmody is not only not required, but is positively erroneous and sinful. That is, the principle of refusing to praise God expressly for all his mighty deeds is itself a violation of both the pattern of scripture and the express teaching of scripture."[56]

However, Psalm 105:2, "Speak of all His wonders," uses a synecdoche (the whole for the part). Calvin interprets the text as using a synecdoche: "He indeed names in general *his works*, and *his wonders*, but he limits both to that spiritual covenant by which God made choice of a church, that might lead on earth a heavenly life."[57] This interpretation is reasonable and sensible approach to the text. How so? John 21:25 answers, "There are also many other things which Jesus did, which if they were written in detail, I suppose that even the world itself would not contain the books that would be written." *All* the deeds of God are not recorded, could not be recorded, and, therefore, cannot be put to song. It should be clear that the Psalmist is using the figure of speech, *synecdoche*.

Believers do sing of the essential deeds of God in Christ using the Psalms. The Psalms lay the foundation of human depravity (Ps. 5:9; 10:7; 14:1-3; 36:1; 51:4; and 140:3). Psalm 32:1-2 leads God's people

---

55. Gordon, "Provisional Thoughts," 1-2.
56. Ibid., 27.
57. Calvin, *Psalms*, 4:173.

in singing of justification by grace through faith in Christ. Psalm 117 leads believers in singing of the gospel going to the nations. Psalm 2 leads worshipers in singing about the opposition of the nations to Christ and His Kingdom. Psalm 22 leads the church in singing about several aspects of Christ's crucifixion. Psalm 16 leads believers in singing about His resurrection. Psalm 110 leads believers in singing about Christ's ascension and heavenly reign. Psalm 68 also leads the church in singing about His ascension. Psalm 118 leads Christians in singing about Christ's coming, and of His coming again. Psalms 2:7, 45:6-7, 102:25-27, and 110:1 lead us in singing of Christ as our God and Creator. Psalm 40:6-8 leads believers to sing of Christ in His active obedience and in His once for all sacrifice for our sins. *The Psalms are sufficient to lead the church in singing in public worship of the essential deeds of God in Christ.*

WHY REGULATE TEACHING, PRAYING, AND SINGING DIFFERENTLY?

Dr. Coppes declares,

> The theological method and conclusions expressed in exclusive psalmody reverse the order of importance of preaching and singing. It does this by its conclusion that God regulates singing more closely than He regulates preaching. Biblically speaking, however, God teaches us that preaching occupies a more central and more important place in Christian worship than does singing.[58]

Professor Poythress understands "teaching-by-singing and teaching-in-the-narrow-sense" as "two forms of teaching."[59] He then draws this line: "We challenge the exclusive psalmist position to prove *from Scripture*, rather than *assume*, that teaching-by-singing and proclamation are 'two separate elements of worship.'"[60]

---

58. Coppes, *Exclusive Psalmody*, 22.
59. Vern S. Poythress, "Ezra 3, Union with Christ, and Exclusive Psalmody (Concluded)," *Westminster Theological Journal* 37:2 (Winter 1975): 225.
60. Ibid.

Professor Gordon points to Acts 16:25 to display the similarity between prayer and praise. "Paul and Silas were praying and singing hymns of praise to God." Literally, the text reads, "praying they hymned to God" [*proseuxomenoi humnoun ton theon*].

> The importance of this relation between song and prayer for the present discussion is significant, because this consideration causes a general problem with exclusive psalmody to be more acute. Generally, it is already problematic that exclusive psalmody argues that the words of songs of praise must be inspired, and restricted to the canonical psalter, while the words of the other elements of worship are not so restricted … But this is even more acute a difficulty when two elements in scripture that are so similar (prayer and praise) are considered to be regulated differently.[61]

Preaching, prayer, and praise are separate and distinct elements of worship. Paul tells Timothy, "I am writing these things to you … so that you will know how one ought to conduct himself in the household of God, which is the church of the living God" (1 Tim. 3:14-15). Paul's purpose was to guide the conduct of the church. He tells Timothy, "Preach the word; be ready in season and out of season; reprove, rebuke, exhort, with great patience and instruction" (2 Tim. 4:2). It seems strange that, in Reformed circles, it is necessary to defend preaching as a distinct element of worship. It will be argued below that the references to singing in both Ephesians 5:19 and Colossians 3:16 have to do with corporate worship. The Westminster Divines appear to have held this position. Public prayer is also an important part of corporate church life:[62] "First of all, then, I urge that entreaties and prayers, petitions and thanksgivings, be made on behalf of all men, for kings and all who are in authority, so that we may lead a tranquil and quiet life in all godliness and dignity" (1 Tim. 2:1-2).

---

61. Gordon, "Provisional Thoughts," 6.
62. John Calvin, *The Second Epistle of Paul to the Corinthians and the Epistles to Timothy, Titus, and Philemon*, trans. T. A. Smail (Grand Rapids: Eerdmans, 1964), 205.

The Westminster Confession of Faith is clear on these matters. "The reading of Scriptures with godly fear; the sound preaching, and conscionable hearing of the Word, in obedience unto God, with understanding, faith, and reverence; singing of Psalms with grace in the heart ... are all parts of the ordinary religious worship of God" (WCF 21:5). "Prayer, with thanksgiving, being one special part of religious worship, is by God required of all men" (WCF 21:3). Following Scripture and our Confession, it is maintained that preaching, prayer, and praise are separate and distinct elements of worship.

Colossians 3:16 makes it clear that preaching and singing in the congregation are equally important: "Let the word of Christ dwell in you richly, [1] *teaching and admonishing* one another in all wisdom, [2] *singing* psalms and hymns and spiritual songs, with thankfulness in your hearts to God" (ESV, italics added). Colossians 1:28 defines *admonishing* and *teaching* as *preaching*. "We proclaim Him, admonishing every man and teaching every man with all wisdom." In the grammatical construction of Colossians 3:16, the two participles, *admonishing* and *teaching*, are parallel to the third participle, *singing*. This construction indicates that preaching, on one hand, and singing, on the other hand, are equally important. Singing is definitely not more important than preaching. Exclusive Psalmody rejects such a notion.

At the same time, note the translation of the English Standard Version. "Let the word of Christ dwell in you richly, [1] *teaching and admonishing* one another in all wisdom, [2] *singing* psalms and hymns and spiritual songs, with thankfulness in your hearts to God" (italics added). The Revised Standard Version is similar. "Let the word of Christ dwell in you richly, [1] *teach* and *admonish* one another in all wisdom, and [2] *sing* psalms and hymns and spiritual songs with thankfulness in your hearts to God." Both of these versions place *psalms and hymns and spiritual songs* with singing. John Eadie supports this approach.

> Our translators, too, so point the verse as to make psalms
> and hymns the material of instruction, whereas, it seems

better, and more appropriate, to keep the clause distinct, thus—"Let the word of Christ dwell in you richly; in all wisdom teaching and admonishing one another: in psalms, hymns, and spiritual songs, singing with grace in your hearts unto the Lord."[63]

Paul therefore restricts singing more than preaching. As just indicated, teaching and admonishing is preaching: "We proclaim Him, *admonishing every man and teaching every man with all wisdom,* so that we may present every man complete in Christ" (Col. 1:28, italics added). From Paul's perspective wisdom comes from the Scriptures. He reminds Timothy, "From childhood you have known the sacred writings *which are able to give you the wisdom* that leads to salvation through faith which is in Christ Jesus" (2 Tim. 3:15, italics added). When Colossians 3:16 exhorts, "Let the word of Christ dwell in you richly, teaching and admonishing one another *in all wisdom,*" the text exhorts teaching and admonishing rooted in Scripture. In other words, preaching must be *Scriptural*.

Second, Paul is more specific when it comes to singing. He not only requires the singing of public worship to be Scriptural, he specifies the Scriptures to be use in this singing; he specifies the psalms, hymns, and songs inspired by the Spirit found in the Book of Psalms. Again, the English Standard Version exhorts, "Let the word of Christ dwell in you richly ... singing *psalms and hymns and spiritual songs,* with thankfulness in your hearts to God" (italics added). What are believers assembled for worship to sing? They are to sing psalms, hymns, and spiritual songs; these are the songs of the 150 Psalms of the Old Testament. In other words, *Paul requires exclusive Psalmody.* The Apostle Paul commands the New Testament church to restrict corporate, public singing to the 150 Psalms of the Old Testament by the power of, and under the inspiration of, the Holy Spirit. Restricting singing more than preaching is not arbitrary. It is Scriptural.

---

63. John Eadie, *Commentary on the Epistle of Paul to the Colossians* (Grand Rapids: Zondervan, 1957), 251. See the complete analysis of Col. 3:16 in Chapter 11 under the heading of "Exclusive Psalmody."

It is also granted that believers pray when they sing the Psalms. In his preface to the Geneva Psalter, Calvin acknowledges that, "As for public prayers, there are two kinds: the ones made with word only, the other with song. And this is not a thing invented a short time ago. For from the first origin of the church, this has been so, as appears from the histories."[64] Believers may pray and earnestly seek God's face when they sing (Acts 16:15). Prayers expressed in song do not eliminate the status of prayers with word only as a separate element of worship. Prayer *with word only* must be according to the will of God (1 John 5:14). Such prayer must be *Scriptural*. As already argued, prayer *with song* is restricted to certain Scripture, the Psalms. God may and does regulate one element of worship differently than the other.

Paul does not explain why he restricts singing more than preaching or prayer. Part Four of this study will investigate the unique power of music. Calvin was deeply concerned about music's penetrating power. "For there is scarcely anything in the world which is capable of turning or moving this way or that the morals of men, as Plato prudently considered it. And in fact we experience that it has a secret and almost incredible power to arouse hearts in one way or the other."[65] The penetrating capacity of music may be a factor in Paul's command in Colossians 3:16.

Another factor may be the Psalter's subjective element. Part of Psalmody's purpose is to guide and train the inner person of believers through singing. Gordon maintains, "The capacity to compose *worthy* devotional material is due to the wonder of being created in God's image; not to the wonder of inspiration."[66] Gordon does not hesitate to indicate "the best work of Donne or Cowper rivals the best work of David ... "[67] He neglects the depth of depravity that yet

---

64. John Calvin, "Calvin's Preface to the Psalter," in Charles Garside, *The Origin of Calvin's Theology of Music* (Philadelphia: American Philosophical Society, 1979), 32.
65. Ibid., 33.
66. Gordon, "Provisional Thoughts," 19. Italics added.
67. Ibid.

remains with converted composers. Calvin's view regarding the material *worthy* of God is more circumspect.

> Now what Saint Augustine says is true, that no one is able to sing things worthy of God unless he has received them from Him. Wherefore, when we have looked thoroughly everywhere and searched high and low, we shall find no better songs nor more appropriate to the purpose than the Psalms of David which the Holy Spirit made and spoke through him.[68]

In Colossians 3:16, therefore, Paul teaches that singing the Psalms is part of the way believers let the word of Christ richly dwell within them.

Another factor in restricting congregational singing to the Psalms may be their universality and staying power. Michael LeFebevre speaks to the universality of the Psalms, including their curses and imprecations, and his experience at a seminar on the Psalms.

> One of the participants was a young priest from the Anglican Church in Rwanda. He spoke of the genocide in Rwanda in 1994, and how most of his own family was brutally slain in that violence. Three of his brothers were killed on the same day. It was painful to talk about those events ... But then he found Psalm 137 in the Bible ... And ironically, he was able to forgive, because of Psalm 137.

> After this young minister from Rwanda spoke, another young minister from Nigeria spoke. He described the unrest and bloodshed which his country has continually experienced over the years. And he spoke of the comfort which believers in that land found in looking to God to bring judgment on the wicked. "We need such Psalms," he concluded ...

---

68. Calvin, "Preface to the Psalter," 33.

Men like these live and serve Jesus in circumstances we, in the West, have not experienced for a long time ... But ... the Psalter is not a hymnal for the affluent churches of the modern West. It is the hymnal for all God's church, in all times and places.[69]

Along with their universality, the staying power of the Psalms is well known. Gordon thus speaks about good hymnody. "I have suggested to my students, for instance, that one of the tests of a hymn is whether it would exist as Christian verse if it were not put to music."[70] The English verse of good hymns has staying power. "This poetry would have survived, indeed has survived, apart from musical settings."[71] Gordon then compares the Psalms. "Totally apart from any musical considerations, both individuals and congregations routinely find the psalms edifying for use in private, family, or corporate worship."[72] The Psalter has exhibited much more staying power than traditional hymns, not only over centuries but over millennia. The Psalter's universality, staying power, subjective element, and the power of music may be reasons why Scripture regulates singing more closely than preaching or prayer.

WHY NOT SING NEW TESTAMENT HYMNS?

The New Testament contains hymns and hymn fragments. Why not sing these Scripture songs along with the Psalms? The New Testament does indeed contain several songs. Why not sing Mary's Song, *The Magnificat* (Luke 1:46-55)? Why not sing Zechariah's Song, *Benedictus* (Luke 1:68-79)? What about the Song of Simeon, the *Nunc dimittis* (Luke 2:29-32). Why not sing the songs of Revelation (Rev 5:9-10, 15:3-4)? What about the widely acknowledged hymn fragments imbedded in the New Testament? Philippians 2:6-11 and 1 Timothy 3:16

---

69. Michael LeFebvre, *Singing the Songs of Jesus* (Fearn: Christian Focus, 2010), 129-130.
70. T. David Gordon, *Why Johnny Can't Sing Hymns* (Phillipsburg: P & R, 2010), 130.
71. Ibid., 131.
72. Ibid., 132.

are outstanding examples. It is, however, quite unlikely that the early New Testament Church sang anything but Psalms.

The tradition of Psalmody is centuries old when we come to the New Testament. "King Hezekiah and the officials ordered the Levites to sing praises to the Lord with the words of David and Asaph the seer" (2 Chron. 29:30). As John Klienig indicates,

> If there was no collection of psalms attributed to David and Asaph, this decree would have authorized such an edition. These were thereafter to be used to praise the Lord as the public burnt offering was presented in the temple ... The words of these songs therefore became an integral part of the whole sacrificial ritual and so achieved their authoritative status from their use within that context.[73]

Hezekiah's decree restricts temple praise to the Psalms. What about other Old Testament songs, such as the songs of Moses (Exod. 15:1-18 and Deut. 32:1-43), the Song of Deborah and Barak (Judg. 5:1-31), the Song of the Bow written in the Book of Jashar (2 Sam. 1:17-18), and the song of Habakkuk (Hab. 3:1-19)? These songs are excluded from the public worship of Israel by Hezekiah's decree. The scope of permissible song is narrowed. This narrowing of permissible songs took place late eighth century or early seventh century B.C. Fast-forward 500 years. "The LXX Psalter, dating probably from the early second century BCE, contains the 150 psalms of the Masoretic Text (MT), in the same sequence ... "[74] The content of the Psalter and the content of Israel's sung praise in worship are settled by this time.

By the time of Christ and the apostles, the traditions surrounding the sacrifices, including Psalmody, are well established. See the discussions of the temple services and associated Psalmody in chapters 5 and 11. Also review the discussion of how temple Psalmody comes into New Testament worship. Given the centuries-old tradition of ex-

---

73. John W. Kleinig, *The Lord's Song* (Sheffield: Sheffield Academic Press, 1993), 68-69.
74. Mitchell, *The Message of the Psalter*, 16, n. 2.

clusive Psalmody and the derivation of New Testament praise from temple Psalmody, there is little reason to think other songs or hymns were used by the New Testament Church.

The *Odes of Solomon* is a collection of 42 psalm-like compositions and is known as the "Earliest Christian Hymnbook."[75] McKinnon notes the possibility of the composition of the *Odes* at the end of the first century.[76] "Specialists on the *Odes* now agree that the collection was completed in the early second century, and most likely before 125 CE."[77] In addition, The *Odes* are quoted only in the early fourth century by Lactantius [ca. 240 – ca. 320] ... "[78] In addition, the first known extra-biblical hymn that continues in use, in the Greek Orthodox tradition, is *Phos Hilaron*, "Hail Gladsome Light," and was composed about the third century.[79] There are, therefore, no extant manuscripts of hymns or hymn fragments that date back to the early first century. There are also no known extra-biblical hymns or songs that date to this time.

Paul likely wrote Philippians in 60 or 61 A.D. and his first letter to Timothy in the early 60s.[80] It is, therefore, unlikely that Philippians 2:5-11 and 1 Timothy 3:16 are early hymn fragments. Gordon Fee suggests pause on several additional counts regarding the former passage.

> First, if originally a hymn, it has no correspondence of any kind with Greek hymnody or poetry; therefore it would have to be Semitic in origin. But the alleged Semitic parallelism of this piece is unlike any *known* example of Hebrew psalmody ... Second, exalted—even poetic—*prose* does not necessarily mean that one is dealing with a hymn ... Third, the ... connection of the "hymn" with its antecedent is not at all smooth ... Fourth, as

---

75. James H. Charlesworth, *The Earliest Christian Hymnbook* (Eugene, OR: Cascade, 2009), xxi.
76. James McKinnon, *Music in the Early Christian Church* (Cambridge: Cambridge University Press, 1987), 23.
77. Charlesworth, *Early Christian Hymnbook*, xxii.
78. Ibid., xxi.
79. M. Eleanor Irwin, "Phos Hilaron: The Metamorphoses of a Greek Christian Hymn," *The Hymn* 40:2 (April, 1989): 7.
80. D. A. Carson and Douglas Moo, *An Introduction to the New Testament* (Grand Rapids: Zondervan, 2005), 506, 571.

pointed out in the commentary, these sentences, exalted and rhythmic as they are, follow one another in perfectly orderly prose—all quite in Pauline style ... Fifth, many of the alleged lines are especially irregular if they are intended to function as lines of Semitic poetry ... It should be noted finally that any excision of words or lines, so as to reproduce the "original" hymn, is an exercise in exegetical futility.[81]

First Timothy 3:16 is a much more likely candidate to be a hymn fragment, given its poetic structure.[82] Philip Towner, however, counters, "Unfortunately, despite the generous amounts of attention given to the source and background of this piece, nothing can be said about its origin or structure."[83] Commenting on "literary-critical attempts to discern its source and internal structure," Towner goes on to say, "These disciplines might indeed shed some light on the meaning of the lines and their interrelation, but all too often they give the impression that the piece, as employed here, has a life of its own."[84] It does not. There is no evidence that it is an independent hymn.

Surely 1 Corinthians 14:15 and 26 speak of the church singing newly-inspired hymns. "What is the outcome then? I will pray with the spirit and I will pray with the mind also; I will sing [*psalō*] with the spirit and I will sing [*psalō*] with the mind also ... What is the outcome then, brethren? When you assemble, each one has a psalm [*psalmon*] ... " Calvin disagrees with the supposition that these texts refer to newly-inspired hymns. "When he says, 'I shall sing the Psalms,' or *I shall sing*, he is speaking specifically instead of generally. For, since the Psalms had as their themes the praises of God, he uses 'singing psalms' [*psalein*] for *blessing* or giving thanks to God."[85] Calvin goes on to affirm that the Corinthians sang Psalms.

---

81. Gordon D. Fee, *Paul's Letter to the Philippians* (Grand Rapids: Eerdmans, 1995), 41-43.
82. Philip H. Towner, *The Letters to Timothy and Titus* (Grand Rapids: Eerdmans, 2006), 277, 284.
83. Ibid., 277.
84. Ibid., 284.
85. John Calvin, *The First Epistle of Paul to the Corinthians*, trans. John W. Fraser (Grand Rapids: Eerdmans), 292-293.

From this verse we also gather, however, that at that time the custom of singing was already among believers. That is also established by Pliny, who, writing at least forty years after the death of Paul, tells us that the Christians were in the habit of singing hymns to Christ before daylight.[86] And indeed I have no doubt that from the very beginning they adopted the usage of the Jewish Church in singing psalms.[87]

Therefore, the conclusion is that, on the one hand, there was a centuries-old tradition of Psalmody excluding other songs from public worship, which carried over to the infant New Testament church. On the other hand, the existence of New Testament era extra-biblical hymns quoted by Paul in his letters to Timothy and the Philippians is unlikely.

BUT PAUL'S PSALMS, HYMNS, AND SONGS INVOLVE PRIVATE WORSHIP

Although some maintain that Ephesians 5:18-19 involves private worship, this text more likely refers to the corporate setting. "And do not get drunk with wine, for that is dissipation, but be filled with the Spirit, speaking to one another in psalms and hymns and spiritual songs, singing and making melody with your heart to the Lord." Paul is speaking to the church as a whole. The people hear Paul's letter read to them in gathered assembly. He addresses his letter: "To the saints who are at Ephesus and who are faithful in Christ Jesus" (Eph. 1:1). The saints (plural) hear Paul in the corporate context.

Paul greets the saints at Ephesus with these words: "Blessed *be* the God and Father of our Lord Jesus Christ, who has blessed us with every spiritual blessing in the heavenly *places* in Christ" (Eph. 1:3). Paul was trained as a Jewish rabbi. This blessing is reminiscent of the

---

86. Pliny's 'Letter to Emperor Trajan' will be discussed in the next chapter.
87. Calvin, *First Corinthians*, 293.

prescribed blessings and benedictions pronounced at the beginning of the Synagogue services.[88] Paul is speaking to the church as a body.

Although Paul makes application to individuals and families in his Epistle, he also makes frequent reference to the local church in the context of the church at-large. Paul reminds the local body that it is a temple taking its place as part of the greater temple of the church (Eph. 2:19-22). Paul connects the blessing of the local Christians with the blessing of the whole church body saved by Christ: "That He would grant you [*plural*] ... that Christ may dwell in your [*plural*] hearts through faith ... to comprehend with *all* the saints" (Eph. 3:14-19, italics added). Paul speaks to individuals, but in the corporate context. Paul reminds the Ephesians, that because there is one God and one Spirit, there is one body. The purpose of spiritual gifts is the building up of the body. The unity of faith in the body is in view (Eph. 4:4-13). The corporate idea continues in Ephesians 5:18-19. "You [*plural*] don't get drunk with wine. But you [*plural*] be filled with the Spirit." Paul's injunction is for Christians individually *and* corporately. The tendancy is to approach Paul's words from the individualistic perspective only. The corporate setting and approach of the apostle is too often neglected, especially because English language Bibles cannot distinguish between the singular and plural "you."

Paul now indicates ways in which the fullness of the Spirit is manifest among God's people. Hearing these words in the corporate setting and grasping other injunctions regarding the local church body, how would the Ephesians understand Paul? "You [plural] be filled with the Spirit, speaking to one another in psalms and hymns and spiritual songs, singing and making melody with your [plural] heart to the Lord." Paul speaks these words to the body. The outcome is communication with *one another*. The outcome is singing. Again, in the phrase, with your heart, *your* is plural. The phrase might be translated, "singing with the heart of each of you" or "singing and making

---

88. Review the discussion of synagogue worship in chapter 5.

melody to the Lord with each of your hearts." Paul exhorts collective singing not silent meditation and thanksgiving. Paul's exhortation most naturally applies to the worship setting.

The phrase "in your heart" or "with your heart" is an instrumental dative. That is, the heart is the instrument through which the Spirit expresses praise. This comports with Hebrews 13:15, "Through Him then, let us continually offer up a sacrifice of praise to God, that is, the fruit of lips that give thanks to His name." Note again the corporate emphasis, "let us." Believers' sacrifice is praise, which comes from their lips. They sing. They should sing from the heart.

Charles Hodge indicates this passage "proves singing was from the beginning a part of Christian worship."[89] Referring to the second clause Hodge says, "[T]he great majority of commentators make this clause subordinate to the preceding and descriptive of the kind of singing required."[90] Westcott adds, "Men whose spirits are kindled by noble emotion express themselves in the highest forms of speech, and their hearts are in harmony with their words ... The Christian congregation as Christian joins in various forms of praise; and the same strains which set forth aspects of God's glory elevate the feelings of those who join in them."[91] Ephesians 5:18-19 refers to corporate, public worship.

Colossians 3:16 also involves the corporate setting. Paul writes to the church: "To the saints and faithful brethren in Christ who are at Colossae" (Col. 1:2). The people hear Paul's Letter read to them as they are gathered in sacred assembly. With this corporate setting in view, note the plurals in Colossians 3:16. "Let the word of Christ dwell in you [*plural*] richly, teaching [*masculine plural nominative participle*] and admonishing [*masculine plural nominative participle*] one another [*plural*] in all wisdom, singing [*masculine plural nominative participle*] psalms and hymns and spiritual songs, with thankfulness in

---

89. Charles Hodge, *Commentary on the Epistle to the Ephesians* (Grand Rapids: Eerdmans, 1966), 303.
90. Ibid., 505.
91. Brooke Foss Westcott, *St. Paul's Epistle to the Ephesians* (London: Macmillan, 1906), 82.

your [*plural*] hearts [*plural*] to God" (Col 3:16, ESV).

Note also the plurals within the immediate context. "Therefore if you [*plural*] have been raised up with Christ" (Col. 3:1). "[*You plural*] Set your mind on the things above" (Col. 3:2). "For you [*plural*] have died and your [*plural*] life is hidden with Christ in God" (Col. 3:3). And so on throughout the passage.

Recall that Paul refers to teaching and admonishing and uses these terms in Colossians 1:28. There, he defines teaching and admonishing as preaching or proclamation. "We proclaim Him, admonishing every man and teaching every man with all wisdom." Proclamation consisting of teaching and admonition is a corporate activity. The singing, teaching, and admonishing Paul discusses in Colossians 3:16, therefore, is of the worship setting.

14

A Brief History of Psalmody:
The First Five Centuries

Let us shout joyfully to Him with psalms.
~ Ps. 95:2

INTRODUCTION

FROM THE DAY OF PENTECOST, Christianity began to spread into all parts of the known world. "Parthians and Medes and Elamites [Modern Iran], and residents of Mesopotamia [Ancient Babylon and Modern Iraq], Judea and Cappadocia [Central Turkey], Pontus and Asia [Northern Turkey], Phrygia and Pamphylia [Central and Southern Turkey], Egypt and the districts of Libya around Cyrene [Northern Africa], and visitors from Rome" heard the gospel on that day (Acts 2:9-10). Paul preached in Damascus, Syria (Acts 9). He took the gospel into what is now Turkey (Acts 16). Although forbidden to enter Bithynia (Acts 16:7), this area of Northern Turkey near Pontus had no doubt already heard the gospel (1 Pet. 1:1). The gospel entered Greece in Corinth, Thessalonica, and other cities. The gospel pressed across North Africa through Alexandria to Cyrene by the end of the first century. By the end of the second century, the church found a home in Carthage and the gospel also penetrated what is now Spain and France.[1]

---

1. Barry J. Beitzel, *The Moody Atlas of Bible Lands* (Chicago: Moody Press, 1985), 188-189.

In 1959, Eric Werner wrote, "The paramount importance of the Psalter for the evolution and structure of Christian as well as Jewish liturgy is too well known to warrant special elaboration."[2] Decades later, it is difficult to hold Professor Werner's perspective. Chapter 11 attempted to elaborate on the place of Psalmody in the infant New Testament church. This chapter extends the discussion through the first five centuries. Part of the difficulty facing good analysis is terminology. From a twenty-first century perspective, a hymn is a hymn is a hymn, and a Psalm is a Psalm is a Psalm. The two are distinct, even to the most casual Christian observer. However, pressing back fifteen to twenty centuries, this contemporary distinction does not hold. As will be seen, the church fathers often spoke of the Psalms of Scripture as hymns. The discussion of the terms *psalms, hymns, and songs*, in chapter 11, showed that the New Testament writers considered Psalms to be hymns. In what follows, it will be shown that the identity of Psalms with hymns continues. This brief review will also show Psalmody's rich history in the first through the fifth centuries.

THE BEGINNINGS

As has been argued, Psalmody prevails in the New Testament. At the conclusion of the first celebration of the Lord's Supper, "after singing a hymn," Jesus and the disciples, "went out to the Mount of Olives" (Matt. 26:30; Mark 14:26). The words *singing a hymn* are "in Greek a single word, *hymning* (or *having hymned*), referring no doubt to the series of psalms usually chanted at the Passover and known in the latter Jewish ritual as the Great Hallel."[3] Alexander goes on to say, "There is of course no allusion to the modern distinction between psalms and hymns ... "[4] Acts 16:25 also mentions singing hymns: "About midnight Paul and Silas were praying and singing hymns of praise to God." Ralph Martin declares,

---

2. Eric Werner, *The Sacred Bridge* (New York: Schocken, 1970), 133.
3. J. A. Alexander, *Commentary on the Gospel of Mark* (Minneapolis: Klock and Klock, 1980), 382.
4. Ibid.

> There is no means of knowing the genre of the hymns which Paul and Silas sang in the Philippian jail, but if we are correct in reasoning that the human spirit, under duress and trial, turns instinctively to what is familiar and well-known, there is nothing to deny that the Psalms of the Old Testament rang through the dark prison, greatly to the interest of the missionaries' fellow-captives.[5]

In both of these Biblical examples, singing hymns means singing the Psalms. This conclusion is logical when it is realized that Psalmody derives from the temple and now, as the New Testament church, "We are the temple of the living God" (2 Cor. 6:16). It is in this light that Heb. 13:15 commands: "Through Him then, let us continually offer up a sacrifice of praise to God, that is, the fruit of lips that give thanks to His name."

> The sacrifice of thanksgiving had once been accompanied by an animal sacrifice in the temple—it was in the form of a peace-offering, according to Lev. 7:12. Animal sacrifices had been rendered forever obsolete by the sacrifice of Christ, but the sacrifice of thanksgiving might still be offered to God, and indeed should be offered to Him by all who appreciated the perfect sacrifice of Christ. No longer in association with animal sacrifices, but through Jesus, the sacrifice of praise was acceptable to God ... The sacrifice of praise is further described as "the fruit of lips which make confession of his name"... [6]

Since Psalms accompanied the animal sacrifices in the temple, it makes sense that the sacrifices of praise in the New Testament temple are the Psalms. As God specified the temple sacrifices in the Old Testament, God specifies the New Testament sacrifices of thanksgiving. Paul reminds the Ephesian Christians, "You also are being built together into a dwelling of God [a temple] in the Spirit" (Eph. 2:21-22)

---

5. Ralph P. Martin, *Worship in the Early Church* (Westwood, NJ: Fleming H. Revell, 1964), 43.
6. F. F. Bruce, *The Epistle to the Hebrews* (Grand Rapids: Eerdmans, 1964), 405.

and, in the early 60s,[7] he enjoins the practice of Psalmody among the Ephesians and Colossians (Eph. 5:19; Col. 3:16). Review the arguments in chapter 11.

As the church spread, Psalmody also spread. Peter's first letter was directed to Christians "scattered throughout *Pontus*, Galatia, Cappadocia, Asia, and *Bithynia*" (1 Pet. 1:1, italics added), and "almost surely was written in A.D. 62-63."[8] Christianity was therefore well established in Bithynia and Pontus by the end of the first century. "During the brief period that Pliny the Younger was governor of Bithynia and Pontus, in 111-12, he interrogated a group of Christian prisoners ... "[9] He is "the earliest independent witness to Christian ritual singing."[10] Writing to Emperor Trajan, Governor Pliny says of the Christians he interrogated, "They affirmed, however, the whole of their guilt, or their error, was, that they were in the habit of meeting on a certain fixed day before it was light, when they sang in alternate verses a hymn to Christ, as to a god, and bound themselves by a solemn oath, not to any wicked deeds ... "[11]

What was this hymn to Christ? Pliny does not say, and would not have known. With a twenty-first century reading, we presume a hymn is a hymn is a hymn. What else could it be? A first century reading indicates the real possibility, yes, probability, that the hymn is a Psalm. Here is Calvin's thinking. "Pliny ... writing at least forty years or so after the death of Paul, tells us that the Christians were in the habit of singing hymns to Christ before daylight. And indeed I have no doubt that from the very beginning they adopted the usage of the Jewish Church in singing psalms."[12] In Calvin's mind, Pliny's hymnody is a reference to Psalmody.

---

7. D. A. Carson and Douglas Moo, *An Introduction to the New Testament* (Grand Rapids: Zondervan, 2005), 487, 523.
8. Ibid., 646.
9. Christopher Page, *The Christian West and Its Singers: The First Thousand Years* (New Haven: Yale University Press, 2010), 10.
10. Ibid., 60.
11. Pliny the Younger, *Pliny Letters* (Cambridge: Harvard University Press, 1985), 2:403.
12. John Calvin, *The First Epistle of Paul to the Corinthians*, trans. John W. Fraser (Grand Rapids: Eerdmans), 293.

From what has just been observed, the church and Psalmody pressed north from Jerusalem into modern Turkey. It is also well known that Paul took the gospel into Greece, then on to Rome. The church and Psalmody also advanced to the south and west. Christopher Page indicates, "By approximately 200, significant traces of psalm-singing appear along the Mediterranean littoral [region along the coastline] of Africa, from Alexandria to Carthage ... "[13]

THE SECOND AND THIRD CENTURIES

Speaking of post-apostolic worship, Professor John Wilson says, "We are confronted, at the outset of this period, with the presumption in favor of the Psalms of the Bible. There is absolutely not an iota of evidence that any other songs were used in worship in Apostolic times."[14] Looking back over the church's first three centuries, Philip Schaff confesses,

> [W]e have no complete religious song remaining from the period of persecution, except the song of Clement of Alexandria [c. 150 - c. 215] to the divine Logos—which, however, cannot be called a hymn, and was probably never intended for public use—the Morning Song and the Evening Song in the Apostolic Constitutions [ca. 380] ... [15]

If Psalmody is assumed during the second and third centuries, detailed arguments in favor of Psalmody would not be expected. Quite to the contrary, one would expect to find occasional references to the use of Psalms. For example, Clement of Alexandria [c. 150 - c. 215] exhorts, "[L]et hymns to God be our songs."[16] Clement immediately

---

13. Page, *The Christian West*, 67.
14. John A. Wilson, "The Psalms in the Post-Apostolic Church," *The Psalms in Worship*, ed. John McNaugher (Pittsburgh: United Presbyterian Board of Publication, 1907), 159.
15. Philip Schaff, *History of the Christian Church* (Grand Rapids: Eerdmans, 1960), 3:578. Schaff indicates the Evening Song is "Phos Hilaron" (n. 2).
16. James McKinnon, *Music in Early Christian Literature* (Cambridge: Cambridge University Press, 1987), 34. Hereafter, MECL with item number. In this case: *Paedagogus* II, iv in *MECL* 55, with the place in Clement given first. Other footnotes, citing McKinnon's comments not found within numbered items, are given as follows: McKinnon, *MCEL*, with page number.

quotes the Psalms. "'Let them praise his name in dancing,' it is said; 'let them play to him on typmanum and psaltry' (Ps. 149.3). And who is this singing chorus? The Spirit will explain it to you. 'His praise is in the assembly of the faithful; let them rejoice in the king' (Ps 149.1-2). And again he adds, 'that the Lord takes pleasure in his people' (Ps 149.4)."[17] Here, Clement indicates that the hymns of God are the Psalms.

Clement also speaks about the importance of Psalmody in the life of the believer, whose "entire life is a sacred festival. His sacrifices are prayers and praise, converse with the Scriptures before the banquet, *psalms and hymns* at the banquet and before bed, and prayers again during the night" (italics added).[18] The doublet *psalms and hymns* is a hendiadys, a very frequently used figure of speech in which two words connected by *and* are employed, but only one thing, or idea, is intended.[19] For example, Peter speaks of Christ's *power and coming* (2 Pet. 1:16). Peter is speaking of one thing, that is, Christ's *powerful coming*.[20] Because of the historical situation within second century Christianity, Clement appears to be speaking of *psalms which are also hymns*.

Moving from Alexandria west into Carthage, one finds Tertullian (c. 155 - c. 223). "A native and life-long resident of Carthage, he was the most powerful and original Christian author writing in Latin before Augustine."[21] Tertullian refers to corporate Psalmody and to a charismatic. "There is among us today a sister favored with gifts of revelation which she experiences through an ecstasy of the spirit during the Sunday liturgy ... The material for her visions is supplied as the scriptures are read, psalms are sung, the homily delivered and prayers are offered."[22] J. A. Lamb adds, "In his *Ad Uxorem* ii, 8, he says

---

17. Ibid.
18. *Stromata* vii, vii, 49; *MECL*, 61. Italics added.
19. E. W. Bullinger, *Figures of Speech Used in the Bible* (Grand Rapids: Baker, 2004), 670. See pages 657-658 for examples from Latin and Greek Classics.
20. Ibid.
21. *McKinnom, MCEL*, 42.
22. *De anima* IX, 4; *MCEL*, 82.

that the psalms are sung alternately and even competitively by two cantors between the lessons and the sermon."[23] Note that the following quotation begins with an hendiadys. "Psalms and hymns sound between the two of them, and they challenge each other to see who sings better to the Lord. Seeing and hearing this, Christ rejoices."[24] Tertullian also makes the point that Psalms are read responsively. "The more exacting in their prayers are accustomed to add to their prayers an Alleluia and that sort of a psalm in which those present can respond with the closing verse … "[25] Finally, Tertullian makes it clear that the Psalms of David are sung in sacred assembly. "The psalms come to our aid on this point ... those of the most holy and illustrious prophet David. He sings among us of Christ, and through him Christ indeed sang of Himself."[26]

Moving back to the east is Syrian Antioch and Caesarea in Palestine. Paul of Samosata became Bishop of Antioch in 260. He was a unitarian, denying the deity of Christ and the Holy Spirit. "To introduce his Christology into the mind of the people, he undertook to alter the church hymns … "[27] He was deposed by a Synod at Antioch in 269.[28] Eusebius of Caesarea (c. 260 - c. 340) records one of the accusations, "He put a stop to those psalms addressed to our Lord Jesus Christ, on the grounds that they were new and composed by recent authors, and instead trained the women to sing to himself in the middle of the church on the great day of the Pascha—everyone hearing them would shudder."[29] Wilson asks, "What does such language mean, if not that Paul of Samosata's crime lay in setting aside the songs of inspiration as though they were of merely human authority, and substituting hymns of human composition?"[30]

---

23. John Alexander Lamb, *The Psalms in Christian Worship* (London: Faith Press, 1962), 27.
24. *Ad Uxorem* II, viii, 8-9; *MECL*, 80.
25. *De oration* XXXVII; *MCEL*, 78.
26. *De carne* Christi XX, 3; *MCEL*, 84.
27. Schaff, *History of the Christian Church*, 2:575.
28. Ibid.,576.
29. *Ecclesiastical History* VII, XXX, 10, *MECL* 211.
30. Wilson, "Psalms in the Post-Apostolic Church," 162.

Philip Schaff notes an earlier statement from Eusebius, *Ecclesiastical History* V, 8, referring to the same period. Schaff indicates that no extra-biblical hymns but only the Psalms plus certain other New Testament Scripture songs are sung in the church at Rome.

> This passage is sometimes interpreted as indicating that hymns written by Christians themselves were sung in the Church of Rome at this time. But this is by no means implied. So far as we are able to gather from our sources, nothing except Psalms and the New Testament hymns (such as Gloria in Excelsis, the Magnificat, the Nunc Dimitis, et cetera) was the rule in public worship before the fourth century.[31]

We should also recognize that Eusebius spoke of Psalms in worship as hymns. Commenting on Psalm 91:1 he says, "When formerly the people of the circumcision worshipped through symbols and types, it was not unreasonable that they raised hymns to God ... "[32] Of course, the Old Testament people of God sang Psalms in the temple liturgy. Note this connection in Eusebius's following remarks. He clearly says singing Psalms is singing hymns. Italics added.

> Formerly, when we learned the miraculous signs of God and the benefits secured for men by wondrous deeds of the Lord by hearing the divine Scriptures being read, we could raise hymns and canticles and say as we were taught: *"We have heard with our ears, O God; our fathers have told us what work thou didst perform in their days, in the days of old"* (Ps 43:1). But now as we learn of the uplifted arm and heavenly right hand of our all gracious God, not from hearsay or word of mouth, but by observing in deeds, as one might say, and with our very eyes what had been recorded as faithful and true, we can raise a

---

31. Philip Schaff in McNaughter, *Psalms in Worship*, 163.
32. *In psalmum* XCI, 4; *MECL*, 206.

second hymn of triumph, and sing out clearly, saying:
"As we have heard, so have we seen, in the city of the Lord of hosts, in the city of our God" (Ps 47.8).[33]

Eusebius therefore says, "The command to sing psalms in the name of the Lord was obeyed by everyone in everyplace ... "[34]

THE FOURTH CENTURY (PART ONE)

The fourth century is covered in two parts. First, a list of various quotations supporting Psalmody follows. The quotations are from scholars circling the Mediterranean from Alexandria, Egypt to Jerusalem and Syrian Antioch, then into what is now central Turkey, and finally to Milan in Northern Italy. Second, there is a brief review of fourth century desert monasticism, and the coordinate emphasis on Psalmody.

Athanasius (c. 295 - 373) resided in Alexandria in North Africa. He attended the Council of Nicea, Bithynia, in 325. He became bishop of Alexandria in 328. Athanasius has been quoted extensively regarding the subjective element of Psalmody, which is beneficial to the soul for two reasons. For Athanasius, hymning to God is Psalmody.

> First, because it was proper for Divine Scripture to hymn God not only with continuity but with expanse of voice ... Secondly, because as harmony creates a single concord in joining together the two pipes of the aulos, so ... reason wills that a man be not disharmonious with himself ... Hence to recite the psalms with melody is not done from a desire for pleasing sound, but is a manifestation of harmony among the thoughts of the soul. And melodious reading is a sign of the well-ordered and tranquil condition of the mind.[35]

---

33. *Ecclesiastical History* X, iv, 5-6; MECL, 214.
34. Mary Berry, "Psalmody," *Westminster Dictionary of Liturgy and Worship*, ed. J. G. Davis (Philadelphia: Westminster Press, 1986), 450.
35. *Epistula ad Marcellinum* 27, 29; MECL, 98, 100.

Moving north to Jerusalem, there is Cyril (c. 315 - 386), who was appointed bishop of Jerusalem about 349. He indicates that Psalm 32:1 [*Latin*, 31:1] celebrates Christian salvation. "Even now let there ring in your ears that sweet sound which you desire to hear the angels sing after your salvation: 'Blessed are they whose iniquities are taken away and whose sins are covered' (Ps 31.1) ... "[36] John Chrysostom (c. 347 - 407) preached in the principal church of Syrian Antioch for a decade beginning in 386 and became patriarch of Constantinople in 397. Commenting on Psalm 1, Chrysostom speaks of *melody with prophecy*. Prophecy is the Psalms, which he also calls sacred hymns. "When God saw that the majority of men were slothful, and that they approached spiritual reading with reluctance and submitted to the effort involved without pleasure—he mixed *melody with prophecy*, so that enticed by rhythm and melody, all might raise *sacred hymns* to him with great eagerness."[37] Chrysostom also speaks of the profit of Psalms in contrast to *licentious songs*. "But from the spiritual psalms can come considerable pleasure, much that is useful, much that is holy, and the foundation of all philosophy, as these texts cleanse the soul and the Holy Spirit flies swift to the soul who sings such songs."[38] Chrysostom expects the Spirit's blessing on the Psalms, the Spirit's inspired songs. And so he exhorts congregational Psalmody.

> They went out at that time holding palm branches, and they cried out and said: "Hosanna in the highest! Blessed is he who comes in the name of the Lord" (Mt 21.9). Let us also go out, and displaying in place of palm branches blossoming good intentions, let us cry out as we sang today in response: "Praise the Lord, O my soul! I will praise the Lord as long as I live" (Ps 145.2) ... But let us see what he says, "Praise the Lord, O my soul!" Let us also sing these words today along with David.[39]

---

36. *Procatechesis* XV; MECL, 155.
37. *In psalmum* i, 1; MECL, 164.
38. *In psalmum* xli, 1; MECL, 165.
39. *Homilia habita in magnum hebdomadam* 2; MECL, 175.

Now swing northwest into modern Turkey. The Council of Laodicea (c. 363-365), in Canon 59, charged, "One must not recite privately composed psalms nor non-canonical books in the church ... "[40] Gregory (c. 329 - 389) hailed from Nazianzus, in Cappadocia in what we call central Turkey. Gregory became bishop of Constantinople in 381 and was a contemporary of Basil the Great (c. 330 - 379). Basil became bishop of Caesarea, the capital of Cappadocia, in 370. Gregory reported the experience of Valens, Eastern Roman Emperor, when he visited Basil's church at Caesarea. "He entered the temple with his entire retinue about him—it was the day of Epiphany, and there was a great crowd—and he took his place among the people ... When he got inside, he was struck by the thunderous sound of the psalmody ... "[41]

Basil explains the virtue of congregational Psalmody in his homilies on the Psalms.

> What did the Holy Spirit do when he saw that the human race was not led easily to virtue, and that due to our penchant for pleasure we gave little heed to an upright life? He mixed sweetness of melody with doctrine so that inadvertently we would absorb the benefit of the words through the gentleness and ease of hearing ... Thus he contrived for us these harmonious psalm tunes, so that those who are children in actual age as well as those who are young in behavior, while appearing only to sing would in reality be training their souls. For not one of these many indifferent people ever leaves church easily retaining in memory some maxim of either the Apostles or the Prophets, but they do sing the texts of the Psalms at home and circulate them in the marketplace.[42]

> A psalm is a tranquility of soul and the arbitration of peace; it settles one's tumultuous and seething thoughts.

---
40. Quoted in *MECL*, 261.
41. *Oration* XLIII; *MECL*, 148.
42. *Homilia in psalmum* I; *MECL*, 130.

> It mollifies the soul's wrath and chastens its recalcitrance. A psalm creates friendships, unites the separated and reconciles those at enmity. Who can still consider one to be a foe with whom one utters the same prayer to God! Thus psalmody provides the greatest of all goods, charity, by devising in its common good a certain bond of unity, and by joining together the people into the concord of a single chorus.[43]

Remesiana is modern Bela Palanka, Serbia, in southern Europe. Niceta of Remesiana (c. 335 - 414) speaks to the profound usefulness of Psalmody.

> For a psalm is sweet to the ear when sung, it penetrates the soul when it gives pleasure, it is easily remembered when sung often, and what the harshness of the Law cannot force from the minds of man it excludes by the suavity of song. For whatever the Law, the Prophets and even the Gospels teach is contained as a remedy in the sweetness of these songs.[44]

Ambrose (c. 339 - 397) became bishop of Milan in northern Italy in 374. He too emphasizes the subjective element in Psalmody.

> It softens anger, it gives release from anxiety, it alleviates sorrow; it is protection at night, instruction by day, a shield in time of fear, a feast of holiness, the image of tranquility, a pledge of peace and harmony, which produces one song from various and sundry voices ... The Apostle admonishes women to be silent in church, yet they do well to join in a psalm; this is gratifying for all ages and fitting for both sexes ... Kings put aside the arrogance of power and sing a psalm, as David himself was glad to be observed in this function; a psalm, then, is sung by emperors and rejoiced in by the people ... A

---

43. *Homilia in psalmum* i, 2; MECL, 131.
44. *De ultimate hymnorum* 5; MECL, 306.

> psalm joins those with differences, unites those at odds and reconciles those who have been offended, for who will not concede to him with whom one sings to God in one voice? It is after all a great bond of unity for the full number of people to join in one chorus.[45]

This section of the discussion ends with a reference to fourth century Psalmody by William Clebsch. "By Athanasius's time the memorization of the Psalms by many Christians and their habitual use as songs in worship by all Christians we know about were matters of long standing tradition."[46] Psalmody was a regular feature of Christian worship through the fourth century.

THE FOURTH CENTURY (PART TWO)

> St. Antony, a Christian ascetic of Alexandria, left the city about 285 to live in the desert as a hermit. After some twenty years of solitary existence ... he organized a number of other hermits into a loosely knit community; at that moment, one might say, Christian monasticism was born ... Monasticism spread rapidly from its Egyptian cradle to the deserts of Palestine and Syria ... [47]

James McKinnon links monasticism with "an unprecedented wave of enthusiasm for the singing of psalms that swept from east to west through the Christian population in the closing decades of the fourth century."[48] Christopher Page argues that monastic Psalmody was a natural outgrowth of a centuries-old emphasis on Psalmody.

> This suggests that the psalmodic movement was not necessarily a new wave of enthusiasm for psalmody, but rather a movement that took ascetics long accustomed

---

45. *Explanatio psalmi* i, 9; *MECL*, 276.
46. William Clebsch, "Preface," in Athanasius, *The Life of Anthony and the Letter to Marcellinus* (New York: Paulist Press, 1980), xviii.
47. James W. McKinnon, "Desert Monasticism and the Later Fourth-Century Psalmodic Movement," *Music and Letters* 75:4 (1994): 505.
48. Ibid.

to make psalmody part of their domestic round into a new predominately rural environment. Once there, their lives attracted an unprecedented amount of comment from two generations of writers including Athanasius (d. 373), Basil (d. 379), Gregory of Nyssa (d. 395), Ambrose (d. 397), John Chrysostom (d. 407), Jerome (d. 420), and Augustine (d. 430) ... The enthusiasm of this group for psalmody reveals the desire to extol the life of desert monks, which developed among a remarkable group of intellectuals who were mostly so inspired by the monastic life of the desert that they chose to experience it for a time themselves and regarded it as an ideal which all Christians could use to measure their weaknesses and sharpen their aspirations.[49]

"As the fourth century progressed, the desert monks came to participate in what might properly be called an Office."[50] The Divine Office states the hours for daily prayers and psalmody to be followed by members of religious orders or by individuals. "Two times each day were singled out for special prayer and psalmody, morning and evening, times sanctified in Christian tradition and in Judaism as well."[51] Much of the information we have about monastic Psalmody comes from John Cassian (c. 360 - 435). "Believed to have been born in Scythia—modern Rumania—he is first observed as a monk at Bethlehem. In about 385 he left to spend several years studying monasticism in Egypt."[52] Cassian writes, "Thus, as we have said, the number of twelve psalms is preserved throughout all Egypt and the Thebaid at the evening and the night offices, in such a way that afterwards two readings follow, one each from the Old and New Testaments."[53] As Old observes, "By chanting twelve psalms per service, the monks

---

49. Page, *The Christian West*, 136.
50. McKinnon, "Desert Monasticism," 507.
51. Ibid.
52. McKinnon, *MECL*, 146.
53. *De instetutis* II, 4; *MECL*, 337.

would recite the entire Psalter each week."⁵⁴ This Psalmody used the *lectio continua* method. "What is certain about the authentic Egyptian Office is the continuous psalmody, interspersed with prayer ... "⁵⁵ At the same time, each Psalm was broken down into segments. "And therefore they do not even try to complete the very psalms they sing at their assembly in an unbroken recitation, but work through them section by section, according to the number of verses, in two or three segments with prayers in between ... "⁵⁶

"A host of eminent ecclesiastical figures visited Egypt to admire and study the heroic lives of the monks and nuns in residence there ... They helped to foster the dramatic development of monasticism as it spread from east to west, and from the deserts to the cities."⁵⁷ In the cities, the monastic example affected the churches. McKinnon puts it this way: "After the emancipation of the Church in 313, however, public morning and evening Offices became normalized to constitute the so called 'cathedral office' of the fourth century."⁵⁸ In this context are found Chrysostom's well-known words:

> In the churches there are vigils, and David is first and middle and last. In the singing of early morning hymns David is first and middle and last. In the tents at funeral processions David is first and last ... In the monasteries there is a holy chorus of angelic hosts, and David is first and middle and last. In the convents there are bands of virgins who imitate Mary, and David is first and middle and last. In the deserts men crucified to this world hold converse with God, and David is first and middle and last.⁵⁹

---

54. Hughes Oliphant Old and Robert Cathart, "From Cassian to Cranmer: Singing the Psalms from Ancient Times until the Dawning of the Reformation," *Sing a New Song*, ed. Joel Beeke and Anthony T. Selvaggio (Grand Rapids: Reformation Heitage, 2010), 3.
55. McKinnon, "Desert Monasticism," 507.
56. *De instetutis* II, 11; *MECL* 342.
57. McKinnon, "Desert Monasticism," 508.
58. Ibid., 509-510. "The [Milan] edict of 313 not only recognized Christianity within existing limits, but allowed every subject of the Roman Empire to choose whatever religion he preferred" (Schaff, 3:29-30).
59. McKinnon, "Desert Monasticism," 509 and *MECL* 195.

The *Apostolic Constitutions* give us a look at the liturgy of late fourth century Syrian Antioch. Introducing Book VIII, Section xiii, of the *Constitutions*, McKinnon says, "There are two points of musical significance here: Psalm 33 with its highly relevant verse 8, 'O taste and see that the Lord is good,' is sung during the distribution of Communion; and the cantor (*psaltes*) is listed among the clerical orders receiving."[60] The cantor, *psaltes*, is the song leader or precentor. Here is another place where the Psalms are called hymns: "After two readings let someone else sing the hymns of David."[61] The *Apostolic Constitutions* also encouraged the daily offices.

> As you teach, O bishop, order and exhort the people always to assemble in the church morning and evening each day ... For it is said not only of priests, but rather each of the laity must hear it and consider it for himself ... But you must assemble each day, morning and evening, singing psalms and praying in the houses of the Lord, saying the sixty-second psalm in the morning, and in the evening the hundred and fortieth ... [62]

McKinnon adds this description of the fourth century liturgy.

> In the morning, a careful selection of psalms was sung, always including Psalm 62 [*Latin*], "Oh God my God, I rise before thee at the break of day"; in several liturgies, the "Gloria in excelsis" was also sung, while virtually all of them concluded with intercessory prayers and the blessing of the bishop. At some point in the fourth century (whether earlier or later is disputed) were added Psalms 148-50, the set of alleluia psalms that would eventually become the Lauds psalms par excellence. The evening service opened with the lucernarium, the ceremony of lamp-lighting, which was accompanied in

---

60. McKinnon, *MECL*, 109.
61. *Apostolic Constitutions* II, lvii, *MECL* 233.
62. *Apostolic Constitutions* II, lix, *MECL* 236.

some localities by "Phos hilaron," the hymn that celebrates Jesus Christ as light. The obligatory psalm of the evening service was Psalm 140 [*Latin*], with its appropriate second verse, "Let my prayer be directed to thee as incense, and the lifting up of my hands as an evening sacrifice."[63]

Although other songs and hymns were beginning to creep into the cathedral office, "the hallmark of monasticism remained psalmody," and it can also "be said that the cathedral Office was imbued with the continuous psalmody of monasticism."[64]

FIFTH CENTURY

John Cassian (c. 360-435) sojourned in Egypt for fifteen years to study monasticism there and later established a monastery and convent in Marseilles in present day France in 415. Cassian wrote two important works on monasticism, the *De institutis* and the *Collationes partum*.[65] "Books II and III of *De institutis* give detailed information for the order of psalmody to be followed in the monastic office."[66] Cassian implemented the Egyptian model for the monastic office including the use of twelve Psalms *lectio continua*. He observed: "This arrangement, established long ago, has endured intact in all the monasteries of those regions through so many ages up to the present day, because it is said by the elders not to have been established by human invention but to have been brought down to the fathers from heaven through the agency of an angel."[67] Cassian's placement of the doxological response to the Psalms is a change from what he observed in Egypt: "And what we have seen in this province, that after one sings to the end of the psalm, all stand and sing aloud, 'Glory be to the Father and to the Son, and to the Holy Spirit,' we have never heard

---

63. McKinnon, "Desert Monasticism," 507.
64. Ibid., 510.
65. McKinnon, *MECL*, 146.
66. Ibid.
67. *De institutis* II, 4; *MECL*, 337.

throughout the entire east."⁶⁸ As in the case of many others, Cassian speaks of the Psalms as hymns.

> We ought to know this, that nothing concerning the ancient custom of psalmody was changed by our elders ... For the hymns which they have adopted in this region at the morning office ... that is the one hundred and forty-eighth, which begins, 'Praise the Lord from the heavens,' and the rest which follow ... Finally, the fiftieth psalm is sung today after the completion of the morning hymns in every church throughout Italy, a practice I do not doubt derived from no other source but here.⁶⁹

Residents of the monasteries and other devout Christians also kept the daily offices, along with the morning and evening offices. Cassian indicates that the morning offices were, however, conflated on the Lord's Day: "But one ought also to know that on the Lord's Day only one office is conducted before mealtime. Out of respect for this meeting itself as well as the Lord's communion they employ at it a more solemn and extended form of psalmody, prayers and readings ... "⁷⁰ Cassian speaks of similar practices in "the monasteries of Palestine, Mesopotamia and all of the east."⁷¹ From east to west, devotions and worship were Psalm-filled in the fifth century churches and monasteries.

Egeria was a Spanish nun who recorded her pilgrimage to Jerusalem. McKinnon dates her journey to the beginning of the fifth century.⁷² She describes the daily and cathedral offices. In her descriptions, Egeria refers to the *Anastasis*, the Church of the Holy Sepulcher in Jerusalem called the Church of the Resurrection by the Eastern Church. It is built over the site of the crucifixion and tomb of Christ. The *monazontes*, those living alone, are monks. The *parthenae*, virgins, are

---

68. *De institutis* II, 8; *MECL*, 340.
69. *De institutis* III, 6; *MECL*, 348.
70. *De institutis* III, 3; *MECL*, 350.
71. *De institutis* III, 11; *MECL*, 346.
72. McKinnon, *MECL*, 112.

nuns. The *cave* is Christ's tomb. Considering what has been already shown, it is not unusual for her to speak of Psalms as hymns. Speaking of the fifth century use of *antiphons*, McKinnon notes, "By this time it was customary to use the term in virtually every passage that mentioned extended psalm singing, particularly in monastic rules where references to 'antiphons,' 'psalms' and 'responses' meant, apparently, that psalms were sung in a variety of ways ... "[73] Egeria reports:

> Each day before cockcrow, all the doors of the Anasatsis are opened, and all the *monazontes* and *parthenae*, as they are called here, come down, and not only they, but also those lay people, men and women, who wish to keep vigil at so early an hour. From that hour until light, hymns are sung and psalms responded to, and likewise antiphons; and with every hymn there is a prayer.[74]

At this time, there does not seem to have been a strong push away from Psalmody and toward hymnody, as understood from a twenty-first century perspective. The Council of Chalcedon, a city in Bithyinia in what is now northern Turkey, met in 451. The Council summarily reaffirmed the prohibition of the use of "privately composed psalms" by the Council of Laodicea (c. 363-365).[75] "We have judged it right that the canons of the Holy Fathers made in every synod even until now, should remain in force" (Canon 1). The habit of thought and speech was that Psalms were called hymns. "Indeed, the psalms had in earlier centuries been regarded as hymns ... "[76] Concerning hymnody, Schaff reports that with minor exceptions, "the Greek church of the first six centuries produced nothing in this field which has had permanent value or general use. It long adhered almost exclusively

---

73. McKinnon, "Desert Monasticism," 515. See also Robert F. Taft, "Liturgical Christian Psalmody: Origins, Development, Decomposition, Collapse," *Psalms in Community*, ed Harold W. Attridge and Margot E Fassler (Atlanta: Society of Biblical Literature, 2003), 17-20.
74. *Itinerarium Egeriae* xxiv, 1; *MECL*, 242.
75. Schaff, *History of the Christian Church*, 3:579.
76. Berry, "Hymns," 262.

to the Psalms of David ... "[77] Egeria's reports are consistent with this generalization.

Egeria also gives us a look at the beginning of the Lord's Day. It was the practice of the clergy to sing and the people to observe during part of the Lord's Day activities.

> On the seventh day, however, that is the Lord's Day... as soon as the first cock crows, straightway the bishop comes down and enters the cave of the Anastasis. All the gates are opened, the entire throng enters the Anastasis, where already countless lamps are burning, and when the people are within, one of the priests sings a psalm and all respond, after which there is prayer. Then one of the deacons sings a psalm, similarly followed by prayer, and a third psalm is sung by some cleric, followed by a third prayer and the commemoration by all ... As soon as the bishop withdraws to his house, the monks right from that very hour return to Anastasis and psalms and antiphons are sung until it is light ... When it is light, however, because it is the Lord's Day, they go to the greater church, which Constantine built, the church on Golgotha [adjacent to Anastasis] ... Indeed, since the custom here is such that as many of the priests sitting in attendance preach as wish to, and after all of them the bishop preaches ... [78]

Augustine (354-430) was born in Thagaste, studied rhetoric in Carthage, moved to Rome, and began to teach rhetoric in Milan in 384. He came under the influence of Ambrose who had become the bishop of Milan a decade earlier. Returning to Thagaste, he formed a monastery and then became bishop of Hippo in 396 where he labored for the next thirty-five years. Thagaste is in northeast Algeria, about 150 miles west of the ancient site of Carthage in Tunisia. Hippo, modern

---

77. Schaff, *History of the Christian Church*, 3:579.
78. *Itinerarium Egeriae* xxiv; *MECL*, 247-250.

Annaba, is roughly 60 miles north northwest of Thagaste on the Mediterranean coast. Augustine expresses the "intense pleasure he experienced in listening to the psalmody in Ambrose's church at Milan ... "[79]

> How much I wept at your hymns and canticles, deeply moved by the voices of your sweetly singing church. Those voices flowed into my ears, and the truth poured into my heart, whence a feeling of piety surged up and my tears down ... Not long since had the church at Milan begun this mode of consolation and exhortation, with the brethren singing zealously together with voice and heart.[80]

Augustine beautifully sets forth the subjective element of Psalmody and his own wrestling with truth versus the gratifications received from the melody of the songs. There will be further discussion of the priority of text over tune in Part Four of this study.

> Now I confess that I repose just a little in those sounds to which your words give life, when they were sung by a sweet and skilled voice; not such that I cling to them, but I rise out of them when I wish. But it is with the words by which they have life that they gain entry into me, and seek in my heart a place of some honor, even if I scarcely provide them a fitting one. Sometimes I seem to myself to grant them more respect than is fitting, when I sense that our souls are more piously and earnestly moved to the ardor of devotion by these sacred words when they are thus sung than when not thus sung, and that all the affections of our soul, by their own diversity, have their proper measures in voice and song, which are stimulated by I know not what secret correspondence. But the gratification of my flesh—to which I ought not to surrender my mind to be enervated—frequently leads me

---

79. McKinnon, "Desert Monasticism," 518.
80. *Confessions* IX, vi, 14 - vii, 15; *MECL*, 351.

astray, as the senses do not accompany reason in such a way as patiently to follow; but having gained admission only because of it, seek even to run ahead and lead it. I sin thus in these things unknowingly, but afterward I know.

Sometimes, however, in avoiding this deception too vigorously, I err by excessive severity, and sometimes so much so that I wish every melody of the sweet songs to which the Davidic Psalter is usually set, to be banished from my ears and from the church itself …

However, when I recall the tears which I shed at the song of the church in the first days of my recovered faith, and even now as I am moved not by the song but by the things which are sung, when sung with fluent voice and music that is most appropriate, I acknowledge again the great benefit of this practice. Thus I vacillate between the peril of pleasure and the value of experience, and I am led more … to endorse the custom of singing in church so that by the pleasure of hearing the weaker soul might be elevated to an attitude of devotion. Yet when it happens to me that the song moves me more than the thing which is sung, I confess that I have sinned blamefully … O Lord my God, give ear, look and see, have pity and heal me, in whose sight I have become an enigma unto myself; and this itself is my weakness.[81]

Augustine also finds the eschatological thrust of the Psalter in their titles. An example is his comment on Psalm 67:1 (LXX), in which he reminds his congregation of the meaning of "in the end" [*eis to telos*].

The title of this psalm seems not to require laborious discussion, but appears to be simple and easy. For it stands thus: "In the end, for David himself, a psalm of a song."

---

81. *Confessions* X, xxxii, 49-50; *MECL*,352.

A BRIEF HISTORY OF PSALMODY: THE FIRST FIVE CENTURIES 331

> In many psalms already, we have advised you what "in the end" means, since "Christ is the end of the Law, that everyone who has faith may be justified" (Rom 10.4); he is the end who perfects, not who consumes or destroys.[82]

In his expositions of the Psalms, Augustine also frequently refers to having just sung a portion or a response from a Psalm. "The psalm which we have just now heard sung and responded to in singing, is short and highly beneficial."[83] "We sang to the Lord and said, 'To thee the poor man left; thou will be a helper to the orphan' (Ps 9.14 [10:14 MT])."[84] "For you were singing this, 'Save us, O Lord our God, and gather us from among the heathen, then we may give thanks to your holy name' (Ps 105.47 [LXX])."[85] "The voice of the penitent is recognized in the words with which we respond to the singer (*psallenti*): 'Hide thy face from my [sins], and blot out my iniquities' (Ps 50.11 [LXX])."

Finally, we note that Augustine continues the Biblical practice of referring to Psalms as songs or canticles, and also as hymns. "This indeed we have sung: 'I will extol thee, O Lord, for thou hast drawn me up, and hast not let my foes rejoice over me' (Ps 29.1 [LXX]). If we have learned from the Holy Scriptures who are our enemies, we know the truth of this canticle … "[86] "Meanwhile a certain Hilary … attacked the custom which had begun then in Carthage … of singing at the altar hymns from the Book of Psalms … "[87]

CONCLUSION

A has been seen, Psalmody accompanied the expansion of the church all around the Mediterranean from Palestine into Asia Minor, Southern Europe, Italy, and North Africa. Schaff points out that the Greek church in the East "long adhered almost exclusively to the Psalms of

---

82. *In psalmum* lxvii, 1; MECL, 359.
83. *In psalmum* cxix, 1; MECL, 364.
84. *Sermo* XIV, *de uerso* 14, *psalmi* ix, 1; MECL, 369.
85. *Sermo* CXCVIII, *de calendis Januariis* II, 1-2; MECL, 372.
86. *In psalmum* xxix, II, 1; MECL, 354.
87. *Liber retractationum* II, 37; MECL, 385.

David ..."[88] He then adds, "After the fifth century, the Greek church lost its prejudice against poetry, and produced a great but slightly known abundance of sacred songs for public worship."[89] Up to this time, "biblical psalmody was seen as the antidote to 'private psalms' [*psalmoi idiotikoi*]—that is, non-biblical refrains and hymns—often used by heretics to propagate their doctrine."[90] Recall that these 'private psalms' were prohibited by the councils of Laodicea and Chalcedon.

Schaff is generous in his assessment of the development of hymnody in the West. "More important than the Greek hymnology is the Latin from the fourth to the sixteenth century ... The two patriarchs of Latin church poetry, Hilary and Ambrose, were the champions of orthodoxy against Arianism in the West."[91] Hilary (c. 300-c. 368), Bishop of Poitiers, France, may have been the first hymn writer of the Latin church, but Ambrose (c. 339-397), Bishop of Milan, is the most well known.[92] Although credited with thirty to one hundred hymns, only twelve are considered genuine; the most famous being *Te Deum laudimous*.[93]

It appears that toward the end of the fifth century and the beginning of the sixth century and into the seventh century, communion cathedral psalmody became overgrown with non-biblical hymns and responses. "This strangling, in favor of the ecclesiastical refrain, of what was the most important element of the whole liturgical movement, the scriptural text, is a common phenomenon throughout the history of liturgical hymnody."[94] Even though this "strangling" may have occurred, liturgical scholar Robert Taft assures us, "By all accounts, Christian liturgical psalmody was a huge success, if we can believe the patristic witnesses of late antiquity."[95] The history of

---

88. Schaff, *History of the Christian Church*, 3:579.
89. Ibid., 580.
90. Taft, *Liturgical Christian Psalmody*, 24.
91. Schaff, *History of the Christian Church*, 3:585.
92. Ibid., 589-590.
93. Ibid., 591-592.
94. Taft, *Liturgical Christian Psalmody*, 31.
95. Ibid., 23.

Psalmody continues in the next chapter with a look at the declension in the medieval church and its restoration in the time of the Reformation.

15

A Brief History of Psalmody: Medieval Declension and Reformation Restoration

Sing unto him, sing psalms unto Him. ~ Ps. 105:2

SOME HISTORICAL CONTEXT

THE MEDIEVAL PERIOD or the Middle Ages span the thousand years from the fall of Rome in the West (476) to the fall of Constantinople in the East (1435). Constantine (272-337) was Emperor in the West from 306 to 337. Licinus (c. 263-325) was Emperor in the East from 308 to 324. When Licinus married Constantine's half sister in Milan, the emperors jointly issued the Edict of Milan (313) granting religious tolerance. Civil war then ensued, and Constantine defeated Licinus. In 330, Constantine moved the imperial capital to Byzantium and renamed it Constantinople. It proved impossible to hold the Empire together. Theodosius (347-395) was the last Emperor to rule over both the eastern and western portions of the Roman Empire (379-395). Romulus Augustus (c. 460-c. 500) was the last emperor of the Western Empire. Germanic tribes sacked the city of Rome in 476. Rome's fall marked the beginning of the Middle Ages. Augustine wrote his *City of God* in the aftermath of, and in response to, the fall of Rome. Ecclesiastical strains paralleled political tensions, in part, because Latin prevailed in the Western Empire while Greek prevailed in the Eastern Empire.

The Church recognized by the Empire formally divided in 1054. This divided church then formed what became the Latin-based Roman Catholic Church and the Greek-based Eastern Orthodox Church. Constantinople fell to the Turks in 1435, marking the end of the Roman Empire in the East.[1]

Recent Reformed writers reviewing Psalmody gloss over this thousand-year period. Terry Johnson devotes two short paragraphs out of twenty pages.[2] In the seventeen pages of a chapter titled "The Ministry of Praise," Hughes Oliphant Old devotes one paragraph to the Middle Ages.[3] Michael Bushell devotes a paragraph to the Middle Ages as he begins a discussion of "Calvin and the Origin of Reformed Psalmody."[4] He says, "By the time of the Reformation, vernacular Psalm-singing was all but dead. We cannot stop here to trace the decline, because it has no direct bearing on our own practice or on our understanding of the practice of the Apostolic Church."[5] Part of the difficulty in looking at the middle Ages is that the traditions of both the Roman Catholic Church and the Eastern Orthodox Churches, which emerge in the Middle Ages, are very foreign to contemporary Reformed and Evangelical churches. However, understanding the reasons behind the decline in Psalmody during this period is helpful in evaluating its status in the church today. It will be seen *why* and *how* Psalmody, over time, was removed from the people. Seeing this picture provides a frame of reference for the restoration of Psalmody among the Reformed churches of the Reformation, and the pursuit of modern hymnody in the Lutheran Churches.

SOME BASIC DISTINCTIONS

Taft says, "Essential to any understanding of Christian liturgical psalmody is the by now classic distinction of Christian liturgy and

---

1. Philip Schaff, *History of the Christian Church* (Grand Rapids: Eerdmans, 1960), 4:5-7; William L.Holladay, *The Psalms through Three Thousand Years* (Minneapolis: Fortress, 1996), 161-162.
2. Terry Johnson, "The History of Psalm Singing," *Sing a New Song*, ed. Joel R. Beeke and Anthony T. Selvaggio (Grand Rapids: Reformation Heritage, 2010), 46-47.
3. Hughes Oliphant Old, *Worship That Is Reformed According to Scripture* (Atlanta: John Knox, 1984), 47.
4. Michael Bushell, *The Songs of Zion* (Norfolk, VA: Norfolk Press, 2011), 259-260.
5. Ibid.

its attendant psalmody into monastic and cathedral."[6] We discussed this distinction in chapter 14, noting two other distinctions. First, the monastic's "interest was ... in conforming their hearts to the word of God. This is quite different from cathedral offices, in which the psalmody is our praise of God rather than his saving word to us."[7] Recall that Michael Lefebvre makes this distinction.[8] Second, the *enarxis*, sometimes referred to as the *synaxis*, is distinguished from the Eucharist in the East or the Mass in the West. What is the *enarxis* or *synaxis*? "This is the preliminary office attached to the Eucharist ... "[9] Or, as the *Catholic Encyclopedia* puts it, "We must distinguish the liturgical (eucharistic) from the aliturgical Synaxis, which consisted only of prayers, readings, psalms, out of which our Divine Office evolved." In other words, the cathedral office became a meeting before and attached to the Mass or Eucharist. There were thus three entities: one, monastic devotions performed at prescribed times or the monastic daily offices; two, similar worship performed corporately in the cathedrals at prescribed times or the cathedral daily offices; and three, celebrations of the Lord's Supper or the Latin Mass in the West and the Eucharist in the East.

A SNAPSHOT OF MEDIEVAL PSALMODY

As Robert Taft rightly observes, "Psalmody of some sort was a factor in Christian worship from the start ... "[10] In the West, the "Rule" formulated by St. Benedict became the standard for monasticism. Joseph Dyer says, "Every monk was expected to memorize all 150 psalms ... St. Benedict [c. 480-547], taking as his model the monasteries attached to the Roman basilicas, recommended the weekly recitation of the psalter ... "[11] Taft also reminds us that when Latin or Syriac texts

---

6. Robert F. Taft, "Christian Liturgical Psalmody: Origins, Development, Decomposition, Collapse," *Psalms in Community*, ed. Harold W. Attbridge and Margot E. Fassler (Atlanta: Society of Biblical Literature, 2003), 9.
7. Ibid., 11.
8. Michael LeFebvre, *Sing the Songs of Jesus* (Fearn: Christian Focus, 2010), 15ff.
9. John Alexander Lamb, *The Psalms in Christian Worship* (London: Faith Press, 1962), 50.
10. Taft, "Christian Liturgical Psalmody," 8.
11. Joseph Dyer, "The Singing of Psalms in the Early Medieval Office," *Speculum* 64:3 (July, 1989), 535.

"refer to the psalms being 'said,' this simply means they are executed aloud orally; it in no way implies that they are 'spoken' as opposed to 'chanted' or 'sung'... "[12] In fact, "The psalms, in contrast to the prayers and readings of the Office, were performed nearly always in a manner resembling singing rather than nonmusical recitation."[13] As for the Benedictine Rule, "[I]n the ninth century, its plan for the weekly recitation of the psalter became the norm of the monastic Office."[14] These recitations involved two or more monks taking turns chanting the Psalms. "This solo psalmody ... was normative in early-medieval monasticism in the West, just as it was in the East."[15] However, "By the ninth century choral psalmody seems to have become more common ... "[16] As Dyer adds, "The simultaneous singing of psalm verses by a large group of untrained singers demanded the development of some general principles that could be followed by the entire choir ... Standardization and discipline became high priorities."[17]

This move toward standardization resulted in new developments in singing the Psalms. Dyer describes the situation this way: "The advent of choral psalmody stimulated theorists to standardize the melodies to which the psalms were sung and to prescribe the class of antiphons with which each formula should properly be used."[18] Antiphons are short sentences sung before or after a psalm portion used "as a simple frame for the singing of the psalm."[19] As Holladay indicates, "In the centuries that followed, recitation of the Divine office became the regimen of prayer not only for monks and nuns but for secular [non-monastic or cathedral] priests as well."[20]

Eastern monastic Psalmody for use in the daily offices developed in a similar way. In what follows, *Kathismata* are divisions of the Psalter

---

12. Taft, "Christian Liturgical Psalmody," 8, n. 3.
13. Dyer, "The Singing of Psalms," 538.
14. Ibid.
15. Ibid., 544.
16. Ibid., 546.
17. Ibid
18. Ibid., 568.
19. Ibid.
20. Holladay, *The Psalms Through Three Thousand Years*, 177.

used in the Eastern Orthodox Church. *Stasies* are subdivisions. "The Psalter is divided into twenty *Kathismata*, each of which consists of three *Stasies* ... When the *Kathismata* are recited, *Gloria Patri* is said, not at the end of each psalm, but at the end of each *Stasis*."[21] As these developments occurred in monastic psalmody, they followed in cathedral psalmody. "By the fifth century, Palestinian monks were even assisting in the performance of the cathedral offices ... "[22] Therefore, Taft indicates, "Furthermore, cathedral offices were popular services for nonprofessionals ... The psalmody of these cathedral services was designed for popular participation by the ordinary laity, many of whom were illiterate."[23]

In the meantime, books were developed for monastic libraries, with summaries of what should be recited in the divine office each day for an entire year. These books were called *breviaries* and they offered opportunity for some lay people to recite the divine office.[24] "On the continent of Europe the use of such books by lay people as well as clerics was encouraged by the new literacy that came during the Carolingian period [750-987][25] (that is, after Charlemagne)."[26] Holladay, therefore, concludes, "The Psalms, then, were perceived to be the property of lay Christians in a way that the rest of the Scriptures were not ... The 'Earlier Rule' of St. Francis (1221) offers the following on the divine office: 'All the brothers, whether clerical or lay, should celebrate the Divine Office, the praises and prayers, as is required of them.'"[27]

Turning to the Mass and Eucharist, Lamb points out, "By the fifth century, certain formulas of the Canon of the Mass were in existence ... By a.d. 1000 the Roman rite was pretty well fixed apart from minor details ... Between a.d. 1000 and 1570 small changes continued to

---

21. Lamb, *The Psalms in Christian Worship*, 61-62; Holladay, *The Psalms Through Three Thousand Years*, 182-183.
22. Taft, "Christian Liturgical Psalmody," 13.
23. Ibid., 16-17.
24. Holladay, *The Psalms Through Three Thousand Years*, 177.
25. Schaff, *History of the Christian Church*, 4:615-620.
26. Ibid., 178.
27. Holladay, *The Psalms Through Three Thousand Years*, 178.

take place."[28] As for the Psalms, "Their place is normally between the lections [Scripture readings], which has been a place for psalmody as far back as records can take us. At this point nothing else is being done; the psalms are sung, not as an accompaniment to other rite or ceremony, but as themselves a vital part of the service."[29] Lamb adds, "Another important psalmody is sung during the communion of the people, or of the priest if the people do not communicate."[30]

There were also various liturgies used in the East. The Eucharist was in two parts, one for catechumens preparing for baptism and the other only for communicants. In the former, "lections were read ... sermons were delivered partly to interpret and expound the Scriptures, partly to teach the people the Christian faith. This was also a regular place for psalmody, which appears consistently between the lessons, but in some forms also at other points."[31] Again in another liturgy, "The customary place for the psalms in this section is clearly between the lessons... "[32] What about the second part of the Eucharist? "It is during the Communion that psalms are commonly sung."[33]

DEVELOPMENTS SQUEEZING OUT PSALMODY

There can be little doubt that Psalmody was the backbone of the divine office, both monastic and cathedral, in the early Middle Ages.[34] As has been seen, Psalmody was also imbedded in the celebration of the Mass in the West and the Eucharist in the East. Both cultural and liturgical developments served to squeeze out popular Psalmody and to deprive the people of involvement in this aspect of worship. There are three developments in particular that have the consequence, perhaps unintentional, of silencing popular Psalmody. First, the development of language differences between the church and the people.

---

28. Lamb, *The Psalms in Christian Worship*, 80.
29. Ibid., 82.
30. Ibid., 97.
31. Ibid., 51.
32. Ibid., 53.
33. Ibid.
34. Holladay, *The Psalms Through Three Thousand Years*, 182.

Second, the proliferation of the use of antiphons that squeeze out the Psalms. And third, the use of antiphons that interpret and frame the Psalms and thus tend to change their meaning. The church in the twenty-first century is subject to each of these developments in varying degrees. These three developments are examined in detail.

First, the development of language differences between the church and the people. The early Middle Ages (c. 500-1000) witnessed the decline of the Western Roman Empire. Church historian Kenneth Latourette calls this period the "Great Recession."[35] Except for the Carolingian renaissance under Charlemagne (c. 742-814), this period is known by others as the Dark Ages.[36] "In much of the West, the common Latin speech was the basic means of communication … "[37] However, the literacy of the people depended upon the presence of state funded "grammar masters" in various cities.[38] What happened when this system disintegrated with the decline of the Western Empire? "The task of giving an authoritative example of proficient Latin speech, as of accomplished Latin writing, principally fell to the bishops and higher clergy."[39] Christopher Page argues that "all the essential conditions were present for the rise of diglossia: a state when 'two or more varieties of the same language are used by some speakers under different conditions.'"[40]

The church liturgy was set forth in what we may call *high* Latin, rather than in the *vernacular*. Page points out: "No manuscript of chant has been found which provides substantial evidence for the liturgy being sung in anything other than a hypercorrect Latin with most developments in the common speech or *sermo vulgaris* diligently suppressed."[41] Page assesses this result:

---

35. Kenneth Scott Latourette, *A History of Christianity* (New York: Harper and Row, 1953), 269-277.
36. B. K. Kuiper, *The Church in History* (Grand Rapids: Eerdmans, 1973), 54.
37. Christopher Page, *The Christian West and its Singers* (New Haven: Yale University Press, 2010), 205.
38. Ibid., 198.
39. Ibid., 200.
40. Ibid., 205.
41. Ibid., 207.

> As many linguists have observed, in situations where the higher register of the language in a diglossic situation is required, speakers who cannot wield it cannot simply use their colloquial idiom and get by. *The expectation is that they will remain silent.* In most chants of the Eucharistic liturgy, it seems, that is exactly what happened.[42]

Remember, there was no printing during this period and there were no printed books. The access the common people had to the Psalms and to Psalmody was principally through the church's liturgy. As a language difference developed, it deprived the people of the Psalms and of participation in Psalmody. As Page observes, "If this is correct, then the silencing of the laity belongs in the political and social context of the Empire."[43]

Second, the use of antiphons tended to squeeze out the Psalms. This squeezing out of the Psalms was true East and West, in cathedral worship and in the Eucharist or Mass. Of Eastern cathedral worship, Taft says,

> The psalmody of these cathedral services was designed for popular participation by the ordinary laity, many of whom were illiterate. In any case, before the advent of printing they would not have owned psalters, nor, unlike the monks and professional psalmists, did they know the psalter by heart. Thus their active participation in the psalmody was assured by providing them with short, easily remembered responses or refrains that they could repeat after the psalm verses chanted aloud by a professional soloist. This psalmody took two forms: responsorial psalmody and its later elaboration, antiphonal psalmody ... Responsorial psalmody consists in the congregation repeating a "respond"—a psalm verse or a short exclamation such as Alleluia—after each segment

---

42. Ibid., 197-198. Italics in the original.
43. Ibid., 207.

> or verse of the psalm intoned by the soloist ... Antiphonal psalmody, from the Greek verb [*antophōnein*], to respond alternately, is an elaboration of the responsorial method ... The people, divided into two choirs, respond alternately—hence the name "antiphonal"—to the verses of the psalm chanted by a soloist ... [44]

Alexander Lingas describes what commenced to take place in Eastern cathedral services. "Beginning in the seventh century, the churches of Jerusalem and the nearby monastery of Saint Sabas fostered the composition of hymns for intercalation [insertion] between the biblical psalms and canticles of the Horologon (the 'Book of Hours' containing the Palestinian Divine Office)."[45] The insertion of these hymns was a clear devolution of the liturgy.

> By the twelfth century the process of farcing [padding] Studite[46] psalmody with hymnody was virtually complete, bequeathing to subsequent generations over sixty-thousand proper hymns ... Hymnody thereafter was assimilated so completely to the concept of Greek Orthodox *psalmōdia* that it became customary in many places to abridge or even omit the scriptural texts that the hymns were meant to adorn.[47]

The same devolution was true for Eastern communion psalmody.

> The custom of chanting psalmody during the communion rite emerges in the East in the second half of the fourth century, where we see it for the first time almost simultaneously in Palestine and the environs of Antioch. In its earliest form this communion chant comprised simple responsorial psalmody, initially, it seems, LXX Ps 33, with verse 9, "Taste and see that the Lord is good!"

---

44. Taft, "Christian Liturgical Psalmody," 17, 20.
45. Alexander Lingas, "Tradition and Renewal in Contemporary Greek Orthodox Psalmody," *Psalms in Community*, ed. Harold W. Attbridge and Margot E. Fassler (Atlanta: Society of Biblical Literature, 2003), 344.
46. The reference is to the rule of the *Monastery of Stoudios*, historically the most important monastery of Constantinople.
47. Lingas, "Tradition and Renewal," 345.

as respond. However, communion antiphons develop by late antiquity, with the first appearance of liturgical books ... [and] collections of non-biblical Christian liturgical chant texts ... This shows that early on the communion psalmody, originally responsorial, had been "antiphonalized" via the addition of an entire repertory of non-biblical refrains, a process clearly observable in the sources of Antioch, Jerusalem, and, somewhat later, Constantinople.[48]

Taft calls this addition of hymnody to the Eucharist *strangling*. "This strangling, in favor of the ecclesiastical refrain, of what was the most important element of the whole liturgical unit, the scriptural text, is a common phenomenon throughout the history of liturgical hymnody."[49] For this reason, Westermeyer says, "In contrast to the West where psalmody flourished over hymnody, in the East, hymnody flourished over psalmody."[50] *Hymns squeezed out Psalms.*

However, the same developments do occur in the Western Church. As indicated above, Psalmody was closely associated with the readings of the lessons in the mass. "But before long, this psalmody, like that of the Introit, began to be shortened."[51] A little known fact about the offertory is that

> in early custom the people brought bread and wine as offerings, and out of these offerings what was required for the Communion was taken, and the remainder was distributed among the poor ... In the case of a large congregation this offering would take a long time, and during the period of waiting, the singing of psalms was introduced.[52]

"Later, the Offertory like other psalmody was shortened, this ap-

---

48. Taft, "Christian Liturgical Psalmody," 27-28.
49. Ibid., 31.
50. Paul Westermyer, *Te Deum: The Church and Music* (Minneapolis: Fortress, 1998), 101.
51. Lamb, *The Psalms in Christian Worship*, 90.
52. Ibid., 93-94.

parently taking place about the eleventh or twelfth century ... The shortening was due to the discontinuance of the people's offering."[53] Other developments also altered the communion mass. "As ceremonies were multiplied and the ritual added to, the service tended to become overlong, and the compensation was found in the abbreviation of psalmody."[54] Lamb comments, "This was in many respects unfortunate, as this was the one thing in which the people could join, though it is true that participation in what psalmody was left was withdrawn from them."[55] Psalmody was strangled in the cathedral office and the mass. As a result, the people were deprived of the Psalms.

The Western Church's daily offices were also adversely affected by the same crowding out of the Psalms. For example, "As the number of Saint's Days multiplied, the ordinary recitation of the psalms was interfered with more and more ... The consequence was that the whole Psalter was no longer said weekly, as had been the original intention ... The matter was complicated by the introduction of hymns ... "[56] The introduction of breviaries also offered the opportunity to shorten the offices. It seems this shortening became the custom under Innocent III (1198-1216) and the "abbreviated Office was adopted by the Franciscans shortly after their foundation [1239] ... "[57]

Third, the use of antiphons to interpret and frame the psalms tended to change their meaning and thus to subtly deprive the people of authentic Psalmody. Margot Fassler outlines the procedure.

> One of the best ways to understand the complexities of medieval Christian psalmody is by analyzing the relationships of Office psalms to their antiphons. Antiphons are sung texts of several kinds: they may consist of a particular psalm verse chosen to comment upon the whole

---

53. Ibid.
54. Ibid., 98.
55. Ibid.
56. Ibid., 104.
57. Ibid., 106.

psalm; they may be newly written texts created to link a given psalm to a particular hour of the day, to a feast, or to a season ... This way of singing the psalms has long been central to the Christian understanding of these poems ... In addition to this, the custom in many psalmodic practices—and throughout the Latin Middle Ages—was to seal the text with the lesser doxology, "Glory be to the Father and to the Son and to the Holy Spirit, as it was in the beginning and will be now and forever. Amen." Thus the texts were sung according to the formula: antiphon, intoned psalm with the doxology as its final verse, and a repeat of the antiphon.[58]

What was the result of this relationship between Psalm and antiphon? "By framing the text of the psalm an antiphon transforms it in several ways. The antiphon comments upon the psalm text, transforming its meaning in the process."[59] Fassler adds, "The composer of the antiphon texts and music was a creator of commentary as well, in this case, of exegesis of the texts of the psalter. Of all the commentaries, those sung in community were the most influential, shaping minds, hearts, and human relationships in conjunction with the psalm texts themselves."[60]

Fassler's example comes from the Office for Morning Prayer during the time between Easter and Pentecost and was used in western Germany in the twelfth century. A look at only one Psalm with its antiphon will suffice. "The psalms are divided into lines according to the chanted practice, with a pause at the asterisk. In this practice the lines are sung by alternate choirs."[61]

> Antiphon 1: Today a closed gate has opened to us, that which the serpent choked in a woman. So the flower

---

58. Margot Fassler, "Hildegard and the Dawn Song of Lauds: An Introduction to Benedictine Psalmody," *Psalms in Community*, ed. Harold W. Attbridge and Margot E. Fassler (Atlanta: Society of Biblical Literature, 2003), 219-220.
59. Ibid., 220.
60. Ibid., 222.
61. Ibid., 226.

A Brief History of Psalmody: Medieval Declension and Reformation Restoration   347

from the Virgin Mary gleams in the dawn.

> Psalm 92 [*Dominis regnavit* (the Lord is King)]
> The Lord hath reigned, he is clothed with beauty: *
> the Lord is clothed with strength and hath girded himself.
> For he hath established the world * which shall not be moved.
> Thy throne is prepared from of old: * thou art from everlasting.
> The floods have lifted up, O Lord, * the floods have lifted up their voice.
> The flood have lifted up their waves, * with the noise of many waters.
> Wonderful are the surges of the sea: * wonderful is the Lord on high.
> Thy testimonies are become exceedingly credible: holiness becometh thy house, O Lord, unto length of days.
> Doxology
> Repeat Antiphon 1.[62]

Psalm 92 [Latin/LXX] is clearly a song in praise of God's kingship. Paul applies this kingship to Christ (Isa. 52:7; Rom. 10:9-15). The Psalm is, therefore, a Gospel song exhorting believers to recognize the Lord Jesus Christ as King (Rom. 10:9). However, here is the explanation of the above framing.

> Antiphon 1, when sung with Ps 92 [93 MT], reworks the incarnation, reshaping the verses of the text through allusion to Mary and the virgin birth. In this new guise, "The Lord is clothed with beauty" is the flower gleaming in the dawn, the Christ who has come clothed with human flesh. The throne prepared from of old is the

---

62. Ibid.

Virgin Mary, who becomes here *sedes sapientiae*, the throne of wisdom.⁶³

Fassler confirms the outcome of such framing.

> Meanings, then, were made in several ways in monastic psalmody: by the way antiphons interacted with each other; by the way they framed the particular psalm texts with which they were associated (as well as with other psalm and canticle texts sung during the same day or hour); by the way the antiphons and psalm texts were tied to themes found elsewhere in the liturgy, especially as found in the Office readings or in the Mass liturgy; and by the overarching character of particular hours, feast days, and seasons.⁶⁴

Overall, there was a silencing of *popular* Psalmody. First, language differences developed between church and people. Second, the proliferation of antiphons and hymns tended to squeeze out Psalmody. Third, framing the Psalms with antiphons changed the meanings of the Psalms. James McKinnon's perspective is pertinent.

> It is hardly an exaggeration to say that the Western medieval liturgy consisted in the public singing of the Psalter. The entire cursus of 150 was chanted each week in the Office, and the five principal sung items of the Mass—the introit, gradual, alleluia, offertory, and communion—all came into existence as psalms, even if the responses and antiphons that accompanied the original psalms eventually achieved a musical prominence beyond that of their progenitors. *We may be inclined to take this overwhelming psalmodic presence for granted, but we should not; it was by no means inevitable.*⁶⁵

---

63. Ibid., 235.
64. Ibid., 231.
65. James W. McKinnon, "The Book of Psalms, Monasticism, and the Western Liturgy," *The Place of the Psalms in the Intellectual Culture of the Middle Ages*, ed. Nancy Van Deusen (Albany: State University of New York, 1999), 43. Italics added.

LEARNING FROM HISTORY

Twenty-first century Psalm-singing churches must learn from history. What about language differences? The language and images of the Psalms go back three millennia. They differ dramatically from twenty-first century vernacular languages and images. The use of technical theological language by professionals to explain the Psalms can exacerbate the situation. Haddon Robinson warns preachers about the use of technical language. "It takes a man three years to go through seminary, but it takes seven or eight years to get over seminary."[66] There is also a need to return to the tradition of Psalm Explanations. In adding this material to already crowded times of worship, however, churches must ensure that Psalm Explanations do not become sermon length expositions that squeeze out the singing of the Psalms. Churches must maintain the Pauline perspective on the equal ultimacy of teaching and singing in worship. Review the earlier exposition of Colossians 3:16. Since Psalm explanations or introductions frame Psalms in preparation for singing, much like ancient antiphons, pastors must take care to offer solid Biblical-theological commentary in understandable terms. Contemporary Psalm singing churches also may be subject to medieval failures leading to reduced popular Psalmody.

PSALMODY AND THE PRINTING REVOLUTION

"In 1453, Constantinople, long a bulwark of Christendom against the Moslem advance, fell to the Ottoman Turks."[67] While the tide of Islam was rising, in the West, another event had equally transformative effects. Living in Strasbourg in 1440, Johannes Gutenberg perfected a movable type printing system and in 1455 he completed his 42-line Bible, known as the Gutenberg Bible. He printed about 180 copies of this Latin Vulgate Bible in three volumes each. On the one hand,

---

66. Haddon Robinson, *Biblical Preaching* (Grand Rapids: Baker, 2001), 190.
67. Latourette, *History of Christianity*, 613.

Schaff aptly states, "In Western Asia and North Africa, the Cross was supplanted by the Crescent ... "[68] Latourette adds, "In the closing years of the fifteenth century and in the sixteenth century the Turkish empire continued to expand."[69] On the other hand, while the Ottoman Empire restrained the Eastern Orthodox Church within its confines, printing provided the Western Church a new technology for the advancement of Christianity. In the opening years of the sixteenth century, the Reformation spread over Europe and was a reformation in worship as much as a doctrinal renewal. For present purposes, the printing and publication of Psalters and hymnals indicates the place of Psalmody within the church. What follows is a brief review of Psalter publication leading to the Reformation and then to the contemporary church.

CATHOLIC PSALTERS

> In the first decades of printing, hundreds of editions of the complete collection of 150 psalms were printed in the liturgical psalter that includes in print or manuscript rubrics for singing the psalms in the services of the hours of the Divine Office. Copies of eighty such psalters [were] printed in German speaking lands and eastern Europe between 1455 and 1500 ... [70]

Interestingly enough, these Psalters demonstrate a change and movement from the "traditional sung Latin liturgy ... to printed dual-language Latin/German or solely vernacular translations ... "[71] In this form, the early printed Catholic Psalter "was transformed from a service book for religious [monastic] and secular [non-monastic] clergy to a book for participants and observers at services and for private use."[72]

---

68. Schaff, *History of the Christian Church*, 4:5.
69. Latourette, *History of Christianity*, 614.
70. Mary Kay Dugan, "The Psalter on the Way to the Reformation: The Fifteenth Century Printed Psalter in the North," *The Place of the Psalms in the Intellectual Culture of the Middle Ages*, ed. Nancy Van Deusen (Albany: State University of New York, 1999), 154.
71. Ibid.
72. Ibid.

At the same time, it appears that the effects of the Renaissance were being felt.

> [T]he proliferation of thousands of printed Latin liturgical psalters in the late fifteenth century suggests a new pious audience dissatisfied with the breviary. That audience was literate and desirous of participating in Catholic church services based on the psalms and antiphons with the Latin (and very soon the vernacular) text in hand. While at the outset printed liturgical psalters were intended for religious and clerical users, the proliferation of printed copies were increasingly sold to a broader audience that included lay [parishioners].[73]

LUTHERAN HYMNODY

It is well-known that the Reformation erupted in Germany in 1517.

> Accordingly, on the memorable thirty-first day of October, 1517, which has ever since been celebrated in Protestant Germany as the birthday of the Reformation, at twelve o'clock [Martin Luther] affixed (either he himself or another) to the doors of the castle-church at Wittenberg, ninety-five Latin Theses on the subject of indulgences, and invited public discussion.[74]

Luther had a high regard for the Psalms. "Of the more than thirty hymns of Luther's which have come down to us we have German versions of Psalms 12, 14, 46, 67, 124, 128, and 130."[75] At the same time, Luther wrote, "I plan after the example of the prophets and ancient fathers of the Church to make German psalms [hymns] for the people, that is to say, spiritual songs, so that the Word of God may dwell among the people by means of song also."[76] Alexander Lamb

---

73. Ibid.
74. Schaff, *History of the Christian Church*, 7:155-156.
75. Old, *Worship That Is Reformed*, 48.
76. Quoted in Lamb, *The Psalms in Christian Worship*, 134.

indicates that, "When worked out in practical terms, the result was that much of the psalmody of the Roman services disappeared from the Lutheran services, being replaced by German hymns."[77] The first Protestant hymnal, published in 1524 under Luther's supervision, and containing eight hymns, became know as the *Achtleiderbuch, Eight Song Book*.[78] "Before Luther's death (1546), there appeared no less than forty-seven Lutheran hymn- and tune-books."[79]

It also appears that Luther understood the *subjective element* of singing discussed above. However, he related it to the music, not the words.

> We can mention only one point (which experience confirms), namely, that next to the Word of God, music deserves the highest praise. She is a mistress and governess of those human emotions—to pass over the animals—which as masters govern men or more often overwhelm them. No greater commendation than this can be found—at least not by us. For whether you wish to comfort the sad, to terrify the happy, to encourage the despairing, to humble the proud, to calm the passionate, or to appease those full of hate—and who could number all these masters of the human heart, namely, the emotions, inclinations, and affections that impel men to evil or good?—what more effective means than music could you find?[80]

Calvin's view of the priority of text over tune in Psalmody, and his view of the necessity of music appropriate to the themes of the Psalms will be reviewed in Part Four of this study.

---

77. Ibid.
78. Westermeyer, *Te Deum*, 142, n. 5.
79. Schaff, *History of the Christian Church*, 7:506.
80. Martin Luther, *Luther's Works: Liturgy and Hymns*, ed. Ulrich S. Leupold (Philadelphia: Fortress, 1965), 323.

REFORMED PSALMODY

In the Churches of the Reformation there have been two main streams of church-song. On the one hand, there has been hymnody, with Luther as its fountainhead; on the other hand, metrical psalmody, after the example set by Calvin. Luther carried on the tradition established by the Latin hymn; his exemplars were the Breviary. Calvin gave his adhesion to a still older tradition, which the Roman Church had maintained by the use of the prose psalms in its Daily Office; he went back to the primitive days when the church had no other means than the psalms for the singing of praise. These two streams ran parallel for many generations ... [81]

"The *Strasbourg German Service Book* of 1525, the first attempt at a 'Reformed' service of worship, appeared with a number of metrical psalms to be sung by the congregation. Metrical psalmody was a part of Reformed worship from the very beginning."[82] Banished from Geneva and discouraged, Calvin took refuge in Strasbourg in 1538. In the meantime, "With each succeeding edition of the Strasbourg Psalter the number of psalms is augmented."[83] Once in Strasbourg, "Calvin immediately encountered the vernacular congregational psalmody which had been practiced with Bucer's ideas ever since 1524."[84]

In barely four months, Calvin undertook to prepare a French psalter for the congregation he was serving. "In 1539 the psalter appeared ... It contained nineteen psalms in French translation, all but one of which (No. 113) were rhymed. Thirteen were by Clement Marot, and Calvin was responsible for the remainder."[85] Calvin returned to Geneva in 1541. "In 1541 another collection appeared in Anvers

---

81. Patrick Millar, *The Story of the Church's Song* (Edinburgh: Saint Andrews Press, 1927), 86.
82. Old, *Worship That Is Reformed*, 49.
83. Ibid.
84. Charles Garside Jr., *The Origins of Calvin's Theology of Music: 1536-1543* (Philadelphia: American Philosophical Society, 1979), 14.
85. Ibid., 14-15.

[Antwerp], including thirty psalms by Marot and fifteen by other writers."[86] "On these two collections the first edition of the Genevan Psalter was based and was published at Geneva in 1542."[87] It took another twenty years to complete this work.

> Marot's own first publication was in 1542, and the next fifty psalms in August of 1543. At least sixteen editions of this psalter appeared in Paris, Lyons, Strasbourg and Geneva. The remainder of the Psalter was put into meter by Beze. Thirty-four psalms appeared in 1551, and various additions were made till the Psalter was complete in 1562 ... This was known as the Genevan Psalter, and had 125 melodies.[88]

The influence of the Genevan Psalter is nothing short of remarkable. "When the first complete edition was published in 1562 it was immediately consumed, going through twenty-five editions in its first year of publication."[89] The printing and distribution of Psalters was precipitated by the growth of the church. "By 1562 there were estimated to be more than 2,150 churches established in France with approximately three million attending."[90] The printing of the Genevan Psalter increased rapidly.

> In Geneva itself there were nine editions, or rather issues, bearing the imprint of six different printing houses; seven editions at Paris, three at Lyons, one at St. Loo, and five that bear no indication of the place of issue. Fifteen editions of 1563 are known, eleven of 1564 and thirteen of 1565: a total of sixty-four issues within four years of publication.[91]

---

86. Lamb, *The Psalms in Christian Worship*, 141.
87. George Arthur Crawford, "Bourgeois," *Grove's Dictionary of Music and Musicians*, ed. J. A. Fuller Maitland (New York: Macmillan, 1904), 1:374.
88. Lamb, *The Psalms in Christian Worship*, 142.
89. Johnson, "The History of Psalm Singing," 51.
90. Ibid.
91. Louis F. Benson, "John Calvin and the Psalmody of the Reformed Churches," *Journal of the Presbyterian Historical Society* 5:2 (June 1909): 71.

"The Genevan Psalter as it appeared in its final edition in 1562 became the standard not only for all succeeding French Reformed psalm books but for those in Dutch, German, Hungarian, and English."[92] Because fitting tunes were often difficult to put with metricized psalms, "Calvinists of other languages often attempted to translate Marot's and Beza's versions into their own tongues in such a way that they could also use the same tunes."[93] French pastor and historian "Douen [1830-1896] lists 1400 editions of French metrical Psalters, and in addition there were many translations from the French into German, Dutch, Italian, Spanish, Bohemian, Polish, Latin, and even Hebrew, as well as English."[94]

As to actual practice, the psalms were sung in unison with the melody in the tenor, later put in the soprano.[95] "The singing by the congregation, led by a precentor, was without instrumental accompaniment. The Psalms were sung right through the Psalter from beginning to end, without selection or omission, within a given period."[96] This *lectio continua* method, however, was discontinued in France around the end of the sixteenth century.[97]

ENGLISH PSALTERS

In the interim, after England broke from Papal authority, Thomas Cranmer (1489-1556) "desired to liberate the Daily Office for the laity. He aimed to create truly *common* prayer ... written in the vernacular ... Essentially, he returned to the type of service that Cassian observed in the Egyptian desert."[98] The connection with the past was from the ancient Divine Office through the more recent Breviary or abbreviated Office to the Book of Common Prayer (1549 and 1552).

---

92. W. Sanford Reid, "The Battle Hymns of the Lord, Calvinist Psalmody of the Sixteenth Century," *Sixteenth Century Essays and Studies* 2 (1971): 42.
93. Ibid.
94. Lamb, *The Psalms in Christian Worship*, 142.
95. Reid, "The Battle Hymns of the Lord," 42.
96. Benson, "John Calvin and the Psalmody of the Reformed Churches," 72.
97. Louis F. Benson, "John Calvin and the Psalmody of the Reformed Churches," *Journal of the Presbyterian Historical Society* 5:3 (September 1909): 110.
98. Hughes Oliphant Old and Robert Cathart, "From Cassian to Cranmer," *Sing a New Song*, ed. Joel R. Beeke and Anthony T. Selvaggio (Grand Rapids: Reformation Heritage, 2010), 11.

"Cranmer's Book of Common Prayer slows down the pace considerably, dividing the Psalms evenly between morning and evening so that they are completed in thirty days [rather than weekly]."[99] In addition, "A major difference between the Anglican prayer book and the *Strasbourg Psalter* is that the singing of metrical psalms, rather than the chanting of psalms takes center stage."[100]

The first complete English metrical psalter was produced by Robert Crowley in 1549 and was based upon the Latin *Biblia sacrosancta*.[101] Crowley's Psalter had only one tune, "a plainsong chant in tenor, harmonized for four voices."[102] Thomas Sternhold (1500-1549) was a gentleman servant of King Henry VIII and, once converted, undertook to put some of the Psalms in English meter. Sternhold had 37 of his translations published in 1549, and dedicated them to King Edward VI, who heard them rehearsed by Sternhold when he was younger.[103]

> Within a few months Sternhold was dead. But his friend John Hopkins (d. 1570), a clergyman and schoolmaster in Suffolk, took up the task ... During the persecutions under Queen Mary, many of the leaders of the Reformation took refuge in Geneva. There, in 1556, a collection of *One and Fiftie Psalmes of Dauid in Englishe Metre* was published, containing the forty-four versions of Sternhold and Hopkins then available, but with seven others ... The next edition, appearing in 1558, was distinguished by the fact that it contained twenty-four versions by William Kethe,[104] among them the world-famous version of the 100th Psalm ... When the exiles returned to [England] after the death of Mary, they brought the psalm-singing practice with them ... The complete metrical

---

99. Ibid.
100. Ibid., 12.
101. "Psalms," *The New Cambridge Bibliography of English Literature*, ed. George Watson (Cambridge: University Press, 1974), 1899.
102. Charles L. Etherington, *Protestant Worship Music* (Westport, CT: Greenwood, 1978), 100.
103. Millar, *The Story of the Church's Song*, 96.
104. The tune, "Old One Hundredth," was originally arranged by Louis Bourgeois for Psalm 134 in the Genevan Psalter. Kethe used the same tune for his own rendering of Psalm 100.

Psalter, known as the old Version, but more popularly as "Sternhold and Hopkins" was published in 1562 by John Day, who himself had been an exile for the faith, and was licensed for use in public worship.[105]

When the work of Sternhold and Hopkins was first published for use in the English-speaking congregation in Geneva, the Psalters were known as Anglo-Genevan Psalters. At the same time, "the Marian exiles decided to translate a complete version of their own [Bible] into English."[106] The Sternhold and Hopkins Psalter was bound with the *Geneva Bible* published in London in 1599, as was the Book of Common Prayer.[107] This Psalter enjoyed tremendous popularity in England. For example, Lamb quotes John Strype's *Annals of the Reformation and Establishment of Religion, and Other Various Occurrences in the Church of England*, "You may now sometimes see at St Paul's Cross after the service, six thousand persons, young and old, of all sexes, singing together."[108] As mentioned above, this Psalter became known as the "Old Version."

Frequent revisions and perfections were attempted. Francis Rous, a member of the Westminster Assembly, published his own work in 1641.[109] A second Rous edition appeared in 1646 and a third edition, thoroughly revised, in 1647.[110] Millar says, "This, after a great deal of amendment, the house of Commons, in 1646, ordered—it 'and none other'—to be used in all churches and chapels within the kingdom."[111] Nathan Tate and Nicholas Brady published a version in 1696; the Tate and Brady version was also sanctioned for use in churches and a Supplement was published in 1703.[112] Tate and Brady became known as the "New Version" and, although not as popular

---

105. Millar, *The Story of the Church's Song*, 96-98.
106. Michael Brown, "Preface," *The Geneva Bible: A Facsimile of the 1599 Edition with Undated Sternhold and Hopkins Psalms* (Ozark, MO: L. L. Brown, 1990), ii.
107. Lamb, *The Psalms in Christian Worship*, 149. Compare the previous note.
108. Ibid.
109. Millar, *The Story of the Church's Song*, 98.
110. Henry Alexander Glass, *The Story of Psalters* (London: Kegan Paul, Trench, 1888), 84-85.
111. Ibid.
112. Ibid., 98-99.

as Sternhold and Hopkins, it "continued to be used in many places until the middle of the nineteenth century."[113] Between 1549 and 1863, there were 601 editions of Sternhold and Hopkins, and 303 editions of Tate and Brady.[114]

SCOTTISH PSALTERS

John "Knox was minister to the congregation of English-speaking refugees in Geneva for two years. When he returned to Scotland in 1559, he brought with him the *Anglo-Genevan Psalter*."[115] To better serve the growing Reformed church in Scotland, two Edinburgh ministers, John Craig and Robert Pont, produced a revised edition of this psalter. "Their revision was published in Edinburgh in 1564 as part of the Book of Common Order, and it remained the Scottish Psalter till 1650."[116]

When the Westminster Assembly began to meet in 1643, its charge was enlarged to seek "'uniformity in religion, confession of faith, form of church-government, directory for worship and catechizing ... ' in the three kingdoms of England, Scotland and Ireland."[117] The results of much of the Assembly's work are well known: the Westminster Confession of Faith, the Larger and Shorter Catechisms, the Form of Presbyterian Church-Government, and the Directory for the Public Worship of God.

> In addition to all this, they [the Westminster Divines] also went to great lengths to produce a metrical Psalter that was to be part of the uniformity they sought. In so doing, they wanted to produce a Psalter that was not only more accurate and more smoothly running than those in existence, but also simpler in metre so as to be more easily used by all. Francis Rous, who was not a

---

113. Ibid., 100.
114. Glass, *The Story of Psalters*, 10.
115. Millar, *The Story of the Church's Song*, 103.
116. Lamb, *The Psalms in Christian Worship*, 152.
117. David Silversides, "The Development of the Scottish Psalter" (Paper, The Scottish Reformation Society, 2002), 2.

minister but a member of both Parliament and the Westminster Assembly, had produced a version of the Psalter in 1643 and this was to form the basic starting point for the Assembly.[118]

The work was accomplished as follows: "The Assembly was divided into three committees, each responsible for the scrutiny of 50 Psalms. All 150 were subsequently read line by line before the whole Assembly. The Assembly included some excellent Hebrew scholars ... "[119] The revised versions were then sent in batches to Scotland for further examination. The Church of Scotland took several steps before granting approval of a new Psalter.

> The General Assembly of the Church of Scotland in 1647 appointed four men to take an initial look at the version sent north by the Westminster Assembly ... The General Assembly of 1648 appointed that the version should be examined first by the Edinburgh ministers, then by seven more ministers ... A Commission of Assembly ... appointed another Committee ... to have yet another look at the draft. The draft version was sent to the presbyteries of the Church in 1648 with instructions from the General Assembly to send any suggested corrections to the Committee of Public Affairs. In June 1649 an Assembly Commission appointed certain members to go over the material ... Another Commission in November of the same year ... spent five sessions seeking to improve the version ... In 1650, the General Assembly finally approved the Psalter in the form it has come down to us today.[120]

"Like the Authorized Version of the Bible, the Scottish Psalter reigned supreme for generations."[121] Its profound effects are compa-

---

118. Ibid.
119. Ibid., 3.
120. Ibid., 3-4.
121. Ibid., 9.

rable to those of the Genevan Psalter. "Although the psalms roused the Huguenot congregations to public action, they also stimulated and strengthened the Protestant witness of individuals, particularly those who had to face the prospect of death at the stake."[122] In the wars between French Catholics and Protestants (1562-1598), the Psalms understandably became battle hymns. "[O]ne of the most popular psalms of the Huguenot armies was the 68th, 'Let God arise, let his enemies be scattered,' known to the Huguenots as the 'song of battles.'"[123]

The similarity of experience for Scottish Christians during the enormous suffering of the "Killing Times" (1668-1688) is striking. Patrick Millar reminds us that the Psalter "won its place in the people's hearts, and its lines were so deeply imprinted upon their memories that it is always the language thus given them for the expression of their emotions, which in the great hours we find upon their lips."[124] Terry Johnson responds. "Note what he says: the language that they used to interpret and express their experience was the language of the Psalms, which they sang."[125] Johnson quotes Millar, "The Scottish metrical psalms, he says, 'are stained with the blood of martyrs, who counted not their lives dear to them that by suffering and sacrifice they might keep faith with conscience and save their country's liberties from defeat.'"[126]

Since the Psalter of 1650 was rooted in the work of the Westminster Assembly, it is appropriate to note that the Westminster Confession 21:5 requires Psalmody as an element of worship.

> The reading of Scriptures with godly fear; the sound preaching, and conscionable hearing of the Word, in obedience unto God, with understanding, faith, and reverence; *singing of Psalms with grace in the heart*; as also, the

---

122. Reid, "The Battle Hymns of the Lord," 46.
123. Ibid., 47.
124. Quoted by Johnson, "The History of Psalm Singing," 53.
125. Ibid.
126. Ibid.

due administration and worthy receiving of the sacraments instituted by Christ; are all parts of the ordinary religious worship of God ... (italics added).

DUTCH PSALTERS

As Latourette notes, "The Reformation made great strides in the Netherlands ... Between 1513 and 1531 more than a score of translations of the Bible or the New Testament were produced in Dutch, Flemish, or French."[127] The Belgic Confession, "which with some modifications long remained standard in the Dutch Reformed Church," was prepared in 1561 by Guy de Bray, who had studied in Geneva.[128] "The first Dutch metrical Psalter, the *Souterliedekens* [*Psalter-Songs*], was published in Antwerp in 1540 by Symon Cock and employed Dutch and French folk songs. Between 1551 and 1566 Jan Utinhove produced Dutch metrical Psalms, published in London and Emden."[129] The *Souterliedekens* appeared in no fewer than thirty-three editions.[130] "Yet," as Reid observes,

> despite the proliferation of Dutch Psalters, the Marot-Beza psalm-book seems to have been the most popular, even though published in French. In 1562 some of these psalms were translated into Dutch by de Heere and the following year Peter Dathenus, a Reformed minister, brought out another edition that was adopted officially at the Synods of Wesel (1568) and Dortrect (1574).[131]

"These were the metrical Psalms early Dutch immigrants brought to North America and in some parts of the Netherlands they are still sung today."[132]

---

127. Latourette, *A History of Christianity*, 762-763.
128. Ibid., 763.
129. "Psalter," *The Harvard Dictionary of Music*, ed. Don Michael Randel (Cambridge: Harvard University Press, 2003), 692.
130. Reid, "The Battle Hymns of the Lord," 47.
131. Ibid., 48.
132. *Harvard Dictionary of Music*, 692.

THE FIRST AMERICAN PSALTERS

The Pilgrims brought the first Psalter to appear in America in 1620: "In 1612 Henry Ainsworth published *The Book of Psalms, Englished, both in Prose and Metre* for the Separatist Church at Amsterdam whom we often call the 'Pilgrims.'"[133] Richard Appel explains that discontent with the Ainsworth Psalter precipitated what became know as the "Bay Psalm Book":

> Dissatisfied with the authorized English versification of the Book of Psalms, that of Thomas Sternhold and John Hopkins (1562 *et seq.*), and not accepting the version of Henry Ainsworth (1612; 2nd ed. 1618) brought to Plymouth by the Pilgrims in 1620, a group of Massachusetts Bay Colony clerics set about preparing a new translation in the 1630's. The result was *The Whole Booke of Psalmes Faithfully Translated into English Metre*, printed in Cambridge in 1640 ... in a run of 1700 copies ... No music appeared in the first edition. Instead, an "admonition to the reader" ... explained that the newly versified psalms could be sung to some forty tunes printed in Revencroft's English psalter of 1621 and to others in "our english psalm books," i.e. Sternhold-Hopkins.[134]

Appel then spells out the origin of what became known as the "New England Psalter."

> Following the second edition which was merely an English reprinting of the first, the Bay Psalm Book was reissued at Cambridge in 1651 in a third edition, thoroughly revised by Henry Dunster and Richard Lyon, under the new title *The Psalms Hymns and Spiritual Songs of the Old Testament Faithfully Translated into English Metre for the Use, Edification and Comfort of the Saints in Publick and Pri-*

---

133. Westermeyer, *Te Deum*, 179.
134. Richard G. Appel, "The Music of the Bay Psalm Book, 9th Edition," *Institute for Studies in American Music* 5 (1975): 1.

vate, *especially in New England*. The new title and versification (with some 125 psalms in common meter) were to prove definitive, undergoing virtually no change for more than a century. This version came to be called the "New England Psalter."[135]

It appears that this thoroughly-revised "third edition" of the Bay Psalm Book, which became the "New England Psalm-book (1650)[,] was an American version of Rous, intended to take the place of the unsatisfactory Bay Psalm-book."[136] *A Dictionary of Hymnology* states, "This was mainly a revised version of Rous's Psalter made by President Dunster of Harvard College, Richard Lyon, and thirty others. It had a large circulation and was in extensive use for many years."[137] Musical notations were added more than four and a half decades later.

> Not until the ninth edition (Boston: B. Green and J. Allen, 1698) was any music printed in the Bay Psalm Book. In that edition, following some instruction for performance, an eleven-page supplement of thirteen psalm tunes was added after the text of the psalms ... Printed from wood blocks, this was the first music to be published in English-speaking America.[138]

The New England Psalter "went through fifty editions, including those published in Europe."[139] *A Dictionary of Hymnology* also provides a "list of *Complete* and *Partial* versions of the Book of Psalms in English (including those pub. in Scotland and America) ... *from* 1414 *to* 1889."[140] There are no less than 326 entries.[141]

---

135. Ibid., 4.
136. Glass, *The Story of Psalters*, 39.
137. "Psalters, English," *A Dictionary of Hymnology*, ed. John Julian (New York: Dover, 1907), 2:928.
138. Ibid.
139. Ibid., 92.
140. *A Dictionary of Hymnology*, 2:926.
141. Ibid., 926-932.

THE TURNING POINT

The Reformation brought with it a strong resurgence and restoration of Psalmody among Calvinistic Independent, Reformed, and Presbyterian Churches in Europe and England eventually extending into America. There were strains, however. "Baptists in seventeenth-century England were generally opposed to psalm singing in worship. In 1689 the General Baptist Assembly concluded that psalm singing was 'so strangely foreign to evangelical worship that it was not conceived anyways safe to admit such carnal formalities.'"[142] Benjamin Keach (1640-1704) was a Particular Baptist who is generally credited to have "opened the door to English hymnody, as poetry for the congregation to sing that was not restricted to psalmody."[143] Nevertheless, it was Isaac Watts (1674-1748) who opened the sluice-gates of hymnody. Millar gives one of the seeming reasons for this success. "In the grievous plight into which that psalmody had sunk and from no one seemed to be able to raise it, Watts saw with the clear intuition of genius what needed to be done, and alone he did it."[144] Watts himself begins his Preface to *The Psalms of David Imitated* with these words:

> Though the Psalms of David are a Work of admirable and divine Composure, though they contain the noblest Sentiments of Piety, and breathe a most exalted Spirit of Devotion, yet when the best of Christians attempt to sing many of them in our common Translations, that Spirit of Devotion vanishes and is lost, the Psalm dies upon their lips, and they feel scarce any thing of the holy Pleasure.[145]

In the first paragraph of the Preface to his *Hymns and Spiritual Songs*, Watts writes:

> To see the dull Indifference, the negligent and the thoughtless Air that sits upon the Faces of a whole As-

---
142. Westermeyer, *Te Deum*, 188.
143. Ibid.
144. Millar, *The Story of the Church's Song*, 128.
145. Isaac Watts, "Preface," *The Psalms of David Imitated in the Language of the New Testament, and Applied to the Christian State of Worship*, Christian Classic Ethereal Library, accessed January 16, 2012.

sembly, while the Psalm is on their Lips, might tempt even a charitable Observer to suspect the Fervency of inward Religion; and tis much to be feared that the Minds of most of the Worshippers are absent or unconcerned. Perhaps the Modes of Preaching in the best Churches still want some Degrees of Reformation, nor are the Methods of Prayer so perfect as to stand in need of no Correction or Improvement: But of all our Religious Solemnities Psalmodie is the most unhappily managed. That very Action which should elevate us to the most delightful and divine Sensations, does not only flat our Devotion, but too often awakens our Regret, and touches all the Springs of Uneasiness within us.[146]

A change was needed to awaken the praise of people in congregational worship. The argument has the same ring as the debates over contemporary Christian music. It was not, however, only the manner of congregational singing but the matter of many Psalms that Watts vigorously opposed.

I have been long convinced, that one great Occasion of this Evil arises from the Matter and Words to which we confine all our Songs. Some of them are almost opposite to the Spirit of the Gospel: Many of them foreign to the State of the New Testament, and widely different from the present Circumstances of Christians.[147]

CONTINUING MOMENTUM

"From 1620 to 1800, metrical psalmody dominated the American church scene ... Subsequent hymnbooks for the next sixty-five years contained both psalms and hymns, typically with a large opening section of psalms."[148] This combination of Psalms with hymns was true

---

146. Isaac Watts, "Preface," *Hymns and Spiritual Songs* (London: J. Humphreys, 1707), iii.
147. Ibid.
148. Johnson, "The History of Psalm Singing," 55.

in both the Old School and New School Presbyterians in their 1843 *Psalms and Hymns* and *Church Psalmist* respectively.[149] This distinction is no longer evident in the hymnal of the reunited church, *The Presbyterian Hymnal* of 1874.[150] In the meantime, in 1887, the United Presbyterian Church of North America (UPCNA) issued a revised Psalter and in 1901 published *Bible Songs: A Collection of Psalms Set to Music for Use in Church and Evangelistic Services, Prayer Meetings, Sabbath Schools, Young People's Societies, and Family Worship*.

In 1912, the UPCNA published another Psalter. The Preface reads,

> The prime distinction of this Psalter is its use of the metrical version of the Psalms approved September 22d, 1909, by a Joint Committee from nine Churches of the Presbyterian family in Canada and the United States. These Churches are as follows: the Presbyterian Church in the United States of America, the Presbyterian Church in Canada, the Reformed Church in America, the United Presbyterian Church of North America, the Reformed Presbyterian Church, Synod, the Reformed Presbyterian Church, General Synod, the Christian Reformed Church in North America, the Associate Reformed Presbyterian Church, and the Associate Presbyterian Church.[151]

The Preface to both *Bible Songs* (1901) and *The Psalter* (1912) carries these words:

> With this brief preface the book is sent forth upon its sacred mission. It presents anew the immortal songs of the Holy Spirit, those matchless hymns of the Bible which have been sung in far-off countries and centuries, which were chanted by our Lord and His disciples, and which

---

149. Ibid.
150. Ibid., 56.
151. John McNaugher, et al., "Preface," *The Psalter with Responsive Readings* (Pittsburgh: United Presbyterian Board of Publication, 1912), 3.

with their measured language of religious feeling and devotion will abide until the end.[152]

The Christian Reformed Church of North America published its first English language Psalter in 1914 but then approved the use of hymns with the Psalms in 1928.[153] The Protestant Reformed Churches in America, founded in 1924, use the *The Psalter with Responsive Readings* of 1912. The Reformed Presbyterian Church of North America published new Psalters in 1889 (split leaf), 1911, 1920, 1929, 1950, 1973, and 2009. Other denominations holding to exclusive Psalmody today are the American Presbyterian Church, Associated Presbyterian Churches, Australian Free Church, Evangelical Presbyterian Church of Australia, Free Church of Scotland (Continuing), Free Church of Scotland (Continuing) (Presbytery of the United States), Free Presbyterian Church of Scotland, Presbyterian Church of Eastern Australia, Presbyterian Reformed Church, Reformed Presbyterian Church of Australia, Reformed Presbyterian Church of Ireland, Reformed Presbyterian Church of North America (Japan Presbytery), and Reformed Presbyterian Church of Scotland.

Exclusive Psalmody has a venerable heritage growing out of the Old Testament into the New Testament, and into the early New Testament and Patristic Church. Although there was decline in the Middle Ages, Psalmody revived in the Reformation under Calvin, and was standard in Presbyterian and Reformed churches until around 1800 when hymns again began to squeeze out the Psalms.

> At the same time hymns were displacing psalms, most American and British denominations began to use organs in worship, making possible more variety of sound and style. While the "core repertory" of tunes in most hymnals and psalters remains accessible to worshipers,

---

152. Ibid., 5; John McNaugher, et al., "Preface," *Bible Songs* (Pittsburgh: The United Presbyterian Board of Publication, 1901), [4].
153. "Memorable Events in the History of the Christian Reformed Church," Christian Reformed Church, The Official Website of CRCNA Ministries, http://www.crcna.org/pages/memorable_events.cfm, accessed January 16, 2012.

a growing number of tunes popular in denominations using accompaniment have proven too difficult for unaccompanied congregational singing.[154]

At the same time, to many Christians, the language of the Psalms seems distant, its ideas foreign, and its theology archaic. Yet the Psalms, poetic literature loved by devout souls, have proved their worth for millennia. "I have suggested to my students, for instance," says Dr. T. David Gordon, "that one of the tests of a hymn is whether it would exist as Christian verse if it were not put to music."[155] The Psalms have stood the test for nearly three thousand years, far longer than any traditional hymn or contemporary song. The church can fall into *old traps* and deny the Psalms in song to God's people or she can heed Jeremiah 6:16. "Thus says the Lord: 'Stand in the ways and see, / And ask for the *old paths*, where the good way is, / And walk in it; / Then you will find rest for your souls'" (NKJV, Italics added).

---

154. Robert M. Copeland, "The Experience of Singing Psalms," *The Book of Psalms for Worship* (Pittsburgh: Crown and Covenant, 2009), xvi.

155. T. David Gordon, *Why Johnny Can't Sing Hymns* (Phillipsburg: P and R, 2010), 130.

Public Worship 101

PART FOUR:
Instrumental Music in Worship

16

INSTRUMENTAL MUSIC: LAYING THE FOUNDATION

Also in the day of your gladness and in your appointed feasts, and on the first days of your months, you shall blow the trumpets over your burnt offerings, and over the sacrifices of your peace offerings; and they shall be as a reminder of you before your God. I am the LORD your God. ~Num. 10:10

GETTING STARTED

THE CD INTRODUCING a popular sound system opens with the words, "Sound can touch our emotions directly."[1] There is a hen quietly clucking. Then a rooster crows loudly to welcome morning. A horse whinnies, and then dogs howl. Familiar farm scenes race through our minds. The narrator adds, "And different sounds evoke different feelings."[2] The quiet rumble of thunder is heard in the distance. It is coming closer and closer. Suddenly, there is a loud crack of lightning, and then thunder. Your heart jumps. "But there are places in the heart only music can touch."[3] Now, you *feel* the bow on the strings of a bass viola producing deep, sonorous tones.

Discussions about instrumental music in worship tend to be emotional too, and for two reasons. First, music connects with the emotions. Second, believers have an emotional investment in both

---

1. *Presenting the Bose Wave Music System*, Framingham, MA: Bose Corporation, 2004.
2. Ibid.
3. Ibid.

instruments and worship. The two work together. A discussion of the power of music, both instrumental and vocal, is a part of this chapter.

The thesis for this part of the study is simple. *Instrumental music is not integral to Biblical worship but, when introduced, it is incidental, typical, and temporary.* The validation of this thesis is sought in four parts. This chapter is foundational and will review the basic nature of worship, who governs worship, what is essential to worship, and the nature of music and its power.

Chapters 17 and 18 will survey the extensive Biblical and historical data on the use and nonuse of musical instruments in Biblical worship. If musical instruments are neither essential to worship, nor consistently used throughout the history of the worship of the church, what is their status? In chapter 19, it will be seen that they were typical and temporary. History shows their use was temporary. Why? It was their nature as types. In examining this typological perspective, Biblical types will be defined and described. Instrumental music is not part of Biblical worship in the present era, because it was typical and temporary, foreshadowing the Spiritual praise integral to worship today. Putting this material together will confirm this thesis: Instrumental music is not integral to Biblical worship but, when introduced, it is incidental, typical, and temporary.

To round out the discussion of instrumental music in worship, chapter 20 will address several popular objections. What about Israel's celebration of her deliverance from Egypt when Miriam sang and danced and played the tambourine? Is this worship scene not an example for worship today? Many of the Psalms, including Psalm 150, command the use of different types of instruments in worship. How can the church ignore these commands? What about the Book of Revelation? If the saints in heaven use instruments to give praise to God, why can believers not use instruments in the church today? Building on earlier discussions, these objections will be answered and the thesis confirmed. This chapter now briefly reviews the main points from chapters 1, 2, and 4, and examines the nature and power of music.

WHAT IS WORSHIP?

Worship means *fearing the Lord*. Acts 16:14 describes Lydia as "a worshiper [*sebomene*] of God." In Acts 18:7, Paul visits "a man named Titius Justus, a worshiper [*sebomenou*] of God." In other words, these folks are "God-fearing" people (Acts 13:43; 17:17). Joshua 4:24 reminds the people that God delivered them "so that you may fear [LXX *sebesthe*] the Lord your God forever." The principal aspect of worship found here is fear. The one who has a proper fear, reverence, and awe of the Creator and Redeemer is the believer.

Worship means *bowing before the Lord*. The Greek word pictures the worshiper kneeling on the ground and bending forward to touch his forehead to the ground. John 4:20-24 uses this term.

> Our fathers worshiped [*prosekunesan*] in this mountain, and you people say that in Jerusalem is the place where men ought to worship [*proskunein*]. Jesus said to her, "Woman, believe Me, an hour is coming when neither in this mountain nor in Jerusalem will you worship [*proskunesete*] the Father. You worship [*proskuneite*] what you do not know; we worship [*proskunoumen*] what we know, for salvation is from the Jews. But an hour is coming, and now is, when the true worshipers [*proskunetai*] will worship [*proskunesousin*] the Father in spirit and truth; for such people the Father seeks to be His worshipers [*proskunountas*]. God is spirit, and those who *worship* [*proskunountas*] Him must worship [*proskunein*] in spirit and truth.

Abraham uses the same idea when he says, "I and the lad will go over there; and we will worship [*proskunesantes* (LXX)] and return to you" (Gen. 22:5). The principal aspect of worship seen in these cases is that of bowing or prostrating one's self before the Lord. This bowing is in both heart and posture.

Worship also means *service*. Compare the following verses. Hebrews 9:1, "Now even the first covenant had regulations of divine worship [*latreias*]." The KJV reads here, "service." Hebrews 9:6, "The priests are continually entering the outer tabernacle performing the divine worship [*latreias*]." Again, the KJV reads here, "service." Hebrews 9:9, "Both gifts and sacrifices are offered which cannot make the worshiper [*latreuonta*]." The KJV reads here, "him that did the service." Exodus 3:12 uses similar language. God promised Moses, "When you have brought the people out of Egypt, you shall worship [*latreusete* (LXX)] God at this mountain." Again, the KJV says, "Ye shall *serve* God upon this mountain." The principal aspect of worship seen here is that of serving the Lord, carrying out His directions.

There is another Greek word associated with the idea of service. Luke 1:23 says of Zechariah, the father of John the Baptist, "When the days of his priestly service [*leitourgias*] were ended, he went back home." The English word *liturgy* comes from the Greek word translated *priestly service*. In carrying out his service, Zechariah followed a specific order of *worship* or order of *service* within the temple. Worship, therefore, involves a holy reverence, awe, and fear of the Lord in which believers bow before Him and serve Him as He directs them.

What about the English word "worship"? The English word *worship* comes from an archaic word meaning worthy, that is, having worth from the standpoint of dignity, importance, or rank. Just as a king or queen might be called 'your *highness*,' this same king or queen might be called 'your *worth*ship.' Worship is a contraction of worthship. Listen to the worship of Revelation 4:11. "Worthy are You, our Lord and our God, to receive glory and honor and power; for You created all things, and because of Your will they existed, and were created." God has ultimate worth. He has the highest dignity, honor, and rank. Thus, He is worthy, and worship is a response to the dignity, honor, and rank of God. Because He is of infinite worth, He alone is worshiped.

True worship is, therefore, God-centered. God forbids the worship of idols, of other gods. Notice the language of the Second Commandment. "You shall not make for yourself an idol, or any likeness of what is in heaven above or on the earth beneath or in the water under the earth. You shall not *worship* them or *serve* them ... " (Exod. 20:4-5, italics added). Also, note Paul's indictment of unbelievers: "They exchanged the truth of God for a lie, and *worshiped* and *served* the creature rather than the Creator" (Romans 1:25, italics added). In true worship, believers bow before God and serve Him as He directs because they recognize that He alone is worthy of honor, reverence, and fear. This understanding of worship is foundational to the discussion that follows.

WHO GOVERNS WORSHIP?

This question has already been answered. Believers bow before God and serve Him *as He directs*. What does serving God as He directs mean for the church today? The Apostle Paul makes this startling declaration to the church at Corinth. "We are the temple of the living God" (2 Cor. 6:16). The Corinthian people do not receive these words by Email or Twitter or on Facebook. The people hear these words sitting in sacred assembly as Paul's Letter is read to them. Paul likens their gathering to the temple in Jerusalem. That temple was God's special dwelling place. There, God's Shekinah glory took up residence (1 Kings 8:11; Exod. 40:35-38).

Paul affirms the declaration that the gathered church is God's temple by quoting Leviticus 26:11-12. "Moreover, I will make My dwelling among you, and My soul will not reject you. I will also walk among you and be your God, and you shall be My people." In other words, God promises to meet with His people, apply His covenant promises to them, and assure them that they belong to Him.

Paul makes a similar declaration to the church at Ephesus. In Christ, "the whole building [the church], being fitted together, is growing into a holy temple in the Lord" (Eph. 2:21). Yes, the church at large is growing into a temple. Paul does not stop here. He speaks directly to the church at Ephesus, declaring that, "you also are being built together into a dwelling of God in the Spirit" (Eph. 2:22). The people of Ephesus, and present day congregations, are being built together into special dwelling places of God. Peter also uses this temple imagery: "You also, as living stones, are being built up as a spiritual house for a holy priesthood, to offer up spiritual sacrifices acceptable to God through Jesus Christ" (1 Pet. 2:5).

Two other concepts round out the picture. Philippians 3:20 teaches that "our citizenship is in heaven." The true homeland of Christians is heaven. From this perspective, Paul speaks of himself as an ambassador (Eph. 6:20) and He reminds the Corinthians that, "we are ambassadors for Christ" (2 Cor. 5:20). Historically, an embassy is a group of dignitaries sent by a sovereign to represent him in a foreign land. The ambassador is their leader. Believing congregations are embassies of heaven in this world.

Like the word *church*, an embassy is thought of as the building where the ambassador lives and works. When visiting in a foreign land, foreigners can find safe haven in their embassy. The property where the embassy stands is the territory of their homeland. In like manner, as a citizen of heaven, believers regularly repair to their embassy, the church, the gathering of God's people. There, believers meet with their King, and they taste heaven. Therefore, Sabbath worship is an entrance into and a taste of heaven.

But who prescribes how we enter heaven? The answer to this question is simple. God does. Jesus says, "I am the way, and the truth, and the life; no one comes to the Father but through Me" (John 14:6). Peter affirms this. "There is salvation in no one else; for there is no other name under heaven that has been given among men by which we must be saved" (Acts 4:12). The way into heaven is the narrow way, and God prescribes the way.

These points lead to a very simple syllogism. Major premise: God prescribes how we enter heaven. We take this truth for granted. Minor Premise: Sabbath worship is an entrance into and a taste of heaven. This point has been established. Therefore, the conclusion is clear: God prescribes how we worship. Who governs or prescribes how believers worship?

1. God prescribes how we enter heaven.

2. Sabbath worship is an entrance into, and a taste of heaven.

3. God prescribes how we worship.

Keeping this syllogism in mind, there are two approaches to worship. The regulative principle states: In matters of worship, whatever God does not command, He forbids. The normative principle states: In matters of worship, whatever God does not forbid, He permits. The regulative principle is in keeping with the syllogism. This principle is foundational for the discussion that follows.

WHAT IS BASIC TO WORSHIP?

To answer this question, we turn to the early pages of Genesis. Moses uses the word *offering* for the first time in Genesis 4:3-4. "So it came about in the course of time that Cain brought an offering to the Lord of the fruit of the ground. Abel, on his part also brought of the firstlings of his flock and of their fat portions." Moses then indicates, "The Lord had regard for Abel and for his offering" (Gen. 4:4). Calvin says,

> We must, however, notice the order here observed by Moses; for he does not simply state that the *worship* which Abel had paid was pleasing to God, but he begins with the *person* of the offerer; by which he signifies, that God will regard no works with favor except those the doer of which is already previously accepted and approved by him.[4]

Why then does the Lord have regard for Abel? He is a man of faith; he is righteous; he is justified by faith. "By faith Abel offered to God

---

4. John Calvin, *Commentaries on the First Book of Moses Called Genesis*, trans. John King (Grand Rapids: Baker, 1979), 1:194.

a better sacrifice than Cain, through which he obtained the testimony that he was righteous" (Heb. 11:4). The text indicates that faith is essential to worship.

Moving ahead to Genesis 4, Moses points out that when God replaced murdered Abel with Seth, and Seth had a son, Enosh, "men began to call upon the name of the Lord" (Gen. 4:26). Calvin again comments, "But when Seth has children and God blesses that line, it is at that time that there is a 'church apparent.'"[5] In other words, Genesis 4:26 likely marks the beginning of the formal,[6] *public*,[7] stated[8] worship of God. As Calvin goes on to say, God "wanted to have a company of people who would trust him and learn to call upon his name and walk in uprightness."[9]

The Lord is Jehovah, the covenant-keeping God, the promise-keeping God.[10] He is the One who promised the Savior (Gen. 3:15). Worship involves faith, but faith always has an object. In this case, calling on the name of the Lord includes calling with faith in the promise.

Genesis 12:8 also connects calling on the name of the Lord with the altar of burnt offering; Abraham "built an altar to the Lord and called upon the name of the Lord." In the Old Testament, calling on the name of the Lord included sacrifice. Job, who likely lived during the time of the ancient patriarchs, regularly sacrificed for his family and children. "Job would send and consecrate them, rising up early in the morning and offering burnt offerings according to the number of them all; for Job said, 'Perhaps my sons have sinned and cursed God in their hearts'" (Job 1:5). "Sacrifice (which is as old as the sin of mankind) was to Job a means of grace, by which he cleansed himself every week from inward blemish."[11] The sacrifice was, therefore, a

---

5. John Calvin, *Sermons on Genesis 1-11*, trans. Rob Roy McGregor (Carlisle: Banner of Truth, 2009), 477.
6. John Peter Lange, *Genesis*, trans. Tayler Lewis and A. Gosman (Grand Rapids: Zondervan, 1960), 1:262.
7. Martin Luther, *Luther's Commentary on Genesis*, trans. J. Theodore Mueller (Grand Rapids: Zondervan, 1958), 1:116; George Bush, *Notes on Genesis* (Minneapolis: James Family, 1979), 1:108.
8. Bush, *Notes on Genesis*, 1:108.
9. Calvin, *Genesis 1-11*, 477.
10. Lange, *Genesis*, 1:262.
11. F. Delitzsch, *Biblical Commentary on the Book of Job*, trans. Francis Bolton (Grand Rapids: Eerdmans, 1966), 1:51.

means of cleansing from sin by grace through faith in the promised Savior. "When Moses says that men began to call on the name of the Lord, that is rightly referred to Christ."[12]

But there is more. "In the verb 'to call upon' there is a *synecdoche*, for it embraces the whole worship of God."[13] And so what does calling on the name of the Lord include? "We have here an account of the commencement of that worship of God which consists in prayer, praise, and thanksgiving, or in the acknowledgment and celebration of the mercy and help of Jehovah."[14]

At this point you may ask: Is worship with faith in the promised Savior and in atoning sacrifice expressed by way of prayer, praise, and thanksgiving prescribed by God? The very first sacrifice seems to indicate this. Genesis 3:21 says, "The Lord God made garments of skin for Adam and his wife, and clothed them." How did He do so? Calvin answers that God commands Adam and Eve to "put some [animals] to death, in order to cover themselves with their skins ... therefore Moses calls God the Author of it."[15]

> We undoubtedly see then in this incident the *first institution of animal sacrifices*; for that such a rite should have originated in mere human device cannot be maintained with any show of reason. How should it have entered into the mind of man to imagine that the blood of a beast could make satisfaction to God for sin? What conceivable connection is there, apart from divine appointment, between the blood of a brute animal and the sins of a human being? Indeed there was much more reason to think that God would have been displeased with the unauthorized destruction of his creatures, than that he would so accept it as to forgive iniquity on account of it. Such an offering without divine warrant would have

---

12. Luther, *Commentary on Genesis*, 1:116.
13. Calvin, *Commentaries on the First Book of Moses*, 223. Synecdoche is a figure of speech in which the part is put in the place of the whole. Italics in the original.
14. C. F. Keil and F. Delitzsch, *The Pentateuch*, trans. James Martin (Grand Rapids: Eerdmans, 1981), 1:120.
15. Calvin, *Commentaries on the First Book of Moses*, 181.

been at best a mere act of superstitious will-worship ... for what superstition can be more gross than to believe without any authority for so doing, that God will transfer the sins of the sacrificer to the sacrifice, and that thus the sacrificer himself shall be pardoned?[16]

What is basic to worship? From the beginning, worship requires faith in the atoning sacrifice prescribed by God and in the promised Savior. This faith is expressed through prayer, praise, and thanksgiving. This definition is foundational for further discussion.

THE POWER OF MUSIC

Expressing faith with prayer, praise, and thanksgiving raises the topic of music. What is music? The definition of music leads to a discussion of music and emotions. What is the connection between music and emotion? As the door is opened on this question, there is also a need to draw a distinction between vocal and instrumental music as they relate emotion. Understanding in these areas is foundational for the discussion of the thesis: Instrumental music is not integral to Biblical worship but, when introduced, it is incidental, typical, and temporary.

What, therefore, is music? A musician-physicist defines music this way, "All we can safely say is that music is sound which has been organized to stimulate someone—which is a bit feeble really."[17] Perhaps this definition is not so feeble. It has two important ingredients, organized sound connected with emotions. A dictionary definition is similar. Music is "the art and science of combining vocal or instrumental sounds or tones in varying melody, harmony, rhythm, and timbre, especially so as to form structurally complete and emotionally expressive compositions."[18] Both definitions speak of organized sound. In the first case, the sound stimulates or *evokes* feelings. In the

---

16. Bush, *Notes on Genesis*, 90.
17. John Powell, *How Music Works* (New York: Little Brown and Company, 2010), 5.
18. *Webster's New World Dictionary of the American Language* (Cleveland: World Publishing, 1958), 969.

second case, the sound *expresses* emotions. The dictionary definition covers both vocal and instrumental music.

Here is a second dictionary definition. Music is "the art or science of incorporating pleasing, expressive, or intelligible vocal or instrumental tones into a composition having definite structure and continuity."[19] This definition speaks of sounds that are pleasing, evoke pleasurable feelings, and are also expressive and intelligible. To grasp the significance of these definitions, a look at a handful of the basic building blocks of music is in order.

"A musical note consists of four things: a loudness, a duration, a timbre and a pitch."[20] As for duration, "some notes last longer than others."[21] Because of the nature of sound, loudness may relate to duration. "The normal loudness of a note can be heard if it is played for a second or so, but if it is played for a half a second or less, it will sound quieter."[22] Why is this important? "Subtle changes in loudness and duration during a song can carry a lot of emotional information."[23] What is pitch? "The most distinctive property of a musical note is its *pitch* ... "[24] At the same time, "[e]very melody is made up of a string of notes of different pitches."[25] And "the jumps in pitch between the notes in a tune are called *intervals* ... "[26] These definitions seem simple enough. Now we add timbre, which "is the characteristic quality of sound that distinguishes one voice or musical instrument from another."[27] A trumpet and a saxophone may sound the same note but they are distinguished from one another by their distinctive sounds, by their timbre. Different voices sounding the same note are distinguished in the same way, by their timbre. Timbre, however, is more than this distinguishing characteristic. "Timbre adds extra interest to

---

19. *Webster's Third New International Dictionary of the English Language, Unabridged* (Springfield, MA: G. and C. Merriam Company, 1966), 1490.
20. Powell, *How Music Works*, 6.
21. Ibid.
22. Ibid., 89.
23. Ibid., 6.
24. Ibid.
25. Ibid., 7.
26. Ibid., 15.
27. *Webster's New World Dictionary*, 1525.

the situation—in the same way that shading adds information to an outline drawing. This musical shading can have a big impact on the emotional feel of the music ... "[28]

Two other basic building blocks of music are worth mentioning, chords and harmonies. "A chord is the sound made by three or more notes [which sound good together] played at the same time ... A succession of chords produces a harmony. The relationship between chords and harmony is therefore similar to that between words and a sentence."[29] Those who write songs

> usually use harmony to provide background to the melody. This harmony can alter the mood of the melody just as the background of a photograph can make a portrait more or less cheerful. Film music composers often use only three or four tunes for an entire film, and they need to change the feel of the melody to match the moods of the different scenes. Techniques for altering the mood of music include using different instruments [the effect of timbre] ... and playing the melody faster or slower [subtle changes in loudness and duration]. But playing the tune with a different harmony is one of the most effective ways of manipulating our emotions.[30]

Understanding the basic building blocks of music moves the discussion ahead and builds upon the foundation already laid. The basic definitions of music include both the vocal and the instrumental. First, consider instrumental music.

THE POWER OF INSTRUMENTAL MUSIC

As indicated above, "A musical note consists of four things: a loudness, a duration, a timbre and a pitch."[31] Either human voices or

---

28. Powell, *How Music Works*, 40.
29. Ibid., 103.
30. Ibid.
31. Ibid., 6.

musical instruments may produce the sounds. In either case, music involves what are called nonverbals. Public speaking and preaching distinguishes between verbals and nonverbals.

> The use of *words* is spoken language. The topic of *voice* is a reference to paralanguage, how you speak, your tempo, pitch, intonation, and the like. The third element is the use of your *body*, kinesics or body language. How you use your voice, paralanguage, and how you use your body, kinesics, fall in the category of wordless communication. They are nonverbals in contrast to verbal or spoken language.[32]

These nonverbals are an important part of the communication process. Robert Dabney says that the very sound of a voice "suggests often some sentiment, and awakens it in the hearer."[33] In other words, speakers communicate feelings by how they use their voices. It makes a difference how you say, "Shut the door." These words may relay a simple request, "Hey, shut the door." Or they may issue a command, "Shut the door!" There may be urgency in this command. But there may also be anger, "Hey! Shut the door!" Facial expression, use of the eyes, tilt of the head, and hand gestures enter into the communication process too. Nonverbals communicate feelings and emotion. "Generally speaking, we can say that a person's nonverbal behavior has more bearing than his words on communicating feelings or attitudes to others."[34] These nonverbals evoke emotional responses in listeners. In a similar way, instrumental music evokes emotional responses in listeners. However, there are some significant differences.

For example, musical instruments and music do not have emotions. Emotions are a human characteristic. Those hearing a piece of music may say that it is sad. "But the connection is not a literal one, since

---
32. Dennis Prutow, *So, Pastor, What's Your Point?* (Philadelphia: Alliance of Confessing Evangelicals, 2010), 317.
33. Robert L. Dabney, *Sacred Rhetoric* (Carlisle: Banner of Truth Trust, 1979), 314.
34. Albert Mehrabian, *Silent Messages* (Belmont, CA: Wadsworth, 1971), 44.

'the music is sad' seems to attribute a feeling to the music whereas we all know that music, being nonsentient, feels nothing."[35] The key here is that emotions are attributed to that which does not have emotions.

Attributing emotions to the inanimate is common. Take Psalm 98:8 as an example. "Let the rivers clap their hands, / Let the mountains sing together for joy." There are two important figures of speech in this text. Rivers do not have hands but the Bible attributes human hands to them. We call this figure of speech an anthropomorphism.[36] In like manner, the text attributes joy to mountains. In this case, the Bible attributes human emotions to inanimate mountains. This figure of speech is an anthropopathism.[37]

The Bible speaks about musical instruments in the same way. "Therefore my harp is turned to mourning, / And my flute to the sound of those who weep" (Job 30:31).

> Here the meaning is certainly not one of material substance being changed into a non-material entity (emotion). It is rather a poetic and emphatic way of relating that these musical instruments articulated emotional states (in the sphere of sound ordered in time and space) so accurately that they could actually be thought of as becoming those very emotions.[38]

In other words, emotions are attributed to the music of the harp and the flute. Why? "In music we know how certain sounds can 'trigger' a response because the associational value is strong. The national anthem, a favorite hymn, a school song, or even a bugle-call are examples of this kind of direct signal."[39] When musical sounds evoke certain emotions, those emotions are attributed to the music

---

35. Stephen Davies, *Musical Meaning and Expression* (London: Cornell University Press, 1994), 163. Sentient: "capable of feeling or perception," *Webster's New World Dictionary*, 1327.
36. Louis Berkhof, *Principles of Biblical Interpretation* (Grand Rapids: Baker, 1964), 83. The word, anthropomorphism combines *anthropos*, man, and *morphe*, form. An anthropomorphism is a type of metaphor sometimes called a *special metaphor*. A metaphor is an implied comparison.
37. Ibid. The word anthropopathism combines *anthropos*, man, and *pathos*, passion or emotion. An anthropopathism is also a special metaphor.
38. John Makujina, *Measuring the Music* (Willow Street, PA: Old Paths, 2002), 319.
39. William Edgar, *Taking Note of Music* (London: SPCK, 1986), 74.

and to the instruments. The attribution of emotion to music is the idea of an anthropopathism.

Other nonverbals, in addition to the sounds, may also come into play. How musicians address and attack their music affects the sounds they produce with their instruments. Their body language, facial expressions, stance, and gestures all come into play when listening to live performances. All of these elements contribute to how the audience responds, and how instrumental music evokes various emotions.

THE POWER OF VOCAL MUSIC

Everything just said about nonverbals applies also to a cappella vocal music. Everything said about notes, loudness, duration, timbre, and pitch, and about chords and harmonies applies also to vocal music. For example, Robert Dabney observes, "The feeling in a man's voice consists partly in its peculiar timbre ... "[40] On one hand, for listeners, vocal presentations may evoke various emotions in them. On the other hand, when individuals sing, and when congregations sing, vocal music also offers opportunity for expressing emotions.

In vocal music, text is connected with melody and voice. This connection is ancient. "Plato believes that education in music, meaning the unity of melody, poetry, and dance is important, because rhythm and harmony penetrate deeply into the inmost soul and exercise a strong influence upon it."[41] Note two things here: the unity of melody, poetry, and dance; and the penetrating quality of this unity. "Wind instruments are generally criticized by Plato because they also prevent the performer from singing or speaking while playing, thus violating the unity of speech or song, instrumental playing, and dance."[42] This quote indicates that Plato's emphasis is not on performance. "The aim of training in music, however, is not musical expertise but the

---

40. Dabney, *Sacred Rhetoric*, 314.
41. Lelouda Stamou, "Plato and Aristotle on Music and Music Education: Lessons from Ancient Greece," *International Journal of Music Education*, 39 (2002): 5.
42. Ibid., 6.

cultivation of the soul. As he says, 'the vocal aspect reaching the soul we regard as education in virtue and we named it *music*.'"[43]

Calvin agrees with Plato on two counts, the power of music and the importance of the connection of text with music. First, consider these often-quoted words from "Calvin's Preface to the Psalter," dated June 10, 1543. "But there is still more: there is scarcely in the world anything [like music] which is able to turn or bend this way and that the morals of men, as Plato prudently considered it. And in fact, we find by experience that it [music] has a sacred and almost incredible power to move hearts in one way or other."[44] Second, "in speaking now of music, I understand two parts: namely the letter, or the subject matter; secondly, the song, or the melody."[45] Calvin insisted on the superiority of text over music.[46] "Touching the melody, it has seemed best that it be moderated in the manner we have adopted to carry the weight and majesty appropriate to the subject ... "[47] In Calvin's thought, however, the melody is carried by voices, and excludes the use of instruments.[48]

> What about the text connected with vocal music? Calvin answers the question. It is to have songs not only honest, but also holy, which will be like spurs to incite us to pray to and praise God, and to meditate upon his works in order to love, fear, honor and glorify him. Moreover, that which St. Augustine has said is true, that no one is able to sing things worthy of God except that which he has received from him. Therefore, when we have looked thoroughly, and searched here and there, we shall not

---

43. Ibid., 7. "Oddly enough, even the term *music* is derivative of a Greek adjective that means, etymologically, 'produced by the Muse.' In Greek, then, music is a gift from part of the Greco-Roman pantheon, a semi-divine creation. Our verb *muse*, therefore, etymologically meant 'to give careful attention to a matter,' as though it were produced by the semi-divine Muse. The word *a-muse*, then, means just the opposite: 'no-muse,' or 'no serious attention to be given.' A-musement thus puts the divinity in the background – what an oxymoron: *background music*!" T. David Gordon, *Why Johnny Can't Sing Hymns* (Phillipsburg: P & R, 2010), 90-91.
44. John Calvin, "Preface to the Psalter," in Oliver Strunk, *Source Readings in Music History* (New York: W. W. Norton, 1998), 366.
45. Ibid.
46. Robert M. Copeland, *The Direct Path of Music of Louis Bourgeois* (Ottawa: Institute of Mediaeval Music, 2008), 8.
47. Calvin, "Preface to the Psalter," 367.
48. Copeland, *The Direct Path*, 11.

find better songs nor more fitting for the purpose, than the Psalms of David, which the Holy Spirit spoke and made through him.[49]

But why the Psalms? What is it that makes the Psalms so unique as to qualify them to be placed with vocal music for singing in worship? Again, Calvin answers the question.

> I have been accustomed to call this book, I think not inappropriately, "An Anatomy of all the Parts of the Soul"; for there is not an emotion of which any one can be conscious that is not here represented as in a mirror. Or rather, the Holy Spirit has here drawn to the life all the griefs, sorrows, fears, doubts, hopes, cares, perplexities, in short, all the distracting emotions with which the minds of men are wont to be agitated ... It is by perusing these inspired compositions, that men will be most effectually awakened to a sense of their maladies, and, at the same time, instructed in seeking remedies for their cure. In a word, whatever may serve to encourage us when we are about to pray to God, is taught us in this book.[50]

According to Calvin, the Psalms provide believers with a divine guide for expressing their emotions while singing in worship. This position is in keeping with singing as the cultivation of character and of the soul. It is possible that Calvin derives this perspective on the Psalms from Athanasius, who writes:

> And, among all the books, the Psalter has certainly a very special grace, a choiceness of quality well worthy to be pondered; for, besides the characteristics which it shares with others, it has this peculiar marvel of its own, that within it are represented and portrayed in all their great variety the movements of the human soul. It is like

---

49. Ibid.
50. John Calvin, "The Author's Preface," *Commentary on the Book of Psalms*, trans. James Anderson (Grand Rapids: Baker, 1979), 1: xxxviii-xxxix.

a picture, in which you see yourself portrayed, and seeing, may understand and consequently form yourself upon the pattern given ... [I]n the Psalter, besides all these things, you learn about yourself. You find depicted in it all the movements of your soul, all its changes, its ups and downs, its failures and recoveries. Moreover, whatever your particular need or trouble, from this same book you can select a form of words to fit it, so that you do not merely hear and then pass on, but learn the way to remedy your ill ... [I]t is the Psalms that show you how to set about repenting and with what words your penitence may be expressed ... [I]t is in the Psalms that we find written and described how afflictions should be borne, and what the afflicted ought to say, both at the time and when his troubles cease: the whole process of his testing is set forth in them and we are shown exactly with what words to voice our hope in God ... The Psalms not only exhort us to be thankful, they also provide us with fitting words to say ... [T]he Psalms supply words with which both those who flee persecution and those who suffer under it may suitably address themselves to God, and it does the same for those who have been rescued from it ... [H]ere in the Psalms we are shown ... with what sort of words His majesty may meetly be confessed. In fact, under all the circumstances of life, we shall find that these divine songs suit ourselves and meet our own souls' need at every turn.[51]

Yes, with a cappella vocal music, using the Psalms, believers have a divine guide for the proper expression of all their emotions in the public worship of God. What is the power of a cappella vocal music in worship? Using this means, their souls are cultivated and aligned with the Word of God.

---

51. Athanasius, "The Letter to Marcellinus," Fisheaters.com, accessed November 15, 2011.

SUMMARY AND REVIEW

In true worship, believers bow before God and serve Him as He directs, because they recognize that He alone is worthy of honor, reverence, and fear. Since God prescribes how one enters heaven, and corporate, public worship is an entrance into and a taste of heaven, God prescribes how believers are to worship. Worship requires faith in the atoning sacrifice prescribed by God, and in the promised Savior, this faith being expressed by way of prayer, praise, and thanksgiving. Part of the genius of music is to evoke and/or express emotions. In the case of instrumental music, the sounds evoke certain emotions within those listening. Emotions are, therefore, imputed to the music. While the sound of others singing around an individual in the congregation may also evoke emotions, vocal music aligned with text gives worshipers the opportunity to express their emotions. The sounds they hear around them reinforce this expression. Understanding these points provides the foundation for further study. Building on this foundation, it will be seen that the Biblical and historical data shows that instrumental music is not integral to Biblical worship. It will be seen that, when introduced, instrumental music is incidental and temporary, because it is typical.

17

INSTRUMENTAL MUSIC:
THE HISTORICAL PERSPECTIVE
FROM ADAM TO AUGUSTINE

*His brother's name was Jubal; he was the father of
allthose who play the lyre and pipe.* ~ GEN. 4:21

INTRODUCTION

This chapter looks at the Biblical history in both the Old and New Testaments, and in the post-apostolic period regarding instrumental music in worship. Chapter 18 continues the discussion with the Medieval church, the Reformation era, the modern era, and the future as set forth by the Book of Revelation. This historical data will display the transitions that take place in Biblical worship and the corresponding responsibilities of believers living in the respective eras. Chapter 19 entertains a brief discussion of Biblical typology and will show how the instruments in the Old Testament were types foreshadowing aspects of New Testament worship. At various points, reference will be made to the foundation reviewed in chapter 16.

ADAM TO ABRAHAM

In discussing the basics of worship, we examined the worship of Adam and Eve (Gen. 3:21) and of Cain and Abel (Gen. 4:3-4). It was found that worship requires faith in the atoning sacrifice prescribed by God and in the promise of the Savior, this faith being expressed through prayer, praise, and thanksgiving.

Genesis 4:21 introduces the second son of Lamech. His name was Jubal, and "he was the father of all those who play the lyre and pipe." The lyre and pipe may be representative stringed and wind instruments.[1] The invention of musical instruments at this time indicates that they were not essential to the worship carried out by Adam, Eve, Cain, and Abel. Note, too, that Jubal is the son of Lamech, of the line of Cain.

After Moses relates the invention of various arts and crafts including musical instruments (Gen. 4:20-22), the "song of Lamech" is heard.[2] "Adah and Zillah, / Listen to my voice, / You wives of Lamech, / Give heed to my speech, / For I have killed a man for wounding me; / And a boy for striking me; / If Cain is avenged sevenfold, / Then Lamech seventy-sevenfold" (Gen. 4:23-24). "Along with the invention of music (v 21) went the composition of poetry."[3] In this song, "Lamech breaks forth in eulogy and praise of great violence. It is an arrogant boast of the seed of the serpent."[4] And in this first apparent conjunction of instrumental music and song, we see God's good gifts put to evil use.[5]

At this point, Moses interjects, "Then men began to call upon the name of the LORD" (Gen. 4:26). Calling on the name of the LORD was public, and included sacrifice and faith in the promised Savior expressed in prayer, praise, and thanksgiving. The next time Scripture records such worship is immediately after the flood. "Then Noah built an altar to the LORD, and took of every clean animal and of every clean bird and offered burnt offerings on the altar" (Gen. 8:20). "The first thing which Noah did, was to build an altar for burnt sacrifice, to thank the Lord for gracious protection, and to pray for His mercy in

---

1. George Bush, *Notes on Genesis* (Minneapolis: James Family, 1979), 106. John Currid, *A Study Commentary on Genesis* (Webster, NY: Evangelical Press, 2003), 1:154.
2. Gordon J. Wenham, *Genesis 1-15* (Waco: Word Books, 1987), 114.
3. Ibid.
4. Currid, *Genesis*, 1:155.
5. Robert M. Copeland, *The Direct Path of Music of Louis Bourgeois* (Ottawa: Institute of Mediaeval Music, 2008), 10.

time to come."[6] The Lord received the offering as a *"soothing aroma"* (Gen. 8:21, italics added). God, however, did not gladly receive the sacrifice in-and-of-itself. Noah was a man of faith, who received the righteousness of faith (Heb. 11:7). "That the sacrifice of Noah on this occasion prefigured that of Christ is evident from the words of Paul" who uses the same words in Ephesians 5:2.[7] "Christ also loved you and gave Himself up for us, an offering and a sacrifice to God as a *fragrant aroma*."[8]

There is no indication of the use of musical instruments with the above worship. Yes, this is an argument from silence. However, had instrumental music been integral to worship, and necessary to make it whole and complete, surely Scripture would have mentioned the use of instruments and their necessity. It does not.

ABRAHAM TO MOSES

Next is the period of the patriarchs, the times of Abraham, Isaac, Jacob, and Job. Worship continued, as already described, with intimate connections between promise, faith, and sacrifice. It was also a time, as Matthew Henry characterizes it, "before sacrifices were confined to one altar."[9] Job no doubt lived during the patriarchal period.[10] He was a man of faith who believed in the resurrection of the dead, as he himself testified. "As for me, I know that my Redeemer lives, / And at the last He will take His stand on the earth. / Even after my skin is destroyed, / Yet from my flesh I shall see God; / Whom I myself shall behold, / And whom my eyes will see and not another" (Job 19:25-27). Job confirmed his faith with weekly sacrifices on behalf of his children as described above in chapter 16. Job's home was "in the land of Uz" (Job 1:1) which is northern Arabia, east of Palestine.[11]

---

6. C. F. Keil and F. Delitzsch, *The Pentateuch*, trans. James Martin (Grand Rapids: Eerdmans, 1981), 1:150.
7. Bush, *Genesis*, 148. For "fragrant" or "soothing aroma," the LXX reads *osmen euōdias*.
8. Paul uses the same words: *osmen euōdias*.
9. Matthew Henry, *Matthew Henry's Commentary on the Whole Bible* (Grand Rapids: Fleming H. Revell, 1985), 3:1.
10. Gleason L. Archer, *A Survey of Old Testament Introduction* (Chicago: Moody Press, 1964), 440-441; Edward J. Young, *An Introduction to the Old Testament* (Grand Rapids: Eerdmans, 1975), 323.
11. Archer, *A Survey*, 440.

After traveling from Ur of the Chaldeans, Abraham migrated to Shechem, located "in a pass between mounts Ebal and Gerizin, at the crossroads of central Palestine" (Gen. 12:6).[12] "The LORD appeared to Abram and said, 'To your descendants I will give this land.' So he built an altar there to the LORD who had appeared to him" (Gen. 12:7). After responding to God's promise in faith with worship, Abraham moves south. "Then he proceeded from there to the mountain on the east of Bethel, and pitched his tent, with Bethel on the west and Ai on the east; and there he built an altar to the LORD and called upon the name of the LORD" (Gen. 12:8). Review the discussion of this text in chapter 16.

After time spent in Egypt because of famine, Abraham returned to Bethel and worshiped there according to the well-established custom. "He went on his journeys from the Negev as far as Bethel, to the place where his tent had been at the beginning, between Bethel and Ai, to the place of the altar which he had made there formerly; and there Abram called on the name of the LORD" (Gen. 13:3-4). Again, moving south to Hebron, Abraham built another altar to the LORD. "Then Abram moved his tent and came and dwelt by the oaks of Mamre, which are in Hebron, and there he built an altar to the LORD (Gen. 13:18).

When Abraham took Isaac to Mount Moriah to sacrifice him in obedience to the LORD, Genesis 22:13 records, "Then Abraham raised his eyes and looked, and behold, behind him a ram caught in the thicket by his horns; and Abraham went and took the ram and offered him up for a burnt offering in the place of his son."[13] Genesis 22:18 then repeats God's covenant promise, "In your seed all the nations of the earth shall be blessed, because you have obeyed My voice."[14]

---

12. Derek Kidner, *Genesis* (Chicago: Inter-Varsity Press, 1967), 114.
13. "Moriah reappears only in 2 Chronicles 3:1, where it is identified as the place where God halted the plague of Jerusalem and where Solomon built the Temple. In the New Testament terms, this is the vicinity of Calvary" (Kidner, *Genesis*, 143).
14. As indicated, Genesis 22:18 does not teach works righteousness. When God says, "because you have *obeyed* my voice," the text uses a figure of speech called metonymy, where the effect or outcome is put in the place of the instrument or cause. Works are the proper outcome of sincere faith (James 2:26). When God indicates His blessing comes "because you have *obeyed* my voice," the meaning is "because you have *believed* my voice." See, E. W. Bullinger, *Figures of Speech Used in the Bible* (Grand Rapids: Baker, 1968), 538-539, 572.

Abraham's obedience grew out of his belief that God would raise Isaac from the dead in order to fulfill His promise. "By faith Abraham, when he was tested, offered up Isaac, and he who had received the promises was offering up his only begotten son" (Heb. 11:17). Again, sacrifice, promise, and faith are joined in an act of worship.

In Genesis 26:23-25, God renewed his covenant with Isaac. The location was in Beersheba, south of Hebron in the Negev. Isaac followed the family tradition of public worship. Receiving God's promise, he offered sacrifice and called on the Lord.

> Then he [Isaac] went up from there to Beersheba. The Lord appeared to him the same night and said, "I am the God of your father Abraham; Do not fear, for I am with you. I will bless you, and multiply your descendants, For the sake of My servant Abraham." So he built an altar there and called upon the name of the Lord, and pitched his tent there; and there Isaac's servants dug a well.

After his reconciliation with Esau, Jacob returned to Shechem. "Then he erected there an altar and called it El-Elohe-Israel" (Gen. 33:20). Jacob had made a vow to return to Bethel (Gen. 28:18-22). God, therefore, directed him back to Bethel to build an altar and lead in public worship.

> Then God said to Jacob, "Arise, go up to Bethel and live there, and make an altar there to God, who appeared to you when you fled from your brother Esau." So Jacob said to his household and to all who were with him, "Put away the foreign gods which are among you, and purify yourselves and change your garments; and let us arise and go up to Bethel, and I will make an altar there to God, who answered me in the day of my distress and has been with me wherever I have gone." So they gave to Jacob all the foreign gods which they had and the rings which were in their ears, and Jacob hid them under the oak which was near Shechem. As they journeyed, there

was a great terror upon the cities which were around them, and they did not pursue the sons of Jacob. So Jacob came to Luz (that is, Bethel), which is in the land of Canaan, he and all the people who were with him. He built an altar there, and called the place El-bethel, because there God had revealed Himself to him when he fled from his brother (Gen. 35:1-7).

Job, Abraham, Isaac, and Jacob called upon the Lord, trusting His promises. They did so by building altars in various locations to offer sacrifices to the Lord. As will become clear, although musical instruments are commonly used in banquets, weddings, and other community celebrations, there is no evidence that the patriarchs used them with their sacrifices. Had instrumental music been integral to worship, and necessary to make it whole and complete in these cases, Scripture would have so indicated. It does not.

MOSES TO DAVID

Two significant changes to worship took place under Moses. There was a change from various altars in various places to one altar in one place. There was also the specific addition of musical instruments to the sacrifices. (The worship scene in Exodus 15 will be examined, concluding that it is a one time event tied to a specific occasion.)

After delivering Israel from bondage in Egypt (Exod. 1-18), God formed the people into a covenant community at Sinai (Exod. 19-24). The Lord then formed the people into a worshiping community (Exod. 25-40).[15] God commanded Moses, "Let them build a sanctuary for Me, that I may dwell among them" (Exod. 25:8). The remainder of Exodus details the plan for the tabernacle (Exod. 25-31), Aaron leading the people in idolatry (Exod. 32-34), and the construction of the tabernacle according to God's plan (Exod. 35-40). Moses "erected the court all around the tabernacle and the altar, and hung up the veil

---

15. Tremper Longman and Raymond Dillard, *An Introduction to the Old Testament* (Grand Rapids: Zondervan, 2006), 70-72.

for the gateway of the court. Thus Moses finished the work" (Exod. 40:33). The passage continues,

> Then the cloud covered the tent of meeting, and the glory of the Lord filled the tabernacle. Moses was not able to enter the tent of meeting because the cloud had settled on it, and the glory of the Lord filled the tabernacle. Throughout all their journeys whenever the cloud was taken up from over the tabernacle, the sons of Israel would set out; but if the cloud was not taken up, then they did not set out until the day when it was taken up. For throughout all their journeys, the cloud of the Lord was on the tabernacle by day, and there was fire in it by night, in the sight of all the house of Israel (Exod. 40:33-38).

Once completed, the Tabernacle with its altar of burnt offering was Israel's central place of worship. "During the period from Sinai to Solomon, the tabernacle served as the earthly dwelling of God. It was the place to which the people would go in order to meet with him. As the place of God's special presence, the tabernacle was holy ground."[16] No longer would Israel build altars in different locations. Now the altar traveled with Israel.

As part of the sacrificial worship in the Tabernacle, God ordained the use of two silver trumpets. "The Lord spoke further to Moses, saying, 'Make yourself two trumpets of silver, of hammered work you shall make them; and you shall use them for summoning the congregation and for having the camps set out'" (Num. 10:1-2). God also commanded the priests to use these trumpets with the sacrifices on the altar of burnt offering. Note the exact command of God in Numbers 10:10. "Also in the day of your gladness and in your appointed feasts, and on the first days of your months, you shall blow the trumpets over your burnt offerings, and over the sacrifices of your peace offerings ... "

---

16. Ibid., 77.

For the first time, musical instruments were used with the sacrifices on the altar. The trumpets did not accompany any singing. There was no singing with the sacrifices. The trumpets simply accompanied the sacrifices on the altar. This practice continued until the time of David. There was, therefore, a transition in Biblical worship that God commanded. There was now sacrifice on one altar, with trumpets accompanying the sacrifice.

DAVID TO NEHEMIAH

After the Philistines captured and released the ark of the covenant (1 Sam. 4-6), the ark of the covenant remained at Kiriath-jearim for 20 years (1 Sam. 7:2). The tabernacle remained at Shiloh and then found its way to Nob (1 Sam. 1:1 and 21:1). "When Nob was destroyed by Saul, the tabernacle was transported to Gibeon, where it remained till the temple was built by Solomon (I Chron. xvi. 39; xxi. 29; I Kings iii. 4; 2 Chron. i. 3)."[17] During this time, the ark of the covenant was separated from the tabernacle. After an unsuccessful effort to relocate the ark of the covenant, David did move it to a tent he erected for it in Jerusalem (2 Sam. 6; 1 Chron. 15).[18]

It was now time for two significant changes to take place in Israel's worship. First, David "appointed some of the Levites as ministers before the ark of the LORD, even to celebrate and to thank and praise the LORD God of Israel" (1 Chron. 16:4). While sacrifices were offered at the Tabernacle in Gibeon, David appointed "Heman and Jeduthun, and the rest who were chosen, who were designated by name, to give thanks to the LORD" (1 Chron. 16:41). The earlier genealogies describe this new service for the Levites. "Now these are those whom David appointed *over the service of song* in the house of the LORD, after the ark rested there. They ministered *with song* before the tabernacle of

---

17. Alfred Edersheim, *Old Testament Bible History, Complete in One Volume* (Grand Rapids: Eerdmans, 1982), 3:78.

18. It is true that David relocated the ark of the covenant with singing and the use of various instruments. This one time event was tied to a specific occasion similar to that of Exodus 15, and it will be reviewed later in the discussion.

the tent of meeting, until Solomon had built the house of the LORD in Jerusalem" (1 Chron. 6:31-32, italics added). David added sacred song to the sacrificial worship of God.

Second, David added the use of "harps, lyres," and "loud sounding cymbals" while "the priests blew the trumpets continually before the ark of the covenant of God" (1 Chron. 16:5-6). In the tabernacle at Gibeon, David appointed "Heman and Jeduthun with trumpets and cymbals for those who should sound aloud, and with instruments for the songs of God" (1 Chron. 16:42). We learn later that David made these specific changes because "the command was from the LORD through His prophets" (2 Chron. 29:25). And so David made these significant changes to the worship of Israel by God's command. He added both vocal and instrumental music to the worship of his time.

This pattern of worship continued under Solomon, and, when abandoned, it was restored, for example, by Hezekiah, who

> then stationed the Levites in the house of the LORD with cymbals, with harps and with lyres, according to the command of David and of Gad the king's seer, and of Nathan the prophet; for the command was from the LORD through His prophets. The Levites stood with the musical instruments of David, and the priests with the trumpets. Then Hezekiah gave the order to offer the burnt offering on the altar. When the burnt offering began, the song to the LORD also began with the trumpets, accompanied by the instruments of David, king of Israel (2 Chron. 29:25-27).

The Jews also observed these standards after the exile. Nehemiah 12:45 reports, "They performed the worship of their God and the service of purification, together with the singers and the gatekeepers in accordance with the command of David and of his son Solomon."

One might ponder the reaction of the Israelites when David added singing and instruments to the worship of God inaugurated under Moses. "Why should this singing and the use of musical instruments be added to God's worship? Why can we not continue worshiping God with the simplicity of former times? Why must we change now?" Of course the change came at God's command. A principle began to emerge. Believers are responsible to worship the LORD, in the era in which they live, according to the standards He gives to them for that era. The people of David's time were not free to worship according to the standards for worship for the previous era under Moses. With the new era, there were new standards for worship they were to follow.

NEHEMIAH TO CHRIST

The Babylonians destroyed the Temple in 586 B.C., taking most of the Jews into captivity. When the people returned to Palestine after the captivity, they rebuilt the temple (Ezra 6:13-15). By this time, two institutions stood side by side, the temple and the synagogue. "The origin of the synagogue is uncertain."[19] As pointed out in this study, the traditional position was that the origin of the synagogue goes back to Moses and Leviticus 23:3.[20] Many other commentators hold that the development of the synagogue was "forced upon the Jews during the Exile."[21] Others point to Ezra the scribe. "In point of fact, the attentive reader of the books of Ezra and Nehemiah will discover in the period after the return from Babylon the beginnings of the synagogue."[22] Whichever the case, after the exile, "the custom of attending the synagogue on the Sabbath day for instruction in the law and for prayer grew with considerable rapidity."[23]

As a result, during this period, "the devotional form of worship Jeremiah, Ezekiel, and other prophets envisaged became the established pattern of religious activity."[24] What was the significance of this emphasis on the synagogue for the Jews? "Oddly enough, they

---

19. J. Julius Scott, *Customs and Controversies* (Grand Rapids: Baker, 1995), 139.
20. Review the argument presented in chapter 5.
21. R. K. Harrison, *Old Testament Times* (Peabody, MA: Hendrickson, 2001), 299.
22. Alfred Edersheim, *Sketches of Jewish Social Life* (Grand Rapids: Eerdmans, 1993), 252.
23. Harrison, *Old Testament Times*, 299-300.
24. Ibid., 299.

were more distinctively themselves, more Jewish, than at any time of their existence as a sovereign state."[25]

> In short, what we see in Ezra-Nehemiah is an Israel cut down almost to the roots, but drawing a new vitality from its neglected source of nourishment in the Mosaic law and already showing signs, by its new concern for purity, of growing into the Judaism which we meet, both for better and for worse, in the New Testament.[26]

With the temple and synagogue standing side by side, there are two types or forms of worship standing side by side. The temple centered on sacrifice. The synagogue centered on Scripture. Very briefly, the services were as follows.

In the temple, the Levites designated to sing and play their harps and lyres, and the priests ordained to perform the sacrifices gathered at the altar of burnt offering. As a part of the sacrificial service, the head of the Levites stood between the sanctuary and the altar with the cymbals. Two priests stood on either side of him with their trumpets. After the sacrifice was on the altar of burnt offering, the priests gave three blasts on their trumpets. The head of the Levites then clashed the cymbals. As the Chief Priest was pouring out the drink offering of wine on the burnt offering, the Levitical Choir sang the designated Psalm of the day.[27]

The synagogue service was distinct. "It was not a substitute for temple worship and services as such, but a supplement to them."[28] There were no sacrifices. For this reason, "There was no service of 'praise' in the synagogues."[29] Why? The synagogue service was not only distinct from the temple but, "the main object of the synagogue

---

25. Derek Kidner, *Ezra and Nehemiah* (Downers Grove: Inter-Varsity, 1979), 14.
26. Ibid., 23.
27. James W. McKinnon, "The Exclusion of Musical Instruments from the Ancient Synagogue," *Journal of the Royal Musical Association* 106 (1979): 77; John Lightfoot, *The Works of the Reverend and Learned John Lightfoot* (London: Robert Scot, 1684), 1:923.
28. Scott, *Customs and Controversies*, 139.
29. Edersheim, *Sketches of Jewish Social Life*, 268. Those who hold that there was singing in the synagogue argue that since Christian worship is based on the synagogue, the synagogue must have included singing. They read 1 Corinthians 14:26 back into the synagogue, "When you assemble, each one has a psalm, has a teaching ... " For example, see, W. O. E. Oesterley, *The Psalms in the Jewish Church* (London: Skeffington and Son, 1910), 134.

was the teaching of the people."³⁰ The order of worship was, therefore, simple. Worship began with a confession, the Shema, consisting of a recitation of Deuteronomy 6:4-9 and 11:13-21, plus Numbers 15:37-41. Daily prayers followed. "The daily prayer, the *Shemoneh 'Esreh* (Eighteen Benedictions) was an important component of both synagogue worship and private devotion."³¹

> After the appropriate prayers had been recited and the two scripture lessons read—one from the Pentateuch and the other from some place in the prophetical books bearing some relation to the subject of the Pentateuchal reading—an address was normally delivered by some suitable member of the congregation.³²

A translator-interpreter also stood by during the Scripture readings to translate the Hebrew text into the local language spoken by the people and to offer brief explanations of the text.³³

In summary, temple and synagogue stood as two complementary institutions. In temple worship, the sacrifices were accompanied by the singing of Psalms and instrumental music. The instruments were the two silver trumpets, ordained by God through Moses, and the use of cymbals, harps, and lyres ordained by God through David. In the synagogue, the primary feature was the reading and teaching of Scripture. "[T]here was no singing of psalms in the ancient Synagogue … "³⁴ Those who were "sympathetic to the idea that the origins of the Christian liturgy were to be sought in the Synagogue, simply assumed that Christian psalmody must have stemmed from Synagogue psalmody."³⁵ Since there was likely no singing in the ancient synagogue, instrumental music was also absent from its worship. Musical instruments were reserved for the temple. "The writers who have most carefully investigated Jewish antiquities, and have writ-

---

30. Ibid., 267.
31. Scott, *Customs and Controversies*, 141.
32. F. F. Bruce, *Commentary on the Book of Acts* (Grand Rapids: Eerdmans, 1970), 267-268.
33. Scott, *Customs and Controversies*, 142. See also Edersheim, *Sketches of Jewish Social Life*, 265-280.
34. McKinnon, "Exclusion of Musical Instruments," 84.
35. Ibid.

ten learnedly and elaborately in regard to the synagogue, concur in showing that its worship was destitute of instrumental music."[36]

THE NEW TESTAMENT ERA

Entering the New Testament, it is clear that the temple and synagogue are both firmly established institutions. They continue to complement each other. Christ frequented the temple and regarded it as His Father's house (Luke 2:49; John 2:16). Christ also frequently taught in the synagogue (Matt. 4:23; 9:35; Luke 4:15; 13:10). It was also His custom to attend Sabbath worship in the synagogue (Luke 4:16).

The Romans destroyed the temple in 70 A.D., thus closing the era of the temple. After lamenting His rejection by the Jews, Christ predicted its final destruction. "Jerusalem, Jerusalem, who kills the prophets and stones those who are sent to her! How often I wanted to gather your children together, the way a hen gathers her chicks under her wings, and you were unwilling. Behold, your house is being left to you desolate" (Matt. 23:37-38). Christ, the glory of God, then walked away from the temple. As Calvin writes, "He proclaims the razing of the temple and the ruin of the whole people."[37] As Calvin sees it, Christ predicted the permanent destruction of the temple. "This was a dreadful act of God's vengeance, that a place He had so magnificently embellished He should abandon and wish utterly destroyed; yes, and to the end of the world, subject to extreme ignominy."[38] Matthew Henry agrees, "Both the city and the temple, God's house and their own, all shall be laid waste."[39] Again, the destruction of the temple took place at the hand of the Romans in 70 A.D.

In Hebrews 10:5-9, the writer reveals the ultimate reason the temple sacrifices were set aside. He contrasts the temporary temple sacrifices

---

36. John L. Girardeau, *Instrumental Music in Public Worship* (Havertown, PA: New Covenant Publication Society, 1983), 39.
37. John Calvin, *A Harmony of the Gospels, Matthew, Mark, and Luke*, trans. A. W. Morrison, ed. David W. Torrance and Thomas F. Torrance (Grand Rapids: Eerdmans, 1972), 3:70.
38. Ibid.
39. Henry, *Commentary on the Whole Bible*, 5:343.

with the permanency of the sacrifice of Christ. He puts the words of Psalm 40 into the mouth of Christ.

> Therefore, when He comes into the world, He says, "SACRIFICE AND OFFERING YOU HAVE NOT DESIRED, BUT A BODY YOU HAVE PREPARED FOR ME. IN WHOLE BURNT OFFERINGS AND SACRIFICES FOR SIN YOU HAVE TAKEN NO PLEASURE. THEN I SAID, 'BEHOLD I HAVE COME (IN THE SCROLL OF THE BOOK IT IS WRITTEN OF ME) TO DO YOUR WILL, O GOD.'"

The writer to the Hebrews then interprets Psalm 40; that is, he interprets the words of Christ recorded in Psalm 40. The writer to the Hebrews identifies the sacrifices and offerings as those offered according to the Law of Moses. Christ thus came to do the will of God.

> After saying above, "SACRIFICE AND OFFERING YOU HAVE NOT DESIRED, BUT A BODY YOU HAVE PREPARED FOR ME. IN WHOLE BURNT OFFERINGS AND sacrifices FOR SIN YOU HAVE TAKEN NO PLEASURE in them" (which are offered according to the Law), then He said, "BEHOLD I HAVE COME TO DO YOUR WILL."

Hebrews 10:9-10 identifies the "will of God" Christ accomplishes. Verse 9 observes that, "He takes away the first in order to establish the second." Christ took away the temple sacrifices, the first. He did so in order to establish His own sacrifice, the second. Verse 10 indicates that the second sacrifice is "the offering of the body of Jesus Christ once for all." The term "once for all" means "once for all time." The contrast is between the repeated daily sacrifices performed in the temple and the "once for all sacrifice" of Christ. The single sacrifice of Christ replaced the repeated temple sacrifices. They were permanently done away with.

Why is the destruction of the temple so significant for the purposes of this study? Remember, in temple worship, the sacrifices were accompanied by the singing of psalms and instrumental music. The instruments were the two silver trumpets ordained by God through

Moses, and the use of cymbals, harps, and lyres ordained by God through David. The singing of Psalms and the use of these musical instruments were part of the sacrifices offered in the temple. Second Chronicles 29:25-28 is confirmation.

> He [Hezekiah] then stationed the Levites in the house of the LORD with cymbals, with harps and with lyres, according to the command of David and of Gad the king's seer, and of Nathan the prophet; for the command was from the LORD through His prophets. The Levites stood with the musical instruments of David, and the priests with the trumpets. Then Hezekiah gave the order to offer the burnt offering on the altar. When the burnt offering began, the song to the LORD also began with the trumpets, accompanied by the instruments of David, king of Israel. While the whole assembly worshiped, the singers also sang and the trumpets sounded; all this continued until the burnt offering was finished.

Since the singing of Psalms and the use of these musical instruments were part of the sacrifices offered in the temple, when the temple and its sacrifices were set aside, the singing of psalms and the use of the musical instruments accompanying the sacrifices were also set aside. *A profound and fundamental transition in worship took place.* Since God set aside the temple and its worship in favor of the sacrifice of Christ, He also set aside the use of musical instruments in worship. Remember, God directs how believers worship. This reasoning is the historic Biblical argument for the nonuse of instrumental music in the worship of God.[40]

An important question now arises. If what has been said is true, why is singing part of the worship of the church today? The answer is that the *New Testament* commands it. "Let the word of Christ dwell

---

40. Girardeau, *Instrumental Music*, 80ff; John Price, *Old Light on New Worship* (Avinger, TX: Simpson, 2005), 39-44; Brian Schwertley, *Musical Instruments in the Public Worship of God* (Haslett, MI: Covenant Reformed Press, 2003), 100-104.

in you richly, teaching and admonishing one another in all wisdom, singing psalms and hymns and spiritual songs, with thankfulness in your hearts to God" (Col. 3:16, ESV). "Be filled with the Spirit, addressing one another in psalms and hymns and spiritual songs, singing and making melody to the Lord with your heart" (Eph. 5:18-19). "Through Him then, let us continually offer up a sacrifice of praise to God, that is, the fruit of lips that give thanks to His name" (Heb. 13:15).

It has already been seen that Paul connects the temple and the church, writing, "We are the temple of the living God" (2 Cor. 6:16). God's removal of the physical temple accentuates the significance of the spiritual temple, the church. Similarly, as members of the spiritual temple, what are believers to do? "You also, as living stones, are being built up as a spiritual house for a holy priesthood, to offer up spiritual sacrifices acceptable to God through Jesus Christ" (1 Pet. 2:5). Note the language taken from the temple sacrifices. Hebrews 13:15 makes a similar connection; remember, this connection is with the peace offerings.

The peace offerings were placed on top of the daily whole burnt offerings (Lev. 3:5). The symbolism is significant. As the daily sacrifices offered morning and evening, the whole burnt offerings were the basic offerings to make atonement or propitiation for the sins of the people (Lev. 1:4). They pointed to Christ, who is our propitiation (Rom. 3:25; Heb. 2:17; 1 John 2:2, 4:10). Placing the peace offering on top of the whole burnt offering recognized that peace with God is through Jesus Christ (Rom. 5:1). Leviticus 7:15-16 indicates that there were three types of peace offerings. They included the thank-offering and the votive or vow-offering. "These two, together with the freewill-offering, made up three classes within the peace-offering proper ... "[41] Hebrews 13:15 uses the specific language of the thank-offering.

---

41. R. J. Thompson, "Sacrifice and Offering," *The New Bible Dictionary*, ed. J. D. Douglas (Grand Rapids: Eerdmans, 1964), 1120.

The same words "sacrifice of praise"[42] in Hebrews 13:15 are translated "sacrifice of thanksgiving" in the Old Testament (LXX). Leviticus 7:13 speaks of the worshiper's "sacrifice of his peace offerings for thanksgiving."[43] Leviticus 7:15 speaks of "the flesh of the sacrifice of his thanksgiving peace offerings."[44] Psalm 50:14 refers to both the thank-offering and the votive-offering. "Offer to God a sacrifice of thanksgiving / And pay your vows to the Most High."[45] The animal "sacrifice of thanksgiving" in the Old Testament becomes the "sacrifice of praise" which is "the fruit of lips that give thanks to His name" in the New Testament. Psalm 116:17 connects the Old Testament sacrifice of thanksgiving with calling on the name of the LORD. "To You I shall offer a sacrifice of thanksgiving, / And call upon the name of the LORD."[46]

Finally, using the language of Hebrews 13:15, Psalm 107:22 connects the animal sacrifices of thanksgiving with joyful singing. "Let them also offer sacrifices of thanksgiving, / And tell of His works with joyful singing."[47] This connection is natural. As has been seen, singing always accompanied the animal sacrifices in the temple. Since temple worship no longer exists, Hebrews 13:15 naturally transforms the Old Testament animal "sacrifice of thanksgiving" into the New Testament "sacrifice of praise," which is the "fruit of lips that give thanks to His name." Just as the Levites sang Psalms to the LORD over the animal sacrifices in the temple, so we now sing Psalms of praise remembering the sacrifice of Christ. "You also, as living stones, are being built up as a spiritual house for a holy priesthood, to offer up spiritual sacrifices acceptable to God through Jesus Christ" (1 Pet. 2:5). Although God set aside all Old Testament sacrificial temple worship, including the use of musical instruments, God's people continue to sing God's

---

42. The Greek for "sacrifice of praise" in Hebrews 13:15 is *thusian aineseōs*.
43. The Greek Old Testament (LXX), *thusia aineseōs*, uses the same language as Hebrews 13:15.
44. Again, the LXX, *thusias aineseōs*, uses the same language as Hebrews 13:15.
45. The Old Testament Greek (LXX) for "sacrifice of thanksgiving" is again exactly the same as the New Testament Greek for "sacrifice of praise" in Hebrews 13:15, *thusian aineseōs*.
46. Compare Psalm 116:17 (LXX), *thusian aineseōs*, with the Greek of Hebrews 13:15, *thusian aineseōs*.
47. Compare Psalm 107:22 (LXX), *thusian aineseōs*, with the Greek of Hebrews 13:15, *thusian aineseōs*.

praise in the church, the New Testament spiritual temple, because the New Testament commands them to do so.

THE FIRST FIVE CENTURIES

As has been seen, the practice of singing Psalms in the early church, although sung without instruments, comes from the temple. If there was singing in the synagogue, as many assume, it too was without instruments. "The basic musical implication is simple enough: the synagogue service is not a sacrificial rite and hence it lacks the instrumental music that accompanies such a rite."[48]

When the Church Fathers speak about musical instruments, it is in either or both of two ways. First, they contrast the bloody sacrifices of the Old Testament with the spiritual sacrifices of the New Testament. The Church Fathers indicate that ancient Israel engaged in those bloody sacrifices, accompanied by musical instruments, because those Old Testament worshipers were weak (Heb. 5:2), and the law was weak (Heb. 7:18). Why was the law weak, and why were the Old Testament worshipers weak? Jerome (340-420) says, "The Law of Moses, which before was rich, affluent and illustrious, became after Christ's advent and in comparison with him weak and beggarly ... "[49] Chrysostom (349-407), therefore, says of the Old Testament ceremonies, "All were figures, all shadows: circumcision, sacrifice, sabbath. Therefore they could not reach through the soul, and thus they pass away ... "[50] Theodoret (c. 393-c. 458) adds, "It must be noted, of course, that he [the writer to the Hebrews] refers to obsolete prescriptions of the law as ineffective and useless—circumcision, sabbath observance and similar things ... "[51] From this perspective, the law is weak, and the Old Testament worshipers are weak.

---

48. James W. McKinnon, "The Church Fathers and Musical Instruments" (Ph.D. Diss., Columbia University, 1965), 105-106. See also Girardeau, *Instrumental Music*, 46.

49. *Ancient Christian Commentary on Scripture, New Testament: Galatians, Ephesians, Philippians*, ed. Mark J. Edwards (Downers Grove: InterVarsity Press, 1999), 60.

50. *Ancient Christian Commentary on Scripture, New Testament: Hebrews*, ed. Eric M. Heen and Philip D. W. Krey (Downers Grove: InterVarsity Press, 2005), 116.

51. Ibid.

Second, the Church Fathers speak of musical instruments figuratively, not literally. Some relegate this approach to the allegorical interpretation used by the Church Fathers. However, "the most important influence on the development of allegorical exegesis is Christian belief itself."[52] Allegories are stories like fables; they are extended metaphors. In the case of the musical instruments, it is more proper to speak of the use of metaphors. However this may be, the figurative interpretation of the instruments arises from the belief that, when Christ came in fulfillment of the ceremonial law, God permanently set aside the ceremonial law, including the instruments associated with the sacrifices. As the following quotations from the Church Fathers are reviewed, keep these two points in mind.

There is little or nothing said against the use of instrumental music in Christian worship in the first century. The reason is quite simple, "the issue of instruments in church was never raised."[53] It was never raised because the common practice was singing without instruments, and there was no effort to introduce instrumental music into Christian worship. Ignatius of Antioch (c. 35-c. 110) refers to the harp, not as an instrument used in worship, but by way of comparison with worshipers. "For your justly renowned presbytery, worthy of God, is fitted as exactly to the bishop as the strings are to the harp. Therefore in your concord and harmonious love, Jesus Christ is sung."[54]

In the second century, Justin Martyr (c. 100-c. 165) contrasts bloody sacrifices with prayers and hymns in worship.

> We have been instructed that only the following worship is worthy of him, not the consumption by fire of those things created by him for our nourishment but the use of them by ourselves and by those in need, while in

---

52. McKinnon, "The Church Fathers," 215.
53. Ibid., 263.
54. David W. Music, *Instruments in Church: A Collection of Source Documents* (Lanham, MD: Scarecrow Press, 1998), 28.

gratitude to him we offer solemn prayers and hymns for his creation and for all things leading to good health.[55]

Martyr notes that Christian worship does not offer bloody sacrifices. Rather, such worship involves spiritual sacrifices, including the fruit of lips. Contrasting Christian worship with Old Testament worship, the assumption is the nonuse of instrumental music. For this reason, he also says, "The use of singing with instrumental music was not received in the Christian churches as it was among the Jews in their infant state, but only the use of plain song."[56] Following the now standard interpretation, Martyr freely connects the use of musical instruments with the ceremonial law: "Musical organs pertain to the Jewish ceremonies and agree no more to us than circumcision."[57] The argument is clear. The Old Testament ceremonies have ceased. The use of instrumental music, being part of that ceremonial worship, also ceases.

Clement of Alexandria (c. 150-c. 215): The following quote is from Clement's *Protrepticus* [*Exhortation to the Greeks*]. "The trumpet of Christ is his Gospel: he has blown it and we have heard."[58] Clement's reference to a trumpet is "[p]ossibly the first use of the metaphor of the Gospel as a trumpet."[59] The next comment indicates how to conduct oneself at banquets and comes from Clement's *Paedagogus* [*The Instructor*].

> Let the syrinx [pipe] be assigned to shepherds and the aulos [flute] to superstitious men who are obsessed with idolatry. In truth these instruments must be excluded from our sober symposium; they are less suitable for men than for beasts and the bestial portion of mankind.[60]

---

55. James W. McKinnon, *Music in Early Christian Literature* (Cambridge: Cambridge University Press, 1987), 20. Hereafter, the reference to the ancient writer is given and *MECL* plus the item number: *Apology* I, 13, *MECL*, 24. References to the comments of McKinnon rather than to the ancient writers are cited as follows: McKinnon, *MECL*, [page number].
56. Charles Spurgeon, *A Treasury of David* (Newark, DE: Cornerstone, n.d.), 2:123.
57. Williams Ames, *A Fresh Suit Against Human Ceremonies in God's Worship* (Rotterdam: Johannes A. Lasco, 1633), 405. Organs refers to musical instruments in general not to modern church organs.
58. *Protrecticus* XI, 116, 2-3; *MECL*, 49.
59. McKinnon, *MECL*, 49.
60. *Paedagogus* II, iv; *MECL*, 32.

Following these comments, Clement compares pagan banquets and divine worship.

> The Spirit, distinguishing the divine liturgy from this sort of revelry, sings: "Praise Him with the sound of the trumpet," and indeed he will raise the dead with the sound of the trumpet. "Praise Him with psaltery [harp]," for the tongue is the psaltery [harp] of the Lord; "And praise him with the cithara [lyre]," let the cithara [lyre] be taken to mean the mouth, played by the Spirit as if by a plectrum [pick] ... "Praise him on strings and the instrument" refers to our body as an instrument ... [61]

Origen (c. 185-c. 265), like Clement, speaks of the trumpet of the gospel.

> First Matthew sounded the priestly trumpet of his gospel; and Mark too, and Luke and John played their own priestly trumpets. Peter also plays the two trumpets of his epistles, and likewise James and Jude. And John plays the trumpet yet again through his epistles and apocalypse. And finally he comes who said, "I believe God has shown us as the last Apostles", and blasting forth on the trumpets of his fourteen epistles, he toppled the walls of Jericho to their very foundations and all the schemes of idolatry and the tenets of philosophy.[62]

Eusebius (c. 260-c. 339) compares the symbols and types of Old Testament worship using instruments with the spiritual New Testament worship, which is more pleasing to God. Here is a portion of his commentary on Psalm 91:4:

> When formerly the people of the circumcision worshipped through symbols and types, it was not unreasonable that they raised hymns to God with psalteries and cithara, and that they did this on the days of the

---

61. *Paedagogus* II, iv; MECL, 52.
62. *In librum Jesu Naue homilia* VII, I; MECL, 67.

Sabbath days ... We, however, maintain the Jewish law inwardly according to the saying of the apostle: "For he is not a real Jew who is one outwardly, nor is real circumcision something external and physical, but he is a Jew who is one inwardly, and real circumcision is a matter of the heart, spiritual not literal (Romans 2:28-9); and it is upon a living psaltery and an animate cithara and in spiritual songs that we render the hymn. And so more sweetly pleasing to God than any musical instrument would be the symphony of the people of God, by which, in every church of God, with kindred spirit and single disposition, with one mind and unanimity of faith and piety, we raise melody in unison in our psalmody.[63]

Athanasius of Alexandria (293-373) compares rescue from Egypt to rescue by Christ and to the use of the gospel trumpet. Here is a portion of his commentary on Psalm 80:4:

"Blow the trumpet at the new moon" (Ps 80.4). Just as Israel in ancient times took sensible trumpets and blew them at the new moon (an ordinance given by God and a witness to their being freed from the Egyptian servitude), so too the new people, using the Gospel trumpet, whose sound has gone forth into the whole world, are called to blow a trumpet at the new moon, that is, the renewal of their mind, giving witness that it has been rescued from the figurative Egypt, that is from the power of darkness.[64]

The following is a short excerpt from Athanasius's "Letter to Marcellinus on the Interpretation of the Psalms." In it, Athanasius indicates that the music of the voice should accompany the Psalms. The effect is harmony in the soul, like the harmony of flutes.

It is important not to pass over the question of why words of this kind [the Psalms] are chanted with melo-

---

63. *In psalmum* xci, 4; MECL, 206.
64. *Expositio in psalmum* lxxx, 4; MECL, 101.

> dies and strains. For some of the simple among us, although they believe indeed that the phrases are divinely inspired, imagine, however, on account of the sweetness of sound, that also the psalms are rendered musically for the sake of the ear's delight. But this is not so ... First, because it is fitting for the Divine Scripture [the Psalms] to praise God not in compressed speech alone, but in voice richly broadened ... The second is that, just as harmony that unites flutes effects a single sound ... man [is] neither to be discordant in himself, nor to be at variance with himself.[65]

Basil the Great (330-379) also sees praising God on the harp as singing from the heart using the voice. The following are excerpts from his Homilies on Psalms 15:2 and 19:2.

> It is necessary to praise the Lord on the harp; that is, to render harmoniously the actions of the body. Since, indeed we sinned in the body, "when we yielded our members as slaves to sin, to lawlessness," let us give praise with our body, using the same instruments for the destruction of sin ... One, therefore who observes all the precepts and makes, as it were, harmony and symphony from them, this one, I say, plays for God on a ten stringed psaltery.[66]

> The psaltery is a musical instrument that gives out its sounds harmoniously with the melody of the voice. Accordingly, the rational psaltery is opened especially at that time when actions in harmony with words are displayed. And he is a spiritual psaltery who has acted and has taught. He it is who opens the proposition in the psalms, setting forth the possibility of the teaching from

---

65. Athanasius, *The Life of Antony and the Letter to Marcellinus*, trans. Robert C. Gregg (New York: Paulist Press, 1980), 123-124.
66. *Ancient Christian Commentary on Scripture, Psalms 1-50*, ed. Craig A. Blaising and Carmen S. Hardin (Downers Grove: InterVarsity Press, 2008), 246-247. Hereafter: *ACCS*, OT VII.

> his own example ... There is nothing incongruous or out of tune in his life.⁶⁷

Ambrose, Bishop of Milan (340-397), speaks of the life of the Apostle Paul as an excellent harp in his comments on Psalm 49:7 in the *Commentary on Twelve Psalms*.

> The Lord opens up a theme or problem that has been closed when he finds an apt organ and a chosen instrument. Call it a harp. Such as this was Paul. He rang out the sweet canticle of grace, awakening all the strings of his harp in harmonious sound; plucking the inner chords by grace of the Holy Spirit and playing in ringing tones both interiorly and exteriorly ... Excellent harp, where a person's life is in tune with his faith ... Sweet harp, where discipline of lifestyle sings a canticle.⁶⁸

Evagrius Ponticus (349-399) understands the musical instruments of the Old Testament to be unsuitable for us.

> "Praise the Lord on the cithara, sing to him on the psaltery of ten strings, etc." The cithara [lyre] is the practical soul put in motion by the commandments of God; the psaltery [harp] is the pure mind set in motion by spiritual knowledge. The musical instruments of the Old Testament are not unsuitable for us if understood spiritually.⁶⁹

Chrysostom (349-407) opposes the allegorical interpretation of the Old Testament and teaches that the use of instruments in the Old Testament was a concession to the Spiritual weakness of the people. His comments on Psalm 149:2 follow.

> Some also take the meaning of these instruments allegorically ... But I would say this: that in ancient times, they were thus led by these instruments due to the slowness of their understanding, and were gradually drawn

---

67. *ACCS*, OT VII, 375.
68. *ACCS*, OT VII, 375-376
69. *Selecta in psalmos* XXXII, 2-3; *MECL*, 68.

from idolatry. Accordingly, just as he allowed sacrifices, so too he did permit instruments, making concession to their weakness.[70]

Augustine (354-430) also teaches that Christians are the true instruments of praise. He does so in his *Exposition of the Psalms*, on Psalm 33:6. "Take up the psaltery and sing psalms to God on this psaltery with its ten strings. There are ten commandments in the law, and in these ten commandments you find the psaltery ... Pluck your psaltery and fulfill the law ... "[71] In his exposition of Psalm 150, Augustine declares, "Ye are *trumpet, psaltery, harp, timbrel, choir, strings, and organ, cymbals of jubilation* sounding well, because sounding in harmony. All these are ye ... "[72]

Niceta of Remesiana (died c. 414) was "born in Dacia in the second quarter of the century," and he "was named bishop of Remesiana (present-day Bela Palanka, Yugoslavia) in about 370."[73] Niceta held that the spiritual sacrifice of praise is better than the physical bloody sacrifice. "Behold, what is superior, behold the spiritual sacrifice, greater than all the sacrifices of victims. And justly so, if there indeed the irrational blood of animals was poured out, here is offered the reasonable praise of the soul itself and a good conscience."[74] Following the Old Testament standards for worship is also fleshly or carnal.

> For what is carnal has been rejected, for example, circumcision, the Sabbath, sacrifices, discrimination among foods, trumpets, citharas, cymbals, and tympana, all of which are understood to reside now in the bodily members of man and there better to sound ... The other things which are spiritual faith, piety, prayer, fasting, patience, chastity, praise—have been increased, not diminished.[75]

---

70. *In psalmum* cxlix, 2; *MECL*, 173.
71. *ACCS, OT VII*, 247.
72. Quoted by McKinnon, "The Church Fathers and Musical Instruments," 236.
73. McKinnon, *MECL*, 134.
74. *De utilitate hymnorum* 7; *MECL*, 306.
75. *De utilitate hymnorum* 9; *MECL*, 137.

Isidore (d. 440) was from Pelusium, east of the present day Port Said in northern Egypt.

> Isidore of Pelusium, who lived since Basil, held, [in book 2 and epistle 176] that music was only allowed the Jews by God, in a way of condescension to their childishness: "If God," he says, "bore with bloody sacrifices, because of men's childishness at that time, why should you wonder he bore with the music of a harp and a psaltery."[76]

Theodoret of Cyrrus (c. 393-c. 458) became Bishop of Cyrrus, a small town close to Syrian Antioch in 423. In his *Cure of the Greek Maladies*, he speaks of the weakness of Israel. "What he [God] ordained in the Law, then, concerning these things, was because of their [Israel's] weakness ... "[77] In his *Questions and Responses*, Theodoret asks, since "those under grace have adopted better practices, unlike those customs" observed by Israel, "why have they used these songs in the churches as did the children of the Law?"[78] The same question was asked above. Theodoret responds, "It is not singing as such which benefits the childish, but singing with lifeless instruments ... wherefore the use of such instruments and those things appropriate to those who are childish is dispensed with in the churches and singing alone has been left over."[79]

In concluding these comments from the first five centuries of the church, also consider two church councils. "The Council of Laodicea (367) forbid the use of musical instruments in worship, and this has remained the policy of the Eastern Orthodox Church to the present day."[80] The Orthodox Church in America also continues this practice. The Council of Carthage (416) declared, "On the Lord's day let all instruments of music be silenced."[81]

---

76. Girardeau, *Instrumental Music*, 158.
77. *Graecarum affectionum curatio, de sacrificiis* 34-5; MECL, 231.
78. *Quaestiones et responsiones ad orthodoxos* CVII; MECL, 232.
79. Ibid.
80. Price, *Old Light on New Worship*, 80.
81. Girardeau, *Instrumental Music*, 67.

This review of the Church Fathers indicates that the nonuse of musical instruments was the position of the church during the first five centuries of her existence.

> It provides the most convincing historical evidence that musical instrumentation was not commanded by the apostles or practiced in the churches of their time. If the apostles had commanded and used musical instruments in the early church, then surely this practice would have been carried on by the Church Fathers. But here we have seen that musical instruments had no place in Christian worship for centuries after the apostles.[82]

---

82. Price, *Old Light on New Worship*, 81.

18

Instrumental Music: The Historical Perspective from Cassiodorus to Girardeau

Surely my soul remembers and is bowed down within me. ~ Lam. 3:20

THE MEDIEVAL PERIOD

THE MIDDLE AGES span the time from roughly 500 A.D. until 1500 A.D. Rome declined and collapsed. Darker times crossed Europe. Finally, the Renaissance emerged. Then came the Reformation. Cassiodorus (485-585) continued the positions of the other Church Fathers concerning musical instruments in worship in his *Explanation of the Psalms*, on Psalm 15:2. "The harp and the psaltery lie within us, or rather we ourselves are the instruments when like them we sing through the quality of our actions by means of the Lord's grace."[1] The first organ introduced into Christian worship was in a Roman Catholic Church in Rome about 670 A.D.[2] The second use of an organ in a church in worship occurred when Charlemagne had one made for the Roman Catholic Cathedral in Aix-la-Chapelle in 812 A.D.[3] The first organ in England made its appearance in the ninth century.[4]

---

1. *Ancient Christian Commentary on Scripture, Old Testament, Vol. VII*, ed. Craig A. Blaising and Carmen S. Hardin (Downers Grove: InrterVarsity Press, 2008), 246. Hereafter: *ACCS, OT VII*.
2. M. C. Kurfees, *Instrumental Music in Worship* (Nashville: Gospel Advocate, 1950), 152.
3. John Price, *Old Light on New Worship* (Avinger, TX: Simpson Publishing Co., 2005), 84.
4. Ibid.

"From the eighth century onward, we also occasionally find the harp, violin, and cithern depicted in some Western musical manuscripts"[5] as being used in worship.

The growing use of instruments in worship seems to have been scattered and isolated.[6] "When the organ was introduced into worship it encountered strong opposition, and made its way but slowly to general acceptance."[7] So much so was slow acceptance of the organ and opposition to it the case that Thomas Aquinas (1225-1274) declares, "Our church does not use musical instruments, as harps and psalteries, to praise God withal, that she may not seem to Judaise."[8] Aquinas rejected musical instruments because they introduce into the worship of the church a part of the Old Testament ceremonial law, much like requiring circumcision. Broadly speaking, it therefore appears "that the Christian church did not employ instrumental music in its public worship for 1200 years after Christ."[9]

Aquinas continues with reasons for this rejection of musical instruments.

> As Aristotle says, "We must not introduce flutes into teaching, nor any artificial instrument such as the harp, nor anything of the kind, but only such things as make people morally good." For musical instruments usually move the soul more to pleasure than create inner moral goodness. But in the Old Testament, they used instruments of this kind, both because the people were more coarse and carnal, so they needed to be aroused by such instruments and with worldly promises, and also because bodily instruments were symbolic of something. (*Summa theologica* part 2.2, Q 91 art. 2).[10]

---

5. Nick R. Needham, "Worship Through the Ages," *Give Praise to God*, ed. Philip Ryken, Derek Thomas, and Ligon Duncan (Phillipsburg: P & R, 2003), 392.
6. Ibid., 393.
7. John L. Girardeau, *Instrumental Music in Public Worship* (Havertown, PA: New Covenant Publication Society, 1983), 161.
8. John M'Clintock and James Strong, *Cyclopaedia of Biblical, Theological, and Ecclesiastical Literature* (New York: Harper, 1879), 8:739.
9. Girardeau, *Instrumental Music*, 161.
10. Needham, "Worship Through the Ages," 393.

Note four things packed together in this comment. First, instrumental music tends to evoke emotion and pleasure-seeking. Review the discussion of instrumental music. Second, on the other hand, vocal music's purpose is to assist in forming and expressing inner moral goodness. Compare the discussion of vocal music. Third, there is the weakness and childishness of the Old Testament economy as discussed earlier. Fourth, there is the fact that the musical instruments, along with the other parts of the sacrificial system, were symbolic of something. They looked forward to something better. They were types, and were to be left behind when the reality came. An examination of this symbolism and typology follows, in chapter 19.

In spite of opposition, "the organ, during the fourteenth and fifteenth centuries, steadily made its way toward universal triumph in the Romish church."[11] And despite Biblical and historical precedents, the church in the Middle Ages moved from the apostolic and post-apostolic standards of worship to embrace instrumental music in worship. The Eastern Orthodox Churches, however, continued to worship without organs or other musical instruments.[12] In making comments on 1 Corinthians 14:19, Erasmus (1466-1536) said of his times,

> We have brought into our churches a certain operose and theatrical music; such a confused, disorderly chattering of words, as I hardly think was ever heard in any of the Grecian or Roman theaters. The church rings with the noise of trumpets, pipes and dulcimers; and human voices strive to bear their part with them ... Men run to church as to a theater, to have their ears tickled.[13]

THE REFORMATION AND FOLLOWING

"The Protestant Reformation of the sixteenth century was just as much

---

11. Girardeau, *Instrumental Music*, 161.
12. Needham, "Worship Through the Ages," 394.
13. Girardeau, *Instrumental Music*, 162.

a reformation of worship as it was a reformation of [the teaching of salvation]."[14] Because of his own personal struggle and anguish, "Luther never considered the reformation of worship a matter of priority as did the other leading reformers."[15] "This led to the development of two new and vibrant traditions in Christian worship: the Lutheran and Reformed traditions."[16] Luther followed the normative principle of worship. "He believed that unless a practice was expressly forbidden by the Word of God it could be allowed."[17] Review the discussion in chapter 16, Who Governs Worship?

In his commentary on Psalm 32, Luther says, "God is to be praised and is being praised today by both and many other musical instruments."[18] In the preface to his *German Mass and Order of God's Service*, Luther points to the needs of "the simple and the young people ... for the sake of such, people must read, sing, preach, write, and compose, and if it is helpful and conducive to growth, for that reason I would make all the bells to ring and all the organs to pipe, and use every sound that can sound."[19]

Huldreich Zwingli (1484-1531), the leader of the Swiss Reformation, went to the other extreme. He "remove[d] not only musical instruments but all vocal singing from the churches in Zurich."[20] Zwingli was succeeded by Heinrich Bullinger (1504-1575) as pastor in Zurich. In his history of the Swiss Reformation, Bullinger records the destruction of church organs. "Organs in the church are not of particular antiquity, especially in these lands. Since they also are not in accord with the Apostle's teaching in 1 Corinthians 14, the organs in the great cathedral of Zurich were demolished on the 9th of December in this year of 1527."[21] Bullinger also wrote the Second Hel-

---

14. Needham, "Worship Through the Ages," 396.
15. Price, *Old Light on New Worship*, 91.
16. Needham, "Worship Through the Ages," 396.
17. Price, *Old Light on New Worship*, 91.
18. David W. Music, *Instruments in Church: A Collection of Source Documents* (Lanham, MD: Scarecrow Press, 1998), 56.
19. Ibid., 57.
20. Price, *Old Light on New Worship*, 95.
21. Music, *Instruments in Church*, 58.

vetic Confession (1566), one of the important Reformed confessions of that era. Chapter 23 states,

> If there are churches which have a true and proper sermon but no singing, they ought not to be condemned. For all churches do not have the advantage of singing. And it is well known from testimonies of antiquity that the custom of singing is very old in the Eastern Churches whereas it was late when it was at length accepted in the West.

From the destruction of organs, it is clear that such singing was obviously without instrumental accompaniment.

John Calvin (1509-1564) followed the regulative principle of worship set forth above under Who Governs Worship?

> Thus, though Calvin did not object to the private use of musical instruments, his views of them as a part of public worship essentially followed the familiar argument of the Church Fathers: instruments were characteristic of the "infant church" (i.e., the Old Testament Jews), but their use was a ceremony that was no longer necessary in the New Dispensation.[22]

Along this line, note Calvin's comments on those Psalms that speak of using instruments in worship. In his commentary on Psalm 33:2, Calvin speaks of the need of instruments to stimulate the ancient people of God to praise and evoke strong affections toward God.

> It is evident that the Psalmist here expresses the vehement and ardent affection which the faithful ought to have in praising God, when he enjoins musical instruments to be employed for this purpose. He would have nothing omitted by believers which tends to animate the minds and feelings of men in singing God's praises. The name of God, no doubt, can, properly speaking, be cel-

---

22. Ibid., 59

ebrated only by the articulate voice; but it is not without reason that David adds to this those aids by which believers were wont to stimulate themselves the more to this exercise; especially considering that he was speaking to God's ancient people.[23]

Calvin points to the fact that what applied to the ancient Jews no longer applies to the New Testament church. As part of the ancient temple worship, the use of musical instruments was set aside by God in the sacrifice of Christ. Calvin therefore teaches the nonuse of instrumental music in worship.

> There is a distinction, however, to be observed here, that we may not indiscriminately consider as applicable to ourselves, every thing which was formerly enjoined upon the Jews. I have no doubt that playing upon cymbals, touching the harp and the viol, and all that kind of music, which is so frequently mentioned in the Psalms, was a part of the education; that is to say, the puerile [childish] instruction of the law: I speak of the stated service of the temple. For even now, if believers choose to cheer themselves with musical instruments, they should, I think, make it their object not to dissever their cheerfulness from the praises of God. But when they frequent their sacred assemblies, musical instruments in celebrating the praises of God would be no more suitable than the burning of incense, the lighting up of lamps, and the restoration of the other shadows of the law... Men who are fond of outward pomp may delight in that noise; but the simplicity which God recommends to us by the apostle is far more pleasing to him.[24]

There is also Calvin's reference to 1 Corinthians 14, which may

---

23. John Calvin, *Commentary on the Book of Psalms*, trans. James Anderson (Grand Rapids: Baker, 1979), 1: 538.

24. Ibid., 1:538-539.

seem odd to contemporary believers. "Paul allows us to bless God in the public assembly of the saints only in a known tongue (1 Corinthians 14:16)."[25] Paul requires believers to sing with their minds and understanding. Because instruments are inanimate and give off sounds without words, they do not communicate with understanding (1 Cor. 14:14-16). For this reason, they are also rejected in New Testament worship.

When Calvin speaks to Psalm 71:22, he points out that the musical instruments used by the ancient Jews were but shadows and figures, not suitable for today. He goes on to say that because believers cannot interpret the sounds of musical instruments as understandable languages, Paul forbids them.

> In speaking of employing the psaltery and the harp in this exercise, he alludes to the generally prevailing custom of that time. To sing the praises of God upon the harp and psaltery unquestionably formed a part of the training of the law, and of the service of God under that dispensation of shadows and figures; but they are not now to be used in public thanksgiving. We are not, indeed, forbidden to use, in private, musical instruments, but they are banished out of the churches by the plain command of the Holy Spirit, when Paul, in 1 Cor. xiv. 13, lays it down as an invariable rule, that we must praise God, and pray to him only in a known tongue.[26]

Finally, consider Calvin's comments on Psalm 92:4. He points out that musical instruments were used by the ancient Jews as people under age, restricted to these childish ways, in order to help stimulate them to proper worship.

> In the fourth verse, he more immediately addresses the Levites, who were appointed to the office of singers, and calls upon them to employ their instruments of music—

---
25. Ibid., 1:539.
26. Ibid., 2:98.

> not as if this were in itself necessary, only it was useful as an elementary aid to the people of God in these ancient times. We are not to conceive that God enjoined the harp as feeling a delight like ourselves in mere melody of sounds; but the Jews, who were yet under age, were astricted [restricted] to the use of such childish elements. The intention of them was to stimulate the worshippers, and stir them up more actively to the celebration of the praise of God with the heart. We are to remember that the worship of God was never understood to consist in such outward services, which were only necessary to help forward a people, as yet weak and rude in knowledge, in the spiritual worship of God.[27]

Calvin then reminds believers that the church in this New Testament age buries the light of the gospel if the church falls back to employing the shadows and figures of the Old Testament. He gives the example of the use of instrumental music by the Roman Catholic Church. This delight in Old Testament ways of worship, he says, was ended by the gospel.

> A difference is to be observed in this respect between his people under the Old and under the New Testament; for now that Christ has appeared, and the Church has reached full age, it were only to bury the light of the Gospel, should we introduce the shadows of a departed dispensation. From this, it appears that the Papists, as I shall have occasion to show elsewhere, in employing instrumental music, cannot be said so much to imitate the practice of God's ancient people, as to ape it in a senseless and absurd manner, exhibiting a silly delight in that worship of the Old Testament which was figurative, and terminated with the Gospel.[28]

---

27. Ibid., 3:494-495.
28. Ibid., 3:495.

Calvin follows Eusebius and Chrysostom in interpreting the Old Testament ceremonies, including the musical instruments, as shadows, figures, and types.

At the same time, the Anabaptists followed the now standard Protestant interpretation regarding instrumental music in worship.

> Menno Simons (1496-1561), the wise and peace-loving leader of the Anabaptists, believed that what is not expressly commanded in the New Testament should not be permitted in Christian worship. Menno applied this principle to musical instruments and wrote, "There is not a word to be found in Scripture concerning their anointing, crosses, caps, togas, unclean purifications, cloisters, chapels, organs, choral music, masses offerings, ancient usages, etc."[29]

Richard Mather (1596-1659) was the father of Increase Mather (1639-1723) and the grandfather of Cotton Mather (1663-1728). In 1640, he wrote the preface to the Bay Psalm Book, the first book printed in North America. Speaking of worship in the Old Testament temple, he says, "Some things in it were ceremonial, as their musical instruments ... "[30] Then speaking of praise directly, Mather asks,

> What type can be imagined in making use of his [David's] songs to praise the Lord? If they [David's psalms] were typical because the ceremony of musical instruments were joined with them, then their prayers were also typical, because they had that ceremony of incense mixed with them: but we know that prayer then was a moral duty, notwithstanding the incense, and so singing those psalms [was a moral duty] notwithstanding their musical instruments. Besides, that which was typical (as that they were sung with musical instruments, by the

---

29. Price, *Old Light on New Worship*, 104.
30. Richard Mather, "Preface," *The Whole Booke of Psalmes Faithfully Translated into English Metre* (Cambridge: Riverside Press, 1640), 2. Rendered into modern English.

twenty-four orders of Priests and Levites, 1 Chron. 25:9) must have the moral and spiritual accomplishment in the New Testament, in all the churches of the Saints ... with hearts and lips, instead of musical instruments, to praise the Lord ... [31]

Samuel Mather (1650-1727), another son of Richard Mather, wrote a classic and influential work, *The Figures and Types of the Old Testament*, in 1683. "We do not find," he says, "that these musical instruments among the Jews were part of their *Synagogue* worship, which was moral and perpetual; but rather of their *Temple* worship, which was *Ceremonial*, and is now vanished away."[32] Samuel Mather also lists the prominent theologians from Zwingli to his own day who held to the view that the musical instruments of Old Testament worship were part of the ceremonial law.

> There was a *typical signification in them*. And upon this account they are not only rejected and condemned by the whole army of Protestant Divines; as for instance, by
>
> > [Huldreich] *Zwingli* [1484-1531],
> > [John] *Calvin* [1509-1564],
> > *Peter Martyr* [1499-1562],
> > [Wilhelm] *Zepperus* [1550-1607],
> > [David] *Pareus* [1548-1622],
> > [Andrew] *Willet* [1562-1622],
> > [Henry] *Ainsworth* [1571-1622],
> > [William] *Ames* [1567-1633],
> > [David] *Calderwood* [1575-1650], and
> > [John] *Cotton* [1584-1652] ...
>
> who do by one mouth testify against them, most of them expressly affirming, that they are part of the abrogated legal pedagogy [method of teaching]; so that we might

---

31. Ibid.
32. Samuel Mather, *The Figures and Types of the Old Testament* (New York: Johnson Reprint Corporation, 1969), 479. Rendered into modern English.

as well recall the incense, tapers, sacrifices, new moons, circumcision, and all the other shadows of the law into use again.³³

The popular Matthew Henry (1662-1714) comments on David's celebration when he moved the ark of the covenant into Jerusalem with instruments, song, and dancing.

> This way of praising God by musical instruments had not hitherto been in use. But David, being a prophet, instituted it by divine direction, and added it to the other carnal ordinances of that dispensation, as the apostle calls them, Hebrews 9:10. The New Testament keeps up singing of psalms, but has not appointed church-music.³⁴

In like manner, commenting on Psalm 81:2, Henry contrasts, on the one hand, Old Testament praise with various instruments, with, on the other hand, New Testament praise with the joy and godly fear that are signified by the instruments.

> It was then to be done by musical instruments, *the timbrel, harp, and psaltery*; and by blowing *the trumpet*, some think in remembrance of the sound of the trumpet on Mount Sinai, which waxed louder and louder. It was then and is now to be done by singing psalms, singing *aloud*, and making *a joyful noise*. The pleasantness of the harp and the awfulness of the trumpet intimate to us that God is to be worshipped with cheerfulness and joy with reverence and godly fear.³⁵

THE EIGHTEENTH AND NINETEENTH CENTURIES

Amazingly, Isaac Watts (1674-1748), the great hymn writer, rejected the use of musical instruments in worship indicating that "we can

---

33. Ibid., 480. Rendered into modern English. For clarity, first names and dates added.
34. Matthew Henry, *Matthew Henry's Commentary on the Whole Bible* (Grand Rapids: Fleming H. Revell, 1985), 2:875.
35. Ibid., 3:548.

never suppose the primitive church in those days [of the apostles] had instruments of worship."³⁶ Commenting of Revelation 15:3, Watts also writes,

> The church now under the salvation and instruction of the Lamb, sings *with the voice* to the glory of the vengeance and the grace of God, as Israel under the conduct of Moses *sung with harps* ... it would be as unreasonable to prove from this text, that we must sing the very words of the 15th of Exodus in a Christian church, as to prove from this book of Revelation that we must use *harps* and altars, censers, fire and incense.³⁷

The Methodist scholar, Adam Clarke (1762–1832), agreed with John Wesley (1703-1791), the founder of Methodism, and opposed musical instruments in worship.

> The late venerable and most eminent divine, the Rev. John Wesley, who was a lover of music, and an elegant poet, when asked his opinion of instruments of music being introduced into the chapels of the Methodists said, in his terse and powerful manner, "I have no objection to instruments of music in our chapels, provided they are neither HEARD nor SEEN." I say the same, though I think the expense of purchase had better be spared.³⁸

John L. Dagg (1794-1884), a prominent Baptist theologian in America, wrote in his *Manual of Church Order*, "Instrumental music formed a part of the temple worship; but it is nowhere commanded in the New Testament; and it is less adapted to the more spiritual service of the present dispensation."³⁹

The great Baptist preacher, Charles Spurgeon (1834-1892), led the congregation of the Metropolitan Tabernacle in London to sing with-

---

36. Quoted in Price, *Old Light on New Worship*, 124.
37. Ibid. Italics added.
38. Adam Clarke, *Adam Clarke Commentaries*, StudyLight.org, Accessed March 18, 2011.
39. John L. Dagg, *Manual of Theology: Second Part, A Treatise on Church Order* (Harrisonburg, VA: Gano Books, 1990), 240.

out instrumental accompaniment. "There was no organ or choir. A precentor set the pitch of each hymn with a tuning fork and led the singing with his own voice."[40] The reasoning behind Spurgeon's non-use of musical instruments reflects the thinking of the Church Fathers and the Reformers. Commenting on Psalm 33:2-3 Spurgeon says,

> Men need all the help they can get to stir them up to praise. This is the lesson to be gathered from the use of musical instruments under the old dispensation. Israel was at school, and used childish things to help her learn; but in these days, when Jesus gives us spiritual manhood, we can make melody without strings and pipes. We do not believe these things are expedient in worship, lest they should mar its simplicity ... We do not need them, they would hinder than help our praise ... [41]

Under Psalm 71:22, Spurgeon also quotes John Cotton with approval.

> Suppose singing with instruments were not typical, but only an external solemnity of worship, fitted to the solace of the outward senses of children under age, such as the Israelites were under the Old Testament (Gal. iv. 1, 2, 3); yet now in the grown age of the heirs of the New Testament, such external pomp and solemnities are ceased, and no external service reserved, but such as hold forth simplicity and gravity; nor is any voice to be heard in the church of Christ, but such as is significant and edifying by signification (1 Cor. xiv. 10, 11, 26), which the voice of instruments is not.[42]

Spurgeon also gives this graphic pastoral advice applying Psalm 92:3, "It is, however to be feared that attention to the mere mechanism of music, noting keys and strings, bars and crotchets [quarter notes],

---

40. Arnold Dallimore, *Spurgeon* (Chicago: Moody Press, 1984), 98.
41. Charles Spurgeon, *A Treasury of David* (Newark, DE: Cornerstone, n.d.), 2:115.
42. Ibid., 3:313.

has carried many away from the spiritual harmony which is the soul and essence of praise. Fine music without devotion is but a splendid garment upon a corpse."[43]

The first organ used in church worship in America was the "Brattle organ," the personal property of Thomas Brattle (1658-1713), a successful Boston merchant.[44] The organ was likely procured in England during or before 1708.[45] Upon his death, Brattle bequeathed the organ to the Congregational Church of which he was a founding member. According to the terms of the will, if the Congregational church did not accept the organ within a year, it was to go to the Anglican parish.[46] On June 26, 1883, an article in *The New York Times* reports, "Brattle-Street Church refused the gift, the opposition to organs in dissenting churches being then as great as it is in the churches in Scotland. But the Parish of Kings Chapel (Stone Chapel) accepted the gift."[47] In the late nineteenth century, it appears, the Congregational Church opposed instrumental music in worship; Scottish Presbyterianism continued its opposition; but the Anglicans, like the Roman Catholics, embraced the organ. As Girardeau indicates, the organ regularly met strong opposition.[48]

In 1843, *The Biblical Repertory and Princeton Review* published an article on "Church Music" which states, "It cannot be denied that instruments do render essential aid correcting, purifying and sustaining the vocal tones."[49] Charles Hodge and his coeditor footnote this statement:

> The opinions expressed above, on the subject of instrumental music, are adverse, as is well known, to those which have prevailed, and continue to prevail in the Presbyterian church [Presbyterian Church in the USA].

---

43. Ibid., 4:264.
44. Music, *Instruments in Church*, 136.
45. Ibid.
46. Ibid.
47. "The First Organ Brought to America," *The New York Times*, June 26, 1883.
48. Girardeau, *Instrumental Music*, 161.
49. *The Biblical Repertory and Princeton Review for the Year 1843*, ed. Charles Hodge and Lyman Atwater, Vol. 15, No. 1 (Philadelphia: M. B. Hope, 1843), 97.

As a calm and guarded vindication of a practice which we would by no means be understood to recommend, we have given place to expressions from which our readers, no less than ourselves, may choose to dissent.[50]

The Directory for Worship of the United Presbyterian Church of North America, founded in 1858, also declares, "As the use of musical instruments in the worship of the New Testament Church has no sanction in the Bible, they shall not be introduced, in any form, in any of our congregations."[51] The church later voided this directive. "This Assembly hereby ratifies the decision of the Presbyteries, and declares Sec. 5. Art. 2, Chap. 3 of the Directory for Worship repealed. – *Minutes. General Assembly of 1882*, page 525."[52]

On August 23, 1860, the Free Methodist Church was organized. One of the points of the *Discipline* of the new denomination was, "Doctrines and usages of primitive Methodism such as the witness of the Spirit, entire sanctification as a state of grace distinct from justification, attainable instantly by faith; free seats, *congregational singing, without instrumental music in all cases*; plainness of dress."[53] Writing in 1915, Free Methodist historian, Wilson Hogue, says,

> These differences have characterized it from the beginning, however; free seats in all its Churches; simplicity and inexpensiveness in the erection of Churches; no kind of entertainments allowed for the purpose of raising funds for religious purposes; *neither instrumental music nor choir singing permitted in public worship*."[54]

In 1888, the Southern Presbyterian, John L. Girardeau, published his classic defense of the nonuse of instruments in worship, *Instrumental Music in Public Worship*. A year later, a Southern Presbyterian col-

---

50. Ibid.
51. Quoted in Brian Schwertley, *Musical Instruments in the Public Worship of God* (Haslett, MI: Covenant Reformed Press, 2003), 129; *The Directory for Worship of the United Presbyterian Church of North America* (Pittsburgh: United Presbyterian Board of Publication, 1882), 676.
52. *The Directory for Worship of the United Presbyterian Church of North America*, 676, note.
53. Wilson Thomas Hogue, *History of the Free Methodist Church of North America*, Vol.1 (Chicago: Free Methodist Publishing House, 1915), 320. Italics added.
54. Ibid., 334.

league, Robert L. Dabney (1820-1898), wrote a review of Girardeau's book. "Dr. Girardeau is supporting the identical position held by all the early fathers, by all the Presbyterian reformers, by a Chalmers, a Mason, a Breckenridge, a Thornwell, and by a Spurgeon."[55] Dabney lists these adherents to the nonuse of instruments: Thomas Chalmers (1780-1847) of the Free Church of Scotland; the Reformed Presbyterian, Archibald Mason (1753-1831); a fellow Southern Presbyterian, Robert J. Breckinridge (1800-1871); another Southern Presbyterian, James Henley Thornwell (1812-1862), and the great Baptist preacher, Charles Spurgeon (1834-1892).

Another article from *The New York Times*, June 4, 1883, reports, "That particular branch of the Presbyterian family in this country which calls itself the 'United Presbyterian Church' is just now torn with controversy over the question of the introduction of instrumental music into its form of worship. At the same time the same question is agitating the Free Kirk [Church] of Scotland."[56] This article indicates that opposition to the organ continued in Presbyterian circles in both America and Scotland. *The New York Times* article advises, "The organ will undoubtedly triumph, both in the Free Church and among United Presbyterians, and the wisest thing the advocates of the organ could do would be to moderate their zeal and trust to time to vindicate the innocence of church instrumental music."[57]

Not everyone saw the introduction of instrumental music into the worship of God as innocent. As has been seen, a host of scholars, churchmen, and churches followed the now traditional understanding that the Old Testament instruments used in worship were reserved for Israel as a church weak and underage and were also types and shadows of the good things to come (Heb. 8:5). Dabney, following Girardeau, puts it way: "For as the temple-priests and animal sacrifices typified Christ and his sacrifice on Calvary, so the musical instruments of

---

55. Robert L. Dabney, "Girardeau's 'Instrumental Music in Public Worship,'" *The Presbyterian Quarterly*, 3 (1889): 463.
56. "The Organ Controversy," *The New York Times*, June 4, 1883.
57. Ibid.

David in the temple-service only typified the joy of the Holy Ghost in his pentecostal effusions."[58] As already indicated, the next chapter will deal with the musical instruments of the temple as specific types.

OVERVIEW

All of the men of God mentioned heretofore, from apostolic times through the nineteenth century, taught that instrumental music in worship ceased with the death and resurrection of Christ, along with all the other ceremonies and sacrifices. Instrumental music was not used in the New Testament church. Ralph P. Martin, retired Scholar in Residence, Fuller Theological Seminary, concedes, "While there are allusions made to certain instruments (for example, the harps and lyres, the pipe, the cymbal, the trumpet—and possibly the 'noisy gong' of 1 Corinthians xiii, 1), there is no certainty that any of these were actually used. The balance of probability is against such use."[59]

The prediction of *The New York Times* proved correct. In the face of "so great a cloud of witnesses surrounding us" (Heb. 12:1), the greater part of the church abandoned Biblical and apostolic principles. As far as the organ is concerned, "The Latin church [Roman Catholicism] introduced it pretty generally ... The Lutheran church retained [it], the Calvinistic churches rejected it, especially in Switzerland and Scotland [including Baptists, Presbyterians, and Independents]; *but in recent times the opposition has largely ceased.*"[60]

There are exceptions. "It was never adopted by the Eastern Church."[61] Eastern Orthodoxy in its various forms rejects instrumental music in worship for the reasons outlined above. It is well known that the Churches of Christ do not use instrumental music in worship, also for the reasons outlined above. Smaller Presbyterian denominations, such as the Reformed Presbyterian Churches of North America, Scotland, Ireland, Australia, and Japan maintain the historic standard.

---

58. Dabney, "Girardeau's 'Instrumental Music in Public Worship,'" 463.
59. Ralph P. Martin, *Worship in the Early Church* (Westwood, NJ: Fleming H. Revell, 1964), 134.
60. Philip Schaff, *History of the Christian Church* (Grand Rapids: Eerdmans, 1910), 4:439. Italics added.
61. McClintock and Strong Cyclopaedia, 4:425.

The question remains. Why the movement away from Biblical and apostolic principles regarding instrumental music in worship? There appear to be five interconnected reasons. *First,* there is ignorance of the historic Biblical position regarding musical instruments in worship. Because the church at large now embraces instrumental music in worship, the position of the apostles and the early church is not taught today in the church, in seminary theology courses, or in Bible classes at Christian schools and colleges. As a result, there is growing and spreading ignorance regarding the worship of the New Testament church and the Biblical principles of worship held by her.

Second, because the church at large has embraced instrumental music in public worship, there is also ignorance of "the great cloud of witnesses" (Heb. 12:1) rejecting musical instruments in the public worship of God. Good Christian people are simply ignorant of the long history of church worship without instruments rooted in the New Testament. They do not know that the Biblical and apostolic position has been held unvaried for centuries, and cuts a wide swath across many denominations.

Third, there are pragmatic reasons leading the church to embrace instrumental music and to ignore her Biblical and historical roots. There is the so-called effort to retain and appease the youth of the church. Rather than teaching and training her youth to appreciate her Biblical roots and history, the church has sought to please. F. Carlton Booth, a Free Methodist, musician and song leader, and retired professor of evangelism, speaks about this tension in his own church.

> There were things about our church in my day which I know seemed strange to people outside, and perhaps to some inside as well. *Many of the rules and regulations were looked down upon by the younger generation. For example, musical instruments were not permitted in the church.*[62]

---

62. F. Carlton Booth, *On the Mountain Top* (Wheaton: Tyndale House, 1984), 58. Italics added.

Booth is looking back to around 1925.⁶³ Dabney gives a similar testimony about young people.

> The first organ I ever knew of in a Virginia Presbyterian church was introduced by one of the wisest and most saintly pastors, a paragon of old school doctrinal rigor. But he avowedly introduced it on an argument the most unsound and perilous for a good man to adopt—that *it would be advantageous to prevent his young people from leaving his church to run to the Episcopal organ in the city.*⁶⁴

This argument is often heard today. Booth counters the sentiment. He relates that the nonuse of instrumental music, although tightly held in his own church, was at the same time a great blessing.

> I was even criticized on occasion for using a concealed pitch pipe to sound the key note for our quartet to sing. Yet I must add at once that I have never heard more inspiring, and spirit-filled singing than we had in our church in those days. *Without piano or organ to carry the music,* the voices were left alone to do it, and they did.⁶⁵

Fourth, there is a sincere but misguided desire to enhance worship and assist men, women, and young people in praise. Note the comment from Booth just above and relevant to this point. Both Calvin and Spurgeon state the reasons behind the use of instruments *in the Old Testament*. "David adds to this [worship] those aides by which believers were wont to stimulate themselves the more to this exercise."⁶⁶ "The intention of them was to stimulate the worshippers, and stir them up more actively to the celebration of the praise of God with the heart."⁶⁷ "Men need all the help they can get to stir them up to praise."⁶⁸ These references are to Old Testament Israel, a people

---

63. Ibid., 59.
64. Dabney, "Girardeau's 'Instrumental Music in Public Worship,'" 468-469. Italics added.
65. Booth, *On the Mountain Top.*, 58. Italics added.
66. Calvin, *Commentary on the Book of Psalms*, 1:538.
67. Ibid., 3:495
68. Spurgeon, *A Treasury of David*, 2:115.

bound to rituals and ceremonies pointing forward to Christ, "things which are a mere shadow of what is to come" and "a copy and shadow of the heavenly things" (Col. 2:17; Heb. 8:5). "Israel was at school, and used childish things to help her learn; but in these days, when Jesus gives us spiritual manhood, we can make melody without strings and pipes."[69] In other words, if believers have the gospel of grace and the gift of the Holy Spirit, do they need the external inducements of musical instruments to evoke praise? Is the work of the Holy Spirit within them insufficient so that they must add to His work to sing the praise due to God?

In this context, Dabney cautions us. "Once more, man's [fleshly] nature is sensitive, through the ear, to certain sensuous, aesthetic impressions from melody, harmony and rhythm."[70] Recall what was said about the emotional effects of background harmonies under the heading What Is Music? Dabney's concern is that of people "mistaking the sensuous impressions for, and confounding them with, spiritual affections ... because they have sensual [fleshly] feelings, in accidental juxtaposition with religious places, words, or sights."[71] In other words, do those pleading the propriety of instrumental music in worship properly discern the Spirit? Do they discern the effects of the Spirit or the subtle effects of instrumental music? Considering the historical position of Christianity, Dabney's concern is worth pondering.

Fifth, to support their position, the proponents of instrumental music in worship must reject the regulative principle of worship, with its Biblical and historical roots, and embrace the normative principle of worship. Recall the syllogism undergirding the fundamental truth of the regulative principle: *God prescribes how we enter heaven; Sabbath worship is an entrance into and a taste of heaven; God prescribes how we worship.* Keeping this syllogism in mind, there are two proposed approaches to worship. The regulative principle is: *In matters*

---

69. Ibid.
70. Dabney, "Girardeau's 'Instrumental Music in Public Worship,'" 467.
71. Ibid. Also see Dennis Prutow, "Adrenaline Addiction, Spirituality, and Worship" (Paper, Orlando, FL: Reformed Theological Seminary, 1995).

of worship, whatever God does not command He forbids. The normative principle states: *In matters of worship, whatever God does not forbid He permits*. The regulative principle is in keeping with the syllogism. It is the Biblical and historical position applied by all those quoted in this part of this study.

Sadly, John Frame, a prominent, influential, conservative Presbyterian theologian of today, takes issue with the regulative principle. In his forward to, *Covenantal Worship: Reconsidering the Puritan Regulative Principle*, he urges readers to "thoughtfully and prayerfully" consider its message. The author wants us "to observe the way God regulates worship in Scripture itself and to follow the biblical pattern, commanding what God commands, forbidding what God forbids, and leaving to the liberty of the church what God neither commands nor forbids."[72] This comment is simply a rejection of the Biblical and historical regulative principle of worship, and the rewording of the normative principle.

To support the Biblical position, the witness of those quoted above, and the many more who stand with them, it is time to validate the truth that the instruments of Old Testament stated worship were Biblical types looking forward to spiritual realities. The next chapter will briefly define and explain Biblical types; describe the Old Testament services of animal sacrifice; and then explain the significance of the trumpets, cymbals, and harps and lyres used in these services of animal sacrifice. The use of instruments in the celebration after the Red Sea crossing will be discussed in chapter 20.

---

72. John M. Frame, "Forward," *Covenantal Worship: Reconsidering the Puritan Regulative Principle* (Phillipsburg, NJ: P & R, 2002), x.

19

INSTRUMENTAL MUSIC: THE TYPOLOGICAL PERSPECTIVE

Adam, who is a type of Him who was to come
~ ROM. 5:14

TYPES AND THEIR IDENTIFICATION[1]

To understand types, it is helpful to go back to a basic figure of speech, the *simile*. A simile is a formal comparison using *like* or *as*. Isaiah 1:9 makes the comparison: "Unless the Lord of hosts had left us a few survivors, / We would be *like* Sodom, / We would be *like* Gomorrah." Isaiah 53:6 makes the comparison: "All of us *like* sheep have gone astray." Emphasis added. These comparisons are similes.

A parable is an expanded simile. "He spoke another parable to them, 'The kingdom of heaven is *like* leaven, which a woman took and hid in three pecks of flour until it was all leavened'" (Matt. 13:31, italics added). The simile is expanded into a short story and becomes a parable. There are two important characteristics of parables. First, the parables are little stories that could take place. Second, like similes, parables have a central comparison. When interpreting them,

---

1. For helpful discussions of Biblical typology, see: Milton S. Terry, *Biblical Hermeneutics* (Grand Rapids: Zondervan, 1974), 334-346; and Louis Berkhof, *Principles of Biblical Interpretation* (Grand Rapids: Baker, 1964), 144-148.

look for the central comparison. The parable about the leaven describes the growth of the kingdom of God.

Types are in the same literary family as parables. That is, types involve formal comparisons, often identified with *like* or *as*. There are four additional, special features of types. First, types always involve persons, offices, institutions, or special events. Second, types are dynamic rather than static. They are more like demonstrations than displays. Seeing a car on display is not enough; you want to drive it, you want a demonstration. Third, types always look forward from the Old Testament to something in the gospel age. Fourth, types are prophetic. Because types look forward, a type always has an antitype, that is, an answer to the type. Therefore, a type in the Old Testament *foreshadows* an antitype in the New Testament. When a Biblical type comes on the scene, the antitype *must* later appear. Given these features, types involve preordained relationships between persons, events, institutions, or offices in the Old Testament and corresponding persons, events, institutions, or offices revealed in the New Testament.

Observing the formal connections between type and antitype, using a simile, may be the best way to identify a type in the Bible. Since types are in the same literary family as similes and parables, to interpret a type, seek to understand the central comparison between the type and antitype. For example, Romans 5:14 speaks of "Adam, who is a type of Him who was to come." Here, there are two persons taking certain actions. That is, Christ is *like* Adam. Romans 5 defines the similarity between Adam, the type, and Christ, the antitype. The comparison is that of representative headship. Adam is the head of all humanity; he represents all humanity. Christ is the head of the new humanity; He represents the new humanity, His church. Adam and Christ also differ. Adam sins; Christ never sins.

Similarly, Deuteronomy 18:15 presents Moses as a type of Christ. "The Lord your God will raise up for you a prophet *like* me from among you, from your countrymen, you shall listen to him" (italics added). Here, Scripture establishes a formal connection by way of simile. The connection or comparison is between two men. Moses holds the office of prophet, as will Christ. Deuteronomy 18:15 is also a prophetic word. Peter specifically confirms the connection between Moses and Christ in Acts 3:19-22. Moses is clearly a type of Christ.

Speaking of Christ, Isaiah 53:7 declares, "He was oppressed and He was afflicted, / Yet He did not open His mouth; / *Like* a lamb that is led to slaughter, / And *like* a sheep that is silent before its shearers, / So He did not open His mouth" (italics added). Isaiah compares Christ with sacrificial sheep and lambs. Philip shows the Ethiopian that this text speaks of Christ (Acts 8:32-36). John the Baptizer makes this same connection. "Behold the lamb of God" (John 1:29, 36). Clearly the Old Testament sacrifices foreshadow Christ; they are types of Christ. "You were not redeemed with perishable things like silver or gold from your futile way of life inherited from your forefathers, but with precious blood, *as of a lamb unblemished and spotless*, the blood of Christ" (1 Pet. 1:18-19, italics added).

With this brief explanation and these examples, the musical instruments of Old Testament worship can be examined to see how they fit into the sacrificial system and what their significance is.

MOSES'S TWO SILVER TRUMPETS

The discussion of the Old Testament, God-ordained musical instruments, begins by looking first at Moses's two silver trumpets. Consider Numbers 10:10: "In the day of your gladness and in your appointed feasts, and on the first days of your months, you shall blow the trumpets over your burnt offerings, and over the sacrifices of your peace offerings; and they shall be as a reminder of you before your God."

God instructed Moses to fabricate two silver trumpets (Numbers 10:2). These trumpets had a variety of uses, including worship. Leviticus 23 stipulates the appointed times or appointed feasts. The first appointed time was the weekly Sabbath. "My appointed times are these: For six days work may be done, but on the seventh day there is a Sabbath of complete rest, a holy convocation" (Lev. 23:2-3).

The burnt offerings were the basic offerings of Israel. God required these offerings continually morning and evening every day (Num. 28:3-6). They were doubled on the Sabbath Day (Num. 28:9-10). The fire on the altar of burnt offering was fire from heaven; it was the fire of God (Lev. 9:24). The uniqueness of the burnt offering was that, except for the skin, it was wholly consumed on the altar of burn offering. "The priest shall offer all of it" (Lev. 1:13). The burnt offerings were also an atonement offered on behalf of sinners (Lev. 1:4). The word *atonement* comes into the New Testament as *propitiation*, a sacrifice that consumes God's fiery wrath. Jesus Christ "Himself is the propitiation for our sins" (1 John 2:2).

The peace offerings were placed on top of the burnt offerings (Lev. 3:5). If the burnt offerings symbolized the propitiation of Christ, the peace offerings indicated "we have peace with God through our Lord Jesus Christ" (Rom. 5:1).

Numbers 10:10 further dictates that the trumpets were blown "over the sacrifices." The priests carried out this task (1 Chron. 16:6). Thus the trumpets accompanied the sacrifices. They were never designed to accompany the singing of praise. It was not until the time of David that God introduced praise into the worship of Israel. These trumpets, therefore, give no basis for the use of instruments in New Testament worship.

If the sacrifices foreshadowed Christ, what did the trumpets typify? Numbers 10:10 states that they were a reminder or a memorial. The King James Version indicates their purpose with these words: "that they may be to you for a memorial." Blown over the sacrifices, the trumpets reminded the people of their sins covered by the sacrifices and the peace they had with God. Isaiah 58:1 points in the same direction. "Cry loudly, do not hold back; raise your voice *like a trumpet*, and declare to My people their transgression and to the house of Jacob their sins" (italics added). Scripture makes a formal connection and comparison between the trumpet and preaching. Isaiah therefore raised His voice *like a trumpet* to remind the people of their sins. This trumpet call was not only negative. God also called the prophet to remind the people of the remedy for their sins (Isa. 40:1-2).

The burnt offerings and peace offerings both pointed to Christ. The sounding of the trumpet is likened to the preaching of the word about Christ, the great and final sacrifice. Pastors must raise their voices like a trumpet over the sacrifice of Christ. They must remind the members of their congregations of their sin, the remedy for sin in the sacrifice of Christ, and the resultant peace they have with God.

The trumpets used in Old Testament worship do not provide a rationale for the use of instrumental accompaniment in praise. Rather, the Bible likens those Old Testament trumpets to gospel preaching. This understanding of Moses's two silver trumpets is an historic position among interpreters. "The Silver Trumpets then are conceived to hold forth the Promulgation [communication] of the Gospel, the Preaching of the Pure Word of God by his Messengers."[2] "The sound of the trumpet, then, was symbolic [typological] of the majestic, omnipotent voice or word of God ... "[3] "So preaching the Word in the Old Testament is compared to blowing a trumpet."[4] "Therefore the Preaching of the Word, is compared to the sounding of a trumpet, *Isa 58. Lift up thy voice like a trumpet*, that is, powerfully and distinctly ... "[5] Yes, the preaching of Christ is likened to the Old Testament trumpets blown over the sacrifices. They are types pointing forward to the gospel preaching of Christ. Because the trumpets are types associated with the Old Testament sacrifices, they pass away with those Old Testament sacrifices. Because the trumpets are types that foreshadow gospel preaching, they do not provide a basis for using instruments in the worship of the New Testament church.

---

2. Samuel Mather, *The Figures and Types of the Old Testament* (New York: Johnson Reprint Corporation, 1969), 480.
3. Patrick Fairbairn, *The Typology of Scripture* (Welwyn, Herts: Evangelical Press, 1975), 2:395.
4. Jonathan Edwards, *Typological Writings* (New Haven: Yale University Press, 1993), 253.
5. James Durham, *A Commentary upon the Book of Revelation* (Willow Street, PA: Old Paths, 2000), 42.

DAVID'S CYMBALS

God instituted the use of trumpets in worship through Moses. God commanded, "You shall blow the trumpets over your burnt offerings, and over the sacrifices of your peace offerings" (Num. 10:10). As just said, the trumpets foreshadow the voice of Christ sounding forth the gospel. God commands Isaiah, "Raise your voice like a trumpet" (Isa. 58:1). When John heard a voice "like a trumpet," he "turned to see the voice that was speaking" and "saw one like the Son of Man" (Rev. 1:10, 12-13). Again, trumpets foreshadow gospel preaching. Furthermore, they foreshadow the voice of Christ heard in *gospel preaching*. As Paul asks in Romans 10:14, "How shall they believe *him* of whom they have not heard?"[6]

God instituted the use of cymbals in worship through David (1 Chron. 16:4-5; 29:25). First Chronicles 16:42 indicates that the "trumpets and cymbals [were] for those who should sound aloud." That is, the cymbals were used along with the trumpets during the daily sacrifices. David also appointed "instruments for the songs of God," the harps and lyres (1 Chron. 29:42).

As a part of the sacrificial service, the head of the Levites stood in the court of the temple in front of the holy place, between the sanctuary and the altar, with the cymbals. The two priests stood on either side of him with their trumpets. After the sacrifice was on the altar of burnt offering, the priests gave three blasts on their trumpets. The head of the Levites then clashed the cymbals. As the chief priest was pouring out the drink offering of wine on the burnt offering (Num. 15:5), the Levitical choir sang the designated Psalm of the day.[7]

There is no indication that cymbals were used to accompany the singing that took place in conjunction with the sacrifices. Their function was similar to that of the trumpets. The cymbals were to "sound

---

6. This translation is suggested by John Murray, *The Epistle to the Romans* (Grand Rapids: Eerdmans,1973), 2:58, n. 16. Italics added.
7. For further descriptions of how these sacrifices were conducted, see: James W. McKinnon, "The Exclusion of Musical Instruments from the Ancient Synagogue," *Journal of the Royal Musical Association*, 106 (1979): 77; and John Lightfoot, *The Works of the Reverend and Learned John Lightfoot* (London: Robert Scot, 1684), 1:923.

aloud." They are called "loud-sounding cymbals" (1 Chron. 15:16, 28; 16:5). To sound aloud is to cause to hear, to proclaim, or to announce. Isaiah and Nahum use the same word to describe God's messengers. "How lovely on the mountains are the feet of him who brings good news, who announces peace and brings good news of happiness, who *announces* salvation, and says to Zion, 'Your God reigns!'" (Isa. 52:7, italics added). Similarly, Nahum 1:15 reads, "Behold, on the mountains the feet of him who brings good news, who *announces* peace" (italics added).

The loud sounding cymbals were therefore announcing or proclaiming cymbals. What did they announce? "The practical function of the cymbals was to call for the attention of the congregation to the performance of sacred song."[8] They were a signal to the choir to begin singing. They did not accompany the Levitical choirs. "Contrary to popular opinion, the cymbals were not used by the precentor [song leader] to conduct the singing by beating out the rhythm of the song, but rather to announce the beginning of the song or a stanza in the song."[9] In other words, the cymbals, along with the trumpets, announced the response to the sacrifice on the altar, praise with Psalms.

Notice the prominent features in this worship setting. The burnt offerings and peace offerings foreshadowed Christ and pointed worshipers to Christ. The trumpets foreshadowed gospel preaching about the sacrifice of Christ. However, the loud sounding cymbals were *not* types. They simply announced the time for the Levitical choirs to begin their songs of praise in response to the grace of Christ foreshadowed in the sacrifices and the call of the trumpets. "[T]hey called for the attention of the congregation to the performance of praise during the presentation of burnt offerings ... "[10] This use of cymbals in Old Testament worship does not provide any grounds for the use of instruments in worship today.

---

8. John W. Kleinig, *The Lord's Song* (Sheffield: Sheffield Academic Press, 1993), 83.
9. Ibid., 82.
10. Ibid., 84.

DAVID'S HARPS AND LYRES

When King David appointed Levitical singers to accompany the sacrifices at the altar, they were to sing with stringed instruments, harps and lyres. "David spoke to the chiefs of the Levites to appoint their relatives the singers, with instruments of music, harps, lyres, loud-sounding cymbals, to raise sounds of joy" (1 Chron. 15:16).

These harps and lyres were not ordinary instruments. David did not go out to the local harp and lyre shop to buy instruments for the temple. He created special harps and lyres for use in the temple, just like Moses made the instruments or vessels for the tabernacle.[11] First Chronicles 23:5 mentions "the instruments which David made for giving praise." John Owen comments on this text,

> And he [David] speaks expressly, in 1 Chron. xxiii. 5, of praising God with instruments of music, "which," he says, "I made [KJV]." He did it by the direction of the Spirit of God; otherwise he ought not to have done it: for so it is said, 1 Chron. xxviii. 12, when he had established all the ordinances of the temple—*the pattern of all that he had by the Spirit* [KJV].[12]

Second Chronicles 7:6 confirms Owen's exposition: "The priests stood at their posts, and the Levites also, with the instruments of music to the Lord, which King David *had made* for giving praise to the Lord" (italics added).

The instruments of David were the harps, lyres, and cymbals, in distinction from the instruments of the priests, the trumpets. "The Levites stood with the musical instruments of David, and the priests with the trumpets" (2 Chron. 29:26). Only the harps and lyres actually accompanied the sacred song. "And with them were Heman and Jeduthun with trumpets and cymbals for those who should sound aloud, and with instruments for the songs of God" (1 Chron. 16:42).

---

11. John Price, *Old Light on New Worship* (Avinger, TX: Simpson Publishing Co., 2005), 58-65.
12. John Owen, *The Works of John Owen*, ed. William H. Goold (London: Johnstone and Hunter, 1851), 9:463.

As has been seen, the trumpets foreshadowed proclamation or the preaching of the Word accompanying the sacrifice. The cymbals announce the response of praise with Psalms, now accompanied by harps and lyres. As part of the Old Testament ceremonial system, what do the harps and lyres foreshadow? The visions of the Book of Revelation give the needed help. Harps are mentioned first in Revelation 5:8. "When He [Christ] had taken the book, the four living creatures and the twenty-four elders fell down before the Lamb, each one holding a harp and golden bowls full of incense, which are the prayers of the saints."

The visions of Revelation are not reality; rather, they portray reality. In Revelation 5:8, the twenty-four elders represent the church, both Old and New Testament. Each of them has a harp in one hand and a bowl of incense in the other. The vision itself gives a word of interpretation: the bowls of incense portray the prayers of the saints. What about the harps? The text continues, "And they [the elders] sang a new song" (Rev. 5:9). In this vision, it is unlikely that the elders, representing the church of all ages, hold a *portrayal* of prayer in one hand, but hold *literal* harps in the other hand. Rather, if the bowls of incense portray prayer, the harps portray singing praise. "The redeemed Church begin[s], and they sing ... Again, their work here, is, not only to praise, but to pray; for they have vials full of odours, as well as harps, *vers*. 8."[13]

Revelation 14:2 confirms this thinking. Note the similes. Note also that the text does not speak of actual harps but of sounds *like* harps. "I heard a voice from heaven, like the sound of many waters and like the sound of loud thunder, and the voice which I heard was *like the sound of harpists playing on their harps*" (italics added). Verse 3 follows, "And they sang a new song before the throne." The voice is a heavenly choir. This vision portrays the united voice of the choir sounding *like* "harpists playing on their harps." Again, there are no

---

13. Durham, *Revelation*, 364.

actual harps, but the united voice of the choir sounds *like* harps. The harps portray the singing of sacred song.

The vision also describes the sound of the choir as being *like* the sound of "many waters." Revelation 1:15, part of the vision of Christ, indicates that "His voice was like the sound of many waters." Therefore, in Revelation 14:2, the choir sings with the spiritual power and voice of Christ. The harps not only portray singing, they portray Spirit-empowered sacred song.

Here is something else to remember. Because no one has been to the future, the only way the Biblical writers can speak about the future is to use images from the past and their own present.[14] In the case of the Book of Revelation, the imagery comes from the temple. Old Testament temple worship included singing accompanied by harps and lyres. Given the formal comparison the Book of Revelation makes between Spirit empowered-singing and the Old Testament temple harps, it is clear that these harps foreshadow New Testament, Spirit-empowered singing. They are types. The Old Testament Levitical choir singing in response to the sacrifices with harps and lyres, therefore, typifies *Spirit-empowered* singing.

The use of harps and lyres in Old Testament temple worship is not a reason to go back to the things of the ceremonial law and use various stringed instruments in corporate worship today. God gives believers the Holy Spirit to fill their hearts to sing songs fit for the realm of the Spirit. The Apostle Paul enjoins, "Be filled with the Spirit ... singing and making melody with your heart to the Lord" (Eph. 5:18-19). *Believers are, therefore, the true instruments of praise.*

In this light, consider Colossians 3:16. "Let the word of Christ dwell in you richly, teaching and admonishing one another in all wisdom, singing psalms and hymns and spiritual songs, with thankfulness in your hearts to God" (ESV). Believers must let the message of the sacrifice of Christ live within them. They let the word of Christ dwell

---

14. Walter Kaiser, *Back Toward the Future* (Grand Rapids: Baker, 1990), 51-52.

within them when they take heed to the teaching and counsel they receive from Scripture as they worship together in the church. Believers also let the word of Christ dwell richly within them when they offer praise to God with Psalms in their corporate worship. The Old Testament harps accompanying the songs of the Lord in temple sacrificial worship foreshadowed New Testament, Spirit-empowered praise. These instruments were types. The use of harps in Old Testament temple worship provides no ground to use stringed instruments in the worship of the church today.

TRUE INSTRUMENTS OF THE SPIRIT

As has been seen, the use of musical instruments in Old Testament worship does not provide warrant for the use of musical instruments in New Testament worship. As a part of the formal and ceremonial worship of Israel, the musical instruments were symbolic and typical. Yes, the Bible likens those Old Testament trumpets to gospel preaching. In addition, the trumpets, standing with the cymbals, typified the preaching of the word accompanying the sacrifice. This gospel preaching and proclamation is Spirit-empowered preaching. Jesus Christ declares, "The Spirit of the Lord God is upon me, because the Lord has anointed me to bring good news" (Isa. 61:1, Luke 4:18). The Apostle Paul confesses, "My message and my preaching were not in persuasive words of wisdom, but in demonstration of the Spirit and of power" (1 Cor. 2:4).

As has also been seen, the harps are types of Spirit-empowered singing. The Old Testament Levitical choir singing in response to the sacrifices with harps and lyres, therefore, typifies Spirit-empowered, sacred song. The Apostle Paul teaches us that truly singing praise to God is the result of the fullness of the Spirit in the heart. He enjoins, "Do not get drunk with wine, for that is dissipation, but be filled with the Spirit ... singing and making melody with your heart to the Lord" (Eph. 5:18-19). The thread connecting and running through the typology of the Old Testament musical instruments used in stated worship is the Holy Spirit. Getting this connection is to understand God's rationale for ordaining instrumental worship in the Old Testament, and then removing these instruments from the stated worship of God's people in the New Testament.

In addition, "That music evokes emotion is a well-known and uncontested fact. Rather more contentious have been the numerous attempts by philosophers, writers and musicians over the centuries to explain the phenomenon."[15] We recognize the emotional affect of instrumental music in movie soundtracks. Recall the discussion under Instrumental Music. Music evokes fear, sympathy, awe, and other emotions in response to the action in the movie. The emotions portrayed in the film are more successfully evoked among the audience through the music. There is little trouble making this connection.

In the gospel era, after the coming of Christ and the pouring out of the Holy Spirit, it is not instrumental music that should evoke emotional responses to the gospel and to Christ. Instruments that stir the emotions are but a dim reflection of the Holy Spirit who changes and bridles the emotions and brings believers into conformity to Jesus Christ. Instrumental music may evoke various emotions, but the Holy Spirit works proper emotions within the believer. God guides them in the expression of their emotions with a use of the Psalms. Calvin says, "I have been accustomed to call this book, I think not inappropriately, 'An Anatomy of all the Parts of the Soul'; for there is not an emotion of which any one can be conscious that is not here represented as in a mirror."[16] In the Psalms, believers find a Holy Spirit-given guide for the expression of their emotions in worship.

However, although Spirit-empowered and Spirit-guided praise in worship is an important outlet for the emotions of believers, God does not ordain praise primarily to satisfy *their* emotions. Look again at Colossians 3:16. "Let the word of Christ dwell in you richly, teach-

---

15. Matthew M. Lavy, "Emotion and the Experience of Listening to Music: A Framework for Empirical Research" (Ph.D. dissertation, University of Cambridge, Jesus College, 2001), 6.
16. John Calvin, "The Author's Preface," *Commentary on the Book of Psalms* (Grand Rapids: Baker, 1979), 1:xix.

ing and admonishing one another in all wisdom, singing psalms and hymns and spiritual songs, with thankfulness in your hearts to God" (ESV). Again, Paul is pointing out the two primary ways you "let the word of Christ dwell within you." The first means is through the teaching and admonishing received each Lord's Day. Simply put, Paul has preaching in mind. Compare Colossians 1:28. Paul explains, we *proclaim* Christ, "admonishing every man and teaching every man." Listening to Spirit-empowered preaching is one of God's primary means of forming Christ in you. Singing praise is the second primary means God uses to form Christ in you, when this praise is empowered and guided by the Spirit through the Psalms.

Therefore, the use of musical instruments in praise falls away in the New Testament. The musical instruments employed in Old Testament worship point to the Holy Spirit who makes use of both preaching and singing as the primary means to let the word of Christ dwell richly within the believer. "They were therefore fit resemblances to [foreshadow] that heavenly music and inward melody of the joys and graces of God's Spirit in the hearts of his people."[17] Believers, themselves, then become the instruments of the Holy Spirit in singing praise to God. This teaching is the Biblical, apostolic, and historic position of the church of Jesus Christ.

CONCLUSION: CHRIST CONTINUES TO SING IN HIS CHURCH

As instruments of the Holy Spirit, when believers lift their voices in praise to God, Jesus Christ continues His songs of praise to the Father. How so? Thanksgiving is covenant praise for covenant grace. David enjoined the Levites, in their singing, "Remember His covenant forever, the word which He commanded to a thousand generations" (1 Chron. 16:15). The words of 1 Chronicles 16:7-36 provide a sample of the praise David ordained. Verse 34 says specifically, "O give thanks

---

17. Mather, *Figures and Types*, 481.

to the Lord, for He is good; For His lovingkindness is everlasting." Lovingkindness is covenant love. When the "Levitical singers" lifted their voices and "praised the Lord," they sang, "He indeed is good for His lovingkindness is everlasting" (2 Chron. 5:13). This refrain, "His lovingkindness is everlasting," epitomized the praise appointed by David (2 Chron. 7:6).

The sample of the praise in 1 Chronicles 16:7-36 prescribed by David includes Psalm 105:1-15, Psalm 96:1-13, and Psalm 106:1 and 47-48. This Psalmody was later formalized. "King Hezekiah and the officials ordered the Levites to sing praises to the Lord with the words of David and Asaph the seer (2 Chron. 29:30). David appointed "Asaph the chief" Levitical singer (1 Chron. 16:5). Asaph was David's servant as both an author and a singer of Psalms. David, therefore, appointed both the singers and the songs for covenant praise.

Not only so, even as Moses made the tabernacle vessels, David made the instruments of song for this covenant praise. "The priests stood at their posts, and the Levites also, with the instruments of music to the Lord, which King David *had made* for giving praise to the Lord" (2 Chron. 7:6, italics added). What David did was similar to what Moses did in two ways. First, the word *instruments* may be translated *vessels* or *utensils*, as in the vessels of the tabernacle ordained through Moses. Exodus 27:19 speaks about, "All the utensils [vessels, KJV] of the tabernacle … " Second, David did not take common instruments for use in the worship of God. The word *made* in 2 Chronicles 7:6 is the same word used in Genesis 1:31. "God saw all that He had made, and behold, it was very good." It is the same word God uses in the crucial command He gave to Moses in Exodus 25:8. "Let them make me a sanctuary; that I may dwell among them." Moses *made* the tabernacle and all its utensils for the worship of God. David *made* the instruments for use in praise before God. David therefore appointed the songs, the singers, and the instruments for singing praise to God.

Second Chronicles 7:6 speaks of God's priests standing before the

Lord with David's instruments. The text indicates, "David praised by their ministry" (KJV). That is, although David was dead (1 Chron. 29:28-29), he continued to give covenant praise to God through the ministry of the Levites. How so? David appointed the Levites as singers. He appointed their songs. He also made and appointed the instruments of covenant praise.

Make this connection. David is a type of Christ.[18] Long after David's death, Ezekiel 37:24 promises, "My servant David will be king over them, and they will all have one shepherd; and they will walk in My ordinances and keep My statutes and observe them." Jesus Christ fulfills these words. He is the one *like* David whom Ezekiel promises will shepherd His people.

Fast forward. Jesus Christ makes His people "new creatures" (2 Cor. 5:17). He makes them "vessels of mercy" (Rom. 9:23). He gives them His inspired songs, the Psalms, to sing. "From You comes my praise in the great assembly" (Ps. 22:25; Col. 3:16; Eph. 5:19). God's people are "a kingdom of priests and a holy nation" (Exod. 19:6, 1 Pet. 2:9). Their task is praise. "Through Him then, let us continually offer up a sacrifice of praise to God, that is, the fruit of lips that give thanks to His name" (Heb. 13:15). Jesus Christ, the greater David, appoints believers His singers. He makes believers His instruments. He gives them His songs. In their praise to God, Jesus Christ continues to offer His songs of covenant praise to His Father by making us both His instruments and His singers, with His songs.

Because the Old Testament temple instruments are *types*, pointing ahead to preaching and praise, they present no ground for using musical instruments in the worship of the church today. It is not the prerogative of God's people to go back to the sacrifices, ceremonies, types, and shadows of Old Testament worship, as though those types and shadows are still applicable. God makes believers His instruments of praise. They offer Spirit-empowered praise to God by the

---

18. Fairbairn, *Typology*, 1:114; Mather, *Figures and Types*, 53.

breath of the Spirit working in and through them. This teaching is the historic, Biblical position regarding the nonuse of instrumental music in the church.

20

INSTRUMENTAL MUSIC: BASIC OBJECTIONS

> *Miriam the prophetess, Aaron's sister, took the timbrel in her hand, and all the women went out after her with timbrels and with dancing.* ~ Exod. 15:20

OLD TESTAMENT CELEBRATIONS

God ordained the use of trumpets in the stated worship of Israel through Moses (Num. 10:2, 10). God also ordained the use of cymbals, harps, and lyres through David (2 Chron. 29:25). As has been seen, these instruments had symbolic and typological significance. Their use in Old Testament *temple* worship is, therefore, no warrant for the use of musical instruments in New Testament *church* worship. What about the use of musical instruments in other Old Testament worship settings? That the Old Testament saints used musical instruments in celebrations of praise before God is clear. What prohibits contemporary believers doing the same?

The following short study answers this question. One of the popular instruments in the Old Testament was the timbrel or tambourine. The first mention of tambourines is in Genesis 31:27. Jacob's father-in-law, Laban, complains that he has not been given an opportunity to properly send away his daughters with a banquet. "Why did you flee secretly and deceive me, and did not tell me so that I might have sent you away with joy and with songs, with timbrel and with lyre?"

Stereotypical banquets or wedding feasts of that time featured singing and dancing with timbrel and lyre.

Job 21:12 speaks similarly of the revelry of unbelievers. "They sing to the timbrel and harp and rejoice at the sound of the flute." This text again pictures a *secular* celebration. Israel was prone to engage in such revelry and to ignore God. "Their banquets are accompanied by lyre and harp, by tambourine and flute, and by wine; but they do not pay attention to the deeds of the Lord, nor do they consider the work of His hands" (Isa. 5:12). The contemporary culture of the time celebrated various events with banquets, singing, and playing various instruments. Banquets, singing, and playing musical instruments were not sinful in themselves. The problem in Israel was a failure to acknowledge God. The result was judgment.

When judgment comes, "The gaiety of tambourines ceases, / The noise of revelers stops, / The gaiety of the harp ceases" (Isa. 24:8). Judgment cuts off joy, celebration, banquet, and party. On the other hand, when Israel's enemies face God's judgment, it is time to celebrate. Israel will rejoice at the demise of Assyria. "Every blow of the rod of punishment, / Which the Lord will lay on him, / Will be with the music of tambourines and lyres" (Isa. 30:32). In like manner, the restoration of Israel from exile meant the restoration of banquet, joy, celebration, and party. "Again you will take up your tambourines, / And go forth to the dances of the merrymakers" (Jer. 31:4). These texts all make statements regarding *culturally-conditioned, secular and occasional celebrations*.

Given the common use of tambourines in the culture of the time, it is not surprising that Miriam took up the timbrel to celebrate the crossing of the Red Sea and the destruction of the Egyptians. The people naturally would have celebrated a great occasion in this manner. "Miriam the prophetess, Aaron's sister, took the timbrel in her hand, and all the women went out after her with timbrels and with dancing" (Exod. 15:20). In this case, Miriam gave thanks to the Lord. "Miriam answered them, 'Sing to the Lord, for He is highly exalted;

the horse and his rider He has hurled into the sea'" (Exod. 15:21).

This *celebration* had a worshipful component. However, it differed from the tabernacle worship and temple worship later ordained by God. This difference is crucial. Regular worship, stated for each Sabbath or Lord's Day, is God-ordained and heaven-directed. Miriam's celebration occasioned by God's deliverance was a one-time event and culturally-conditioned. It provides no warrant for us to use instrumental music in regular, stated New Testament worship today. The distinction is *regular, weekly, stated, heaven-directed worship versus occasional, culturally-conditioned celebrations.*

Continuing the discussion of culturally-conditioned, occasional celebrations, turn to Judges 11:34. "When Jephthah came to his house at Mizpah, behold, his daughter was coming out to meet him with tambourines and with dancing." Jephthah's daughter celebrated his victory in battle over Ammon. Scripture records a similar circumstance regarding David. "It happened as they were coming, when David returned from killing the Philistine, that the women came out of all the cities of Israel, singing and dancing, to meet King Saul, with tambourines, with joy and with musical instruments" (1 Sam. 18:6). As in the case of Miriam, this celebration involved special circumstances rather than regular, stated, weekly meetings established by God. Further, these celebrations were *culturally-shaped*. As argued in part one of this study, regular tabernacle and temple worship was God-directed and heaven-filled.

There are two other important incidents in the Old Testament manifesting an air of celebration *and* having a worshipful component. The first is 1 Chronicles 13:8, where David celebrated the return of the ark of God from the Philistines. "David and all Israel were celebrating before God with all their might, even with songs and with lyres, harps, tambourines, cymbals and with trumpets." Again, this celebration is *culturally-shaped*. And, as in the case of Miriam, this celebration involved a special circumstance; it was occasional. It differed from the weekly, regular, stated meetings established by God. In addition, as a culturally-shaped celebration, it stood in sharp contrast to the regular, stated worship of God in the tabernacle and temple. The latter is specifically God-directed and heaven-imbued.

In 1 Samuel 10:5, Saul met a band of prophets prophesying and using tambourines and other instruments. Samuel made this prediction. "You will come to the hill of God where the Philistine garrison is; and it shall be as soon as you have come there to the city, that you will meet a group of prophets coming down from the high place with harp, tambourine, flute, and a lyre before them, and they will be prophesying." The prophets were prophesying; "in a condition of ecstatic inspiration, in which singing or speaking, with accompaniment of music, they gave expression to the overflowing feeling with which their hearts were filled from above by the controlling Spirit."[1]

These ministers of God were singing with musical accompaniment; they were doing so under the influence of the Spirit. On one hand, there was a combination of instruments and singing, as found later in the temple. However, as has been observed, the musical instruments are typological. They point to Spirit-empowered proclamation and praise, the exact circumstance of 1 Samuel 10:5. On the other hand, the celebratory activity of the prophets was clearly shaped by their contemporary culture. This again contrasted with the regulated, God-ordained, stated worship of the tabernacle and the temple.

The temple and its services, not the occasional celebrations of the Old Testament, form the basis for New Testament worship. The New Testament repeatedly compares the church with the temple (2 Cor. 6:16; Eph. 2:21-22; 1 Pet. 2:5). The temple was the Old Testament designated place for regular, corporate, stated worship. Today, the church assembled is the designated place for regular, corporate, stated worship.

The celebrations of Miriam, Jephthah's daughter, David, and Saul do not provide an apologetic for the use of instruments in the gath-

---

1. David Erdmann, *The Books of Samuel: Lange's Commentary on the Holy Scriptures*, trans. C. H. Troy and John A. Broadus (Grand Rapids: Zondervan, 1960), 5:153.

erings of God's people for regular, stated, worship in the present era. These celebrations were culturally-conditioned and culturally-shaped. These celebrations involved special circumstances and not stated meetings. Scripture shows them to be distinct from regular, corporate, stated worship instituted by God in the tabernacle and temple.

Contemporary Christians have celebrations: patriotic remembrances, special banquets, and weddings, all of which are culturally-shaped. However, believers properly maintain that these celebrations are quite distinct from the regular worship of God, from which they properly exclude instrumental music.

THE MEANING OF THE WORD "PSALM"

Supporters of instrumental music in worship point to the Greek word for psalm, *psallō*. The root for the word means, they say, *to play on a stringed instrument, to play the harp*. The Greek word for Psalm refers to "striking the chords of a musical instrument."[2] To sing Psalms therefore means to sing "to the accompaniment of a harp."[3] End of argument.

This argument, however, is "one of the most enduring errors"[4] in Biblical interpretation, the root fallacy. "In this view, meaning is determined by etymology; that is, by the root or the roots of a word."[5] Any dictionary shows that most words have a range of meanings. As a result, word meaning depends upon the context of its use.[6]

Isaiah 55:8 is good example of this phenomenon. "'For My thoughts are not your thoughts, / Nor are your ways My ways,' declares the Lord." The note in *The Reformation Study Bible* reads as follows, "My thoughts are not your thoughts. Specifically, God's thoughts concerning grace exceed human imagination ... "[7] An examination of the context leads to a different interpretation.

---

2. *A Greek-English Lexicon of the New Testament*, trans. Joseph H. Thayer (New York: American Book Company, 1889), 675.
3. William F. Arndt and F. Wilbur Gingrich, *A Greek-English Lexicon of the New Testament* (Grand Rapids: Zondervan, 1963), 899.
4. D. A. Carson, *Exegetical Fallacies* (Grand Rapids: Baker, 2004), 28.
5. Ibid.
6. Milton Terry, *Biblical Hermeneutics* (Grand Rapids: Zondervan, 1974), 181.
7. *The Reformation Study Bible*, ed. R. C. Sproul (Orlando: Ligonier Ministries, 2005), 1031.

Isaiah 55:7 says, "Let the wicked forsake his way / And the unrighteous man his thoughts; / And let him return to the Lord, / And He will have compassion on him, / And to our God, / For He will abundantly pardon." The wicked have wicked thoughts. The unrighteous have unrighteous thoughts. God's thoughts and ways are holy and righteous.

Isaiah 55:8 does not teach God's transcendence. The immediate context indicates that the text speaks about God's righteous thoughts and ways. The proper meanings of the words "thoughts" and "ways" are derived from the context. The note in the *The Reformation Study Bible* is misleading.

Context also governs the meaning of the word "psalm." A quick review of the titles to the Psalms in the Old Testament reveals that fifty-four of them are called "A Psalm of David." Sixteen psalms are called both "a psalm" and "a song." Six psalms are called "hymns" in the Greek version of the Old Testament. Psalm 67 is titled "a song and a psalm among the hymns." In each of these cases, the titles refer to the *content* of the Psalms. The psalms and songs are the lyrics given in each of the Psalms. These lyrics, these psalms and hymns and songs, can be sung with or without instrumental accompaniment.

Consider context when interpreting Colossians 3:16. "Let the word of Christ dwell in you richly, teaching and admonishing one another in all wisdom, singing psalms and hymns and spiritual songs, with thankfulness in your hearts to God" (ESV). Since the Old Testament refers to the Psalms as songs and hymns, when Paul speaks of "psalms and hymns and spiritual songs," he most likely has in mind the Psalms of the Old Testament.

Paul's grammatical construction also points in this direction. The Greek underlying the English is without the conjunctions. Paul packs the three terms together: psalms, hymns, songs. He uses a figure of speech, asyndeton, without conjunctions. It "ordinarily join[s] coordinate words or clauses … "[8] In this case, where psalms, hymns, and

---

8. James D. Hernando, *Dictionary of Hermeneutics* (Springfield: Gospel Publishing House, 2005), 111.

songs are joined as one, the grammatical construction is a *conjunctive asyndeton*.[9] Paul has one thing in mind, the Psalms of the Old Testament. He thus outlines the *content* of congregational singing. Context rules; etymology does not rule.

In their celebration of the Passover, Matthew 26:30 indicates Christ and His disciples went out to the Mount of Olives, "after singing a hymn." Once again, consider context. The hymn was a selection from Psalms 113 through 118, the Egyptian Hallel. The content of this hymn is well known because of the Passover context in which it was sung.

In Scripture, the word "psalm" most often refers to the *content* of the songs. The root meaning of the word is not an argument for the use of instrumental accompaniment in singing the Psalms. Remember the root fallacy. Context is king.

THE COMMANDS IN THE PSALMS TO USE INSTRUMENTS

One of the arguments favoring the use of musical instruments in worship points to the commands in the Psalms. How do both Spurgeon and Calvin approach these commands? Do they see them as valid for the New Testament church? If not, why not? Psalm 33:2 is an example. "Give thanks to the Lord with the lyre; / Sing praises to Him with a harp of ten strings." Spurgeon comments:

> Men need all the help they can get to stir them up to praise. This is the lesson gathered from the use of musical instruments under the old dispensation. Israel was at school, and used childish things to help her to learn; but in these days, when Jesus gives us spiritual manhood, we can make melody without strings and pipes. We do not believe these things expedient in worship, lest they should mar its simplicity ... [10]

---

9. E. W. Bullinger, *Figures of Speech Used in the Bible* (Grand Rapids: Baker, 2004), 138.
10. Charles Spurgeon, *A Treasury of David* (Newark, DE: Cornerstone, n.d.), 2:115.

Spurgeon draws a distinction between the New Testament age and the Old Testament age under David and Solomon. As a result, Spurgeon "practiced what he preached" in his Metropolitan Tabernacle in London. "There was no organ and no choir. A precentor set the pitch of each hymn with a tuning fork and led the singing with his own voice."[11] As God ordered the use of musical instruments in the stated worship of Israel under David, a transition from the standards of worship under Moses, so God again altered the standards for worship for the New Testament church.[12]

Calvin was of like mind.

> I have no doubt that playing upon cymbals, touching the harp and the viol, and all that kind of music, which is so frequently mentioned in the Psalms, was a part of the education; that is to say, the puerile [childish] instruction of the law: I speak of the stated service of the temple. For even now, if believers choose to cheer themselves with musical instruments, they should, I think, make it their object not to dissever their cheerfulness from the praises of God. But when they frequent their sacred assemblies, musical instruments in celebrating the praises of God would be no more suitable than the burning of incense, the lighting up of lamps, and the restoration of the other shadows of the law.[13]

For Calvin, the use of musical instruments in corporate worship was a retreat from the New Testament, and a reinstitution of the ceremonial law of the Old Testament. The instrumental music in the Old Testament temple, as we have seen, was part of the ceremonies associated with the sacrifices. Thomas Aquinas earlier declared "the Church in his time did not use them lest they should seem to judaize."[14] What

---

11. Arnold Dallimore, *Spurgeon* (Chicago: Moody, 1984), 98.
12. Review chapters 17 and 18: "The Historical Perspective."
13. John Calvin, *Commentary on the Book of Psalms*, trans. James Anderson (Grand Rapids: Baker, 1979), 1:538.
14. Samuel Mather, *The Figures and Types of the Old Testament* (New York: Johnson Reprint Corporation, 1969), 480.

he means is that seeking to introduce musical instruments into New Testament worship is no different than seeking to restore circumcision to the church. It means following Jewish customs and religious rites. It is a retreat from Christianity, and a return to Judaism.

Psalm 71:22 announces, "I will also praise You with a harp, / *Even* Your truth, O my God; / To You I will sing praises with the lyre, / O Holy One of Israel." Again, Spurgeon commented on this use of instruments: "There was a typical signification in them; and upon this account they are not only rejected and condemned by the whole army of Protestant divines ... so that we might as well recall the incense, tapers, sacrifices, new moons, circumcision, and all the other shadows of the law into use again."[15] Instrumental music was therefore "part of the abrogated legal pedagogy [method of teaching]."[16] As types looking forward to something better in the New Testament, when the reality of Spirit-empowered singing arrives, the types fall away. If instrumental music is restored to New Testament worship, the other Old Testament ceremonies might just as well be restored. If instrumental music is restored to New Testament worship, the church expresses a preference for the shadows pointing to Christ rather than the reality of Christ.

Calvin agreed. "In speaking of employing *the psaltery* and the *harp* in this exercise, he alludes to the generally prevailing custom of that time. To sing the praises of God upon the harp and psaltery unquestionably formed a part of the training of the law, and of the service of God under that dispensation of shadows and figures; but they are not now to be used in public thanksgiving."[17]

Again, the inclination is to go back to the ways of Old Testament worship, to the ceremonial types and shadows pointing forward to Christ and all He accomplished. However, believers ought to worship, not by acting out the Old Testament types, but as those caught

---

15. Spurgeon, *Treasury of David*, 3:313.
16. Ibid.
17. Calvin, *Psalms*, 3:98.

up in the fulfillment of those types. A proper interpretation of the Psalms means understanding that the commands in the Psalms regarding the use of musical instruments are directed to the Old Testament people of God and not to the New Testament church. These commands are not a reason to use musical instruments in worship today.

BUT PSALMODY ITSELF IS A RETURN TO OLD TESTAMENT WORSHIP

As has been observed, continued Psalmody is indeed tied back to Old Testament temple worship. However, several other points have also been stressed. First, the New Testament commands the continued use of the Psalms in worship.[18] Second, Psalmody, although associated with the Old Testament typical and ceremonial sacrifices, was not itself a type.[19] The use of Psalms in New Testament worship is therefore not a return to Old Testament types and shadows. Third, we grant that the Psalms speak of the future using types and symbols.[20] Remember, the only way the Biblical writers could speak about the future was by using imagery from their own past or present.[21] This use of imagery includes the New Testament writers who describe the work of Christ using terms from the Old Testament sacrifices. They also discuss the church using terms from Old Testament temple worship. Fourth, remember the genius of Psalmody, the subjective element.[22] "Subjective responsiveness is the specific quality of these songs."[23] The language of the Psalms is therefore useful and suitable and functional for all peoples in all times.

> At first sight, this may easily seem strange to us when we remember that the Psalmists lived under the conditions of a typical and preparatory dispensation; that on

---

18. Review the discussion under, "Psalms, Hymns, Songs."
19. Review the discussion answering the objection that, "Psalmody is Typological."
20. Ibid.
21. Ibid.
22. Review the discussion under, "The Genius of Psalmody: The Subjective Element."
23. Geerhardus Vos, "Eschatology of the Psalter," *The Pauline Eschatology* (Grand Rapids: Baker, 1979), 324

many points they saw through a glass darkly, whereas we, who live in the full light of the complete gospel, see face to face. But for the very reason that the Psalms reflect the experimental religion of the heart, which is unvarying at all times and under all circumstances, we need not greatly wonder at this.[24]

Present day Psalmody is not a rationale for the contemporary use of musical instruments that were associated with Old Testament temple Psalmody.

PSALM 150 COMMANDS INSTRUMENTS

What about the explicit commands of Psalm 150? Surely this Psalm directs believers to use musical instruments in worship. Before agreeing with this assertion, an analysis of Psalm 150, in context, is in order. Each of the five books of the Psalms ends with a doxology: Psalm 41:13; Psalm 72:18-19; Psalm 89:52; Psalm 106:48; and Psalm 150. Psalms 146-150 offer a crescendo of praise at the end of the Psalter. There is also a general movement through the five books of the Psalms. The movement is from a contrast between the righteous and wicked (Ps. 1), the warfare of the wicked with the righteous (Pss. 2 and 3), through the coming and victory of Messiah (Pss. 22, 45, 110, and 118), to the praise of God (Pss. 146-150).

Many of the Psalms are tied to specific occasions and situations. Psalms 51, 57, and 137 are good examples. In addition, God's ancient people used certain Psalms on a regular basis in their worship. The titles indicate this: Psalm 92:1, Sabbath Day; 24:1, First Day (LXX); 48:1, Second Day (LXX); 82:1, Third Day; 94:1, Fourth Day (LXX); 81:1, Fifth Day; and 93:1, Sixth Day (LXX). Sets of Psalms were also sung on certain occasions: Psalms 113-118, the Egyptian Hallel, at Passover; Psalms 120-134, the Psalms of Ascent, journeying to the temple; Psalms 146-150, the Great Hallel, at the morning temple services, etc.[25]

---

24. Ibid.
25. John Lightfoot, *The Works of the Reverend and Learned John Lightfoot* (London: Scot, Basset, and Chiswell, 1684), 2:922-923.

Psalm 150 has a similar, occasional emphasis. It speaks of the occasions on which believers ought to express praise. "Praise the Lord!" or "Hallelujah" in verses 1 and 6 form bookends for the Psalm. Verse 1 continues, "Praise God in His sanctuary; / Praise Him in His mighty expanse." Believers must praise God in His sanctuary, that is, in their regular, stated worship. The mighty expanse is the vault of heaven. Believers do not enter heaven, but they certainly live under heaven. They carry out all their earthly lives under heaven. They are to give praise to God in all of life under heaven. Psalm 150, therefore, outlines the *occasions* when believers are to give praise to God. These occasions are in regular, weekly, stated worship *and* in all of life.

Psalm 150:2 informs believers *why* they ought to give praise to God. "Praise Him for His mighty deeds; / Praise Him according to His excellent greatness." Worshipers raise their voices in praise to God because of who He is; He is their Creator. Worshipers also praise Him for what He has done; He is their Redeemer.

It might be thought that Psalm 150 goes on to direct believers *how* they are to give praise God. Verses 3-5 read, "Praise Him with trumpet sound; / Praise Him with harp and lyre. / Praise Him with timbrel and dancing; / Praise Him with stringed instruments and pipe. / Praise Him with loud cymbals; / Praise Him with resounding cymbals." The Psalm, however, returns to the theme of the occasions *when* we give praise to God. The parallel is in verse 1.

Verse 3 speaks of the trumpet, the harp, and the lyre. As has been seen, the trumpet was used primarily in the temple and blown over the sacrifices. There were only two trumpets blown, and the priests used them. The trumpets and cymbals were never intended for use as musical accompaniment *with* singing. At the same time, the Levitical choirs in the temple were accompanied with harps and lyres. Mention of the trumpet sound and the harps and lyres is a reference to stated worship in the temple. The people in the temple were to worship when they heard the sound of the trumpets, harps, and lyres. Verse 3 does not require the use of wind or stringed instruments by all the people. Neither does it require the use of wind or stringed instruments in present-day worship. Rather, it reminds God's people of the stated meetings of the church, the *occasions* when God calls them to worship and to praise.

The argument is that Psalm 150 enjoins praise on various *occasions*. It does not command the use of instrumental music in the regular stated meetings of worship in the church. As just noted, verse 3 requires the praise of God to accompany David's harps and lyres after the trumpets sound over the sacrifice. Verse 5 is parallel in thought. "Praise Him with loud cymbals; / Praise Him with resounding cymbals." During the sacrifices, a priest with cymbals stood between two priests with trumpets. After the sounding of the trumpets, there came a clash of the cymbals. The Levitical choir then began to sing. As discussed above, the use of cymbals was restricted to one priest; the cymbals did not accompany the singing. Psalm 150, therefore, did not command all the people to use cymbals *with* their singing in the public worship of God. This use of the cymbals would have been contrary to the ceremonial law. As with the trumpets, harps, and lyres, on the *occasion* of the clashing of the cymbals, God's people, assembled in the court of the temple, joined in singing praise to God. Psalm 150 did not and does not command the use of cymbals in public worship to accompany singing.

While verses 3 and 5 of Psalm 150 refer to public worship in the temple, verse 4 refers to other occasions. "Praise Him with timbrel and dancing; / Praise Him with stringed instruments and pipe." Genesis 31:27 speaks of the timbrel or tambourine, and the common lyre, not the instrument designed by David for the temple. See the earlier discussion of David's harps made especially for temple worship. Laban upbraids Jacob, "Why did you flee secretly and deceive me, and did not tell me so that I might have sent you away with joy and with songs, with timbrel and with lyre." In other words, why did you not allow me to have a going away wedding reception for you and my daughter? Job 21:12 says something similar regarding the wicked. "They sing to the timbrel and harp and rejoice at the sound of the flute." Both believers and unbelievers have their parties and dances. On such occasions, God commands, "Whether, then, you eat or drink or whatever you do, do all to the glory of God" (1 Cor. 10:31).

When the people of Israel celebrated their salvation after crossing the Red Sea, "Miriam the prophetess, Aaron's sister, took the timbrel in her hand, and all the women went out after her with timbrels and with dancing. Miriam answered them, 'Sing to the Lord, for He is highly exalted; the horse and his rider He has hurled into the sea'" (Exod. 15:20-21). Here was a very special occasion for praise. Psalm 150 enjoins praise to celebrate special occasions of deliverance. There is, however, no indication that timbrels or dancing were part of the regular stated times of worship in the temple. Introducing timbrel and dancing into this worship would have been contrary to the ceremonial law. Psalm 150 is, therefore, not instructing Israel to use timbrel and dancing with their regular worship. Psalm 150 is not enjoining present day believers to do so either.

Finally, although the preposition *with* in Psalm 150 may refer to "the instrument or means," it may also be used of "accompaniment" as in traveling *with* others; that is, accompanying them.[26] Therefore, Psalm 150:3-5 may refer to praise accompanying the sound of the instruments rather than the other way around. As a result, Psalm 150 exhorts worshipers to give praise to God on all *occasions*, including public worship. Psalm 150 is not directing worshipers to use musical instruments in their worship.

THE INSTRUMENTS IN BOOK OF REVELATION

An argument for the use of musical instruments in public worship comes from the Book of Revelation. Since the saints in heaven use musical instruments, the argument goes, following their example, New Testament believers should use instrumental music in their

---

26. Francis Brown, S. R. Driver, Charles Briggs, *A Hebrew and English Lexicon of the Old Testament* (New York: Oxford University Press, 1962), 89.

public worship. Before looking at the three texts in Revelation referring to harps, note something important about the book itself.

Revelation is a series of visions. These visions are *portrayals* of reality, not the reality itself. For example, Revelation portrays Jesus Christ as a "Lamb standing, as if slain, having seven horns and seven eyes, which are the seven Spirits of God, sent out into all the earth" (Rev. 5:6). Slain lambs do not stand. Neither do lambs have seven horns and seven eyes. Further, Jesus Christ is not a strange looking lamb having seven horns and seven eyes. This *portrayal* of Christ is not the reality itself. Interpreters must take care to make this important distinction.

With this distinction in mind, look at Revelation 14:2-3 which reads as follows:

> I heard a voice from heaven, like the sound of many waters and like the sound of loud thunder, and the voice which I heard was like the sound of harpists playing on their harps. And they sang a new song before the throne and before the four living creatures and the elders; and no one could learn the song except the one hundred and forty-four thousand who had been purchased from the earth.

Verse 3 shows us 144,000 singers who represent the saints of God.[27] This number forms a great choir singing before the throne of God. Verse 2 describes the sound of the choir. "The voices are so loud they echo throughout the halls of heaven. They are *likened* to 'the sound of many waters' and 'the sound of great thunder.'"[28] Christ empowers these voices. Revelation 1:15 says of Christ, "His voice was like the sound of many waters." The voice of the choir is also a harmonious whole; it is "like the sound of harpists playing on their harps." Notice that there are not real harps in use in the vision. Rather, the choir sounds *like* a huge number of harps. It should therefore be plain that

---

27. G. K. Beale, *The Book of Revelation* (Grand Rapids: Eerdmans, 1999), 735.
28. Ibid., 736. Italics added.

this text does not support the use of musical instruments in the public worship of God.

Revelation 15:2-3 says:

> I saw something like a sea of glass mixed with fire, and those who had been victorious over the beast and his image and the number of his name, standing on the sea of glass, holding harps of God. And they sang the song of Moses, the bond-servant of God, and the song of the Lamb, saying, "Great and marvelous are Your works, O Lord God, the Almighty; Righteous and true are Your ways, King of the nations!"

Here, a great choir of saints is giving praise to God. These saints are holding harps designated as the "harps of God." Again, this vision is a portrayal of reality, not reality itself. The harps are symbolic. Compare Revelation 5:8 where "the twenty-four elders fell down before the Lamb, each one holding a harp and golden bowls full of incense, which are the prayers of the saints." Here, the elders around the throne have harps and bowls of incense. The sacred text points out that the incense represents the prayers of the saints. As indicated before, since the bowls of incense held by the elders represents the prayers of the saints, the harps are not literal harps. What do the harps represent? Revelation 14:2, quoted above, gives the answer. There, the choir sounds like harps. In other words, in both Revelation 5:8 and 15:3, the harps represent sacred praise to God. These harps are not literal but symbolic. This *symbolic* use of harps in the Book of Revelation is not an argument for the use of musical instruments in worship today.

The other instrument the Book of Revelation mentions is the trumpet. In Revelation 1:10, Christ has "a loud voice like the sound of a trumpet." In Revelation 4:1, a voice *like* a trumpet summons John. In both these cases a voice is compared to a trumpet. The remaining references to trumpets in Revelation are to the seven angels given seven trumpets to announce God's judgment (Rev. 8:2, 6, 13; 9:14).

"The trumpets portray judgment upon unbelievers because of their hardened attitude."[29] The symbolic use of trumpets in the Book of Revelation is also not an argument for the use of musical instruments in public worship today.

THE USE OF MUSICAL INSTRUMENTS IS A CIRCUMSTANCE OF WORSHIP

The argument that the use of musical instruments is a circumstance of worship rests upon the Westminster Confession of Faith 1:6. In part, this paragraph of the Westminster Confession teaches "that there are some *circumstances* concerning the worship of God, and government of the Church, *common to human actions and societies,* which are to be ordered by the light of nature, and Christian prudence, according to the general rules of the word, which are always to be observed" (italics added). As Girardeau states, these circumstances include matters such as the time and place of assembly.

> But these *circumstances* are declared to be *common* to *human societies,* to societies of all sorts—political, philosophical, scientific, literary, mercantile, agricultural, mechanical, industrial, military, and even infidel. Time and place, costume and posture, sitting or standing, and the like, are circumstances common to *all* societies, and therefore pertain to the church as a society.[30]

The use of instrumental music in the worship of the church does not fit this definition of *circumstances*. The circumstances to which the confession refers are *common* to human societies or organizations. In other words, these circumstances, as the Westminster Confession of Faith uses the term, involve *all* organizations, religious and secular. Therefore, as Girardeau contends, "If, however, the action of singing praise in God's worship is *peculiar* to the church as a *particular* kind

---

29. Ibid., 472.
30. John R. Girardeau, *Instrumental Music in the Public Worship of the Church* (Havertown, PA: New covenant Publication Society, 1983), 139. Italics added.

of society, the circumstance of instrumental music as attending it cannot be common to human actions and societies. It is therefore ruled out by the language of the Confession."[31] In addition, Girardeau observes that, "instrumental music is a condition peculiar to the act of singing praise in *some* particular churches."[32] And since

> instrumental music is a circumstance which is not common to even particular churches. Some have it, and some do not. How can it be common to all societies, when it is not common to churches themselves? How can the conclusion be avoided, that it is *not* one of the circumstances designated by the Confession of Faith?[33]

From the perspective of the Westminster Confession of Faith, instrumental music in worship is therefore *not a circumstance of worship*.

That the use of instrumental music in the Old Testament economy is not a circumstance of worship is also evident from the fact that, God commanded the use of specific musical instruments in worship. God commanded Moses to use two silver trumpets in the sacrificial services of the tabernacle (Num. 10:2, 10). God also commanded David to add cymbals and harps and lyres to the worship of God (2 Chron. 29:25). It is quite clear that the use of these musical instruments was not something that was "common to human actions and societies, which are to be ordered by the light of nature, and Christian prudence." To the contrary, God *commanded* the use of specific musical instruments, in a specific place, at specific times.

Some still insist that the use of musical instruments was common to human institutions. In fact, as already argued in this study, instrumental music was used in weddings, banquets, and patriotic and religious celebrations. Since instrumental music was used in these other *circumstances*, including worshipful *circumstances*, the use of musical instruments, it is argued, is a *circumstance* of worship. The argu-

---

31. Ibid., 140. Italics added.
32. Ibid. Italics Girardeau's.
33. Ibid. Italics added.

ment is ambiguous and equivocal; it uses the term *circumstances* in two different ways. Just because musical instruments may have been used in different *circumstances*, or on different occasions, in the Old Testament, does not identify their use as a circumstance of worship as defined by the Westminster Confession of Faith.

It is true that the *circumstances* concerning the worship of God, being discussed, are *common to human actions and societies*. However, although many human actions and societies do not involve the use of musical instruments, many do. Suppose that many human actions and societies do include the use of musical instruments. Also suppose that the use of musical instruments is a circumstance of worship. These suppositions place the church on the same cultural level as other organizations and societies. However, the objective of Biblical worship is not to seek common ground with other human actions and societies but to recognize the fact that, because the church is in the world, the church already does have certain things in common with other human societies. The visible church is in the world, but the church is not of the world. As emphasized in this study, the objective of corporate worship in the church is not to be more culturally-connected but to be God-directed and heaven-imbued.

Finally, the musical instruments used in connection with Old Testament tabernacle and temple worship were prophetic types. As discussed above, types were persons, offices, institutions, or special events in the Old Testament, which foreshadowed persons, offices, institutions, or special events in the New Testament. "[T]he types were [also] prophecies and promises presented concretely, and not merely in words, to the ancient worshiper."[34] Being prophetic, the emergence of a type in the Old Testament demanded the appearance of the anti-type, answer to the type, in the New Testament. For example, Paul tells us that Adam was a type of Christ (Rom. 5:14). The creation of Adam therefore predicted the later and inevitable appear-

---

34. Ibid., 51.

ance of Christ. The Old Testament temple and all of its ceremonies was a type pointing forward to Christ and the Holy Spirit. As argued above, this typology included the musical instruments used in the worship of God.

Therefore, if the musical instruments used in the stated worship of Israel were types, commanded by God, and pointing forward to the New Testament and to Spirit-empowered, a cappella psalmody, they cannot be circumstances of worship in either the Old Testament or the New Testament. In addition, "when the Antitype has come, the types must be abolished."[35] Again, [T]he sacrifices, being types and peculiar to the temple service, were necessarily abolished by the coming of the Antitype."[36] Since the musical instruments used in temple worship were part of the ceremonial and typical worship of Israel, they passed away with the temple and its sacrifices (Heb. 10:8-9). The use of musical instruments in worship cannot, therefore, be considered as circumstances of worship as set forth by the Westminster Confession of Faith.

---

35. Robert L. Dabney, "Girardeau's 'Instrumental Music in Public Worship,'" *The Presbyterian Quarterly*, 3 (1889): 463.
36. Ibid., 464.

21

Instrumental Music: Thesis Confirmed

*Now therefore, O Lord God, the word that You
have spoken concerning Your servant and his house,
confirm it forever.* ~ 2 Sam. 7:25

INTRODUCTION

Here is the thesis for this part of this study: *Instrumental music is not integral to Biblical worship but, when introduced, it is incidental, typical, and temporary.* First, the foundation for the discussion of the use of instrumental music in worship included a review of the nature of worship, the regulative principle, and the basic nature of music, both instrumental and vocal. Second, a Biblical and historical review of the use of musical instruments followed, in order to show the transitions that took place and will take place in worship. Third, the study showed that the musical instruments used in the sacrificial worship of the Old Testament were Biblical types pointing to New Testament preaching and Spirit-empowered singing. Finally, various objections to the nonuse of musical instruments were addressed. Now, the following short review shows that the thesis is, indeed, confirmed.

BIBLICAL TRANSITIONS IN THE PLACE OF WORSHIP

Biblical transitions in worship involve significant changes in both the *places* of God-ordained worship and the *manner* of God-ordained worship. Consider the successive changes in the places of Biblical worship. Early in this study, the three main aspects to worship were covered: an altar, a sacrifice, and calling upon the Lord. It was because of sin that worship centered on an altar and a sacrifice where the people called on the name of the Lord.

Before Moses, and during the lives of the patriarchs, worship was performed before God with sacrifices on altars built by the patriarchs at places, seemingly, of their own choosing. When Abraham entered Canaan, he came to a place "with Bethel on the west and Ai on the east; and there he built an altar to the LORD and called upon the name of the LORD" (Gen. 12:8). Similarly, Isaac, when near Bethel, "built an altar there and called upon the name of the LORD" (Gen. 26:25). From the perspective of worship, the period from Adam to Moses can be called *Phase One*.

When God redeemed the people of Israel and brought them out of Egypt under Moses (Exod. 1-18), He formed them into a covenant community (Exod. 19-24), and into a worshiping community (Exod. 25-40). God commissioned the building of the tabernacle as a place of worship. "Let them construct a sanctuary for Me, that I may dwell among them" (Exod. 25). God commanded sacrifices morning and evening in the tabernacle on an altar built specifically for this purpose (Num. 28:3). Thus, God formalized the place of sacrifice and consecrated His house of worship. "The glory of the LORD filled the tabernacle" (Exod. 40:35). From the perspective of worship, the period from Moses to David can be called *Phase Two*.

Moses then declared that when Israel entered Canaan, God would require the people to make their sacrifices in the place of His choosing. "You shall seek the LORD at the place which the LORD your God will choose from all your tribes ... and there you shall come" (Deut. 12:5). When God directed David to sacrifice on the threshing floor of Ornan the Jebusite in order to deal with David's sin of numbering the people, He revealed this chosen location (1 Chron. 21:18). God accepted David's sacrifice with fire from heaven (1 Chron. 21:26). David responded, "This is the house of the LORD God, and this is the altar of burnt offering for Israel" (1 Chron. 22:1).

"Solomon began to build the house of the LORD in Jerusalem on Mount Moriah, where the LORD had appeared to his father David, at the place that David had prepared on the threshing floor of Ornan the Jebusite" (2 Chron. 3:1). The place of worship shifted to this more permanent location. God again consecrated His house of worship and "the glory of the LORD filled the house of the LORD" (1 Kings 8:11). From the perspective of worship, the period from David to Christ can be called *Phase Three*.

Much later, the Samaritan woman at the well challenged Jesus regarding the proper place of worship. "Jesus said to her, 'Woman, believe Me, an hour is coming when neither in this mountain [the place of Samaritan worship] nor in Jerusalem [the place of Jewish worship] will you worship the Father ... An hour is coming, and now is, when the true worshipers will worship the Father in spirit and truth'" (John 4:21, 23). Profound change was again taking place.

The Apostle Peter speaks of this change. "Coming to Him as to a living stone ... you also, as living stones, are being built up as a spiritual house for a holy priesthood, to offer up spiritual sacrifices acceptable to God through Jesus Christ" (1 Pet. 2:4-5). All the former Old Testament places of worship looked forward to more spiritual worship in living temples, congregations of the New Testament church. Our places of worship are therefore *not* Old Testament temple-like buildings with ceremonies, robes, bells, and smells. God now gives us simpler, yet much more profoundly spiritual, places of worship. Our congregations, spiritual houses, gather around His word and offer up spiritual sacrifices of praise (Heb. 13:15). From the perspective of worship, the period between the first coming of Christ and His second coming can be called *Phase Four*.

There will no doubt come another dramatic change in worship when Christ comes a second time in glory and the dead are raised incorruptible. It will be worship around God's heavenly throne, in one assembly rather than in many, and there, the sacrifice of the Christ, God's Lamb, will be celebrated.

> Then I looked, and I heard the voice of many angels *around the throne* and the living creatures and the elders; and the number of them was myriads of myriads, and thousands of thousands, saying with a loud voice, "Worthy is *the Lamb that was slain* to receive power and riches and wisdom and might and honor and glory and blessing." And every created thing which is in heaven and on the earth and under the earth and on the sea, and all things in them, I heard saying, "To Him who sits on the throne, and to the Lamb, be blessing and honor and glory and dominion forever and ever" (Rev. 5:11-13, italics added).

The worship of God's people around God's throne in heaven can be called *Phase Five*. These God-ordained changes in the place of worship are Biblical transitions in worship.

BIBLICAL TRANSITIONS IN THE MANNER OF WORSHIP

Now, look at these same Biblical transitions in worship from the perspective of the manner of worship established by God. The manner of worship from Adam forward was simple, an altar, a sacrifice, and calling on the name of the Lord. There is no indication of the use of musical instruments in this worship. At the same time, as seen under the heading of Old Testament Celebrations, musical instruments were used widely in the culture. They were used on various occasions such as banquets and weddings, God's victories in war and God's deliverances. These celebrations were all culturally-conditioned. There is no witness in Scripture that these musical instruments were used around the altars of sacrifice while the people called on the name of the Lord. The use of instruments was not integral to worship. *Phase One* in the manner of worship was simple and solemn.

In *Phase Two*, God inaugurated Israel's ceremonial worship under Moses. In *Phase Three*, the Lord instituted significant changes under David and brought this worship to fruition with the building of the temple under Solomon. From their beginning, these God-ordained ceremonies always looked forward to the work of Christ and to heaven.

Two of the ceremonial offerings directed by God under Moses were the whole burnt offering and the peace offering. Recall the *manner* of these two offerings. Whole burnt offerings were sacrificed every morning and evening (Num. 28:3-6). God commanded the doubling of this morning and evening sacrifice on the Sabbath (Num. 28:9-10). The whole burnt offerings, which were fully consumed except for the skin, were for atonement. They were propitiations pointing to Christ who is the propitiation for the believer's sins (Lev. 1:4; 1 John 2:2, 4:10). Peace offerings were placed on top of the whole burnt offerings. "Then Aaron's sons shall offer it up in smoke *on* the altar *on* the burnt offering, which is *on* the wood that is *on* the fire" (Lev. 3:5, italics added). The placement of peace offerings on the burnt offerings signified "we have peace with God through our Lord Jesus Christ" (Rom. 5:1).

In *Phase Two*, under Moses, God commanded the use of two trumpets with these blood sacrifices. "In the day of your gladness and in your appointed feasts, and on the first days of your months, you shall blow the trumpets over your burnt offerings, and over the sacrifices of your peace offerings; and they shall be as a reminder of you before your God" (Num. 10:10). These two trumpets are the first musical instruments used with the ceremonial sacrifices. In *Phase Two*, God changed the *manner* of worship.

In *Phase Three*, there was another radical change in the *manner* of worship under David. "David spoke to the chiefs of the Levites to appoint their relatives the singers, with instruments of music, harps, lyres, loud-sounding cymbals, to raise sounds of joy" (1 Chron. 15:16). Like the trumpets ordained through Moses, David now associated sacred song and specific musical instruments with the sacrifices (1

Chron. 16:40-42). This transition took place "according to the command of David and of Gad the king's seer, and of Nathan the prophet; for the command was from the Lord through His prophets" (2 Chron. 29:25). The additional musical instruments and the singing of Psalms with the sacrifices ordained through David was a radical change in the *manner* of worship.

In *Phase Four*, another significant change in the *manner* of worship occurred when Christ "offered Himself without blemish to God" (Heb. 9:14). With this sacrifice, God set aside Israel's ceremonial system, that is, all the sacrifices and the things accompanying them including the musical instruments. As Hebrews 10:9 indicates, "He takes away the first [all the sacrificial ceremonies] in order to establish the second [the sacrifice of Christ]."

Singing continues in the New Testament church, because the New Testament commands it. "Let the word of Christ dwell in you richly, teaching and admonishing one another in all wisdom, singing psalms and hymns and spiritual songs, with thankfulness in your hearts to God" (Col. 3:16, ESV). "Through Him then, let us continually offer up a sacrifice of praise to God, that is, the fruit of lips that give thanks to His name" (Heb. 13:15). The use of musical instruments was never integral to worship. When added, they were typical, foreshadowing gospel preaching and Spirit-empowered singing. The use of musical instruments was, therefore, temporary.

In *Phase Five*, a final transition and change in the form and manner of worship will occur when Christ comes again in glory. Glimpses of this transition are seen in the Book of Revelation. However, we cannot remove the veil to fully reveal worship in the life to come.

Now, imagine people questioning the changes in worship that David made. "Why did David add singing and musical instruments to the sacrifices of Moses? Can't we go back to the old ways? Can't we continue to worship in the simplicity of Moses?" No! It was not possible to do so. God made the changes. Also, recognize the great change in worship God made with the coming of Christ. Some insist on going back to the older ways of worship, seeking the feel of something ancient. It is not proper to go back. *God made the changes.*

What if people in the time of Moses had a book giving them a preview of the temple, its choirs, and its instruments? Imagine them saying, "Let's add some musical instruments to the sacrifices, and let's set up some choirs to sing in the tabernacle while we offer the sacrifices. Hey, Moses, the people during David's time will be doing this, what's wrong with doing it now? Why wait?" It can be said with surety that Moses, under God, would have rejected such an idea.

In like manner, the Book of Revelation does not set the standard for worship in this age. As with prior transitions, there will be a final step forward in worship. All believers will gather before God's throne in heaven. Old Testament worship prefigured this worship. New Testament worship provides a foretaste of it. Believers cannot step back into the shadows of Old Testament worship. Neither can believers step forward into the full glory of heavenly worship. God must make the change. It is not ours to do.

THE RESPONSIBILITIES OF BELIEVERS

There are God-ordained Biblical transitions in worship. It is the obligation of believers to recognize and observe them. Believers must maintain the standards for worship God gives them in this New Testament age. It is not their right to go back to the era of those living after Adam and worship like Abraham, calling upon the Lord with altars and sacrifices. Nor may believers reinstitute the ceremonies instituted through Moses for the tabernacle or the ceremonies instituted through David for the temple. It is their responsibility to maintain God's standards of worship for the age in which they live.

Too often, the cry is that the church must be more culturally relevant. Professor Frame says, "I shall present the regulative principle as one that sets us free, within limits, to worship God in the language of our own time, to seek those applications of God's commandments *which most edify worshipers in our contemporary cultures.*"[1] Applying his principle, imagine Aaron saying to Moses, "We need to spice up this tabernacle worship a little. Remember how Miriam led us in a celebration when God brought us through the Red Sea? Let's add some tambourines and singing and dancing to our worship. We can make this worship much more edifying and culturally relevant." Sadly, Aaron did have experience with making worship culturally relevant with the golden calf incident. In no way would Moses find Aaron's suggestion acceptable.

Remember the distinction between culturally-conditioned celebrations and God-ordained worship. As has been seen, worship should connect believers to and give them a taste of heaven. Its objective is not cultural relevance. The more fully worship is directed by God, and permeated by heaven, the more culturally relevant it will really be. True cultural relevancy occurs when churches take their responsibility seriously, the responsibility to maintain the standards of worship God gives them for this present era.

THESIS CONFIRMED

Remember this thesis: *Instrumental music is not integral to Biblical worship but, when introduced, it is incidental, typical, and temporary.* Does what has been learned support this thesis?

That instrumental music is not integral to worship means that such music is not fundamental to or necessary for worship. It is incidental; it may accompany worship but it is certainly not a necessary part of it. Adam and Eve and the patriarchs centered their worship on an altar, a sacrifice, and calling on the name of the Lord. Although musical instruments were a part of the culture around them, there is no indication that they were a part of the worship of Adam and Eve or of the patriarchs.

---

1. John M. Frame, *Worship in Spirit and Truth* (Phillipsburg, NJ: P & R, 1996), 46. Italics added.

When God instituted the ceremonial worship of Israel, altar and sacrifice and calling on the Lord continued. In addition, God commanded Moses to fashion two silver trumpets. The priests were to blow these trumpets over the sacrifices. The trumpets reminded the people of their sins and the significance of the sacrifice. The trumpets were announcements. As has been seen, these trumpets were types foreshadowing gospel proclamation, announcing the sacrifice of Christ. The trumpets were, therefore, typical and temporary.

When the temple was built, the tasks of the Levites changed. Their job of disassembling, transporting, and reassembling the tabernacle was no longer needed. Their new task was, in part, to form choirs to accompany the sacrifices in the temple. God also ordained the use of cymbals through David. The cymbals, sounding with the trumpets, gave the signal for the Levitical choirs to begin their songs before the Lord. Finally, God ordained the use of harps to accompany the Levitical choirs. These harps were also types, and therefore, temporary. The harps represented Spirit-empowered praise before God, fulfilled in the New Testament through Christ and His Spirit. Therefore, believers singing before the Lord are God's instruments of praise.

When Christ sets aside the ceremonial worship of Israel by His own sacrifice, the sacrifices pass away, along with the instruments accompanying them. Thus, the use of these instruments is typical and, therefore, temporary. Their typical and temporary nature confirms the fact that they are not integral to worship, but incidental to it.

Those who argue that the use of instruments is integral to worship also argue that they are needed to assist worship, to stir up worshipers, and to evoke praise. That instrumental music can and often does evoke various emotions is one of the reasons that the Church Fathers and Reformers prohibited their use. Review the discussion of the power of music, both instrumental and vocal. In addition, the harps especially prefigure the Spirit. If believers have new life in the Spirit, do they really need external means to evoke praise? The answer ought to be a resounding, No!

Vocal music continues in the New Testament church by the command of God (Heb. 13:15). This singing is tied to texts, but not to musical instruments. This singing is one of the ways believers let the word of Christ dwell richly within them. They themselves become the instruments of praise God uses for His glory. Again, the use of musical instruments in worship is typical and temporary. Instrumental music is not integral to Biblical worship but, when introduced, it is incidental, typical, and temporary.

That instrumental music is not integral to Biblical worship but, when introduced, is incidental, typical, and temporary is confirmed by the Biblical transitions in worship, the use of instrumental music in the Old Testament, the profound effects of the work of Christ, the stance of the New Testament church, and Church history. Thesis confirmed: *Instrumental music is not integral to Biblical worship but, when introduced, it is incidental, typical, and temporary.*

Summing-Up

To sum up… ~ 1 Pet. 3:8

Public Worship 101 develops a Biblical theology of worship, and based upon this theology of worship, explores the Biblical elements of worship, including exclusive, a cappella Psalmody. This is done in four parts: The Theology of Worship; The Elements of Worship; The Element of Praise, Psalmody; and The Element of Praise, Instrumental Music.

Part One, the Theology of Worship, answers four questions: What is worship? What is the church? What is the Sabbath? Who prescribes how we worship? The Biblical answers to these four questions form the *theology* of worship.

Chapter 1 defines worship as the reverent fear and awe of God expressed by bowing to Him in heart and soul and determining to serve Him because He alone is worthy. The Father seeks such worship as a response to His worthiness as the Creator and Redeemer. In truly spiritual worship, believers approach the Father, through the Son, by the power of the Spirit. As they do so, they delight in God, and He delights in them. They enjoy Him and pause to find rest in Him. This worship is the corporate, public approach to God and the response to God's initiative.

Chapter 2 describes the church assembled for worship as the New Testament temple in which God graciously dwells for the purpose of renewing His covenant with His people. As citizens of heaven, God's people form embassies of heaven in this world. God commits himself to his worshiping assemblies for the purpose of renewing His covenant with His people. This aspect of worship is God's approach to believers as they gather before Him in sacred assembly. As God meets with his people, and they enjoy His presence, they enter into and taste of heaven.

Chapter 3 teaches that, as there is a stated place of worship, the gathered church, the Biblical data shows that there is also a stated day of worship, the Christian Sabbath. Sabbath rest is a perpetual, moral obligation and the Sabbath is changed from the seventh to the first day of the week. In it, God pledges to assure His people that they belong to Him and that He is indeed their God. Thus, the theology of worship is derived from the temple and the Sabbath.

Chapter 4 seeks to validate this syllogism: God prescribes how we enter heaven; public worship is an entrance into and a taste of heaven; God prescribes how we worship. This syllogism is a restatement of the regulative principle of worship: In worship, whatever God does not command, He forbids. The alternative is the normative principle: In worship, whatever God does not forbid He permits. The normative principle is the default position of many churches. The theology of worship, built, as it is, on the temple and the Sabbath, supports the regulative principle of worship. The church's worship ought not to be built on Old Testament occasional, culturally-conditioned, celebrations. Biblical worship seeks to strengthen a congregation's connection with heaven and its distinctiveness from fallen cultural influences.

Part Two, The Elements of Worship, undertakes a study of the *elements* of worship. While the theology of worship derives from the *temple* and the *Sabbath*, the elements of worship arise from the *temple* and the *synagogue*.

Chapters 5-7, show that Psalmody derives from praise in the Old Testament temple, and that there is direct exegetical connection between the Old Testament thank offering and the New Testament sacrifice of praise, which is the fruit of lips giving thanks to God. The offering and benediction can also be traced back to the temple. The synagogue was the teaching institution in Israel. There, the people confessed their faith with the *Shema*, recited prescribed prayers, heard the Scriptures read, and also heard an exhortation based upon Moses, as seen through the eyes of the prophets. The New Testament confirms the above-mentioned elements of worship. Chapters 8-10 discussed the propriety and administration of the sacraments.

Although the New Testament does not set forth a formal order of worship, Old Testament temple worship serves as a pattern for approaching God. This approach to God includes the recognition and confession of sin, trust in the promised Savior through sacrifice, and cleansing from sin. Since, in worship, God renews His covenant with His people, and they respond to Him, worship is dialogical. Praise, then, becomes one of the means of response. Considering the nature of worship, the approach to God in worship, and the individual elements of worship, "by good and necessary consequence" an order of worship "may be deduced from Scripture" (WCF 1:6).

Part Three, The Element of Praise: Psalmody, developed the element of praise, argued for the propriety of Psalmody and exclusive Psalmody, answered objections to Psalmody, and completed a brief historical review of Psalmody. Psalmody has a venerable history of some 3000 years. On one hand, a rejection of Psalmody must ignore this history. On the other hand, a rejection of Psalmody fails to grasp both the *subjective element* and the *eschatological thrust* of the Psalms.

Part Four, Instrumental Music in Worship, begins with a simple thesis: Instrumental music is not integral to Biblical worship but, when introduced, it was incidental, typical, and temporary. Chapters 16-21 sought to validate this thesis. Chapter 16 reviewed the theology of worship and did a short study of music and emotions. Chapter 17 revealed that from the beginning, worship required faith in the atoning sacrifice prescribed by God and in the promised Savior with this faith expressed through prayer, praise, and thanksgiving. Instrumental music was not integral to this worship.

Chapter 17 also demonstrated that God took His people through various transitions in worship. He introduced more regulated ceremonial worship with Moses, Psalmody with various instruments with David, and then abrogated the sacrificial system, including the use of musical instruments, with the once for all sacrifice of Christ. Chapters 17 and 18 continued the historical perspective showing that a cappella worship was the standard approach in the church for over eighteen hundred years.

Chapter 19 discussed the typological perspective, showing that God set aside the use of musical instruments with the setting aside of the ceremonial sacrifices, and that the musical instruments were temporary, because they were Biblical types. Psalmody continued because it is commanded in the New Testament. That instrumental music was typical and therefore temporary confirms the fact that it is incidental to worship, not integral to it. Chapter 20 reviewed basic objections to not using musical instruments in worship. Chapter 21 reviewed the argument of part four in order to confirm the thesis: Instrumental music is not integral to Biblical worship but, when introduced, it was incidental, typical, and temporary.

Here is the one-point summation of this study as a whole. Whether this purpose has been accomplished is for you, the reader, to judge. The purpose of *Public Worship 101* has been to demonstrate that in

Biblical worship, God renews His covenant with His people as they draw near to Him in the *place* He prescribes, on the *day* He prescribes, in the *manner* He prescribes, with the *elements* He prescribes, including the *praise* He prescribes both in content, *exclusive Psalmody*, and manner, *a cappella Psalmody*, using an *order* properly deduced from Scripture. *To God alone be the glory.*

Bibliography

Adams, Jay E. *Essays on Biblical Preaching*. Grand Rapids: Zondervan, 1983.

_____. *Preaching With Purpose*. Grand Rapids: Zondervan, 1982.

Alexander, J. A. *Commentary on the Acts of the Apostles*. Carlisle, PA: Banner of Truth, 1980.

_____. *Commentary on the Gospel of Mark*. Minneapolis: Klock and Klock, 1980.

Alford, Henry. *Alford's Greek Testament*. Grand Rapid: Guardian, 1976.

Ames, William. *A Fresh Suit Against Human Ceremonies in God's Worship*. Rotterdam: Johannes A. Lasco, 1633.

Annotations Upon All the Books of the Old and New Testament. London: Evan Tyler, 1657.

Appel, Richard G. *The Music of the Bay Psalm Book*, 9th Edition. New York: Institute for Studies in American Music, 1975.

Archer, Gleason L. *A Survey of Old Testament Introduction*. Chicago: Moody, 1964.

Arndt, William F., and F. Wilbur Gingrich, *A Greek-English Lexicon of the New Testament*. Grand Rapids: Zondervan, 1963.

Athanasius. "The Letter to Marcellinus." Fisheaters.com. Accessed November 15, 2011.

_____. *The Life of Antony and the Letter to Marcellinus*. Translated by Robert C. Gregg. New York: Paulist Press, 1980.

Auberlen, C. A., and C. J. Riggenbach. *The Two Epistles of Paul to the Thessalonians*. Translated by John Lillie. Grand Rapids: Zondervan, 1960.

Augustine. *Expositions on the Book of Psalms*. Oxford: John Henry Parker, 1857.

Bannerman, James. *The Church of Christ*. Carlisle, PA: Banner of Truth, 1960.

Barnett, Paul. *The Second Epistle to the Corinthians*. Grand Rapids: Eerdmans, 1997.

Barrett, C. K. *The New Testament Background: Selected Documents*. London: SPCK, 1961.

———. *The Second Epistle to the Corinthians.* New York: Harper and Row, 1973.

Beale, G. K. *The Book of Revelation.* Grand Rapids: Eerdmans, 1999.

Beale, G. K., and D. A. Carson. *Commentary on the New Testament Use of the Old.* Grand Rapids: Baker, 2007.

Beitzel, Barry J. *The Moody Atlas of Bible Lands.* Chicago: Moody Press, 1985.

Benson, Louis F. "John Calvin and the Psalmody of the Reformed Churches." *Journal of the Presbyterian Historical Society* 5:2 (June 1909): 55-87; 5:3 (September 1909): 107-118.

Berkhof, Louis. *Principles of Biblical Interpretation.* Grand Rapids: Baker, 1964.

———. *Summary of Christian Doctrine.* Grand Rapids: Eerdmans, 1969.

Berry, Mary. "Hymns." *Westminster Dictionary of Liturgy and Worship.* Edited by J. G. Davis. Philadelphia: Westminster Press, 1986.

Blaising, Craig A., and Carmen S. Hardin. ed. *Ancient Christian Commentary on Scripture: Psalms 1-50.* Downers Grove: InterVarsity Press, 2008.

Booth, F. Carlton. *On the Mountain Top.* Wheaton: Tyndale House, 1984.

Broadus, John A. *Lectures on the History of Preaching.* New York: A. C. Armstrong and Son, 1893.

Bromiley, G. W. *The Baptism of Infants.* London: Church Book Room Press, 1955.

Brown, Francis, S. R. Driver, Charles Briggs. *A Hebrew and English Lexicon of the Old Testament.* New York: Oxford University Press, 1962.

Brown, Michael. "Preface." *The Geneva Bible: A Facsimile of the 1599 Edition with Undated Sternhold and Hopkins Psalms.* Ozark, MO: L. L. Brown, 1990.

Brubaker, Joanne, Robert Clark, and Roy Zuck. *Childhood Education in the Church.* Chicago: Moody Press, 1975).

Bruce, F. F. *Commentary on the Book of Acts: The English Text with Introduction, Exposition, and Notes.* Grand Rapids: Eerdmans, 1970.

———. *Exposition of the Epistle to the Hebrews.* Grand Rapids: Eerdmans, 1964.

———. *The Acts of the Apostles: The Greek Text with Introduction and Commentary.* Grand Rapids: Eerdmans, 1968.

Bullinger, E. W. *Figures of Speech Used in the Bible.* Grand Rapids: Baker, 1968.

Bullock, C. Hassell. *An Introduction to the Old Testament Prophetic Books.* Chicago: Moody Press, 2007.

Bush, George. *Commentary on Exodus.* Grand Rapids: Kregel, 1993.

_____. *Notes, Critical and Practical, on the Book of Leviticus*. Minneapolis: James Family, 1979.

_____. *Notes on Genesis*. Minneapolis: James Family, 1979.

Bushell, Michael. *The Songs of Zion*. Fourth Edition. Norfolk, VA: Norfolk Press, 2011.

Buswell, James Oliver. *A Systematic Theology of the Christian Religion*. Grand Rapids: Zondervan, 1972.

Calvin, John. *A Harmony of the Gospels: Matthew, Mark, and Luke*. Translated by A. W. Morrison. Edited by David W. Torrance and Thomas F. Torrance. Grand Rapids: Eerdmans, 1972.

_____. *Commentaries on the Catholic Epistles*. Translated by John Owen. Grand Rapids: Baker, 1979.

_____. *Commentaries on the First Book of Moses Called Genesis*. Translated by John King. Grand Rapids: Baker, 1979.

_____. *Commentaries on the Four Last Books of Moses in the Form of a Harmony*. Translated by Charles William Bingham. Grand Rapids: Baker, 1979.

_____. *Commentaries on the Twelve Minor Prophets*. Translated by John Owen. Grand Rapids: Baker, 1979.

_____. *Commentary on the Prophet Isaiah*. Translated by William Pringle. Grand Rapids: Baker, 1979.

_____. *Commentary on the Book of Psalms*. Translated by James Anderson. Grand Rapids: Baker, 1979.

_____. "Epistle to the Reader," In Charles Garside. *The Origin of Calvin's Theology of Music, 1536-1543*. Philadelphia: American Philosophical Society, 1979.

_____. *Institutes of the Christian Religion*. Translated by Ford Lewis Battles. Edited by John T. McNeill. Philadelphia: Westminster Press, 1960.

_____. "Preface to the Psalter." In Oliver Strunk. *Source Readings in Music History*. New York: W. W. Norton, 1998.

_____. "'Preface' to the Geneva Psalter (1545)," Charles Garside, *The Origins of Calvin's Theology of Music, 1536-1543*. Philadelphia: American Philosophical Society, 1979.

_____. *Selected Works of John Calvin: Tracts and Letters*. Edited and Translated by Henry Beveridge. Grand Rapids: Baker, 1983.

_____. *Sermons on Deuteronomy*. Translated by Arthur Golding. Carlisle, PA: Banner of Truth, 1987.

_____. *Sermons on Genesis 1-11*. Translated by Rob Roy McGregor. Carlisle, PA: Banner of Truth, 2009.

―――――. *Sermons on 2 Samuel, Chapters 1-13*. Translated by Douglas Kelly. Carlisle, PA: Banner of Truth, 1992.

―――――. *The Acts of the Apostles*. Translated by John Fraser and W. J. G. McDonald. Edited by David W. Torrance and Thomas F. Torrance. Grand Rapids: Eerdmans, 1973.

―――――. "The Author's Preface." *Commentary on the Book of Psalms*. Translated by James Anderson. Grand Rapids: Baker, 1979.

―――――. *The Epistle of Paul the Apostle to the Hebrews and the First and Second Letters of St. Peter*. Translated by William B. Johnston. Edited by David W. Torrance and Thomas F. Torrance. Grand Rapids: Eerdmans, 1970.

―――――. *The Epistles of Paul the Apostle to the Galatians, Ephesians, Philippians, and Colossians*. Translated by T. H. L. Parker. Edited by David W. Torrance and Thomas F. Torrance. Grand Rapids: Eerdmans, 1972.

―――――. *The First Epistle of Paul to the Corinthians*. Translated by John W. Frazer. Edited by David W. Torrance and Thomas F. Torrance. Grand Rapids: Eerdmans, 1973.

―――――. *The Gospel According to John, 1-10*. Translated by T. H. L. Parker. Edited by David W. Torrance and Thomas F. Torrance. Grand Rapids: Eerdmans, 1959.

―――――. *The Second Epistle of Paul to the Corinthians and the Epistles to Timothy, Titus, and Philemon*. Translated by T. A. Smail. Edited by David W. Torrance and Thomas F. Torrance. Grand Rapids: Eerdmans, 1973.

―――――. *Theological Treatises*. Translated by J. K. S. Reid. Philadelphia: Westminster, 1954.

Carson, D. A. *Exegetical Fallacies*. Grand Rapids: Baker, 2004.

―――――. *The Cross and the Christian Ministry*. Grand Rapids: Baker, 2002.

―――――. *Worship by the Book*. Grand Rapids: Zondervan, 2002.

Carson, D. A., and Douglas Moo. *An Introduction to the New Testament*. Grand Rapids: Zondervan, 2009.

Charlesworth, James H. *The Earliest Christian Hymnbook*. Eugene, OR: Cascade, 2009.

Charnock, Stephen. *The Existence and Attributes of God*. Minneapolis: Klock and Klock, 1977.

Christian Reformed Church. "Memorable Events in the History of the Christian Reformed Church." The Official Website of CRCNA Ministries. Accessed January 16, 2012.

Clarke, Adam. *Adam Clarke Commentary*. StudyLight.org. Accessed March 28, 2011.

Clebsch, William. "Preface," Athanasius. *The Life of Anthony and the Letter to Marcellinus*. Translated by Robert C. Gregg. New York: Paulist Press, 1980.

Cohen, A. *The Psalms*. New York: Soncino, 1992.

Cohen, Frances L. "Ancient Musical Traditions of the Synagogue." *Journal of the Royal Musical Association*. 19 (1892): 135-158.

Cole, R. Alan. *Exodus*. Downers Grove: Inter-Varsity, 1973.

Copeland, Robert M. *The Direct Path of Music of Louis Bourgeois*. Ottawa: Institute of Mediaeval Music, 2008.

_____. "The Experience of Singing Psalms." *The Book of Psalms for Worship*. Pittsburgh: Crown and Covenant, 2009.

Coppes, Leonard J. *Exclusive Psalmody and Doing God's Will as It Is Fulfilled in Christ*. NP: The Author, n.d.

Crawford, George Arthur. "Bourgeois." *Grove's Dictionary of Music and Musicians*. Edited by J. A. Fuller Maitland. New York: Macmillan, 1904.

Currid, John. *A Study Commentary on Genesis*. Webster, NY: Evangelical Press, 2003.

Dabney, Robert L. "Girardeau's 'Instrumental Music in Public Worship,'" *The Presbyterian Quarterly* 3 (1889): 462-469.

_____. *Sacred Rhetoric*. Carlisle, PA: Banner of Truth, 1979.

Dagg, John L. *Manual of Theology, Second Part: A Treatise on Church Order*. Harrisonburg, VA: Gano Books, 1990.

Dallimore, Arnold. *Spurgeon*. Chicago: Moody Press, 1984.

Dawn, Marva. *Reaching Out Without Dumbing Down*. Grand Rapids: Eerdmans, 1995.

Delitzsch, Franz. *Biblical Commentary on the Book of Job*. Translated by Francis Bolton. Grand Rapids: Eerdmans, 1966.

Davies, Stephen. *Musical Meaning and Expression*. London: Cornell University Press, 1994.

Davis, H. Grady. *Design for Preaching*. Philadelphia: Fortress, 1958.

DeVries, Mark. *Family Based Youth Ministry*. Downers Grove: InterVarsity Press, 1994.

Downs, David. *The Offering of the Gentiles*. Tübingen: Mohr Siebeck, 2008.

Dugan, Mary Kay. "The Psalter on the Way to the Reformation: The Fifteenth Century Printed Psalter in the North." *The Place of the Psalms in the Intellectual Culture of the Middle Ages*. Edited by Nancy Van Deusen. Albany: State University of New York, 1999.

Durham, James. *A Commentary upon the Book of Revelation*. Willow Street, PA: Old Paths, 2000.

Dyer, Joseph. "The Singing of Psalms in the Early Medieval Office." *Speculum* 64:3 (July 1989), 535-578.

Eadie, John. *Commentary on the Epistle of Paul to the Colossians*. Grand Rapids: Zondervan, 1957.

_____. *Commentary on the Epistle to the Ephesians*. Minneapolis: James and Klock, 1977.

Edersheim, Alfred. *Old Testament Bible History*, Complete in One Volume. Grand Rapids: Eerdmans, 1982.

_____. *Sketches of Jewish Social Life*. Grand Rapids: Eerdmans, 1993.

_____. *The Life and Times of Jesus the Messiah*. Peabody, MA: Hendrickson, 2000.

_____. *The Temple, Its Ministry and Services*. Peabody, MA: Hendrickson, 1994.

Edgar, William. "Reformed Systematic Theology Textbooks: Hand Maiden to the Enlightenment Privatization of Faith." Paper, Reformed Presbyterian Theological Seminary, 2010.

Edgar, William. *Taking Note of Music*. London: SPCK, 1986.

Edwards, Mark J., ed. *Ancient Christian Commentary on Scripture: Galatians, Ephesians, Philippians*. Downers Grove: InterVarsity Press, 1999.

Edwards, Jonathan. *Typological Writings*. New Haven: Yale University Press, 1993.

Engelsma, David J. "Forward." *Sermons on Election and Reprobation by John Calvin*. Audubon, NJ: Old Paths Publications, 1996.

Erdman, David. *The Books of Samuel*. Translated by C. H. Troy and John Broadus. Grand Rapids: Zondervan, 1960.

Etherington, Charles L. *Protestant Worship Music*. Westport, CT: Greenwood, 1978.

Fairbairn, Patrick. *The Typology of Scripture*. Welwyn, Herts: Evangelical Press, 1975.

Fassler, Margot E. "Hildegard and the Dawn Song of Lauds: An Introduction to Benedictine Psalmody." *Psalms in Community*. Edited by Harold W. Attbridge and Margot E. Fassler. Atlanta: Society of Biblical Literature, 2003.

Fawcett, Cheryl L. *Understanding People*. Wheaton: Evangelical Training Association, 2001.

Fee, Gordon D. *Paul's Letter to the Philippians*. Grand Rapids: Eerdmans, 1995.

Feinberg, C. L. "Synagogue." *The New Bible Dictionary*. Edited by J. D. Douglas. Grand Rapids: Eerdmans, 1964.

Frame, John M. "Forward." *Covenantal Worship: Reconsidering the Puritan Regulative Principle*. Phillipsburg, NJ: P & R, 2002.

———. *Worship in Spirit and Truth*. Phillipsburg, NJ: P & R, 1996.

Futato, Mark D. *Interpreting the Psalms*. Grand Rapids: Kregel, 2007.

———. *Transformed by Praise*. Phillipsburg, NJ: P & R, 2002.

Garside, Charles Jr. *The Origins of Calvin's Theology of Music, 1536-1543*. Philadelphia: American Philosophical Society, 1979.

Gingrich, F. Wilbur, and Frederick W. Danker. *Shorter Lexicon of the Greek New Testament*. Chicago: University of Chicago Press, 1983.

Girardeau, John L. *Instrumental Music in Public Worship*. Havertown, PA: New Covenant Publication Society, 1983.

Glass, Henry Alexander. *The Story of Psalters*. London: Kegan Paul, Trench, 1888.

Godet, F. L. *Commentary on the Gospel of Luke*. Grand Rapids: Zondervan, 1956.

Godwyn, Thomas. *Moses and Aaron*. London: R. Rayston, 1631.

Gordon, T. David. "Some Provisional Thoughts on Exclusive Psalmody." Grove City, PA: The Author, n.d.

———. *Why Johnny Can't Sing Hymns*. Phillipsburg, NJ: P & R, 2010.

Gouge, William. *Commentary on Hebrews*. Grand Rapids: Kregel, 1980.

Greenhill, William. *Exposition of Ezekiel*. Carlisle, PA: Banner of Truth, 1994.

Grimm, Carl L. W. *A Greek-English Lexicon of the New Testament*. New York: American Book Company, 1889.

Grosheide, F. W. *Commentary on the First Epistle to the Corinthians*. Grand Rapids: Eerdmans, 1972.

Hammond, Henry. *A Paraphrase and Annotations Upon the Book of Psalms*. London: R. Norton, 1659.

Harper, Norman E. *Making Disciples*. Memphis: Christian Studies Center, 1981.

Harrison, Everett F. *Introduction to the New Testament*. Grand Rapids: Eerdmans, 1964.

———. "The Influence of the Septuagint on the New Testament Vocabulary." *Bibliotheca Sacra* 113 (January 1956): 37-45.

Harrison, R. K. *Old Testament Times*. Peabody, MA: Hendrickson, 2001.

Harrisville, R. A. "The Concept of Newness in the New Testament." *Journal of Biblical Literature* 74:2 (June 1955): 69-79.

Hart, D. G., and John R. Muether. *With Reverence and Awe*. Phillipsburg, NJ: P & R, 2002.

Hebrew-English Edition of the Babylon Talmud: Tamid. Translated by Maurice Simons. Edited by I. Epstein. London: Soncino, 1989.

Heen, Eric M., and Philip D. W. Krey, ed. *Ancient Christian Commentary on Scripture; Hebrews*. Downers Grove: InterVarsity Press, 2005.

Hendriksen, William. *Exposition of the Gospel of John*. Grand Rapids: Baker, 1972.

_____. *Exposition of the Gospel According to Luke*. Grand Rapids: Baker, 1978.

_____. *Exposition of the Gospel According to Mark*. Grand Rapids: Baker, 1976.

_____. *Exposition of the Gospel According to Matthew*. Grand Rapids: Baker, 1973.

Henry, Matthew. *Matthew Henry's Commentary on the Whole Bible*. Grand Rapids: Fleming H. Revell, 1985.

Hernando, James D. *Dictionary of Hermeneutics*. Springfield: Gospel Publishing House, 2005.

Hoekema, Anthony A. *The Bible and the Future*. Grand Rapids: Eerdmans, 1979.

Hodge, A. A. *Outlines of Theology*. Grand Rapids: Zondervan, 1976.

_____. *The Confession of Faith*. Carlisle, PA: Banner of Truth, 1978.

Hodge, Charles. *An Exposition of the First Epistle to the Corinthians*. Grand Rapids: Eerdmans, 1965.

_____. *Commentary on the Epistle to the Ephesians*. Grand Rapids: Eerdmans, 1966.

Hodge, Charles and Lyman Atwater, eds. *The Biblical Repertory and Princeton Review for the Year 1843* 15:1 (1843).

Hogue, Wilson Thomas. *History of the Free Methodist Church of North America*. Chicago: Free Methodist Publishing House, 1915.

Holladay, William L. *The Psalms through Three Thousand Years*. Minneapolis: Fortress, 1996.

Horton, Michael. *A Better Way*. Grand Rapids: Baker, 2003.

Hughes, Philip E. *Commentary on the Second Epistle to the Corinthians*. Grand Rapids: Eerdmans, 1973.

Irwin, Eleanor M. "Phos Hilaron: The Metamorphoses of a Greek Christian Hymn," *The Hymn* 40:2 (April 1989): 7-12.

Johnson, Terry. "The History of Psalm Singing." In *Sing a New Song*. Edited by Joel R. Beeke and Anthony T. Selvaggio. Grand Rapids: Reformation Heritage, 2010.

Josephus, Flavius. *The Works of Flavius Josephus*. Translated by William Whiston. Grand Rapids: Baker, 1974.

Julian, John, ed. *A Dictionary of Hymnology*. New York: Dover, 1907.

Kaiser, Walter. *Back Toward the Future*. Grand Rapids: Baker, 1990.

Keil, C. F., and F. Delitzsch. *The Books of the Chronicles*. Translated by Andrew Harper. Grand Rapids: Eerdmans, 1982.

_____. *The Pentateuch*. Translated by James Martin. Grand Rapids: Eerdmans, 1981.

Kidner, Derek. *Ezra and Nehemiah*. Downers Grove: Inter-Varsity Press, 1979.

_____. *Genesis*. Chicago: Inter-Varsity Press, 1967.

_____. *Psalms 73-150*. Downers Grove: Inter-Varsity Press, 1973.

Kittredge, George Lyman, and Frank E. Farley. *Advanced English Grammar*. New York: Ginn and Company, 1913.

Kuiper, B. K. *The Church in History*. Grand Rapids: Eerdmans, 1973.

Kuiper, R. B. *The Glorious Body of Christ*. Carlisle: Banner of Truth, 1967.

Kistemaker, Simon. *Exposition of the Epistle to the Hebrews*. Grand Rapids: Baker, 1984.

Kleinig, John W. *Leviticus*. St. Louis: Concordia, 2003.

_____. *The Lord's Song: The Basis, Function and Significance of Choral Music in Chronicles*. Sheffield: Sheffield Academic Press, 1993.

Kurfees, M. C. *Instrumental Music in Worship*. Nashville: Gospel Advocate, 1950.

Ladd, George Eldon. *A New Testament Theology*. Grand Rapids: Eerdmans, 1993.

Lamb, John Alexander. *The Psalms in Christian Worship*. London: Faith Press, 1962.

Lane, William. *Word Biblical Commentary: Hebrews 9-13*. Dallas: Word, 1991.

Lange, John Peter. *Genesis*. Translated by Tayler Lewis and A. Gosman. Grand Rapids: Zondervan, 1960.

_____. *Exodus*. Translated by Charles M. Meade. Grand Rapids: Zondervan, 1960.

_____. *Numbers*. Translated by Samuel T. Lowrie and A. Grosman. Grand Rapids: Zondervan, 1960.

Latourette, Kenneth Scott. *A History of Christianity*. New York: Harper and Row, 1953.

Lavy, Matthew M. "Emotion and the Experience of Listening to Music, A Framework for Empirical Research." Ph.D. Diss., University of Cambridge, Jesus College, 2001.

LeFebvre, Michael. *Sing the Songs of Jesus*. Fearn: Christian Focus, 2010.

_____. "The Shape of the Psalter." Paper, International Christian College, 2000.

Lewis, C. S. *The Abolition of Man*. New York: Macmillan, 1966.

Lightfoot, J. B. *Saint Paul's Epistles to the Colossians and to Philemon*. Grand Rapids: Zondervan, 1965.

Lightfoot, John. *A Commentary on the New Testament from the Talmud and Hebraica*. Peabody, MA: Hendrickson, 2003.

_____. *The Works of the Reverend and Learned John Lightfoot*. London: Robert Scot, 1684.

Lingas, Alexander. "Tradition and Renewal in Contemporary Greek Orthodox Psalmody." *Psalms in Community*. Edited by Harold W. Attbridge and Margot E. Fassler. Atlanta: Society of Biblical Literature, 2003.

Longman, Tremper, and Raymond Dillard. *An Introduction to the Old Testament*. Grand Rapids: Zondervan, 2006.

Lucarini, Dan. *Why I Left the Contemporary Christian Music Movement*. Webster, NY: Evangelical Press, 2010.

Luther, Martin. *Luther's Commentary on Genesis*. Translated by J. Theodore Mueller. Grand Rapids: Zondervan, 1958.

_____. *Luther's Works: Liturgy and Hymns*. Edited by Ulrich S. Leupold. Philadelphia: Fortress, 1965.

Makujina, John. *Measuring the Music*. Willow Street, PA: Old Paths, 2002.

Marshall, I. Howard. *The Acts of the Apostles*. Grand Rapids: Eerdmans, 1982.

Martin, Ralph. *Worship in the Early Church*. Westwood, NJ: Fleming H. Revell, 1964.

Mather, Richard. Preface to *The Whole Booke of Psalmes Faithfully Translated into English Metre*. Cambridge: Riverside Press, 1640.

Mather, Samuel. *The Figures and Types of the Old Testament*. New York: Johnson Reprint Corporation, 1969.

McCullough, W. S. "Goat." *The Interpreter's Dictionary of the Bible*. New York: Abingdon, 1962.

M'Clintock, John and James Strong, eds. *Cyclopaedia of Biblical, Theological, and Ecclesiastical Literature*, Vol. 8. New York: Harper and Brothers, 1879.

McKinnon, James W. "Desert Monasticism and the Later Fourth-Century Psalmodic Movement." *Music and Letters* 75:4 (1994): 505-521.

_____. *Music in Early Christian Literature*. Cambridge: Cambridge University Press, 1987.

_____. "On the Question of Psalmody in the Ancient Synagogue." *Early Music History* 6 (1986): 159-191.

_____. "The Book of Psalms, Monasticism, and the Western Liturgy." *The Place of the Psalms in the Intellectual Culture of the Middle Ages*. Edited by Nancy Van Deusen. Albany: State University of New York, 1999.

_____. "The Church Fathers and Musical Instruments." Ph.D. Diss., Columbia University, 1965.

_____. "The Exclusion of Musical Instruments from the Ancient Synagogue." *Journal of the Royal Musical Association* 106 (1979): 77-87.

McNaugher, John, et al. "Preface." *Bible Songs*. Pittsburgh: United Presbyterian Board of Publication, 1901.

_____. "Preface." *The Psalter with Responsive Readings*. Pittsburgh: United Presbyterian Board of Publication, 1912.

Mitchell, David C. *The Message of the Psalter: An Eschatological Programme in the Book of Psalms*. Sheffield: Sheffield Academic Press, 1997.

Mehrabian, Albert. *Silent Messages*. Belmont, CA: Wadsworth, 1971.

Meyer, Jeffrey J. *The Lord's Service*. Moscow, ID: Canon Press, 2003.

Millar, Patrick. *The Story of the Church's Song*. Edinburgh: Saint Andrews Press, 1927.

Motyer, J. A. "Name." *The New Bible Dictionary*. Edited by J. D. Douglas. Grand Rapids: Eerdmans, 1962.

Moulton, Harold K. *The Analytical Greek Lexicon Revised*. Grand Rapids: Zondervan, 1977.

Morris, Leon. *The First Epistle of Paul to the Corinthians*. Grand Rapids: Eerdmans, 1979.

Murray, John. *Christian Baptism*. Philadelphia: Presbyterian and Reformed, 1972.

_____. *The Epistle to the Romans*. Grand Rapids: Eerdmans,1973.

Music, David W. *Instruments in Church: A Collection of Source Documents*. Lanham, MD: Scarecrow Press, 1998.

Nägelsbach, Carl W. E. *The Prophet Isaiah*. Translated by Samuel Lowrie and Dunlop Moore. Grand Rapids: Zondervan, 1960.

Needham, Nick R. "Worship Through the Ages." In *Give Praise to God*. Edited by Philip Ryken, Derek Thomas, and Ligon Duncan. Phillipsburg, NJ: P & R, 2003.

North, Gary. *Crossed Fingers: How Liberals Captured the Presbyterian Church*. Tyler, TX: Institute for Christian Economics, 1996.

Oesterley, W. O. E. *The Psalms in the Jewish Church*. London: Skeffington and Son, 1910.

Old, Hughes Oliphant. *Worship That Is Reformed According to Scripture*. Atlanta: John Knox, 1984.

_____, and Robert Cathart, "From Cassian to Cranmer: Singing the Psalms from Ancient Times until the Dawning of the Reformation." In *Sing a New Song*. Edited by Joel R. Beeke and Anthony T. Selvaggio. Grand Rapids: Reformation Heritage, 2010.

O'Neill, Jerry. *Roman Catholic Baptism. Memorandum to Reformed Presbyterian Students Under Care of Presbytery*, Pittsburgh: Reformed Presbyterian Theological Seminary, 2011.

Orthodox Presbyterian Church. *The Standards of Government, Discipline, and Worship of the Orthodox Presbyterian Church*. Philadelphia: Committee on Christian Education, 1965.

Owen, John. *The Works of John Owen*, Volume 9. Edited by William H. Goold. London: Johnstone and Hunter, 1851.

Packer, J. I. *A Quest for Godliness: The Puritan Vision of the Christian Life*. Wheaton: Crossway Books, 1990.

Page, Christopher. *The Christian West and Its Singers*. New Haven: Yale University Press, 2010.

Parker, T. H. L. *Calvin's Preaching*. Louisville: Westminster/John Knox. 1992.

_____. *John Calvin: A Biography*. Philadelphia: Westminster Press, 1975.

Pipa, Joseph A. *The Lord's Day*. Fearn: Christian Focus, 1997.

Pliny the Younger, *Pliny Letters*. Cambridge: Harvard University Press, 1985.

Plumer, William S. *Psalms*. Carlisle: Banner of Truth, 1975.

Powell, John. *How Music Works*. New York: Little Brown, 2010.

Poythress, Vern S. "Ezra 3, Union with Christ, and Exclusive Psalmody," *Westminster Theological Journal* 37:1 (Fall 1974): 74-94; 37:2 (Winter 1975): 218-235.

Presenting the Bose Wave Music System. Framingham, MA: Bose Corporation, 2004.

Price, John. *Old Light on New Worship*. Avinger, TX: Simpson Publishing, 2005.

Prutow, Dennis. "Adrenaline Addiction, Spirituality, and Worship." Paper, Orlando, FL, Reformed Theological Seminary, 1995.

———. *So, Pastor, What's Your Point?* Philadelphia: Alliance of Confessing Evangelicals, 2010.

———. "The Eucharist at Corinth." Paper submitted to Dr. George Eldon Ladd, Fuller Theological Seminary, 1968.

"Psalms." In *The New Cambridge Bibliography of English Literature*, vol. 1. Edited by George Watson. Cambridge: University Press, 1974.

"Psalter." In *The Harvard Dictionary of Music*. Edited by Don Michael Randel. Cambridge: Harvard University Press, 2003.

"Psalters, English." In *A Dictionary of Hymnology*. Edited by John Julian. New York: Dover, 1907.

Quigley, Andrew. *Giving in the Church*. Airdrie: In the Pew Publications, 1997.

Rabbinowitz, J. *The Book of Exodus: The Soncino Chumash*. Edited by A. Cohen. New York: Soncino, 1993.

Reid, W. Stanford. "The Battle Hymns of the Lord: Calvinist Psalmody of the Sixteenth Century." *Sixteenth Century Essays and Studies* 2 (1971): 36-54.

Reformed Presbyterian Church of North America. *1985 Minutes of the Synod and Yearbook*. Pittsburgh: Board of Education and Publication, 1985.

Reformed Presbyterian Church of North America. *The Book of Psalms for Worship*. Pittsburgh: Crown and Covenant, 2009.

Reformed Presbyterian Church of North America. "The Committee to Study the Contents of the Cup in the Lord's Supper." In *Minutes of the 2010 Synod of the Reformed Presbyterian Church of North America*. Pittsburgh: Crown and Covenant, 2010.

Reformed Presbyterian Church of North America. *The Constitution of the Reformed Presbyterian Church of North America*. Pittsburgh: Crown and Covenant, 2010.

Robertson, A. T. *Word Pictures in the New Testament*. Nashville: Broadman, 1932.

Robinson, Haddon W. *Biblical Preaching*. Grand Rapids: Baker, 2001.

Robson, Edward A. "Interpretation of the Two-Kai Configurations of the Greek New Testament." *Semper Reformanda* 7:2 (Summer 1998): 1-88.

Runesson, Anders. *The Origin of the Synagogue: A Socio-Historical Study*. Stockholm: Almqvist and Wiksell, 2001.

Sanborn, Scott F. "Inclusive Psalmody: Why 'Psalms, Hymns, and Spiritual Songs' Refer to More than the Old Testament Psalter." *Kerux* 23:3 (December 2008): 13-50.

Schaff, Philip. *History of the Christian Church*. Grand Rapids: Eerdmans, 1910.

Schaeffer, Francis A. *Baptism*. Wilmington: TriMark, 1976.

Schroeder, Wilhelm Julius. *Deuteronomy*. Translated by A. Gosman. Grand Rapids: Zondervan, 1960.

Schultz, W. *The Book of Esther*. Translated by James Strong. Grand Rapids: Zondervan, 1960.

Schwertley, Brian. *Musical Instruments in the Public Worship of God*. Haslett, MI: Covenant Reformed Press, 2003.

Scott, J. Julius. *Customs and Controversies*. Grand Rapids: Baker, 1995.

Silversides, David. "The Development of the Scottish Psalter." Paper presented to The Scottish Reformation Society, 2002.

Shaw, Robert. *An Exposition of the Westminster Confession of Faith*. Fearn: Christian Focus, 1998.

Slotki, I. W. *Chronicles*. New York: Soncino, 1985.

_____, and A. J. Rosenberg. *Isaiah*. New York: Soncino, 1983.

Smith Frank J., and David Lachman, eds. *Worship in the Presence of God*. Greenville, SC: Greenville Seminary Press, 1992.

Smith, John. "The Ancient Synagogue, the Early Church and Singing." *Music and Letters* 65 (1984): 1-16.

Sproul, R. C., ed. *The Reformation Study Bible*. Orlando: Ligonier Ministries, 2005.

_____. "The Teaching Preacher." In *Feed My Sheep: A Passionate Plea for Preaching*. Orlando: Reformation Trust, 2008.

Spurgeon, Charles. *A Treasury of David*. Newark, DE: Cornerstone, n.d.

Sternhold, Thomas, and John Hopkins. *The Booke of Psalmes Collected into English Meeter*. Bound with *The 1599 Geneva Bible, Facsimile Edition*. Ozark: L. L. Brown, 1995.

Stamou, Lelouda. "Plato and Aristotle on Music and Music Education: Lessons from Ancient Greece." *International Journal of Music Education* 39 (2002): 3-16.

Taft, Robert F. "Liturgical Christian Psalmody: Origins, Development, Decomposition, Collapse." In *Psalms in Community*. Edited by Harold W. Attridge and Margot E. Fassler. Atlanta: Society of Biblical Literature, 2003.

Terry, Milton S. *Biblical Hermeneutics*. Grand Rapids: Zondervan, 1974.

The Greek New Testament. Stuttgart: United Bible Societies, 1983.

The New York Times, "The First Organ Brought to America," June 26, 1883.

The New York Times, "The Organ Controversy," June 4, 1883.

Thomas, Derek W. H. "Expository Preaching." In *Feed My Sheep: A Passionate Plea for Preaching*. Orlando: Reformation Trust, 2008.

Thompson, J. A. *Deuteronomy*. London: Inter-Varsity Press, 1974.

Thompson, R. J. "Sacrifice and Offering." In *The New Bible Dictionary*. Edited by J. D. Douglas. Grand Rapids: Eerdmans, 1964.

Towner, Philip H. *The Letters to Timothy and Titus*. Grand Rapids: Eerdmans, 2006.

Turretin, Francis. *Institutes of Elenctic Theology*. Edited by George Musgrave Giger. Translated by James T. Dennison. Phillipsburg, NJ: Presbyterian and Reformed Publishing, 1992.

United Presbyterian Church of North America. *The Directory for Worship of the United Presbyterian Church of North America*. Pittsburgh: United Presbyterian Board of Publication, 1882.

Ursinus, Zacharius. *The Commentary on the Heidelberg Catechism*. Phillipsburg, NJ: Presbyterian and Reformed, 1980.

Venema, Cornelius P. *The Promise of the Future*. Carlisle: Banner of Truth, 2000.

Verhoef, Pieter A. *The Books of Haggai and Malachi*. Grand Rapids: Eerdmans, 1987.

Vos, Geerhardus. "Eschatology of the Psalter." In *The Pauline Eschatology*. Grand Rapids: Baker, 1979.

———. "Songs from the Soul." In *Grace and Glory*. Carlisle: Banner of Truth, 1994.

———. "The Doctrine of the Covenant in Reformed Theology." In *Redemptive History and Biblical Interpretation*. Edited by Richard B. Gaffin. Phillipsburg, NJ: Presbyterian and Reformed, 1980.

Warfield, B. B. "Pneumatikos and Its Opposites in the Greek New Testament." *The Presbyterian Review* 1:3 (1880): 561-565.

Watts, Isaac. "Preface." *Hymns and Spiritual Songs*. London: J. Humphreys, 1707.

———. "Preface." In *The Psalms of David Imitated in the Language of the New Testament, and Applied to the Christian State of Worship*. Christian Classic Ethereal Library. Accessed January 16, 2012.

Watts, Malcolm H. "The Case for Psalmody." In *Sing a New Song*. Edited by Joel R. Beeke and Anthony T. Selvaggio. Grand Rapids: Reformation Heritage, 2010.

Wenham, Gordon J. *Genesis 1-15*. Waco: Word Books, 1987.

Werner, Eric. *The Sacred Bridge*. New York: Schocken, 1970.

Westcott, Brooke Foss. *St. Paul's Epistle to the Ephesians*. London: Macmillan, 1906.

Westermyer, Paul. *Te Deum: The Church and Music*. Minneapolis: Fortress, 1998.

Westminster Confession of Faith. Glasgow: Free Presbyterian Publications, 1997.

Williamson, G. I. *The Westminster Confession of Faith for Classes*. Philadelphia: Presbyterian and Reformed, 1964.

Wilson, John A. "The Psalms in the Post-Apostolic Church." In *The Psalms in Worship*. Edited by John McNaugher. Pittsburgh: United Presbyterian Board of Publication, 1907.

Young, Edward J. *An Introduction to the Old Testament*. Grand Rapids: Eerdmans, 1975.

_____. *The Book of Isaiah*. Grand Rapids: Eerdmans, 1981.

Index of Persons

Aaron 77, 190, 484
Aaron's sons 190, 481
Abel, son of Adam 5-6, 10, 377-378, 391, 392
Abihu, son of Aaron 77-78
Abraham 51, 145, 283, 373, 378, 393, 394-395, 396, 478, 483
Abraham's children 193
Adam 379, 391, 392, 441, 443, 475, 480, 483
Adam and Eve 391, 484
Adams, Jay E. 162, 261
Adeh, wife of Lamech 392
Ainsworth, Henry 362, 428
Alexander, J. A. 237, 238, 310
Ambrose, of Milan 320, 332, 414
Ames, William 428
Antony, the mystic 321
Appel, Richard G. 362
Aquinas, Thomas 420, 464
Aristotle 420
Asaph, the psalmist 236, 282, 302, 454
Athanasius, of Alexandria 255, 256, 258, 259, 290, 317, 322, 387, 412
Augustine, of Hippo 64, 180, 216, 250, 264, 266, 300, 314, 322, 328-331, 386, 391, 415
Bannerman, James 42-43
Barak, general of Israel 302
Barnabas, companion of Paul ... 154, 186-187
Basil, pope 319, 322, 413, 416
Baum, Frank viii

Beale, G. K. 22
Benedict, the monastic 337
Berkhof, Louis 179
Beze, Theodore de 355
Bonhoeffer, Dietrich 258
Booth, F. Carlton 436-437
Brady, Nicholas 357
Brattle, Thomas 432
Breckinridge, Robert J. 434
Broadus, John 165
Bruce, F. F. 58, 116, 118, 198
Bucer, Martin 353
Bullinger, E. W. 174, 245
Bullinger, Heinrich 422
Bush, George 74
Bushell, Michael 336
Calderwood, David 428
Cain, son of Adam .. 5-6, 10, 391, 392
Calvin, John 6, 13, 30, 57-58, 61, 111, 113, 125-127, 149, 151, 163, 180, 181, 184, 195, 198, 208, 212, 216, 217, 223, 234, 239, 250, 253, 255, 258, 282, 289, 294, 299, 300, 304, 312, 352, 353, 367, 377, 378, 386, 387, 403, 423, 424, 425, 426, 427, 428, 437, 452, 463, 464
On Exodus 12:43-48 212
On Exodus 20:8 61
On Deut. 33:10 11
On Psalm 22:25 234
On Psalm 71:22 425
On Psalm 105:2 .... 289, 294
On Malachi 2:7 113
On John 4:23 13
On 1 Cor. 10:16 208

On 1 Cor. 11:28 217
On 1 Cor. 14:15, 26 304
On Hebrews 3:12-19 57-58
Apostolic authority.................. 151
Application in preaching........ 163
Baptism.............. 184, 195, 198, 216
Benediction 149
Hymn-singing 312
Instruments in worship .. 424, 426
Instruments as aids to worship ... 43
Instruments commanded in the Psalms........................... 463, 464
Instruments as shadows 427
Lord's Supper 217, 223
New songs 282
Preaching....................................111
Psalms... 239
Psalms, Subjective element in...... 253, 255, 258
Psalm-Singing 250, 289, 299, 300, 367, 387, 452
Psalters 352, 353
Regulative principle of worship.. 423
Sacraments........................ 180, 181
Teaching priests.........................113
Temple, destruction of 403
Temple, true............................... 30
Worship, Abel's 377
Worship, early 378
Worship, order of 125-127
Worship, true............................... 6
Worship and Plato 386
Carson, D. A................... 22, 33, 42, 83
Cassian, John 322, 325, 326
Cassiodorus 419
Chalmers, Thomas....................... 434
Charlemagne 341, 419
Charnock, Stephen......................... 43
Chrysostom................... 408, 414, 427
Clarke, Adam................................ 430
Clebsch, William 321
Clement, of Alexandria 313-314, 410, 411
Cock, Symon................................. 361
Constantine, emperor of Rome.. 335
Coppes, Leonard .. 276, 279, 284, 295
Cotton, John 428, 431
Cowper, William 299
Craig, John 358
Cranmer, Thomas......................... 355
Crowley, Robert............................ 356
Cyprian, early church father 216
Cyril, of Jerusalem 318
Dabney, Robert Lewis 383, 385, 433-435, 437, 438
Dagg, John L. 430
Dathenus, Peter 361
David, King of Israel, 29-30, 41, 234-236, 263-264, 266, 282, 283, 284, 285, 288, 302, 315, 323, 330, 398-400, 402, 423-424, 429, 437, 444, 448-451, 453-454, 455, 459, 460, 464, 469, 478, 481, 483, 485
Added musical instruments to worship............ 402, 423-424, 437, 448-451, 454
And musical instruments 464
And Psalm 72 266
Appointed Asaph 454
Author of the Psalms............... 285
Change of worship in his time 481
Christ fulfilled his ordinances 288
Commands concerning worship 234-236, 283, 284, 398-400
Confidence in God............ 263-264
Covenant promises to 29-30
Desire to worship....................... 41
Early church sang David's Psalms...................... 315, 323, 330
Introduced sung praise into worship..................................... 444
King Hezekiah sang David's Psalms....................................... 302
Moved the ark of the covenant.... 429

Prophetic songs of 282
Remembered the covenant...........
   453-454
Returned from killing the
   Philistines........................ 459, 460
Sin of numbering the people.. 478
Type of Christ 455
Use of musical instruments... 469,
   483, 485
Dawn, Marva................................ 91
Day, John 357
De Bray, Guy.................................. 361
De Heere... 361
Deborah, judge of Israel.............. 302
Delitzsch, Franz.................... 150, 236
Dick, John...................................... 174
Dix, Dom Gregory 105
Donne, John 299
Dorothy, of the Wizard of Oz viii
Douen, Orentin............................ 355
Dugmore, Clifford 105
Dunster, Henry 362-363
Dyer, Joseph............................337-338
Eadie, John 247, 248, 297
Edersheim, Alfred........ 105, 106, 119,
   121, 204, 236, 237
Edward VI, king of England 356
Egeria, the Spanish nun 326, 327,
   328
Enosh, son of Seth 378
Erasmus, of Rotterdam 420
Esau, son of Isaac 395
Esther, queen of Persia 74-75
Ethiopian eunuch......................... 443
Eusebius, of Caesarea..........315-317,
   411, 427
Evagrius Ponticus 414
Eve... 379, 392
Ezekiel, the prophet........ 36, 177, 400
Ezra, the scribe 284, 285, 400
Fassler, Margot 345, 347, 348
Fee, Gordon................................... 303
Frame, John M. 80-83, 439, 483
Futato, Mark D. 265, 271, 272

Gad, the king's seer 482
Gamaliel II, leader of the Sanhedrin
   119
Girardeau, John L................ 419, 432,
   433-434, 473
Godwyn, Thomas 109
Gordon, T. David 91, 276, 283,
   293, 294, 296, 299, 301, 368
Gouge, William............................. 156
Greenhill, William........... 36, 143, 179
Gregory, of Nazianzus 319
Gregory, of Nyssa......................... 322
Grotius, Hugo............................... 108
Gutenberg, Johannes 349
Hammond, Henry 109
Harper, Norman........................... 192
Harrison, Everett.......... 240, 241, 243
Harrisville, R. A............................ 280
Hart, Daryl 92
Hebrews, writer to the 403-404,
   408
Heman, the Levite.........398-399, 448
Hendriksen, William 237
Henry, Matthew 43-44, 68, 106,
   107, 232, 238, 239, 285, 291, 393,
   403, 428
Henry VIII, king of England 356
Hezekiah, king of Israel 235,
   243-244, 302, 399, 405, 454
Hilary, of Poitiers 332
Hodge, A.A. 37-38, 82, 136,
   196, 214
Hodge, Charles..... 144, 209, 307, 432
Hogue, Wilson.............................. 432
Holdeman, Richard ....ix, xii
Holladay, William L...................... 338
Hopkins, John............................... 356
Horton, Michael 91
Ignatius, of Antioch 409
Innocent III, pope......................... 345
Isaac, son of Abraham 393, 395,
   396, 478
Isaiah, the prophet 443, 444-445,
   446, 447

Isidore, of Pelusium 416
Jacob, son of Isaac 73-74, 393, 395, 396, 444, 469
James, the epistle writer 411
Jeduthun, the Levite 398-399, 448
Jephthah, the judge 87, 88, 459
Jephthah's daughter 87, 89, 459, 460
Jeremiah, the prophet 400
Jerome 322, 408
Jesus Christ 6-7, 34-35, 41, 55-56, 66, 69, 71, 72, 74, 76-77, 122, 139-140, 147, 152, 154, 164-166, 175, 179, 180, 184, 185, 187, 188, 197, 202, 204-212, 214, 220-222, 237-238, 277, 278, 331, 403-405, 409, 442-443, 445, 447, 449, 453, 455, 463, 475-476, 479, 482, 487, 490
   And church discipline 214
   And sacraments 179, 180
   And signs and seals 175
   And synagogue 404-405
   And temple 403-405
   Anointed for death 204
   Appointed Paul as a steward. 187
   As Jacob's ladder 74
   As Lord 41
   As Savior 185
   As the only way to heaven 74
   As the temple 34-35
   Blood of 443
   Commanded baptism 184
   Commanded preaching 154
   Commanded the Lord's Supper.. 204-212
   Commended justice, mercy, and faith 147
   Commissioned His apostles 76-77
   Commissioned the church... 76-77
   Communicated the benefits of redemption 152
   Compared to Moses 55-56
   David as a type of 455
   Death of 208-209, 220-222
   Drank the cup of God's wrath..... 220-222
   End of the law 331
   Entry into Jerusalem 204
   Fulfilled the ceremonial law .. 409
   In the Book of Revelation 449
   In the synagogue of Capernaum 122
   Is Yahweh 277
   Moses as a type of 442-443
   On the Mount of Olives 463
   Peace with God through.. 139-140
   Preaching 445
   Predicted the destruction of Jerusalem 403
   Prepared the church for heaven.. 164-166
   Prescribed how we enter God's presence 72
   Presence in the Lord's Supper 209-210
   Psalms speak of 278
   Required public confession of faith 188
   Resurrection 69
   Sacrifice of 404-405, 407, 482, 485, 490
   Sang Psalms 237-238
   Second coming 479, 482
   Seventh-day Sabbath passed away with 66
   Singing 453
   Teaching 204
   Temptation by Satan 6-7
   Typology..... 442-443, 445, 447, 455
   Worship offered through.. 71, 487
   Wrong views of 197
Job, the patriarch 378, 393, 396
John Chrysostom 318, 322, 323
John, the apostle 205, 237, 411
John, the baptizer 443
Johnson, Terry 336, 360
Josephus, the historian 116
Jubal, the first instrumentalist... 391, 392

Index of Persons

Jude, the epistle writer 411
Justin Martyr...........................409-410
Keach, Benjamin............................ 364
Keil, Karl Friedrich 150, 235
Kethe, William 356
Kidner, Derek................. 268, 271, 272
King of Persia 75
Kleinig, John 26, 236, 302
Knox, John...................................... 358
Kuiper, R. B. 44
Laban, father-in-law of Jacob 85, 457, 469
Ladd, George Eldon 280
Lamech, father of Jubal 392
Lamb, John Alexander 314, 340, 345, 351-352
Latourette, Kenneth Scott .. 341, 350, 361
Lefebvre, Michael........ 241, 252, 258, 272, 273, 300, 337
Lewis, C. S. 14-15
Licinius, emperor of Rome 335
Lightfoot, J. B. 248
Lightfoot, John....... 68, 108, 109, 110, 112, 117
Lingas, Alexander 343
Lot, nephew of Abraham............. 145
Lucarini, Dan 90
Luke, the gospel writer 181, 411
Luther, Martin 351-352, 353, 422
Lydia, of Thyatira................. 188, 373
Lyon, Richard 362-363
Malachi, the prophet 145
Marcel, Pierre................................. 192
Marcellinus 255
Mark, the gospel writer................411
Marot, Clement 353, 355
Marshall, I. Howard 192
Martin, Ralph P..... 145, 239, 310, 435
Mary, mother of Jesus.................. 301
Mary, queen of England.............. 356
Mason, Archibald......................... 434
Mather, Cotton............................. 427
Mather, Increase 427
Mather, Richard............ 285, 427, 428
Mather, Samuel............................. 428
Matthew, the gospel writer 411
McKinnon, James W. 100, 105, 118, 119, 303, 321, 323, 324, 326, 327, 348
Melchizedek, king of Salem 145
Millar, Patrick 357, 360, 364
Miriam, sister of Moses.... 86, 87, 89, 372, 457, 458, 459, 460, 470, 484
Mitchell, David C......................... 266
Morris, Leon 144
Moses 7, 55-56, 111, 116, 257, 377, 379, 392, 396-397, 442-443, 445, 446, 454, 457, 464, 478, 481, 482, 483, 484, 485, 489, 490
  And Abel's worship 377
  And Adam and Eve................. 379
  And arts and crafts 392
  And calling upon the Lord..... 392
  And ceremonial law 481, 490
  And Promised Land 55-56
  And silver trumpets 445, 446, 457, 485
  And synagogue worship 489
  And tabernacle worship 484
  And transitions in commanded worship.....396-397, 464, 482, 483
  Commissioned by God 7
  Established weekly teaching...116
  Led Israel................................... 478
  Made the tabernacle vessels... 454
  Read in the synagogues...........111
  Type of Christ 442-443
  Words of 257
Mowinckel, Sigmund 105, 237
Muether, John 92
Murray, John 155, 210
Nadab, son of Aaron 77-78
Nahum, the prophet.................... 447
Nathan, the prophet 29, 399, 482
Negoita, Anastasie 273
Niceta, of Remesiana 320, 415
Noah.. 392

North, Gary 214, 215
Oesterley, W. O. E. 105
Old, Hughes Oliphant......... 322, 336
O'Neill, Jerry.....................................xii
Origen, the church father.............411
Ornan, the Jebusite 478
Owen, John 448
Packer, J. I. 44
Page, Christopher 106, 237, 313, 321, 341, 342
Pareus, David 428
Parker, T. H. L. 126, 163
Paul, of Sarasota........................... 315
Paul, the apostle 27, 29-31, 38-39, 122-123, 145, 148-149, 151, 154, 157, 158-159, 161, 163, 184-185, 186-187, 188, 189, 197-198, 208, 209, 217, 221, 238, 241, 248, 254-255, 256, 258, 276, 277, 278, 292, 296, 298, 303, 305-308, 309, 373, 375, 393, 425, 451, 453, 462-463
  And baptism............. 184-185, 189, 197-198
  And Barnabas..................... 186-187
  And benedictions...... 122-123, 151
  And God's covenant............. 29-31
  And God's temple 27
  And justification....................... 278
  And Passover 208
  And pastors as shepherds 186-187
  And preaching.......................... 453
  And Psalm titles....................... 241
  And the fullness of the Holy Spirit.. 451
  And the Lord's Supper 208, 209, 217, 221
  And the mystery of Christ...... 292
  And the sacrifice of Noah....... 393
  And the subjective element in the Psalms 258
  And tithing 145
  And tribulation 256
  Charge to elders 158-159
  Charge to preach.............. 161, 163
  Charge to Timothy 154, 161
  Circumscribed singing more than teaching 248, 298
  Described Jesus Christ 276-277
  Formed churches 188
  Grammar of 462-463
  Guarded the conduct of the churches 296
  Indicted unbelievers................. 375
  Instructions to the Corinthian church 425
  Preaching in Damascus........... 309
  Preached in Philippi 157
  Salutations of 148-149
  Sang the Psalms 238
  Teaching of......................... 186-187
  Used ambassadorial language..... 38-39
  Visited Titius Justus................. 373
  Wrote Ephesians and Colossians for a corporate setting 305-308
  Wrote Philippians 303
Peter, the apostle 34, 157, 186, 192, 205, 237, 312, 376, 411
Philip, the deacon 194, 443
Philo, of Alexandria......................115
Plato 299, 385-386
Pliny the younger......................... 312
Plumer, William S. 37
Pont, Robert 358
Poythress, Vern S.. 276, 288, 293, 295
Prutow, Dennis J...........................viii
Quigley, Andrew 143, 144, 146
Reid, Thomas..................................xii
Reid, W. Stanford 361
Robertson, A. T. 13, 65
Robinson, Haddon............... 168, 349
Robson, Edward........................... 244
Romolus Augustus, emperor of Rome... 335
Rous, Francis..........357, 358-359, 363
Samaritan woman....................... 479
Sanborn, Scott 276, 290, 291, 292
Saul, king of Israel 88, 89, 398,

Index of Persons

459, 460
Schaeffer, Francis 194
Schaff, Philip 313, 316, 327, 331, 332, 349-350
Sennacherib, king of Assuria 16
Seth, son of Adam 378
Silas, companion of Paul 248, 296
Simeon, Charles 301
Simons, Menno 427
Smith, Frank J. 44
Smith, John 105
Solomon, king of Israel 145, 283, 397, 398, 399, 464, 481
Sproul, R. C. 158, 162
Strype, John 357
Spurgeon, Charles Haddon 20, 430-431, 434, 437, 463-464, 465
Sternhold, Thomas 356
Taft, Robert F. 332, 336-337, 339, 342, 344
Tate, Nathan 357
Terry, Milton 135, 284
Tertullian, of Carthage 314-315
Theodoret, of Cyrrus 408, 416
Theodosius, emperor of Rome ... 335
Thomas, the disciple 69
Thornwell, James Henley 434
Timothy, early church pastor 140, 154, 188, 296
Titius Justus, worshiper of God 373

Towner, Philip 304
Trajan, Emperor 312
Troup, Lee xii
Turretin, Francis 44-45, 198
Tweed, Robert Bruce xii
Ursinus, Zacharias 65-66
Utinhove, Jan 361
Valens, Eastern Roman Emperor 319
Vermigli, Peter Martyr 428
Vos, Geerhardus 31, 252, 258, 262, 263, 264, 272, 273, 274, 279, 280
Warfield B. B. 245
Warren, Rick 90
Watts, Isaac 364-365, 429-430
Watts, Malcolm 249
Werner, Eric 310
Wesley, John 430
Westcott, Brooke Foss 207
Westermann, Claus 265
Westermyer, Paul 344
Willet, Andrew 428
Williamson, G. I. 251
Wilson, John 313, 315
Young, Edward J. 28
Zacharias, the priest 78, 301, 374
Zepperus, Wilhelm 428
Zillah, wife of Lamech 392
Zwingli, Huldreich 422, 428

Index of Scripture Verses

Genesis
1:27-28 48-49
1:31 454
2:1-3 48
2:2-3 67
3:15 .... 35, 378
3:21 .... 379, 391
4 378
4:3-4 .... 377, 391
4:4 377
4:4-5 5-6
4:6 150
4:20-22 392
4:21 .... 391, 392
4:26 .... 378, 392
8:20 392
8:21 393
12:6 394
12:7 394
12:8 .... 378, 394
13:3-4 394
13:18 394
14:18-19 128
14:19 145
14:20 145
17:7 26
17:7-8 26
17:9-10 51
17:10 51
17:10-12 193
17:11 51
22:5 .... 5, 373
22:13 394
22:18 .... 292, 394
26:23-25 395

26:25 478
28:10-17 73
28:12 170
28:18-22 395
31:27 .... 85, 457, 469
33:20 395
35:1-7 396
41:42 23
49:7 111-112
49:9 286
49:10-11 220
49:11 20

Exodus
1-18 .... 23, 396, 478
1-40 23
3:3 374
3:12 7
4:22 166
4:27-31 9
12 215
12:3-4 216
12:21 216
12:26 216
12:38 150
12:47 213
14:13-14 19
15 .... 396, 430
15:1-18 302
15:20 .... 85, 457, 458
15:20-21 470
15:21 .... 86, 458, 459
16:26 48
16:29 48
19-24 .... 23, 396, 478

19:6	286, 455
20	141
20:3	6
20:4-5	288, 375
20:5	6
20:8	61
20:8-10	54
20:8-11	49, 61
23	53
23:1-3	53
24:7	27
25-31	392
25-40	23, 396, 478
25	478
25:8	27, 35, 76, 129, 396, 454
25:8-9	71
25:9	35
25:40	76
26	25
26:1	23
26:11-12	23
26:14	23
26:15-30	23
26:35	130
27:9-18	23
27:19	454
30:14	133
30:18	129
30:19	129, 190
30:20	130
31:12-13	51
31:13	52, 63
31:16	51, 61
32-34	396
32:8	9
33:14	133
33:15-16	133
34:22	270
34:28	135, 136
35-40	396
40:5	130
40:33	397
40:33-38	397
40:35	478
40:35-38	375

Leviticus

Whole book	23
1:3	444
1:4	129, 406, 444, 481
1:9	130
3	103
3:5	406, 444, 481
3:12	103
3:13	103
3:15	103
7	103
7:12	233, 311
7:12-15	233
7:13	102, 233, 407
7:15	102, 233, 407
7:15-16	406
9:24	444
10:1-3	77-78
11:45	23
19:2	23
20:26	23
23	443
23:2	109-110
23:2-3	110, 115, 443-444
23:2-4	108
23:3	108, 400
23:4	109-110
23:9-11	68
26:2	27
26:3	26, 65-66
26:3-13	26
26:11	35
26:11-12	26, 129, 375
26:12	22
26:13	26
26:34	60
26:35	60
26:34-35	60
26:43-45	28

Numbers

6:22-26	150

6:22-27	148, 149
6:23-24	122
6:24-27	128
6:27	150
10:1	98
10:1-2	397
10:2	443, 457, 474
10:10	98, 371, 397, 443, 444, 446, 457, 474, 481
15:5	446
15:32	63
15:37-41	119, 402
18:7	77
28:3	478
28:3-4	106
28:3-6	444, 481
28:4	106
28:9-10	106, 481
29:16	106
29:19	106
29:22	106
29:25	106
29:28	106
29:31	106
29:34	106
29:38	106

Deuteronomy

4:13	50, 136
5:12-15	49-50
5:15	70
6:4-9	119, 402
10:4	136
11:13-21	402
12:5	478
12:5-7	145
12:10-11	55
16:10	147
16:16-17	143
16:17	147
18:15	177, 442, 443
30:6	189
32:1-43	302
33:8-10	114
33:10	112

Joshua

1:12-15	54
4:24	373
22:4	55

Judges

5:1	302
7:1	110, 113
11:34	85, 87, 459

I Samuel

1:1	398
4-6	398
5:17	234
7:1-2	234
7:2	398
9:19	110
10:5	85, 88, 110, 460
18:6	85, 87, 459
21:1	398

II Samuel

1:17-18	302
6	398
7:8	29
7:12-14	29
7:14	22, 29
7:16	29
7:25	477

I Kings

3:4	110, 398
8:11	375, 479
8:22-30	128

II Kings

12:2	110
14:4	110
15:4	110

I Chronicles

1-9	243

6:31-32 243
13:1-3 234
13:8 .... 85, 87, 459
15 398
15:16 .... 447, 448, 481
15:28 447
16 284
16:1 234
16:1-4 235
16:4 .... 234, 398
16:5 .... 447, 454
16:5-6 399
16:6 444
16:40-42 481-482
17:7-36 .... 453, 454
16:8-26 235
16:15 453
16:31 235
16:32 235
16:34 453
16:37 234
16:37-42 235
16:39 .... 234-235, 398
16:41-42 235
16:42 .... 243, 399, 446, 448
16:48 235
21:18 478
21:26 478
21:29 398
22:1 479
22:6-11 29
23-26 235
23:5 448
25:1 99
25:6 99
25:9 .... 285, 428
28:12 448
29:28-29 455
29:42 446

II Chronicles
1:3 398
1:3-4 234
3:1 479

4:1 99
5:4-5 234
5:12 101
5:13 453
7:6 .... 448, 453, 454-455
7:17 150
15:3 .... 113, 114
29:25 .... 98-99, 235, 399, 457, 474, 482
29:25-27 399
29:25-28 .... 98, 102, 405
29:26 448
29:27 243
29:30 ... 235, 236, 243, 284, 302, 454
31:2 102
36:20-21 60
36:21 60
36:22 161

Ezra
Whole book 401
1:3 28
1:5 28
3:10-11 236
6:13-15 400
7:1f 28

Nehemiah
Whole book 401
8:1-8 127
12:45 399
12:45-46 236
12:46 243

Esther
4:11 75
5:2 75

Job
1:1 393
1:5 378
11:12 250
14:4 250
19:25-27 393

21:12 .... 85, 457, 469-470
30:31 384

Psalms
Whole book 242-243, 284-285,
293, 298, 424, 452, 464
1 .... 4, 265, 266, 273, 318
2 ... 137-138, 265, 266, 278, 295, 467
2:2-3 271
2:6 266
2:7 .... 278, 295
2:8 .... 266, 271, 292
3 467
4:1 .... 241, 264
5:9 .... 278, 294
6:1 241
6:3 267
9 293
9:14 331
10:7 .... 278, 294
12 351
13:1 261
13:1-2 267
14 351
14:1-3 .... 277, 294
15:2 .... 413, 419
16 .... 278, 295
17:15 264
18:19 16
19:2 413
22 .... 278, 293, 295, 467
22:1 221
22:3 .... 128, 232
22:25 .... 234, 455
23:4 263
26:12 108-109
27:4 12
29:1 331
31:1 318
32 422
32:1 .... 129, 318
32:1-2 .... 141, 278, 294
33:2 .... 423, 463
33:2-3 431

33:3 279
33:6 415
33:8 324
33:9 343
35:28 273
36:1 278
37:4 .... 15, 16
40 .... 293, 404
40:6-8 .... 278, 295
41 266
41:13 .... 266, 467
43:1 316
45 467
45:6-7 .... 278, 295
46 351
46:1-3 17
46:4-7 17
46:8-11 18
46:10 .... 16, 19
47:8 317
48:1 467
49:7 414
50:11 331
50:14 .... 103-104, 407
50:23 .... 104, 233
51 .... 141, 264, 467
51:4 .... 277, 294
52:7 347
57 467
61:1 241
62 324
65:1 241
66:1 242
67 .... 351, 462
67:1 .... 242, 330
68 .... 278, 295, 360
68:1 242
68:26 108-109
71:22 .... 425, 431, 465
72 .... 242, 266
72:2 242
72:18-19 467
72:19 266
72:20 242

73:25-26	12
73:26	264
74:8	109-110
74:10	267
75:1	242
76:1	242
79:5	267
80:4	267, 412
81:1	467
81:2	85, 429
82:1	467
84:1-3	41
86:9	271, 287
89	267, 293
89:46	267
89:49	267
89:52	266, 467
90-106	267
90:1	267
91:1	316
91:2	267
91:4	411
92	15, 346-348
92:1	467
92:3	431
92:4	15, 425
93:1	267, 467
94:1	467
95	56-57
95:1-2	40-41, 132-133
95:2	309
95:6	128
95:11	58
96:1	277
96:1-13	235, 454
96:10	267
96:10-13	268
97:11	267
98:2	287
98:8	384
98:8-9	268
99:1	267
100	41, 132, 356
100:1-4	41
101	264
102:25-27	278, 295
105	293
105:1-15	235, 454
105:2	293, 294, 335
105:47	331
106:1	235, 236, 454
106:46-47	235
106:47-48	454
106:48	266, 467
107	293
107-150	268
107:1	236
107:22	104, 407
110	278, 295, 467
110:1	268, 278, 295
113-114	237
113-118	205, 237, 268, 285, 463, 467
113	206, 268
114	206, 268
115	268
115-118	207, 208, 237
115:17-18	264
116	268
116:15	264
116:17	104, 407
117	268, 278, 291, 295
117:1	232
118	204, 205, 207, 208, 268, 269, 295, 467
118:1	236, 268
118:22-23	204
118:26	204, 268, 278
118:29	236
119	268
120-134	268, 269, 271, 467
122:1	129
122:4	269
124	351
126:6	270
127:3-5	270
128	351
128:3	270

129:6-7	269
130	351
132:15	270
134	270
134:1	270
136:1	236
137	300, 467
139:7-8	36-37
140	325
140:3	278, 294
145:2	318
146-150	265, 268, 271, 467
148-150	324
149:1	140, 279
149:1-2	314
149:2	414
149:3	85, 314
149:4	314
149:6-8	271
150	264, 372, 415, 467-470
150:1	468
150:2	468
150:3	468, 469
150:3-5	468
150:4	85
150:5	469
150:6	266, 468

Proverbs
1:7	4
3:12	16
9:10	4

Isaiah
Whole book	242-243
2:2	271
2:3	271
5:1-7	204
5:12	85, 457
9:12	141
11:1	286
18:6	277
24:8	85, 86, 458
29:13	4
30:32	85, 86, 458
40:1-2	444
42:1	279
42:9	279
42:10	279, 280, 282, 283
45:21-23	277
45:23	276
52:7	161, 447
52:11	22, 27, 28, 135
53:4	207
53:6	441
53:7	207, 443
55:6	152
55:7	462
55:8	461-462
56:7	119
58	445
58:1	444, 446
58:13	64
58:13-14	54
61:1	161, 451
62:4	16
63:2	220
63:3-4	220
66:22-24	18-19

Jeremiah
6:16	368
17:24	63
31:4	85, 86, 458

Lamentations
3:20	419

Ezekiel
4:1-3	177
20:12	52, 63
20:20	52
20:21	63
20:34	22, 29
22:8	63
23:38	63
28:13	85
37:24	455

Daniel
9:19 150

Hosea
11:1 166
11:2-5 166

Joel
2:32 277

Micah
4:1 271
4:2 271

Nahum
1:15 447

Habakkuk
3:1-19 302

Zechariah
9:9 269
14 270
14:16 270
14:16-19 270
14:17 270
14:18 270
14:19 270

Malachi
2:7 --113
3:6-12 137
3:8 147
3:10 .... 146, 147

Matthew
2:11 .... 4, 9
2:14-15 167
3:11 199
4:10 7
4:17 161
4:23 403
6:9 142
6:9-15 142

7:13-14 ....
9:35 403
9:56 165
10:32 188
11:17 119
11:28-29 132
11:28-30 42
13:18-23 138-139
13:31 441
15:7 4
15:8-9 4
16:21 177
18:15-17 214
21:5 269
21:9 .... 204, 269, 318
21:12 204
21:17 204
21:22 142
21:43 204
21:45 204
22:40 136
23:37-38 403
23:38 204
23:39 .... 204, 269, 278
24-25 204
26:3-5 204
26:6-13 204
26:14-16 204
26:26 .... 207, 227
26:27 227
26:29 .... 219, 222
26:30 .... 208, 237, 241, 310, 463
26:39 219
27:46 278
28:9 10
28:18-20 76
28:19 .... 174, 183, 184, 187, 266
28:19-20 .... 18, 128, 185

Mark
1:8 183
1:15 211
6:32 164
6:33 164

6:34	164, 165
7:3	190
7:4	191
8:21	177
10:18	249
11:17	119
14:25	219
14:26	237, 244, 310
14:36	219
15:34	221, 278
16:15	154

Luke

1:8	100
1:10	101
1:23	7, 78, 374
1:46-55	301
1:68-79	301
2:29-32	301
2:49	403
4:15	403
4:16	403
4:16-17	140
4:16-18	161
4:16-21	117, 122
4:18	451
9:22	177
11:1	142
11:9	142
13:10	403
18:19	249
19:37	232
22:8	204
22:17	206
22:18	206, 219
22:19	209, 227
22:19-20	179, 212
22:20	227
22:42	219, 221

John

1:29	207, 287, 443
1:36	443
1:51	74
2:13	205
2:16	403
2:18-21	34
2:19-21	35
2:23	205
3:8	211
4:20-24	373
4:21-24	5
4:23	3, 12, 13
4:24	6
6:4	205
10:11	277
10:14	277
10:16	277
13:34	282
14:6	73, 376
17:9	266
17:20	266
19:24	278
20:1	69
20:19	69
20:26	69
21	293
21:25	294

Acts

1:2	265
1:5	183
1:8	266
2:9-10	309
2:17-18	191
2:24	278, 283
2:33	191
2:34-35	278
2:38	184, 188
2:38-39	180, 192, 193
2:38-42	210
2:40	249
2:41	181
2:41-42	128
2:42	125, 181, 223
3:1	117
3:22	177
4:12	73, 376

4:21	479
4:23	479
4:25-26	278
7:42	7
8:12	183, 194
8:13	210
8:32-36	443
8:35-38	210
10:34-38	210
10:45	191
10:47	183-184
10:48	184
11:16	184
11:21	186
11:25-26	154
11:26	186
13:2	78
13:14-15	116
13:15	116, 117
13:35	278
13:43	3, 373
15:11	278
15:21	117, 127, 140
16:14	3-4, 157, 373
16:14-15	188, 210
16:15	299
16:25	238, 244, 296, 310
16:31-33	210
17:4	4
17:17	373
17:26-27	152
18:7	4, 373
18:11	155
19:2-5	197
20:7	70, 155
20:20	155
20:28	153, 164, 187
20:31	155
20:35	147
22:17	117

Romans
Whole book	242
1:7	134
1:16	156
1:25	10, 375
2:4	160
2:28-29	189, 412
2:29	189
3	277
3:1-2	191
3:25	406
4:11	188-189
4:16	145
5	442
5:1	444, 481
5:1-2	139-140
5:5	228
5:14	441, 442, 475
6:4	63
9:23	454
10:4	331
10:9	161, 277, 347
10:9-13	41
10:9-15	347
10:11	277
10:13	277
10:14	127, 155, 446
10:15	161
12:1	7
12:1-2	83
13:9	136, 163
15:11	231
15:20	154

I Corinthians
1:3	134
2:4	451
3:5	199
3:9-17	33
4:1	187
5:7	208, 291
7:14	195
10:16	207, 208
10:16-17	218, 221
10:31	12, 470
11:16	227
11:23-26	127, 223

11:24 209
11:24-25 .... 174, 203, 212
11:25 .... 207, 219
11:26 .... 173, 177, 209, 212
11:27 228
11:28 217
11:29 218
12:13 184
13:4 163-164
13:14 128
14 .... 422, 424
14:10 431
14:11 431
14:13 425
14:14-16 425
14:15 .... 275, 304
14:16 425
14:19 420
14:24-25 40
14:26 .... 275, 304, 431
15:20-23 68
15:23 154
15:27 268
16:2 .... 70, 128, 143, 144, 147

II Corinthians
Whole epistle 122, 375
1:1 157
1:2 134
1:3 .... 122, 148
4:6 150
5:8 264
5:17 .... 281, 455
5:20 .... 75, 376
6:1 25
6:10 311
6:11 25
6:12 25
6:13 .... 22, 25
6:14 .... 22, 25
6:14-16 .... 22, 30-31
6:14-7:1 22
6:14b-16a 22
6:16 .... 1, 21, 25, 75, 88, 128,
146, 155, 375, 406, 460
6:16a 22
6:16-17 134
6:16-18 21
6:16-26 .... 32, 34, 38
6:17 27
6:17-18 28
7:1 22
7:2 22
8:3 147
9:7 147
13:14 .... 150, 151

Galatians
1:1 157
1:3 134
2:20 64
3:7 145
3:8 292
3:16 292
4:1-3 431
5:19-21 139

Ephesians
Whole epistle 306
1:1 .... 157, 305
1:2 128
1:3 .... 122, 134, 148, 305
1:4-5 184
1:6 232
1:7 .... 185, 226
1:12 242
1:13-14 .... 175, 185
1:14 242
2:2 226
2:8 185
2:19-22 306
2:19-23 32-33
2:21 375
2:21-22 .... 75, 88, 155, 311, 460
2:22 375-376
3:3 291
3:4-5 292
3:4-6 290

3:6 .... 291, 292
3:10 156
3:14-19 306
4:4-13 306
4:7-8 278
4:11-12 35
4:15 164
4:18 250
4:30 226
5:12 392
5:18-19 .... 305, 306-307, 406, 450, 451
5:19 .... 123, 244, 245, 251, 276, 296, 312, 455
5:25-27 164
6:20 .... 39, 75, 376

Philippians
Whole epistle 303, 305
1:1 188
1:2 134
1:6 52
1:23 264
2:5-11 303
2:6-11 301
2:9-11 276
2:15 249
3:20 .... 38, 75, 376

Colossians
1:1 157
1:2 .... 134, 307, 308
1:25 187
1:28 ..... 163, 248, 297, 298, 308, 453
2:11 189
2:11-12 .... 67, 193
2:12 189
2:16 67
2:16-17 .... 66, 67
2:17 .... 1, 63, 67, 438
3:2 308
3:3 308
3:16 .... 123, 128, 231, 240, 245, 248, 251, 255, 275, 296, 297, 298, 299, 307, 312, 349, 406, 450, 452, 455, 462-463, 482

I Thessalonians
1:1 134
2:13 156

II Thessalonians
1:9 37
2:2 134

I Timothy
Whole epistle 303, 305
1:1 157
1:4 187
2:1 .... 123, 127, 154
2:1-2 .... 141, 296
3:2-3 .... 158, 159
3:5 154
3:14-15 .... 127, 141, 296
3:15 .... 123, 140, 187, 298
3:16 .... 301, 304
4:13 .... 123, 127, 140, 154
5:17 213

II Timothy
Whole epistle 305
1:1 157
2:23 159
2:24 159
2:24-26 158
3:15 .... 141, 248
4:1-2 154
4:2 .... 127, 158-159, 161, 296

Titus
3:5 .... 183, 189

Hebrews
1 278
1:5 29
1:10 278
2:17 406
3:1-6 56

3:1-4:11	55
3:6	52
3:7-11	56-57
3:11	58
3:12-19	57
3:14	56
3:18	58
4:1	58
4:1-2	58-59
4:1-5	58
4:3	58, 58, 64
4:5	58
4:9	47, 60, 67
4:9-10	59
4:10	58, 64
4:14	56
4:16	142
5:2	408
6:4-5	39, 58-59
7:18	408
7:19	1
8:1-2	78
8:4-5	76
8:5	1, 434, 438
8:6	7
9:1	6, 373-374
9:6	6, 374
9:6-14	189
9:9	6, 374
9:10	189, 429
9:13	189
9:14	482
10	278
10:5-9	403
10:8-9	476
10:9	289, 404, 482
10:9-10	404
10:10	404
10:19-22	1
10:23	56
11:4	377-378
11:7	393
11:4-6	6
11:17	395
12:1	435, 436
12:22-24	38
12:23	196
13:15	97, 103-104, 106, 107, 123, 128, 231, 233, 307, 311, 455, 479, 482, 486
13:20	167
13:20-21	128
13:22	117

James

4:8	1, 42, 128, 133
5:16	142

I Peter

1:1	157, 312
1:3	122, 148
1:18-19	445
2:4-5	34, 479
2:5	1, 75, 88, 376, 406, 407, 460
2:9	455
3:8	487
5:1-2	187

II Peter

1:16	314
2:21	278
3:10	1

James

5:13	239, 251

I John

Whole book	139
1:8	219
1:8-9	219
1:9	139
2:2	406, 444, 481
4:10	406
4:19	97, 228
5:3	228
5:13	139
5:14	142, 299
5:14-15	128

Revelation
  Whole book................vii, 283, 372,
    449, 450, 470-473, 482, 483
  1:3 .... 127, 141
  1:4-6 .... 128, 134-135
  1:10 .... 70, 472
  1:15 .... 450, 471
  4:1 472
  4:8 vii
  4:10 5
  4:11 .... 8, 374
  5:1-14 8-9
  5:2 8
  5:4 8
  5:5 286
  5:6 287
  5:8 .... 449, 472
  5:9 .... 8, 280, 449
  5:9-10 .... 286, 301
  5:11-13 .... 40, 480
  5:12 8
  7:9-12 11
  8:1 19

8:2 472
8:6 472
8:13 472
9:14 472
13:1-4 11
13:4 5
13:6 34
13:8 5
14:2 .... 449, 450, 472
14:2-3 471-472
14:3 .... 280, 449
14:19 226
15:2-3 472
15:3 .... 430, 472
15:3-4 .... 286, 301
19:5 232
19:7 164
19:8 23
19:13 220
19:16 220
21:2 164
22:1-4 17-18

Index of Subjects

Achtleiderbuch (1524) 352
Ai 394, 478
Aineite (Greek word) 231-233
Aix-la-Chapelle, Germany 419
Alexandria, Egypt 115-116
Allegorical interpretation of the Old Testament 409, 414
Altar of burnt offering 401
Altar of incense 77
Altar of sacrifice 394-398, 446, 478, 480, 481, 484-485
Ambassador 38
American Presbyterian Church . 367
Ammon 459
Amsterdam 362
Anabaptists 427
Angels 472, 480
Anger 158
Anglican Church 432
Anthropomorphism 384
Anthropopathy 384-385
Antidote to Trent (1547) 198
Antitype 442
Annals of the Reformation and Establishment of Religion, and Other Various Occurences in the Church of England 357
Anointing in worship 427
Antioch, Syria 154, 186-187, 324
Antiphons 342-348
Antwerp, Belgium 361
Apostolic Constitutions 324
Apprenticeship 186
Arabia 393
Ark of the covenant 398, 429

Associate Presbyterian Church.. 366
Associate Reformed Presbyterian Church 366
Assurance 52, 53-54, 139-140, 258-259
Assyria 458
Asyndeton 462
Atonement 129, 406, 444, 481, 490
Australian Free Church 367
Authorized Version 359
Babylon 28, 29
Babylonian Talmud 99-102, 191
Babylonians 400
Banquets 410, 457-458, 480
Baptism 183-202
    Adult 188, 195
    As seal 188-189
    As sign 188-189
    In Jerusalem 181
    Infant 191-196, 201
    Institution 181
    Practice of 197, 200-201
    Private 197
    Re-baptism 198
    Spiritual 183-184
    Valid 196
    Vows 200-201
    Water 183-184, 185-188, 201
Baptismal regeneration 196-197
Baptismo (Greek Word) 189-191
Baptist churches ... 364, 430, 434, 435
Baptizo (Greek word) 189-191
Bay Psalm Book 240, 285, 362-363, 427
Beersheba 395

Belgic Confession 215, 361
Benediction 120, 127, 148-151, 489
Bethel 394-396, 478
Bible Songs: A Collection of Psalms
  (1901) 366
Bible translations 361
Biblia sacrosancta 356
Biblical Repertory and Princeton
  Review 432
Biblical theology 155
Blessing 149-151
Blood 220
Bodies, Human 34, 383, 385,
  411, 413
Body of Christ 35
Book of Common Prayer (1549,
  1552) 355-356, 358
Book of Psalmes, Englished, both in
  Prose and Metre (1612) 362
Boston, Massachusetts 430
Bowing to God 4-6, 373
Bowl of incense 449
Brattle Street Congregational
  Church (Boston, Mass.) 432
Breviaries 339
Burnt offerings 397, 405, 443-445,
  447, 481
Call to Worship 132-133
Calling on the name of the Lord .....
  407, 478, 480, 483, 484-485
Calvinistic independent churches ...
  364
Camp of Israel 84
Canaan, land of 58, 396, 478
Canticles 331
Caps in worship 427
Catechism for Young Children 171
Cathedral office 337, 342-343
Celebration 84-90, 458-461,
  474, 480, 488
Censers in worship 430
Ceremonial law 66-69, 147, 289,
  409-410, 420, 427-428, 450, 464
Chapels 427

Chief priests 401, 446
Children 167-171, 191-196, 201
Children's church 167-169
Children's sermons 169-171
Choirs 346, 415, 427, 431, 433, 446,
  449-450, 464, 471, 472, 483, 485
Chords, Musical 382
Christian Reformed Church in
  North America 366, 367
Church .... vii-viii, 17, 21-45, 47, 65,
  71-72, 86-87, 88-89, 164, 186-188,
  426, 428, 449, 455, 479, 482, 486,
  487-488
  Gathered church 154
  Growth 311
  Membership 210-215
  Visible church 186-188, 202
"Church" (English word) 376
Church fathers 310, 408-416, 423,
  485
Church of Scotland 359
  General Assembly (1647) 359
  General Assembly (1648) 359
  General Assembly (1650) 359
Church of the Holy Sepulchre,
  Jerusalem 326-328
Church Psalmist (1843) 366
Churches of Christ 435
Circumcision 51, 188-189, 211,
  408, 412, 420, 429, 465
Cithara .... See Lyres
Civil law 289
Cloisters 427
Clothing 379
Commentary on the Book of Psalms
  (John Calvin) 253
Commentary on Twelve Psalms
  (Ambrose) 414
Common meter tunes 363
Confession of faith 210-212
Confession of sin ... 133-134, 142, 402
Congregational churches 432
Congregational singing 353, 355
Conjunctions 462-463

Index of Subjects

Conjunctive asyndeton 245, 463
Constantinople 336, 349
Contemporary Christian music ....
   90-92
Contemporary worship 84
Context, Importance of 461-463
Conversion 211
Corinth, Asia Minor.............. 154-155
Corinthian church 144-145,
   304-305, 375
Council of Carthage (416) 416
Council of Chalcedon 327, 332
Council of Laodicea (367) 319,
   327, 332, 416
Council of Trent 198
Covenant .. x, 21-32, 50, 188-189, 394
Covenant children 191-202
Covenant promises 375
Covenant renewal 27, 28, 31-32,
   226-228, 487-488, 489, 490-491
Covenant sign 51, 53-54
Covenantal Worship: Reconsidering the Puritan Regulative Principle (Gore) 439
Creation ordinance 48-50
Creeds 214-215
Crosses in worship 427
Culture 85-89
Cure of the Greek Maladies (Theodoret) 416
Cymbals 99, 399, 401-402, 405, 415, 435, 439, 446-447, 448-449, 457-458, 464, 468-469, 474, 481, 485
Dancing 86, 87, 429, 457-459, 469, 470, 484
Deborah and Barak's song 302
A Dictionary of Hymnology (1907)..
   363
Directory for Worship of the United Presbyterian Church of North America 433
"Directory of the Public Worship of God" 222, 358

Disciples of Jesus 205, 237-238
Discipleship 185-187
Doxologies 266-267
Drinking 470
Dulcimers 421
Eastern communion psalmody ....
   343-344
Eastern Orthodox Churches 303, 336, 338-339, 416, 420, 435
Eating 470
Edict of Milan (313) 335
Egypt 65, 206, 269, 325, 372, 394, 412, 439, 458-459, 470, 478
Egyptian Hallel 463
Eighth day 69
El-Bethel 396
Elders 197-198, 213-218, 472, 480
Elders, Twenty-four 449
Embassy 38-40, 376, 488
Emden, The Netherlands 361
Emotions, Human 380-381, 383-385, 387, 389, 490
End of time 17
England 355-358, 364
Ephesian church 33, 197-198, 305-307, 311-312, 375-376
Ephesian elders 155
Episcopalians 79, 437
Etymology 463
Eucharist liturgy 340
Europe 364
Evangelical Presbyterian Church of Australia 367
Evangelism 195-196
Evangelistic meetings 40
Exclusive psalmody 249-259
   Objections to 275-308
Exhortations 116-122
Experience 92
Explanation of the Psalms (Cassiodorus) 419
Faith in God 378-380, 395
Fear of God 3-4, 373
Feast days 53, 66-69

Feast of First Fruits 68-69
Feelings, Human ... 380-381, 383-385
Figures and Types of the Old Testament (Samuel Mather) 428
First day sabbath 65-70
Flutes in worship 384, 410, 412, 413, 420, 458, 460
Folk songs 361
Foods 415
Forgiveness 136-139
"Form of Presbyterian Church Government" 358
Franciscans 345
Free Church of Scotland 434
Free Church of Scotland (Continuing) 367
Free Church of Scotland (Continuing), Synod of North America 367
Free Methodist Church 433, 436
Free Presbyterian Church of Scotland 367
Fruit of the vine 219-222
"Fulfilled" (English word) 289
Fuller Theological Seminary 435
Genealogies 398
General Baptists 364
Generosity 147
Geneva Bible (1599) 181
Geneva, Switzerland 126-127, 353-355, 356, 357, 358, 361
Genevan Psalter 299, 354-355, 359-360
Gentiles 290-293
Germany 346
Gibeon (town) 398, 399
Glory 12
God 37, 133, 183-185, 196, 197, 198, 217, 220-221, 264-265, 277, 293-295, 404, 461-462, 470, 472, 478, 479-480, 487, 491
    Deeds of 293-295
    Fear of 487
    Glory of 470, 478, 479, 491
    Judgment of 472

Name Yahweh 277
Omnipresence 37
Presence 133
Throne of 479-480
Transcendence 461-462
Will 404
Wrath 220-221, 264-265
Golden calf 484
Gongs in worship 435
Gospel 410, 445
Gospel songs 274
Government 137-138
Grace 64-66
Great Commission 18, 76-77
Great Hallel 467
Greek church 332
Greek grammar 244-246
Greek New Testament (United Bible Societies) 240
Greek Orthodox tradition 303
Greeting in worship 134-135
Habakkuk's song 302
Harmony (Musical) 382, 413
Harps (or psalteries) 99, 384, 399, 405, 409, 411, 412, 413-414, 415, 416, 419, 420, 425, 429, 430, 435, 439, 448-451, 460, 464, 465, 468, 471, 472, 474, 481, 485
Heaven 38-40, 55-59, 61-64, 73-74, 75, 88, 376, 470-471, 484
Hebron 394, 395
Heirs 38
Hendiatris 244
Holiness 23
Holy Place 130
Holy Spirit 157, 165-166, 176, 183-184, 198, 211, 245, 249, 300, 319, 387, 414, 438, 450, 451-453, 460, 465, 485, 487
    Fullness of the 451
    Gift of the 438
    In baptism 183-184
    In preaching 157, 165-166
    In the Lord's Supper 176

Inspired a band of prophets... 460
Inspired Paul 249
Inspired the Psalms 300, 387
Inspires praise 451-453, 465, 485, 487
Like wind 211
Unknown in Ephesus.............. 198
House of Commons (London, England) 357
Huguenots..................................... 360
Humneo (Greek word) 238
Hymn fragments 275
Hymnals 352
"Hymns" (English word) ... 241-248, 331, 462-463
Hymns and Spiritual Songs (Watts) 364-365
Hymns, Medieval 343-344
Hymns, Reformation............ 351-352
Hymns, Modern.................... 272, 274
Idolatry 10-12, 28, 410
Immersion 189-191, 196
Incense in worship...... 427, 429, 430, 465, 472
Independent churches.................. 435
Individualism 261
Instrumental music......x-xi, 129, 381
Instrumental music in worship 369-486
   As an aid to worship 437-438
   As appealing to the emotions 421
   In Lutheran worship 422
   In the early church............ 408-417
   In the medieval church 419-421
   In the modern church....... 427-435
   In the Reformation............ 421-427
   In the Old Testament........ 391-408
   Objections to a non-use in worship.............................. 457-476
   Reasons for popularity..... 436-439
   To attract youth 436-437
   Typological perspective on........... 441-456
Invocation in worship 133-134

Ireland.. 358
Israel..................... 54-55, 56, 111-112, 399, 478, 485
   Ceremonial worship in 485
   In exile 399
   In the Promised Land........... 54-55
   Levites in 111-112
   Moses as a servant in 56
   Numbering of........................... 478
Jehovah's Witnesses..................... 197
Jericho, walls of 411
Jerusalem............ 17-18, 113, 177-178, 326-328, 479
   City of God 17-18
   Early church worship in .. 326-328
   Fall of 177-178
   Restoration of 113
   Worship in................................ 479
Jerusalem church.................... 186-187
Jesus Christ .... vii, 13, 63, 74, 288, 289, 293-295, 393
   Resurrection........................ 63, 69
   Sacrificial death 424
Jesus Only churches..................... 197
Jews 191, 400, 408, 412, 424-426
   Captivity in Babylon 400
Judgment....................................... 458
Judging the body................... 218-219
Kai (Greek word).................... 244-246
Kathismata (Greek word)..... 338-339
Killing Times (1668-1688) 360
Kings Chapel Episcopal Church (Boston, Mass.) 432
Kiriath-jearim 398
Kneeling before God 373
Koinonia 221-222
Lamb of God ..286-287, 449, 473, 480
Latin language............... 335, 340-341
Latin Vulgate....................... 249, 349
   Printed (1455) by Gutenberg.. 249
Law of God 273, 408
Law of Moses............................... 404
Law, Reading of the.............. 135-139
Levitical choir 401, 446, 448, 450,

451, 468, 485
Levitical system............................ 285
Levites............. 101, 111-112, 398-399, 401, 405, 407, 425, 428, 446, 453, 454, 455, 485
Lilies.. 265
"Liturgy" (English word) 374
London, England 357, 361
Lord's Day........ 70, 328, 416, 453, 459
Lord's Supper 179, 203-228, 237, 340
    Admittance to.....................210-218
    Administration...................218-226
    Fencing 218-219
    Frequency............................222-223
    Institution................................. 179
    Liturgy 340
    Session-controlled.............213-218
Lutheran churches .79, 351-352, 422, 435
Lyons, France.................................. 354
Lyres (or Cithara) .. 99, 392, 399, 405, 411, 412, 414, 415, 420, 448-450, 457-460, 468, 469, 474, 481
Macedonian churches 147
Manual of Church Order (John Dagg) 430
Marriage 48-49
Martyrs 360
Mary's song 301
Mass 337, 342-348, 427
Massachusetts Bay Colony 362
Melody (Musical)........................... 385
Messiah................... 130, 266-267, 283
Metaphors 409
Methodist churches 430, 433
Metonymy....................................... 174
Metropolitan Tabernacle (London, England)......................430-431, 464
Middle Ages............................419-421
Milan, Italy 329
Ministers........................ 187-188, 201
Mishnah............. 99-102, 119, 121-122
Monasticism................... 321-325, 326, 337-339, 348

Moral law 288-289
Mormons 197
Mosaic law 288
Moses's song.................................. 302
Mount Ebal 394
Mount Gerizin 394
Mount Moriah 394, 479
Mount Sinai................................... 429
Music............... 380-389, 452-453, 490
    Definition 380-381
    Notes....................................381-382
    Vocal....................381, 385-389
Musical Instruments.........................
    85-88, 98, 384-385, 392-486, 423, 429, 454-455, 457-460, 464, 469, 474, 481, 485
    Emotions produced by............ 485
    In Davidic worship.................. 399
    Not in Mosaic worship 397-398
    Not in patriarchal worship.... 393, 396
    Origin.. 392
    Power of 485
Narcissism.. 91
Negev desert region 394, 395
"New" (English word) 280-283
New Bible Dictionary 107
New birth 211
New heavens and new earth... 18-19
New moons............................ 429, 465
New School Presbyterians (USA).... 365
"New song" 279-283, 471-472
New Testament.............240, 277-278, 286-289, 301-305, 310-313
    Hymns 301-305
    Old Testament quotations in.. 240
    Psalmody prevalent in 310-313
    Quotations of the Psalms. 277-278
    Songs....................................286-289
"New Version" of the English Bible 357-358
The New York Times 432, 434, 435
Nigeria 300-301

Ninth commandment.................. 163
Nob... 398
"Noisy gongs" 435
Non-Trinitarian churches............ 197
Normative Principle of Worship .....
 ix, 79-84, 377, 422, 439, 488
Noun 35
Noun, Collective singular.............. 35
Oaks of Mamre............................. 394
Oaths.. 82
Object lessons 169-171
Occasional celebration 458-461
Odes of Solomon.......................... 303
Offering 143-148, 406-407, 489
Offertory................................. 344-345
Office for Morning Prayer ... 346-348
Old School Presbyterians (USA) 365
Old Testament quotations in the
 New Testament 240
"Old Version" of the English Bible..
 357
Olivet Discourse........................... 204
*One and Fiftie Psalmes of Dauid in
 Englishe Metre* (1556).............. 356
Organs.................. 367, 410, 415, 419,
 421, 422, 423, 427, 431, 432, 434,
 435, 437, 464
Orthodox Church in America 416
Orthodox Presbyterian Church ....
 199, 223
Ottoman Empire 349-350
Paedagogius (Clement of Alexan-
 dria).. 410
Paedocommunion.................. 215-217
Palestine................................. 394, 400
Parable of the sower 138-139
Parables 441-442
Para-Church organizations . 185-186
Parallelism.............................. 287-288
Paraphrases............................ 250-251
Parents 192, 201
Particular Baptists........................ 364
Passover..........203-208, 237, 463, 467
Passover lamb........................ 204-207

Patriarchs of Israel 257, 393-396,
 478, 484
Peace offerings......102-103, 371, 397,
 406, 443, 444-445, 447, 481
Pentateuch..................................... 402
Pentecost................................. 37, 186
Pharisees............................... 146, 199
Philistines.............................. 398, 459
Pilgrims 362
Pipes in worship 392, 410, 421,
 431, 435, 469
Pouring 189-191, 196
Praise......................229-333, 490, 491
 Subjective element............252-259
Prayer............. 107, 120-121, 133-134,
 138-139, 141-143, 295-301, 402,
 427, 449, 472, 489, 490
 Public ... 133-134, 138-139, 141-143
 Written... 142
Preachers 111-115, 157-159
 Angry... 158
 Human instruments 157-158
 Teachable............................ 158-159
Preaching......................153-167, 172,
 383, 445, 446, 453, 485
 As application 162
 As proclamation 160-161, 164-165
 As shepherding................. 153-167
 Commanded.............................. 154
 Not teaching 162-165
 Primary means of grace ... 155-156
Precentor 431, 447, 464
Presbyterian Church in America 200
Presbyterian Church in Canada 366
Presbyterian Church in the U.S.
 (Southern Presbyterian Church)..
 433, 434
Presbyterian Church in the U.S.A.
 (Northern Presbyterian Church) .
 366, 432-433
Presbyterian Church of Eastern
 Australia.................................... 367
Presbyterian churches 213-214,
 364, 367, 434, 435

The Presbyterian Hymnal (1874)...... 366
Priesthood 77-78, 112-115, 428, 434-435, 444, 446-447, 485
Promised Land 54-59
Prophesying....................................460
Prophets of Israel 88, 114, 399, 400, 405, 406, 442-443, 457, 482
Propitiation 406, 444, 481
Prospects of Israel 88
Protrepticus (Clement of Alexandria).. 410
Protestant Reformed Churches of America 367
Protestant reformers..................... 485
"Psalm" (English word).......461-463
Psalm explanation........................ 349
Psalm of Ascents 467
Psalmes, Hymns, and Spiritual Songs of the Old Testament (1651) 362-363
Psalmody...................... ix-x, 229-368, 466-467, 476, 489-490, 492
   History................................309-368
   Not a circumstance of worship.... 476
   Subjective element in 466-467
Psalms..... 237-239, 386-388, 467, 482
   Alleged insufficiency of...276-279
   Books 1-3 266-267
   Books 4-5 266-267
   Eschatology....... 261-274, 280-281, 330-331
   God-given 249-250
   In temple worship 402
   In the early church, 2nd and 3rd centuries 313-317
   In the early church, 4th Century . 317-325
   In the early church, 5th Century . 325-331
   In the medieval church 335-348
   In the New Testament 310-313, 407
   In the Post-Reformation period... 363-367
   In the Reformation period............ 351-363
   In the Roman Catholic Church.... 336, 350-351
   Inspiration.......... 249-250, 262-263
   Monastic............. 321-322, 337-340
   Popular....................................... 348
   Qualities 387-388
   Staying power 300-301
   Subjective element...........261-274, 299-300, 320-321, 329-330
   Sufficiency...........................292-295
   Sung during New Testament times................................310-313
   Titles.. 241
   Typological.........................283-288
   Uniqueness 252-259
   Universality 300-301
Psalmes and Hymns (1843)......... 366
"Psalms and hymns and spiritual songs" 297-298, 305-308
The Psalms of David Imitated in the Language of the New Testament... 364-365
The Psalter (1912)......................... 366
The Psalter, with Responsive Readings (1912) 367
Psalteries............................see Harps
Psalters, Ancient....................284-285
Psalters, Metrical.. 239-240, 250-251, 350-368
   Anglo-Genevan................ 357, 358
   In Bohemian............................. 355
   In Dutch............................ 355, 361
   In English 355-367
   In French 353-355
   In German 355
   In Hebrew 355
   In Hungarian............................ 355
   In Italian 355
   In Latin 355
   In Polish..................................... 355

In Spanish 355
In vernacular languages .. 350-368
Printed 350-367
Scottish 358-361
Public confession of faith 188
Questions and Responses (Theodoret) 416
Rabbis 305-306
Ravencroft's Psalter (1621) 362
Reading of Scripture 140-141
Red Sea 484
Redemption 28, 49-50, 393
Reformation 125-127, 351-363, 419, 421-429
Reformation Study Bible 461-462
Reformed Church in America 366
Reformed Church of the Netherlands 361
Reformed churches 353-367, 422, 435
Reformed Presbyterian Church of Australia 367, 435
Reformed Presbyterian Church of Ireland 367, 435
Reformed Presbyterian Church of North America 193, 199-200, 213-214, 279, 366, 367, 435
Reformed Presbyterian Church of North America, Japan Presbytery 367, 435
Reformed Presbyterian Church of North America, General Synod ... 366, 434
Reformed Presbyterian Church of Scotland 367, 435
Regeneration 211
Regulative Principle of Worship ...... ix, 74-90, 288-290, 376-377, 423, 438-439, 488
Remesiana (Bela Palanka), Yugoslavia 415
Renaissance 351, 419
Repentance 211
Rest 49, 54, 57-65

Roman Catholicism 79, 196-197, 198-200, 419-421, 432, 433
Roman Empire 419
Rome 316, 419
Root fallacy 461
Rule of St. Benedict 337-338
Rule of St. Francis, Earlier (1221) 339
Rwanda 300-301
Sabbath .... ix, 47-70, 72, 106-108, 146, 400, 408, 411, 443-444, 459, 467, 481, 487, 488
Sabbath-keeping 59-65
Sabbatismos (Greek word) 60-61
Sacred music 91
Sacraments 173-228, 489
"Sacrifice of praise" 406-407, 415, 489
Sacrifices 99-107, 233, 289, 311, 371, 378-380, 393, 395, 401, 406-407, 408, 409-419, 415, 421, 429, 434-435, 439, 443-446, 450, 465, 468, 474, 476, 478, 479-480, 484-485, 489, 490
Daily 406
Spiritual 410
Sadducees 199
Saint Loo 354
Saint Paul's Cross 357
Saints 470-471
Salvation 134-135
Sanctification 52
Entire 423
Samaritans 479
Sanctuary 446
Satan 6-7
Schachan (Hebrew word) 35
Scotland 358-361, 432, 435
Scripture readings 116
Sea of glass 472
Seals 188-189, 226-227
Second commandment 78, 288, 374-375
Second Helvetic Confession 422-423

Chapter 23 423
Seed 35
Selah (Hebrew word) 16-17
Self-examination 216-217
Separatist Church, Amsterdam . 362
Septuagint 240-242, 264, 302
Session-controlled communion ....
  213-217
Seventh-day sabbath 65-70
Shechem 394, 395
Sheep 441, 443
Shekinah 35-36
Shema (Hebrew word) 402, 489
Shemoneh 'esreh (Hebrew expression) 402
Shepherding 228
Shiloh 398
Signs 188-189, 202
Simeon's song 301
Simile 441, 449
Sin 218-219, 413, 445, 478, 481, 485, 189
Sinai desert region 396
Singing 99, 103-106, 295-301, 398, 399-400, 401-402, 405-408, 410, 446-447, 450, 458-459, 463-464, 482, 484
  In celebration 458-459
  In worship 399-400, 401-402, 405-408, 410, 447
Sodom and Gomorrah 441
Song of Lamech 392
Song of the Bow 302
"Songs" (English word) 241-248, 331, 462-463
Sound 371, 380-382
Souterliedekens (1540) 361
Speaking, Public 383
"Spiritual" (English word) 245
Split cup 221-222
Sprinkling 189-191, 196
Sternhold and Hopkins psalter ....
  239-240, 356-358
Stewards 187

Strasbourg, France 126, 349, 353
Strasbourg German Service Book (1525) 353, 356
String instruments 415, 431
Superstition 410
Switzerland 422, 435
Syllogism 72-76, 376-377, 438-439, 488
Synagogue 105, 107-123, 140, 148, 236-237, 400-403, 408, 428, 488, 489
  Origins of 107-111
  Purpose of 111-115
  Worship in 115-123, 140, 148
Synecdoche 294, 379
Synod of Dordrecht (1574) 361
Synod of Wesel (1568) 361
Tabernacle ... 23-26, 32, 35-36, 76, 77, 396-398, 454, 459, 460, 478, 485
Tabernacles, Feast of (Sukkoth) ....
  269-271
Tambourines 85, 458-460, 483
Tapers in worship 429, 465
Tate and Brady psalter 357-358
Teaching 111-115, 295-301
Tehillim (Hebrew word) 274
Temple .... vi, 25-26, 32-35, 36, 41-45, 76, 88, 98-103, 129-130, 204, 231, 237, 375, 400-404, 406, 408, 428, 448, 450, 459, 460, 467, 476, 481, 483, 485, 488-489
  Destruction of 403-404
  Symbolism of 129-130
  Worship in 99-103
Ten Commandments 48, 51, 135
Thank offerings 102-107, 233, 406-407, 489
Thanksgiving 103, 311, 453, 458-459, 490
Theater 421
Throne of God 449
Timbrels 85, 429, 457-460, 469, 470
Tithing 145-147
Tof (Hebrew word) 85

Index of Subjects

Togas in worship 427
Tribes of Israel 54-55
Trinity 183-185, 196, 197, 198
Trumpets 98, 371, 397-398,
    401-402, 404-405, 410, 411, 412,
    415, 421, 429, 435, 439, 443-447,
    457-459, 468, 472, 474, 481, 485
  Silver 397, 443-447, 474, 485
Truth 249-250
Tuning fork 431, 464
Tympana 415
Typology 29-30, 55-56,
    423-429, 441-456, 457, 460, 465-
    466, 475-476, 485, 490
Unclean purifications in worship....
    427
Unitarians 197, 315
United Presbyterian Church of
    North America 366, 433, 434
United States of America 362-367
Ur of the Chaldees 394
Uz, land of 393
Violins (or viols) in worship 420,
    464
Visions 471-473
Vocal music 381, 385-389, 421, 486
Voice, Human 383, 385, 471-472
Votive-offering 407
Vow-offering 406
Vows 82, 200-201, 395
  By Jacob 395
War 480
Washings 129-130, 189-191
Wedding 85, 457-458, 480
Westminster Annotations 110-111
Westminster Assembly 357, 358,
    359, 360
Westminster Assembly divines.. 428
Westminster Confession of Faith .....
    215, 358, 473, 476
  1:6 .... 67-68, 128, 131, 473, 489
  7:1 31
  21:3 297
  21:5 .... 127, 251, 297, 360-361
21:7 53
22:1 82
22:4 81-82
27:3 196
27:4 187-188
28:2 197
28:3 191
Westminster Larger Catechism.. 358
  Question 167 195
Westminster Shorter Catechism 358
  Question 1 12
  Question 41 136
  Question 42 136
  Question 49 78-79
  Question 50 79
  Question 51 .... 79, 288
  Question 88 151-152
Westminster Standards 78-79
Whole Booke of Psalmse Faithfully
Translated into English Metre
(1640) 362
Wilderness Wanderings 50, 57
Wine 458
Wizard of Oz viii
Word of God 388
Words 383
Work 48-49, 54, 61-64
Work, Cessation from 54
Worship
  Act of faith 378-380
  As bowing to God 373
  As Delight 15-16
  As Joy 14-15
  As Pleasure 12
  As Response 9
  As Rest 16-19
  As Service 6-7, 373
  Carnal 415
  Ceremonial 476, 481, 490
  Circumstances ... 128-129, 473-475
  Commanded 283
  Contemporary 90-92
  Corporate 487
  Day of 491

Definition .... viii, 3-20,47, 232, 373-375, 487
Dialogical 131, 489
Due to God 468
Elements ...... ix-x, 98-123, 127-128, 131-152, 488-489
Experience 92
Faith essential to 377-378
Heavenly 482, 483, 484
House of 478
Manner of 477-478, 491
Of the Church vii
Of the Triune God 13-14
Order of 126-127, 129-131, 402, 489
Pattern x
Places of 477-479, 488, 491
Prescribed 72-76
Private 305-308
Public 31, 42-45, 83-90, 119-122, 305-308, 378-380, 395
  By Isaac 395
  By Jacob 395
Sacrificial 397, 401, 403-407
Service .... vii, 77, 92
Simplicity in 463, 479, 482-483
Synagogue 105-123, 401-403
Tabernacle 397
Temple ... 98-103, 401-403, 427-429
Theology .... ix, 21-93, 490
Transitions 490
Without musical instruments 369-486
Youth 436-437
"Worship" (English word) 374
Zechariah's song 301
Zion 145
Zurich, Switzerland 422